Transform Coding of Images

MICROELECTRONICS AND SIGNAL PROCESSING

Series editors: **P. G. Farrell,** University of Manchester, U.K.
J. R. Forrest, University College London, U.K.

About this series:
The topic of microelectronics can no longer be treated in isolation from its prime application in the processing of all types of information-bearing signals. The relative importance of various processing functions will determine the future course of developments in microelectronics. Many signal processing concepts, from data manipulation to more mathematical operations such as correlation, convolution and Fourier transformation, are now readily realizable in microelectronic form. This series aims to satisfy a demand for comprehensive and immediately useful volumes linking microelectronic technology and its applications.

Key features of the series are:
• Coverage ranging from the basic semiconductor processing of microelectronic circuits to developments in microprocessor systems or VLSI architecture and the newest techniques in image and optical signal processing.
• Emphasis on technology, with a blend of theory and practice intended for a wide readership.
• Exposition of the fundamental theme of signal processing; namely, any aspect of what happens to an electronic (or acoustic or optical) signal between the basic sensor which gathers it and the final output interface to the user.

Transform Coding of Images

R. J. CLARKE

Department of Electronic and Electrical Engineering
University of Technology
Loughborough, England

 1985

ACADEMIC PRESS

Harcourt Brace Jovanovich, Publishers
London   Orlando   San Diego   New York
Austin   Montreal   Sydney   Tokyo   Toronto

COPYRIGHT © 1985 BY ACADEMIC PRESS INC. (LONDON) LTD.
ALL RIGHTS RESERVED.
NO PART OF THIS PUBLICATION MAY BE REPRODUCED OR
TRANSMITTED IN ANY FORM OR BY ANY MEANS, ELECTRONIC
OR MECHANICAL, INCLUDING PHOTOCOPY, RECORDING, OR
ANY INFORMATION STORAGE AND RETRIEVAL SYSTEM, WITHOUT
PERMISSION IN WRITING FROM THE PUBLISHER.

ACADEMIC PRESS INC. (LONDON) LTD.
24–28 Oval Road
LONDON NW1 7DX

United States Edition published by
ACADEMIC PRESS, INC.
Orlando, Florida 32887

British Library Cataloguing in Publication Data

Clarke, R.J.
    Transform coding of images.–(Microelectronics
    and signal processing)
    1. Image processing
    I. Title   II. Series
    621.3819'598   TA1632

Library of Congress Cataloging in Publication Data

Clarke, R. J.
    Transform coding of images.

    (Microelectronics and signal processing)
    Includes index.
    1. Image transmission.   2. Bandwidth compression
(Telecommunication)   3. Coding theory.   I. Title.
II. Series.
TK5105.2.C57   1985   621.38'043   85-1379
ISBN 0–12–175730–7 (alk. paper)
ISBN 0–12–175731–5 (paperback)

PRINTED IN THE UNITED STATES OF AMERICA

85 86 87 88   9 8 7 6 5 4 3 2 1

Contents

Preface

Over the past twenty years or so, the field of electrical engineering has been revolutionised by the advent and the subsequent rapidly increasing use of the digital computer. Not only are many analytical operations which were originally carried out in analogue form now performed more conveniently and speedily via the (discrete) digital computation process, but, and perhaps of more significance, procedures can now be executed which were once considered quite impossible, for example, the manipulation or processing of frames of video data on a realtime basis. Even where still images are concerned, the computer now allows complex high-speed processing operations, which typically involve large numbers of non-integer multiplications, to be applied to high-resolution data emanating, for example, from earth satellites. More generally, the development of information provision services (including the transmission of pictorial material) has been fostered by the close relationship between the digital computer and digital communication systems.

Digital communication links, although offering several advantages when compared with their analogue counterparts, do require a much higher equivalent bandwidth, and this is particularly a problem where image data is concerned, since such source material requires a large bandwidth in any case. It is not surprising, therefore, that interest in bandwidth compression techniques, originally analogue but now digital, has a long history, particularly as applied to image communication or storage, and the present volume is concerned with one appropriate procedure — transform coding, which, to risk a sweeping oversimplification, allows the reproduction of images of reasonable quality at average rates of perhaps 0.5 to 1.0 bit/element.

The main part of this book is concerned with the theoretical and practical aspects of transform coding systems intended to process still, or moving sequences of, images. However, two other topics are given more consideration than might, at first sight, seem appropriate. The successful operation of any bandwidth compression system is crucially dependent upon specific properties of the source data, and here such statistical measures are given detailed consideration in the light of their effect on coder performance. Again, there is much interest nowadays in the development of image processing systems having regard to the perception, by an observer, of degradation in the reconstructed picture. Furthermore, it is possible to use simple models of the human visual system within an image coder design in order to improve its performance, and the book, therefore, includes material on these aspects of image coding also.

An attempt has been made to exclude complex mathematical detail except where its presence is unavoidable (in particular, in parts of Chapters 2 and 9) and to demonstrate fundamental relationships via numerical examples. The book is intended for postgraduate students pursuing either course options or research in image coding and for those actively engaged in the design of coding systems, but it is suitable, in part, for final year undergraduate courses which include an image processing element. The list of references has been made as complete as practicable, and suggestions for supplementary reading have been made for those who wish to pursue specific topics in more detail.

Acknowledgements

Naturally, a volume of the present kind would not be possible without the dedicated work, over many years, of all those individuals and research groups throughout the world who have developed the subject to its present level of sophistication and have, moreover, freely published their results. It is also appropriate to acknowledge here the foresight of the electronics division of the Institution of Electrical Engineers (London), who, a few years ago, established professional group E4 (Electronic Image Processing), with whose members I have had many long and fruitful discussions on the topic. More specifically, I should like to thank the Society of Motion Picture and Television Engineers and the British Broadcasting Corporation for allowing me to employ their test-image material and to Taylor and Francis, Ltd., London, for permitting me to make use of the content of the paper "The Application of Image Covariance Models to Transform Coding", which appeared in Volume 56 of the *International Journal of Electronics* in 1984. Acknowledgement is also due to the Ministry of Defence for permitting the reproduction of Fig. 8.1 and to the IEE for allowing me to use material which forms the basis of Section 4.3.

It is worth emphasising that the book could not have been written without the financial support provided by the research laboratories of British Telecom, Martlesham, United Kingdom, which has enabled the author and his research students to pursue an active research programme in transform image coding at Loughborough University over the past six years. In turn, the enthusiastic labours of those students, in particular D. Allott (who carried out the coding simulations described in Chapter 5), W. K. Cham, K. N. Ngan and W. C. Wong, as well as of other members of the image coding research group (M. G. B. Ismail, M. N. Pauls and Badi Moussa), have, it is hoped, contributed usefully to the sum total of knowledge on the subject. Needless to say, any errors, omissions or, equally significant, points of contention concerning the material within the volume remain solely the responsibility of the author.

Finally, it is a pleasure to acknowledge the wholehearted support of the editorial staff of Academic Press and of the editors of the series, Professors J. R. Forrest and P. G. Farrell, in this project.

Symbols

The main symbols used are defined below. All notation employed is defined upon its first appearance, and, of necessity, some symbols are used for more than one quantity.

a_i	Predictor weighting coefficient
$A(f)$	HVS spatial frequency response
A_R	Row transform
$b_{(0,0)}$	Bit allocation for the dc coefficient
b_i	Bit allocation for the ith coefficient
B	Binary wordlength
B	Colour component
B_C	Column transform
$[B_N]$	Matrix in DCT decomposition
c_j	jth transform coefficient
$\hat{c}_j$	Estimated value of c_j
C	Transform coefficient vector
C	Channel capacity
$C(p, q)$	Transform coefficient array
$COR(\cdot)$	Correlation matrix of $(\cdot)$
$COV(\cdot)$	Covariance matrix of $(\cdot)$
D	Distortion parameter
$DCT(\cdot)$	Discrete cosine transform basis matrix of order $(\cdot)$
$DFT(I)$	Imaginary part of the discrete Fourier transform basis matrix
$DFT(R)$	Real part of the discrete Fourier transform basis matrix
$DLB(\cdot)$	Discrete linear basis matrix of order $(\cdot)$

DST($\cdot$)	Discrete sine transform basis matrix of order ($\cdot$)
e	Error term (suitably subscripted and/or indexed)
e	Quantisation distortion
$E(\cdot)$	Expectation operator
f	Spatial frequency (cycles/deg)
f	Data vector
$f(k, l)$	Input array of picture elements
$[F]$	Two-dimensional data array
G	Colour component
$G(\omega)$	Visual contrast sensitivity
$h(\cdot)$	Differential entropy of ($\cdot$)
$h(\theta)$	Line spread function
$[H]$	Horizontal process correlation matrix
$H(\cdot)$	Walsh–Hadamard transform basis matrix of order ($\cdot$)
H_N	Entropy of N level quantiser
$H(x)$	Per-element entropy of data sequence
$H(x, y)$	Joint entropy of two data sequences
$H(y/x)$	Conditional entropy of two data sequences
$H(\omega)$	Spatial frequency response
HA($\cdot$)	Haar transform basis matrix of order ($\cdot$)
HCT($\cdot$)	High-correlation transform basis matrix of order ($\cdot$)
HVS	Human visual system
$i(x)$	Self information of occurrence of event $x = X$
$i(x; y)$	Mutual information between events $x = X$ and $y = Y$
$I(x; y)$	Average mutual information between element sequences
I	Chrominance signal in NTSC system
I_N	Identity matrix of order N
$[J]$	Matrix in the development of the sinusoidal transform family
k	Data or coefficient index
KLT($\cdot$)	Karhunen–Loève transform basis matrix for the first-order Markov process of interelement correlation coefficient ($\cdot$)
$K_{1,2,3}$	Colour conversion components
L	Total number of allowable luminance levels ($L = 2^B$)
L	Luminance (suitably subscripted)
m	Optical contrast
m.s.e	Mean square error
M	Image or sub-block dimension
n_l	Number of image elements taking on luminance level l
N	Transform, image or sub-block dimension
N_B	Number of bits allocated
N_L	Number of quantisation levels
p	Transform coefficient order
p_i	Probability of occupation of the ith quantiser interval

$p(x)$	Probability of element x taking on value X
$p(x, y)$	Joint probability of x and y
$p(y/x)$	Conditional probability of y given x
$P(\omega)$	One-dimensional power spectral density
$P(\omega_h, \omega_v)$	Two-dimensional power spectral density
q	Quantisation error
Q	Chrominance signal in NTSC system
Q	Selectivity factor of human spatial frequency response
Q	Entropy power
R	Colour component
$R(\cdot)$	Correlation function (suitably indexed and subscripted)
$R(D)$	Rate-distortion function
$R_L(D)$	Lower bound on $R(D)$
$R_U(D)$	Upper bound on $R(D)$
$[R_N]$	Matrix in DCT decomposition
$S(\cdot)$	Slant transform basis matrix of order $(\cdot)$
$\mathbf{t}$	Transform basis vector (appropriately subscripted)
$T(\cdot)$	General transform operator
$[T]$	General transform basis matrix (subscripts C = complex, R = real)
$T_{1,2,3}$	Colour conversion components
u	Colour conversion component
$u(i)$	Scaling constant in symmetric cosine transform
U	Colour conversion component
U_d	PAL system colour difference signal
v	Colour conversion component
V	Colour conversion component
V_d	PAL system colour difference signal
$\mathbf{V}$	Correlation separation vector
$[V]$	Vertical process covariance matrix
$\text{VAR}(X)$	Variance matrix of $[X]$
W	Colour conversion component
W	$e^{-2\pi j/N}$
W_k	kth element of window function
$W(x)$	Error weighting function
$W(\omega)$	One-dimensional spectral weighting function
$W(\omega_h, \omega_v)$	Two-dimensional spectral weighting function
x	Arbitrary image element
$\hat{x}$	Predicted value of x
x_D	Data dynamic range
x_i	Quantiser decision level
X	Particular luminance value assumed by x
$\mathbf{X}$	Data column vector

$[X]$	Two-dimensional data array
$\mathbf{X}_C$	$[X]$ in column stacked form
$\mathbf{X}_R$	$[X]$ in row stacked form
y	Arbitrary image element
y_i	Quantiser reconstruction level
Y	Particular value assumed by y
Y	Luminance signal
$\mathbf{Y}$	Transform coefficient vector
α	Parameter in exponential form of the first-order Markov correlation relation
α	One-step prediction coefficient
β	Parameter in sinusoidal transform development
γ	System (non)linearity parameter
$\Gamma(\cdot)$	Gamma function
Δ	Reconstruction error
$\Delta_{h,v}$	Mean square differences between adjacent horizontal or vertical elements
Δ_L	Luminance increment
$\Delta_{x,y,z}$	Inter-element spacing in axial directions
η_C	Transform decorrelation efficiency
η_E	Transform energy packing efficiency
θ	Quantisation/bit allocation parameter
θ	Subtended angle
θ	Distortion parameter
λ	Optimisation multiplier
λ_i	ith eigenvector
$[\Lambda]$	Diagonal matrix of eigenvalues
$[\Lambda]$	DCT matrix
ρ	Inter-element correlation coefficient
ρ_d	One-step diagonal correlation coefficient
ρ_h	One-step horizontal correlation coefficient
$\rho_H(x)$	Horizontal correlation coefficient as a function of x
ρ_k	k-step correlation coefficient
ρ_n	Single letter fidelity criterion
ρ_V	One-step vertical correlation coefficient
$\rho_V(y)$	Vertical correlation coefficient as a function of y
$\rho(x, y)$	Two-dimensional correlation function
σ^2	Variance (appropriately subscripted)
τ	Element delay
ω	Angular frequency
ω_h	Horizontal angular frequency (two-dimensional case)
ω_v	Vertical angular frequency (two-dimensional case)
ω_r	Radial angular frequency

Chapter 1

Image Data Compression:
An Introduction

1.1 Introduction

It is a truism nowadays to say that the advent of the digital computer has revolutionised almost every technological discipline. Not least amongst those affected has been electrical engineering (the very field which itself has been responsible for the myriad advances in computer technology), and there are many who, though working as electrical engineers, now hardly come into the close vicinity of moving electrons in a professional capacity from one year to the next. Within that sphere of interest, arguably one of the most radical changes has taken place in communications, in which the accent is now heavily placed upon representation of the input information in discrete (sampled and quantised) form, leading to a much greater flexibility in the scope and nature of the operations which can subsequently be carried out on the data. In more general terms, the information 'revolution' appears to have created a demand for a wide range of new services, and it is just such a diversity of requirements that can be catered for by the now rapidly evolving networks of digital communications channels. Many of the new services envisaged (or already in operation) require the transmission and/or storage of image detail, and the days when the only pictures to be seen 'at a distance' were those of broadcast television are long past.

Given the more or less continual demand for increased bandwidth (or channel capacity) to enable more users to benefit from communication systems, and also the great demands made upon such systems by the desire to transmit satisfactory moving images, or still images in a reasonable time, it is not surprising that interest in picture transmission at as low a bandwidth or bit rate as is conveniently possible has continued unabated ever since the days when the only means of manipulation of an image or sequence of image frames were analogue in nature. Naturally, technological advances have greatly increased the efficiency of image-processing operations; indeed, little advance would have been possible without the growing availability of large volumes of storage capacity at an economic price, together with the development of algorithms which allow so-called 'fast' processing to be undertaken. In this context it is worth remembering that the data rate for reasonable spatial and temporal quality of a moving image is more than 1000 times that for a speech signal of good intelligibility, and the processing of an image 512×512 elements in extent at a frame rate of $25\,s^{-1}$ has presented the designer of digital systems with an intriguing, if somewhat daunting, task. Nowadays, however, image data compression is an exclusively digital concern, and it has been carried out at all rates from those of standard broadcast television (100–200 Mbit/s), down to those necessary for low-resolution surveillance applications (tens of kilobits per second).

As far as techniques are concerned, there are two basic approaches: predictive coding, carried out in the spatial (data) domain; and transform coding, the subject of this volume, which is, loosely speaking, a frequency domain process. It is also possible to combine the two approaches in a technique called hybrid coding, which may be said to combine the more attractive features of both. Before describing these methods briefly, however, it is appropriate to make one or two more general remarks on the subject of data compression.

1.2 Statistical image data compression

Both of the techniques referred to earlier are statistical in nature. Thus, they make no attempt to code image information in what might be described as a meaningful way, i.e., abstracting those features which the human observer might consider important. They simply operate by virtue of the statistical properties of the image or class of images in question. If those properties are 'appropriate' in some more or less well-defined sense, then the coding performance will be satisfactory, and vice versa. Thus, non-adaptive systems, in particular, may be expected to produce poor results at locations where image properties depart significantly from the average. A good example of this behaviour occurs at edges, whose presence implies large variations in luminance over small distances.

The basic statistical property upon which image compression techniques rely is inter-element correlation. To the extent to which element values in a locality in the spatial domain are similar, the magnitude of one may be estimated from the value(s) of one or more of the others nearby which have been previously coded. Again, high values of correlation imply a power spectral distribution which is strongly low pass in nature, thus requiring little coding capacity for transmission. The degree to which images may be compressed whilst still allowing satisfactory reproduction after storage or transmission in compressed form is, therefore, crucially dependent upon their correlation properties, and it is fortunate that even fairly 'active' images, i.e., those containing a reasonable amount of spatial detail, have quite high values of correlation coefficient. Such images may be successfully coded by transform methods at rates below 1 bit/element compared with an original digital coding requirement of perhaps 8 bits/element [it should be noted here that it is conventional, when considering compression schemes, to quote the coding requirement (rate) in terms of the average number of bits per image element—when transmission time is taken into account this figure may easily be converted into the more usual measure of bits per second]. It is worth mentioning at this point that this method of comparison, although universally used, is in fact open to a misleading interpretation. The preceding figures imply a notional 'compression ratio' of $8:1$, and such a figure seems to suggest that a similar result will be produced when a 16-bit original is coded at a rate of 2 bits/element. In fact the quality of the reproduced image in the latter case will certainly be much better than in the former, even though the variation in quality of the (8- and 16-bit) original images will be barely detectable to the eye, and it is the final rate, rather than the compression ratio, which is the true indicator of the performance capability of the system.

Another general point worth mentioning here briefly is that of the visibility of degradation in the reconstructed image. It has proved notoriously difficult to specify quantitatively and in a consistent manner, even with the help of sophisticated models of the human visual system, the degree of annoyance experienced by the observer in the presence of even simple image impairments. Since all compression schemes introduce imperfections when operation at low coding rates is attempted, there is significant interest in the development of such a numerical measure, but whether this will ever be possible for a wide range and degree of impairment remains to be seen, and for the present we must be satisfied with the results of extensive and closely controlled subjective testing, carried out at considerable cost in terms of time and money.

1.3 Predictive coding

At this point we consider briefly the technique of predictive coding. Although in one respect it is the main alternative to transform coding as a method of image data compression, it is more relevant to this volume than at first appears to be the case, since the two approaches are frequently combined to form a 'hybrid' coding scheme (see the following). The principle is very simply stated. Since the image data source is assumed to be highly correlated, on *average* the picture elements lying in the same neighbourhood will tend to have similar amplitudes. We may therefore use the value(s) of one or more earlier elements (which have been previously coded) in the same line, or in a previous line or lines, or frame(s) to form a prediction of the present element. Given the nature of the image in a statistical context, we expect, again on average, that the prediction will be quite good, and that the magnitude of the difference signal formed by subtracting the prediction from the actual value of the present element will be quite small. This signal is then coded and transmitted or stored. In order to reconstruct the element value, the same prediction is carried out in the decoder, and the difference signal added to it. Carried out properly, the only error (ignoring external channel effects) is that involved in quantising the difference signal. The method is simple, easy to implement, and with an adaptive system gives good quality images in the 1–2 bit/element range. It is, however, quite sensitive to variations in input data statistics and also to channel errors.

1.4   Transform coding

Whilst the mechanism of operation of predictive coding is easy to appreciate, that of transform coding is perhaps more elusive. Possibly the simplest short explanation is to call upon the reader's knowledge of the operation of the Fourier transform, which effects a spectral decomposition of the temporal or spatial domain input signal. In fact the Fourier transform has often been used for image coding, but has now been largely superseded by other transforms which have the advantage of higher coding efficiency and a requirement for real number manipulations only. For an image with high inter-element correlation, many of the higher-order spectral components will be small and may either be coded with very few bits or deleted completely. As an alternative interpretation, the operation of the transform may be seen as producing spectral coefficient sequences which are approximately uncorrelated; in other words, most of the redundancy in the input signal has been removed. Compared with predictive coding the method is relatively complex, and its implementation has benefitted greatly from the recent advances in high-speed digital hardware. An adaptive system will give good image quality (provided that the input data does not have large amounts of intricate spatial detail) at rates between 0.5 and 1.0 bit/element. It is somewhat less sensitive to errors than predictive coding, but since those errors that do influence system performance manifest themselves in a manner completely different from that which obtains for the latter approach, direct comparison is difficult.

1.5   Hybrid coding

It is probably the case that, were the requirements of implementation of transform coding not quite so severe (or had been considered to be so some 10 years ago), hybrid coding would not have achieved the prominence it has. The difficulties of carrying out fast two-dimensional transforms, however, in order to take advantage of the correlation existing in both horizontal and vertical directions in the image, prompted the use of a one-dimensional transform in one axial direction (horizontally, for example), followed by a predictive coding operation carried out between like members of the set of horizontal coefficient vectors. In this case the significant vertical correlation assumed to exist within the image ensures that, on average, the entries in those vectors will have similar values, as do the original spatial domain elements in a given locality. Again, given the availability of fast two-dimensional transform processing, the predictive operation may be carried out between transform coefficients in the same location but situated in different frames, to allow the hybrid coding of moving images. In fact, variations on this theme are possible: the predictive step may, for instance, be carried out first, which requires a rather more complex system. Loosely speaking, the characteristics of such an approach may be said to lie between those of the two constituent methods, and minimum coding rates are not as low as those of pure transform coding but implementation is easier. As in the two previous cases, the use of adaptive techniques is necessary to achieve rates around 1 bit/element with adequate reconstructed image quality.

1.6   Chapter contents

Chapter 2 is entitled Statistical Properties of Images. A knowledge of the statistical properties of the input data is essential for the efficient design of coding schemes of the types discussed earlier. This chapter develops statistical and spectral measures which can be used for the characterisation of images and then applies them to typical scenes in an attempt to indicate the relation between image detail and coding performance.

Chapter 3 is entitled Orthogonal Transforms for Image Coding. This chapter describes in detail one- and two-dimensional transform operations and then considers the specific properties of those transforms used in image coding. The performance of the various transforms is compared using both statistical approaches and actual image data.

Chapter 4 is entitled Transform Coefficient Quantisation and Bit Allocation. For digital transmission or storage, the transform coefficients must be quantised and coded in the most efficient way possible if low data rates are to be achieved. Coefficient sequence distributions are determined for test images and compared with theoretical models in order to allow quantisation procedures to be developed, and methods are described which allow varying numbers of bits to be allocated to the coefficient sequences.

Chapter 5 is entitled Practical Coding Techniques. This chapter is divided into three sections. The first deals with the basic principles of adaptive coding of still images using both two-dimensional and hybrid techniques, and the second considers coding of moving images by three-dimensional or hybrid (two-dimensional transform/predictive coding) methods. Frame difference techniques and motion compensation are also included. The final section covers the transform coding of colour images in both component and composite format.

Chapter 6 is entitled The Human Visual Response. The permissible nature and amount of visible degradation produced when an image is coded at a low data rate are closely connected with the visual properties of the human observer. In this chapter models for the human visual system are developed, and their application in the assessment of image quality and their more direct use as part of a transform coding scheme are described.

Chapter 7 is entitled Fast Transforms and System Implementation. The first part of this chapter details the development of the fast transform, without which the transform coding operation (and many others) would have remained in the realm of computer simulation, and then examines fast algorithms for each of the transforms described in Chapter 3. The second part is concerned with matters of implementation, i.e., the development of coding systems in hardware which, although not so widely reported in the literature as simulation experiments, is the real object of the investigation.

Chapter 8 is entitled Error and Noise Effects. In a practical system, approximations in the implementation of numerical operations and errors in the communication channel or storage process will inevitably influence the quality of the reconstructed image. Such effects are considered here, together with methods by which they may be alleviated.

Chapter 9 is entitled Rate Distortion Theory and Image Coding. Some years ago, Shannon posed a fundamental question in communication theory. Given a prespecified source signal, what is the minimum channel capacity necessary to transmit the information from that source to the receiver with a prescribed degree of fidelity? The general rate-distortion relation has occupied information theoreticians ever since, and this chapter is an attempt, using a minimum of mathematics, to indicate the connection between the one- and two-dimensional forms of the theory and various aspects of image coding.

1.7   Further reading

This chapter has sought, in a very brief fashion, to set the main topic of this book in the more general context of image data compression. Further and more wide-ranging discussion of the subject may be found in two review articles: Jain (1981) and Netravali and Limb (1980).

Chapter 2

Statistical Properties of Images

2.1 Introduction

In the previous chapter stress was laid on the importance of certain image properties in the development of image data compression systems. In the present chapter those properties will be defined, initially in the data domain, and subsequently in the transform domain, and then three more or less 'typical' images will be taken as practical examples to show the range of values which might be expected of those properties in practice. It is appropriate to refer briefly here to another matter discussed in more detail in Chapter 9. The essence of information transmission is the communication to the recipient of material that is previously unknown to him, and it is almost certainly the case that we shall not know precisely, even at the transmitter, the complete statistical representation of the sum total of the image data to be coded (in fact, as it turns out, there are other reasons, explained in detail in the course of this chapter but irrelevant to the present discussion, why this should be so). We must therefore be content to optimise our image coding and transmission system by using what we hope is a representative selection of test image inputs, in which case the statistical characterisations developed in this chapter must be averaged in some predetermined way over the test selection. Furthermore, if a representative set of images is found to have reasonably 'well-behaved' statistical properties, it would seem at first sight (at least in theory) that the possibility exists of using not directly measured numerical data (mean, variance, and so on) but rather a simple model definable in terms of a small number of parameters whose equivalent in the transform domain may be used to determine an appropriate coding strategy. In fact, image data may assume such a wide variety of forms as to make any 'global' model of this type so approximate as to be almost useless. On the other hand, if we restrict the application of such modelling to input data which has little rapidly varying detail (head and shoulders images, for example), it will at least serve as a guide to the subsequent coding of transform coefficients (Clarke, 1984a).

2.2 Image properties in the data domain

Images under consideration here are assumed to be of the kind generated by a digital image processing system, typically a television camera or scanner of some description which operates initially in an analogue fashion and is then followed by a stage of analogue-to-digital conversion which produces binary words B bits in length, in which case we may identify 2^B separate video levels. A frequently chosen value for B is 8, and there are therefore 256 distinguishable levels which the digitised image signal may assume—it being generally considered that if such a signal is processed in this way, i.e., by representation of the real-valued analogue signal using words at least 8 bits in length, then it will not be possible visually to detect any difference between the processed (digital) version and its unprocessed (analogue) counterpart.

We commence, therefore, with a single image field, consisting of a two-dimensional array of picture elements (frequently referred to as pixels, or pels), each of which may take on an integer value in the range $(0, 2^B - 1)$. At this point it may be in order to sound a note of warning in regard to the analogue-to-digital conversion process. If the signal applied to the converter is a conventional video signal emanating from a television camera, it will, of course, consist of segments of active video waveform separated by synchronisation and blanking pulses. If the converter is set to accept the maximum excursion of this 'composite' waveform, then the dynamic range of the active video component will be less by a significant factor than that allowed for the composite signal. What seems, therefore, to be a true 8-bit video signal may be something quite different, and this has important implications where comparisons between systems are concerned, particularly in regard to quoted values of the normalised error between an original image and its necessarily imperfect reconstruction. Thus the average of some function of the numerical difference between original and reconstructed element amplitudes is normalised by the average of the same function of the input signal amplitude; and whereas the former quantity is independent of the reference level the latter is not and is artificially increased if it is measured from the bottom of the video synchronising pulses instead of from the lowest point on the active video waveform. This leads to remarkably small (i.e., good) error figures being quoted for given degrees of data compression. The effect is illustrated in Fig. 2.1. One good reason for making initial statistical measurements on test images (apart from the help that such measurements give in system design) is that one is then under no illusion as to system performance comparisons made using arbitrary test images.

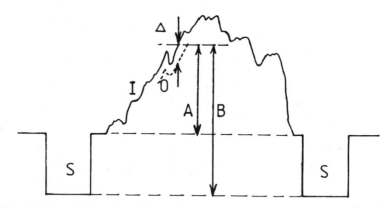

FIG. 2.1. Section of a typical video waveform. Here, A is the actual active input amplitude, B the measured input amplitude, I the input waveform, O the reconstructed waveform, Δ the error in reconstruction, S the synchronising pulses, $f(\cdot)$ the predetermined error measure, $E_1 - f(\Delta, A)$ the correct normalised error measure and $E_2 - f(\Delta, B)$ the incorrect normalised error measure.

We return, then, to our array of picture elements, which we allow to be of extent $N \times M$. Often it is convenient to process images having the same number of elements per row as rows, in which case $N = M$, and a typical value of N is 512, although with the rapidly increasing availability of large image stores, higher values are becoming more common. Furthermore, the fact that the array size is usually an integral power of two is mainly a consequence of the use of fast processing routines, to be discussed in Chapter 7. It will not have escaped the reader's attention that such an array of numbers (which is all that the original scene 'observed' by the camera now is) has the form of a matrix. Indeed, discrete two-dimensinal image fields are ideal from the point of view of manipulation by any of the very extensive range of matrix operations which mathematicians have devised, and this approach will frequently be employed subsequently. For the moment we investigate one or two simple image properties from an information theoretic viewpoint.

2.2.1 Information theory and images

Since the purpose of image coding for storage and/or transmission is the retrieval or communication of information, it is logical to investigate the information content of the source material, as we shall then be in a position to make use of several powerful theoretical results in information theory. The reader is assumed to be conversant with the elements of that theory, and the relevant relationships are introduced briefly later. Good introductions to the subject can be found in Pierce (1962) and Gallager (1968). One result which is immediately of interest is the fact that it is possible, in principle, to calculate the minimum number of bits per image sample necessary (given an optimum encoding scheme) to preserve all the information within the image, i.e., to allow us to reconstruct it without error. An objection may be raised here that transform coding schemes do not operate in this way, coding images at rates below the 'information-preserving' limit in return for an acceptable degree of distortion in reconstruction. This is of course true, but it still remains the case that the figure obtained is a guide to what will happen when a particular image is subjected to a transform coding operation. The lower the figure, the easier the image will be to code at rates below the limit for a predetermined level of distortion. In practice, it is usually difficult to calculate the limiting figure exactly, due to the enormous number of interrelationships between the occurrences of various element values within the image, but measurements on low-order distributions are not too difficult to make and allow an estimate to be made. We begin with the first-order distribution.

2.2.1.1 *The first-order distribution*

The fundamental notion in information theory is that of surprise or uncertainty, unlikely events carrying more information than likely ones, and vice versa. Thus, if event $x = X$ occurs with probability $p(x)$, where x is an arbitary image element in the present context and X a particular luminance value, then the self-information of that occurrence is defined as

$$i(x) = \log[1/p(x)] = -\log p(x) \qquad (2.1)$$

It is inappropriate here to consider in detail the formal establishment of a measure of probability, a comprehensive discussion of which may be found in, for example, Papoulis (1965); it suffices to take the event $x = X$ as the occurrence of one of the 2^B integer outputs of the analogue-to-digital converter, and the probability of occurrence of X, $p(x)$, as the number of times that $x = X$ divided by the total number of occurrences of all possible values of the converter output, i.e., the total number of elements within the image (or in the set of images, if measurements on more than one test image are being carried out). This 'relative frequency' interpretation of probability is, in spite of the existence of more abstruse and perhaps more formally acceptable ones, the only one which is practicable given, as mentioned earlier, only incomplete prior knowledge of the range of images which the coding system is to be called upon to process.

The base of the logarithm in Eq. (2.1) is arbitrary but will, of course, affect the numerical value of $i(x)$. Two bases are in common use. If we employ base 2 then $i(x)$ is expressed in bits, a convenient and easily appreciated unit of information. On the other hand natural logarithms are more convenient in theoretical developments in information theory (the reason being the frequent appearance of exponential terms), in which case $i(x)$ is expressed in natural units, or nats. Conversion between the two is easily carried out by the use of the relation

$$\log_2(\cdot) = \log_2(e) \ln(\cdot)$$
$$= (1/\ln 2) \ln(\cdot)$$
$$= 1.443 \ln(\cdot) \qquad (2.2)$$

where the notation $\log(\cdot)$, etc., implies the logarithm of the term in parentheses.

It is also useful to recall that

$$\log_2(\cdot) = \log_2(10) \log_{10}(\cdot)$$
$$= [1/\log_{10}(2)] \log_{10}(\cdot)$$
$$= 3.322 \log_{10}(\cdot) \qquad (2.3)$$

It will be noted that it is not necessary to consider the value taken on by Eq. (2.1) when $p(x) = 0$. Should all outcomes be equally likely, then, since there are 2^B possibilities, $p(x = X) = 2^{-B}$ and so, assuming base 2 logarithms,

$$i(x) = -\log_2(2^{-B}) = B \qquad \text{bits} \qquad (2.4)$$

and thus a binary word B bits long contains B bits of self-information. It is now necessary to average the value of self-information per picture element over the whole image. Thus

$$H(x) = \sum_{x=1}^{2^B} p(x)i(x) = -\sum_{x=1}^{2^B} p(x) \log_2 p(x) \qquad \text{bits} \qquad (2.5)$$

where we take $0 \log 0 = 0$, if necessary, and note that, although the 2^B analogue-to-digital converter outputs are here indexed from 1 to 2^B, we could equally well have used 0 to $2^B - 1$, for the values of $i(x)$ and $H(x)$ depend solely upon the probabilities of occurrence of the various output levels and *not* upon their numerical values, contrary to other statistical image properties discussed later in this chapter. The quantity $H(x)$ is termed the entropy of the sequence of source outputs which constitutes the image array and is defined as the average value of the self-information of the array. It is not difficult to show that the maximum value of $H(x)$ occurs when all outcomes (possible values of x) are equally likely, in which case

$$H(x) = - \sum_{x=1}^{2^B} 2^{-B} \log_2(2^{-B}) = B \qquad \text{bits} \qquad (2.6)$$

as in Eq. (2.4), in which case the average number of bits per image element needed to represent the array without loss of information is B. All naturally produced images have a probability distribution which departs from this uniform situation, however, and so can be represented by fewer than B bits per element on average. As mentioned previously, the degree to which $H(x)$ is less than B indicates how easy it will be to code the image efficiently, down to a value of $H(x)$ bits per element on average for perfect reconstruction, or below $H(x)$ if a certain amount of distortion is allowable, in each case coding and reconstruction being performed on an element by element basis. Section 2.4 contains practical results of measurements of B and $H(x)$ for typical images and demonstrates, in fact, that the rewards of such an approach hardly justify the effort involved. We therefore consider next a refinement of the measurement of $H(x)$ which will illustrate the advantages of using a system such as transform coding, which operates not on single elements but on several image elements at a time.

2.2.1.2   *The second-order distribution*

The relationship developed in the previous section allows us to determine the average information content of an image on a 'per element' basis, i.e., neglecting any interdependence between image data points. Obviously, since this approach negates the whole rationale of efficient coding as described in Chapter 1, we should expect to be able to do significantly better by taking such interdependence into account, and it is an easily observed fact that most images have considerable areas over which luminance values do not vary to any great extent. A logical continuation of the previous development, then, is to consider elements not singly, but in pairs, and to determine a corresponding value for the entropy of such an arrangement, which should, by the foregoing argument, be smaller than the per element entropy $H(x)$. Accordingly, a joint entropy $H(x, y)$ is defined in a similar way to $H(x)$, where the relevant event is $(x = X, y = Y)$, and the two equalities are to be simultaneously satisfied by x and y, which are the values of adjacent elements in the image array. [Here x and y may be pairs taken horizontally or vertically and, even when the configuration of the sampling lattice is such that the element spacing horizontally is the same as that vertically, there is of course no necessity for the corresponding values of $H(x, y)$ to be the same.] Thus

$$H(x, y) = - \sum_{x,y=1}^{2^B} p(x, y) \log_2 p(x, y) \qquad \text{bits} \qquad (2.7)$$

is the average value of self-information of a pair of image elements. If there was no statistical relationship between the elements of any pair, averaged over the whole image, then we should expect that $H(x, y) = 2H(x)$, i.e., that each element of the pair contained the same amount of information $H(x)$ (convenient expressions for calculating entropies are given in Appendix 1). It is the case in practice, however, that $H(x, y) \leqslant 2H(x)$ and so

$$2H(x) - H(x, y) \geqslant 0 \qquad (2.8)$$

and it follows that, knowing the first element of a pair, the information imparted by a subsequent knowledge of the other element is less than $H(x)$, reflecting the fact that, on average, knowing the value of one element tells us something about its neighbour (the qualification 'on average' is essential since we might just select, as an arbitrary example, a pair of elements one on either side of a sharp luminance transition in the image). The difference between $H(x, y)$ and $H(x)$ is

$$H(y/x) = - \sum_{x,y=1}^{2^B} p(x, y) \log_2 p(y/x)$$

$$= H(x, y) - H(x) \qquad (2.9)$$

where the expression $H(y/x)$ indicates the average self-information in the occurrence of Y(i.e., $y = Y$) given that we know that the previous element has value X, and is termed the conditional entropy of y given x. Two limiting cases may serve to clarify the relationships between Eq. (2.8) and Eq. (2.9). Suppose, first, that Eq. (2.8) is satisfied with equality. Then, from Eq. (2.9)

$$H(y/x) = H(x) \qquad (2.10)$$

and the amount of information needed to specify the value of y is $H(x)$, reflecting the fact that knowledge of the value of x is of no use for this purpose when X and Y are independent. Again, suppose that $H(y/x)$ in Eq. (2.9) is zero. Then

$$H(x, y) = H(x) \qquad (2.11)$$

and *both* element values in the pair are completely specified by the single amount of information $H(x)$. Knowing x therefore informs us of the exact value of y also, or, in other words, every pair of elements has members of the same value. In short, the degree to which first-order statistical dependence within the image reduces the necessary coding rate is

$$2H(x) - H(x, y) = 2H(x) - H(y/x) - H(x)$$

$$= H(x) - H(y/x) \qquad (2.12)$$

It is useful to note that the preceding development is paralleled in many elementary texts on information theory, but usually in the context of information transmission over a noisy channel, where x is the symbol transmitted and y the symbol received. The quantity specified by Eq. (2.8) or Eq. (2.12) is the rate at which information is transmitted by the channel. Again, Section 2.4 presents measurements made on typical images of the various quantities referred to earlier, in order to give some idea of the advantage gained by considering not single elements but pairs of elements in the context of image coding.

2.2.1.3   *Higher-order distributions*

It has been shown in the previous two subsections of this chapter that it is advantageous to consider image elements not singly, but in pairs taken either horizontally or vertically over the image array (it is hardly necessary to carry out a mathematical analysis to be convinced that, since pairs taken diagonally must have a greater separation, and that the greater the separation between the members of any pair the less likely they are to be similar; taking pairs in any direction other than horizontally or vertically will be disadvantageous). Why not, therefore, extend the approach to cover not just pairs of elements, but blocks of several elements taken either in one or two dimensions? This is, of course, exactly what is done when an actual transform coding operation is carried out, as will be described in detail subsequently, and it forms the basis of the other widely investigated form of efficient image coding, i.e., differential pulse code modulation (DPCM) (see Chapter 5). The difficulty is that we are not using such blocks of elements for coding purposes, where we might reasonably expect the relatively straightforward result that the coding efficiency increases with increasing block size, but rather for characterising a test image, and so it is a matter of making detailed measurements of element distribution conditioned upon the state of neighbouring elements. To illustrate the problem consider the measurements necessary for the test images discussed later in this chapter which, in the case of the grey-scale images, have been digitised nominally to an accuracy of 8 bits. The number of possible levels is therefore 256, and $H(x)$ is determined simply by counting the number of times each value between 0 and 255 is encountered within the image. A single graph suffices then to represent completely this histogram distribution. When we move to measurements of $H(x, y)$ the same approach is taken for the values assumed by y, with the important modification that this must be carried out for *each* of the 256 values of x. Thus, 256 curves are now necessary to represent the results of this measurement, and the effort required to carry out the analysis is greater than that needed for the first-order distribution by a factor of 256, or 2^B. In short, increasing the order of the calculation by one increases the computational load by 2^B, and so a move even to a third-order distribution has rarely been reported in the literature. [Note that this is not true for binary images, for which $B = 1$, and for which higher-order distributions can be determined with relative ease; the work of Gabrielli *et al.* (1979) on third-order correlation is also interesting in this respect.]

One such determination is that of Schreiber (1956), whose paper is interesting not only from the point of view of his results but also from that of the special experimental arrangement devised to carry out the measurements. He also makes the significant point that, when considering higher-order distributions, many of the allowable combinations of elements (say perhaps alternating maximum and minimum luminance levels) will occur only rarely and therefore the determination of their probability of occurrence (relative frequency) will be subject to large statistical errors which, of course, may be reduced by increasing the number of images considered, but only with the expenditure of much more computation time. Schreiber concludes that, based on a study of 6-bit (64-level) images, the information content of a picture element given a knowledge of the two preceding elements is lower than that given a knowledge of only one element by a 'significant, though small' amount (something rather less than 0.5 bit) and that attempting to employ higher-order distributions for image coding brings rapidly diminishing returns. This conclusion is challenged, however, by Limb (1968) who determined joint entropies up to the fourth order for 4-bit images of varying degrees of detail. His conclusion is that, for a highly detailed image, there is a distinct fall in entropy as we move from order 3 to order 4 and that, for all types of scene, the fourth-order entropy is about the same. The significant difficulties associated with entropy measurement where both the number of bits per element (say 7–8) and the order ($\geqslant 3$) are large seems to have prevented further work in this area. It is unlikely, too, that the results obtained would justify the expenditure of the high degree of effort necessary.

2.2.2   Other statistical properties of images

Having touched upon one or two information theoretic measures which may be used to characterise images we now move to more generally used properties, developed originally for the statistical representation of random signals, which have the advantage that, by the application of certain results in transform theory, their significance may be carried over in a relatively straightforward way from the data (spatial) domain to the transform domain. For the most useful of these measures, the covariance function, it will be seen that for certain classes of images it is possible, as mentioned in the introduction, to provide a reasonably accurate model which may subsequently be employed in the design of a transform coding scheme. In fact, such characterisation is not entirely unconnected with the material of the previous sections of this chapter, since Elias (1951) has demonstrated the relation, under certain conditions, between autocorrelation and entropy measures. In general such modelling must be based on the average properties of a given set of test images and so will not necessarily 'fit' any individual image particularly well. In Appendix 2 there is a brief discussion of the general statistical properties of signals, with particular reference to those that are stationary and/or ergodic, and to time and ensemble averages. From that discussion it will be appreciated that the formally correct approach to image characterisation would be to assume the existence of a very large set of 'typical' (in some sense) test images, and then to look on the sequence of luminance values at a particular location (fixed over all images) as a member of the 'ensemble' of outputs of the source which was assumed to be responsible for the generation of the test images in the first place. Since such a procedure is quite impractical, however, we are forced to limit our measurements to a relatively small number of 'likely' scenes. In such cases it is only possible to determine the properties of individual (two-dimensional) images, for which we therefore determine the spatial properties. [Note that Hunt and Cannon (1976), Hunt (1980), and Strickland (1983) have attempted to remove the stationary assumption usually made in this context.] This is then the spatial equivalent to the measurement of the properties of a one-dimensional signal source with time as the independent variable, and the only complication which arises is that concerning the properties of image elements in relation one with the other (correlation) for in a two-dimensional image there are, for this purpose, not one but two independent variables. To start with we consider the two most easily measured properties, mean and variance.

2.2.2.1 *Image mean and variance*

The mean of the (two-dimensional) image field is given by the spatial average of the luminance values of all the picture elements. Thus

$$\bar{x} = \frac{1}{N \times M} \sum_{n=1}^{N} \sum_{m=1}^{M} x_{nm} \tag{2.13}$$

where x_{nm} is an arbitrary element of the image field, which contains N rows and M columns. Alternatively, given that we know the probability of occurrence of the various allowable luminance levels l (in the present case 2^B in number, where B is the accuracy of digitisation in bits)

$$\bar{x} = \sum_{l=1}^{2^B} x_l p(x_l)$$ (2.14)

where

$$p(x_l) = n_l/(N \times M)$$ (2.15)

and n_l is the number of image elements taking on value l. Note that, since all image elements are non-negative, this property also applies to $\bar{x}$.

The variance of the image field is the average value of the square of the difference between the value of an arbitrary image element and the mean. Thus

$$\sigma^2 = \frac{1}{N \times M} \sum_{n=1}^{N} \sum_{m=1}^{M} (x_{nm} - \bar{x})^2$$ (2.16)

or

$$\sigma^2 = \sum_{l=1}^{2^B} (x_l - \bar{x})^2 p(x_l)$$ (2.17)

where $p(x_l)$ has the interpretation of Eq. (2.15). The square root of the variance is, of course, the standard deviation. There is a more or less vague relation between image mean and variance which arises because the actual value that any element can assume is constrained by the maximum and minimum output levels of the sensing and digitising device. Suppose, for example, that we find that the mean is near to the upper limit. Then it is not possible for large positive differences between element values and the mean to exist. A similar argument applies to low values of the mean. We therefore expect the variance of the image field (other things being equal) to be greatest for images with mean values around the centre of the analogue-to-digital converter output range and to decrease as the mean moves towards either extreme. There is a further, and more useful, connection between mean and variance which is helpful in the characterisation of image properties. It is conventional to consider the squared value of an image element as a measure of the energy it contains. We can then separate this quantity, when determined over the complete image field, into two parts. Consider the variance as defined either by Eq. (2.16) or Eq. (2.17). Thus

$$\sigma^2 = E(x - \bar{x})^2$$ (2.18)

where, for simplicity, the subscript previously attached to x is omitted, and $E(\cdot)$ is the expectation operator (see Appendix 2) which is used here to define an averaging operation over the whole image. Expanding Eq. (2.18) we have

$$\sigma^2 = E(x^2 + \bar{x}^2 - 2x\bar{x})$$
$$= E(x^2) + \bar{x}^2 - 2\bar{x}E(x)$$
$$= E(x^2) - \bar{x}^2 \qquad (2.19)$$

since $E(\bar{x}^2) = \bar{x}^2$ (the expected value of the mean is the mean itself) and $E(x) = \bar{x}$. The variance σ^2 may thus be considered to be the difference between $E(x^2)$, the average total element energy, and $\bar{x}^2$, the mean energy per element. It is often said, therefore, that

$$E(x^2) \quad = \quad \sigma^2 \quad + \quad \bar{x}^2$$
$$\text{Total energy} = \text{`AC' Energy} + \text{`DC' Energy} \qquad (2.20)$$

We shall have occasion to refer to this relation again in the context of the energy content of blocks of transform coefficients, where it will apply equally well. As far as computation is concerned, Eq. (2.19) allows the determination of the variance of an image field in a single operation, whereas the use of Eq. (2.18) necessitates the prior calculation of the mean.

Thus the variance of the image field (or of a transformed segment of it) gives us information on the degree to which the elements vary in value, i.e., on the image or segment 'activity', the general consequence being that regions of high activity require a greater coding rate (bits per sample) than those of low activity. Unfortunately, whilst variance is frequently used in this context, it is a very insensitive indicator of anything but gross element variations, and the reason is easy to see. Consider the one-dimensional data sub-sequences

$$1 \quad 1 \quad 1 \quad 1 \quad 0 \quad 0 \quad 0 \quad 0 \qquad (2.21a)$$

$$1 \quad 0 \quad 1 \quad 0 \quad 1 \quad 0 \quad 1 \quad 0 \qquad (2.21b)$$

Both have the same variance and so the same 'activity' (see Chapter 5) using that particular measure. The sequences will have completely different sets of AC transform coefficients, however, and although the transform variance will equal that of the data domain, the result will be that the dominant coefficient in (2.21b) will be allocated fewer bits than that in (2.21a), whereas the allocation for both coefficients ought to be the same (see Chapter 4). Simple variance measures, therefore, are not good indicators of specific details of image or block activity.

2.2.2.2   One-dimensional correlation properties of images

The reader will have noticed the emphasis placed upon the properties of image elements, not so much taken in isolation as considered one with another, in the development presented previously. Since such interdependence lies at the heart of any statistical data compression scheme, it follows that the correlation properties of images are of considerable importance in the development of transform processing techniques. We begin their consideration by rewriting Eq. (2.18) as

$$\sigma_{xx}^2 = E(x - \bar{x})(x - \bar{x})$$ (2.22)

where the subscripting is necessary for the following discussion and implies taking the expected value of the termwise product of each element, with the mean subtracted, with itself. In a similar manner, we may form an equivalent operation between two different sequences, thus

$$\sigma_{xy}^2 = E(x - \bar{x})(y - \bar{y})$$ (2.23)

where sequence y has mean $\bar{y}$, and σ_{xy}^2 is termed the covariance of the two sequences. The approach can be extended to define the covariance between any number of sequences, but for the moment we shall include only one more, sequence z with mean $\bar{z}$. There are now three covariance terms, σ_{xy}^2 [in Eq. (2.23)] and

$$\sigma_{xz}^2 = E(x - \bar{x})(z - \bar{z})$$ (2.24)

$$\sigma_{yz}^2 = E(y - \bar{y})(z - \bar{z})$$ (2.25)

and three variance terms σ_{xx}^2, σ_{yy}^2, σ_{zz}^2, all of the form of Eq. (2.22). We now form the vector

$$[\mathbf{X} - \bar{\mathbf{X}}] = \begin{bmatrix} (x - \bar{x}) \\ (y - \bar{y}) \\ (z - \bar{z}) \end{bmatrix}$$ (2.26)

and evaluate the quantity $E\{(\mathbf{X} - \bar{\mathbf{X}})(\mathbf{X} - \bar{\mathbf{X}})^T\}$ to obtain the covariance matrix

$$\mathrm{COV}(\mathbf{X}) = E\begin{bmatrix} (x - \bar{x})(x - \bar{x}) & (x - \bar{x})(y - \bar{y}) & (x - \bar{x})(z - \bar{z}) \\ (y - \bar{y})(x - \bar{x}) & (y - \bar{y})(y - \bar{y}) & (y - \bar{y})(z - \bar{z}) \\ (z - \bar{z})(x - \bar{x}) & (z - \bar{z})(y - \bar{y}) & (z - \bar{z})(z - \bar{z}) \end{bmatrix}$$ (2.27)

which may alternatively be written, employing previously developed equations for the various terms, as

$$\mathrm{COV}(\mathbf{X}) = \begin{bmatrix} \sigma_{xx}^2 & \sigma_{xy}^2 & \sigma_{xz}^2 \\ \sigma_{yx}^2 & \sigma_{yy}^2 & \sigma_{yz}^2 \\ \sigma_{zx}^2 & \sigma_{zy}^2 & \sigma_{zz}^2 \end{bmatrix}$$ (2.28)

Equation (2.28) defines the covariance matrix for the three sequences x, y and z. It can be seen to be a symmetric matrix ($\sigma_{xy}^2 = \sigma_{yx}^2$, etc.), where the diagonal elements represent the variances of the original sequences and the off-diagonal terms represent the covariances between different sequences. In the more general case in which there are K sequences

$$
\text{COV}(X) = \begin{bmatrix} \sigma_{11}^2 & \sigma_{12}^2 & \sigma_{13}^2 & \cdots & \sigma_{1K}^2 \\ \sigma_{21}^2 & \sigma_{22}^2 & \sigma_{23}^2 & \cdots & \vdots \\ \vdots & \vdots & \vdots & & \vdots \\ \sigma_{K1}^2 & \sigma_{K2}^2 & \sigma_{K3}^2 & \cdots & \sigma_{KK}^2 \end{bmatrix} \tag{2.29}
$$

where $X = x_0 \, x_2 \, x_3 \cdots x_{M-1}$
a vector only

We now need to interpret Eq. (2.29) in a way which will allow its application to the inter-element relationships which exist within a single image, initially restricting the treatment to the one-dimensional case. At the moment it relates to K different sequences, each with its own (possibly different) mean and variance. For a single image we wish to use the equation in a way which extracts all K sequences from the one original sequence of picture elements. Consider first a single line of the scanned image containing elements $x_1, x_2, x_3, \ldots, x_M$. The first off-diagonal element in the covariance matrix will be that corresponding to the sequences

$$
\begin{aligned} a &= x_1 \quad x_2 \quad x_3 \quad \cdots \quad x_{M-1} \\ b &= x_2 \quad x_3 \quad x_4 \quad \cdots \quad x_M \end{aligned} \tag{2.30}
$$

if sequence 'x' is $1 * 8 = 8$ will produce 'cov(r)' $.8 * 8 = 64$

and we shall therefore calculate the pointwise products and average

$$
\sigma_{12}^2 = \sigma_{21}^2 = E(a - \bar{a})(b - \bar{b}) \tag{2.31}
$$

For convenience we assume that $\bar{a} = \bar{b} = $ the overall mean $\bar{x}$, and so

$$
\sigma_{12}^2 = \sigma_{21}^2 = \frac{1}{M-1} \sum_{m=1}^{M-1} (x_m - \bar{x})(x_{m+1} - \bar{x}) \tag{2.32}
$$

is the 'one-step' covariance of the image line in question. In general,

$$
\sigma_{1,k+1}^2 = \sigma_{k+1,1}^2 = \frac{1}{M-k} \sum_{m=1}^{M-k} (x_m - \bar{x})(x_{m+k} - \bar{x}) \tag{2.33}
$$

is the 'kth step' covariance of the sequence.

The approach may be extended to cover all lines of the image by considering those lines to be ordered into a single vector of length $N \times M$, where there are N lines in the image, provided that care is taken not to include products involving elements at the end of one line and the beginning of the next in the calculation. Alternatively, results for separate lines may be averaged over the image and, of course, the calculation can also be carried out vertically. Equation (2.33) is sometimes modified, with the purpose of providing a better covariance estimate (one with reduced variance), to the form

$$\sigma^2_{1,k+1} = \sigma^2_{k+1,1} = \frac{1}{M} \sum_{m=1}^{M-k} (x_m - \bar{x})(x_{m+k} - \bar{x}) \tag{2.34}$$

but, as long as $k \ll M$, the difference is marginal (Jenkins and Watts, 1968). Since in the present case we have considered the image as a single sequence of elements it has but one value of variance, and the same applies to the various k-step covariances (thus there are one-step covariances starting with elements x_1 and x_2, x_2 and x_3, and so on). Hence referring to Eq. (2.29)

$$\sigma^2_{11} = \sigma^2_{22} = \cdots = \sigma^2_{KK} \qquad = \sigma^2$$

and

$$\sigma^2_{12} = \sigma^2_{23} = \cdots = \sigma^2_{K-1,K} = \sigma^2_1$$

Thus the mean and variance are now taken to be constant, and the covariance is a function only of relative displacement, and not of actual location within the sequence. The image is therefore considered to be 'wide-sense' stationary (see Appendix 2) and Eq. (2.29) reduces to

$$\text{COV}(\mathbf{X}) = \begin{bmatrix} \sigma^2 & \sigma^2_1 & \sigma^2_2 & \cdots & \sigma^2_{K-1} \\ \sigma^2_1 & \sigma^2 & \sigma^2_1 & \cdots & \sigma^2_{K-2} \\ \vdots & \vdots & \vdots & & \vdots \\ \sigma^2_{K-1} & \sigma^2_{K-2} & \sigma^2_{K-3} & \cdots & \sigma^2 \end{bmatrix} \tag{2.35}$$

Matrices of the form of Eq. (2.35), with diagonal elements equal, are of general importance in signal theory and processing. For a discussion of the properties of such 'Toeplitz' matrices see Kac et $al.$ (1953) and for a more general review see Gray (1972). It is convenient to normalise the matrix entries in Eq. (2.35) by the overall variance to give

$$\text{COV}(\mathbf{X}) = \sigma^2 \begin{bmatrix} 1 & \rho_1 & \rho_2 & \cdots & \rho^{K-1} \\ \rho_1 & 1 & \rho_1 & \cdots & \rho_{K-2} \\ \vdots & \vdots & \vdots & & \vdots \\ \rho_{K-1} & \rho_{K-2} & \rho_{K-3} & \cdots & 1 \end{bmatrix} \tag{2.36}$$

where

$$\rho_k = \begin{cases} 1, & \text{if} \quad k = 0 \\ \sigma^2_{|k|}/\sigma^2 & \text{if} \quad |k| = 1 \to K \end{cases} \tag{2.37}$$

is the k-step correlation coefficient. We note that the direction of relative displacement between the terms in the averaged product in Eq. (2.34) is immaterial. In one important case there is a simple functional relationship between the values of ρ_k which allows even further simplification of Eq. (2.36). In this case, which is very frequently considered to constitute a suitable, if approximate, model for an image field, the correlation coefficient at step k is related to the coefficient at step 1 by

$$\rho_k = \rho^{|k|} \tag{2.38}$$

where $\rho = \rho_1$.

Thus

$$\text{COR}(\mathbf{X}) = \begin{bmatrix} 1 & \rho & \rho^2 & \cdots & \rho^{K-1} \\ \rho & 1 & \rho & \cdots & \rho^{K-2} \\ \vdots & \vdots & \vdots & & \vdots \\ \rho^{K-1} & \rho^{K-2} & \rho^{K-3} & \cdots & 1 \end{bmatrix} \tag{2.39}$$

is the correlation (normalised covariance) matrix of the stationary 'first-order Markov' process. A formal definition of the process is given, for example, by Papoulis (1965). For the present purpose, it is sufficient to recognise that, as far as the influence of the past history of the element sequence upon the value of the present element is concerned, it is contained within the value of the previous element only. In fact, this model is not too inaccurate for the correlation/displacement relationship for images which are 'smooth', i.e., which contain relatively little rapidly varying detail, and it even works fairly well for the first few steps in more active images, but the often expressed criticism (see, e.g., Jain, 1976b; Booton and Ready, 1976; Mauersberger, 1979c) that it does not provide an accurate general representation of the correlation properties of image fields must be upheld; indeed, with only three parameters given (mean, variance and one-step correlation coefficient), it would be surprising if this were not the case.

The covariance/correlation matrix forms an important aspect of image characterisation in one dimension (the two-dimensional case will be dealt with subsequently). In passing, two other points are worth a brief remark. First, even in the one-dimensional case the representation is in matrix, and not vector, form, a point that occasionally causes some confusion; second, the prefix auto- is often used in connection with the terms covariance and correlation, indicating that the 'random' sequences involved, considered originally to emanate from different sources, are in fact all part of the same source output. The first-order Markov model for one-dimensional correlation produces a set of values of the kind defined by the first row or column of Eq. (2.39). Thus, suppose that the one-step correlation coefficient ρ were

0.95 (a typical value for relatively 'inactive' images). The relevant entries will then be

$$\rho_k = \rho^{|k|} = \begin{array}{ccccc} 1.000 & 0.950 & 0.903 & 0.857 & 0.815 \cdots \end{array}$$
$$k = \begin{array}{ccccc} 0 & 1 & 2 & 3 & 4 \end{array}$$

(handwritten annotations above: $\log \rho_k = K \log \rho =$ 0 -0.0223 -0.0443 -0.067 -0.0888)

$$\tag{2.40}$$

and the relationship will be a straight line if log ρ_k is plotted against k. An exponential form can also be used, involving a new parameter, thus

$$\rho_k = e^{-\alpha|k|} \tag{2.41}$$

(handwritten: $\pm \ln \rho^{|k|}$; e)

where $\alpha = -\ln \rho$. In the present example the value $\rho = 0.95$ corresponds to $\alpha = 0.0513$.

In Section 2.4 a modified exponential correlation model will be used in conjunction with a relatively 'well-behaved' test image and shown to give a reasonable fit to the measured values of correlation. This model is of the form

$$\rho_k = e^{-\alpha|k|^r} \tag{2.42}$$

where the parameters α and r may be optimised so that the model fits the measurements as well as possible. It must be reiterated, however, that this approach does not have a great deal of use in the general case.

2.2.2.3 *Two-dimensional correlation properties of images*

In the previous subsection a one-dimensional sequence of data points (in the present context, samples of an image generation process taken either horizontally or vertically across the image) was characterised by the (auto-) correlation properties of the data points within the sequence. Since an image is naturally a two-dimensional (at least) entity it is logical now to consider the equivalent extension of this form of representation. Recall that the one-dimensional covariance matrix has dimension $K \times K$ for a set of K random sequences (the correlation function measured up to a maximum separation between elements of $K - 1$). For an image array it is reasonable to suppose that we shall require to determine the correlation properties over a set of K sequences both horizontally and vertically. We thus have K sequences in the one direction as before, but there are now K of these K-length sequences arranged one after another in the other direction. The total number of sequences is therefore K^2, and we immediately encounter problems relating to the dimensions of the resulting matrix, which is now $K^2 \times K^2$. Thus, dealing with a one-dimensional 8×8 covariance matrix, for example, is one thing, but dealing with its two-dimensional counterpart, which will be 64×64 in extent, is quite another. The development of the two-dimensional case is nevertheless not only interesting, but important from the point of view of the correspondence between image properties in the data domain and in the transform domain, to be considered subsequently.

The technique used is that described by Pratt (1975, 1978) and consists of the conversion of a matrix into an equivalent vector by a rearrangement of the rows or columns. Thus the matrix

$$[X] = \begin{bmatrix} x_{11} & x_{12} & x_{13} \\ x_{21} & x_{22} & x_{23} \\ x_{31} & x_{32} & x_{33} \end{bmatrix} \qquad (2.43)$$

becomes, by row 'stacking',

$$\mathbf{X_R} = [x_{11} \quad x_{12} \quad x_{13} \quad x_{21} \quad x_{22} \quad x_{23} \quad x_{31} \quad x_{32} \quad x_{33}]^{\mathrm{T}} \qquad (2.44)$$

and, by column stacking

$$\mathbf{X_C} = [x_{11} \quad x_{21} \quad x_{31} \quad x_{12} \quad x_{22} \quad x_{32} \quad x_{13} \quad x_{23} \quad x_{33}]^{\mathrm{T}} \qquad (2.45)$$

where the transpose operation is included merely because it is conventional to write vectors as column vectors. Since the treatment becomes unwieldy in the extreme for larger values of K, we restrict ourselves here to the case $K = 3$, although the technique is, of course, applicable for any value, and also in the situation when the array is not square, although in the overwhelming majority of cases, both the image array, and the area over which the covariance products are calculated are indeed so. For convenience, we represent the various products encountered in the construction of the two-dimensional covariance matrix by their subscripts only, hence

$$(32,11) = (11,32) \equiv E(x_{11} - \bar{x}_{11})(x_{32} - \bar{x}_{32}) = \sigma^2_{(11,32)} \qquad (2.46)$$

[see Eq. (2.23)] is the covariance between random sequences (11) and (32), of which x_{11} and x_{32} form explicit samples in the array $[X]$ [Eq. (2.43)]. We now stack the array entries in the form given by Eq. (2.45) and apply the operator of Eq. (2.29) to obtain the array shown in Fig. 2.2, where we note that the matrix is, of course, symmetric, and that the variances of the original sequences appear along the main diagonal. Here $\mathbf{X_C}$ and $\mathbf{X_C^T}$ have been appended to the Figure to clarify the operation. Further examination of Fig.2.2 shows that the array can be expressed in the form

$$\mathrm{COV}(X) = \begin{bmatrix} [c_1 \; c_1^{\mathrm{T}}] & [c_1 \; c_2^{\mathrm{T}}] & [c_1 \; c_3^{\mathrm{T}}] \\ [c_2 \; c_1^{\mathrm{T}}] & [c_2 \; c_2^{\mathrm{T}}] & [c_2 \; c_3^{\mathrm{T}}] \\ [c_3 \; c_1^{\mathrm{T}}] & [c_3 \; c_2^{\mathrm{T}}] & [c_3 \; c_3^{\mathrm{T}}] \end{bmatrix} \qquad (2.47)$$

where terms of the form $c_a \, c_b^{\mathrm{T}}$ $(a = b)$ are the matrices corresponding to the individual columns of Eq. (2.43), for example

$$c_1 c_1^{\mathrm{T}} = \begin{bmatrix} (11) \\ (21) \\ (31) \end{bmatrix} [(11) \quad (21) \quad (31)] = \begin{bmatrix} (11,11) & (11,21) & (11,31) \\ (21,11) & (21,21) & (21,31) \\ (31,11) & (31,21) & (31,31) \end{bmatrix} \quad (2.48)$$

$\mathbf{X}_c \backslash \mathbf{X}_c^T$	(11)	(21)	(31)	(12)	(22)	(32)	(13)	(23)	(33)
(11)	(11, 11)	(11, 21)	(11, 31)	(11, 12)	(11, 22)	(11, 32)	(11, 13)	(11, 23)	(11, 33)
(21)	(21, 11)	(21, 21)	(21, 31)	(21, 12)	(21, 22)	(21, 32)	(21, 13)	(21, 23)	(21, 33)
(31)	(31, 11)	(31, 21)	(31, 31)	(31, 12)	(31, 22)	(31, 32)	(31, 13)	(31, 23)	(31, 33)
(12)	(12, 11)	(12, 21)	(12, 31)	(12, 12)	(12, 22)	(12, 32)	(12, 13)	(12, 23)	(12, 33)
(22)	(22, 11)	(22, 21)	(22, 31)	(22, 12)	(22, 22)	(22, 32)	(22, 13)	(22, 23)	(22, 33)
(32)	(32, 11)	(32, 21)	(32, 31)	(32, 12)	(32, 22)	(32, 32)	(32, 13)	(32, 23)	(32, 33)
(13)	(13, 11)	(13, 21)	(13, 31)	(13, 12)	(13, 22)	(13, 32)	(13, 13)	(13, 23)	(13, 33)
(23)	(23, 11)	(23, 21)	(23, 31)	(23, 12)	(23, 22)	(23, 32)	(23, 13)	(23, 23)	(23, 33)
(33)	(33, 11)	(33, 21)	(33, 31)	(33, 12)	(33, 22)	(33, 32)	(33, 13)	(33, 23)	(33, 33)

FIG. 2.2. Covariance matrix for the two-dimensional case, $K = 3$.

and those of the same form but having $a \neq b$ are the matrices corresponding to the columns of Eq. (2.43) taken in pairs. From the array of Fig. 2.2 the variance array of the process may be extracted in a simple way. Thus

$$\text{VAR}(X) = \begin{bmatrix} \sigma_{11}^2 & \sigma_{12}^2 & \sigma_{13}^2 \\ \sigma_{21}^2 & \sigma_{22}^2 & \sigma_{23}^2 \\ \sigma_{31}^2 & \sigma_{32}^2 & \sigma_{33}^2 \end{bmatrix} \qquad (2.49)$$

where

$$\sigma_{mn}^2 = c_n c_n^T(m, m) \qquad (2.50)$$

is the entry in the mth row and mth column of array $c_n c_n^T$ [using the notation of Eq. (2.47)].

We cannot reduce the preceding expressions to a simpler form unless, as we did in the one-dimensional case, we make certain assumptions about the structure of the underlying processes generating the random sequences in Eq. (2.43). The first of these is that all sequences derive, in fact, from the same source (we are considering here the analysis of a single-image field). Further, we assume that the image field is wide-sense stationary, i.e., that the separate means and variances of the sequences are all the same, and the correlation function depends only on the horizontal and vertical separation of sequences in Eq. (2.41). Returning to that equation once more, this latter restriction is seen to result in the following distinct entries in Fig. 2.2:

Symbol	1	h_1	h_2	v_1	v_2	d_1	d_2	e_1	e_2
Example	(13,13)	(22,23)	(21,23)	(12,22)	(13,33)	(12,23)	(11,33)	(11,23)	(11,32)

with the following relationships:

Any sequence with itself	1
Any sequence with a horizontal neighbour one step distant	h_1
Any sequence with a horizontal neighbour two steps distant	h_2

Any sequence with a vertical neighbour one step distant v_1
Any sequence with a vertical neighbour two steps distant v_2
Any sequence with a diagonal neighbour one step distant d_1
Any sequence with a diagonal neighbour two steps distant d_2
Any sequence with an oblique neighbour, case (1) e_1
Any sequence with an oblique neighbour, case (2) e_2

With this terminology, the matrix of Fig. 2.2 becomes

$$
\text{COV}(X) \equiv
\begin{bmatrix}
\begin{bmatrix} 1 & v_1 & v_2 \\ v_1 & 1 & v_1 \\ v_2 & v_1 & 1 \end{bmatrix} &
\begin{bmatrix} h_1 & d_1 & e_2 \\ d_1 & h_1 & d_1 \\ e_2 & d_1 & h_1 \end{bmatrix} &
\begin{bmatrix} h_2 & e_1 & d_2 \\ e_1 & h_2 & e_1 \\ d_2 & e_1 & h_2 \end{bmatrix} \\
\begin{bmatrix} h_1 & d_1 & e_2 \\ d_1 & h_1 & d_1 \\ e_2 & d_1 & h_1 \end{bmatrix} &
\begin{bmatrix} 1 & v_1 & v_2 \\ v_1 & 1 & v_1 \\ v_2 & v_1 & 1 \end{bmatrix} &
\begin{bmatrix} h_1 & d_1 & e_2 \\ d_1 & h_1 & d_1 \\ e_2 & d_1 & h_1 \end{bmatrix} \\
\begin{bmatrix} h_2 & e_1 & d_2 \\ e_1 & h_2 & e_1 \\ d_2 & e_1 & h_2 \end{bmatrix} &
\begin{bmatrix} h_1 & d_1 & e_2 \\ d_1 & h_1 & d_1 \\ e_2 & d_1 & h_1 \end{bmatrix} &
\begin{bmatrix} 1 & v_1 & v_2 \\ v_1 & 1 & v_1 \\ v_2 & v_1 & 1 \end{bmatrix}
\end{bmatrix}
\tag{2.51}
$$

Considering the nine submatrices as single terms in the larger matrix $\text{COV}(X)$, we see that this latter matrix again has the 'Toeplitz' form referred to earlier. If we now consider that the two-dimensional process may be separated into the product of distinct horizontal and vertical covariance terms, then we obtain

$$
\begin{aligned}
e_1 &= h_2 v_1 \\
e_2 &= h_1 v_2 \\
d_1 &= h_1 v_1 \\
d_2 &= h_2 v_2
\end{aligned}
\tag{2.52}
$$

and Eq. (2.51) becomes

$$
\text{COV}(X) \equiv
\begin{bmatrix}
[V] & h_1[V] & h_2[V] \\
h_1[V] & [V] & h_1[V] \\
h_2[V] & h_1[V] & [V]
\end{bmatrix}
\tag{2.53}
$$

where

$$
[V] =
\begin{bmatrix}
1 & v_1 & v_2 \\
v_1 & 1 & v_1 \\
v_2 & v_1 & 1
\end{bmatrix}
\tag{2.54}
$$

If we write

$$[H] = \begin{bmatrix} 1 & h_1 & h_2 \\ h_1 & 1 & h_1 \\ h_2 & h_1 & 1 \end{bmatrix} \qquad (2.55)$$

then we see that the covariance matrix of the two-dimensional process, $\text{COV}(X)$, can be expressed as the direct matrix product of the separate horizontal and vertical matrices:

$$\text{COV}(X) = [H] \otimes [V] \qquad (2.56)$$

Note that representing the product relationship of any sequence with itself by '1' implies that the overall process variance is unity. The actual value may be taken in with either the vertical or the horizontal covariance matrix; since the process has only one overall value of variance, the term will, of course, only appear in one of the matrices.

Finally, the individual horizontal and vertical covariances may turn out to be closely approximated by those of the first-order Markov process, in which case Eqs. (2.54) and (2.55) will take on the simple forms

$$[V] = \sigma^2 \begin{bmatrix} 1 & \rho_v & \rho_v^2 \\ \rho_v & 1 & \rho_v \\ \rho_v^2 & \rho_v & 1 \end{bmatrix} \qquad (2.57)$$

$$[H] = \begin{bmatrix} 1 & \rho_h & \rho_h^2 \\ \rho_h & 1 & \rho_h \\ \rho_h^2 & \rho_h & 1 \end{bmatrix} \qquad (2.58)$$

where ρ_v and ρ_h are the one-step vertical and horizontal correlation coefficients, respectively, of the image process.

In the one-dimensional case there is not much scope for the development of models of the correlation function which results from actual measurements on real images, a model of the form of Eq. (2.42) sufficing for low-detail scenes (the point here is not so much that more complicated functions cannot be used to model rapidly varying correlation/distance relations accurately as that such relations vary so widely amongst commonly occurring scenes that accurate modelling is just not worthwhile). In the two-dimensional case there are two models which have been fairly widely used in image covariance modelling, the first of which is the separable form referred to earlier. Thus, in this simple case we take the basic one-dimensional expression given in Eq. (2.41) and write

$$\rho_H(x) = e^{-\alpha x}, \qquad x = 0 \rightarrow K \qquad (2.59)$$

$$\rho_V(y) = e^{-\beta y}, \qquad y = 0 \rightarrow K \qquad (2.60)$$

as the relations between horizontal and vertical correlation functions and distances x and y (for brevity, the notation implies the magnitudes of x and y, which may themselves, of course, be negative). In the present application x and y will be measured in integral multiples of the separations between adjacent horizontal and vertical image elements, both of which will be functions of the parameters of the scanning device, i.e., sampling frequency and vertical scanning frequency, respectively, and, in general, different. In this context it should be pointed out that, unless the scanning and digitising processes are accurately set up and calibrated, it is dangerous to 'carry-back' any property which relates the relative magnitudes of horizontal and vertical correlation coefficients as measured on the digitised image to form an assumption about the correlation properties of the image itself.

The separable two-dimensional correlation model is therefore

$$\rho(x,y) = e^{-\alpha x}e^{-\beta y}$$
$$= e^{-(\alpha x + \beta y)} \tag{2.61}$$

reducing to Eq. (2.59) or Eq. (2.60) along the horizontal or vertical axes, respectively. The loci of constant values of Eq. (2.61) as x and y vary are given by

$$\alpha x + \beta y = C \tag{2.62}$$

where the constant C takes on various positive values. It is easy to see that

$$y = (C/\beta) - (\alpha/\beta)x \tag{2.63}$$

and thus the loci are in fact straight lines, as is shown in Fig. 2.3 for the case $\rho_H(1) = 0.95$ and $\rho_V(1) = 0.90$, corresponding to values of α and β of 0.0513 and 0.1054, respectively.

As was the case in one dimension, the model may be modified to provide a better fit with the observed data (i.e., measured correlation values) in the horizontal and vertical directions [see Eq. (2.42)]. Thus

$$\rho(x,y) = \exp[-(\alpha x^{r_1} + \beta y^{r_2})] \tag{2.64}$$

forms what might be called a generalised, separable, two-dimensional correlation model (of course, the loci of constant correlation are here no longer straight lines). More complicated relationships are possible but will naturally exhibit strong image dependence. It turns out that, for most images, the separable model is a poor one (Jain, 1976b, 1977; Natarajan and Ahmed, 1978) the reason being that it causes the diagonal correlation within the image to fall off too rapidly with distance. We therefore turn to a better model, in which the loci of constant correlation are, even in its basic form, not

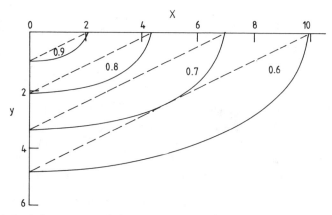

FIG. 2.3. Loci of constant correlation; $\rho_h = 0.95$; $\rho_v = 0.90$; x, horizontal element separation; y, vertical element separation. Dashed line represents the separable model [Eq. (2.61)] and solid line represents the generalised isotropic model [Eq. (2.66)]. The parameter is the actual value of the correlation coefficient.

straight lines but rather, arcs of circles. The basic equation of this 'isotropic' model is

$$\rho(x,y) = \exp[-\alpha(x^2 + y^2)^{1/2}] \tag{2.65}$$

which is immediately seen to impose the restriction that $\rho_H(1) = \rho_V(1)$, i.e., equality of one-step horizontal and vertical correlation coefficients. It may initially be generalised, therefore, to

$$\rho(x,y) = \exp[-(\alpha^2 x^2 + \beta^2 y^2)^{1/2}] \tag{2.66}$$

and in this form has been used, for example, by Natarajan and Ahmed (1978). An example of this relationship is shown in Fig. 2.3. It is tempting to extend the preceding relationship to include accurate modelling of the individual horizontal and vertical correlation structures, as was done in Eq. (2.64) for the separable model using the basic form of Eq. (2.42). Thus

$$\rho(x,y) = \exp[-(\alpha^2 x^{2r_1} + \beta^2 y^{2r_2})^{1/2}] \tag{2.67}$$

reduces to the same, improved, horizontal or vertical model as does Eq. (2.64) when either y or x, respectively, is zero. Whereas, however, the separable model tends to underestimate the diagonal correlation of the image, the reverse is true of this version. As a final step, therefore, we generalise the model still further, to a form which includes both separable and generalised isotropic models and which forms a surprisingly good fit for the image in question

$$\rho(x,y) = \exp\{-[(\alpha x^{r_1})^h + (\beta y^{r_2})^h]^{1/h}\} \tag{2.68}$$

where setting $h = 1$ reduces Eq. (2.68) to the separable form of Eq. (2.64), setting $h = 2$ gives the model of Eq. (2.67), and a best fit to the image mentioned earlier and discussed further in Section 2.4 is given by a value of h of approximately $\sqrt{2}$. A similar generalised model has been used with success by Mauersberger (1979c), but under the constraint $\alpha = \beta$, over a set of 16 test images with optimisation of parameters in the transform domain.

2.3   Image properties in the spectral domain

In the previous sections of this chapter, image properties have been discussed from the point of view of the existence of the image as a set of discrete data samples, arranged in straight lines (where we consider the one-dimensional representation) or, more naturally, in the form of a two-dimensional image field. In the present section, we turn to the characterisation of the image by its one- or two-dimensional power spectrum which, although in a sense generating no new information, by virtue of the equivalence of temporal and spatial, and spectral domains, presents our knowledge of the properties of the image in a new form and, moreover, is particularly appropriate to the present purpose, since transform coding is basically a spectral domain process.

2.3.1   The spectrum of the first-order Markov process

Knowing the covariance (or correlation) properties of a series having time or space as its independent variable, it suffices to employ any of the many readily available techniques to determine the equivalent distribution of power or energy with respect to a new independent variable, i.e., frequency, (the term is used here in its conventional sense of the spectral equivalent of time variations in a signal; it is occasionally referred to as temporal frequency to make this point explicit) or, in the case of spatially varying series, spatial frequency. The more general aspects of image power spectrum determination will be discussed further in subsection 2.3.2 and the technique applied to three test images in Section 2.4, but for the moment we shall examine one extremely important case for which an analytical development is possible, and we may then determine the extent to which the model analysed provides a good representation of image properties in a spectral context. The case to be considered is that of the first-order Markov process, which is characterised by a correlation/distance relation of the form of Eq. (2.38) or Eq. (2.41). Thus, for a continuous signal, which we include here from the point of view of completeness, in one dimension

$$\rho(x) = e^{-\alpha|x|} \tag{2.69}$$

and we may determine the spectrum of the process by employing the continuous Fourier transform, as is implied by the Wiener–Kintchine relation that the power spectral density and autocorrelation form a Fourier transform pair. Three points are worthy of note here; first since the autocorrelation function is real and even, so is the power spectral density; second, perhaps more subtle, we shall take the transform of Eq. (2.69) rather than of the autocorrelation function as the Wiener–Kintchine theorem suggests. The consequences of this step follow from the differences between the autocorrelation function and the correlation coefficient; the latter being calculated on the basis of subtraction of the original data mean and final division by overall variance [see Eqs. (2.33) and (2.36)]. Thus, our spectral function will be that of an effectively zero-mean sequence and consequently will have no zero frequency (DC) term. This does not mean, of course, that a finite spectral power density cannot exist over a frequency range extending to a point arbitrarily close to zero frequency, but rather that there will be no impulse term at $f = 0$. Also, division by the variance in the course of the calculation will normalise the spectrum which is, in fact, an advantage, since different images may then be compared on an equal footing. The third point is that, however sophisticated we might wish to make our image analysis in terms of non-stationary properties, strictly speaking we are allowed only to carry out the present operation under the assumption that it is stationary, for only then does the transform relation apply.

Returning to Eq. (2.69) and applying the transform,

$$P(\omega) = \int_{-\infty}^{\infty} e^{-\alpha|x|} e^{-j\omega x}\, dx$$

$$= \int_{-\infty}^{0} e^{\alpha x} e^{-j\omega x}\, dx + \int_{0}^{\infty} e^{-\alpha x} e^{-j\omega x}\, dx$$

$$= \frac{1}{\alpha - j\omega} + \frac{1}{\alpha + j\omega}$$

$$= \frac{2\alpha}{\alpha^2 + \omega^2} \tag{2.70}$$

where $P(\omega)$ is the power spectral density as a function of ω (which may take on values in the interval $\pm\infty$). Therefore, $P(\omega)$ varies from a maximum of $2/\alpha$ at $\omega = 0$ to a minimum of zero at $\omega = \pm\infty$.

The positive half of this relationship is illustrated in Fig. 2.4 and is, of course, analytically exact. In practice, however, we have to deal with a discrete image, whose sample values are known only at a specific set of points and not as a continuous function. The correlation is therefore also discrete and, in addition, the inherent sampling operation imposes a periodic structure on the spectral response. In short, we should carry out a discrete

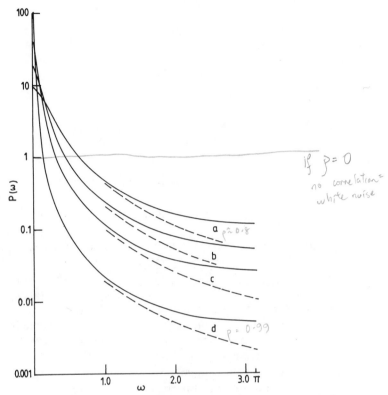

FIG. 2.4. Spectrum of the process $\rho_k = \rho^{|k|}$. Dashed line represents the continuous result [Eq. (2.70)] and solid line represents the discrete result [Eq. (2.73)]. (a) $\rho = 0.80$, (b) $\rho = 0.90$, (c) $\rho = 0.95$ and (d) $\rho = 0.99$.

transform to determine $P(\omega)$, which will now only take on nonredundant values over the range $\omega = \pm \pi (\omega = 2\pi f$, and so the maximum signal frequency represented will be $f/2$ or $\omega = \pi)$, and the degree to which $P(\omega)$ has reached an acceptably small value by the time ω reaches its extreme values will, of course, indicate whether or not the sampling frequency is sufficiently high.

Thus

$$\rho_k = \rho^{|k|} \tag{2.71}$$

where k is now a discrete variable and ρ is the one-step correlation coefficient. Applying the discrete transform

$$P(\omega) = \sum_{k=-\infty}^{\infty} \rho^{|k|} e^{-jk\omega} \qquad -\pi \leqslant \omega \leqslant \pi$$

$$= 1 + \rho e^{-j\omega} + \rho^2 e^{-j2\omega} + \cdots + \rho e^{j\omega} + \rho^2 e^{j2\omega} + \cdots \tag{2.72}$$

Now, since

$$\sum_{r=0}^{\infty} x^r = \frac{1}{1-x}$$

then

$$P(\omega) = \sum_{n=0}^{\infty} (\rho e^{-j\omega})^n + \sum_{n=0}^{\infty} (\rho e^{j\omega})^n - 1$$

$$= \frac{1 - \rho^2}{1 + \rho^2 - 2\rho \cos \omega} \tag{2.73}$$

This relationship also is illustrated in Fig. 2.4 for various values of correlation coefficient. As expected, the two versions (discrete and continuous) are much the same at low frequencies but diverge as ω approaches π. The reason is, as noted earlier, that especially for processes with lower values of ρ (i.e., a wider spectrum, according to the reciprocal relation between temporal and spectral domains), the original sampling frequency is inadequate, the differences between the two representations having the same linear extent but on a logarithmic scale. The remedy is, of course, to sample the image at a higher rate, in which case the sample spacing will be reduced and the inter-element correlation correspondingly higher. In Section 2.4 this simple spectral representation will be compared with actual measured spectra, as determined by the technique described in the next subsection.

2.3.2 Measurement of image spectra

In order to interpret the correlation properties of images, discussed at some length earlier, in the spectral domain, we shall carry out a practical spectral analysis on the measured correlation coefficients of the three test images. It is not the present purpose to investigate different approaches to spectrum analysis, together with their various advantages and disadvantages, which subject has been extensively discussed in many texts in its application to all forms of time series (for a comprehensive review of this topic, the reader is referred to Kay and Marple, 1981). What we shall do is to employ one particular technique and use the results to highlight the spectral properties of images in general, and to assess the validity of modelling images using the simple first-order Markov representation. To do this we transform the correlation coefficient sequence (i.e., the normalised auto-covariance) using an appropriate window function selected as a compromise between spectral resolution and variance (roughly speaking, the uncertainty in the spectral estimate in this context). We start with a modified version of the discrete transform of Eq. (2.72)

$$P(\omega) = \sum_{k=-\infty}^{\infty} \rho_k e^{-jk\omega} \qquad -\pi \leqslant \omega \leqslant \pi \qquad (2.74)$$

where ρ_k now represents the measured values of the correlation coefficient. Since ρ_k is a real and even function the sine terms in the summation will be zero, and we can combine separate sums over $k = -\infty \to 1$ and $1 \to \infty$ to yield

$$P(\omega) = \rho_0 + 2 \sum_{k=1}^{K} \rho_k \cos \omega k \qquad (2.75)$$

where, of course, $e^0 = 1$ and there are only $K - 1$ measured correlation coefficients [the reason that only $K - 1$ coefficients are required in Eq. 2.75) is explained below]. We now 'smooth' the correlation coefficient series with a window function (see, e.g., Jenkins and Watts, 1968; Chatfield, 1980, for a justification of this step). The one chosen in the present case is the Tukey window, defined by

$$W_k = \tfrac{1}{2}[1 + \cos(\pi k/K)], \qquad k = 1 \to K \qquad (2.76)$$

giving an estimate for $P(\omega)$ of

$$P(\omega) = 1 + \sum_{k=1}^{K} \rho_k \left(1 + \cos\frac{\pi k}{K}\right)\cos \omega k \qquad (2.77)$$

where $\rho_0 W_0 = 1$ and $W_K = 0$.

It is not claimed that the preceding spectral estimate is 'best' in any particular sense, but it does provide a convenient way of moving from a spatial domain (correlation sequence) representation to a spectral domain (power spectral density) one, and will be employed in Section 2.4 to determine the properties of three test images.

2.3.3 The equivalence of spatial and spectral domain representations

To complete the theoretical specification of spatial and spectral domains and their inter-relationships we now demonstrate how the properties of the image in that latter domain may be derived from those in the former (i.e., without separately calculating or measuring them) from a knowledge of the transform operation which links the two. This operation may be that of Fourier transformation, in which case quantities defined with the usual notion of frequency as an independent variable will result. Alternatively, and more frequently in the case of transform image coding, the independent variable in the spectral domain will be a generalisation of frequency called 'sequency', which will be defined and explained in Chapter 3.

In the present development the space and spectral indices will merely be represented in symbolic form, as coordinates within a two-dimensional array of data points or spectral coefficients, respectively. It is worth pointing out here that the representation of image properties in the spectral domain is of fundamental importance in the study of transform coding of images, for it is upon the redistribution of coefficient sequence variances (energies) within the spectral array that the whole concept of the method depends. Again, it is useful to recall here that all transform operations discussed in this volume are linear, and so the value of a coefficient in the spectral domain is a linear weighted sum of (usually) all data values in the spatial domain, the exact values of the weighting coefficients in any particular case being determined, naturally, by the transform being used. Although the following discussion may be generalised to input and output arays of any dimension, for convenience and simplicity, and also because the vast majority of transform operations carried out conform to the condition, both will be assumed to be of extent $N \times N$. We therefore define an input array of picture elements $f(k, l)$ where $1 \leqslant k, l \leqslant N$ and an output (transform domain) array $C(p, q)$ where, similarly, $1 \leqslant p, q \leqslant N$. These arrays are represented in Fig. 2.5 where two points in each domain have been identified, the auxiliary data and transform domain coordinates being m, n and r, s, respectively.

The general relationship between transform and image domains is explained fully in the next chapter, and it is only necessary to quote it here. Thus

$$C(p, q) = \sum_{k=1}^{N} \sum_{l=1}^{N} f(k, l)T(p, q; k, l) \qquad p, q = 1 \to N \qquad (2.78)$$

where $T(\cdot)$ is the (as yet unspecified) transform operator and is, of course, a function of both input and output coordinates. We may generate an output array of mean values by determining $E[C(p, q)]$ which results, by the linearity of the operators involved, in

$$E[C(p, q)] = \sum_{k=1}^{N} \sum_{l=1}^{N} E[f(k, l)]T(p, q; k, l) \qquad (2.79)$$

In the stationary case, of course, this relation may be considerably simplified, since the input array has but a single overall value of the mean $E[f(k, l)]$, which applies to all elements.

In a similar fashion, the output array correlation will be

$$R_S = E[C(p, q)C^*(r, s)] \qquad (2.80)$$

where we have allowed for the possibility that $T(\cdot)$ may be complex (of course, the formal definition of correlation or covariance includes the

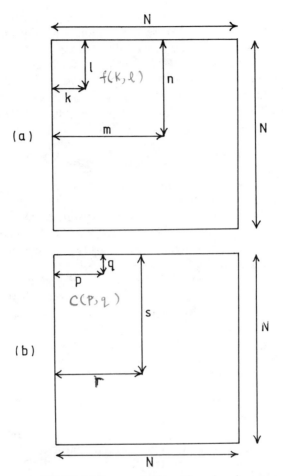

FIG. 2.5. (a) Image and (b) transform domains.

complex conjugate in Eq. (2.80), but since practical data is normally real, this only has significance in a situation such as the present one, in which the transform domain coefficients may be complex). Substitution of $C(p, q)$ and $C^*(r, s)$ yields the output correlation

$$R_S(p, q; r, s) = E\left[\sum_{k=1}^{N}\sum_{l=1}^{N}f(k, l)T(p, q; k, l)\sum_{m=1}^{N}\sum_{n=1}^{N}f(m, n)T^*(r, s; m, n)\right]$$

$$= \sum_{k=1}^{N}\sum_{l=1}^{N}\sum_{m=1}^{N}\sum_{n=1}^{N}R_f(k, l; m, n)T(p, q; k, l)T^*(r, s; m, n)$$

$$(2.81)$$

where $R_f(k, l; m, n) = E[f(k, l)f(m, n)]$ is the correlation function in the data domain. Note that, in the general case, this formulation is quite impractical to evaluate and express (typically N will be, perhaps, 256 or more), and simplifications are necessary—its equivalent in vector-matrix form is the stacking of the data array into an $N^2 \times 1$ vector and its multiplication by an $N^2 \times N^2$ transform matrix. In the wide-sense stationary case, the data correlation $R_f(k, l: m, n)$ is a function only of the spacing between, and not the actual location of, the sequences considered, i.e.,

$$R_f(k; l; m, n) = R_f(|k - m|; |l - n|) \tag{2.82}$$

and the dimension N need now only be that over which determination of the correlation coefficients has been carried out. Even in this case the calculation is of fairly large dimension for if, typically, we measure the coefficients over an array of size 16×16, we shall still have an array 256×256 in extent. Since, however, we are usually more interested in using two-dimensional techniques to determine spectral domain variances rather than covariances or correlations (this will be elaborated upon in Chapter 3), we need only calculate $\sigma_{p,q}^2$, which array will form the main diagonal of the larger matrix obtained by transformation of the data covariance function.

One further simplification is worthy of mention here. The two-dimensional transforms used in transform coding schemes are separable into the sucessive application of first, row, and then, column transforms (or vice versa). Thus, we can write

$$T(p, q; k, l) = A_R(p, k)B_C(q, l) \tag{2.83}$$

where A and B may represent different transform types (which will, however, be the same in the vast majority of cases), and the subscripts R and C refer to row and column transforms, respectively.

Finally, the image data correlation function may itself be separable into the product of row and column correlation functions [see Eq. (2.61)],

$$R_f(k, l; m, n) = R_{f(R)}(k, m)R_{f(C)}(l, n) \tag{2.84}$$

in which case we may transform each separately

$$R_{S(R)}(p, r) = \sum_{k=1}^{N} \sum_{m=1}^{N} R_{f(R)}(k, m)A_R(p, k)A_R^*(r, m) \tag{2.85}$$

and

$$R_{S(C)}(q, s) = \sum_{l=1}^{N} \sum_{n=1}^{N} R_{f(C)}(l, n)B_C(q, l)B_C^*(s, n) \tag{2.86}$$

and then form the product

$$R_S(p, q; r, s) = R_{S(R)}(p, r)R_{S(C)}(q, s) \qquad (2.87)$$

It has been pointed out elsewhere in this chapter, however, that the separable model is generally a poor one for typical images.

2.4 Application of the theory to practical images

In the previous sections we have examined ways in which images may be characterised from a statistical point of view. It is most important that this be done for any so-called 'efficient' coding method, since all such techniques are sensitive to changes in the properties of the input (image) data and the question arises as to just what kind of test images should be used in setting up a coding system and in determining its operating parameters, performance, etc. For the present, however, the task is not to optimise a coding system for a given set of test images but rather to show how the nature of such images affects the operation of transform coding, and to that end this section presents experimental results on three images which may be considered to be representative of widely differing categories of input material. In each case the techniques developed in the preceding sections of this chapter are applied and the results discussed in the context of efficient coding.

2.4.1 Image 1

The male head and shoulders image shown in Fig. 2.6 may be described as 'typical' from the point of view of low-data-rate image communications (videoconference applications, for example). It is one which is expected to be fairly easy to code, with large areas of relatively constant luminance and prominent, but not severe, edge detail. Visual examination leads us to expect that the high spatial frequency content will be small, and this will be borne out by measurements discussed subsequently. The image is 256 × 256 elements in extent, and has been digitised to a nominal accuracy of 8 bits. It is therefore represented within the data store as 64 k (65,536) 8-bit words, corresponding to three-digit integers having any value between 0 and 255. Since it was digitised as a composite video signal, however, the total signal range contains synchronising and blanking information, and it is necessary to exclude this from the signal in order to consider only the 'active' video image (see Fig. 2.1). The first measurement made is therefore a first-order approximation to the image probability density function in the form of a histogram (Fig. 2.7) which is simply a plot of the number of occurrences of each allowed luminance level within the image. In this case the lowest 91 levels are not occupied (corresponding to the height of the synchronising pulses) and have

FIG. 2.6. Image 1—A male 'head and shoulders' image.

been removed from the diagram to leave a total of 165 levels occupied by image information. We might note here that, for this reason, we are not really justified in calling Image 1 an 8-bit image; it has, more accurately, a resolution of $\log_2 165 = 7.37$ bits. The shape of the distribution portrayed in Fig. 2.7 is more or less characteristic of a broad class of low-detail images. There are often two peaks (here there is a third), one in the dark grey region and one near the top of the intensity distribution (Mannos and Sakrison, 1974; Hunt and Cannon, 1976) and the distribution is widely spread, making use of all available levels. This feature may be given quantitative substance by the application of Eq. (2.5) to determine the first-order entropy $H(x)$, which turns out to be 7.13 bits, demonstrating that optimum coding in the Huffman (1952) sense (matching codeword length to probability of use),

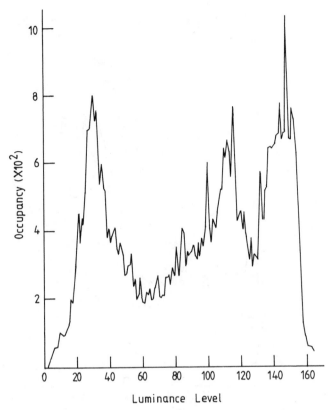

FIG. 2.7. First-order distribution of luminance levels for Image 1.

even if it were practicable, would hardly be worthwhile, resulting in a saving of only 0.24 bit/element.

The next measurement we can make is of the second-order distribution, following which we shall be able to make use of the results of subsection 2.2.1.2. This is a more onerous task, since we now have a total of $165^2 = 27{,}225$ possible combinations of neighbouring element luminance values. If all were used equally the second-order entropy $H(x, y)$ would of course be $2 \times H(x) = 14.26$ bits. To the extent that all allowed combinations are not equally used, $H(x, y)$ will be lower. It turns out that (considering the horizontal direction) only a total of 7060 combinations is used, and the second-order distribution is quite highly peaked as shown in Fig. 2.8 where each of the 165 possible distributions (for clarity, only 16 are shown) corresponds to the distribution of elements throughout the image, given that the previous element has the value corresponding to the ordinate in the

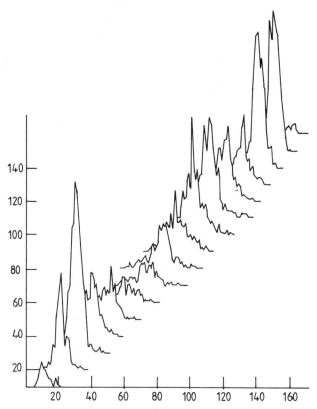

FIG. 2.8. 16 representative second-order luminance level distributions for Image 1. The ordinate is the previous element value and the abscissa is the present element value.

figure. If the 7060 combinations were equally occupied, $H(x, y)$ would be $\log_2 7060 = 12.79$ bits, but the more sharply peaked distribution reduces this figure more than in the first-order case to 11.57 bits. We may use Eq. (2.9) to determine $H(y/x)$, i.e., the conditional entropy of y given x, which turns out to be $11.57 - 7.13 = 4.44$ bits. This is the information needed to specify y exactly after x is known and so, alternatively, knowledge of x imparts $H(x) - H(y/x) = 7.13 - 4.44 = 2.69$ bits of information about y (a result in good agreement with those of Pirsch and Stenger, 1976). We could code the image, therefore, at a rate very close to 4.44 bits/element without incurring any loss of information. The use of dependence extending over a larger distance, 3 or 4 elements, for example, would reduce this figure somewhat. Naturally, we expect to do much better than this by using transform coding schemes which will, however, introduce a finite amount of degradation which must be held to an acceptable upper limit.

We now consider the correlation properties of Image 1. The most basic properties are easily dealt with. The image mean is 93.05 and the variance 2032.81. Since the former figure is roughly half way between the levels corresponding to black and peak white (0 and 164), and the latter figure is quite high, we are led to expect significant areas of both high and low luminance, as is indeed the case. We next determine the variation of correlation coefficient with element separation, initially in the horizontal, vertical and diagonal directions. This behaviour is illustrated in Fig. 2.9. The one-step correlation is very high (reinforcing the initial suspicion that the image will be relatively easy to code) and is slightly greater in the vertical

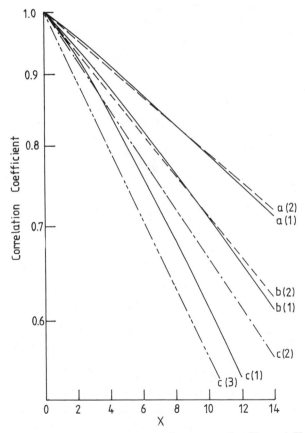

FIG. 2.9. Correlation coefficient/element separation x properties of Image 1. Here, $a(1)$ is the measured values (vertical), $a(2)$ the first-order Markov approximation ($\rho = 0.977$), $b(1)$ the measured values (horizontal), $b(2)$ the first-order Markov approximation ($\rho = 0.967$), $c(1)$ the measured values (diagonal), $c(2)$ the generalised isotropic model [Eq. (2.66)] and $c(3)$ the separable model [Eq. (2.61)].

direction, probably due to the fact that the element separation is slightly less vertically than horizontally (due to restrictions on the choice of sampling frequency, rather than to any inherent image characteristics). Diagonal correlation, as expected, is less than that along either of the coordinate axes owing, of course, to the greater element separation in that direction. Figure 2.9, plotted to a logarithmic scale, naturally portrays the first-order Markov relationship as a straight line. Although this is not the case as far as the actual image results are concerned, it can be seen that reasonable approximations are possible, with one-step correlation coefficients of 0.967 and 0.977 in the horizontal and vertical directions, respectively. Before attempting to model horizontal and vertical correlation functions more accurately, we may consider the modelling of diagonal correlation under the simple assumptions of Eqs. (2.61) and (2.66). These results can also be seen in Fig. 2.9. The separable Markov model gives a correlation/distance relation which underestimates the diagonal correlation significantly, whilst the generalised isotropic model of Eq. (2.66) overestimates it to a similar degree. A relation somewhere between the two would appear to be more appropriate.

In fact, in the present case it is not difficult to generate a model which represents, to a good degree of accuracy, not only horizontal, vertical and diagonal correlation, but the measured values for any combination of horizontal and vertical coordinates as well. We first of all model horizontal and vertical correlation using the following versions of Eq. (2.42), for integral values of x and y

$$\rho_H(x) = \exp\left(-0.025x^{1.137}\right) \tag{2.88}$$

$$\rho_V(y) = \exp\left(-0.019y^{1.090}\right) \tag{2.89}$$

and use them in the model of Eq. (2.68) with the parameter h set at $\sqrt{2}$ to give

$$\rho(x, y) = \exp\left\{-[(0.025x^{1.137})^{\sqrt{2}} + (0.019^{1.090})^{\sqrt{2}}]^{1/\sqrt{2}}\right\} \tag{2.90}$$

The results of applying this model to the image are shown in Fig. 2.10, which also shows measured correlation coefficients and the results obtained with the separable ($h = 1$) and modified isotropic ($h = 2$) versions of Eq. (2.68). It can be seen that Eq. (2.90) does indeed provide a good model for the measured correlation values out to an element separation of perhaps 12 to 14. This model, then, should produce a good representation of the properties of the image in the spectral domain. One further point regarding Fig. 2.10 is worthy of note. Correlation values have been measured not only between elements whose separation vector (see Fig. 2.11) points in a direction lying between 'east' and 'south', but for those directions between 'west' and 'south' also. Since the correlation product is invariant to the order of the

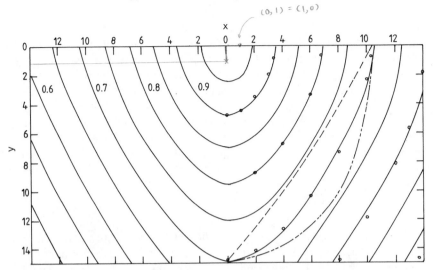

FIG. 2.10. Measured contours of constant correlation coefficient for Image 1. Here, x is the horizontal element separation and y the vertical element separation. Open circles represent calculated values [Eq. (2.90)], solid line represents measured contour, dashed line represents calculated values [Eq. (2.68), $h = 1$] and broken line represents calculated values [Eq. (2.68), $h = 2$]. The lines are single examples for comparison purposes only. Parameter is the actual value of the correlation coefficient.

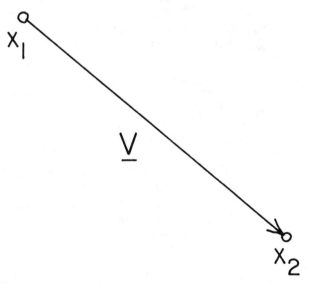

FIG. 2.11. Separation vector for correlation measurement; x_1 and x_2 are typical elements involved in a correlation measurement, and V is the separation vector, directed from the first towards the second.

terms [see Eq. (2.31)], reversing the direction of **V** will make no difference to the result. However, the correlation between elements having separation k and lying on a line directed 'northeast/southwest', say, will not necessarily be the same as that for elements of the same separation but lying in a 'northwest/southeast' direction. Distinct coefficient values exist, therefore, given a maximum element separation of K, over an area $2K \times K$, involving a total of $(K + 1) \times (2K + 1)$ locations in the resulting correlation/separation plot. This property is not at all evident in the case of Image 1, but will be immediately obvious when we examine the correlation properties of the other two test images.

2.4.2   Image 2

This image (Fig. 2.12) has quite different characteristics from those of Image 1. A section of a television test card, it consists predominantly of a rectangular pattern of light and dark areas, and over a large region is confined to a relatively narrow range of luminance levels in the vicinity of mid-grey. Sharp light/dark transitions and a set of resolution bars imply that there will be significant high spatial frequency energy content, and the diagonal bars situated in the top right-hand corner indicate the presence of diagonal frequency components also. To add to the problems of coding, the lower left of the image contains detail of the kind already referred to in connection with Image 1. As before, we commence with an examination of first-order entropy, derived from the histogram of Fig. 2.13, which clearly shows the mid-grey peak. In this case the number of active video levels is 123 and the original resolution is therefore $\log_2 123 = 6.94$ bits. The numerical value of first-order entropy is 6.18 bits; the difference, 0.76 bit/element, is significantly greater than the 0.24-bit difference in the case of Image 1 and is attributable to the sharply peaked distribution. Again, however, coding on this basis gives an improvement which is hardly worth the effort, and the result demonstrates that, in general, it is difficult to achieve a worthwhile result in this way, for the distribution must be very peaked indeed to reduce $H(x)$ significantly from its equal probability value. In the case of the second-order distribution (whose overall characteristics are very similar to those of Image 1, but which are not reproduced here), the total number of possible combinations is $123^2 = 15{,}129$, of which 7540 are actually used (i.e., almost exactly one half, as opposed to just over one quarter in the case of Image 1, reflecting the greater 'activity' of this image). The maximum theoretical value of $H(x, y)$ is thus 13.88 bits but, since only half of the allowable combinations are used, the actual equal probability second-order entropy will be 1 bit less, i.e., 12.88 bits. The measured value of $H(x, y)$ is 10.59 bits, reflecting, as before, the sharply peaked nature of the distribution: $H(y/x)$, from Eq. (2.9), is

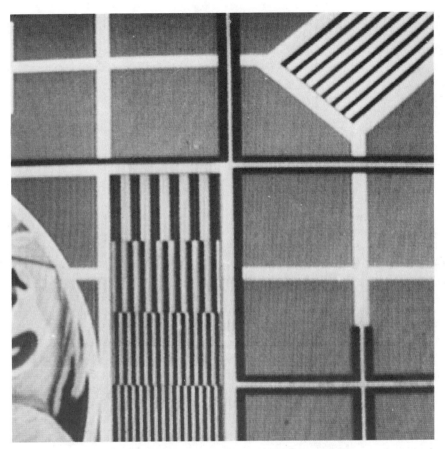

FIG. 2.12. Image 2—section of a television test card.

$10.59 - 6.18 = 4.41$ bits and, equivalently, knowledge of x imparts $6.18 - 4.41 = 1.77$ bits of information about y. Thus, whilst the actual numerical value of $H(y/x)$ is almost identical for Images 1 and 2, the original entropy, and therefore the information gained about y from a knowledge of x are both about 1 bit less in the present case, the latter being a consequence of the less 'predictable' nature of Image 2.

We now consider the correlation properties of Image 2. The mean value is 66.57 and the variance 617.55, the relatively small value of the latter quantity being due to the concentration of luminance levels around the peak evident in Fig. 2.13. Horizontal, vertical and diagonal correlation coefficients up to an element separation of 14 are plotted in Fig. 2.14. It is immediately obvious that the properties of this image are quite different from those of Image 1. The

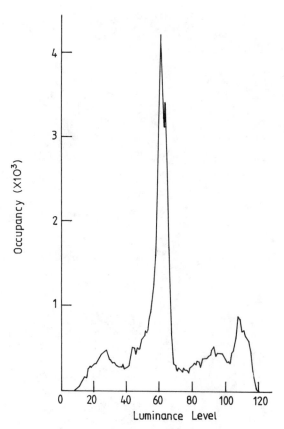

FIG. 2.13. First-order distribution of luminance levels for Image 2.

inter-element correlation decays, at first, in a similar way to that of the latter image, but at a more rapid rate, but after an element separation of 5 or 6 is reached there is no longer any readily discernible pattern to the correlation/ separation relationship. Furthermore, even over that restricted region, horizontal and diagonal correlation functions are almost identical. The reason for the general shape of the relationship is, of course, apparent when the image itself is examined, for it shows pronounced regularities in its structure, particularly in the horizontal direction, and these are naturally represented by the appearance of peaks and troughs in the correlation function. The question now arises as to what to do about accurate modelling of the function in order to determine the equivalent properties in the transform domain, and the short answer to this question is that it is very doubtful whether such an exercise is worthwhile. Naturally the function could be modelled on the basis of an exponential decay of correlation with distance, suitably modified by a

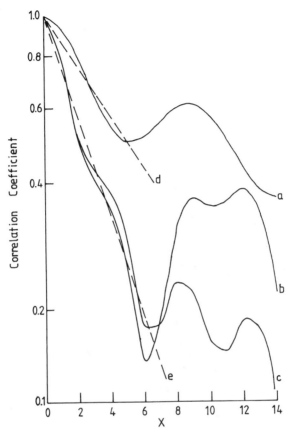

FIG. 2.14. Correlation coefficient/element separation x properties of Image 2. Here, a is the measured values (vertical), b the measured values (horizontal), c the measured values (diagonal), d the first-order Markov approximation to $x = 7$, $\rho = 0.87$ and e the first-order Markov approximation to $x = 7$, $\rho = 0.76$.

polynomial function of element separation, but the model will inevitably be very sensitive to changes in detail in the input data, and this means that it will be of limited use as a model of a class of images (there is not much point in modelling a single image in order to optimise a coding system, since a system intended to process such a limited quantity of data, if needed at all, can operate on the basis of measured image parameters, and a model is not necessary.) The image modelled in the previous subsection, on the other hand, does show features characteristic of a wide class of images not possessing the obvious periodic structure of Image 2, and it seems possible to produce a general model, of reasonable accuracy, for such a class. To indicate the breakdown of the simple first-order Markov model in such a case, we

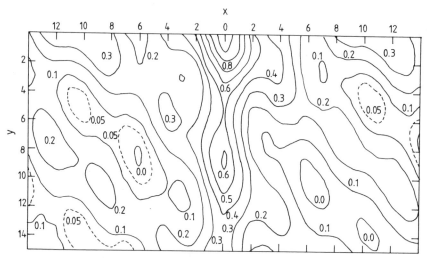

FIG. 2.15. Measured contours of constant correlation coefficient for Image 2. Here, x is the horizontal element separation and y the vertical element separation. Parameter is the actual value of the correlation coefficient.

might here represent the image by that process over a restricted range, in order to assess its defects quantitatively when we come to examine the characteristics of the image in the transform domain. Thus an approximate fit to the horizontal and vertical correlation functions is given, up to an element separation of 7, by $\rho_H(1) = 0.76$ and $\rho_V(1) = 0.87$.

Fig. 2.15 is the counterpart of Fig. 2.10 in the case of Image 1, and the differences between the two are readily apparent. It can be seen that the behaviour characteristic over the whole plotted range in the case of the latter image holds (and then only approximately) over a relatively restricted region around the origin of Fig. 2.15. Further out the two-dimensional correlation/ separation relationship shows no prominent features, apart from the maintenance of relatively high values along the vertical axis, and perhaps an upper-left to lower-right tendency in the contours of equal correlation. Furthermore, the difference between 'northwest/southeast' and 'northeast/ southwest' correlation, referred to in connection with Image 1 is readily apparent here. Overall, the two-dimensional correlation relationship is an interesting one, but not one that can be modelled with any ease or consistency.

2.4.3   Image 3

This image has been included as an example of the class of input data which transform coding schemes do not process well. It is felt, however, that its inclusion is valuable on two grounds. First, its statistical and spectral properties give useful information in general as a comparison with the two preceding cases: second, 'integrated' image coding schemes will inevitably, in the future, be called upon to process a very wide range of input material, including documents as well as grey scale images. It is, therefore, almost as useful to know what material is difficult to process as to know what can be coded without too much difficulty, and what properties lead to that conclusion. Such knowledge may eventually lead to the development of highly flexible coding schemes. Image 3 (Fig. 2.16), then, is simply a segment of a typewritten document which has only two luminance levels, black and white, to which correspond the numerical levels 255 and 32, respectively. These levels are, of course, entirely arbitrary, since the actual value of any level

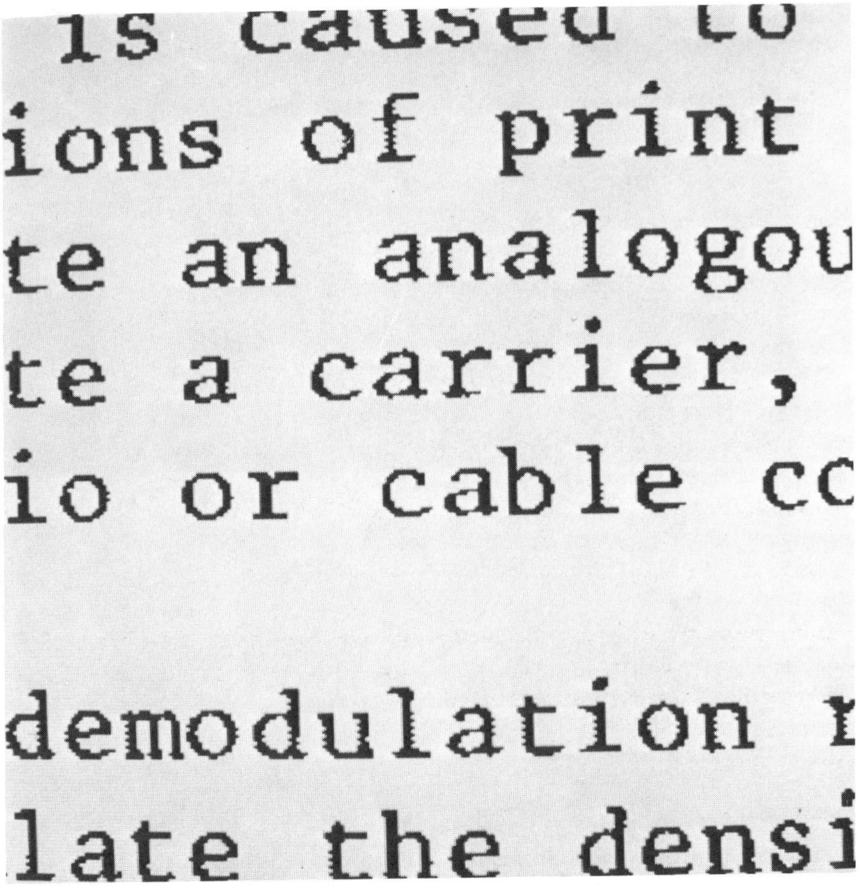
is caused to
ions of print
te an analogou
te a carrier,
io or cable cc
demodulation r
late the densi

FIG. 2.16. Image 3—segment of a typescript document.

assumed by a random variable in no way affects any entropy calculation or measurement, and, in the case of other statistical properties, all transform domain energy values are, in any case, normalised by the original image variance. We expect that a significant property of this image will be the high spatial frequency energy generated by the irregularly spaced black/white transitions.

Of course, entropy figures in this case will be significantly lower than in the previous two. There are only two possible levels, and so the equal probability first-order entropy will be 1 bit. Since there are only 7484 black elements in a total of 65,536, however, the actual first-order entropy turns out to be 0.51 bit. In the second-order case, all four possible combinations are used, and so the maximum theoretical value of $H(x, y)$ is 2 bits. Its actual, measured value

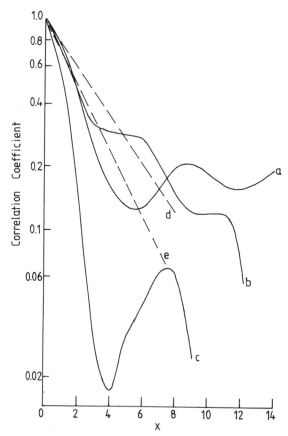

FIG. 2.17. Correlation coefficient/element separation x properties of Image 3. Here, a is the measured values (vertical), b the measured values (horizontal), c the measured values (diagonal), d the first-order Markov approximation to $x = 7$, $\rho = 0.77$ and e the first-order Markov approximation to $x = 7$, $\rho = 0.70$.

is 0.81 bits. Thus $H(y/x)$ is $0.81 - 0.51 = 0.30$ bits, and so a knowledge of the first element in any pair gives us $0.51 - 0.30 = 0.21$ bit of information about the second. Since it is not possible here to make any useful comparison with the entropies in the previous two cases, we now pass on to the correlation and spectral properties, which are of more interest.

In a simple case such as this, the basic properties of the image are easily specified. It turns out that there are 58,052 elements having a value 32 (white), and 7484 of value 255 (black), resulting in values of mean and variance of 57.47 and 5030.38, respectively. The mean value is relatively low because most elements are white, and yet the variance is large because the two allowable levels have been set at almost the full extent of the 8-bit input dynamic range. It is worth re-emphasising that these values are entirely arbitrary, and that in any comparative studies normalised values must be used. Our conclusions with regard to these results are very similar to those relating to Image 2. In this case the correlation (Fig. 2.17) drops off even more rapidly with increasing element separation, until, after a separation of, say, 5 or 6 (less in the case of diagonal correlation), it is not really possible to make any reliable inferences regarding the correlation structure of the image. Again, we may attempt an approximate modelling using a Markov I process with one-step correlation coefficients of 0.70 and 0.77 in the horizontal and vertical directions, respectively.

Figure 2.18 portrays the two-dimensional correlation function of the image. Again it can be seen that any attempt to model this function over a wide range will be fraught with such difficulties as not to make it justifiable,

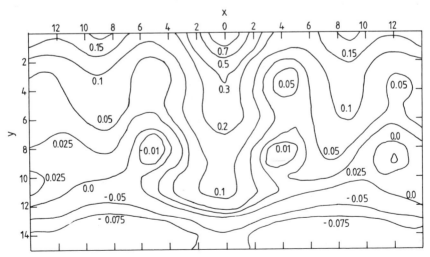

FIG. 2.18. Measured contours of constant correlation coefficient for Image 3. Here, x is the horizontal element separation and y the vertical element separation. Parameter is the actual value of the correlation coefficient.

even though the distribution this time has a degree of left/right symmetry, and lacks the diagonal trend observed in the case of Image 2.

2.4.4. Spectral properties

In the previous three subsections, test images of widely differing character-istics have been examined in terms of their entropy and correlation proper-ties. Both are important in the context of image coding, the former because an entropy measure gives us an absolute indication of the information content of an image, defined in a formal way without any reference to subjective (observer) preferences, and thus provides a figure for comparison between various input sources (the unfortunate fact is, however, that it is impractical to specify the complete joint statistics of any image of any useful size and resolution, and this means that the measure cannot be anywhere as near refined as we would wish), the latter because it is of significance if we wish to use image properties to assess the performance of transform coding schemes or, more narrowly, compare the relative merits of various transforms (see Chapter 3). Here we employ the techniques previously described in Section 2.3 to compare image properties from a spectral point of view, and it is now more convenient to consider all three images together. We begin with an examination of the spatial frequency content of the images determined in the usual sense via the Fourier transform.

2.4.4.1 *Properties in the Fourier transform domain*

Using Eq. (2.74) we may determine the power spectral density of the three test images as a first step in investigating their more general spectral properties. Thus, the measured values of the correlation function/element separation relation are multiplied by the window function [Eq. (2.76)] and transformed to give a curve of $P(\omega)$ against ω for $-\pi \leqslant \omega \leqslant \pi$. Since the curves are always even functions, only the positive halves are shown in the illustrations that follow. To demonstrate the application of the method Fig. 2.19 shows the calculated values of $P(\omega)$, using Eq. (2.77), in comparison with the theoretical values obtained from Eq. (2.73) for a first-order Markov process with one-step correlation coefficient 0.90. It can be seen that the method gives a reasonable approximation to the theoretical discrete spec-trum, although differences between the two are evident at low values of spatial frequency. We note, by comparing Eqs. (2.73) and (2.77), that the method will always underestimate the value of $P(0)$, which should be

$$P(0) = 1 + 2 \sum_{k=1}^{K} \rho_k \tag{2.91}$$

but which is inevitably reduced by the presence of the window term in Eq. (2.77). It is reiterated here that no special degree of accuracy is claimed for

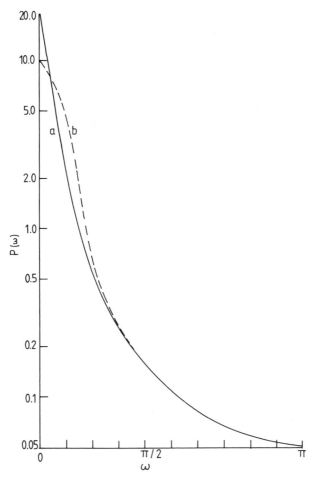

Fɪɢ. 2.19. Theoretical spectra of the first-order Markov process ($\rho = 0.90$). (a) Equation (2.73) and (b) Eq. (2.77).

this approach, particularly in the presence of sharp spectral peaks and troughs.

The measured values of horizontal correlation coefficients have been transformed for each of the test images, and the results are shown in Fig. 2.20. Considering Image 1 first we see that, broadly speaking, it bears out our expectations with regard to its closeness to a first-order Markov process with high inter-element correlation. The spectral estimate falls off smoothly and fairly rapidly and only at the highest frequency is some variation present, due to the content of edge detail in the image. The first-order Markov spectrum corresponding to a one-step correlation coefficient of 0.967 is included for

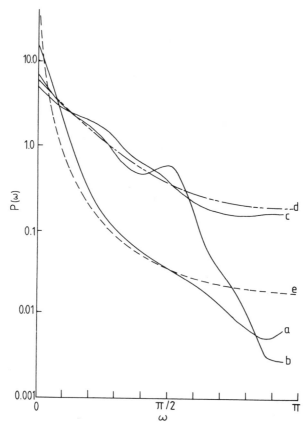

FIG. 2.20. Measured spectra of the test images. (a) Image 1, (b) Image 2, (c) Image 3, (d) first-order Markov process, $\rho = 0.70$ and (e) first-order Markov process, $\rho = 0.967$.

comparison. Not only is this image relatively easy to model, therefore, but we expect that, due to the lack of energy at high spatial frequencies in the spectrum, it will be easy to code efficiently also. For reasons which will shortly become apparent, we next examine the spectrum of Image 3.

As might be expected from a source which has irregularly spaced large-amplitude luminance transitions, the energy content at high frequencies is significantly greater than in the case of the first image, leading to greater difficulty in coding for a given degree of degradation in image quality (in fact, of course, attempting to relate severity of degradation between grey-scale images of the type represented by Image 1 and black/white images as represented by Image 3 is likely to be an impossible task). The spectral response is not unexpected, given the rapid decay of correlation coefficient with increasing element separation (see Figs. 2.17 and 2.18). Somewhat surprisingly, however, the overall shape of the response is not unlike that of a first-order Markov process with an adjacent element correlation coefficient of approximately 0.70, and this fact lends support to the argument that, when considering a relation such as that portrayed in Fig 2.18, more weight should be given to the fact that the correlation function decays rapidly, rather than to the precise magnitude of that function for large values of element separation.

In the spectrum of Image 2 we may expect to detect irregularities due to the periodic detail present in the image itself. Since the image is not completely periodic, however, such detail in the spectrum may well be hidden, partially or completely, by more general characteristics. One such irregularity is apparent, though, following which the energy content falls off with frequency to a value even lower than in the case of Image 1. The general energy level is higher than for that image, though, and again indicates difficulties in coding when compared with Image 1. This conclusion will be borne out when we come to consider the actual spectral coefficients obtained for this image following a transform coding operation. It is apparent that, in this case, any simple first-order Markov model will produce a very poor approximation to the power spectrum/spatial frequency relationship.

2.4.4.2 *Properties in the cosine transform domain*

In the preceding section specimen frequency spectra were determined for the three test images by the normal techniques of spectral analysis, and their characteristics related to the original spatial domain statistics of the input data. There is a most important difference between spectral analysis and transform coding, however (although the latter is a 'frequency domain' technique), which is that in the former case we are concerned with the estimation of the spectral properties of the underlying process generating the image(s), whilst in the latter we start with specific images and seek to code, store and/or communicate them efficiently, and finally reproduce them with as little distortion as is practicable. In spectral analysis, therefore, techniques which improve our estimates (smoothing, or windowing, for example) are not only allowable but desirable. In transform coding, on the other hand, such procedures must not be employed (save in very isolated and specialised instances) since they would lead to severe image distortion, and in the spectral (transform) domain the coefficients which are subsequently to be processed are the unmodified product of the operation of the transform upon the input data. In addition to a knowledge of conventional (Fourier) image spectra, therefore, it is necessary to determine the distribution of coefficient energy in the transform domain following the application of the transform of our choice. To this end we employ the techniques of subsection 2.3.3 to move from the correlation properties of the image in the spatial domain to those of the transform coefficients. Now, whilst it is true that the transform used may very well be the discrete Fourier transform, other transforms are not only easier to employ but are more efficient as well (as will be demonstrated in the next chapter), and we close this chapter, therefore, with an examination of the statistical properties of the transform coefficients of the three test images after they have been processed using the discrete cosine transform, which has the advantage of being a real (as opposed to complex) transform of high efficiency. For the purposes of the present discussion it is not necessary to be familiar with the details of the transform, which is fully described in the next chapter.

One matter worth mentioning briefly here is, however, the size of transform used. In most cases a two-dimensional transform has been taken over a region 8 × 8 elements in extent, although the variance maps of the transform domain are of dimension 16 × 16, the better to correspond with the correlation maps of Figs. 2.10, 2.15 and 2.18. If the transform size is much smaller than 8 × 8, significant effects are not shown very distinctly; on the other hand, a larger size is difficult to manage from the point of view of presentation (recall that it is conventional to perform the transform operation over block sizes which are integral powers of two, to correspond with easy implementation by the use of a fast algorithm of the type discussed in Chapter 7). Naturally the block size does have an influence on the efficiency of the transform operation, but again this is discussed elsewhere.

The procedure which will be used here is as follows: we shall employ the theoretical developments presented earlier in this chapter to transform the correlation properties of the image from the spatial to the transform domain, and then compare the results with actual measured values of, specifically, transform coefficient variance (energy) in order to assess the efficacy of the models considered. For this purpose both separable and non-separable models will be examined.

2.4.5   Transform domain properties based on data correlation models

2.4.5.1   *Image 1*

We now employ the previously developed techniques to determine the transform domain properties of the image, the basic assumption being that if we can reliably model the variances of the transform domain coefficients using the statistical characteristics of the input data suitably transformed, it will be unnecessary to measure, per se, the overall properties in the transform domain (necessary for further operations in the transform coding process) of the set of test images. We first of all consider the separable model for the correlation/separation relation of Image 1. Horizontal and vertical correlation coefficients are given by Eqs. (2.88) and (2.89), respectively, and result in the (stationary) correlation matrices of Tables 2.1 and 2.2.

TABLE 2.1. Horizontal correlation matrix,
separable form, Image 1.[a]

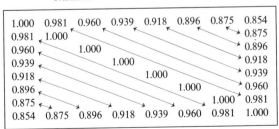

1.000	0.975	0.947	0.917	0.886	0.856	0.826	0.796
0.975	1.000						0.826
0.947		1.000					0.856
0.917			1.000				0.886
0.886				1.000			0.917
0.856					1.000		0.947
0.826						1.000	0.975
0.796	0.826	0.856	0.886	0.917	0.947	0.975	1.000

[a] Based on Eq. 2.88. All values along arrowed lines are
identical.

In terms of this separable model, we may now separately transform each
correlation matrix to the transform domain (using the discrete cosine
transform and the techniques of subsection 2.3.3), to obtain the results shown
in Tables 2.3 and 2.4. It should be noted that the results displayed in Tables
2.1 and 2.2 are conventional (stationary) normalised covariance, i.e., correlation, matrices (notice the unit terms on the main diagonals), whilst those in
Tables 2.3 and 2.4 are (nonstationary) covariance matrices for data having
unit variance. It can be seen that the effect of transformation has been to
'pack' most of the variance (energy), represented by the diagonal terms in
each array into the first coefficient of each matrix whilst significantly reducing
the off-diagonal (residual correlation) components. In order to generate an
array containing the 64 coefficient variances (recall that we are transforming
an 8×8 array) we now form the product

$$\sigma^2(p,q) = C_{\mathrm{T}}(H)_{(q,q)}C_{\mathrm{T}}(V)_{(p,p)} \tag{2.92}$$

i.e., the products of the entries on the main diagonals (variances) of the two
transform domain covariance matrices, to form the variance array of the
transform coefficients shown in Table 2.5. It should be pointed out here that

TABLE 2.2. Vertical correlation matrix.[a]

1.000	0.981	0.960	0.939	0.918	0.896	0.875	0.854
0.981	1.000						0.875
0.960		1.000					0.896
0.939			1.000				0.918
0.918				1.000			0.939
0.896					1.000		0.960
0.875						1.000	0.981
0.854	0.875	0.896	0.918	0.939	0.960	0.981	1.000

[a] Based on Eq. 2.89.

TABLE 2.3. Transform domain covariance matrix (horizontal), Image 1.

$$C_T(H) = \begin{bmatrix} 7.412 & 0 & -0.134 & 0 & -0.030 & 0 & -0.009 & 0 \\ 0 & 0.388 & 0 & 0.001 & 0 & 0 & 0 & 0 \\ -0.134 & 0 & 0.095 & 0 & 0.001 & 0 & 0 & 0 \\ 0 & 0.001 & 0 & 0.041 & 0 & 0 & 0 & 0 \\ -0.030 & 0 & 0.001 & 0 & 0.024 & 0 & 0 & 0 \\ 0 & 0 & 0 & 0 & 0 & 0.016 & 0 & 0 \\ -0.009 & 0 & 0 & 0 & 0 & 0 & 0.013 & 0 \\ 0 & 0 & 0 & 0 & 0 & 0 & 0 & 0.011 \end{bmatrix}$$

this method of determining the transform domain coefficient variances is only applicable to the case of separable correlation. In the general (non-separable) situation we must either form the two-dimensional data covariance matrix (or correlation matrix) and then use the two-dimensional transform techniques to be described in the next chapter, or generate a two-dimensional correlation array for the data (this is not a correlation or covariance matrix of the data, but an array containing, as its ith, jth entry, the value of the correlation coefficient corresponding to that separation vector, as in Fig 2.11, for example, referred to the origin) and use the multiple summation relation of Eq. (2.81).

We can now also determine the transform domain coefficient variance array in the following cases:

(a) The simple first-order Markov model   [Eq. (2.61)]
(b) The generalised isotropic model   [Eqs. (2.66) and (2.67)]
(c) The optimised model   [Eq. (2.68)]
(d) By direct measurement upon the transform domain coefficients themselves

These results are shown in Tables 2.6–2.9, respectively.

TABLE 2.4. Vertical equivalent of Table 2.3.

$$C_T(V) = \begin{bmatrix} 7.572 & 0 & -0.095 & 0 & -0.021 & 0 & -0.007 & 0 \\ 0 & 0.277 & 0 & 0 & 0 & 0 & 0 & 0 \\ -0.095 & 0 & 0.069 & 0 & 0 & 0 & 0 & 0 \\ 0 & 0 & 0 & 0.031 & 0 & 0 & 0 & 0 \\ -0.021 & 0 & 0 & 0 & 0.019 & 0 & 0 & 0 \\ 0 & 0 & 0 & 0 & 0 & 0.013 & 0 & 0 \\ -0.007 & 0 & 0 & 0 & 0 & 0 & 0.010 & 0 \\ 0 & 0 & 0 & 0 & 0 & 0 & 0 & 0.009 \end{bmatrix}$$

TABLE 2.5. Transform domain coefficient variances,
optimum separable model, Image 1.[a]

56.119	2.939	0.717	0.310	0.181	0.125	0.098	0.085
2.056	0.108	0.026	0.011	0.007	0.005	0.004	0.003
0.514	0.027	0.007	0.003	0.002	0.001	0.001	0.001
0.230	0.012	0.003	0.001	0.001	0.001	0.000	0.000
0.137	0.007	0.002	0.001	0.000	0.000	0.000	0.000
0.096	0.005	0.001	0.001	0.000	0.000	0.000	0.000
0.076	0.004	0.001	0.000	0.000	0.000	0.000	0.000
0.067	0.004	0.001	0.000	0.000	0.000	0.000	0.000

[a] Based on Eq. 2.64.

The results for the simple first-order (separable) model are broadly similar to those for the optimised separable model discussed previously. A full discussion will be deferred until results for the other models have been presented. The generalised isotropic model produces quite different results, as might be expected. Horizontal and vertical variances fall off much more rapidly than in the former two cases, but the diagonal terms remain much

TABLE 2.6. Transform domain coefficient variances,
simple first-order model, Image 1.[a]

55.762	2.835	0.810	0.382	0.238	0.172	0.139	0.124
1.990	0.101	0.029	0.014	0.009	0.006	0.005	0.004
0.553	0.028	0.008	0.004	0.002	0.002	0.001	0.001
0.261	0.013	0.004	0.002	0.001	0.001	0.001	0.001
0.162	0.008	0.002	0.001	0.001	0.001	0.000	0.000
0.117	0.006	0.002	0.001	0.001	0.000	0.000	0.000
0.095	0.005	0.001	0.001	0.000	0.000	0.000	0.000
0.084	0.004	0.001	0.001	0.000	0.000	0.000	0.000

[a] Based on Eq. 2.61.

TABLE 2.7. Transform domain coefficient variances,
generalised isotropic model, Image 1.[a]

57.574	2.420	0.383	0.107	0.043	0.022	0.013	0.010
1.416	0.441	0.187	0.081	0.041	0.024	0.016	0.013
0.192	0.136	0.089	0.054	0.033	0.022	0.016	0.013
0.056	0.049	0.041	0.032	0.024	0.018	0.015	0.013
0.024	0.025	0.023	0.020	0.017	0.015	0.013	0.012
0.014	0.015	0.015	0.014	0.013	0.012	0.011	0.011
0.010	0.011	0.011	0.011	0.011	0.010	0.010	0.010
0.008	0.009	0.009	0.009	0.009	0.009	0.009	0.009

[a] Based on Eq. (2.67).

TABLE 2.8. Transform domain coefficient variances,
optimised model, Image 1.[a]

57.064	2.597	0.510	0.183	0.091	0.055	0.039	0.032
1.657	0.293	0.118	0.057	0.033	0.023	0.017	0.015
0.313	0.099	0.053	0.031	0.021	0.015	0.012	0.011
0.115	0.044	0.028	0.019	0.014	0.011	0.009	0.009
0.059	0.025	0.017	0.013	0.010	0.009	0.008	0.007
0.037	0.017	0.012	0.010	0.008	0.007	0.007	0.006
0.027	0.013	0.010	0.008	0.007	0.006	0.006	0.006
0.022	0.011	0.009	0.007	0.006	0.006	0.005	0.005

[a] Based on Eq. 2.68.

higher. It will subsequently be seen that this behaviour is much more in
keeping with that of the actual coefficients. The optimised version of this
model gave a good fit over a wide area to the measured two-dimensional
correlation function, and so we would hope that the results it produces in the
transform domain (Table 2.8) might correspond well with the measured
values. To determine the latter the entire image is divided into 8 × 8 blocks of
data elements, each block is two-dimensionally transformed and the separate
coefficient variances calculated, with the results shown in Table 2.9. Naturally
we would not expect the results obtained by the two approaches to be
identical, owing principally to statistical problems in estimating the covariance parameters of the image data, but if the differences are significant, for
such a 'well-behaved' image as the present one, then the construction of
image correlation models will not be a reliable approach to the optimisation
of a transform coding system.

We see that, whilst all models give reasonable estimates of the variance of
the DC coefficient, the simple and optimum separable models are significantly in error where the higher order coefficients are concerned. The
generalised isotropic models (Tables 2.7 and 2.8) are a much better match to
the measured values, although higher-order estimates are still very poor, even

TABLE 2.9. Transform domain coefficient variances,
direct measurement of Image 1.

58.031	2.700	0.433	0.140	0.045	0.012	0.005	0.002
1.536	0.215	0.113	0.047	0.021	0.010	0.002	0.002
0.187	0.068	0.038	0.024	0.024	0.013	0.002	0.001
0.069	0.027	0.021	0.012	0.010	0.005	0.002	0.002
0.013	0.007	0.007	0.005	0.004	0.002	0.001	0.001
0.012	0.009	0.007	0.006	0.006	0.003	0.001	0.001
0.009	0.006	0.006	0.005	0.007	0.005	0.002	0.002
0.014	0.004	0.005	0.004	0.004	0.003	0.002	0.002

though in this case we are able to model the data correlation array to a good degree of accuracy (see Fig. 2.9). It may be argued, of course, that an important feature of a transform coding scheme is the setting to zero of small, high-order coefficients (or, equivalently, the allocation to them of no bits for transmission, see Chapter 4), and so we need not be too concerned about their accurate estimation. Whilst this is certainly true, we have not yet considered just what should be considered 'small' in this context and, in any case, our present purpose is to consider whether accurate image correlation modelling is even practicable without excessive complication. It is prudent, therefore, at this stage to try to generate a model which is reasonably accurate over as much of the transform block as possible. Without going to the trouble of an exact quantitative analysis, however, the reader may ascertain, by examining the coefficients in the upper left quarter of the various arrays, that the optimised model does indeed give the best overall coefficient variance estimate.

2.4.5.2 *Image 2*

We have seen that, even when the image data correlation function in two dimensions may be modelled accurately, the equivalent relation in the transform domain is still subject to a significant degree of error. We may expect the results, therefore, to be proportionately worse when we can only establish an approximate data domain model.

Such is the case with Image 2, where we were only able to approximate the horizontal and vertical correlation functions with a simple model using one-step correlation coefficients of, respectively, 0.76 and 0.87 out to an element separation of 7. Furthermore, by examining Fig. 2.14, it can be seen that the diagonal and horizontal correlation functions are almost identical over that range. The results of applying a first-order separable Markov model with the preceding parameters are shown in Table 2.10. Table 2.11 contains equivalent results for the generalised isotropic model of Eq. (2.66), and Table 2.12 the

TABLE 2.10. Transform domain coefficient variances,
simple first-order model, Image 2.[a]

25.262	9.517	4.444	2.337	1.514	1.113	0.912	0.812
5.311	2.001	0.934	0.491	0.318	0.234	0.192	0.171
1.965	0.740	0.346	0.182	0.118	0.087	0.071	0.063
0.956	0.360	0.168	0.088	0.057	0.042	0.035	0.031
0.606	0.228	0.107	0.056	0.036	0.027	0.022	0.020
0.439	0.166	0.077	0.041	0.026	0.019	0.016	0.014
0.358	0.135	0.063	0.033	0.022	0.016	0.013	0.012
0.318	0.118	0.056	0.029	0.019	0.014	0.012	0.010

[a] Based on Eq. (2.61.)

TABLE 2.11. Transform domain coefficient variances,
generalised isotropic model, Image 2.[a]

29.425	9.586	3.655	1.473	0.756	0.449	0.313	0.250
4.073	2.242	1.316	0.757	0.476	0.328	0.250	0.212
0.955	0.728	0.558	0.409	0.306	0.240	0.199	0.178
0.324	0.286	0.256	0.222	0.191	0.167	0.151	0.141
0.171	0.160	0.151	0.140	0.130	0.122	0.115	0.112
0.110	0.107	0.104	0.101	0.098	0.095	0.093	0.091
0.085	0.084	0.083	0.082	0.081	0.080	0.079	0.078
0.074	0.073	0.073	0.073	0.072	0.072	0.071	0.071

[a] Based on Eq. (2.66).

TABLE 2.12. Transform domain coefficient variances,
optimised model, Image 2.[a]

27.853	9.538	3.963	1.816	1.051	0.700	0.533	0.453
4.635	2.106	1.117	0.629	0.412	0.300	0.243	0.214
1.366	0.746	0.468	0.307	0.223	0.177	0.150	0.137
0.553	0.335	0.234	0.171	0.135	0.114	0.102	0.095
0.312	0.200	0.147	0.114	0.095	0.084	0.077	0.073
0.206	0.138	0.106	0.086	0.074	0.067	0.062	0.060
0.158	0.109	0.086	0.071	0.063	0.058	0.054	0.053
0.135	0.095	0.076	0.064	0.057	0.053	0.050	0.049

[a] Based on Eq. (2.68).

TABLE 2.13. Transform domain coefficient variances,
direct measurement of Image 2.

29.057	6.087	5.044	3.167	3.798	0.499	0.110	0.035
5.047	2.785	1.376	0.237	0.153	0.032	0.010	0.003
1.758	1.886	0.960	0.145	0.064	0.020	0.007	0.002
0.543	0.251	0.184	0.079	0.030	0.008	0.004	0.001
0.166	0.018	0.029	0.040	0.023	0.009	0.004	0.001
0.031	0.016	0.013	0.011	0.018	0.015	0.004	0.001
0.017	0.007	0.006	0.013	0.018	0.014	0.006	0.001
0.006	0.003	0.003	0.004	0.004	0.006	0.003	0.001

values obtained using the exponent relationship ($h = \sqrt{2}$) which was found to be optimum in the case of Image 1. The actual measured variances are given in Table 2.13.

In this case it is obvious that all models give results for the higher-order coefficients which are grossly in error, the actual variances in that range being very small. This is broadly in agreement with the conventional spectral analysis of the image (Fig. 2.20) which shows significant energy content in the lower part of the spectrum with a sudden drop to much lower values at higher frequencies. None of the models, moreover, can be expected to reproduce the peak evident in the spectral response (see Fig. 2.20, and Table 2.13—row 3, coefficient 2 and row 1, coefficient 5). This image, more than the previous one, shows the inadequacy of simple correlation models for the purpose of accurate transform domain coefficient variance estimation, especially where periodicities in spatial detail generate peaks in either the horizontal or vertical image spectra.

2.4.5.3 *Image 3*

As a generalisation, it is frequently said that transform coding is inefficient as a data compression scheme for two-level images, since the irregularly spaced high amplitude transitions generate substantial frequency components over the whole frequency range. As far as modelling is concerned, however, the horizontal power spectrum, at least, is reasonably well represented by a first-order Markov model with one-step correlation coefficient 0.70, and if we model the vertical process in the same way with a value 0.77 (see Fig. 2.17), the resulting transform domain coefficient variance estimates are as given in Table 2.14. As before, generalised isotropic and optimised versions are included also (Tables 2.15 and 2.16), and the actual measured values in Table 2.17.

This time we see that, as usual, the separable model significantly underestimates higher-order variances, and the best simple model for this image is the generalised isotropic model of Table 2.15, although it tends to overestimate low-order values of variance, and could probably be improved by assuming rather smaller values of correlation coefficients. It should be re-emphasised, however, that the model properties are specific to the image under consideration, and are not of general validity. This fact is brought sharply into focus

TABLE 2.14. Transform domain coefficient variances,
simple first-order model, Image 3.[a]

17.277	7.954	4.139	2.295	1.512	1.123	0.924	0.825
6.259	2.882	1.500	0.831	0.548	0.407	0.335	0.299
2.868	1.320	0.687	0.381	0.251	0.186	0.153	0.137
1.495	0.688	0.358	0.199	0.131	0.097	0.080	0.071
0.967	0.445	0.232	0.128	0.085	0.063	0.052	0.046
0.710	0.327	0.170	0.094	0.062	0.046	0.038	0.034
0.581	0.267	0.139	0.077	0.051	0.038	0.031	0.028
0.517	0.238	0.140	0.069	0.045	0.034	0.028	0.025

[a] Based on Eq. (2.61).

TABLE 2.15. Transform domain coefficient variances, generalised isotropic model, Image 3.[a]

21.307	8.201	3.391	1.410	0.731	0.442	0.313	0.254
5.819	3.136	1.739	0.930	0.554	0.370	0.278	0.234
1.920	1.336	0.929	0.612	0.419	0.308	0.246	0.215
0.712	0.591	0.488	0.383	0.301	0.245	0.209	0.190
0.370	0.330	0.296	0.258	0.223	0.196	0.177	0.167
0.230	0.217	0.205	0.190	0.175	0.163	0.153	0.147
0.171	0.166	0.161	0.154	0.148	0.141	0.137	0.133
0.145	0.142	0.140	0.137	0.133	0.130	0.127	0.125

[a] Based on Eq. (2.66).

TABLE 2.16. Transform domain coefficient variances, optimised model, Image 3.[a]

19.700	8.126	3.719	1.778	1.040	0.698	0.534	0.455
6.066	2.975	1.592	0.875	0.557	0.399	0.318	0.278
2.339	1.317	0.803	0.499	0.346	0.264	0.219	0.196
1.027	0.642	0.435	0.301	0.227	0.184	0.159	0.146
0.589	0.390	0.281	0.208	0.166	0.140	0.125	0.117
0.393	0.272	0.205	0.159	0.132	0.115	0.105	0.100
0.302	0.214	0.166	0.133	0.113	0.101	0.093	0.089
0.258	0.186	0.147	0.120	0.104	0.093	0.087	0.084

[a] Based on Eq. (2.68).

TABLE 2.17. Transform domain coefficient variances, direct measurement of Image 3.

15.214	6.930	5.211	2.326	0.933	0.414	0.257	0.269
4.920	2.469	1.665	0.873	0.456	0.231	0.157	0.162
3.755	1.747	1.133	0.622	0.332	0.181	0.136	0.136
2.431	1.152	0.666	0.418	0.263	0.156	0.117	0.122
1.041	0.490	0.367	0.243	0.202	0.138	0.123	0.128
0.741	0.389	0.282	0.185	0.150	0.121	0.116	0.120
0.404	0.305	0.208	0.176	0.151	0.111	0.128	0.130
0.251	0.252	0.266	0.214	0.195	0.170	0.159	0.161

by considering the three images which have been analysed in this chapter as three images which it is desired to process using the same transform coding system. The model for any one of the images is then seen to be quite unsuitable for the other two. We shall return to this topic, and discuss methods of overcoming the problem when the allocation of coding bits to the various coefficients is considered in Chapter 4.

2.4.6 Equi-variance contours for Images 1, 2 and 3.

As a final comment on the transform domain modelling process we examine plots of equal variance contours for the three images using a block size of 16 × 16, complementing the correlation maps of Figs. 2.10, 2.15, and 2.18. Finite values, of course, only exist at the coefficient locations, but continuous curves calculated by logarithmic interpolation serve to clarify the diagrams. For Image 1 (Fig. 2.21), the variance falls off very rapidly as we move away from the zero frequency (DC) coefficient in the top left-hand corner. Within the upper left-hand quarter of the distribution, the function is more or less 'well behaved', over the remainder of the distribution there is no obvious form or character, even though the correlation function is a smooth function of element separation over the whole area (with an image like this, of course, we would hope, in an efficient transform coding scheme, to eliminate all but a relatively few significant coefficients). Figure 2.22 is interesting, for it clearly shows the influence of periodicities within Image 2, principally by the marked peak at coefficient 4 in the fourth row of coefficients, and in the pronounced diagonal structure of the distribution. Here 'significant' coefficients cover a much more extensive region than was the case for the previous image, and this will naturally be reflected in the coding bit allocations necessary for this image. This is even more the case with the variance distribution of the black and white image shown in Fig. 2.23, where even the highest-order coefficients have relatively large magnitudes, which will certainly influence the coefficient bit allocations. A somewhat rough and ready

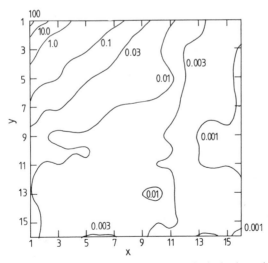

FIG. 2.21. Equi-variance contours for Image 1. Here, x is the horizontal coefficient location and y the vertical coefficient location. Parameter is the actual value of variance.

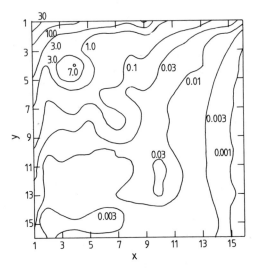

FIG. 2.22. Equi-variance contours for Image 2. Here, x is the horizontal coefficient location and y the vertical coefficient location. Parameter is the actual value of variance.

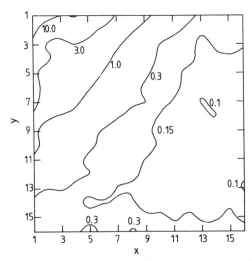

FIG. 2.23. Equi-variance contours for Image 3. Here, x is the horizontal coefficient location and y the vertical coefficient location. Parameter is the actual value of variance.

comparison of image properties (and, in this context, suitability for transform coding) may be made by examining the ratio of maximum to minimum variance over the given block size. For Images 1, 2 and 3 these figures are, to an order of magnitude, 10^5, 10^4 and 10^2, respectively. The corresponding variations in input data energy over the same areas are $\pm 13\%$, $\pm 29\%$ and $\pm 36\%$ for the three images. These figures show at once how much easier it will be to apply transform coding efficiently to Image 1 rather than to Image 3, for instance, and also effectively demonstrate the energy redistribution properties of the transform operation.

2.5 Summary

In the present chapter the fundamental properties of images relevant to their efficient coding have been introduced, both through theoretical development and by the use of experimentally measured results for three widely differing test images. Initial discussions related to information theoretic aspects, where the entropy serves as an indication of the lowest possible coding rate in order that no information be lost in the process. In fact, of course, this approach is seriously hampered by the practical impossibility of measuring joint probability statistics for more than pairs of picture elements when the number of separate grey levels is sufficient to reproduce continuous gradations of intensity acceptably (roughly speaking, a minimum of 7 bits). It does form a useful way of characterising images, however, and serves as a basis for the more potentially valuable area of coding with respect to a fidelity criterion, to be discussed in a later chapter.

Next to be considered were more easily determined properties, acknowledging the difficulties associated with the non-stationary nature of image sources discussed in Appendix 2. Thus we can straightforwardly determine the mean and variance of the three test images, and then define the one-dimensional covariance matrix and estimate values of the correlation function. This characteristic is then extended to its two-dimensional form, and it was shown that, if horizontal and vertical processes could be considered separable, a simplified formulation of what would otherwise become a very large matrix problem was possible. It was then considered useful to attempt to model, as simply as possible, the correlation functions of the test images in order to determine whether this process would be generally successful, and it was found that this could be done with ease only for 'simple' images of the kind represented by Image 1. As an adjunct to the correlation (i.è., spatial) properties of images, their (power) spectral properties were also considered, and it was shown that, in two cases at least, the horizontal process could be modelled reasonably well by the spectrum of a first-order Markov process. In passing we might note here that all images examined have a spectrum which decays in magnitude as the spatial frequency increases, even though Image 2, for example, has a marked periodic structure which appears as a peak in the spectral response.

Of course, although spectral representations are useful in that they give us more information about our basic data, in transform coding schemes they are also important in that they indicate how transmission capacity (i.e., coding bits) should be allocated, and for this reason image modelling is also important, for it is often pointed out that modelling in the spatial domain can, in principle, lead to determination of the transform domain distribution of the variance of the coefficients, without the necessity for their direct measurement, via the equivalence of image representation in the two domains. In fact, as has been demonstrated here, the modelling procedure is not particularly successful, even in the case of Image 1, where an accurate correlation model can be devised, and we are led to the conclusion that the magnitudes of the higher-order coefficients, at least, in the transform domain are very sensitive to the fine structure of the two-dimensional correlation function. These difficulties are emphasised in cases (for example, Image 2) where the correlation function itself cannot be modelled with any degree of confidence.

What broad conclusions, then, may be drawn from the foregoing examination of image properties? First, that entropy measurements indicate a maximum data rate reduction factor of two, or perhaps three, for any compression scheme which is intended to reproduce the input image without any loss of information. Since even a passing acquaintance with the transform coding literature will show that such schemes are intended to produce much higher values than these (for which differential pulse code modulation offers a simpler implementation and excellent reproduced quality; see Musmann, 1979), it is evident that impairments will be present in the reproduced image, and the extent to which these are acceptable is a matter of purely subjective assessment, although we shall have occasion to return to the topic of simple numerical distortion measures subsequently. Second, measurements on test images demonstrate that, even when there is a large amount of rapidly varying detail, high spatial frequency components are significantly smaller in magnitude than those of lower frequencies, and so the general transform coding principle of allocating little, or no, transmission capacity to such coefficients as a means of achieving data compression is sound. Third, attempts to model spatial correlation accurately for an image (Kim and Kim, 1983) or for a set of images (Mauersberger, 1979c) in order to determine an optimised (in some sense) bit allocation scheme in the transform domain are accompanied by uncertainty even if, as in the latter case, a wide selection of images is used and optimisation is carried out in the transform domain. The resulting coding scheme will then be efficient to the extent that images corresponding to those in the test set are used with equal probability, but the technique cannot guarantee that serious degradation will not occur in any particular case. An obvious (partial) solution to the problem is to allow the transmission capacity (bit allocation) to vary on a block by block basis according to localised image 'activity'. This brings with it the problem of variation of instantaneous transmission rate, and takes us into the realm of the material dealt with in Chapter 5.

As a final general comment on image modelling we may contrast the statistical approach presented here (and, of course, appropriate to the coding technique considered in this book) with the 'structural' approach of, for example, Tenenbaum et al. (1981), in which the importance of the underlying structure of a perceived scene is emphasised. There can be little doubt that such modelling concepts hold the key to further significant advances in image data processing, although they will, of necessity, require the associated development of new approaches to the image coding problem.

Chapter 3

Orthogonal Transforms for Image Coding

3.1 Introduction

In any transform coding scheme the central operation is, naturally, the application of the transform to the one-, two- or three-dimensional data array. This step effects a reduction in the correlation which exists between the individual data samples and results in a set of coefficients the members of which may be separately quantised according to their statistical properties (see Chapter 4). Together with the reduction in inter-element correlation there is an equivalent reduction in redundancy which increases the efficiency of the coding operation but, of necessity, leaves the data (in the form of transform coefficients) more 'fragile', i.e., more susceptible to the influence of errors in the storage or transmission medium (this problem will be discussed in more detail subsequently). In the present chapter the fundamental properties of transforms suitable for image coding are presented, together with descriptions and comparisons of the efficiencies (in terms of the reduction in inter-element correlation and ability to 'pack' the signal energy into as few transform coefficients as possible) of those which have been employed for image data compression over the past 10–15 years. One point is immediately worthy of note, and that is that all such transforms are separable; i.e., a two- or three-dimensional transform operation may be factored into the successive application of a one-dimensional transform in the appropriate directions. Specification and comparison of various transforms may therefore, without loss in generality, be carried out with reference to the one-dimensional form. Since, however, the vast majority of transform coding experiments have been carried out in two dimensions and, furthermore, the natural form of an image is a two-dimensional array, a mathematical formulation is developed in this case also.

3.2 The transform operation in one dimension

In describing the transform operation we initially consider only the general case, and leave until later an acknowledgement of the fact that it is desirable, for the purposes of straightforward regeneration of the data from the set of transform coefficients, that the 'forward' and 'inverse' transforms are related in certain specific ways.

Thus the transform operation is that of successive multiplication of the elements of a data vector by those of a set of 'basis' vectors, each of which can be considered as a set of weighting factors, the summing of the values so obtained, and the possible multiplication of the result by a scaling fator, the magnitude of which will be dependent on the number of elements within the data vector, i.e., upon the size of the transform. Suppose, for simplicity, that the data vector is of length four

$$\mathbf{f}^T = [f_1 \quad f_2 \quad f_3 \quad f_4] \tag{3.1}$$

[recall that convention requires that all vectors be written as column vectors—hence the inclusion of the transpose notation in Eq. (3.1)]. The first transform coefficient is given by the product operation described earlier, where the first basis vector is

$$\mathbf{t}_1^T = [t_{11} \quad t_{12} \quad t_{13} \quad t_{14}] \tag{3.2}$$

and so

$$C_1 = f_1 t_{11} + f_2 t_{12} + f_3 t_{13} + f_4 t_{14} \tag{3.3}$$

Similarly, if the second basis vector is

$$\mathbf{t}_2^T = [t_{21} \quad t_{22} \quad t_{23} \quad t_{24}] \tag{3.4}$$

then,

$$C_2 = f_1 t_{21} + f_2 t_{22} + f_3 t_{23} + f_4 t_{24} \tag{3.5}$$

and so on. The operation may therefore be written as

$$C_p = \sum_{k=1}^{4} f_k t_{pk} \qquad p = 1 \to 4 \tag{3.6}$$

and, for a data vector of length, and transform of equivalent size N,

$$C_p = \sum_{k=1}^{N} f_k t_{pk} \qquad p = 1 \to N \tag{3.7}$$

Note that the elements of either, or both, **f** and **t** may be complex, and that the data and basis vector indexing may alternatively cover the range $0 \rightarrow N - 1$. For computer simulation the preceding form is probably more convenient, for certain relationships connected with the development of fast transform algorithms the latter is to be preferred. It is immediately apparent that the transform operation, in one interpretation, may be viewed as a process of feature extraction. A large positive value of the transform coefficient will result when corresponding elements of the data and basis vectors take on similar values and signs; i.e., when the 'shapes' of both vectors (plotted as element amplitude against position within the vector) are alike. Again, if the magnitudes are similar but the signs always different, then the transform coefficient will assume a large negative value. This is, of course, just the way in which Fourier transformation works when carrying out spectral analysis —the basis vectors in that case being sine and cosine functions of increasing frequencies.

The operation of Eq. (3.7) may conveniently be expressed in matrix/vector form thus,

$$\mathbf{C} = [T]\mathbf{f} \tag{3.8}$$

where **C** and **f** are $N \times 1$ matrices (column vectors) containing transform coefficients and data elements, respectively, and $[T]$ is now a 'basis matrix' containing $\mathbf{t}_1^T, \mathbf{t}_2^T, \ldots \mathbf{t}_N^T$, the individual basis vectors written in row form, i.e., in the case $N = 4$,

$$\begin{bmatrix} C_1 \\ C_2 \\ C_3 \\ C_4 \end{bmatrix} = \begin{bmatrix} t_{11} & t_{12} & t_{13} & t_{14} \\ t_{21} & t_{22} & t_{23} & t_{24} \\ t_{31} & t_{32} & t_{33} & t_{34} \\ t_{41} & t_{42} & t_{43} & t_{44} \end{bmatrix} \begin{bmatrix} f_1 \\ f_2 \\ f_3 \\ f_4 \end{bmatrix} \tag{3.9}$$

The practical implementation of this operation requires, for the determination of N transform coefficients, N^2 (complex) multiplications and $N(N - 1)$ (complex) additions, and is, for a large data array, a considerable computational load. This has led to the development of many so-called 'fast' algorithms (discussed in Chapter 7), the most well known of which is, of course, the fast Fourier transform (FFT).

It is appropriate here, in a discussion of elementary transform properties, to consider another interpretation of the transform operation, described in its original form by Wintz (1972), which clearly highlights the correlation-reducing properties of the approach. Suppose that we observe elements of the image data in sets of three (normally larger data vectors are chosen but, since the number of dimensions in the resulting interpretation is equal to the number of elements, three is the maximum number which allows a simple mental 'picture' to be formed). Suppose, further, that the image data has reasonably high correlation between elements, which is, in any case, a necessary condition for data compression schemes to function effectively. It is likely, then, that any three adjacent elements will have similar values and, conversely, very unlikely that they will have widely differing values. If we now plot the observed values of the elements in the length three data vectors in a three-dimensional coordinate system as shown in Fig. 3.1, we shall expect the region occupied by the majority of the points to lie close to the line $x = y = z$, forming, as illustrated in the figure, the elongated, roughly cigar-shaped volume. Furthermore, all of the elements within the data vector are likely to have more or less the same energy (taken as the square of the element amplitude). Consider now the data vector transformed by coordinate rotation to axes u, v and w. In this new coordinate set, the elements all have u components which are much larger than those in the v and w directions (if the correlation within the original data were perfect, the v and w components would be zero). We can now specify the data (now in the transform domain)

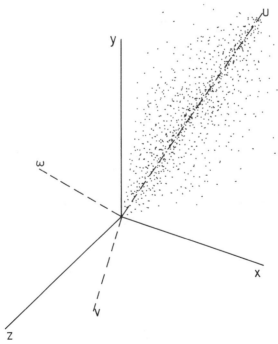

FIG. 3.1. Representation of 'likely' locations of three element image vectors in three dimensions.

by transmitting, or storing, only one component (u) accurately and, depending on requirements, retaining v and w components in approximate form or even not at all. On an energy basis, we now have one high-energy component and two of much lower energy. This interpretation may easily be extended conceptually to a vector of, say, 8 or 16 elements, as is more usual in transform coding, but a pictorial representation is naturally no longer possible. In passing, we may note that such coordinate transformations are well known in geometry (see, e.g., Pettofrezzo and Lacatena, 1970) and that one important property of such rotations is that the scalar (inner) product remains invariant under such an operation (see Appendix 6). This immediately leads to the important property of energy invariance between data and transform domains discussed in more detail subsequently.

To conclude this section a simple example is given which demonstrates some of these properties. We take the 4×4 Walsh–Hadamard matrix (for a theoretical development of this transform see Subsection 3.5.3), and data vector $[5\ 6\ 4\ 8]^T$. Thus, in the notation of Eq. (3.9),

$$\begin{bmatrix} C_1 \\ C_2 \\ C_3 \\ C_4 \end{bmatrix} = \frac{1}{2} \begin{bmatrix} 1 & 1 & 1 & 1 \\ 1 & 1 & -1 & -1 \\ 1 & -1 & -1 & 1 \\ 1 & -1 & 1 & -1 \end{bmatrix} \begin{bmatrix} 5 \\ 6 \\ 4 \\ 8 \end{bmatrix} \qquad (3.10)$$

giving,

$$\mathbf{C}^T = [11.5\ \ -0.5\ \ \ 1.5\ \ -2.5] \qquad (3.11)$$

The total energy in the data domain is $5^2 + 6^2 + 4^2 + 8^2 = 141$ and in the transform domain is $11.5^2 + 0.5^2 + 1.5^2 + 2.5^2 = 141$. Thus four data elements of reasonably similar magnitudes have been transformed into four coefficients, one of which is large and the others relatively small. Furthermore, in this case the first coefficient is just the scaled average of the data (5.75), and, to return to the data domain, all we need do is apply Eq (3.9) once more, but this time replacing the data vector by the transform coefficient vector. The reader may thus easily show that if we now choose to transmit or store only the two dominant coefficients (setting the two smallest to zero), the resulting reconstructed data vector is now $[4.5\ 7.0\ 4.5\ 7.0]^T$.

3.2.1   Mathematical properties of one-dimensional transforms

It was pointed out earlier that the one-dimensional transform operation could be elegantly expressed using matrix/vector notation. Since we shall eventually be applying transform coding techniques to images, which are themselves naturally two-dimensional arrays, it is not surprising that the properties of matrices and manipulations involving them are extensively employed in image processing theory. Here we develop the relevant properties of those matrices suitable for carrying out image transformations, recalling that, for the most part, data values are purely real, as are the elements of the transform basis matrix. Of course, the most well known transform of all, the Fourier transform, has a complex basis matrix and, further, in its two-dimensional form involves the manipulation of complex data values also. It is therefore necessary to develop the general theory taking this into account although, apart from the specific case just referred to, either the basis matrix or the data, but not both, is complex, allowing some simplification in manipulation.

The property of 'orthogonality' is fundamental to the representation of a data vector in terms of a set of predetermined basis vectors and the associated transform coefficients. To return briefly to the feature extraction interpretation of the transform operation mentioned earlier in the present chapter, it is desirable that the individual basis vectors 'identify' totally different types of detail within the data vector. Thus, to take a simple example, consider the analysis of a single sine wave using a (co)sinusoidal set of basis vectors, just one sine/cosine pair of which have the same frequency as that of the input data. Obviously we shall expect to find finite values of the weighting coefficients (of relative magnitude dependent upon the phase relationship between the data and basis vectors) for the basis pair of the correct frequency and zero response at all other frequencies. The element-by-element product and subsequent sum between all other basis vectors and the data vector should therefore be zero. This can only be the case, however, if the process produces zero resultant when applied between any pair of basis vectors, independent of the data vector. If this condition is satisfied, the basis vectors are said to be mutually orthogonal. In the case of complex-valued basis elements the product involves the complex conjugate of the values within one of the vectors. The basis matrix is then said to be unitary. These results are usually expessed mathematically as follows. Consider, for the moment, a continuous data vector $\mathbf{f}_k$ represented over any interval of length K as the sum of a set of basis functions t_{qk} multiplied by the appropriate weighting functions (coefficients), C_q, i.e.,

$$\mathbf{f}_k = \sum_{q=1}^{\infty} C_q t_{qk} \qquad (3.12)$$

To determine the coefficients C_q, we multiply both sides of Eq. (3.12) by t_{pk}^* [where $(\cdot)^*$ denotes complex conjugate], and integrate over K, thus

$$\int_K \mathbf{f}_k t_{pk}^* \, dk = \int_K \sum_{q=1}^{\infty} C_q t_{qk} t_{pk}^* dk \qquad (3.13)$$

The orthogonality condition must now result in zero contribution to the summation except in the case $p = q$, i.e.,

$$\int_K t_{qk} t_{pk}^* \, dk = \begin{cases} 0 & p \neq q \\ A & p = q \end{cases} \tag{3.14}$$

where A is a constant (if $A = 1$ the basis functions are termed orthonormal), and so,

$$C_p = \frac{1}{A} \int_K \mathbf{f}_k t_{pk}^* \, dk \qquad p = 1 \to \infty \tag{3.15}$$

The orthogonal set of basis vectors $[T] = [t_{pk}]$ has the property that, if we initially wish to approximate the desired function $\mathbf{f}_k$ with a limited number of basis vectors and their associated weighting coefficients C_p, the addition of further terms in order to reduce subsequently the approximation error entails no modification to the previously determined values of C_p, since by virtue of the orthogonality property of Eq. (3.14), the cross-product terms which appear are automatically zero [this property is clearly demonstrated and explained by Lynn (1982)]. Furthermore, if the basis set has the property of 'completeness' [which implies that, with a finite number of terms, it is always possible to represent a continuous signal with an approximation which differs from the original by an amount less than ϵ, however small ϵ may be; for a further discussion of this point see Ahmed and Rao (1975), Gallager (1968), or Courant and Hilbert (1953)], then the data vector may be exactly represented by a finite number of basis vectors and weighting factors only. Hence Eq. (3.12) may be modified to

$$\mathbf{f}_k = \sum_{q=1}^{N} C_q t_{qk} \tag{3.16}$$

In the preceding equation, the data $\mathbf{f}_k$ is still continuous. In the discrete case, of course, $\mathbf{f}_k$ represents the sampled data input and, given a data vector of length N (i.e., N separate values), there will be N basis vectors and N transform (weighting) coefficients. A complete orthogonal basis will then allow exact representation of the N values of the data vector in the transform domain, as in the simple example of Section 3.2, where $N = 4$, and the value of A given by Eq. (3.14) in its discrete form in the case $p = q$ is

$$A = \sum_{k=1}^{4} t_{qk} t_{qk} = 1 \qquad q = 1 \to 4 \tag{3.17}$$

The basis matrix in Eq. (3.10) is therefore orthonormal.

As pointed out earlier, transform relationships are concisely expressed in matrix form, as in the case of Eq. (3.8), and using this formulation we may consider how to return from the transform domain to the reconstructed data domain, following processing or storage of the coefficients. To do this we need to be able to invert the relationship expressed by Eq. (3.8) with as little difficulty as possible. Thus, premultiplying both sides of the equation by the inverse of the transform matrix gives

$$[T]^{-1}\mathbf{C} = [T]^{-1}[T]\mathbf{f}$$

$$= [I_N]\mathbf{f} \tag{3.18}$$

where $[I_N]$ is the unit, or identity, matrix of order N. Thus

$$\mathbf{f} = [T]^{-1}\mathbf{C} \tag{3.19}$$

We need therefore to form the inverse of the transform matrix $[T]$, and it turns out that, for orthogonal and unitary matrices, inversion is particularly straightforward. In the case of a unitary matrix (having complex terms), the appropriate relation may, in a simple manner, be shown to be

$$[T_C]^{-1} = [T_C^*]^T \tag{3.20}$$

i.e., the basis matrix inverse is the transpose of its complex conjugate (the subscript merely denoting that the elements of the matrix are complex numbers). In this case the unitary matrix has also been taken to be orthonormal. In the general real orthogonal case

$$[T_R]^{-1} = \frac{1}{A}[T_R]^T \tag{3.21}$$

and, of course, $A = 1$ if orthonormality holds. The original data then, or an approximation in the case of efficient coding and transmission or storage of the coefficient set, is obtained by multiplying the transform coefficient vector by the transpose of the original basis matrix. The relation between forward and inverse operations is further exemplified in Appendix 3.

Since multiplying a matrix by its inverse results in the identity matrix

$$[T][T]^{-1} = [I] \tag{3.22}$$

then multiplying an orthonormal (real) basis matrix by its transpose,

$$[T_R][T_R]^T = [I] \tag{3.23}$$

or a unitary (complex) basis matrix by the transpose of its complex conjugate

$$[T_C][T_C^*]^T = [I] \tag{3.24}$$

will do so also, and this forms a useful check on the correctness (or otherwise!) of the basis functions generated in a transform coding simulation programme. It is worthwhile recalling also that the use of basis matrices in orthonormal form results in energy invariance between transform and data domains, and this property can be used as a further check on a coding simulation. It should be borne in mind, however, that a practical implementation of a transform coding operation will employ the basis matrix in a form most suited to easy computation, and scaling factors introduced to ensure theoretical orthonormality are not necessary in such a context.

3.3   The transform operation in two dimensions

As has been previously discussed, the basic discrete transform operation consists of the term-by-term multiplication of the elements of a data vector with those of one of a set of basis vectors, the latter having clearly defined properties of orthogonality (or orthonormality) and completeness, subsequent summation and possibly scaling. The result, which will be elaborated upon later, is a set of weakly correlated transform coefficients which may be further processed and then transmitted or stored for later inverse transformation. As has been shown in the previous chapter, however, much image data has strong inter-element correlation in more than one direction, and a one-dimensional transform will only take account of correlation between the individual elements of a data vector (strictly speaking, between the sequences formed by like elements in an ensemble of data vectors), and not between adjacent vectors. This is most easily demonstrated by returning to the example of Section 3.2 [Eq. (3.10)] and extending the data vector to form what might be a typical small block of data, thus

$$[F] = \begin{bmatrix} 5 & 6 & 8 & 10 \\ 6 & 6 & 5 & 7 \\ 4 & 5 & 3 & 6 \\ 8 & 7 & 5 & 5 \end{bmatrix} \tag{3.25}$$

Here $[F]$ is now a two-dimensional array of data vectors, of which our original example forms one. We initially carry out the previous one-dimensional transform operation of Eq. (3.10) once again, but this time on all four vectors separately, to obtain a set of four transform coefficient vectors, the first of which is as before [Eq. (3.11)]. Thus

$$[C'] = \frac{1}{2} \begin{bmatrix} 1 & 1 & 1 & 1 \\ 1 & 1 & -1 & -1 \\ 1 & -1 & -1 & 1 \\ 1 & -1 & 1 & -1 \end{bmatrix} \begin{bmatrix} 5 & 6 & 8 & 10 \\ 6 & 6 & 5 & 7 \\ 4 & 5 & 3 & 6 \\ 8 & 7 & 5 & 5 \end{bmatrix}$$

$$= \begin{bmatrix} 11.5 & 12.0 & 10.5 & 14.0 \\ -0.5 & 0.0 & 2.5 & 3.0 \\ 1.5 & 1.0 & 2.5 & 1.0 \\ -2.5 & -1.0 & 0.5 & 2.0 \end{bmatrix} \tag{3.26}$$

where $[C']$ denotes the first-stage result in the two-dimensional transform operation. Note that the total energy in each domain (the sum of the squares of the terms) is the same, namely 620. It is also worth observing that, whereas in the data domain the energy is, roughly speaking, evenly distributed over the array, in the transform domain one quarter of the coefficients contain 94% of the total. It is usual, in fact, for the majority of image energy to reside within the overall mean value, and this is reflected in the large magnitudes of the lowest-order coefficients.

It is obvious that the coefficient array obtained by one-dimensional transformation still contains significant 'structure' in the horizontal direction, and this may be removed by a further one-dimensional transformation, this time performed upon the rows of $[C']$. We could now, if we wished, transpose the elements of $[C']$ and reapply Eq. (3.8) in its original form, but this would result in an array which would require a further transposition to obtain the final result. Instead, therefore, we now postmultiply by the transpose of the basis matrix i.e., $[T]^T$, thus

$$[C] = [C'][T]^T$$
$$= [T][F][T]^T \qquad (3.27)$$

i.e.,

$$[C] = \frac{1}{2}\begin{bmatrix} 11.5 & 12.0 & 10.5 & 14.0 \\ -0.5 & 0.0 & 2.5 & 3.0 \\ 1.5 & 1.0 & 2.5 & 1.0 \\ -2.5 & -1.0 & 0.5 & 2.0 \end{bmatrix}\begin{bmatrix} 1 & 1 & 1 & 1 \\ 1 & 1 & -1 & -1 \\ 1 & -1 & -1 & 1 \\ 1 & -1 & 1 & -1 \end{bmatrix}$$

$$= \begin{bmatrix} 24.0 & -0.5 & 1.5 & -2.0 \\ 2.5 & -3.0 & 0.0 & -0.5 \\ 3.0 & -0.5 & -0.5 & 1.0 \\ -0.5 & -3.0 & 0.0 & -1.5 \end{bmatrix} \qquad (3.28)$$

There is now only a single dominant coefficient compared with the four in Eq. (3.26), the two-dimensional transform having significantly reduced the data array correlation in both horizontal and vertical directions. That single coefficient now contains 93% of the energy in the original data array and represents the scaled mean value of the data [note incidentally that, in this case, since the matrix of Eq. (3.10) is symmetric, its transpose is equal to itself—this is not true generally of basis matrices].

All the basis matrix vectors here have zero average value, with the exception of the first, and this fact ensures that all transform coefficients will be unaffected in value, again with the exception of the term in the upper left-hand corner, if we convert the data to zero mean form before transformation.

To illustrate this point, we first calculate the mean value of the data array,

$$F_{\text{mean}} = \frac{1}{16} \sum_{j=1}^{4} \sum_{k=1}^{4} F_{jk} = 6.0$$

and subtract it from every data point to give

$$[F_0] = \begin{bmatrix} -1 & 0 & 2 & 4 \\ 0 & 0 & -1 & 1 \\ -2 & -1 & -3 & 0 \\ 2 & 1 & -1 & -1 \end{bmatrix} \tag{3.29}$$

where $[F_0]$ is now the equivalent zero-mean data array. The total energy is now separated into a DC (mean) component equal to 16×6.0^2, and an AC component [the sum of the squares of the entries in (Eq.3.29)] equal to 44, giving a total of 620, as before. Two-dimensional transformation of the zero-mean array $[F_0]$ results in the coefficient array

$$[C_0] = \begin{bmatrix} 0.0 & -0.5 & 1.5 & -2.0 \\ 2.5 & -3.0 & 0.0 & -0.5 \\ 3.0 & -0.5 & -0.5 & 1.0 \\ -0.5 & -3.0 & 0.0 & -1.5 \end{bmatrix} \tag{3.30}$$

which is the same as that of Eq. (3.28) except that the DC coefficient is now zero, as expected.

Equation (3.27), then, expresses the widely used two-dimensional transform coding result, premultiplication of the data array by $[T]$ performing a one-dimensional transform on the columns within $[F]$ and postmultiplication by $[T]^{\text{T}}$ carrying out the equivalent operation upon the data rows. It may be noted here that two-dimensional transform coding schemes are by far the most widely reported types in the literature, but the one-dimensional operation is useful in the context of so-called 'hybrid' coding, and the three-dimensional extension has been used in connection with the coding of moving, or multi-spectral data. These operations will be discused subsequently.

As far as carrying out the two-dimensional inverse transform is concerned, we need only extend the formulation developed in the one-dimensional case. Thus, in one-dimension, inverse transformation requires premultiplication of the transform coefficient vector (or matrix) by the inverse (i.e., the complex conjugate transpose) of the basis matrix, i.e.,

$$[F'] = [T^*]^{\text{T}}[C] \tag{3.31}$$

and to complete the two-dimensional transform we postmultiply by the transpose of the first basis matrix, i.e.,

$$[F] = [T^*]^\mathrm{T}[C][T^*] \tag{3.32}$$

Should, as most often is the case, the elements of $[T]$ be real, then

$$[F] = [T]^\mathrm{T}[C][T] \tag{3.33}$$

It was shown in the preceding section of this chapter that the one-dimensional matrix formulation of Eq. (3.8) was equivalent to the series summation form of Eq. (3.7). In the same way the two-dimensional matrix formulation of Eq. (3.27) has its similar counterpart, which is an extension of Eq. (3.7). Thus,

$$C_{pq} = \sum_{l=1}^{N} \sum_{k=1}^{N} f_{kl} t_{pk} t_{ql} \qquad p,q = 1 \to N \tag{3.34}$$

There is also, of course, a similar representation of the two-dimensional inverse transform of Eq. (3.33), although in practice it is more convenient to generate a single basis array (as will be done in the following sections of this chapter on individual transforms) and then take advantage of the matrix formulations previously described for one- and two-dimensional forward and inverse transformation. It might be pointed out here that, in two-dimensional processing, it is not necessary for both horizontal and vertical transforms to be the same. There seems, however, little point in employing different basis matrices in the two directions, and such a step has rarely been reported in the literature.

In the case of the one-dimensional operation the image vector is reconstructed by summing the various basis vectors which make up the orthogonal transform, each weighted according to the individual transform coefficients which have been determined during the forward transform operation. This interpretation can be extended to the two-dimensional case as a similar weighted sum of components, which are not, in this case, basis vectors, but basis 'pictures'. Thus, if we reconsider Eq. (3.33),

$$[F] = [T]^\mathrm{T}[C][T]$$

and take a simple example

$$[F] = \begin{bmatrix} t_{11} & t_{21} \\ t_{12} & t_{22} \end{bmatrix} \begin{bmatrix} C_{11} & C_{12} \\ C_{21} & C_{22} \end{bmatrix} \begin{bmatrix} t_{11} & t_{12} \\ t_{21} & t_{22} \end{bmatrix}$$

then we may expand the coefficient matrix as follows,

$$[C] = \begin{bmatrix} C_{11} & 0 \\ 0 & 0 \end{bmatrix} + \begin{bmatrix} 0 & C_{12} \\ 0 & 0 \end{bmatrix} + \begin{bmatrix} 0 & 0 \\ C_{21} & 0 \end{bmatrix} + \begin{bmatrix} 0 & 0 \\ 0 & C_{22} \end{bmatrix} \tag{3.35}$$

The first matrix multiplication will then result in

$$[T]^T[C] = \begin{bmatrix} t_{11}C_{11} & 0 \\ t_{12}C_{11} & 0 \end{bmatrix} + \begin{bmatrix} 0 & t_{11}C_{12} \\ 0 & t_{12}C_{12} \end{bmatrix} + \begin{bmatrix} t_{21}C_{21} & 0 \\ t_{22}C_{21} & 0 \end{bmatrix} + \begin{bmatrix} 0 & t_{21}C_{22} \\ 0 & t_{22}C_{22} \end{bmatrix}$$

and so

$$[T]^T[C][T] = C_{11}\begin{bmatrix} t_{11}t_{11} & t_{11}t_{12} \\ t_{11}t_{12} & t_{12}t_{12} \end{bmatrix} + C_{12}\begin{bmatrix} t_{11}t_{21} & t_{11}t_{22} \\ t_{12}t_{21} & t_{12}t_{22} \end{bmatrix}$$

$$+ C_{21}\begin{bmatrix} t_{21}t_{11} & t_{21}t_{12} \\ t_{22}t_{11} & t_{22}t_{12} \end{bmatrix} + C_{22}\begin{bmatrix} t_{21}t_{21} & t_{21}t_{22} \\ t_{22}t_{21} & t_{22}t_{22} \end{bmatrix}$$

$$(3.36)$$

Each of the four matrices on the right-hand side of Eq. (3.36) can be written as the outer product of the corresponding basis vectors [see Appendix 6). Thus, for example,

$$\begin{bmatrix} t_{11} \\ t_{12} \end{bmatrix}\begin{bmatrix} t_{11} & t_{12} \end{bmatrix} = \begin{bmatrix} t_{11}t_{11} & t_{11}t_{12} \\ t_{12}t_{11} & t_{12}t_{12} \end{bmatrix}$$

$$\begin{bmatrix} t_{11} \\ t_{12} \end{bmatrix}\begin{bmatrix} t_{21} & t_{22} \end{bmatrix} = \begin{bmatrix} t_{11}t_{21} & t_{11}t_{22} \\ t_{12}t_{21} & t_{12}t_{22} \end{bmatrix}$$

and so on. The image may therefore be reconstructed as the weighted sum of basis pictures in the form of Eq. (3.36). If we allow the matrix in this simple example to be, as before, the Hadamard matrix and, for simplicity, ignore the scaling factor, then

$$\begin{bmatrix} t_{11} & t_{12} \\ t_{21} & t_{22} \end{bmatrix} = \begin{bmatrix} 1 & 1 \\ 1 & -1 \end{bmatrix} \qquad (3.37)$$

and the basis pictures are

$$\begin{bmatrix} 1 & 1 \\ 1 & 1 \end{bmatrix} \quad \begin{bmatrix} 1 & -1 \\ 1 & -1 \end{bmatrix} \quad \begin{bmatrix} 1 & 1 \\ -1 & -1 \end{bmatrix} \quad \begin{bmatrix} 1 & -1 \\ -1 & 1 \end{bmatrix} \qquad (3.38)$$
$$\quad\;\text{(a)} \qquad\qquad \text{(b)} \qquad\qquad \text{(c)} \qquad\qquad \text{(d)}$$

Picture (a) represents the DC or average intensity level of the four image elements, picture (b) the detail consisting of one horizontal zero crossing, but no change in the vertical direction, picture (c) the complement of picture (b), and picture (d) one zero-crossing in both horizontal and vertical directions. This result is generally true, and for an image of dimension $N \times N$, there will be N^2 basis pictures which, together with the appropriate weighting factors, may be summed to reconstruct the original image. If we denote a general basis vector by

$$\mathbf{t}_a = [t_{a1} \quad t_{a2} \quad t_{a3} \quad \cdots \quad t_{aN}]^{\mathrm{T}} \qquad a = 1 \to N \tag{3.39}$$

Then,

$$[F] = \sum_{a=1}^{N} \sum_{b=1}^{N} C_{ab} \mathbf{t}_a \mathbf{t}_b^{\mathrm{T}} \tag{3.40}$$

is the reconstructed image array. Figure 3.2 shows the complete set of basis pictures for the 4 × 4 Walsh–Hadamard case, where white corresponds to +1 and black to −1. As a further example, Fig. 3.3 depicts the 8 × 8 basis set for the discrete cosine transform (see subsection 3.5.6) in its complete form and showing the low-order region expanded in order to try to clarify the variations in level between elements. For a more detailed discussion of the outer product representation of images see Andrews and Patterson (1976a, c). It can also be shown (although it does not appear that it has any useful significance) that the coefficient array may be constructed from a set of basis 'pseudo-pictures' formed from the columns of the basis matrix and weighted

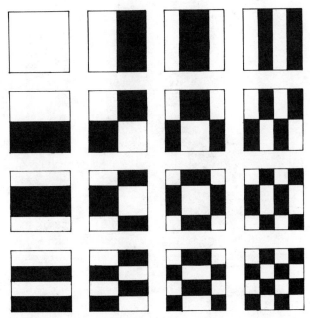

FIG. 3.2.   4 × 4 basis picture set for the Walsh–Hadamard transform, white ≡ +1, black ≡ −1.

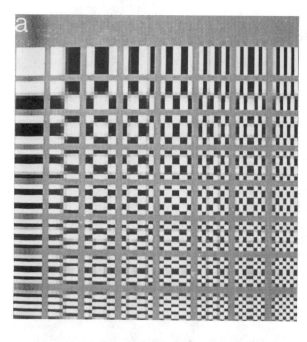

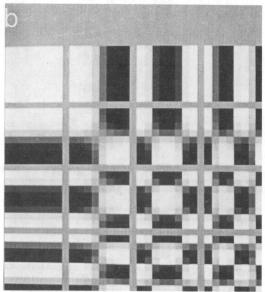

FIG. 3.3. (a) 8 × 8 basis picture set for the discrete cosine transform and (b) expanded view of the low-order region of (a).

by the data values. In the case of the Hadamard matrix the two are, of course, the same. The basis picture interpetation of the decomposition of an image into a set of 'primitive' images is illuminating, since it enables immediate visualisation of the effect of deleting, or approximately coding, a particular coefficient, that coefficient representing just how much of the corresponding basis picture is present in the image.

3.4 Determination of transform efficiency

It has been pointed out that the application of a one- or two-dimensional transform to a vector or array of image elements effects a reduction in correlation and thereby, with appropriate coding of the transform coefficients, allows data compression to be achieved. Since there are many orthogonal transforms which may be used for this purpose, the question arises as to which is the 'best', and the answer is, of course, dependent upon the criteria applicable in any particular case. Thus, if the simplest possible processing is essential, the transform chosen will be different from that selected if the maximum decorrelation is desired, and processing complexity is of less importance. Problems of implementation are dealt with elsewhere in this book, and in this section we concentrate exclusively upon the ability of various transforms to remove correlation from the data source, and to 'pack' the signal energy into as small a number of coefficients as possible, in the same way as exemplified earlier in Section 3.3, where, after two-dimensional transformation, only one dominant coefficient remained.

In the general case, of course, an image is made up of many blocks which are sequentially transformed, and so we are more interested in the overall properties of the sequences of coefficients of various orders, rather than of individual coefficients themselves. In order to compare transforms in this way, we could determine experimental performance on a representative set of images, but this brings with it the problems already touched on in the previous chapter. We shall therefore take the alternative approach and employ the first-order Markov model, which has the virtues of simplicity and analytical tractability. Furthermore, it does represent the gross behaviour of image sources moderately well, even though it fails if accurate modelling is required. The technique used is to assume that the first-order Markov model, with a specified value of inter-element correlation coefficient, represents, in one dimension, the second-order properties of the data. In that domain, then, we have the $N \times N$ covariance matrix, given, as discussed in the previous chapter, by

$$\text{COV}(\mathbf{X}) = E[(\mathbf{X} - \bar{\mathbf{X}})(\mathbf{X} - \bar{\mathbf{X}})^{\mathrm{T}}] \qquad (3.41)$$

where $\mathbf{X}$ is a general data vector and $\bar{\mathbf{X}}$ the mean vector [see Eq. (2.26)]. The right-hand side of Eq. (3.41) may be expanded to yield

$$\begin{aligned}
\text{COV}(\mathbf{X}) &= E(\mathbf{XX}^\mathrm{T} + \bar{\mathbf{X}}\bar{\mathbf{X}}^\mathrm{T} - \bar{\mathbf{X}}\mathbf{X}^\mathrm{T} - \mathbf{X}\bar{\mathbf{X}}^\mathrm{T}) \\
&= E(\mathbf{XX}^\mathrm{T}) + \bar{\mathbf{X}}\bar{\mathbf{X}}^\mathrm{T} - \bar{\mathbf{X}}E(\mathbf{X}^\mathrm{T}) - E(\mathbf{X})\bar{\mathbf{X}}^\mathrm{T} \\
&= E(\mathbf{XX}^\mathrm{T}) - \bar{\mathbf{X}}\bar{\mathbf{X}}^\mathrm{T}
\end{aligned}$$
(3.42)

as an alternative form.

We similarly define the transform domain covariance matrix

$$\text{COV}(\mathbf{Y}) = E[(\mathbf{Y} - \bar{\mathbf{Y}})(\mathbf{Y} - \bar{\mathbf{Y}})^\mathrm{T}]$$
(3.43)

where $\mathbf{Y}$ in this case represents the transform coefficient vector and $\bar{\mathbf{Y}}$ the coefficient mean vector, in which case

$$\text{COV}(\mathbf{Y}) = E(\mathbf{YY}^\mathrm{T}) - \bar{\mathbf{Y}}\bar{\mathbf{Y}}^\mathrm{T}$$
(3.44)

and, of course,

$$\mathbf{Y} = [T]\mathbf{X}$$
(3.45)

$[T]$ being the orthogonal transform matrix. From Eqs. (3.44), (3.45) and (3.42) we obtain the relation between data and transform domain covariance matrices

$$\text{COV}(\mathbf{Y}) = [T][\text{COV}(\mathbf{X})][T]^\mathrm{T}$$
(3.46)

which has just the same form as the two-dimensional transform relationship applied to image data blocks; see Eq. (3.27). To sum up the previous discussion, we shall determine transform decorrelation efficiency by calculating the decrease in inter-element correlation in the transform domain covariance matrix compared with that in the data domain equivalent, recalling that the diagonal terms in such a matrix represent the variances of the relevant sequences and the off-diagonal terms the covariances between sequences. The most desirable transform domain covariance matrix will have a diagonal form, and this will correspond with an efficiency of 100%. The transform which produces no reduction in intersequence covariance will have an efficiency of 0%. To demonstrate the approach we take the example of the discrete cosine transform (the theory for which is developed in Subsection 3.5.6), a block size of $N = 8$, and a first-order Markov inter-element correlation coefficient of 0.91. The data domain covariance matrix is shown in Eq. (3.47), where all values along the arrowed lines are identical, and we have assumed a unit variance, zero-mean input sequence. The corresponding transform domain covariance matrix appears in Eq. (3.48). It should be noted that the computational load of this calculation, even when COV($\mathbf{X}$) is given, is equivalent to that of a normal two-dimensional transform, and Fino and

Algazi (1975) have defined a recursive technique for fast computation of the transform domain covariance matrix. From Eqs. (3.47) and (3.48) the following quantities may be calculated, where X_{jk} and Y_{jk} represent, respectively, the individual terms in the two functions

$$
COV(X) =
\begin{bmatrix}
1.000 & 0.910 & 0.828 & 0.754 & 0.686 & 0.624 & 0.568 & 0.517 \\
0.910 & 1.000 & & & & & & 0.568 \\
0.828 & & 1.000 & & & & & 0.624 \\
0.754 & & & 1.000 & & & & 0.686 \\
0.686 & & & & 1.000 & & & 0.754 \\
0.624 & & & & & 1.000 & & 0.828 \\
0.568 & & & & & & 1.000 & 0.910 \\
0.517 & 0.568 & 0.624 & 0.686 & 0.754 & 0.828 & 0.910 & 1.000
\end{bmatrix}
$$

(3.47)

$COV(Y) =$

$$
\begin{bmatrix}
6.344 & 0.000 & -0.291 & 0.000 & -0.066 & 0.000 & -0.021 & 0.000 \\
0.000 & 0.930 & 0.000 & -0.027 & 0.000 & -0.008 & 0.000 & -0.002 \\
-0.291 & 0.000 & 0.312 & 0.000 & -0.001 & 0.000 & 0.000 & 0.000 \\
0.000 & -0.027 & 0.000 & 0.149 & 0.000 & -0.001 & 0.000 & 0.000 \\
-0.066 & 0.000 & -0.001 & 0.000 & 0.094 & 0.000 & 0.000 & 0.000 \\
0.000 & -0.008 & 0.000 & -0.001 & 0.000 & 0.068 & 0.000 & 0.000 \\
-0.021 & 0.000 & 0.000 & 0.000 & 0.000 & 0.000 & 0.055 & 0.000 \\
0.000 & -0.002 & 0.000 & 0.000 & 0.000 & 0.000 & 0.000 & 0.049
\end{bmatrix}
$$

(3.48)

$$
\sum X = \sum_{\substack{j,k=1 \\ j \neq k}}^{N} |X_{jk}| = 42.748 \quad \text{Total sum of data covariance entries}
$$

$$
\sum Y = \sum_{\substack{j,k=1 \\ j \neq k}}^{N} |Y_{jk}| = 0.835 \quad \text{Total sum of transform covariances}
$$

where $N = 8$, in this case, and the summations exclude the diagonal (variance) terms for which $j = k$. The decorrelation efficiency is then

$$
\eta_C = 1 - \left(\sum Y / \sum X \right) \tag{3.49}
$$

or, in this example, 98.05 %. This measure will be determined subsequently for each transform individually discussed in the following sections. It is worth noting, in passing, that the sum of all entries (excluding diagonal terms) in COV(**X**) is given by $2\rho[N(1 - \rho) + \rho^N - 1]/(1 - \rho)^2$.

We now turn to an examination of the diagonal elements of the transform domain covariance matrix, i.e, the variances of the coefficient sequences themselves. Note, first of all, that all diagonal elements in the data domain covariance matrix are unity, and that we have therefore assumed a stationary process as the input. This does not apply to the transform domain coefficients, however, which can be seen to have widely differing variances, and now represent a non-stationary process. Second, the sum of the diagonal elements in the data domain matrix is, of course N, and the same will be found to be true in the transform domain (in mathematical terms, the trace of the matrix is invariant under an orthonormal transformation). This fact provides a convenient check on transform calculations. The majority of the data energy has therefore been transferred to one or two low-order coefficients (those towards the upper left-hand corner of the matrix), and the remainder may be retained, in a coding application, with reduced accuracy or even omitted altogether when the data source is reconstructed upon inverse transformation. This is the basic principle of the process of transform coding, and the so-called 'energy-packing' property of various transforms is another feature by which they may be quantitatively compared. In this case we determine the relative amount of energy in the first M of the total of N diagonal components, i.e.,

$$\eta_E = \sum_{\substack{j=1 \\ k=j}}^{M} Y_{jk} \Bigg/ \sum_{\substack{j=1 \\ k=j}}^{N} Y_{jk} \tag{3.50}$$

where, for an orthonormal transform, the denominator in Eq. (3.50) equals N. In this case there is no need for us to take the magnitude of the terms since, being variances, they can never be negative [a relation that is occasionally useful in this context is that, for an orthonormal transform with a constant zero-order basis vector, the first diagonal term in COV(**Y**) is N^{-1} multiplied by the sum of all the terms in COV(**X**)].

This result for the discrete cosine transform with the same conditions as in the example of decorrelation given earlier is

M	1	2	3	4	5	6	7	8	
η_E(%)	79.3	90.9	94.8	96.7	97.9	98.7	99.4	100	(3.51)

The large values of η_E even for relatively small values of M are characteristic of all transforms and are the result of high inter-element correlation within the data. Thus retaining one quarter of the coefficients means discarding only about 9% of the total data energy, and so on.

3.5 Specific transforms for image processing

We now turn to the consideration of individual transforms which have been used for image data compression. As has been previously pointed out, transform efficiency and ease of implementation are to a large extent mutually incompatible, and we are, for the moment, solely concerned with their mathematical properties—defining relationships, efficiency, and so on. One question of some importance, at least theoretically, is that of the existence, or otherwise, of an optimum transform, in the sense of completely decorrelating the data and maximising the amount of energy 'packed' into the lowest-order coefficients. The answer to the question is that such a transform does exist, but it is difficult to use and therefore has been applied relatively rarely in data compression schemes. Since it obviously sets a standard by which the performance of all other transforms may be measured, however, we consider it first, followed by the only complex transform used in image compression schemes—the Fourier transform. Subsequently, attention is given to the other, more commonly used, real transforms, before examining transform efficiency on a rather wider basis.

3.5.1 The Karhunen–Loève transform

Once again it is necessary to refer briefly to the underlying basis of transform coding—to allow image data to be represented by a restricted set of transform coefficients which can be transmitted or stored for subsequent inverse transformation and image reconstruction. Obviously the most efficient transform is that which has the maximum energy packing capability: i.e., if we choose to retain only M out of N coefficients, then the fraction of the total energy retained within those coefficients will be a maximum over all transforms. The problem is therefore one of minimising the error introduced by retaining only a reduced number of coefficients.

Given a real, orthonormal transform matrix $[T]$, we know that we can represent an image vector

$$\mathbf{f}^{\mathrm{T}} = [f_1 \quad f_2 \quad f_3 \quad \cdots \quad f_N] \tag{3.52}$$

by a suitably scaled combination of basis vectors, i.e.,

$$\mathbf{f} = C_1 \mathbf{t}_1 + C_2 \mathbf{t}_2 + \cdots + C_N \mathbf{t}_N \tag{3.53}$$

where $\mathbf{t}_1, \mathbf{t}_2, \ldots, \mathbf{t}_N$ are basis vectors written in column form, i.e.,

$$\mathbf{t}_1^{\mathrm{T}} = [t_{11} \quad t_{12} \quad t_{13} \quad \cdots \quad t_{1N}]$$
$$\mathbf{t}_2^{\mathrm{T}} = [t_{21} \quad t_{22} \quad t_{23} \quad \cdots \quad t_{2N}] \tag{3.54}$$

and so on, and $C_1, C_2, C_3, \ldots, C_N$ the appropriate transform coefficients. (It may be remarked here that there is a certain lack of clarity concerning the transposition notation just used—certainly it is conventional to write vectors as column vectors, but, in any transform matrix, they naturally appear in row form for the row/column vector multiplication—it is unwise to adhere 100% to convention!) We now choose to represent $\mathbf{f}$ by only M of the basis vectors, replacing the remaining transform coefficients by constants k_j, i.e.,

$$\hat{\mathbf{f}}_M = \sum_{j=1}^{M} C_j \mathbf{t}_j + \sum_{j=M+1}^{N} k_j \mathbf{t}_j \tag{3.55}$$

where $\hat{\mathbf{f}}_M$ is the approximate value of $\mathbf{f}$, retaining coefficients up to order M. The resulting error is

$$\mathbf{f}_{eM} = \mathbf{f} - \hat{\mathbf{f}}_M \tag{3.56}$$

where $\mathbf{f}_{eM}$ is the error vector. Therefore

$$\mathbf{f}_{eM} = \sum_{j=M+1}^{N} C_j \mathbf{t}_j - \sum_{j=M+1}^{N} k_j \mathbf{t}_j$$

$$= \sum_{j=M+1}^{N} (C_j - k_j) \mathbf{t}_j \tag{3.57}$$

We now determine the average error energy within $\mathbf{f}_{eM}$:

$$e_M = E\left\{ \sum_{j=M+1}^{N} [(C_j - k_j)\mathbf{t}_j]^2 \right\} \tag{3.58}$$

In order to clarify the next step, consider a simple example, in which $N = 4$ and we retain the first two components only. Then,

$$\mathbf{f}_{e2} = (C_3 - k_3)\mathbf{t}_3 + (C_4 - k_4)\mathbf{t}_4 \tag{3.59}$$

The squaring operation in Eq. (3.58) introduces cross-product terms into the calculation resulting in

$$\sum_{j=3}^{4} [(C_j - k_j)\mathbf{t}_j]^2 = (C_3 - k_3)^2 \mathbf{t}_3^T \mathbf{t}_3 + (C_4 - k_4)^2 \mathbf{t}_4^T \mathbf{t}_4$$

$$+ (C_3 - k_3)(C_4 - k_4)\mathbf{t}_3^T \mathbf{t}_4 + (C_4 - k_4)(C_3 - k_3)\mathbf{t}_4^T \mathbf{t}_3 \tag{3.60}$$

The orthonormal property of the transform now ensures that $\mathbf{t}_3^T \mathbf{t}_3 = \mathbf{t}_4^T \mathbf{t}_4 = 1$, and that $\mathbf{t}_3^T \mathbf{t}_4 = \mathbf{t}_4^T \mathbf{t}_3 = 0$, and so

$$\sum_{j=3}^{4} [(C_j - k_j)\mathbf{t}_j]^2 = (C_3 - k_3)^2 + (C_4 - k_4)^2 \tag{3.61}$$

The general relation of Eq. (3.58) may therefore be written as

$$e_M = \sum_{j=M+1}^{N} E((C_j - k_j)^2) \tag{3.62}$$

and e_M is thus determined by the choice of transform (via the coefficients C_j) and the selection of the as yet arbitrary constants k_j. We obviously wish to minimise the value of e_M, and this is easily done with respect to the k_j by differentiation, i.e.,

$$\frac{\partial}{\partial k_j} E((C_j - k_j)^2) = -2(E(C_j) - E(k_j))$$

$$= -2(E(C_j) - k_j) = 0 \tag{3.63}$$

(since the expected value of constant k_j is just k_j). Therefore

$$k_j = E(C_j) \tag{3.64}$$

Now, since

$$C_j = \mathbf{t}_j^T \mathbf{f} \tag{3.65}$$

(this is the basic forward transform relationship)

$$k_j = E(\mathbf{t}_j^T \mathbf{f})$$

$$= \mathbf{t}_j^T E(\mathbf{f}) \tag{3.66}$$

where, of course, $E(\mathbf{f})$ is the data mean vector. Thus setting the data mean vector to zero results in the optimum value of $k_j, j = M + 1 \rightarrow N$ being zero, and the corresponding terms in Eq. (3.55) may simply be omitted. For this reason it is extremely common to consider the data source to be a zero-mean process, by initially calculating the mean value and then subtracting it from each data point, if necessary.

Now, from Eqs. (3.65) and (3.66),

$$C_j - k_j = \mathbf{t}_j^T(\mathbf{f} - E(\mathbf{f})) \tag{3.67}$$

and so, using Eq. (3.62)

$$e_M = \sum_{j=M+1}^{N} E((C_j - k_j)^2)$$

$$= \sum_{j=M+1}^{N} \mathbf{t}_j^T E((\mathbf{f} - E(\mathbf{f}))(\mathbf{f} - E(\mathbf{f}))^T)\mathbf{t}_j$$

$$= \sum_{j=M+1}^{N} \mathbf{t}_j^T (\mathrm{COV}(\mathbf{f}))\mathbf{t}_j \tag{3.68}$$

where $COV(\mathbf{f})$ is the covariance matrix of the input data. We may therefore determine the error energy e_M without explicitly calculating transform domain properties. It is now necessary to minimise e_M with respect to the basis vectors $\mathbf{t}_j$ whilst maintaining the orthonormal property $\mathbf{t}_j^T \mathbf{t}_j = 1$. We therefore minimise

$$e'_M = e_M - \sum_{j=M+1}^{N} \lambda_j(\mathbf{t}_j^T \mathbf{t}_j - 1)$$

$$= \sum_{j=M+1}^{N} \mathbf{t}_j^T (COV(\mathbf{f}))\mathbf{t}_j - \lambda_j(\mathbf{t}_j^T \mathbf{t}_j - 1) \qquad (3.69)$$

with respect to $\mathbf{t}_j$, where λ_j is the Lagrangian multiplier. Using the results of Appendix 4, we obtain, for each value of j,

$$GRAD_{(\mathbf{t}_j)} e'_M = 2(COV(\mathbf{f}))\mathbf{t}_j - \lambda_j(2\mathbf{t}_j) = 0$$

and so

$$COV(\mathbf{f})\mathbf{t}_j = \lambda_j \mathbf{t}_j \qquad (3.70)$$

when solved for $\mathbf{t}_j$ and λ_j will result in the jth component of the optimum transform. It is worth reiterating here that the analysis has been carried out by minimising the mean square error [Eq. (3.58)] incurred by omitting certain coefficients. It is by no means certain that minimisation of this particular function of the error is the most appropriate or advantageous for image coding, particularly where the human observer is concerned, and this matter is considered further in Chapter 6. To return to the present discussion, $COV(\mathbf{f})$ is an $N \times N$ matrix (we are considering the one-dimensional case), $\mathbf{t}_j$ is an N-dimensional column vector and λ_j is a scalar constant. Thus $\mathbf{t}_j$ is an eigenvector of the covariance matrix and λ_j is the corresponding eigenvalue (note, in passing, that the covariance matrix is real and symmetric and so will always have all real eigenvalues; see, e.g., Barnett, 1979).

The value of $e_{M(\min)}$ is now obtained by substituting Eq. (3.70) into Eq. (3.68), i.e.,

$$e_{M(\min)} = \sum_{j=M+1}^{N} \mathbf{t}_j^T \lambda_j \mathbf{t}_j = \sum_{j=M+1}^{N} \lambda_j \qquad (3.71)$$

where $e_{M(\min)}$ is the minimum possible error incurred in retaining only M out of N transform coefficients. Furthermore, transforming the covariance matrix using a transform consisting of the N eigenvectors $\mathbf{t}_j$, $j = 1 \rightarrow N$ of that matrix results in a diagonal matrix consisting of the corresponding eigenvalues

$$[T][COV(\mathbf{f})][T]^T = \Lambda \qquad (3.72)$$

where

$$\Lambda = \text{diag}(\lambda_1, \lambda_2, \ldots, \lambda_N) \qquad (3.73)$$

The covariance matrix is therefore diagonalised by the transformation.

It might be pointed out here that this transform is not exclusively associated with signal processing or image coding. It originated in the analysis of statistical data (Hotelling, 1933) and is referred to by a variety of names—the Hotelling, principal component, eigenvector or Karhunen–Loève transformation (KLT in abbreviated form). As a brief recapitulation on the properties of this transform, it is obtained by determining the basis vector set which diagonalises the data covariance matrix (no mean computational task, incidentally), and it results in a transform domain covariance matrix the components of which are uncorrelated. It is also optimum, in an energy 'packing' sense, if a mean square (i.e., energy) criterion is employed. For a further discussion on this topic, see Fukunaga (1972) or Ahmed and Rao (1975). There are various matters connected with the KLT which make it less than ideal for image processing, notwithstanding its theoretical superiority. First, it is necessary to estimate the data covariance matrix, a task which, even with fast processing techniques, is not insignificant. Furthermore, if the transform is to retain its optimal nature, this needs to be done for both row and column processing operations in a two-dimensional coding scheme, for the horizontal and vertical image correlation will almost certainly be different. Then the actual eigenvector determination must be carried out to generate the basis matrix [a simplified procedure for performing this step is described by Shanmugam and Haralick (1973)]. All this must be done, of course, prior to any actual image coding, and done anew for any other image or set of images, since the basis vectors of the transform are specific to the data source via the correlation measure. In a transmission system employing this type of coding, the basis vectors also need to be sent to the receiver along with the coded data. All these drawbacks would be a matter of research interest, were the efficiency of the KLT significantly greater than that of other transforms. In fact, for data having reasonably high inter-element correlation this is not the case, the difference sometimes being marginal, and so the transform remains of more theoretical than practical interest as far as image coding for transmission or storage is concerned.

To turn now to the matter of the transform itself, it is obtained, in the general case, by determining the eigenvectors of the image data covariance matrix. Since we intend to use a first-order Markov model as a basis for transform comparisons, however, the determination of the basis vectors is somewhat simplified. Ray and Driver (1970) have shown that, in this case, solution of the equation

$$\tan N\omega_p = \frac{-(1 - \rho^2) \sin \omega_p}{(1 + \rho^2) \cos \omega_p - 2\rho} \qquad (3.74)$$

where N is the order of the transform and ρ the inter-element correlation yields N values of ω_p which may be substituted in

$$\lambda_p = \frac{1 - \rho^2}{1 + \rho^2 - 2\rho \cos \omega_p} \qquad (3.75)$$

How to find we?

to generate the N eigenvalues. The basis vector terms are then given by

$$t_{pk} = \left(\frac{2}{N + \lambda_p}\right)^{1/2} \sin\left[\omega_p\left(k - \frac{(N-1)}{2}\right) + \frac{(p+1)\pi}{2}\right] \qquad 0 \leqslant p,k \leqslant N - 1 \qquad (3.76)$$

The resulting eighth-order basis matrix for inter-element correlation coefficient 0.91 is

KLT (0.91) =

$$\begin{bmatrix}
0.3266 & 0.3492 & 0.3645 & 0.3722 & 0.3722 & 0.3645 & 0.3492 & 0.3266 \\
0.4732 & 0.4239 & 0.2925 & 0.1042 & -0.1042 & -0.2925 & -0.4239 & -0.4732 \\
0.4694 & 0.2183 & -0.1692 & -0.4510 & -0.4510 & -0.1692 & 0.2183 & 0.4694 \\
0.4278 & -0.0756 & -0.4832 & -0.2788 & 0.2788 & 0.4832 & 0.0756 & -0.4278 \\
0.3655 & -0.3411 & -0.3576 & 0.3495 & 0.3495 & -0.3576 & -0.3411 & 0.3655 \\
0.2878 & -0.4863 & 0.0914 & 0.4151 & -0.4151 & -0.0914 & 0.4863 & -0.2878 \\
0.1985 & -0.4626 & 0.4590 & -0.1896 & -0.1896 & 0.4590 & -0.4626 & 0.1985 \\
0.1012 & -0.2793 & 0.4154 & -0.4890 & 0.4890 & -0.4154 & 0.2793 & -0.1012
\end{bmatrix}$$

$$(3.77)$$

and the basis vectors are shown in Fig. 3.4. The corresponding eigenvalues are

$$\lambda_j = 6.358 \quad 0.931 \quad 0.298 \quad 0.148 \quad 0.093 \quad 0.068 \quad 0.055 \quad 0.049 \quad (3.78)$$

and form the diagonal entries in the transformed covariance matrix [see Eq. (3.72)], all other entries being, in this case, zero. The decorrelation efficiency, as determined by Eq. (3.49), is, of course, 100%, and the energy packing ability of the KLT, defined in Eq. (3.50), is, for various values of M, the number of coefficients retained

M	1	2	3	4	5	6	7	8
$\eta_E(\%)$	79.5	91.1	94.8	96.7	97.9	98.7	99.4	100

$$(3.79)$$

Comparison of these figures with those for the discrete cosine transform, given in Eq. (3.51), will demonstrate how well the latter performs, with the added advantage that it is data independent (see Subsection 3.5.6), and, of

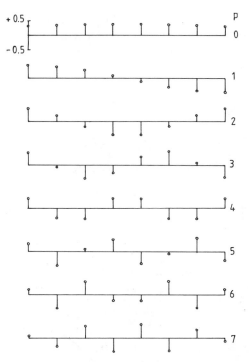

FIG. 3.4. Karhunen–Loève transform basis vectors; $N = 8$; $\rho = 0.91$; p denotes coefficient order.

course, employing the KLT optimised for a particular value of inter-element correlation coefficient with data having other values of correlation will result in degradation of performance, particularly in regard to decorrelation. For a further discussion of this matter, see Clarke (1983c).

Electron Letter 19, 251-253.

3.5.2 The discrete Fourier transform

This transform is the only complex transform used in data coding schemes, and brings with it the attendant disadvantages of storage and manipulation of (albeit a reduced number of) complex quantities. It is, of course, well known in connection with the operations of spectral analysis and filtering, indeed the literature concerning its 'fast' implementation is extremely extensive (see Chapter 7). By applying a two-dimensional discrete Fourier transform to an image array we are, in fact, carrying out a two-dimensional spectral analysis of the data, and this interpretation, approximately at least, carries over into the application of all image transforms for, as we have seen in the last chapter, highly correlated data contains little energy at high spatial frequencies.

The defining relationships for the forward and inverse one-dimensional discrete Fourier transforms (DFT) of order N are,

$$C_p = \frac{1}{\sqrt{N}} \sum_{k=0}^{N-1} f_k e^{(-2\pi jpk)/N} \qquad p = 0 \rightarrow N - 1 \qquad (3.80)$$

$$f_k = \frac{1}{\sqrt{N}} \sum_{p=0}^{N-1} C_p e^{(2\pi jpk)/N} \qquad k = 0 \rightarrow N - 1 \qquad (3.81)$$

where $j = \sqrt{-1}$. The basis matrix therefore consists of the terms

$$\cos(2\pi pk/N) - j \sin(2\pi pk/N) \qquad (3.82)$$

for the forward transform, scaled by $N^{-1/2}$.

For clarity the real and imaginary basis arrays for the case $N = 8$ are shown separately in Eqs. (3.83) and (3.84).

DFT(R) =

$$
\begin{bmatrix}
0.3536 & 0.3536 & 0.3536 & 0.3536 & 0.3536 & 0.3536 & 0.3536 & 0.3536 \\
0.3536 & 0.2500 & 0.0000 & -0.2500 & -0.3536 & -0.2500 & 0.0000 & 0.2500 \\
0.3536 & 0.0000 & -0.3536 & 0.0000 & 0.3536 & 0.0000 & -0.3536 & 0.0000 \\
0.3536 & -0.2500 & 0.0000 & 0.2500 & -0.3536 & 0.2500 & 0.0000 & -0.2500 \\
0.3536 & -0.3536 & 0.3536 & -0.3536 & 0.3536 & -0.3536 & 0.3536 & -0.3536 \\
0.3536 & -0.2500 & 0.0000 & 0.2500 & -0.3536 & 0.2500 & 0.0000 & -0.2500 \\
0.3536 & 0.0000 & -0.3536 & 0.0000 & 0.3536 & 0.0000 & -0.3536 & 0.0000 \\
0.3536 & 0.2500 & 0.0000 & -0.2500 & -0.3536 & -0.2500 & 0.0000 & 0.2500
\end{bmatrix}
$$

$$(3.83)$$

DFT(I) =

$$
\begin{bmatrix}
0.0000 & 0.0000 & 0.0000 & 0.0000 & 0.0000 & 0.0000 & 0.0000 & 0.0000 \\
0.0000 & 0.2500 & 0.3536 & 0.2500 & 0.0000 & -0.2500 & -0.3536 & -0.2500 \\
0.0000 & 0.3536 & 0.0000 & -0.3536 & 0.0000 & 0.3536 & 0.0000 & -0.3536 \\
0.0000 & 0.2500 & -0.3536 & 0.2500 & 0.0000 & -0.2500 & 0.3536 & -0.2500 \\
0.0000 & 0.0000 & 0.0000 & 0.0000 & 0.0000 & 0.0000 & 0.0000 & 0.0000 \\
0.0000 & -0.2500 & 0.3536 & -0.2500 & 0.0000 & 0.2500 & -0.3536 & 0.2500 \\
0.0000 & -0.3536 & 0.0000 & 0.3536 & 0.0000 & -0.3536 & 0.0000 & 0.3536 \\
0.0000 & -0.2500 & -0.3536 & -0.2500 & 0.0000 & 0.2500 & 0.3536 & 0.2500
\end{bmatrix}
$$

$$(3.84)$$

Since $\cos 0 = 1$ and $\sin 0 = 0$, all terms in the first row and column of the real array are $1/\sqrt{N}$; in the imaginary array, 0. Further, the remainder of each array shows the expected even (real) and odd (imaginary) symmetry, and the complex matrix as a whole is symmetric. Separate cosine and sine

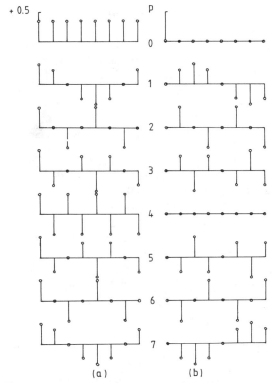

FIG. 3.5.   Fourier transform basis vectors; $N = 8$; p denotes coefficient order. (a) Real part and (b) imaginary part.

basis terms are shown in Fig. 3.5 where the symmetry can clearly be seen. In this case the relevant transform operations are given by Eqs. (3.27) and (3.32), where $[T]^T = [T]$ and $[T^*]^T = [T^*]$.

When the two-dimensional forward transform is applied to the covariance matrix of the first-order Markov model with adjacent element correlation coefficient 0.91 the following transform domain covariance matrix results.

$$
\text{COV}(\mathbf{Y}) =
\begin{bmatrix}
6.344 & 0.206 & 0.047 & 0.015 & 0.000 & 0.015 & 0.047 & 0.206 \\
0.206 & 0.534 & 0.120 & 0.092 & 0.085 & 0.092 & 0.121 & 0.223 \\
0.047 & 0.120 & 0.160 & 0.050 & 0.047 & 0.051 & 0.066 & 0.121 \\
0.015 & 0.092 & 0.050 & 0.094 & 0.036 & 0.039 & 0.051 & 0.092 \\
0.000 & 0.085 & 0.047 & 0.036 & 0.080 & 0.036 & 0.047 & 0.085 \\
0.015 & 0.092 & 0.051 & 0.039 & 0.036 & 0.094 & 0.050 & 0.092 \\
0.047 & 0.121 & 0.066 & 0.051 & 0.047 & 0.050 & 0.160 & 0.120 \\
0.206 & 0.223 & 0.121 & 0.092 & 0.085 & 0.092 & 0.120 & 0.534
\end{bmatrix}
$$

$$(3.85)$$

Note that in this case the diagonal terms are not present in order of decreasing magnitude, and that, with the exception of the lowest-order coefficient, the entries occur in pairs. In this case the decorrelation efficiency $\eta_C = 89.48\%$ and η_E is given, with respect to the number of retained coefficients, as

$$
\begin{array}{ccccccccc}
M & 1 & 2 & 3 & 4 & 5 & 6 & 7 & 8 \\
\eta_E(\%) & 79.3 & 86.0 & 92.7 & 94.7 & 96.7 & 97.8 & 99.0 & 100
\end{array}
\tag{3.86}
$$

where the coefficients are deleted in increasing order of magnitude.

As pointed out earlier, the Fourier transform is inconvenient to use as a result of the necessity to process both real and imaginary components. In one respect, however, it does have an advantage not possessed by other transforms used in image processing, and that results from its property that a shift of the original data within the transform window is reflected solely in a change in the phase of the transform coefficients and not in their magnitude (the so-called Fourier 'shift' theorem see, e.g., Brigham, 1974). Thus, in the case of an image containing objects moving in simple translation, only the changing phases of the components need be monitored from frame to frame (see Chapter 5).

3.5.3 The Walsh–Hadamard transform

So far we have considered transform basis functions which are either (co)sinusoidal, i.e., the Fourier transform, or quite good approximations to sinusoidal functions, i.e., the KLT (the apparently regular nature of the basis vectors in Fig. 3.4 is no accident, and will be referred to again in Subsection 3.5.6 on the discrete cosine transform). The class of complete, orthogonal functions encompasses a far wider set of basis vector 'shapes' than these, however, including various types of polynomial and, significant from the point of view of image processing, rectangular functions, since such latter kinds only take on a restricted number of amplitude values and so are attractive from the standpoint of implementation, where many mathematical operations may have to be carried out in a limited time.

It is convenient at this point to define a quantity often referred to in connection with transforms other than the Fourier transform, which, as noted previously, converts the spatial image domain into coefficients of increasing *frequency*, in the manner of a conventional operation on a data input whose independent variable is time. In the case of other transforms the conventional definition of frequency (one half of the number of zero-crossings of the waveform per unit time) does not apply since the zero-crossings of the functions are not equally spaced along the axis of the independent variable (which, of course, may or may not be time). To deal with this situation Harmuth (1977) has defined a generalisation of the concept of frequency which is called *sequency*. If the function is periodic, the sequency is one half the number of sign changes per period. If the function is aperiodic, then the sequency is one-half of the number of sign changes in unit interval along the axis of the independent variable. It is worth noting here that colloquial usage takes sequency to be the number of zero-crossings in a basis vector, which is not in accordance with the original definition.

It is unnecessary here to recount in detail the history of rectangular orthogonal functions, further details of which may be found in Beauchamp (1984) and Ahmed and Rao (1975). Suffice it to say that two sets of complete orthonormal functions are of interest to us. The first, proposed by Haar (1910), will be dealt with in Subsection 3.5.4; the second, due to the work of Walsh (1923), is based on an incomplete set of functions developed by Rademacher (1922), and consists of a set of rectangular waves of gradually increasing sequency and of amplitude ± 1. These form an orthogonal set which, when correctly scaled, become orthonormal. Although Walsh ordered his functions according to the number of zero-crossings, it is perhaps easier to consider their construction in a different form (it should be noted that the original functions were continuous but, since we are concerned here solely with the digital processing of discrete signal samples, we only require to know the values which the functions take on when they themselves are similarly sampled). Thus, the lowest-order Hadamard matrix is

$$H(2) = \frac{1}{\sqrt{2}} \begin{bmatrix} 1 & 1 \\ 1 & -1 \end{bmatrix} \tag{3.87}$$

and can be seen to satisfy the orthonormality criteria discussed earlier in this chapter. The general relation between Hadamard matrices of orders N and $N/2$ is given by the direct (Kronecker) product operation

$$H(N) = \frac{1}{\sqrt{2}} \begin{bmatrix} H(N/2) & H(N/2) \\ H(N/2) & -H(N/2) \end{bmatrix} \tag{3.88}$$

where $H(1) = 1$, and $N = 2^n$, where n is an integer. Thus, for example,

$$H(4) = \frac{1}{\sqrt{4}} \begin{bmatrix} 1 & 1 & 1 & 1 \\ 1 & -1 & 1 & -1 \\ 1 & 1 & -1 & -1 \\ 1 & -1 & -1 & 1 \end{bmatrix} \tag{3.89}$$

and

$$H(8) = \frac{1}{\sqrt{8}} \begin{bmatrix} 1 & 1 & 1 & 1 & 1 & 1 & 1 & 1 \\ 1 & -1 & 1 & -1 & 1 & -1 & 1 & -1 \\ 1 & 1 & -1 & -1 & 1 & 1 & -1 & -1 \\ 1 & -1 & -1 & 1 & 1 & -1 & -1 & 1 \\ 1 & 1 & 1 & 1 & -1 & -1 & -1 & -1 \\ 1 & -1 & 1 & -1 & -1 & 1 & -1 & 1 \\ 1 & 1 & -1 & -1 & -1 & -1 & 1 & 1 \\ 1 & -1 & -1 & 1 & -1 & 1 & 1 & -1 \end{bmatrix} \begin{matrix} 0 \\ 7 \\ 3 \\ 4 \\ 1 \\ 6 \\ 2 \\ 5 \end{matrix} \qquad (3.90)$$

and so on. The figure on the right-hand side of Eq. (3.90) indicates the number of zero-crossings within each vector, and it is obvious that these are, in general, unequally spaced. Note that, in this case, matrices of all orders are symmetric and therefore that, in terms of the transform coding operation, the matrix, its transpose and inverse are all the same.

It is possible to generate the terms of the Hadamard matrix in an alternative fashion as follows: Let a, b be integers in the range $0 \rightarrow N - 1$. Then

$$a = a_{n-1} \quad a_{n-2} \quad \cdots \quad a_1 \quad a_0$$
$$b = b_{n-1} \quad b_{n-2} \quad \cdots \quad b_1 \quad b_0 \qquad (3.91)$$

where the subscripted coefficients are terms in the n ($=\log_2 N$) bit binary representation of a and b. Then a general term in the matrix is (see, e.g., Pratt, 1978)

$$h_{ab} = (-1)^{\sum_{k=0}^{n-1} a_k b_k} \qquad (3.92)$$

Thus, suppose $N = 8$. Then $n = 3$ and

$$a = a_2 \quad a_1 \quad a_0$$
$$b = b_2 \quad b_1 \quad b_0$$

giving

$$h_{ab} = (-1)^{(a_0 b_0 + a_1 b_1 + a_2 b_2)} \qquad (3.93)$$

If, for example, $a = 7$ and $b = 3$ (or vice versa), then

$$a = 1 \quad 1 \quad 1$$
$$b = 0 \quad 1 \quad 1$$

and $h_{73} = (-1)^2 = 1$. Similarly $h_{56} = (-1)^1 = -1$ and so on.

In the transform domain, it is conventional to consider the coefficients generated in correspondence with increasingly rapid variation of spatial detail (the usual notion of frequency in the case of the Fourier transform), and it is therefore advantageous to modify the array of Eq. (3.90), for instance, to satisfy this convention. Thus

$$
H(8) = \frac{1}{\sqrt{8}}
\begin{bmatrix}
1 & 1 & 1 & 1 & 1 & 1 & 1 & 1 \\
1 & 1 & 1 & 1 & -1 & -1 & -1 & -1 \\
1 & 1 & -1 & -1 & -1 & -1 & 1 & 1 \\
1 & 1 & -1 & -1 & 1 & 1 & -1 & -1 \\
1 & -1 & -1 & 1 & 1 & -1 & -1 & 1 \\
1 & -1 & -1 & 1 & -1 & 1 & 1 & -1 \\
1 & -1 & 1 & -1 & -1 & 1 & -1 & 1 \\
1 & -1 & 1 & -1 & 1 & -1 & 1 & -1
\end{bmatrix}
\begin{matrix}
0 \\ 1 \\ 2 \\ 3 \\ 4 \\ 5 \\ 6 \\ 7
\end{matrix}
\qquad (3.94)
$$

is the 'sequency'-ordered Hadamard matrix for $N = 8$ (we use the same notation as in Eq. (3.90) since there will rarely be any occasion for confusion between the two forms). The scaled basis vectors are shown in Fig. 3.6 and

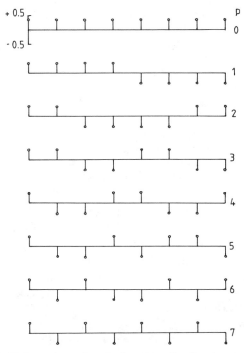

FIG. 3.6. Walsh–Hadamard transform basis vectors; $N = 8$; p denotes coefficient order.

may be compared to those of the KLT in Fig. 3.4. It can be seen that they form 'rectangular' approximations to those of the latter set.

Again, the individual terms in the array may be found via a relation similar to that of Eq. (3.92). Thus,

$$h_{ab} = (-1)^{\sum_{k=0}^{n-1} c_k b_k} \qquad (3.95)$$

where, this time, we need to modify a_k in Eq. (3.91) to account for the interchange of row vectors (b_k, the column index, remains the same); c_k is given by a bit reversal and summation operation as follows

$$c_0 = a_{n-1}$$
$$c_1 = a_{n-1} + a_{n-2}$$
$$\vdots \qquad (3.96)$$
$$c_{n-1} = a_1 + a_0$$

In fact, the summation should formally be the exclusive OR operation but, since we only require to know whether the result is even or odd, ordinary addition will suffice. Taking the previous example, $a = 7$, $b = 3$ again,

$$a = 1 \quad 1 \quad 1$$

i.e.,

$$c = 2 \quad 2 \quad 1 \qquad (\text{or} \quad 0 \quad 0 \quad 1)$$
$$b = 0 \quad 1 \quad 1$$

and so $h_{73} = (-1)^3 = -1$ (or $(-1)^1$) and $h_{56} = 1$ and so on.

It should be pointed out here that this discussion of the properties of the Hadamard matrix has been rather brief. There are many interesting facets to the general theory of such matrices which are not directly relevant to the present purpose and have thus been omitted. For practical purposes, a knowledge of $H(4)$, $H(8)$ and $H(16)$ are, in fact, all that is required to carry out Walsh–Hadamard transformations on image data. We now turn to the question of transform efficiency, which is determined in exactly the same way as for the two previous transforms. In this case, of course, the transform operation is very simple, and the only multiplication needed is that of the final scaling operation to give the following transform domain covariance matrix:

$COV(Y) =$

$$\begin{bmatrix} 6.344 & 0.000 & -0.261 & 0.000 & -0.066 & 0.000 & -0.131 & 0.000 \\ 0.000 & 0.796 & 0.000 & 0.261 & 0.000 & -0.091 & 0.000 & 0.131 \\ -0.261 & 0.000 & 0.275 & 0.000 & -0.001 & 0.000 & 0.091 & 0.000 \\ 0.000 & 0.261 & 0.000 & 0.226 & 0.000 & 0.001 & 0.000 & 0.066 \\ -0.066 & 0.000 & -0.001 & 0.000 & 0.094 & 0.000 & -0.001 & 0.000 \\ 0.000 & -0.091 & 0.000 & 0.001 & 0.000 & 0.094 & 0.000 & 0.001 \\ -0.131 & 0.000 & 0.091 & 0.000 & -0.001 & 0.000 & 0.091 & 0.000 \\ 0.000 & 0.131 & 0.000 & 0.066 & 0.000 & 0.001 & 0.000 & 0.080 \end{bmatrix}$$

$$(3.97)$$

The decorrelation efficiency $\eta_C = 94.86\%$, and η_E depends on the number of retained coefficients as follows:

M	1	2	3	4	5	6	7	8
$\eta_E(\%)$	79.3	89.3	92.7	95.5	96.7	97.9	99.0	100

$$(3.98)$$

These figures compare favourably with those for the Fourier transform and, together with the ease with which the transform may be implemented, have led to its widespread use in image coding schemes. One or two other interesting properties of the transform are given in Appendix 5.

3.5.4 The Haar transform

This transform, like the Walsh–Hadamard transform discussed in the previous section, also uses 'rectangular' basis functions. It is periodic, orthonormal and complete (see, e.g., Shore, 1973: Ahmed and Rao, 1975), and may be generated from the relations

$$HA(0, 0, x) = \frac{1}{\sqrt{N}}$$

$$HA(r, m, x) = \begin{cases} \dfrac{2^{r/2}}{\sqrt{N}} & \dfrac{m-1}{2^r} \leqslant x < \dfrac{m-\frac{1}{2}}{2^r} \\[2mm] -\dfrac{2^{r/2}}{\sqrt{N}} & \dfrac{m-\frac{1}{2}}{2^r} \leqslant x < \dfrac{m}{2^r} \\[2mm] 0 & \text{elsewhere} \end{cases}$$

$$(3.99)$$

over the range $0 \leqslant x < 1$, where $0 \leqslant r < \log_2 N$ and $1 \leqslant m \leqslant 2^r$.

These relations may best be illustrated with a practical example. If we take $N = 8$, then possible values of r are 0, 1 and 2 and corresponding values of m are 1, 1 and 2; and 1, 2, 3 and 4. Thus,

$$HA(0, 0, x) = 1/\sqrt{8}$$

$$HA(0, 1, x) = \begin{cases} 1/\sqrt{8}, & 0 \leqslant x < \frac{1}{2} \\ -1/\sqrt{8}, & \frac{1}{2} \leqslant x < 1 \end{cases}$$

$$HA(1, 1, x) = \begin{cases} 2^{1/2}/\sqrt{8}, & 0 \leqslant x < \frac{1}{4} \\ -2^{1/2}/\sqrt{8}, & \frac{1}{4} \leqslant x < \frac{1}{2} \\ 0. & \text{elsewhere} \end{cases} \qquad (3.100)$$

$$HA(1, 2, x) = \begin{cases} 2^{1/2}/\sqrt{8}, & \frac{1}{2} \leqslant x < \frac{3}{4} \\ -2^{1/2}/\sqrt{8}, & \frac{3}{4} \leqslant x < 1 \\ 0 & \text{elsewhere} \end{cases}$$

and so on, for the other four functions $HA(2, 1, x)$, $HA(2, 2, x)$, $HA(2, 3, x)$ and $HA(2, 4, x)$. Sampling these eight functions at the locations $x = p/N$, $p = 0 \rightarrow N - 1$, results in the following basis matrix:

$HA(8) =$

$$\begin{bmatrix} 0.3536 & 0.3536 & 0.3536 & 0.3536 & 0.3536 & 0.3536 & 0.3536 & 0.3536 \\ 0.3536 & 0.3536 & 0.3536 & 0.3536 & -0.3536 & -0.3536 & -0.3536 & -0.3536 \\ 0.5000 & 0.5000 & -0.5000 & -0.5000 & 0.0000 & 0.0000 & 0.0000 & 0.0000 \\ 0.0000 & 0.0000 & 0.0000 & 0.0000 & 0.5000 & 0.5000 & -0.5000 & -0.5000 \\ 0.7071 & -0.7071 & 0.0000 & 0.0000 & 0.0000 & 0.0000 & 0.0000 & 0.0000 \\ 0.0000 & 0.0000 & 0.7071 & -0.7071 & 0.0000 & 0.0000 & 0.0000 & 0.0000 \\ 0.0000 & 0.0000 & 0.0000 & 0.0000 & 0.7071 & -0.7071 & 0.0000 & 0.0000 \\ 0.0000 & 0.0000 & 0.0000 & 0.0000 & 0.0000 & 0.0000 & 0.7071 & 0.7071 \end{bmatrix}$$

$$(3.101)$$

the individual basis vectors of which are shown in Fig. 3.7. It is often pointed out that the fact that some of the basis vectors have finite values over only a small part of their range makes the transform 'locally, as well as globally' sensitive to image detail (Pratt, 1978). This feature does not prevent its performance from being relatively poor, however, and, despite the ease with which it may be implemented (see Chapter 7) it has only rarely been used for image coding. For the first-order Markov data model with inter-element

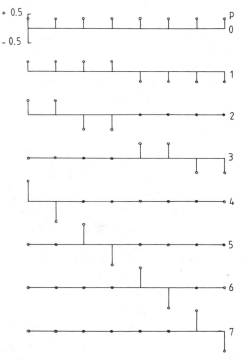

FIG. 3.7. Haar transform basis vectors; $N = 8$; p denotes coefficient order.

correlation coefficient 0.91, the corresponding transform domain covariance matrix for $N = 8$ is

$$COV(\mathbf{Y}) =$$

$$\begin{bmatrix}
6.344 & 0.000 & -0.184 & 0.184 & -0.098 & -0.032 & 0.032 & 0.098 \\
0.000 & 0.796 & 0.184 & 0.185 & 0.020 & 0.111 & 0.111 & 0.020 \\
-0.184 & 0.184 & 0.250 & -0.025 & 0.055 & 0.055 & -0.010 & -0.008 \\
0.184 & 0.184 & -0.025 & 0.250 & -0.008 & -0.010 & 0.055 & 0.055 \\
-0.098 & 0.020 & 0.055 & -0.008 & 0.090 & -0.004 & -0.003 & -0.003 \\
-0.032 & 0.111 & 0.055 & -0.010 & -0.004 & 0.090 & -0.004 & -0.003 \\
0.032 & 0.111 & -0.010 & 0.055 & -0.003 & -0.004 & 0.090 & -0.004 \\
0.098 & 0.020 & -0.008 & 0.055 & -0.003 & -0.003 & -0.004 & 0.090
\end{bmatrix}$$

$$(3.102)$$

Here η_C is 92.70% and the relation between η_E and M is

M	1	2	3	4	5	6	7	8
$\eta_E(\%)$	79.3	89.3	92.4	95.5	96.6	97.8	98.9	100

$$(3.103)$$

3.5.5　The slant transform

It has been conjectured that much commonly occurring image detail consists of regions of smoothly varying luminance having various values of slope. In fact, however, there seems to be little hard evidence for this assertion, and the balance of opinion tends to be that images, by and large, contain areas of relatively constant luminance separated by sharp discontinuities. Thus entropy measurements made on the first differences of image data elements tend to show a marked decrease from those made on the original images. Similar measurements made on the second difference signal, however (Clarke, 1981b), tend to show a reversal of this change (note that, whereas taking the first difference will remove a mean, or DC, value, taking second differences will remove a trend, i.e., a variation of constant slope).

On the basis of the conjecture, however, Enomoto and Shibata (1971) introduced the slant transform, in an attempt to match basis vectors to areas of constant luminance slope. Their work was subsequently extended by Pratt *et al.* (1974). The lowest-order slant matrix is

$$S(2) = \frac{1}{\sqrt{2}} \begin{bmatrix} 1 & 1 \\ 1 & -1 \end{bmatrix} \tag{3.104}$$

which is identical to the first Walsh–Hadamard matrix H(2) [Eq. (3.87)]. If we now consider the next Walsh–Hadamard matrix H(4), given in Eq. (3.89), we can attempt to replace the second basis vector with a sampled version of a continuous vector of constant slope and zero mean

$$\mathbf{h}_2^T = (a + b), (a - b), -(a - b), -(a + b) \tag{3.105}$$

such that (a) we retain the orthonormality of the matrix and (b) $\mathbf{h}_2$ has a constant step size.

It is obvious that a constant interval between four adjacent levels is obtained if the full range $(a + b)$ to $-(a + b)$ is divided into three, thus,

$$(a + b) - (a - b) = (a - b) - (-(a - b)) = -(a - b) - (-(a + b))$$
$$= \tfrac{2}{3}(a + b)$$

or,

$$2b = a \tag{3.106}$$

and therefore,

$$\mathbf{h}_2^T = \frac{b}{\sqrt{4}} (3 \quad 1 \quad -1 \quad -3) \tag{3.107}$$

where b is chosen to retain the orthonormality property

$$\mathbf{h}_2^T \mathbf{h}_2 = 1$$

i.e.,

$$20b^2/4 = 1 \qquad \text{or} \qquad b = \frac{1}{\sqrt{5}} \qquad \text{and so} \qquad a = \frac{2}{\sqrt{5}}$$

likewise

$$\mathbf{h}_4^T = \frac{b}{\sqrt{4}} (1 \quad -3 \quad 3 \quad -1) \tag{3.108}$$

and so

$$S(4) = \frac{1}{\sqrt{4}} \begin{bmatrix} 1 & 1 & 1 & 1 \\ \dfrac{3}{\sqrt{5}} & \dfrac{1}{\sqrt{5}} & -\dfrac{1}{\sqrt{5}} & -\dfrac{3}{\sqrt{5}} \\ 1 & -1 & -1 & 1 \\ \dfrac{1}{\sqrt{5}} & -\dfrac{3}{\sqrt{5}} & \dfrac{3}{\sqrt{5}} & -\dfrac{1}{\sqrt{5}} \end{bmatrix} \tag{3.109}$$

is an orthonormal matrix, with basis vectors ordered in terms of increasing number of sign changes.

Now S(4) may be written

$$S(4) = \frac{1}{\sqrt{2}} \begin{bmatrix} 1 & 0 & 1 & 0 \\ a_4 & b_4 & -a_4 & b_4 \\ 0 & 1 & 0 & -1 \\ -b_4 & a_4 & b_4 & a_4 \end{bmatrix} \begin{bmatrix} S_2 & 0 \\ 0 & S_2 \end{bmatrix} \tag{3.110}$$

where a_4 and b_4 are a and b defined earlier, the subscript being added to identify them with the matrix of order 4. The relation of Eq. (3.110) may be extended to higher orders, as in Eq. (3.111), where I denotes the appropriate identity matrix, i.e.,

$$S(N) = \frac{1}{\sqrt{2}} \left[\begin{array}{cc:cc:c} 1 & 0 & 1 & 0 & \\ a_N & b_N & -a_N & b_N & 0 \\ \hdashline 0 & I & 0 & I \\ \hdashline 0 & 1 & 0 & -1 & \\ -b_N & a_N & b_N & a_N & 0 \\ \hdashline 0 & I & 0 & I \end{array}\right] \begin{bmatrix} S_{N/2} & 0 \\ 0 & S_{N/2} \end{bmatrix} \tag{3.111}$$

and the values of a_N and b_N are given by

$$a_{2N} = \left(\frac{3N^2}{4N^2 - 1}\right)^{1/2} \tag{3.112}$$

$$b_{2N} = \left(\frac{N^2 - 1}{4N^2 - 1}\right)^{1/2} \tag{3.113}$$

(Pratt et al., 1974).

When $N = 8$ the resulting basis matrix is

$S(8) =$

$$
\begin{bmatrix}
0.3536 & 0.3536 & 0.3536 & 0.3536 & 0.3536 & 0.3536 & 0.3536 & 0.3536 \\
0.5402 & 0.3857 & 0.2316 & 0.0771 & -0.0771 & -0.2316 & -0.3857 & -0.5402 \\
0.4745 & 0.1580 & -0.1580 & -0.4745 & -0.4745 & -0.1580 & 0.1580 & 0.4745 \\
0.2415 & -0.0346 & -0.3104 & -0.5865 & 0.5865 & 0.3104 & 0.0346 & -0.2415 \\
0.3536 & -0.3536 & -0.3536 & 0.3536 & 0.3536 & -0.3536 & -0.3536 & 0.3536 \\
0.3536 & -0.3536 & -0.3536 & 0.3536 & -0.3536 & 0.3536 & 0.3536 & -0.3536 \\
0.1580 & -0.4745 & 0.4745 & -0.1580 & -0.1580 & 0.4745 & -0.4745 & 0.1580 \\
0.1580 & -0.4745 & 0.4745 & -0.1580 & 0.1580 & -0.4745 & 0.4745 & -0.1580
\end{bmatrix}
$$

$$\tag{3.114}$$

where the individual basis vectors are shown in Fig. 3.8. The transformed model covariance matrix is ($\rho = 0.91$)

$COV(Y) =$

$$
\begin{bmatrix}
6.344 & 0.000 & -0.292 & 0.000 & -0.066 & 0.000 & 0.000 & 0.000 \\
0.000 & 0.915 & 0.000 & -0.080 & 0.000 & -0.078 & 0.000 & -0.009 \\
-0.292 & 0.000 & 0.311 & 0.000 & -0.001 & 0.000 & -0.019 & 0.000 \\
0.000 & -0.080 & 0.000 & 0.131 & 0.000 & 0.045 & 0.000 & -0.016 \\
-0.066 & 0.000 & -0.001 & 0.000 & 0.094 & 0.000 & 0.000 & 0.000 \\
0.000 & -0.078 & 0.000 & 0.045 & 0.000 & 0.094 & 0.000 & 0.000 \\
0.000 & 0.000 & -0.019 & 0.000 & 0.000 & 0.000 & 0.056 & 0.000 \\
0.000 & -0.009 & 0.000 & -0.016 & 0.000 & 0.000 & 0.000 & 0.055
\end{bmatrix}
$$

$$\tag{3.115}$$

Here $\eta_C = 97.16\%$ and the $\eta_E : M$ relationship is

M	1	2	3	4	5	6	7	8
$\eta_E (\%)$	79.3	90.7	94.6	96.3	97.4	98.6	99.3	100

$$\tag{3.116}$$

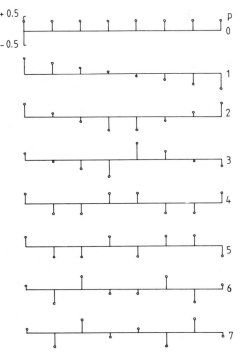

F<small>IG</small>. 3.8. Slant transform basis vectors; $N = 8$; p denotes coefficient order.

3.5.6   The discrete cosine transform

The discrete cosine transform (DCT) is one of an extensive family of 'sinusoidal' transforms documented by Jain (1976b) and discussed generally in Subsection 3.5.8. In their discrete form the basis vectors consist of sampled sinusoidal or cosinusoidal functions, and the DCT has been singled out for special attention by workers in the image processing field since its introduction by Ahmed *et al.* (1974), due to the fact that, for conventional image data having reasonably high inter-element correlation, its performance is virtually indistinguishable from that of the KLT. The DCT is a real transform generated by a procedure which alleviates some of the problems which arise in the application of the discrete Fourier transform to a data series. Briefly, the problem stems from the discrete nature of the transform, for it is of course the case that numerical (i.e., computer) determination of the Fourier spectrum can only be carried out on a sampled data input, and results in the calculation of the transform coefficients at a (finite) number of discrete frequencies. Thus, in each domain, the data which exists is the product of that data in its continuous form and a suitable sampling (in time or frequency, when considering the conventional Fourier transform) function. The sampling of the input data results, of course, in 'repeat' spectra in the transform domain centred about integral harmonics of the sampling frequency, and the relation between that frequency and the upper frequency limit of the input signal must be such that aliasing does not occur. Conversely, the fact that transform components also are 'sampled', i.e., calculated at a finite number of frequencies means that we have generated not a continuous, but a line spectrum, and so have carried out the analysis in the form of a series, rather than a true transform. The input must have been periodic, therefore, to generate such a spectrum, and the conclusion is that the transform domain representation is not that of an isolated segment of the input waveform, but is of that segment periodically repeated (Fig. 3.9). Such a waveform contains, in general, severe discontinuities between the segments (where the start and finish of the repeated segment are next to one another) and these result in spurious spectral components. A more detailed discussion of this point may be found in Beauchamp and Yuen (1979). As far as the DCT is concerned, the discontinuity is eliminated by making the data to be transformed symmetric, i.e., by folding it about the vertical axis as shown in the figure, and then possibly overlapping the two halves by one picture element. These two operations give rise, respectively, to the even and odd forms of the transform (Pratt, 1978). In fact the overlapping process creates the need for amplitude scaling of the overlapped data point in the one-dimensional form, and of the two mutually perpendicular lines of overlapping data points in the two-dimensional version of the transform, before the coefficients can be evaluated and so, since the odd DCT has no clear advantage in terms of coding efficiency, the even form has usually been preferred (the odd DCT has been implemented in one rather specific way, however, and this is described in the section on practical techniques in Chapter 7).

To return to the even version of the DCT. Folding the data has now given us a (real) even function to transform, and we now apply a Fourier transform of length $2N$ to the data f_k, where $k = 0 \to N - 1$ (note that values of k refer to the data samples themselves, and that the axis of symmetry in Fig. 3.9d therefore lies at the point $k = -\frac{1}{2}$). Thus

$$C_p = \frac{1}{\sqrt{2N}} \sum_{k=-N}^{N-1} f_k \exp\left[-\frac{2\pi j}{2N} \left(p\left(k + \frac{1}{2}\right)\right)\right] \qquad (3.117)$$

which, by virtue of the real and even symmetry of the transform, becomes

$$C_p = C_0 \sqrt{\frac{2}{N}} \sum_{k=0}^{N-1} f_k \cos\left(p\left(k + \frac{1}{2}\right)\frac{\pi}{N}\right) \qquad p = 0 \to N - 1 \quad (3.118)$$

where $C_0 = \frac{1}{\sqrt{2}}$ if $p = 0$, and 1 otherwise. The constant is not part of the

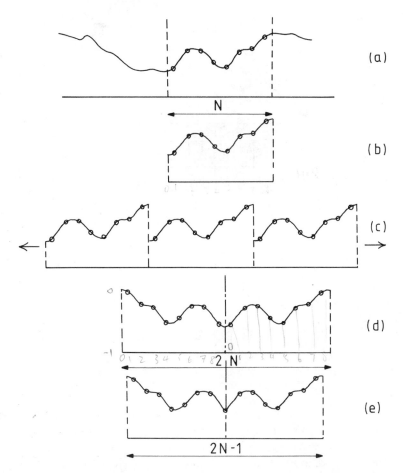

FIG. 3.9. Sampled data and even and odd forms of the discrete cosine transform. (a) Continuous data sampled over a window of length N, (b) segment for analysis, (c) data domain equivalent of sampled (line) spectrum, (d) data folded to eliminate discontinuity (even version, length $2N$) and (e) data folded and overlapped (odd version, length $2N - 1$).

development of the transform as such but is necessary to ensure that the basis set is orthonormal. In the case of Eq. (3.118) the un-normalised basis vector elements for $p = 0$ are each of magnitude $\sqrt{2/N}$ ($\cos 0 = 1$), and so the sum of the squares is $N \times (\sqrt{2/N})^2 = 2$. Since the sum of the squares of all the elements in any basis vector must equal unity [see Eq. (3.17)], each element in the first must be multiplied by $\dfrac{1}{\sqrt{2}}$. The basis vectors for the case $N = 8$ are given in Eq. (3.119) and are shown in Fig. 3.10. In passing we may note that the basis vectors are generated by sampling at N points a set of cosine waves

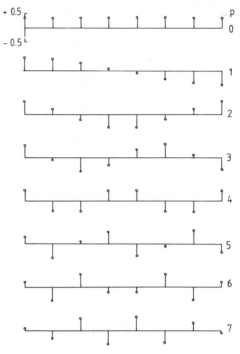

FIG. 3.10. Discrete cosine transform basis vectors; $N = 8$; p denotes coefficient order.

of increasing frequency. Thus we take p ($p = 0 \rightarrow N - 1$) half cycles of the cosine function and sample N times, starting one half a sample interval from the origin. In the case $p = 7$, for example, we take 8 samples of 7 half cycles of a cosine wave and, in Fig 3.10, the low-frequency envelope (beat pattern) can clearly be seen.

$$\text{DCT(8)} =$$

$$
\begin{bmatrix}
0.3536 & 0.3536 & 0.3536 & 0.3536 & 0.3536 & 0.3536 & 0.3536 & 0.3536 \\
0.4904 & 0.4157 & 0.2778 & 0.0975 & -0.0975 & -0.2778 & -0.4157 & -0.4904 \\
0.4619 & 0.1913 & -0.1913 & -0.4619 & -0.4619 & -0.1913 & 0.1913 & 0.4619 \\
0.4157 & -0.0975 & -0.4904 & -0.2778 & 0.2778 & 0.4904 & 0.0975 & -0.4157 \\
0.3536 & -0.3536 & -0.3536 & 0.3536 & 0.3536 & -0.3536 & -0.3536 & 0.3536 \\
0.2778 & -0.4904 & 0.0975 & 0.4157 & -0.4157 & -0.0975 & 0.4904 & -0.2778 \\
0.1913 & -0.4619 & 0.4619 & -0.1913 & -0.1913 & 0.4619 & -0.4619 & 0.1913 \\
0.0975 & -0.2778 & 0.4157 & -0.4904 & 0.4904 & -0.4157 & 0.2778 & -0.0975
\end{bmatrix}
$$

$$(3.119)$$

It can be seen that the vectors do indeed form a good approximation to those of the KLT in Fig. 3.4, and there is therefore a good case to be made for the preferential use of the DCT in transform coding schemes, since the vectors depend only on the selected order of the transform, and not upon the statistical properties of the input data. It is not surprising that the close comparison should obtain, since it can be shown that, for the first-order Markov source at least, the DCT becomes the KLT of the source data in the limit as the adjacent element correlation coefficient tends to unity (Clarke, 1981a).

The transform domain covariance matrix for inter-element correlation 0.91 is shown in Eq. (3.48), and η_C and the η_E/M relationship have been given previously also. The latter, naturally, is virtually the same as that for the KLT.

3.5.7 The discrete sine transform

This transform is a further example of the (co)sinusoidal set defined by Jain (1976b), the general properties of which are described in the next subsection. It is, however, of sufficient importance to warrant separate discussion here. The basis vector set for the sine transform is given by

$$C_{pk} = \sqrt{\frac{2}{N+1}} \sin\left(\frac{(p+1)(k+1)}{N+1}\pi\right) \qquad p, k = 0 \to N - 1 \quad (3.120)$$

Taking the case $N = 8$ gives the basis vectors of Eq. (3.121) shown in Fig. 3.11.

DST(8) =

$$\begin{bmatrix}
0.1612 & 0.3030 & 0.4082 & 0.4642 & 0.4642 & 0.4082 & 0.3030 & 0.1612 \\
0.3030 & 0.4642 & 0.4082 & 0.1612 & -0.1612 & -0.4082 & -0.4642 & -0.3030 \\
0.4082 & 0.4082 & 0.0000 & -0.4082 & -0.4082 & 0.0000 & 0.4082 & 0.4082 \\
0.4642 & 0.1612 & -0.4082 & -0.3030 & 0.3030 & 0.4082 & -0.1612 & -0.4642 \\
0.4642 & -0.1612 & -0.4082 & 0.3030 & 0.3030 & -0.4082 & -0.1612 & 0.4642 \\
0.4082 & -0.4082 & 0.0000 & 0.4082 & -0.4082 & 0.0000 & 0.4082 & -0.4082 \\
0.3030 & -0.4642 & 0.4082 & -0.1612 & -0.1612 & 0.4082 & -0.4642 & 0.3030 \\
0.1612 & -0.3030 & 0.4082 & -0.4642 & 0.4642 & -0.4082 & 0.3030 & -0.1612
\end{bmatrix}$$

$$(3.121)$$

The covariance matrix (for inter-element correlation 0.91) of the transform coefficients is shown in Eq. (3.123): η_C is 84.97%, and the η_E: M relation is

M	1	2	3	4	5	6	7	8	
$\eta_E(\%)$	73.6	84.3	92.5	95.0	97.4	98.4	99.4	100	(3.122)

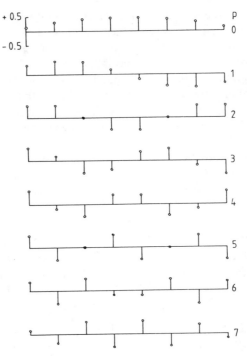

FIG. 3.11. Discrete sine transform basis vectors; $N = 8$; p denotes coefficient order.

It may be seen, therefore, that the efficiency of the DST is not particularly good, and there seems little reason for its use in practice, without some prior modification of the input data. Thus Jain (1976b) and, for example, Zvi-Meiri and Yudilevich (1981) decompose the input data sequence into a 'boundary' and a 'residual' process, and Jain demonstrates that the sine transform is then the optimal (KL) transform of the latter. The sine transform thus takes on the role of a 'fast' version of the KLT in this situation, and the procedure is discussed further in Chapter 7.

$$
\mathrm{COV}(\mathbf{Y}) = \begin{bmatrix}
5.884 & 0.000 & 1.439 & 0.000 & 0.700 & 0.000 & 0.304 & 0.000 \\
0.000 & 0.858 & 0.000 & 0.203 & 0.000 & 0.099 & 0.000 & 0.030 \\
1.439 & 0.000 & 0.655 & 0.000 & 0.228 & 0.000 & 0.099 & 0.000 \\
0.000 & 0.203 & 0.000 & 0.203 & 0.000 & 0.043 & 0.000 & 0.013 \\
0.700 & 0.000 & 0.228 & 0.000 & 0.191 & 0.000 & 0.048 & 0.000 \\
0.000 & 0.099 & 0.000 & 0.043 & 0.000 & 0.084 & 0.000 & 0.006 \\
0.304 & 0.000 & 0.099 & 0.000 & 0.048 & 0.000 & 0.074 & 0.000 \\
0.000 & 0.030 & 0.000 & 0.013 & 0.000 & 0.006 & 0.000 & 0.051
\end{bmatrix}
$$

$$(3.123)$$

There is a further problem with the application of the DST to image coding. Since the zero-order (DC) basis vector is not constant, the requirement that all basis vectors be orthogonal, implying, as it does, that all finite order (AC) vectors should be orthogonal to the DC vector, leads to the result that certain of those vectors have non-zero mean values (the same situation obtains, to a lesser extent, in the case of the KLT). If the transform is applied to data having a finite mean value, the AC coefficients corresponding to those AC basis vectors with finite mean values will contain a contribution due to the mean energy of the data, and this energy is thus undesirably spread through the higher-order coefficients. Since the object of transformation is to compact the data energy into a small set of low-order coefficients, this suggests that, at the very least, data to be transformed using the DST should have its mean value removed, an added complication not necessary with any transform having a constant DC basis vector. The matter is discussed further by Clarke (1983a).

3.5.8 Other sinusoidal transforms

As mentioned earlier, Jain has defined a family of sinusoidal transforms based upon the properties of a set of matrices related to the covariance matrix of a stationary first-order Markov process of the kind used to assess the efficiency of the various transforms described in this chapter. Such a covariance matrix, as shown, for example, in Eq. (2.39), can be written (the overall scaling constant—the variance of the data sequence, is omitted here for simplicity) as

$$[R(i,j)] = \rho^{|i-j|} \qquad i,j = 1 \to N \qquad (3.124)$$

It is a property of the matrix $[R]$ that the eigenvectors of its inverse, $[R]^{-1}$, are the same as those of itself. If we do invert $[R]$ we obtain

$$[R]^{-1} = \frac{1}{1-\rho^2} \begin{bmatrix} 1 & -\rho & & & 0 \\ -\rho & 1+\rho^2 & & & \\ & & 1+\rho^2 & & \\ & & & 1+\rho^2 & -\rho \\ 0 & & & -\rho & 1 \end{bmatrix} \qquad (3.125)$$

Jain now considers the matrix

$$\beta^2 [R]^{-1} = \frac{1}{1+\rho^2} \begin{bmatrix} 1 & -\rho & & & 0 \\ -\rho & 1+\rho^2 & & & \\ & & 1+\rho^2 & & \\ & & & 1+\rho^2 & -\rho \\ 0 & & & -\rho & 1 \end{bmatrix} \qquad (3.126)$$

where $\beta^2 = (1 - \rho^2)/(1 + \rho^2)$, and writes

$$
J(k_1, k_2, k_3, k_4) =
\begin{bmatrix}
(1 - k_1\alpha) & -\alpha & & & k_3\alpha \\
-\alpha & 1 & & & \mathbf{0} \\
& & 1 & & \\
& & & 1 & -\alpha \\
k_4\alpha & & & -\alpha & (1 - k_2\alpha)
\end{bmatrix}
\tag{3.127}
$$

where $\alpha = \rho/(1 + \rho^2)$, and k_1, k_2, k_3, k_4 are $0, +1$ or -1 according to the transform concerned. The set of sinusoidal transforms is then generated by the eigenvectors of the $[J]$ matrices, and each is the optimal (KL) transform of a data sequence with different statistical properties. For example, setting $k_1 = k_2 = k_3 = k_4 = 0$ results in the tridiagonal matrix

$$
J(0, 0, 0, 0) =
\begin{bmatrix}
1 & \dfrac{-\rho}{1 + \rho^2} & & \\
\dfrac{-\rho}{1 + \rho^2} & & & \mathbf{0} \\
& & & \\
\mathbf{0} & & &
\end{bmatrix}
\tag{3.128}
$$

the eigenvectors of which form the sine transform discussed in the previous subsection. Again, setting $k_1 = k_2 = 1$, $k_3 = k_4 = 0$ results in the discrete cosine transform of Subsection 3.5.6.

Jain's development of the sinusoidal transform family is, without doubt, extremely ingenious. There is a problem with this approach, however, and that is that there is no guarantee that the (non-stationary) input sequences of which the various transforms form the optimal transforms actually correspond with typical image data. This can readily be seen if, for example, the matrix of Eq. (3.128) is inverted and scaled so that its largest value is unity. Whether the resulting covariance matrix corresponds with that of 'typical' image data is doubtful. The result in the case of the DCT, as might be expected, does seem to be more in keeping with that expected of common types of image source.

In so far as we are justified in using the first-order Markov model as a valid one for image data we can test the efficiencies of the various members of the sinusoidal set as has been done with the more conventional transforms. Thus measurements have been made on five members of the set excluding the DCT and DST already treated. In no case does the performance of any of the transforms even approach that of the Walsh–Hadamard transform, and it is suggested, therefore, that they will be useful only for transforming very restricted classes of image data, those for which, indeed, they diagonalise exactly, or approximately, the corresponding covariance matrix. Furthermore, not all members of the set are distinct in their transform domain variance performance.

Kitajima (1980) has employed a technique similar to that of Jain to develop a symmetric version of the cosine transform, where the basis matrix elements are given by

$$\psi(i,j) = \sqrt{\frac{2}{N-1}}\, u(i)u(j) \cos\left(\frac{ij\pi}{N-1}\right) \qquad (3.129)$$

where $u(i) = 1/\sqrt{2}$ for $i = 0$, $N-1$; $u(i) = 1$ otherwise. The transform requires fewer multiplications to compute than the basic DCT (see Chapter 7) and the off-diagonal elements of the transform domain covariance matrix can be significantly reduced by windowing the data with the function $W_0 = W_N = 1\sqrt{2}$, $W_k = 1$ otherwise.

It is perhaps worth mentioning here that Srinivasan and Rao (1983) and Kwak et al. (1983) have developed approximations to the DCT which only involve integer arithmetic, as a method of easing the otherwise significant computational load which the general matrix/vector operation poses (see Chapter 7).

3.5.9   The high-correlation transform (HCT)

This transform is intended to provide a compromise between the ease of implementation of the WHT and the theoretical efficiency of the DCT (Cham and Clarke, 1983; Nicol et al., 1983) and is one of a pair of transforms, the other having an improved performance at lower values of inter-element correlation and, for that reason, designated the low correlation transform (LCT). The basis matrix is shown in Eq. (3.130) for the case $N = 8$, and it can be seen to be a modification of the WHT matrix intended to 'smooth out' the sharp changes between elements in that transform, whilst only employing the values ± 1, $\pm \frac{1}{2}$, and so requiring, at most, binary shifts in implementation, together with a scaling operation. The scaling constants for orthonormality are shown on the right of the matrix in Eq. (3.130), and it can be seen that only two vectors require separate scale factors to render the matrix orthonormal to within a constant. The orthonormal basis vectors are shown in Fig. 3.12.

$$\text{HCT(8)} = \begin{bmatrix} 1 & 1 & 1 & 1 & 1 & 1 & 1 & 1 \\ 1 & 1 & \frac{1}{2} & \frac{1}{2} & -\frac{1}{2} & -\frac{1}{2} & -1 & -1 \\ 1 & \frac{1}{2} & -\frac{1}{2} & -1 & -1 & -\frac{1}{2} & \frac{1}{2} & 1 \\ \frac{1}{2} & \frac{1}{2} & -1 & -1 & 1 & 1 & -\frac{1}{2} & -\frac{1}{2} \\ 1 & -1 & -1 & 1 & 1 & -1 & -1 & 1 \\ 1 & -1 & -\frac{1}{2} & \frac{1}{2} & -\frac{1}{2} & \frac{1}{2} & 1 & -1 \\ \frac{1}{2} & -1 & 1 & -\frac{1}{2} & -\frac{1}{2} & 1 & -1 & \frac{1}{2} \\ \frac{1}{2} & -\frac{1}{2} & 1 & -1 & 1 & -1 & \frac{1}{2} & -\frac{1}{2} \end{bmatrix} \begin{matrix} 1/\sqrt{8} \\ 1/\sqrt{5} \\ 1/\sqrt{5} \\ 1/\sqrt{5} \\ 1/\sqrt{8} \\ 1/\sqrt{5} \\ 1/\sqrt{5} \\ 1/\sqrt{5} \end{matrix} \qquad (3.130)$$

For inter-element correlation coefficient 0.91 the transform domain covariance matrix is

$\text{COV}(\mathbf{Y}) =$

$$\begin{bmatrix} 6.344 & 0.000 & -0.289 & 0.000 & -0.066 & 0.000 & -0.042 & 0.000 \\ 0.000 & 0.896 & 0.000 & 0.037 & 0.000 & -0.035 & 0.000 & 0.164 \\ -0.289 & 0.000 & 0.311 & 0.000 & -0.001 & 0.000 & 0.018 & 0.000 \\ 0.000 & 0.037 & 0.000 & 0.126 & 0.000 & 0.035 & 0.000 & 0.011 \\ -0.066 & 0.000 & 0.001 & 0.000 & 0.094 & 0.000 & 0.000 & 0.000 \\ 0.000 & -0.035 & 0.000 & 0.035 & 0.000 & 0.093 & 0.000 & -0.004 \\ -0.042 & 0.000 & 0.018 & 0.000 & 0.000 & 0.000 & 0.055 & 0.000 \\ 0.000 & 0.164 & 0.000 & 0.011 & 0.000 & -0.004 & 0.000 & 0.081 \end{bmatrix}$$

$$(3.131)$$

The value of η_C is 96.72%, and the $\eta_E : M$ relationship is

M	1	2	3	4	5	6	7	8
η_E(%)	79.3	90.5	94.4	96.0	97.1	98.3	99.3	100

$$(3.132)$$

3.5.10 Singular value decomposition

Equation (3.40) expresses the reconstruction of an image (or image subblock) as a sum of basis 'images' formed from the outer products (see Appendix 6) of pairs of basis vectors, $\mathbf{t}_a \mathbf{t}_b^T$ weighted by the appropriate transform coefficient (note that in this representation the basis vectors are written in column form, i.e., the collection of such vectors making up the basis matrix is written as the transpose of that matrix in its normal form). In

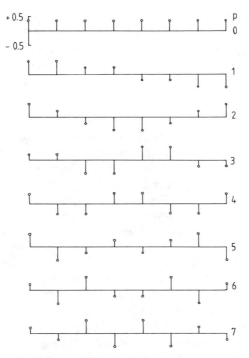

FIG. 3.12. High-correlation transform basis vectors; $N = 8$; p denotes coefficient order.

accordance with conventional notation in the present context, the general two-dimensional image transformation may be written (Andrews and Patterson, 1976a, b, c) as

$$[\alpha] = [U]^{\mathrm{T}}[F][V] \tag{3.133}$$

where $[U]$ and $[V]$ are unitary transform matrices (written in the above sense) and $[F]$ is the $N \times N$ image or block matrix (here assumed square purely for convenience). The equivalent relation to that expressed in Eq. (3.40) is then

$$[F] = \sum_{i=1}^{N} \sum_{j=1}^{N} \alpha_{ij} \mathbf{u}_i \mathbf{v}_j^{\mathrm{T}} \tag{3.134}$$

Where $\mathbf{u}_i$ and $\mathbf{v}_j$ are column vectors within $[U]$ and $[V]$ respectively. If we now define $[U]$ and $[V]$ such that

$$[U][\Lambda][U]^{\mathrm{T}} = [F][F]^{\mathrm{T}} \tag{3.135}$$

and

$$[V][\Lambda][V]^{\mathrm{T}} = [F]^{\mathrm{T}}[F] \tag{3.136}$$

where $[\Lambda]$ is the diagonal matrix of eigenvalues of $[F][F]^T$ and the columns of $[U]$ and $[V]$ are, respectively, the eigenvectors of $[F][F]^T$ and $[F]^T[F]$ (left and right singular vectors of $[F]$), then the only terms appearing in the reconstruction of $[F]$ in Eq. (3.134) will be those for which $i = j$, i.e.,

$$[F] = \sum_{i=1}^{N} \lambda_i \, \mathbf{u}_i \, \mathbf{v}_i^T \tag{3.137}$$

where $\lambda_i = \alpha_{ii}^2$ is the ith eigenvalue of $[F]$, and its square root the ith singular value (Golub and Reinsch, 1970). In theoretical terms Eq. (3.137) may be restricted to that over only R finite terms, where $R \leqslant N$ is the rank of the matrix $[\alpha]$. In practice the set of α_{ii} typically falls off rapidly in magnitude as i increases, in the same way as the coefficient variances following a conventional transform. The present situation is different from both that involving deterministic transforms (the DCT and WHT, for example) and that employing the KLT, however, although it has similarities with the latter in that determination of eigenvalues and vectors is required. The important feature is that, just as the KLT is the most efficient transform for processing a class of images or sub-blocks defined by the appropriate covariance matrix and thereby giving minimum mean square error averaged over the class, the singular value decomposition operates on a single image or block basis and results in the least square error for that image or block of any possible transform (provided that the eigenvalue set is ordered according to decreasing magnitude of the terms). Naturally, it is necessary to code and transmit the singular values of significant magnitude and the corresponding vectors in order that inverse transformation may be carried out at the receiver.

Specific coding implementations are described in Chapter 5 whilst a more general tutorial review, also dealing with the computational requirements, is given by Klema and Laub (1980).

3.5.11   The discrete linear basis

From the point of view of implementation, basis matrices having integer terms have advantages (at least in principle) over those with real number entries (sinusoidal transforms, for example). One such is the discrete linear basis (DLB) described by Haralick and Shanmugam (1974). The basis matrix is generated by requiring that the **N** vectors be mutually orthogonal, have integer components and be either odd or even (describing the symmetry of the vectors about the centre point). Thus, for example, for $N = 4$,

$$\mathrm{DLB}(4) = \begin{bmatrix} 1 & 1 & 1 & 1 \\ 3 & 1 & -1 & -3 \\ 1 & -1 & -1 & 1 \\ 1 & -3 & 3 & -1 \end{bmatrix} \tag{3.138}$$

Constructions for larger values of N, both odd and even, result from applications of the relations given by the authors, and fast algorithms can also be devised (if an orthonormal form is desired, then scaling of some individual basis vector elements will be required).

Although there have been other integer transform developments subsequently, the recent rapid advance in the processing speed and power of digital integrated circuits has meant that problems of implementation have become less prominent, and the importance of such forms has consequently diminished.

3.6 General comparison of transforms

In this section a general comparison is made, again using the first-order Markov model, between the more commonly used transforms on the bases of energy packing and decorrelation efficiency [results for other transforms have been excluded on the grounds of (a) small degree of transform usage and (b) in the case of other sinusoidal transforms, much poorer performance]. Previously the energy packing efficiency η_E has been determined for the case $N = 8$ and $\rho = 0.91$, and it is now considered over a wide range of values of correlation coefficient ($-0.96 - +0.99$) and for $N = 4$, 8 and 16. Similarly we consider the decorrelation efficiency η_C for the same range of parameters. Of course, the number of possible combinations of transform, block size, correlation coefficient and energy packing criteria is extremely large, and so only the most significant comparative features can be included here. Thus the (admittedly arbitrary) criterion of the percentage energy retained in the largest $N/2$ transform coefficients is used to define η_E, and, where the correlation coefficient is not the independent variable, $\rho = 0.91$ is selected. Also, a word concerning some of the graphical scales used here is perhaps in order. It is the case that, whilst the performance of a transform over the whole range of correlation coefficients is of some interest, attention is usually focussed upon the range which corresponds to that of typical image detail, i.e., 0.9 upwards. Furthermore, in this region the various efficiency measures usually take on values not far from 100%. The scales reflect these characteristics in that, whilst they allow wide ranging properties to be portrayed they are expanded, by using an offset reference point and logarithmic representation, over the regions of greater interest.

3.6.1 Transform energy packing efficiency

Figure 3.13 portrays the energy packing efficiency of various transforms for the case $N = 8$. The best performance is given by the DCT, and it is indistinguishable from that of the KLT(0.91) (the notation implies that the KLT basis vectors have been calculated for a first-order Markov process of

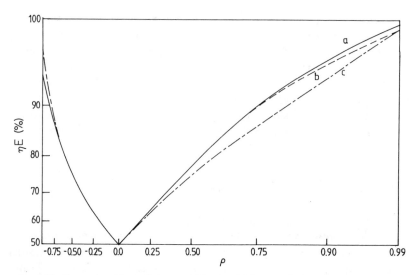

FIG. 3.13. Energy 'packing' efficiency η_E ($N = 8$, with four coefficients retained) as a function of correlation coefficient. (a) Discrete cosine transform (DCT), (b) KLT(0.36) and (c) discrete Fourier transform (DFT).

inter-element correlation 0.91). The associated curve for the KLT(0.36) shows how insensitive the latter transform is, in an energy packing sense, to variations in data correlation coefficient. The transform with the poorest performance is the DFT, the curves for all other transforms (WHT, DST, Haar and slant) lying between the two shown. In any case, the difference between them is, at most, only a few percent (in fact the 50% truncation criterion corresponds to quite severe coefficient deletion and is not a particularly sensitive test, and a better one is described subsequently). Two further points are of interest with regard to this figure. First, both the data and transform covariance matrices are diagonal in form with all values equal when $\rho = 0$, and so the minimum value of η_E is 50% (the same in both domains) and is obtained for that value of correlation. Second, the region $\rho = -0.96$-0 is included in the comparison, since the degree of data compression obtainable depends only on the magnitude of the correlation coefficient and not its sign. Thus data having $\rho = -0.96$ is just as 'predictable' as that having $\rho = +0.96$. That we do not wish to compress data with such values of correlation coefficient does not affect the principles involved, it is simply that such data does not have any interesting features or visible long-range structure. In comparison with typical image data, which is markedly 'low pass' in nature, data with high negative values of ρ is 'high pass', and the large magnitude transform coefficients are packed into the high, instead of low, sequency region of the array.

Figures 3.14 and 3.15 show the values of the coefficient variances for
$N = 16$ and $\rho = 0.91$ for, respectively, the DCT, DFT and DST, and the WH,
Haar and slant transforms. Good energy packing efficiency demands that the
magnitudes of the variances fall off rapidly with increasing coefficient order
and, of course, the DCT is again best in this sense and also has, in contrast
with the other transforms, a smooth decay of variance with order. Owing to
the symmetry inherent within the basis matrix, the DFT has pairs of
coefficients of equal variance, and this accounts for the step-like trend of the
relationship, whilst the DST has the most erratic behaviour of the first three

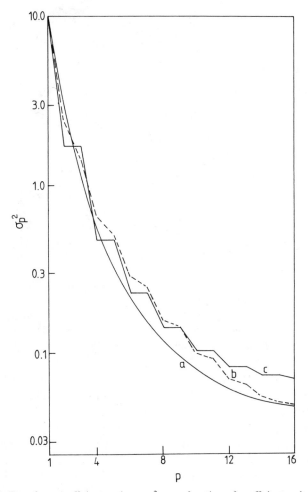

FIG. 3.14. Transform coefficient variance σ_p^2; as a function of coefficient order $p; \rho = 0.91$;
$N = 16$. (a) DCT, (b) DFT and (c) DST.

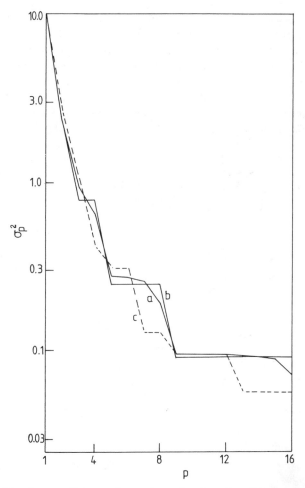

FIG. 3.15. Transform coefficient variance σ_p^2 as a function of coefficient order p; $\rho = 0.91$; $N = 16$. (a) Walsh–Hadamard transform (WHT), (b) Haar transform and (c) slant transform.

transforms, middle-order variances being larger than those of either of the other two, whilst the highest-order terms are almost as small as those of the DCT. The curves for the other three transforms show a more variable trend, the WH and Haar transforms in particular having many high-order terms of similar magnitude, leading to a less flexible coefficient truncation performance. If the degree of truncation is fairly small, however, the performance of the slant transform approaches that of the DCT. As a somewhat crude generalisation, all curves are quite similar, and even the Haar transform manages to achieve a significant reduction in the magnitude of high-order terms.

The truncation behaviour of the various transforms is brought out more clearly in Fig. 3.16 which shows the error incurred in deleting differing numbers of coefficients for the same values of N and ρ. It may therefore be looked on as a 'cumulative' representation of the previous two figures. The best (lowest) result is for the DCT and the worst, over most of the range, is for the Haar transform although as can be seen, if severe truncation is envisaged, the DST then has the highest error. This form of representation is perhaps a more sensitive indication of relative transform behaviour, for it can be seen that, for small degrees of coefficient omission, the Haar transform incurs approximately twice the mean square error of the DCT. In this range the

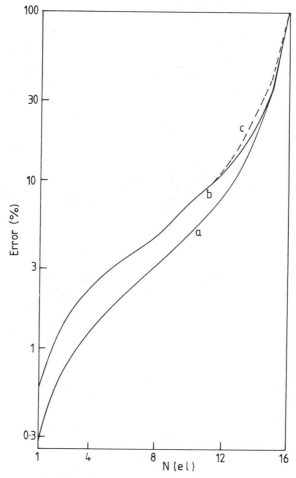

FIG. 3.16. Transform coefficient truncation error as a function of the number of coefficients eliminated N(el); $\rho = 0.91$; $N = 16$. (a) DCT, (b) Haar transform and (c) DST.

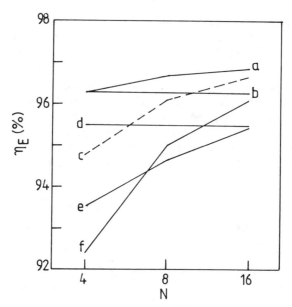

FIG. 3.17. Energy 'packing' efficiency η_E as a function of transform block size, $\rho = 0.91$. (a) DCT and KLT(0.91), (b) slant transform, (c) KLT(0.36), (d) WHT and Haar transforms, (e) DFT and (f) DST.

slant transform compares well with the latter transform, whilst the WHT and DFT results lie closer to those of the Haar transform.

As far as block size effects are concerned Fig. 3.17 shows the variation in η_E as the value of N is increased from 4 to 8 and then 16. As a result of the blockwise nature of the variance/coefficient order relation for the WH, Haar and slant transforms, η_E is independent of the value of N, whilst for all other transforms it increases with N. The greatest improvement occurs in the case of the DST and DFT, and, as before, the result for the DCT is virtually indistinguishable from that for the KLT, whilst the KLT(0.36) curve again shows how insensitive its energy packing performance is to the exact value of ρ for which the eigenvectors (basis vectors) and values (coefficient variances) are determined.

3.6.2. Transform decorrelation efficiency

The other property inherent in the operation of the orthogonal transform is that of decorrelation. Thus, whereas in the data domain the (image) elements are normally highly correlated, implying the presence of redundancy and 'predictability', these properties should not be evident in the transform domain, i.e., the redundancy should no longer be present, and the

coefficient sequences may then be subjected independently to further processing. The degree to which the transform successfully carries out the decorrelation process is, of course, indicated by the transform domain covariance (or
correlation) matrix which, in the case of perfect decorrelation, will have a
diagonal structure. The magnitudes of the off-diagonal terms in any covariance matrix are indicative of the correlation between the various sequences
involved and, as before, the ratio of the summations of such terms in
transform and data domains demonstrates the degree to which the transform
is successful in suppressing the correlation inherent in the data. It is worth
noting here that other measures of decorrelation performance have been
proposed (see, e.g., Yip and Hutchinson, 1982; Hamidi and Pearl, 1976) and
that the one presented here (see also Clarke, 1983c) is chosen for its simplicity
and ease of interpretation—perfect decorrelation is represented by a figure of
100%, no reduction in correlation by 0%. Figures 3.18 and 3.19 show the
behaviour of several transforms with respect to input data correlation
coefficient for $N = 8$. It can be seen that all transforms are reasonably
efficient in this sense when the value of ρ is greater than about 0.9 with the
exception of the sine transform, which performs best in the region of small
correlation. In this area, too, results are subject to error, since as ρ tends to
zero identically, both summations in Eq. (3.49) also tend to zero, leading to
an indeterminate (limiting) result. As in the case of η_E, the decorrelation
efficiency of the transformation process is not particularly interesting in this

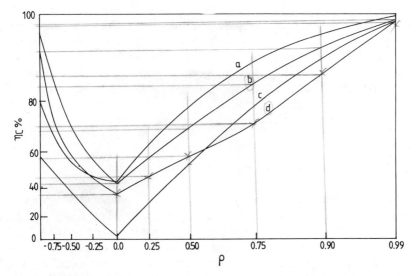

FIG. 3.18.   Decorrelation efficiency $\eta_C(N=8)$ as a function of correlation coefficient. (a) Slant
transform, (b) WHT, (c) Haar transform and (d) DFT.

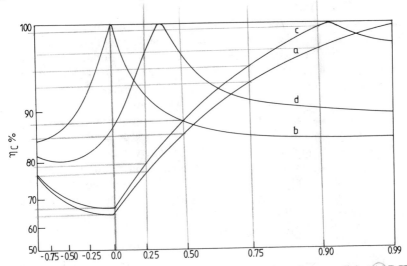

FIG. 3.19. Decorrelation efficiency η_C ($N = 8$) as a functon of correlation coefficient (a) DCT, (b) DST, (c) KLT (0.91) and (d) KLT (0.36)

range, at least from a practical point of view. As usual, the best transform is the DCT which, however, now has a performance measurably different from that of the equivalent optimum transform (KLT). For comparison the curve for the KLT(0.36) is included also, and these results demonstrate that, generally, there is a greater variation in decorrelation performance as the type of transform and the operating parameters are varied than is the case for the energy packing behaviour. Figure 3.20 shows selected decorrelation results in an expanded form over a reduced range of ρ. The effect of block size variation upon η_C is shown in Fig. 3.21. In general, larger block sizes reduce the transform performance in this respect, although this is not always true for the DST and KLT [the result for the KLT(0.91) is, of course, 100% for all N]. For the better transforms, however, the effect is small.

3.7   Transform comparison based on image data

In the previous sections of this chapter the efficiencies of various transforms which have been used for image coding have been compared using the criteria of decorrelation and 'energy packing'. In this section the behaviour of three of the transforms is demonstrated for the three test images introduced in the previous chapter. The transforms chosen are representative of the multiplicity of those available—the Walsh–Hadamard transform (WHT), whose ease of implementation has made it very attractive from the practical

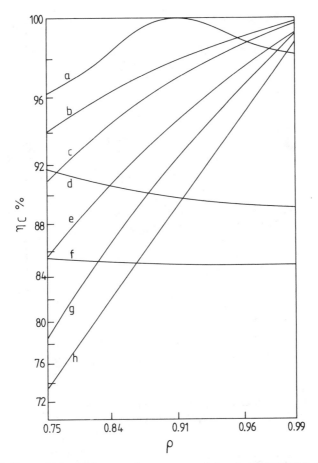

FIG. 3.20. Decorrelation efficiency results on an expanded scale. (a) KLT(0.91), (b) DCT, (c) slant transform, (d) KLT(0.36), (e) WHT, (f) DST, (g) Haar transform and (h) DFT.

point of view, the discrete cosine transform (DCT), having better performance than the WHT but requiring several real multiplications to transform each data block, and the discrete sine transform (DST), the latter chosen to illustrate the behaviour of a less frequently used transform, and one, moreover, with a non-constant DC basis vector.

Transforms are compared on the basis of the fraction of total energy occurring in the first (i.e., DC) coefficient, and in the four lowest-order coefficients in the case of the 8×8 transform, and the 16 lowest-order coefficients for the 16×16 transform. Numerical results appear in Table 3.1. It can be seen that, in the case of Image 1, the DCT and WHT are markedly more efficient than the DST at compacting the data energy into the first few

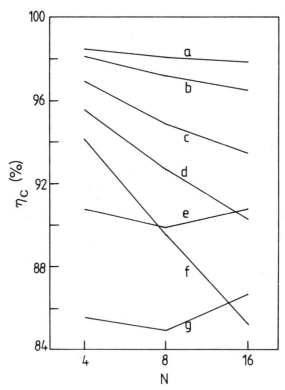

FIG. 3.21. Decorrelation efficiency η_C as a function of transform block size, $\rho = 0.91$. (a) DCT (b) slant transform, (c) WHT, (d) Haar transform, (e) KLT (0.36), (f) DFT and (g) DST.

coefficients, and the reason is that the image mean energy 'leaks' into the higher-order coefficients when using the latter transform, for reasons discussed previously. It can be seen that the effect is not so noticeable in the case of Image 2, where the higher degree of detail in the image results in a much wider spread of energy in the transform domain in all cases. In the case of the 16×16 transform of Image 3 the DST has an even better performance than the DCT—a curious result probably brought about by the low value of inter-element correlation for this image, combined with the relatively good decorrelation efficiency of the DST in such a situation. However, in all cases compaction of energy into the first coefficient is worst in the case of the sine transform and it follows that, since the total energy is always constant for a normalised transform, if there is less in the DC coefficient there must, correspondingly, be more in the higher-order coefficients.

TABLE 3.1. Practical energy compression results for the WHT, DCT and DST.[a]

Transform	Image 1 (a)	Image 1 (b)	Image 2 (a)	Image 2 (b)	Image 3 (a)	Image 3 (b)
WHT $N = 8$	90.70	96.54	45.45	64.70	23.78	44.96
DCT $N = 8$	90.70	97.65	45.45	67.22	23.78	46.17
DST $N = 8$	73.77	79.45	42.08	63.81	22.67	45.47
WHT $N = 16$	82.65	96.86	30.28	64.71	11.24	44.99
DCT $N = 16$	82.65	98.23	30.28	71.59	11.24	48.57
DST $N = 16$	64.28	89.15	25.47	71.27	10.56	49.32

[a] (a) represents the percentage energy compacted into the first coefficient, and (b) represents the percentage energy compacted into the first four coefficients ($N \times N = 8 \times 8$) or 16 coefficients ($N \times N = 16 \times 16$).

3.8 Summary

We have considered, in this chapter, the basic operation of a transform coding scheme: the application of the transform itself to a one-dimensional data vector or, as is more usual, to a two-dimensional array of image elements. A simple numerical example serves to show that transformation of a set of image luminance values, not too dissimilar from each other, results, in the transform domain, in a group of coefficients of widely differing values, and which therefore need not all be retained to the same accuracy in order to allow acceptable reconstruction of the original data via inverse transformation. A similar property will, subsequently, be found to apply to those coefficient sequences obtained by successive transformation of an image divided into sub-blocks, a more usual approach to the transform operation in practice.

In order to compare the various transforms actually used for image processing, numerical measures of energy 'packing' and decorrelation performance have been introduced, followed by individual descriptions of each of the transforms, starting with one which is conveniently used (theoretically at

least) as a standard of 'goodness' against which all others may be assessed—the Karhunen-Loève transform. The numerical measures of efficiency are then used to compare transform performances over a wide range of
data correlation coefficient as well as for different data vector lengths and, on
this basis, as well as on that of application of the transforms to actual image
data, the conclusion is drawn that, for practical purposes, the discrete cosine
transform (DCT) has the best performance of all data-independent transforms (being very close to that of the KLT as long as the data correlation
coefficient is fairly high), whilst the Walsh–Hadamard transform has a
performance which is measurably inferior but whose use may be made
attractive by the ease with which it may be implemented. As an alternative to
the DCT and WHT the high-correlation transform (HCT) provides a
compromise between efficiency and ease of implementation, since it is
composed of basis vectors with a very restricted set of values particularly
amenable to high-speed digital operation. Given the recent rapid improvements in the processing power of integrated circuitry, however, it is quite
likely that the DCT will become the generally accepted transform for coding
applications—even those in which the data rate is very high. The other
transforms described in this chapter will then, except possibly in very
specialised applications, have a significance which is more historical than
practical.

Chapter 4

Transform Coefficient Quantisation and Bit Allocation

4.1 Introduction

The reader who has studied the previous two chapters might well assume that, having ensured that the input data is suitable for transform coding (i.e., has significant inter-element correlation in at least one direction) and having selected a transform which represents a satisfactory compromise between efficient decorrelation and energy packing ability on the one hand and practicability of implementation on the other, there remains little to do but store or transmit the resulting coefficients as simply as possible. In fact, it has been forcefully argued (Tescher, 1979) that the next step in the process is more important than the choice, for example, of transform type or block size, and that more research into the matters dealt with in this chapter and the next, i.e., the selection and efficient quantisation of those coefficients which are to be retained for transmission or storage, would have produced more impressive results than has the extensive work carried out upon the development of more and more (marginally) efficient transforms. It is worth emphasising this point here and also stressing, at the same time, that much more attention should be given to the processing of transform coefficients in the context of the human visual response, a subject taken up again in Chapter 6.

In the present chapter, then, the first topic dealt with is the distribution of coefficient energy and its relation to that in the data domain. Thereafter, the statistical distribution of transform coefficients is discussed, together with methods of selecting and quantising the coefficients in a non-adaptive fashion, i.e., disregarding the fact that different regions of the image have markedly different statistical properties. The matter of more efficient adaptive techniques is considered in Chapter 5 but naturally relies strongly on the basic techniques developed in this chapter.

4.2 Transform coefficient energy distribution

It has been pointed out previously that, following the application of an orthonormal transformation, the total energy in the coefficient domain will equal that of the original data. Thus, to take the simple example of Eqs. (3.25) and (3.28), in each case the total energy, represented by the sum of the squares of the data values or of the transform coefficients, is the same. Furthermore, it is open to us to process the block of data after subtraction of the mean value, in which case all 'AC' coefficients remain unaltered in value but the magnitude of the 'DC' coefficient now becomes zero [Eq. (3.30)]. Thus, the DC and AC energy terms equate separately, and the DC coefficient becomes N times the data mean value, where N is the (two-dimensional) block size. In the example quoted $N = 4$, and so

$$\text{Data mean value} \quad \bar{x} = 6$$

$$\text{Transform DC coefficient} = 6N = 24$$

$$\text{Data DC energy} = \bar{x}^2 N^2 = 36 \cdot 16 = 576$$

This is represented in the transform domain by

$$(\text{DC coefficient})^2 = 24^2 = 576$$

And for the AC terms by

$$\text{Data AC energy} = \sum_{\text{block}} (x - \bar{x})^2 = 44$$

$$\text{Transform domain AC energy} = \sum_{\text{block}} y^2 - (\text{DC coefficient})^2$$

$$= 620 - 576 = 44$$

where x and y are arbitrary entries in the data and transform arrays, respectively.

We may now extend the preceding relationships to the more typical situation in which an image is processed by initial subdivision into smaller blocks for more convenient manipulation. The significant features of such an extension are two. First, it is no longer practical to set the mean value of every block to zero, though we may do so for the image as a whole if we wish. Second, what were individual, single values (the coefficients of various orders) now become sequences of random variables, each with their own value of mean, variance and so on measured over the ensemble of blocks making up the whole image. Appreciation of this point is particularly important in the case of the DC coefficient, since by setting the whole image mean value to zero we shall produce a DC coefficient sequence in the transform domain which itself has zero mean but whose variance is unaffected by such a step and which, typically, will be the largest of the whole coefficient set. (It is worth recalling here the generalisation that the transform operation results in a redistribution of data energy into the low-order transform coefficients—what this means in the case of the DC coefficient is that the various individual block means vary significantly about the overall mean of the image, giving a DC coefficient of large variance.)

The preceding relationships are best illustrated by an actual example. We consider here Image 2 again, with a block size of $N = 8$, and processed using the two-dimensional Walsh–Hadamard transform. The input data has an overall mean value of 67.57 and a variance of 617.55. Originally 256 × 256 elements in extent, it is divided into 1024 blocks of dimension 8 × 8. The transform domain therefore consists of 64 sequences, each containing 1024 samples, and each with its own mean and variance, given in Tables 4.1 and 4.2, respectively.

From Table 4.1 it can be seen that the AC coefficients all have mean values which are approximately zero, whilst the DC coefficient has a mean value N times that of the data, as expected (note that neither of these results is true if the AC basis vectors have mean values different from zero, as in the case of the sine transform). The values in Table 4.2 are each normalised by the input data variance, in order to make the distribution easier to interpret, for the sum of all the entries in the table will always be very nearly N^2, the difference being due to the small, but finite, amount of energy residing in the non-zero

TABLE 4.1. Coefficient mean array, Image 2.[a]

540.54	−1.75	0.31	1.86	−1.82	0.39	−0.52	0.61
1.88	0.56	−0.45	0.23	−0.37	−0.28	−0.28	0.08
4.51	−0.28	0.03	0.02	0.22	0.14	0.17	0.03
1.09	−0.03	−0.10	0.11	−0.33	0.06	0.07	0.02
−0.47	0.04	0.06	−0.05	−0.13	−0.02	0.02	0.01
0.05	−0.20	0.13	0.13	0.00	0.08	0.19	0.02
1.65	−0.08	0.04	0.09	0.11	0.06	−0.01	−0.05
0.11	0.05	0.10	−0.01	−0.09	−0.04	0.11	0.03

[a] $N = 8$, Walsh–Hadamard transformation.

TABLE 4.2. Normalised coefficient variance array, Image 2.[a]

29.057	5.297	4.378	3.069	3.798	1.064	0.776	0.359
4.623	2.387	1.099	0.300	0.117	0.130	0.226	0.055
1.494	1.478	0.693	0.185	0.065	0.088	0.142	0.029
0.614	0.159	0.112	0.093	0.062	0.034	0.019	0.009
0.166	0.018	0.027	0.033	0.023	0.013	0.006	0.003
0.317	0.175	0.094	0.030	0.017	0.016	0.021	0.005
0.280	0.246	0.115	0.039	0.018	0.018	0.028	0.006
0.115	0.034	0.020	0.015	0.010	0.009	0.006	0.002

[a] $N = 8$, Walsh–Hadamard transformation.

mean values of the AC coefficient sequences. The relevant figures are as follows:

Total average energy (DC) per data block $= N^2 \bar{x}^2$

$$= 64 \cdot (67.57)^2 = 2.922 \times 10^5$$

Equivalent value in the transform domain $= \bar{x}^2 = 2.922 \times 10^5$

Total average energy (AC) per data block $= N^2 \sigma^2$

$$= 64 \cdot 617.55 = 39{,}523$$

Equivalent value in the transform domain $=$ variance sum $\cdot \sigma^2$

$$= 63.935 \cdot 617.55 = 39{,}483$$

$$\text{Difference} = 40$$

where the 'variance sum' is that of the entries in Table 4.2. The difference is just the sum of the squares of all the AC entries in Table 4.1. The energy residing in the mean values of the AC coefficient sequences is thus very small. In the case of the sine transform, the coefficient sequences corresponding to those basis vectors having finite mean values contain spurious DC energy, and the value of the true mean coefficient is correspondingly reduced (in the present case, to 481.62).

The use of the normalised variance distribution, as in Table 4.2, allows easy comparison between the transform properties of various images which may have different values of mean and variance (see Section 2.4 of Chapter 2). We can also compare images on the basis of AC energy content, which in the present case will be

$$\frac{N^2 \sigma^2}{N^2 \sigma^2 + N^2 - \bar{x}^2} = \frac{617.55}{617.55 + 67.57^2} = 11.9\%$$

TABLE 4.3. Energy properties of Images 1, 2 and 3.

Parameter	Image 1	Image 2	Image 3
AC energy content (%)	19.4	11.9	87.8
Variance in lowest four terms (%)	96.5	64.7	45.0

The fraction of the total transform domain variance in the four lowest-order terms is 64.7%. Similar figures may be determined for the other two test images, and all are given in Table 4.3.

The fractional variance figure indicates how easy it will be to code any particular image, and the typescript (black and white) image will obviously be the most difficult of the three. It has, in addition, a high AC energy content, although the two quantities are not necessarily closely related (had all the black elements been clustered in one corner of the image, the overall correlation would have been high, and transform processing would then have been a suitable coding technique).

4.3 The dynamic range of transform coefficients

In the most general case, the transform operation consists of pointwise multiplication of a set of data sample values (which may take on any value whatsoever between zero and the maximum allowable within the system, the latter being determined by such considerations as maximum scanning device output level, system overload restrictions, and so on) by a set of weighting coefficients, and subsequent summation of the products so formed. Once the transform type and block size have been selected, the maximum possible value of any transform coefficient may easily be calculated. In the case of continuous-valued data, the smallest coefficient value (or, equivalently, the minimum separation between allowable values) will be zero. In the more usual case, the input data will already be in quantised form (typically to 8-bit accuracy, i.e., taking on one of 256 possible levels) and, although this will not affect the maximum coefficient amplitude calculated as for continuous data, it will impose a limiting value on the allowable coefficient difference, one, moreover, which will vary markedly with the actual transform selected. The determination of the relevant values is most easily carried out by considering the DC and AC coefficients separately. Here we examine the two-dimensional case, although the theory is of course applicable to transformations of any dimension (Clarke, 1985).

Consider the general two-dimensional transformation

$$[C] = [A][X][B]^{\mathrm{T}} \tag{4.1}$$

where $[X]$ is the $N \times M$ data array and different row and column transformations are used. If all elements of $[X]$ are zero then naturally so will be all elements of $[C]$, the set of coefficients. As long as all elements of $[X]$ are equal, all elements of $[C]$, other than the DC term, C_{DC}, will remain zero. The value of C_{DC} under these conditions is determined as follows.

The first stage of the transform is

$$[C']_{DC} = \begin{bmatrix} a_{11} & \cdots & a_{1N} \end{bmatrix} \begin{bmatrix} x_{11} & \cdots & x_{1M} \\ \vdots & & \vdots \\ x_{N1} & \cdots & x_{NM} \end{bmatrix}$$

$$= \begin{bmatrix} c_{11} & \cdots & c_{1M} \end{bmatrix} \tag{4.2}$$

where

$$c_{1m} = \sum_{n=1}^{N} a_{1n}x_{nm} \qquad m = 1 \rightarrow M \tag{4.3}$$

and the data array consists of N rows and M columns. The second stage is

$$C_{DC} = \begin{bmatrix} c_{11} & \cdots & c_{1M} \end{bmatrix} \begin{bmatrix} b_{11} \\ \vdots \\ b_{1M} \end{bmatrix}$$

$$= \sum_{m=1}^{M} c_{1m}b_{1m} \tag{4.4}$$

The largest value of the DC coefficient will be generated when all $x_{nm} = x_{max}$. Thus, from Eq. (4.3)

$$c_{1m(max)} = x_{max} \sum_{n=1}^{N} a_{1n}$$

and so

$$C_{DC(max)} = x_{max} \sum_{n=1}^{N} a_{1n} \sum_{m=1}^{M} b_{1m} \tag{4.5}$$

The smallest value of the DC coefficient will result when only one of the x_{nm} is finite and equal to x_{min} (the smallest quantisation increment in the input data) and, furthermore, corresponds to the location of the smallest elements in the DC basis vectors in both transforms (the elements in such basis vectors are usually, but not necessarily, the same—in the case of the sine transform, for example). In this latter case the AC coefficients will be finite, but this will not affect the value of the DC coefficient. Thus,

$$C_{DC(min)} = x_{min} a_{1n(min)} b_{1m(min)} \tag{4.6}$$

If the dynamic range of the data is x_D ($= x_{max}/x_{min}$), then the dynamic range of the DC coefficient is

$$C_{DC(D)} = x_D \sum_{n=1}^{N} a_{1n} \sum_{m=1}^{M} b_{1m}/(a_{1n(min)} b_{1m(min)}) \qquad (4.7)$$

(This equation may easily be modified to apply to the one- or three-dimensional case.)

In the vast majority of cases, the transforms chosen for $[A]$ and $[B]$ will have constant basis vectors for the DC term which will therefore have all elements of magnitude $1/\sqrt{N}$ or $1/\sqrt{M}$ for $[A]$ or $[B]$, respectively. In this case, Eq. (4.7) simplifies to

$$C_{DC(D)} = x_D \frac{N(1/\sqrt{N})M(1/\sqrt{M})}{(1/\sqrt{N})(1/\sqrt{M}}$$

$$= x_D NM$$

$$= x_D N^2 \qquad \text{if} \quad N = M \qquad (4.8)$$

This latter result is the one usually quoted, i.e., that a two-dimensional transform of order N will result in a DC coefficient dynamic range that is N^2 times that of the input data [note that this factor corresponds to the possible range of the data mean: $x_{max}/(x_{min}/N^2)$]. An extra $2 \log_2 N$ bits is therefore necessary to retain the original accuracy.

If we now consider the discrete sine transform, for which the DC basis vector is not constant, we find that the dynamic range of the coefficient has increased. Thus, for $N = 8$, the smallest element in the DC basis vector is 0.1612, and the sum of the elements is 2.6732. The dynamic range is therefore $4.30N^2 x_D$, and for $N = 16$ the factor becomes 5.48. The dynamic range expansion is thus some five times greater in the case of the DST than for the DCT, or WHT (or any transform with a constant DC basis vector), implying that extra care is necessary, when using the transform, in subsequent coefficient processing.

In the case of the AC coefficients the same approach is valid, noting now that, although the image data values are always non-negative, the transform coefficients can now take on negative values since the basis vectors contain negative elements. The maximum positive value of a first stage coefficient therefore occurs when maximum data values correspond with positive elements of a given basis vector and zero values with negative elements. The equivalent equation to Eq. (4.3) is then

$$c_{km} = \sum_{n=1}^{N} a_{kn} x_{nm} \qquad m = 1 \to M \quad k = 2 \to N \qquad (4.9)$$

where k $(k \neq 1)$ represents an arbitrary AC basis vector. The maximum positive values of c_{km} result when $x_{nm} = x_{max}$ for those values of a_{kn} which are positive and is zero otherwise

$$c_{km}(\text{max } +) = x_{max} \sum_{n=1}^{N} \text{MAX}(+a_{kn}, 0) \qquad (4.10)$$

similarly

$$c_{km}(\text{max } -) = -x_{max} \sum_{n=1}^{N} \text{MAX}(-a_{kn}, 0)$$

Continuing the procedure we find that the maximum positive value of the (k, l)th transform coefficient is

$$C_{k, l(\text{max } +)} = x_{max} \sum_{n=1}^{N} \text{MAX}(+a_{kn}, 0) \sum_{m=1}^{M} b_{lm(+)}$$

$$- x_{max} \sum_{n=1}^{N} \text{MAX}(-a_{kn}, 0) \sum_{m=1}^{M} b_{lm}(-) \qquad (4.11)$$

where $b_{lm(+)}$ represents a positive, and $b_{lm(-)}$ a negative, basis vector element in $[B]$. Due to the symmetry inherent in the basis vectors of most commonly used transforms, the magnitudes of the sums over N, and over M, turn out to be (separately) equal, and the range of the transform coefficient then becomes

$$C_{k, l(R)} = x_{max} \sum_{n=1}^{N} |a_{kn}| \sum_{m=1}^{M} |b_{lm}| \qquad (4.12)$$

For the WHT (for which all elements have equal magnitude), this becomes, for all k, l

$$C_{(R)} = x_{max} N(1/\sqrt{N}) M(1/\sqrt{M})$$

$$= x_{max}\sqrt{NM}$$

$$= x_{max} N \qquad \text{if} \quad N = M \qquad (4.13)$$

For the DCT the scale factor (N in Eq. 4.13) is not constant but is a function of k and l. Thus, for $N = 8$, it varies over the range 6.568–8.000. For the DST the range is 6.000–8.000.

The minimum value which an AC coefficient may attain is, in general, difficult to determine. Since AC basis vector elements may be positive or negative, combinations of (integer) data values with basis vector terms of opposite sign may create very small coefficients indeed. Without undertaking an exhaustive search through all data and basis vector element values, we can perhaps obtain a rough idea of the likely minimum magnitude by using a similar method to that employed for the DC coefficient. Thus

$$C_{k,l(\text{min})} = x_{\text{min}} |a_{kn(\text{min})}| |b_{lm(\text{min})}| \qquad (4.14)$$

and the dynamic range of the AC coefficients is then

$$C_{k,l(\text{D})} = x_{\text{D}} \sum_{n=1}^{N} |a_{kn}| \sum_{m=1}^{M} |b_{lm}| / |a_{kn(\text{min})}| |b_{lm(\text{min})}| \qquad (4.15)$$

Once again, in the case of the WHT, the values are easy to calculate, and simple substitution produces, for all k, l, the identical result to Eq. (4.8), which represents the true coefficient dynamic range. In the case of other transforms, the dynamic range of the AC coefficients is, generally speaking, much larger. Thus, for the DCT, coefficient (2, 2) has a dynamic range $10.8N^2$ compared with the value of N^2 for the WHT, for the case $N = 8$. As the order of the transform increases, the disparity gets worse. As far as practical transform coding is concerned, the preceding matters are of little more than theoretical interest, since AC coefficients are typically quantised using not more than 8 bits. To the author's knowledge, however, no systematic study has ever been carried out to determine whether the very large dynamic range of such a significant coefficient as that referred to earlier for the DCT does affect the performance of a transform coding scheme in terms of the visibility of image degradation at low data rates, and it may be that the allocation of transmission bits to the various coefficients ought to take more account of such factors.

4.4 Theoretical models for coefficient probability density functions

In Chapter 2 reference was made to the probability density function (pdf) of the input data to a transform coding system, and histograms (Figs. 2.7 and 2.13) given for the data of test images 1 and 2. That of Image 1 shows the characteristic distribution for a relatively 'inactive' image, with peaks corresponding to both the light and dark areas of the picture. That of Image 2 contains, in addition, an uncharacteristic peak in the mid-grey region, representing the large proportion of picture area having a single value of intensity. In general terms, efficient coding of a data source implies a recognition of its pdf, since the more uniform a distribution, the more difficult is it to code at a predetermined rate with a prescribed degree of fidelity (see Chapter 9). Conversely, a highly non-uniform distribution will allow the coding rate to be significantly reduced, and in this context entropy measurements are useful since they indicate both the degree of non-uniformity (when compared with the quantity $\log_2 L$, where L is the number of allowable levels in the source output) and the minimum allowable rate, measured in bits per sample, for perfect data reconstruction.

As far as transform coding is concerned, attention at this point centres upon the AC coefficients, since although the DC coefficient has, naturally, to be coded, its distribution is simply that of the original image data (multiplied by a scale constant) and thus shows no marked non-uniformity which the data does not possess. As a general rule, therefore, there is nothing to be gained by trying to match the quantiser characteristic to anything other than a uniform distribution for this coefficient, although occasionally a Rayleigh distribution has been employed. Furthermore, it is usual to quantise the DC coefficient quite accurately (at least 8, and often more, bits) since coarse quantisation results in visible block structure in the reconstructed image. Again, there is only one DC coefficient per block, and little advantage results, in terms of data compression, in trying to reduce the bit allocation. As far as the AC coefficients are concerned, the situation is entirely different, and the whole benefit of the transform coding system results from the deletion, or coarse quantisation, of the higher-order transform terms. This is possible since many of the coefficients are small, and all have non-uniform probability densities as a result of the successive multiplication of data vector elements with the weighting coefficients in the basis vectors, and subsequent summation. To take a trivial example, transformation of a data sequence using the basis vector $[1 \ -1]$ (Walsh–Hadamard transformation of order 2) is equivalent to taking the first difference of successive elements in blocks of two, and results in a distribution which has a mean value which is nominally zero and is highly non-uniform (we could also look on such a scheme as implementing a simple form of one-step predictive coding—see Chapter 5).

We shall commence, therefore, by examining a general model for the pdf of the AC transform coefficients, and then test it against a representative selection of coefficients obtained by actual coding of the three test images discussed in previous chapters. The model chosen has the advantage that, by suitable choice of parameters, it assumes the forms of several well-known and widely used distributions—uniform, Gaussian and exponential (Laplacian). In addition, an alternative model with somewhat similar characteristics will also be described.

4.4.1   The generalised Gaussian distribution

The reader will undoubtedly be familiar with the Gaussian distribution, in which the random variable is distributed proportionally to $e^{-\alpha x^2}$, where α is a constant, and the range of x is that of the variable itself. In the generalised Gaussian distribution (Mauersberger, 1979c; Miller and Thomas, 1972; Kanefsky and Thomas, 1965) the distribution is of the form

$$p(x) = A \exp-(\alpha x)^r \qquad (4.16)$$

In order to determine the constant A we use the fact that, if $p(x)$ is a true probability distribution

$$\int_{-\infty}^{\infty} p(x)\, dx = 1 \tag{4.17}$$

and so, for a symmetrical distribution

$$2A \int_{0}^{\infty} \exp[-(\alpha x)^r]\, dx = 1$$

or

$$2A\,(1/\alpha r)\, \Gamma(1/r) = 1$$

where $\Gamma(\cdot)$ is the gamma function, $\Gamma(n) = \int_{0}^{\infty} x^{n-1} e^{-x}\, dx$. Thus

$$A = \alpha r/2\Gamma(1/r)$$

and so

$$p(x) = [\alpha r/2\Gamma(1/r)]\, \exp[-(\alpha x)^r] \tag{4.18}$$

The variance of $p(x)$ is

$$\sigma^2 = 2 \int_{0}^{\infty} p(x) x^2\, dx$$

$$= \frac{\alpha r}{\Gamma(1/r)} \int_{0}^{\infty} x^2 \exp[-(\alpha x)^r]\, dx$$

$$= \frac{\alpha r}{\Gamma(1/r)} \frac{1}{r\alpha^3} \Gamma\!\left(\frac{3}{r}\right) = \frac{1}{\alpha^2} \frac{\Gamma(3/r)}{\Gamma(1/r)}$$

Thus

$$\alpha = \frac{1}{\sigma} \left(\frac{\Gamma(3/r)}{\Gamma(1/r)}\right)^{1/2}$$

and so

$$p(x) = \frac{r}{2\sigma} \frac{\Gamma(3/r)^{1/2}}{\Gamma(1/r)^{3/2}} \exp\!\left[-\left(\frac{x}{\sigma}\right)^r \left(\frac{\Gamma(3/r)}{\Gamma(1/r)}\right)^{r/2}\right] \tag{4.19}$$

Although this appears, at first sight, a trifle complicated, its usefulness will soon become apparent. Suppose we set $r = 1$, then we obtain

$$p(x) = (1/2\sigma)\sqrt{2} \exp(-(x/\sigma)\sqrt{2})$$

$$= (1/\sigma\sqrt{2}) \exp[-\sqrt{2}(x/\sigma)] \tag{4.20}$$

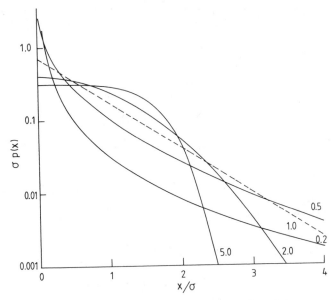

FIG. 4.1. The generalised Gaussian distribution for various values of the parameter r in Eq. (4.19).

the exponential (Laplacian) distribution. If we allow r to equal 2, then

$$p(x) = \frac{1}{\sigma} \frac{(\sqrt{\pi/2})^{1/2}}{(\sqrt{\pi})^{3/2}} \exp\left[-\left(\frac{x}{\sigma}\right)^2 \frac{\sqrt{\pi}}{2} \frac{1}{\sqrt{\pi}} \right]$$

$$= \frac{1}{\sigma\sqrt{2\pi}} \exp\left[-\left(\frac{x}{\sigma}\right)^2 \frac{1}{2} \right] \qquad (4.21)$$

the Gaussian (normal) distribution. Furthermore, it can be shown that, if $r \to 0$ we obtain a distribution tending to an impulse at $x = 0$ and, if $r \to \infty$, we obtain the uniform distribution. Five typical distributions are plotted in Fig. 4.1 where these characteristics are illustrated [note that plotting in the form $\sigma p(x)$ as a function of (x/σ) allows convenient comparison of the various distributions].

4.4.2 The gamma distribution

An alternative relation which has been successfully used to describe the pdf of typical transform coefficients is the gamma distribution (Ghanbari and Pearson, 1978; see also Abut and Erdol, 1979)

$$p(x) = Ae^{-\alpha x}x^{n-1} \qquad (4.22)$$

defined for positive values of x and values of n between 0 and 1. Using Eq. (4.17), and considering $p(x)$ as a symmetrical distribution,

$$2A \int_0^\infty e^{-\alpha x} x^{n-1} \, dx = 1 \tag{4.23}$$

and so

$$A = \tfrac{1}{2} [\alpha^n / \Gamma(n)]$$

Thus

$$p(x) = [\alpha^n / 2\Gamma(n)] \, e^{-\alpha x} x^{n-1} \tag{4.24}$$

and

$$\sigma^2 = 2 \int_0^\infty p(x) x^2 \, dx$$

$$= \frac{\alpha^n}{\Gamma(n)} \int_0^\infty e^{-\alpha x} x^{n+1} \, dx$$

$$= \frac{\alpha^n}{\Gamma(n)} \frac{\Gamma(n+2)}{\alpha^{n+2}} = \frac{1}{\alpha^2} n(n+1) \tag{4.25}$$

and therefore

$$\alpha = \frac{1}{\sigma} [n(n+1)]^{1/2} \tag{4.26}$$

Giving

$$p(x) = \frac{1}{2\Gamma(n)} \frac{1}{\sigma^n} [n(n+1)]^{n/2} \exp\{-x/\sigma[n(n+1)]^{1/2}\} x^{n-1} \tag{4.27}$$

Multiplying numerator and denominator by σ^{n-1} allows us to write Eq. (4.27) in normalised form

$$p(x) = \frac{[n(n+1)]^{n/2}}{2\Gamma(n)\sigma} \exp\left\{-\frac{x}{\sigma}[n(n+1)]^{1/2}\right\} \left(\frac{x}{\sigma}\right)^{n-1} \tag{4.28}$$

If $n = 1$ this reduces to

$$p(x) = \frac{1}{2\sigma} \sqrt{2} \exp\left(-\frac{x}{\sigma}\sqrt{2}\right) = \frac{1}{\sigma\sqrt{2}} \exp\left(-\frac{x}{\sigma}\sqrt{2}\right) \tag{4.29}$$

the Laplacian distribution. Typical gamma distributions are plotted in Fig. 4.2.

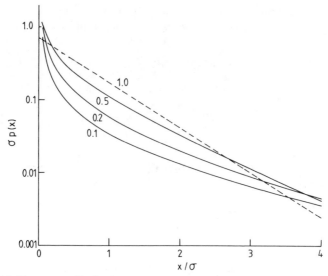

Fig. 4.2. The gamma distribution for various values of the parameter n in Eq. (4.28).

4.5 The coefficient distribution of the test images

In this section we shall examine the distribution of both the DC and AC transform coefficients of the test images which have been referred to in previous sections of this book. As mentioned earlier, we shall expect the DC and AC results to be markedly different, and those obtained for the AC coefficients will enable us to comment further on the widely expressed opinions that such distributions are either of a Gaussian, or a Laplacian, nature. For the moment, however, we confine our attention to the DC coefficient.

4.5.1 The distribution of the DC coefficient

Image 1, it may be recalled, contains 165 separate luminance levels after the removal of blanking and synchronisation signals, and so $x_{min} = 1$, $x_{max} = 165$. Using the WHT or DCT, with $N = 8$, results in maximum and minimum theoretical DC coefficient values, after two-dimensional transformation, of

$$C_{DC(max)} = 8 \times 165 = 1320 \qquad (4.30)$$

$$C_{DC(min)} = 8 \times 1 = 8 \qquad (4.31)$$

If we now consider all elements in a block to be the same, save that one has a value one greater than the remainder, then we may determine the minimum possible difference ($\frac{1}{8}$) between the values of adjacent coefficient levels. If, for convenience, we omit the orthonormal scaling, then the possible coefficient range is 64 to 10,560. The actual range obtained by measurement is 424 to 9490, and although the maximum is nearly attained, the minimum practical and theoretical values are far apart. Another feature is worth noting, and that is that since there are only 1024 DC coefficients in the distribution, the latter is quite sparse, and many available levels in the distribution remain unused. Furthermore, the difference between the actual and equi-probability entropies is very small (0.04 bit), again indicating that the distribution is widely spread. If we now reintroduce the orthonormal scaling (i.e., dividing throughout by $N = 8$) we find that about half of the available levels remain unused, and the entropy difference is still only 0.18 bit, i.e., it is still closely uniform. It is not possible to make general inferences about the formal statistical nature of the distribution, of course, since each possible interval contains relatively few samples, but it is worth noting that even when they are widened until the total number is only 75, i.e., the average occupancy is 13 samples per interval, the entropy differs from that of a uniform distribution by no more than 0.25 bit. Modelling of the DC coefficient distribution for this image, at least, with anything other than a uniform pdf, therefore, seems hardly worthwhile. Indeed, since the coefficient is merely a scaled blockwise average of the image luminance levels, there is no *a priori* reason why its distribution should exhibit any well-defined statistical characteristics, as can be seen from Fig. 4.3.

Image 2 contains 123 levels and therefore the theoretical (integer) limits on the DC coefficient are 64 and 7872. Again, the maximum value is nearly attained (7436) but the minimum measured level is once more relatively high (1486). Under the same conditions as were applied to Image 1, the entropy difference is 0.79 bit, but this merely reflects the highly peaked nature of the initial image data distribution (see Fig. 2.13). The coefficient distribution is plotted in Fig. 4.4.

Image 3 is something of a special case, since its data can assume only one of two possible (arbitrarily set) levels, here taken as 224 and 1. In this case, then, the maximum value of the DC coefficient is $224 \times 8 = 1792$, and we can easily determine all other possible integer levels. Thus, in an 8×8 block, suppose that n elements are black (224). The block DC level will be

$$\bar{x}_{(n)} = \tfrac{1}{64}(n \times 224 + (64 - n) \cdot 1) \tag{4.32}$$

and, after transformation and scaling, the possible integer levels in the resulting distribution will have the values $223n + 64$ and, of course, cover the range 64 to 14,336. The maximum value achieved in practice is 9207, corresponding to a block with 41 black, out of a total of 64 elements. In this case, by far the majority of blocks are all white, and so the distribution shows

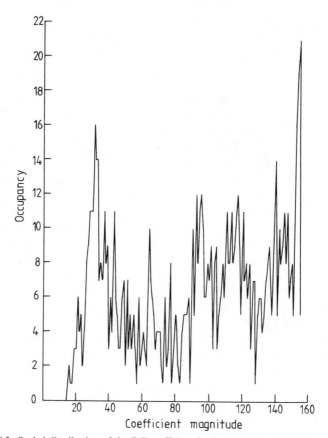

FIG. 4.3. Scaled distribution of the DC coefficient for Image 1; $N = 8$, WHT or DCT.

a predominance of the lowest possible DC coefficient (53 % of all coefficients). Apart from this property, which is likely to obtain whenever black and white documents are transform coded using a manageable block size, owing to the high resolution of such input data (approximately 200 elements/in. or 8 elements/mm), no special features are present. Over a wide range of quantisation accuracies, the difference between the entropy of the distribution and the equal probability entropy is approximately 2 bits (due to the predominance of all white blocks referred to earlier). In fact, there are much more efficient methods of coding such material, and the application of transform techniques in this area is not recommended. The results included in this volume are for comparison only.

As a final general comment on the DC coefficient distribution, it is a smoothed version of that of the input data. Since that data may have a very wide range of ill-defined distributions, so may the DC coefficient, but it is

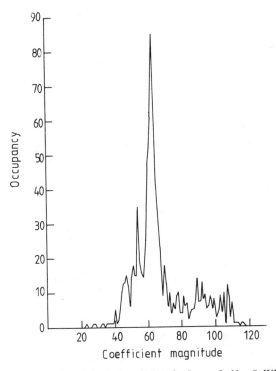

FIG. 4.4. Scaled distribution of the DC coefficient for Image 2; $N = 8$, WHT or DCT.

unlikely that those distributions will often be highly peaked enough to make using anything other than a uniform quantiser worthwhile. Thus the transform operation does not impose any particular pdf upon the DC coefficient, in the way that, for example, taking successive data element differences does on the signal so formed by that operation. The situation is rather different in the case of the AC coefficient distribution.

4.5.2 The distribution of the AC coefficients

In contrast to that of the DC coefficient, the distribution of the AC transform coefficients is interesting in a statistical sense. Since the DC basis vector of those image transforms with good coding efficiencies consists of elements all of the same value (we exclude here the KLT when applied to data having finite mean value as a special case), the orthogonality criterion implies that all AC basis vectors will have zero mean values, which in turn indicates that the coefficient mean values themselves will be close to zero. An example of this behaviour can be seen in Table 4.1. A typical AC coefficient distribution, then, will be at least approximately symmetrical about zero, and

TABLE 4.4. Ratio of the half width of distribution
to standard deviation.

Coefficient	Image 1	Image 2	Image 3
1, 1	1.73	2.78	2.07
1, 2	5.63	4.30	3.74
6, 6	6.68	4.94	4.50

it tends to have a sharply peaked distribution rapidly falling off as the amplitude value increases, but nevertheless with a long 'tail' which extends out to several times the coefficient standard deviation. Thus, using the two-dimensional WHT of block size 8×8, the ratio of half width of the distribution to standard deviation is shown in Table 4.4, for various coefficients of the three transformed test images where coefficient (1, 1) is the DC coefficient.

The influence of the shape of the distribution upon coefficient quantisation strategy will be dealt with subsequently; for the moment we examine a representative selection of coefficient distributions, all determined using the WHT, DCT or DST two-dimensional transformations with $N = 8$, and the three test images, in the light of the various distribution models discussed earlier in the present chapter. As mentioned in Subsection 4.4.1, results are presented in normalised form, i.e., as

$$\sigma p(x) = f(x/\sigma) \qquad (4.33)$$

where σ is the coefficient standard deviation, x is the coefficient amplitude, and $f(\cdot)$ denotes the dependence of the product of σ and $p(x)$ on the normalised abscissa. Whatever their variance, then, all may be plotted over a range of $\sigma p(x)$ of approximately 1.5×10^{-3} to 5 (most conveniently in logarithmic form) and of (x/σ) from 0 to 3, although it must be emphasised that the distribution does extend further, and, in the context of coding with respect to a visual fidelity criterion, it is the isolated large-value coefficients which, if reproduced inaccurately by the quantisation/coding process, will give rise to localised regions of image degradation.

The first coefficient to be examined is (1, 2) for Image 1. The most significant difference to be observed when comparing these results with those for the DC coefficient of this image is the way in which, as the quantisation intervals are widened, the difference between the actual and equal probability entropies increases to approximately 1.5 bits, indicating a significant departure from uniformity in the distribution. The variation of $\sigma p(x)$ with (x/σ) is plotted in Fig. 4.5 for the three transformations, and it can be seen that there are only minor differences between the separate results. Note that, since the distributions are almost exactly symmetrical, only one side is plotted.

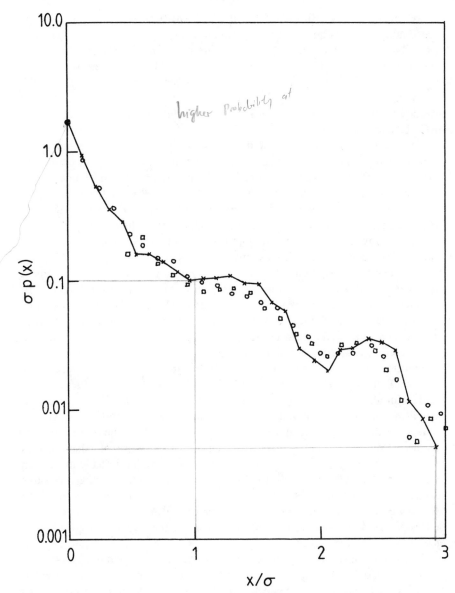

FIG. 4.5. Distribution of coefficient (1, 2) for Image 1; $N = 8$; —×—, DCT; ○, WHT and □, DST.

$$\delta_c^2 \qquad \sum_{n=1}^{M} (x_n - \bar{x})^2 \, p(x_n)$$

When compared with Figs. 4.1 and 4.2, the distribution can be seen to be reasonably fitted using either the gamma density with $n = \frac{1}{2}$ or the generalised Gaussian density with the same value of r. This is in agreement with results reported by Ghanbari and Pearson (1978), who measured WHT statistics for a variety of images. The significant feature to be noted is that the curve is definitely more highly peaked than the Gaussian or Laplacian distributions, which have frequently been suggested as suitable models for the AC coefficients.

In a sense, of course, coefficient (1, 2) is the result of a one-dimensional transform only, and the first true two-dimensional coefficient in the transform array is (2, 2) the results for which are shown in Fig. 4.6. The entropy difference in this case is about 1.75 bits, and, again, all three transforms give very similar results. The curve is still more highly peaked than either those of the Gaussian or Laplacian densities, although this time the maximum value is somewhat lower. Here again the gamma or generalised Gaussian distributions fit the measured results reasonably well with n or $r = \frac{1}{2}$.

It is possible in principle, of course, to examine all N^2 ($= 64$) coefficients in this way. The difficulty with the higher-order coefficients is that they tend to have very small variances, and there are therefore fewer data points available. It is necessary to give at least one more example, however, since in the case of such coefficients a change becomes evident in the shape of the distribution. We therefore now consider coefficient (6, 6), for which the measured values are plotted in Fig. 4.7. In this case the trend is quite different. The results for the WHT diverge from those for the DCT and DST at higher values of (x/σ) and, significantly, the distribution is now well approximated by a Gaussian profile, whilst the entropy difference is still higher (approximately 2 bits). The reason for the change in shape is possibly the way in which the coefficients are formed. Low-order coefficients are generated by the use of basis vectors containing relatively few sign changes. Higher-order vectors have more sign changes and so, whereas the lowest-order AC basis vector of length N sums adjacent weighted samples over length $N/2$ and then subtracts the sum of the following $N/2$ terms, the highest-order vector will take the weighted differences of adjacent samples, since each term in the basis vector has a different sign from that of its neighbour.

The results of similar experiments with Image 2 are shown in Figs. 4.8, 4.9 and 4.10. Coefficient (1, 2) is not fitted well by any of the theoretical distributions, and shows the effect of the pdf of the original data in the sharp peak at the origin—the result of having a predominance of a single background luminance level in the (test card) image. The structure inherent in the data is also reflected in the presence of ripples within the distribution at larger values of (x/σ), resulting from the repetition of certain amplitude patterns throughout the picture.

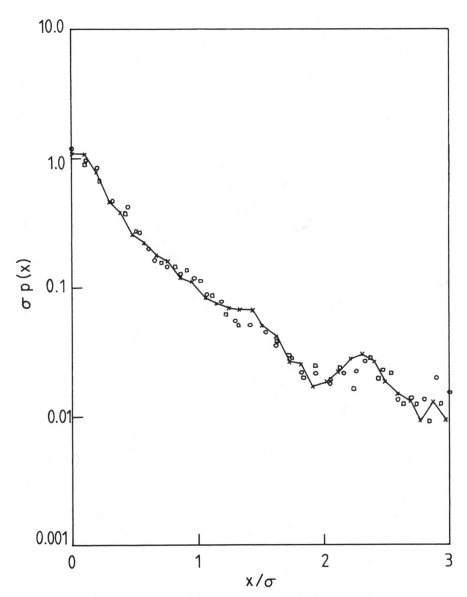

FIG. 4.6. Distribution of coefficient (2, 2) for Image 1; $N = 8$. Symbols are defined in Fig. 4.5.

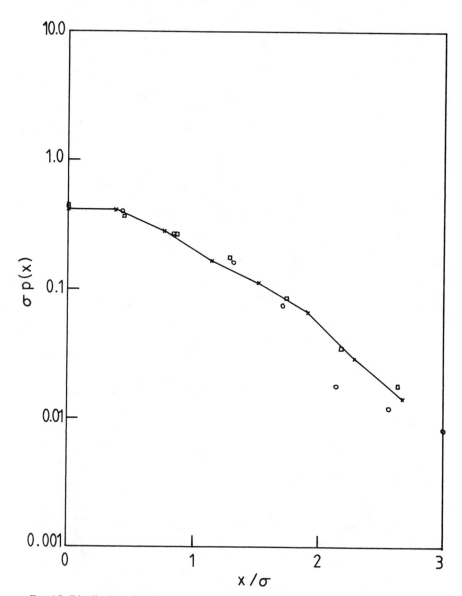

FIG. 4.7. Distribution of coefficient (6, 6) for Image 1; $N = 8$. Symbols are defined in Fig. 4.5.

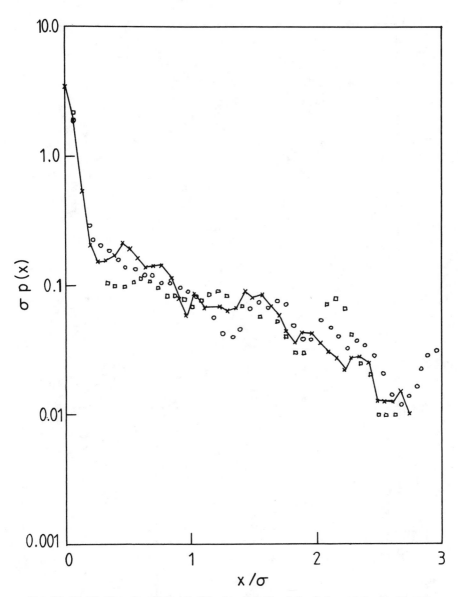

FIG. 4.8. Distribution of coefficient (1, 2) for Image 2; $N = 8$. Symbols are defined in Fig. 4.5.

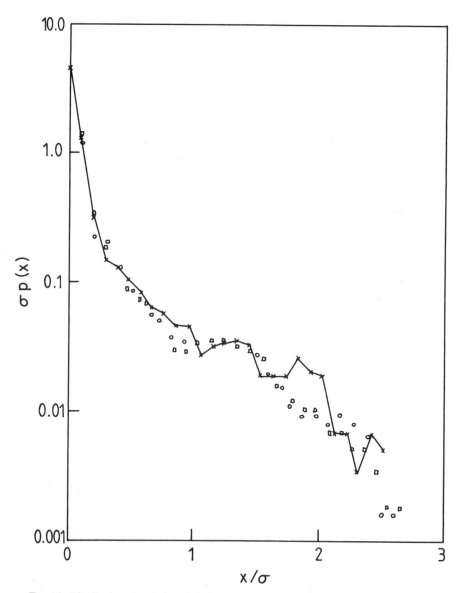

FIG. 4.9. Distribution of coefficient (2, 2) for Image 2; $N = 8$. Symbols are defined in Fig. 4.5.

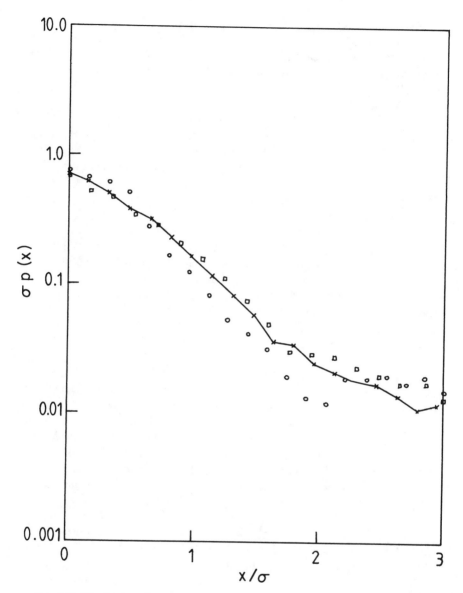

FIG. 4.10. Distribution of coefficient (6, 6) for Image 2; $N = 8$. Symbols are defined in Fig. 4.5.

Coefficient (2, 2) shows more homogeneity in the results for the various transforms, and is fitted moderately well over most of its range by a high-order gamma ($n = \frac{1}{10}$) or generalised Gaussian ($r = \frac{1}{5}$) distribution. Again the higher-order coefficient (6, 6) has a different density profile (in spite of the quite different nature of the input data), and this time approximates the Laplacian distribution.

The result for coefficient (1, 2) of Image 3 (Fig. 4.11) shows an effect similar to that of Image 2, where a majority of values are zero as a result of the presence of regions of uniform luminance. The remainder of the curve falls off approximately linearly [on the logarithmic $\sigma p(x)$ scale], but is not fitted at all well by any of the theoretical distributions. The distribution of coefficient (6, 6) is approximately Laplacian (Fig. 4.12), but since so few data points are available, little can be said with confidence about this result.

What are we to conclude, then, about the likely distribution of transform coefficients? In the first place, the DC term shows no clear statistical properties, and reasons for this have been advanced earlier. It is usual to allocate at least 8 bits to this coefficient and not to bother about optimising its quantisation in the way that is done for the AC coefficients, since this move cannot be justified on the grounds of entropy, and, in any case, there are $N^2 - 1$ AC coefficients for every DC coefficient, and so the few bits that might be saved in this way represent a negligible modification to the average bit rate.

As far as the AC coefficients are concerned, the first point to note is that all of the three transforms give roughly the same results in terms of coefficient distribution. The advantage of one transform over another results from its efficiency in 'packing' data energy into the lower-order coefficients, therefore, and little if any accrues from the imposition of any more or less 'well-defined' statistical distribution. Furthermore, the generally held opinion that low-order distributions are Laplacian cannot be upheld on the basis of the evidence presented here (still less can they be said to be Gaussian, but this view is no longer widely held). Low-order coefficients appear to be reasonably well modelled by gamma or generalised Gaussian distributions, higher-order ones by true Gaussian profiles. Occasionally, the relationship for a higher-order coefficient will be approximately Laplacian. Again, the influence of a high degree of structure in the original image will make itself felt in the coefficient distribution. Finally, and perhaps most important from the point of view of coding images which are to be observed by the eye (as opposed to being subjected to some form of luminance level measurement, for example), all AC coefficient distributions have long 'tails' out to perhaps 4 or 5σ (see Table 4.4) or more, and any 'classical' quantisation technique (to be discussed in the next section) always allows approximate quantisation only in this region. It can be argued that since large coefficients, even if relatively few

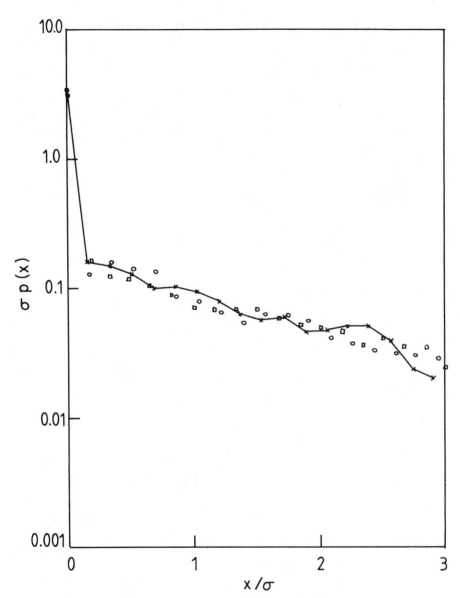

FIG. 4.11.   Distribution of coefficient (1, 2) for Image 3; $N = 8$. Symbols are defined in Fig. 4.5.

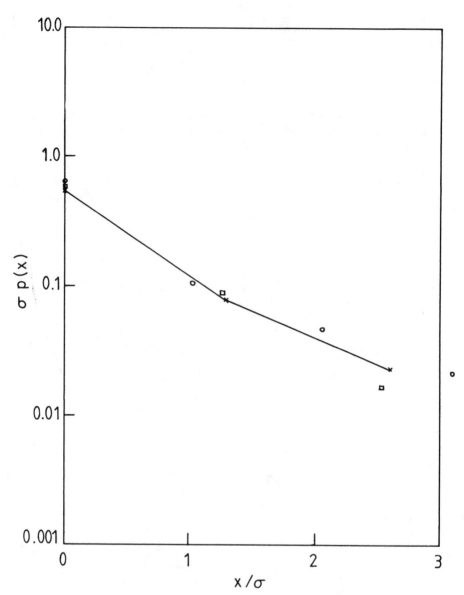

Fig. 4.12. Distribution of coefficient (6, 6) for Image 3; $N = 8$. Symbols are defined in Fig. 4.5.

in number, form an important component of image reconstruction, they should be considered carefully in subsequent stages of the coding process.

4.6 Coefficient quantisation

Any analogue signal must, of necessity, be quantised before it can be coded for transmission or storage in digital form. The process inevitably causes errors due to the representation of analogue values occurring over a finite interval by a single output level, and this error must be maintained within the bounds of acceptability. Arguably, these errors are the most significant factor causing degradation in the reconstructed image (assuming error-free transmission or storage) and are unavoidable (Tescher, 1979). The quantisation of the coefficients resulting from a transform coding operation according to a measure of the visual fidelity of the reconstructed image has been almost completely neglected in the literature (but see Mounts *et al.*, 1977) in contrast to the situation in the case of predictive coding (differential pulse code modulation), where the influence of the properties of the human visual system (HVS) upon the perception of quantisation errors is more easily definable (Limb, 1978; Netravali and Limb, 1980). This subject will be discussed at greater length in Chapter 6 and, for the present, 'classical' quantisation techniques only will be considered in the light of the various probability distributions, defined in the previous sections, which the coefficients may assume.

4.6.1 Classical quantisation techniques

The quantisation of transform coefficients is an essential step in their representation by a binary word of finite length, and it is intriguing that a process that at first sight seems relatively simple should have generated such a vast body of literature dealing with quantiser design, optimisation and optimum characteristics, some of it extremely abstruse. Practically all transform schemes reported to date, however, employ designs which accord with well-known and established principles, and it is those which are reviewed now. One point is worth mentioning in passing here, and that is that the transform operation is normally (but not exclusively) carried out digitally, and therefore the input data is already in (linearly) quantised form. Not every real number is a valid transform output value, then, even when it lies within the maximum and minimum limits of transform coefficient output. Whether or not this has any effect upon the following quantisation operation does not seem to have been investigated. Additionally, since the input data is already quantised, some authors refer to the coefficient quantisation step as 're-quantisation'.

The first workers to show that modification of the step size of the quantiser according to the probability distribution of the input signal was advantageous were Panter and Dite (1951), who developed the basic theory and showed how to design such a system in an approximate fashion. The universally quoted reference in the image coding literature on quantiser design is, however, that of Max (1960), who showed how to minimise the distortion of a quantiser having a fixed number of output levels for a signal of known probability distribution. His paper includes tabulated results in the case of a Gaussian signal and a mean-square-error (mse) criterion, for both uniform and non-uniform level spacing. The procedure is first to establish the error criterion, which is almost always taken to be mse, and then to determine input and output levels through a process of error minimisation. Although the results of Max apply to any number of output levels, practical design considerations will normally constrain that number to be even and, moreover, to be of the form $N = 2^n$, where n is an integer. In fact, there is subjective evidence to show that an even number of output levels in not necessarily a good choice, since the minimum output level(s) is not zero, and better results can be obtained when the quantiser is arranged to have one output level at level zero, in which case a symmetrical characteristic will have an odd number of levels. Max's results can, of course, be applied to the uniformly distributed case, i.e., for the DC coefficient (see Subsection 4.5.1), but more interest, in terms of efficient coefficient quantisation, attaches to the AC coefficients, whose distributions have been shown to be highly non-uniform and are also quite closely symmetrical about zero.

Thus we consider the case shown in Fig. 4.13 as an example, where one side of a symmetrical 8-output quantisation characteristic is shown. For an even number of output levels, one of the input (decision) levels will lie at $x = 0$, and the most distant are assumed to lie at $\pm \infty$. Any input signal within the range x_i to x_{i+1} will result in a fixed output y_i, and Max's procedure determines the location of the x_i and y_i such that the overall quantisation error will be a minimum. The instantaneous distortion occurring in interval i (i.e., when $x_i < x \leqslant x_{i+1}$) will be

$$d_i = f(x - y_i) \tag{4.34}$$

where $f(\cdot)$ is suitably chosen to characterise the quantisation error. Naturally $f(0) = 0$, and it is reasonable to assume that, since the signal pdf is an even function, so will be $f(\cdot)$; i.e.,

$$f(-x) = f(x) \tag{4.35}$$

Furthermore, it is logical to assume that the distortion measure is an increasing function of its argument, i.e., that $f(x)$ increases with x in a monotonic fashion.

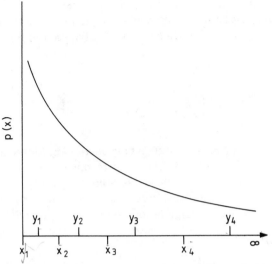

FIG. 4.13. Symmetrical eight-output quantiser characteristic; x_i, decision levels and y_i, reconstruction levels.

The total distortion occurring for values of x in interval i will be

$$e_i = \int_{x_i}^{x_{i+1}} d_i p(x)\, dx$$

$$= \int_{x_i}^{x_{i+1}} f(x - y_i) p(x)\, dx \tag{4.36}$$

and the total distortion is then given by summation over all possible levels, i.e.,

$$e = \sum_i e_i \tag{4.37}$$

The separate e_i of Eq. (4.36) are now minimised with respect to all of the decision (input) and reconstruction (output) levels x_i and y_i. Thus, setting $\partial e_i / \partial x_i = 0$:

$$f(x_i - y_{i-1}) p(x_i) - f(x_i - y_i) p(x_i) = 0 \tag{4.38}$$

Given the previously discussed properties of $f(\cdot)$, Eq. (4.38) results in

$$|x_i - y_{i-1}| = |x_i - y_i|$$

or

$$x_i = \tfrac{1}{2}(y_i + y_{i-1}) \tag{4.39}$$

and the decision levels are situated half-way between the corresponding reconstruction levels [note that Panter and Dite's result is the reverse of this due to their approximation of constant $p(x)$ between any pair of decision levels].

Setting $\partial e_i / \partial y_i = 0$ gives

$$\int_{x_i}^{x_{i+1}} f'(x - y_i)p(x)\, dx = 0 \tag{4.40}$$

and Eqs. (4.39) and (4.40) constitute a pair of coupled equations which must be solved numerically for the decision and reconstruction levels.

Mean square error (or distortion) has been widely used as a criterion for the optimisation of quantiser structures and, whilst not correlating well with perceived (visual) image degradation, does allow a simple geometrical interpretation of Eq. (4.40). Thus we shall set $f(\cdot) = (\cdot)^2$, giving

$$\int_{x_i}^{x_{i+1}} (x - y_i)p(x)\, dx = 0 \tag{4.41}$$

Then y_i becomes the centroid of the area under $p(x)$ between the relevant decision levels

$$\int_{x_i}^{x_{i+1}} xp(x)\, dx = y_i \int_{x_i}^{x_{i+1}} p(x)\, dx$$

or

$$y_i = \int_{x_i}^{x_{i+1}} xp(x)\, dx \Big/ \int_{x_i}^{x_{i+1}} p(x)\, dx \tag{4.42}$$

It has been shown by Limb (1967, 1978) that Eqs. (4.39) and (4.41) also hold for a weighted measure of mse, where Eq. (4.41) becomes

$$\int_{x_i}^{x_{i+1}} (x - y_i)p(x)W(x)\, dx = 0 \tag{4.43}$$

with $W(x)$ a suitable weighting function.

Knowledge of the various levels x_i and y_i allows us to determine two further quantiser parameters. The mse is, using Eqs. (4.36) and (4.37),

$$\text{mse} = 2 \sum_{i=1}^{N/2} \int_{x_i}^{x_{i+1}} (x - y_i)^2 p(x)\, dx \tag{4.44}$$

where the distribution is symmetric and $x_{(1 + N/2)} = +\infty$. Expanding Eq. (4.44) and using Eq. (4.42) results in

$$\text{mse} = 2 \sum_{i=1}^{N/2} \left[\int_{x_i}^{x_{i+1}} x^2 p(x) \, dx - y_i^2 \int_{x_i}^{x_{i+1}} p(x) \, dx \right]$$

$$= E(x^2) - 2 \sum_{i=1}^{N/2} y_i^2 p_i \qquad (4.45)$$

where p_i is the probability that quantisation interval i is occupied by the signal, i.e., $x_i < x \leqslant x_{i+1}$. It is not possible, in general, to develop closed form expressions for the variation of quantiser mse with number of levels and probability distribution, and numerical or approximate solutions must be sought. It is worth examining a simple example, however, before considering the general form of the relationship. Thus, if we apply a uniform quantiser to a signal of amplitude A and pdf $p(x)$, and there are sufficient quantisation levels to allow us to assume that $p(x)$ is approximately constant within any single quantisation interval, then the mean square distortion in interval i is

$$e_i = p(x_i) \int_{y_i - \Delta/2}^{y_i + \Delta/2} (x - y_i)^2 \, dx$$

$$= p(x_i) \int_{-\Delta/2}^{\Delta/2} z^2 \, dz = \frac{p(x_i)\Delta^3}{12} \qquad (4.46)$$

where Δ is the size of the quantiser interval and $p(x_i)$ the value of $p(x)$ within the interval. Since the probability that interval i is occupied is

$$p_i = \int_{y_i - \Delta/2}^{y_i + \Delta/2} p(x) \, dx \sim p(x_i)\Delta$$

then

$$e_i = p_i(\Delta^2/12) \qquad (4.47)$$

and the total error over all intervals is

$$e = \sum_i p_i \frac{\Delta^2}{12} = \frac{\Delta^2}{12} \qquad (4.48)$$

a standard result.

For the uniform quantiser $\Delta = 2A/N$ and so, since $\sigma^2 = A^2/3$,

$$e = (4A^2/N^2)\tfrac{1}{12} = \tfrac{4}{12}(3\sigma^2/N^2) = \sigma^2 N^{-2} \qquad (4.49)$$

If we consider a triangular pdf (again a straightforward case analytically), then $\sigma^2 = A^2/6$ and

$$e = 2\sigma^2 N^{-2} \tag{4.50}$$

For a unit variance input, therefore, we may expect that the relationship between the mean square error and the number of quantisation levels will be of the form

$$e = kN^{-p} \tag{4.51}$$

where, in more complex situations than those shown earlier, the value of p will not necessarily be 2. Thus Max determined the relation between e and N to be

$$e = 1.32N^{-1.74}$$
$$e = 2.21N^{-1.96} \tag{4.52}$$

for values of N in the region of 4 and 36, respectively, for the optimum non-uniform case, and

$$e = 1.47N^{-1.74} \tag{4.53}$$

for $N = 36$ in the uniform case. Roe (1964) has shown that the decision levels which minimise the distortion when using error criteria of the form $|x - y_k|^\theta$ are given to a good approximation by

$$\int_0^{x_n} p(x)^{1/(\theta+1)} \sim 2C_1 n + C_2 \tag{4.54}$$

which leads to Wood's (1969) approximation for the mse of the optimum quantiser for large N as

$$e = \tfrac{2}{3}C_1^3 N \tag{4.55}$$

For the Gaussian distribution $C_1 = 1.5936/(N + 0.8532)$, and so

$$e = 2.698N/(N + 0.8532)^3 \tag{4.56}$$

which tends to approximately $2.7N^{-2}$ as $N \to \infty$. Segall (1976) suggests an approximation of Max's results when N is small and Wood's asymptotic limit when N is large, i.e.,

$$e = N^{-1.57} \tag{4.57}$$

up to $N = 5$ and Eq. (4.56) thereafter in the optimum nonuniform case. For the uniform quantiser

$$e = N^{-1.6} \qquad N \leqslant 4$$
$$e = 1.66N^{-2} \qquad N > 4 \tag{4.58}$$

are applicable.

The majority of reported results apply to signals having a Gaussian distribution. However, Mauersberger (1981) has used the generalised Gaussian distribution [see Eq. (4.19)] to develop a useful expression which may be used to determine the mse/N relation for more general distributions. Thus, taking $p = 2$ in Eq. (4.51), the constant k for $N \rightarrow \infty$ is given by

$$k = a(v) = \sqrt[v]{27} \frac{\Gamma^3(1 + 1/v)}{\Gamma(1 + 3/v)} \tag{4.59}$$

where $v = 1$ and $v = 2$ correspond to the Laplacian and Gaussian distributions, respectively. The mean square error is then

$$e = \sigma^2 N^{-2}\{1 + [a(v) - 1](1 - e^{-b_1 t} - b_2 t^{b_3} e^{-b_4 t})\} \tag{4.60}$$

where $N = 2^t$ and

$$b_1 = 1.103 \qquad b_2 = 0.938 \qquad b_3 = 0.922 \qquad b_4 = 0.868$$

minimise the approximation error over the range $0.3 \leqslant v \leqslant 2.0$.

Knowledge of x_i and y_i allow us to determine, to a greater or lesser degree of accuracy, the actual quantisation error, providing that we also know $p(x)$. The other quantity which we may calculate is the quantiser entropy H_N from the relation

$$H_N = -2 \sum_{i=1}^{N/2} p_i \log_2 p_i \tag{4.61}$$

A comparison between this figure and $H_{max} = \log_2 N$ will then allow us to estimate the degree to which the output levels are unequally occupied. Typical figures are shown in Table 4.5 for 5- and 9-bit quantisers employing both optimum mean-square-error uniform and non-uniform quantisation (in the former case the step size is forced to be constant as an additional optimisation constraint) for Gaussian and Laplacian inputs.

On reflection, it is not surprising that the optimum uniform quantisers have the greatest range of output level occupancy, and so the lowest entropy, and in fact the difference between the above figures and $\log_2 N$ increases with

TABLE 4.5. Quantiser entropy.

Entropy	Gaussian		Laplacian	
	5-bit	9-bit	5-bit	9-bit
Optimum non-uniform	4.73	8.38	4.43	8.69
Optimum uniform	4.45	7.97	3.78	6.96

N. If the quantiser is designed on the basis of equal level occupancy (see, e.g., Andrews and Pratt, 1968; Pratt *et al.*, 1969), then of course $H_N = \log_2 N$. To the extent that the value of H_N is lower, efficient (entropy, or Huffman) coding can be used to reduce the overall data rate still further. Thus, a very efficient scheme might be (if variable length coding is acceptable) a uniform quantiser combined with Huffman coding. Indeed, the uniform quantiser can be shown to be asymptotically optimal (in an information theoretic sense) as the mean square or absolute error becomes very small (Gish and Pierce, 1968; Berger, 1972; Gray and Gray, 1977).

Typical quantisation results are given in Tables 4.6–4.9 for both optimum uniform and non-uniform quantisers, and Fig. 4.14 indicates the way in which the spacing between decision and reconstruction levels expands as the pdf of the input signal becomes more sharply peaked in moving from a Gaussian to a Laplacian and then to a gamma density. In this connection, it is of interest to know what the result will be if a quantiser optimised for a given probability distribution and variance is used to quantise a signal where either or both of these properties is different, and both Gray and Davisson (1975) and Mauersberger (1979a) have examined such a situation.

In the literature tabulated results have been given by Max (1960) for the optimum uniform and non-uniform Gaussian case, for N up to 36, Paez and Glisson (1972) for Gaussian and Laplacian distributions and also for the $\Gamma(\frac{1}{2})$ case, for $N = 2^n$, where n is integral and of maximum value 5. Adams and Giesler (1978) present values for the uniform Laplacian quantiser for N up to 32, and for the non-uniform case for $N = 4$–16 and 32, also correcting some of Paez' results. Wang and Jain (1979) have extensively tabulated both uniform and non-uniform Gaussian and Laplacian results.

TABLE 4.6. Optimum uniform quantisers.

N_B^a	N	Gaussian			Laplacian			Gamma ($\frac{1}{2}$)	
		Step size	mse	H_N	Step size	mse	H_N	Step size	mse
1	2	1.60	0.36	1.00	1.41	0.50	1.00	1.15	0.67
2	4	1.00	0.12	1.91	1.09	0.20	1.75	1.06	0.32
3	8	0.59	0.037	2.76	0.73	0.07	2.39	0.80	0.13
4	16	0.34	0.012	3.60	0.46	0.03	3.06	0.54	0.05
5	32	0.19	0.0035	4.45	0.28	0.009	3.78	0.35	0.02
6	64	0.10	0.0010	5.31	0.17	0.003	4.54		
7	128	0.06	0.0003	6.18	0.10	0.001	5.32		
8	256	0.03	0.0001	7.07	0.06	0.0003	6.13		

^{a} N_B = number of bits.

TABLE 4.7. Gaussian non-uniform quantisation decision and reconstruction levels.

N_B				
1	2	3	4	5
0.0	0.0	0.0	0.0	0.0
0.80	0.45	0.25	0.13	0.07
∞	0.98	0.50	0.26	0.13
0.36[a]	1.51	0.76	0.39	0.20
1.00[b]	∞	1.05	0.52	0.27
	0.12[a]	1.34	0.66	0.33
	1.91[b]	1.75	0.80	0.40
		2.15	0.94	0.47
		∞	1.10	0.54
		0.04[a]	1.26	0.61
		2.82[b]	1.44	0.68
			1.62	0.75
			1.84	0.82
			2.07	0.90
			2.40	0.97
			2.73	1.05
			∞	1.13
			0.01[a]	1.21
			3.77[b]	1.30
				1.39
				1.48
				1.58
				1.68
				1.79
				1.91
				2.03
				2.17
				2.32
				2.51
				2.69
				2.98
				3.26
				∞
				0.003[a]
				4.73[b]

[a] mse value.
[b] H_N value.

TABLE 4.8. Laplacian non-uniform quantisation decision and reconstruction levels.

N_B				
1	2	3	4	5
0.0	0.0	0.0	0.0	0.0
0.71	0.42	0.23	0.12	0.06
∞	1.13	0.53	0.26	0.13
0.50^a	1.83	0.83	0.41	0.20
1.00^b	∞	1.25	0.57	0.27
	0.18^a	1.67	0.73	0.35
	1.73^b	2.38	0.92	0.43
		3.09	1.11	0.50
		∞	1.36	0.59
		0.05^a	1.58	0.67
		2.57^b	1.88	0.76
			2.18	0.86
			2.60	1.00
			3.02	1.06
			3.72	1.17
			4.43	1.28
			∞	1.40
			0.02^a	1.53
			3.47^b	1.67
				1.81
				1.97
				2.13
				2.32
				2.51
				2.75
				2.98
				3.28
				3.58
				4.00
				4.42
				5.13
				5.83
				∞
				0.004^a
				4.43^b

[a] mse value.
[b] H_N value.

TABLE 4.9. Gamma ($\frac{1}{2}$) non-uniform quantisation decision and reconstruction levels.

		N_B		
1	2	3	4	5
0.0	0.0	0.0	0.0	0.0
0.58	0.30	0.15	0.07	0.03
∞	1.21	0.50	0.23	0.10
0.67ᵃ	2.11	0.86	0.39	0.17
	∞	1.40	0.59	0.25
	0.23ᵃ	1.94	0.79	0.33
		2.87	1.04	0.43
		3.80	1.30	0.52
		∞	1.62	0.63
		0.07ᵃ	1.95	0.74
			2.37	0.86
			2.80	0.98
			3.41	1.11
			4.02	1.25
			5.05	1.40
			6.09	1.55
			∞	1.72
			0.02ᵃ	1.89
				2.09
				2.29
				2.52
				2.75
				3.02
				3.30
				3.63
				3.97
				4.40
				4.84
				5.44
				6.05
				7.05
				8.04
				∞
				0.005ᵃ

ᵃ mse value.

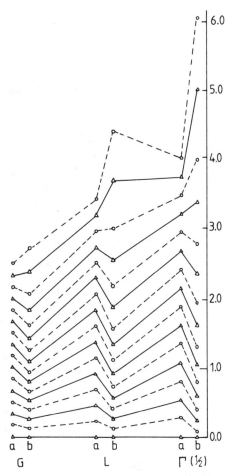

Fig. 4.14. Four-bit quantiser level spacings for various signal distributions. Here G is the Gaussian distribution, L the Laplacian distribution, $\Gamma(\tfrac{1}{2})$ the gamma $(\tfrac{1}{2})$ distribution, a the optimum uniform case and b the optimum non-uniform case. Solid lines represent decision levels and dashed lines represent reconstruction levels.

One or two general remarks on the subject of quantisation may now be appropriate. It has been pointed out earlier that, for all but the most simple cases, analytical results for quantisation error are not possible, and this has led to both approximate designs and the use of numerical methods for level calculation. Thus Roe's approximate procedure for error measures of the form $|x - y_i|^K$ produces results that, for $K = 2$ and N as low as 6, are still within 3% of the exact values. Algazi (1966) similarly considers approximate formulations for step size and distortion of both uniform and non-uniform quantisers, and Lanfer (1978) presents a closed form solution for the particular case of the minimum mean-square-error Laplacian quantiser. For a brief but intriguing review of early published work on quantisers, the reader is referred to Elias (1970). Netravali and Saigal (1976) have considered the general problem of optimisation and the computational requirement therein, and Sharma (1978) has examined the case in which the error weighting function is influenced by the quantiser input as well as the quantisation error. Gallagher (1978) and Bucklew and Gallagher (1979) have investigated the quantisation of Fourier transform coefficients of certain sequences in terms of the relative significance of rectangular and polar representations.

With regard to quantiser implementation, both simulation and hardware systems generally apply 'look-up' table techniques. An alternative, sometimes more practicable, is companding (Smith, 1957) which has, of course, a long history in the communications field in general, and is also discussed by Panter and Dite (1951). In this technique the input signal is compressed so that the design values of the (normally widely spaced) outer levels of the quantiser are effectively brought to the same separation as the innermost levels. The compressed signal is then uniformly quantised and subsequently expanded again. The appropriate non-linear input and inverse relations for this process can be found in Pratt (1978) for commonly used pdfs.

Finally, it is worth pointing out that, on the assumption that all AC transform coefficients have the same form of distribution (which is, of course, questionable), it is not necessary to design separate quantisers for each of the $N^2 - 1$ coefficients in a block of size $N \times N$. All that is needed is a single unit variance quantiser for each integer bit allocation—a total of perhaps seven in all. Each separate coefficient value is divided by a normalisation factor equal to the measured, or estimated, standard deviation of that particular coefficient, giving a random variable of unit variance, which is then routed to the appropriate quantiser. Knowledge of the value of the normalisation factor is naturally necessary for correct coefficient reconstruction and so, in an image transmission system, it must be conveyed to the reciever, although some more sophisticated coder designs enable it to be estimated from other received data.

4.7   Bit assignment procedures

The transform coding operation converts originally highly correlated image samples into sets of transform coefficients which are, at most, only weakly correlated. As has been shown previously, the random variables so obtained have values of variance which may range over several orders of magnitude, and they should, even on an intuitive basis, be coded for digital transmission or storage taking this into account. It will subsequently be seen, in fact, that this variance redistribution is fundamental to the efficient coding (in the transform domain) of the data block. The actual process of assigning, or allocating, coding bits to the transform coefficients will determine their accuracy of representation and so strongly affect the overall system error. Put simply, the basic problem is as follows: given, say, a 512×512 element image originally quantised to an accuracy of 8 bits, and desiring to transmit that image at an overall rate of perhaps 1 bit/element, how should the 512^2 bits available for coding be allocated to the 512^2 transform coefficients in order that the fidelity of the reproduced image be maximised? The short answer to this question is that there *is* no one answer which is satisfactory under any general set of circumstances. Minimising the total average error between original and reproduction will lead to quite a different solution to the problem compared with, say, maximising the visual acceptability of the received image as an image in its own right, independent of the original. These matters are dealt with in more detail in Chapter 6 and, for the moment, we shall concentrate upon the theoretical development of the minimisation of the mean square error between output and input, as has been done in the vast majority of work on the topic. In general terms, there are two basic approaches to the allocation of coding capacity, and they depend upon the allowable complexity of the system. We may opt for a fixed average transmission rate over all the blocks in a single image, say, and then, for a constant transmission rate, allocate the same number of bits to each block. Since image activity (detail) will almost certainly vary very widely from one region to another, this approach, at least in terms of coding efficiency, will be sub-optimum, and we shall benefit by acknowledging the variation of detail from block to block and employing an adaptive scheme which will allocate many bits to blocks having high activities and vice versa. Now the data rate will be non-uniform, and buffering between the variable rate coder and fixed rate channel will be necessary (possibly we may still wish to maintain some overall constraint upon the data rate, such as keeping it constant from image to image, rather than from block to block—the feasibility of such a step will depend upon the buffer capacity available). Given the improved coding efficiency of adaptive systems, and the rapid advance in capacity and fall in cost of hardware memory, it is difficult to see the buffering problem as a major bar to the implementation of such techniques. In either approach, we wish to allocate a total of M bits to a set of n variables (in the present context, transform coefficients) with known variances, such that the overall mse is a minimum.

Early work on this topic is reported by Huang and Schultheiss (1963) who consider blocks of correlated Gaussian variables which are processed using the optimum transform (the KLT) to generate equivalent blocks of coefficients which are uncorrelated and then efficiently quantised. In fact, they implement a transform coding scheme, considering optimum forward and inverse transforms, and practical examples of the technique. Their bit allocation scheme is developed as follows.

Allocating b_i bits to the ith of n variables produces a distortion (or error) of

$$e_i = kN^{-p} = k2^{-pb_i} \tag{4.62}$$

where k and p take on the values quoted in the previous section (the number of levels $N = 2^{b_i}$). Huang and Schultheiss assume that $p = 2$ and that, as a first approximation, k is constant. The average error is then, approximately,

$$e_{av} = \frac{1}{n} \sum_{i=1}^{n} \sigma_i^2 k2^{-2b_i} \tag{4.63}$$

(note that, since Huang and Schultheiss use the optimum transform in their analysis, the variances σ_i^2 in Eq. (4.63) will in fact be the eigenvalues, λ_i, of the data covariance matrix—see Chapter 3); e_{av} is now minimised subject to the constraint

$$\sum_{i=1}^{n} b_i = M \tag{4.64}$$

to yield

$$\sigma_i^2 2^{-2b_i} = c \tag{4.65}$$

where c is a constant, each coefficient contributing an equal amount of error. Then

$$b_i = \tfrac{1}{2}(\log_2 \sigma_i^2 - \log_2 c)$$

and so, using Eq. (4.64)

$$2M = \sum_{i=1}^{n} (\log_2 \sigma_i^2 - \log_2 c)$$

$$= \sum_{i=1}^{n} \log_2 \sigma_i^2 - n \log_2 c$$

giving

$$b_i = \frac{1}{2}\left[\log_2 \sigma_i^2 - \frac{1}{n}\left(\sum_{i=1}^{n} \log_2 \sigma_i^2 - 2M \right) \right]$$

$$= \frac{M}{n} + \frac{1}{2}\left(\log_2 \sigma_i^2 - \frac{1}{n} \sum_{i=1}^{n} \log_2 \sigma_i^2 \right)$$

[Kamangar and Rao (1981) suggest that, in this form, the bit allocation is applicable to the Laplacian distributed error signal in their interfield hybrid coding scheme—see Chapter 5.] Thus

$$b_i = \frac{M}{n} + \frac{1}{2}\left[\log_2 \sigma_i^2 - \frac{1}{n}\log_2\left(\prod_1^n \sigma_i^2\right)\right] \qquad (4.66)$$

Once the b_i are known, the average distortion may be obtained by substitution Eq. (4.63). In the optimum case considered by Huang and Schultheiss, it is a standard result that

$$\text{DET(COV(X))} = \prod_1^n \lambda_i \qquad (4.67)$$

i.e., the determinant of the covariance matrix is the product of its eigenvalues, and the final result is therefore,

$$b_i = \frac{M}{n} + \frac{1}{2}\log_2\left(\frac{\lambda_i}{\text{DET(COV(X))}^{1/n}}\right) \qquad (4.68)$$

Note that, if all $\sigma_i^2 = \sigma^2$, then $b_i = M/n$, the average bit allocation. The second term in Eq. 4.66 is therefore a 'correction' term accounting for the unequal variance distribution. For another approach to this analysis, see that of Goodman (1967) who utilises the WHT in connection with speech coding.

An approximate measure of the benefit of block coding and quantisation may be obtained as follows. Writing Eq. (4.66) as

$$b_i = b_{av} + b_{si} + b_x \qquad (4.69)$$

(where, for no coding, all the σ_i^2 are equal, and made unity, say, in which case $b_i = b_{av} = M/n$). The total error is, from Eq. (4.63)

$$e = k\sigma_i^2/4^{b_i}$$

(the minimisation process ensuring that all error contributions are equal). Since $\frac{1}{2}\log_2 \sigma_i^2 = b_{si}$, then,

$$\sigma_i^2 = 2^{2b_{si}} = 4^{b_{si}}$$

and so

$$e = k4^{(b_{si} - b_i)} = k4^{-(b_x + b_{av})}$$

If block processing has not been performed the error will be

$$e_0 = k/4^{b_{av}}$$

since $b_i = b_{av}$, and so the reduction in error through coding is

$$\frac{e_0}{e} = 4^{b_x} \qquad \text{where} \qquad b_x = -\frac{1}{2n} \log_2 \prod_1^n \sigma_i^2 \qquad (4.70)$$

i.e.,

$$2nb_x = -\log_2 \prod_1^n \sigma_i^2$$

or

$$4^{-nb_x} = \prod_1^n \sigma_i^2$$

giving

$$\frac{e_0}{e} = 4^{b_x} = \left(\prod_1^n \sigma_i^2 \right)^{-1/n} \qquad (4.71)$$

into which, in the optimum case, Eq. (4.67) may be substituted.

As usual, a simple example may serve to clarify the method. Consider coding a stationary random signal with adjacent element correlation coefficient $\rho = 0.91$. On an element-by-element basis we allocate, say, 6 bits/element and thereby achieve an overall mean square error of

$$e_0 = k/4^6$$

Alternatively, we can divide the signal into blocks of length 8 and carry out a Karhunen–Loève transform, resulting in a set of eight random variables with the following variances (normalised to the input signal variance)

6.358   0.931   0.298   0.148   0.093   0.068   0.055   0.049

We have $6 \times 8 = 48$ bits available per block, and so $M/n = 6$ and $\sum_{i=1}^n b_i = 48$. The eigenvalue product is

$$\prod_1^n \sigma_i^2 = 4.45 \times 10^{-6}$$

and so

$$b_x = -\tfrac{1}{16} \cdot 3.322 \cdot \log_{10}(4.45 \times 10^{-6}) = 1.11 \qquad \text{bits}$$

Thus

$$b_i = 7.11 + \tfrac{1}{2} \log_2 \sigma_i^2$$

Giving allocations of

8.44   7.06   6.24   5.73   5.40   5.17   5.02   4.93   bits the sum of which is, to within the accuracy of calculation, 48. The individual terms $\sigma_i^2/4^{b_i}$, are all equal to 5.2×10^{-5} and thus the average coded error overall is

$$e = 5.2 \times 10^{-5} k$$

and the coding 'gain' is

$$\frac{e_0}{e} = \frac{10^5}{4^6 \times 5.2} = 4.70$$

(comparative figures for the DCT and WHT are 4.63 and 3.86, respectively). In practice, of course, the figure attainable will not be quite as great as this since integer bit allocations are necessary.

Returning to our analysis, for a given overall average bit rate (M/n) and set of variances σ_i^2 we may write Eq. (4.66) as

$$b_i = \frac{1}{2} \log_2 \sigma_i^2 - \frac{1}{2n} \left(\log_2 \prod_1^n \sigma_i^2 - 2M \right) \tag{4.72}$$

which is of the form

$$b_i = \tfrac{1}{2} \log_2(\sigma_i^2/D) \tag{4.73}$$

where

$$\log_2 D = \frac{1}{n} \left(\log_2 \prod_1^n \sigma_i^2 - 2M \right) \tag{4.74}$$

Equation (4.73) is interesting in two ways. First, it indicates that bits should be allocated to the various variables in proportion to the logarithms of their variances, or, more straightforwardly, the number of quantisation levels allocated should be proportional to the standard deviations or amplitudes of the components—a result which might have been expected on intuitive grounds. Second, it is none other than Shannon's famous rate distortion equation (Shannon, 1959) for coding Gaussian variables with distortion D under a mean square error criterion. In this form it has been widely used for bit allocation purposes (see the following).

We shall now examine one or two other formulations of the bit allocation rule which have been reported in the literature. Wintz and Kurtenbach (1968) employ a slightly different version of Eq. (4.51). They use an optimum uniform quantiser and suggest an error/quantisation bit allocation relation of the form

$$e = \exp[-\tfrac{1}{2}b_i \ln(10)] \tag{4.75}$$

which, for comparison with the result of Huang and Schultheiss, may be written in the form (assuming unit variance)

$$e = \{\exp[\ln(10)]\}^{-b_i/2} = 10^{-b_i/2}$$

$$= (10^{1/4})^{-2b_i} = 1.778^{-2b_i} = 2^{-1.66b_i} = N^{-1.66} \tag{4.76}$$

i.e., approximately Segall's small N result [Eq. (4.57)]. Their bit allocation relation is the same as that of Huang and Schultheiss with the exception that the factor $\frac{1}{2}$ becomes 0.6 (note their use of natural logarithms). Both treatments minimise the distortion by regarding b_i as a continuous variable, followed by rounding to the nearest integer and subsequent arbitrary adjustments to satisfy Eq. (4.64). Campanella and Robinson (1971) use Eq. (4.51) with $p = 2$ and k a factor which varies with i to examine the performance of transforms in speech processing applications in comparison with conventional PCM coding, and Habibi and Wintz (1971) quoting Kurtenbach and Wintz (1969) give the optimum uniform quantisation error/bit allocation relation as

$$e = \begin{cases} \sigma_i^2(16)^{-b_i/2} & \text{uniform pdf} \\ \sigma_i^2(10)^{-b_i/2} & \text{Gaussian pdf} \end{cases} \tag{4.77}$$

For comparison with previous results, setting $\sigma_i^2 = 1$,

$$e_{\text{uniform}} = 2^{-2b_i} = N^{-2}$$
$$e_{\text{Gaussian}} = 1.778^{-2b_i} \tag{4.78}$$

The former result is just that for the basic uniform quantiser [Eq. (4.76)] and the latter is that used by Wintz and Kurtenbach (note, however, that there are typographical errors in the quoted bit allocation rule).

It is worth pointing out here that assignment rules which, at first sight, seem quite dissimilar, often prove on closer examination to be very much the same or even identical since, for example, there is no consistency in the use of any particular logarithmic base. Thus Habibi (1971) quotes an assignment rule from Wintz and Kurtenbach (1968) and Huang and Schultheiss (1963) which does not appear to be in accord with the given references, and in his 1974 paper (Habibi, 1974), he uses natural logarithms together with a factor $1/a$ where $a = 0.5 \ln(10)$. This is somewhat confusing since, of course, $\exp[-0.5 \ln(10) b_i] = 10^{-b_i/2}$, which is the uniform result given by Wintz and Kurtenbach [Eq. (4.76)]. Ploysongsang and Rao (1982) use Habibi's result but ignore the fact that this expression originated with Wintz and Kurtenbach for the uniform quantiser. Essman et al. (1976) use Habibi's result also but multiply by a factor 'b' which is given as 20 [their Eq. (2.29)] and should almost certainly be 2.0.

Segall, whose quantisation results have already been mentioned, presents a general theory of minimum mean-square-error bit allocation to uncorrelated (i.e., independent) Gaussian variables (Segall, 1976). He uses his quantisation error/number of levels relations to generate bit assignments of the form $b_i = f[\log(\sigma_i^2, \theta)]$ where θ solves a total bit allocation constraint. In this case dependence of the functional relationship of error on the number of quantisation levels is allowed for in the form of Eqs. (4.56) and (4.57). His results are also applied to the rate distortion allocation scheme described later. He also suggests a scheme for moving from a continuous representation of b_i in the minimisation process to integer values for coding purposes by calculating the marginal returns (i.e., reduction in distortion) obtained by unit increase in each bit assignment and then assigning bits in the decreasing order of these returns (Fox, 1966). Pratt (1978) points out that the widely used algorithm (Huang and Schultheiss' result with the coefficient 0.6) is dependent upon an approximate relation between e and b_i which is poor if b_i is small, and suggests as an alternative an algorithm which sequentially assigns bits to variables with the largest differential error in the manner of the marginal return approach of Segall. Thus, the reduction in error obtained by increasing allocation b_i by one bit is calculated over all variables to be quantised and bits allocated accordingly. An alternative technique is described by Ghanbari (1979) in which bits are assigned in sequence to the variable (i.e., coefficient) currently possessing the largest quantisation error, until the total allocation is complete. There are several other methods which have been described in the literature (see, e.g., O'Neal and Natarajan, 1977; Baronetti et al., 1979; Pearlman and Jakatdar, 1981).

An alternative approach to the allocation of bits for quantisation is via rate distortion theory. This will be discussed in more detail in Chapter 9, although we have already seen the usual result, which applies to Gaussian random variables under the constraint of minimum mean square error. Thus (Berger, 1971), the coding requirement in bits for such a variable i of variance σ_i^2 and incurring mse D_i is

$$R(D_i) = \tfrac{1}{2} \log_2(\sigma_i^2/D_i) \qquad D_i \leqslant \sigma_i^2 \tag{4.79}$$

[Note that, if $D_i > \sigma_i^2$; i.e., the allowable distortion is greater than the signal variance (energy), then there is no point in bothering to code it!] This relation has been used by many workers for bit allocation in transform coding schemes (see, e.g., Tasto and Wintz, 1971; Pratt et al., 1974; Chen and Smith, 1976, 1977; Cox and Tescher, 1976; Melzer, 1978; McWhirter et al., 1981) and, whilst its ancestry in rate distortion theory apparently imparts to it a very specific theoretical significance, it has been employed in the coding of transform coefficients which are neither distributed according to a Gaussian pdf nor totally uncorrelated. Furthermore, it can be seen to be a general relation, of which the rule developed by Huang and Schultheiss is a particular example, which assigns coding capacity to the coefficients in a way which allows the number of levels to be proportional to the amplitude of any given term, as might well have been done on a 'rule of thumb' basis. The important fact to be borne in mind in the general application of Eq. (4.79) is that, unless the statistical constraints specified by Shannon for its use are observed, D_i will not be the (numerical) mean square distortion. As far as variation in coefficient pdf is concerned, the value of D_i obtained in the Gaussian case will form an upper bound to that obtaining in the case of any other pdf (see Chapter 9). In practice, a nominal overall data rate, for example 1 bit/ element, is chosen, and D_i (the same value for all coefficients) iteratively adjusted until Eq. (4.79) is satisfied. It is instructive, finally, to solve Eq. (4.79) for D_i and to compare the result with Eq. (4.65). Thus

$$D_i = \sigma_i^2 2^{-2R(D_i)} \tag{4.80}$$

and, with the above constraints satisfied, the constant 'c' and the distortion parameter D_i are identical.

4.8 Summary

In order to transmit or store, in digital form, the real number output of the transform operation it is necessary to apply the procedures of quantisation and bit allocation. It is well known that, for practical purposes, the former operation must be carried out bearing in mind the distribution of the variables to be processed, and the first part of this chapter examines the dynamic range and probability density of transform coefficient sequences, and then defines the more useful theoretical cases, using them as a comparative basis for measured results taken from the test images. It is seen that the significant, low-order AC coefficients have distributions which are, in general, more highly peaked than the Laplacian relation usually assumed, whilst high-order coefficients, whose distributions can only be measured with difficulty, appear to follow a Gaussian profile. What effect exact adherence to any 'standard' profile would have on system performance is unclear, however, especially as visual considerations are neglected in what may be called 'classical' quantisation techniques such as those examined here.

As in the case of quantisation, the matter of optimum bit allocation to a set of variables of differing energies has been extensively treated in the literature. Here standard techniques and variations upon them which have been employed in transform coding schemes are reviewed and compared, and simple calculations for the 'gain' (reduction in error for a given bit allocation due to the application of the transform operation) carried out. Finally, the connection between bit allocation and the subject of Chapter 9, rate distortion theory, is briefly introduced and the application of one basic relation derived by the use of that theory to the allocation of coding capacity is compared with the standard approach of the present chapter.

Chapter 5

Practical Coding Techniques

5.1 Intraframe coding

5.1.1 Introduction

The previous two chapters have considered the steps necessary to generate a set of transform coefficients in a form suitable for storage or transmission either directly, or perhaps after further digital processing. It is possible, of course, to retain all of the coefficients to any desired level of accuracy, but to do so to an arbitrarily high degree would certainly require a number of bits exceeding that used to code the image in its original (spatial) form. The benefits of transform coding, after all, derive from the statistical characteristics of the input data, in that they allow us to reproduce the original image with an acceptable degree of fidelity whilst employing significantly fewer bits for the process, by retaining only 'important' coefficients. The efficient selection of those coefficients which are to be retained, and the allocation to them of an appropriate number of bits, lie at the heart of successful transform coding, and the comments of Tescher (1979) to the effect that the great amount of research work and effort spent in the last decade or so searching for transforms with just that little extra degree of energy packing or decorrelation performance would have been better spent on the alternative task of improving coefficient selection and bit allocation rules have been mentioned previously. Indeed, it is difficult to disagree with his assertion, since there is relatively little to choose in performance (details of implementation apart) between the more efficient transforms, especially when compared with the advantages to be gained by moving from non-adaptive to adaptive techniques (Murphy, 1981).

In this chapter attention is devoted to both adaptive and non-adaptive techniques, although the necessarily poorer performance of the latter has meant that the majority of reported work has been concerned with the former type of algorithm. We shall thus consider the problem in a general context only briefly before turning to study, in detail, adaptive procedures. Furthermore, one-dimensional coding techniques for processing still images will not be discussed here. Their efficiency is poor since they do not take into account the two-dimensional correlation properties of the image, and they have been completely superseded by two-dimensional approaches. Again, consideration is first given to the processing of images on an individual basis (*intra*frame coding) before examining the benefits (and difficulties) associated with the coding of image frames as members of a moving sequence, taking into account the relationships which exist in the temporal direction (*inter*frame coding).

The reader may notice a difference in emphasis when comparing this chapter with those earlier and later in this book. Whereas in those chapters the material discussed has, for the most part, a firm basis in well-developed and substantiated mathematical theory, in the case of the design of practical coding schemes the situation is somewhat different. There is no one best way of developing a coder for a particular application, and this has resulted in a proliferation of approaches which, whilst usually paying at least lip-service to one or two broad principles, almost inevitably differ in significant points of detail. It has been thought more appropriate, therefore, to examine the development of practical coding methods on a semi-historical basis, particularly as that line of advance, from the earliest designs of the mid and late 1960s to the present day, is reasonably clearly drawn in the literature.

5.1.2   General considerations

We have seen that, for 'typical' source images, the transform operation results in a drastic redistribution of image energy into relatively few, low-order coefficients. Although this is still the case (albeit to a rather lesser degree) with input data having significant high-frequency detail, it is worth re-emphasising in passing that this redistribution is a consequence of the assumption of a reasonable level of data correlation, and it would not obtain in the case of an uncorrelated source. To this extent we are constrained in our choice of image data for transformation. Fortunately, meaningful images usually do contain a high degree of long-range structure which renders them amenable to such manipulations. Furthermore, the techniques detailed in the previous chapter enable us to assign an appropriate number of bits to each of a set of coefficients of known variances such that the overall error is minimised. It is important to note here that, whether or not we apply block quantisation rules for bit allocation or, more or less arbitrarily, decide to transmit or store only a subset of the coefficient array, a so-called 'variance criterion' operates; i.e., we always try to choose the m out of M coefficients with the largest variances, in order to minimise the overall error magnitude for a given value of m (with certain of the simpler coefficient selection schemes, this may not always be possible, however, as will be pointed out in more detail later in this chapter). Armed with this knowledge, an initial approach to coefficient selection and coding is to process the full $(N \times N)$ image as a single entity using an $N \times N$ two-dimensional transform and subsequently to apply a bit allocation procedure of the kind already described. Since for a single image there is only one coefficient of each order when full image transforms are used, the separate coefficient variances must be estimated on the basis of results obtained from a series of test images (it is unlikely that we shall want to design a system simply to transmit one image). Such full-image coding has been carried out by Andrews and Pratt (1968), Anderson and Huang (1971), Claire et al. (1971), and Pearlman and Jakatdar (1981), amongst others, and it has the obvious advantage that there is no block structure visible in the reconstructed image, as happens at low data rates with the more usual spatially adaptive systems to be described subsequently. There are two disadvantages, however, the first being that the technique cannot be made spatially adaptive, since the transform is taken over the whole of the image as a single step. The second is that the possible range of coefficient magnitude increases with transform order (see Chapter 4) and so, for a 256×256 or 512×512 transform, is very large indeed. The alternative, and more usual, approach is to divide the image into blocks of dimension $M \times M$, where $nM = N$, and there are then n^2 blocks, and individual coefficients of any given order, per image (it is not necessary, of course, that the blocks be square, although this is the case in the vast majority of reported schemes, and rectangular blocks have occasionally been used). A typical example is of a 512×512 image divided into 1024 blocks each 16×16. With either scheme, the bit allocation is fixed, for a series of full single-image transforms in the first case, and for all sub-blocks in an image in the second, and based on an average measure of data statistics calculated over all partitions. The result is a fixed data rate system, in which the image-to-image or block-to-block distortion is uncontrolled, since, inevitably, some coefficients will require either more, or fewer, bits than the number allocated. In the full-image case, the scheme can be made image (though not spatially) adaptive, by utilising one of a restricted range of predetermined bit allocations, indicated to the decoder by a 2- or 3-bit code word, the decision as to which to employ being based upon a measure of image activity. In this case, of course, the data rate will vary from image to image.

Simpler selection methods may be used also. For example, we might decide to retain only those coefficients lying within a prespecified zone of the variance array (perhaps the upper left-hand quarter, i.e., 4×4 coefficients in an 8×8 sub-block scheme, or the first 5, 4, 4, 3 and 1 coefficients on rows 1 to 5, respectively), on the assumption that they will be those having the largest variances in any case. This procedure is called 'zonal sampling' and may be represented by the product of the coefficient array and a sampling function which has the value unity over the group of coefficients it is desired to retain and zero otherwise (Wintz, 1972; Pratt, 1978). Again, more than one zone may be established, each with a prespecified bit allocation constant over the zone. If all integer allocations up to a convenient maximum (say, 8) are allowed, then this scheme, called 'zonal coding', becomes very similar to the general approach described in Chapter 4, although the actual allocations will probably be based on somewhat *ad hoc* assumptions about the relationship between coefficient variance and order, rather than on actual variance measurement. If coefficient standard deviations are used as scaling (normalisation) factors at the coding stage so that all coefficients having the same pdf and bit allocation can be processed with the same unit variance quantiser, the scaling operation being reversed at the decoder prior to inverse transformation, then the decoder must have available information on the variances of the individual transform coefficients, measured over the appropriate image or block ensemble. For a non-adaptive scheme the amount of overhead information that this requires is small, provided that the image or block sequence is fairly substantial, since only one word per coefficient (suitably error protected, of course), is required. Thus, for 16×16 blocks, at most 256 words will be required which, for a 512×512 image, represents only 0.02 bit/element at 20 bits/word. In view of this low figure, it hardly seems worthwhile to attempt to implement parameter estimation schemes at the decoder to avoid the transmission of overhead information, at least in the case of non-adaptive coding, since such schemes inevitably lead to increased error in image reconstruction.

It is evident, then, that non-adaptive coding of the kind portrayed in Fig. 5.1, which allocates a fixed number of bits (i.e., a fixed quantisation accuracy) to a given coefficient, is very inefficient. The basic reason for this is the variation in picture detail over the n^2 blocks which make up the single image (or over the various images used for variance estimation in the case of full image coding—in the following treatment we shall, however, concentrate on sub-block, rather than full-image processing, as has been done in the majority of reported work). Thus, the presence of several highly 'active' blocks will lead to the overall allocation of several bits to, say, a low order AC coefficient, and if a specific coefficient to be coded is small (occurring, perhaps, in a block with little detail), it will be inefficiently quantised, particularly when the

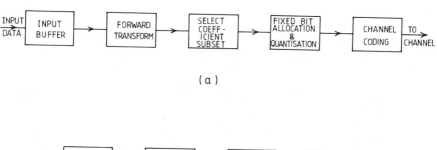

(a)

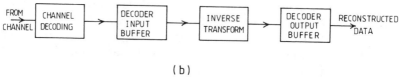

(b)

FIG. 5.1. Non-adaptive transform coding. (a) Coder and (b) decoder.

coding scheme uses the technique of scaling together with a single unit variance quantiser, since then the scale factor will be large, the normalised coefficient of very low amplitude, and after quantisation, coding and transmission, multiplied by the same large factor before inverse transformation. The visual result is then quite likely to be unacceptable, since the eye is sensitive to relatively small quantisation errors in low-detail regions of the image. It is apparent that what should be done is to modify the bit allocation and quantisation scheme according to the amount of block activity, and this is what adaptive techniques attempt to do. In such schemes it is now essential that information be provided at the decoder so that correct processing and image reconstruction can be carried out, and the matter of whether it is better to transmit this as an unavoidable overhead or to use estimation methods is more of an open question than in the case of non-adaptive coding. In fact, there are two good reasons why, even in the adaptive case, the transmission of coding parameters directly is not such a bad idea. The first is that, in a well-designed scheme, the overhead load will still be small compared with the channel allocation necessary for the transmission of data (coded image) information. The second is that estimation schemes inevitably introduce reconstruction errors, as pointed out earlier in relation to non-adaptive coding, since no such technique can be correct 100% of the time. At present, there is a clear division between ideas which are desirable in principle—of which 'intelligent' parameter estimation by the decoder is one, and practical considerations of simple and efficient implementation, in this case the use of (error-protected) overhead transmission. Accepting the need for extra information transmission to the decoder, then, the question arises as to just how 'adaptive' the system should be. The two extremes are, on the one hand, the non-adaptive case, which in its simplest form requires no overhead information transmission at all, and on the other, separate optimum bit allocation and quantisation of every block. The latter option will, however, require a data rate far in excess of that required for transmission of the image by more conventional means, and in any case is not necessary, since even very active images have significant areas over which the the same coding parameters represent a negligible deviation from the optimum. As will be seen in the next section, several practical options are open to the system designer. One quite popular scheme, however, is that due to Chen and Smith (1977) who divide their images into four classes, each of which contains the same number of sub-blocks. This represents a good compromise between the inefficiency of the non-adaptive scheme and the improvement to be obtained from highly complex approaches.

As a very rough generalisation, it may be said that, for a given image and average error in reconstruction, non-adaptive systems need twice the transmission rate or storage capacity of a reasonably efficient adaptive scheme, and it is therefore not surprising that the last 10 years or so have seen a proliferation of such latter designs in the literature. A typical adaptive coding scheme is shown diagrammatically in Fig. 5.2. It differs from the non-adaptive scheme in that the image sub-blocks are sorted (using either data or transform domain numerical estimates) into categories having varying degrees of activity. Each category is then allocated a separate bit-allocation map (see for example Tables 5.2–5.5), and individual blocks are processed accordingly. Thus, the number of bits allocated to a specific coefficient in a given class is used to determine a coefficient normalisation (or scaling) factor, which then allows all AC coefficients to be quantised with the same unit variance quantiser. Naturally the decoder needs to be informed of the various sub-block classification and bit-allocation parameters, which are transmitted as data 'overhead', i.e., an extra rate requirement. We now examine the development of adaptive techniques in more detail.

5.1.2.1 *Adaptive coding techniques*

By far the most frequently reported transform image coding schemes have been those applied to the sub-block coding of single images, and it is with this type of system that this section is almost exclusively concerned (the coding of image sequences is discussed elsewhere in this book).

Even a cursory examination of virtually any randomly selected image will disclose the fact that the spatial distribution of its visual characteristics—luminance, colour, etc.—is highly non-uniform. Thus, some regions many elements in extent may have a non-varying luminance level which needs only a single digital word for its specification, others will have many sharp transitions in luminance which form edges, both straight and irregular,

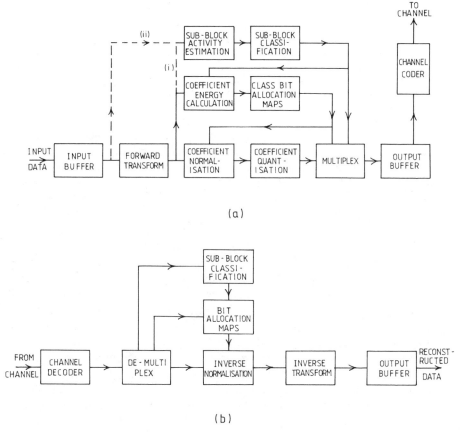

FIG. 5.2. Adaptive transform coding. (a) Coder and (b) decoder. Also included are alternative sub-block classification methods (i) using transform coefficients and (ii) using original data.

directed in more or less arbitrary fashion, and which may need an individual word per element for correct representation. Such regions are often described as having low or high 'activity', respectively, and there will, in general, be regions within the image which correspond to activities anywhere between the two extremes. Efficient coding schemes have been devised which take advantage of such properties by locating and defining the extent of low-activity areas, which need few bits for correct representation, and preferentially allocating more coding capacity to the other, higher-detail areas, and such area-adaptive approaches have been the subject of much research interest, not only in the context of transform coding. In this respect the latter technique is at a distinct disadvantage, since the requirements of the orthogonal transform dictate the arbitrary division of the data into, at best, rectangular blocks (which are, in fact, square in the overwhelming majority of cases) which, in order to allow efficient fast implementation of the transform, have a linear dimension which is an integral power of two (4×4, 8×8, 16×16, etc.). It is impracticable, therefore, to 'fit' the imposed block structure to the regions of differing activities which occur within the actual image. Thus, in a typical case (Image 1, for example), some blocks are located in regions which are part high, part low luminance, and in which the dividing edge is roughly diagonal, and such blocks are difficult to code efficiently. Again, Image 2 contains, over a significant area, a regular structure to which one might be able to fit a sub-block arrangement for transformation, but such niceties are hardly feasible on a consistent practical basis. The problem is partially solved by making the block size as small as possible; where simple edges are concerned the number of blocks which then contain elements of more or less constant luminance values will become a larger fraction of the total, and the average block detail will be more highly responsive to spatial variations in image activity. Two drawbacks may now make themselves felt, however. First, the transform acts to decorrelate the image data present within each individual sub-block. For the typical low-activity image, such correlation is present, and significant, over an element separation of perhaps 15–20 (see the results for Image 1 in Chapter 2), and some of this benefit is lost when using a small block size, since most elements with separations up to the above figure will reside in adjacent, rather than in the same, block(s). Second, some adaptive schemes require the transmission of overhead information on a block-by-block basis. Thus threshold coding, in which coefficients are selected for retention according to their magnitude relative to a preset, or itself adaptive, threshold level, requires that the location (address) of each retained coefficient be transmitted or stored, together with its quantised and coded representation. For a block size $m \times m$, therefore, the address information requirement will be of the order of $2 \log_2 m$ bits. The number of blocks will be proportional to m^{-2} and so the total address overhead will be proportional to $m^{-2} \log_2 m$. Thus, reducing the linear block dimension by a factor of four results in an eightfold increase in overhead transmission. There are therefore both restrictions on allowable block dimension from the point of view of carrying out the transform operation, and drawbacks to the use of very large or very small blocks. The majority of designs reported in the literature, as a result, employ sizes of 4×4, 8×8 or 16×16, although more specialised applications have used 2×2 and 64×64 blocks.

Faced with the practical necessity of an arbitrary division of the image into sub-blocks, then, for the purpose of employing adaptive techniques, are there any other modifications which might be made to match the operation of the transform to the specific properties of individual blocks? It is well known, of course, that the KLT diagonalises the covariance matrix of the input data, and so advantage might be gained by matching the corresponding basis set to groups of blocks with similar statistical properties. Such a method is described in more detail in the following. An even better approach, in principle, is via the use of SVD (see Chapter 3). The problem with such techniques is that, not only is the computational load very great, but additional coding information (basis vectors, etc.) has to be relayed to the decoder without error so that image reconstruction can be carried out. In the case of SVD coding, there is some disagreement as to whether its overall efficiency is greater than that of more commonly used methods (Garguir, 1979; Murphy, 1981). We now examine several adaptive coding schemes which have been proposed for two-dimensional processing of single images, few of which, however, attempt the degree of sophistication of those just mentioned.

5.1.2.1.1 *Early approaches to adaptive transform coding*

Anderson and Huang (1971) employ the DFT to encode three 256×256 images of varying degrees of activity using sub-block sizes of 8×8, 16×16 and 32×32 (finding, incidentally, that for a moderately detailed image the first two sizes require approximately the same data rate whilst the last requires somewhat more). Each block of data has its standard deviation calculated, and this is used to determine how many of the largest Fourier coefficients are to be transmitted, by visual inspection of selected blocks and determination of the number of coefficients needed for high quality reproduction as a function of σ. All block coefficients are linearly quantised with the same number of bits (between 2 and 5) which is made a function of σ by comparison with three predetermined thresholds. Seven bits are used to code the DC coefficient and the maximum AC coefficient magnitude, which influences the maximum sub-block quantisation level, is represented by a 10-bit word. Run-length coding based on measured statistics is used to code the locations of the coefficients retained. The scheme was found to be superior to both full-frame (256×256) and one-dimensional entire line transforms, with high quality reconstruction at a rate of 1.25 bits/element. It is interesting that the scheme takes into account certain of the properties of the human visual response (see Chapter 6), for example, by processing not the values of element luminance directly but rather their logarithms, a compensating exponentiation operation being carried out at the receiver. Threshold coding is also used by Bowyer (1971) who employs the WHT and a 32×32 computer-generated test array. Again the coefficient set is compared against a threshold and the addresses of the retained coefficients specified by run-length coding. Rather more comprehensive WHT results are given by Claire *et al.* (1971) who use a detailed aerial image and both full frame (256×256) and sub-block (64×64

and 16×16) transforms. Coefficients are retained on the basis of their magnitude as compared with that of all coefficients from all sub-blocks, and their results indicate that the best performance both numerically (i.e., as measured mean square error) and visually, is produced by the 16×16 sub-block transformation.

Of course, the classical method of completely decorrelating the sequence of blocks comprising an image is by the use of the KLT, and this transform, together with the Fourier and Hadamard transforms, was used by Habibi and Wintz (1971) to code 16×16 sub-blocks derived from the same images as those of Anderson and Huang (see the preceding), and also from a 6-bit moon picture. A separable first-order Markov model was established for two dimensional image correlation and the appropriate parameters estimated. Quantisation and bit allocation followed the procedures described in Chapter 4. The system was made adaptive by estimating the two correlation parameters for each sub-block and classifying the pair of parameters into one of 16 possible categories. The appropriate transformation (in the case of the KLT) and quantiser were then used for coding. The system thus adaptively allocates coding bits (and, of course, transformation, in the case of the KLT) as a function of block detail. Somewhat surprisingly, only a marginal improvement in performance over that of the non-adaptive system was obtained. This is possibly due to the inexact estimation of correlation parameters based on the limited amount of data in a small sub-block and, of course, the separable first-order correlation is not particularly accurate in the general case (see Chapter 2). The authors point out that a classification scheme based on pattern recognition techniques produces improved results. The KLT is also used by Tasto and Wintz (1971) in an adaptive block quantisation scheme. The three images (256×256, and quantised to an accuracy of 8 bits) used previously in the work described earlier were divided into 6×6 blocks which were each reordered into a vector 36 elements long. The total of 5292 vectors formed the data sample. Three classes were then established via rate distortion theory (Tasto and Wintz, 1972), each containing one-third of the data samples, and each class had its own KLT and quantiser. The block classes had the following properties: (1) highly detailed, (2) little detail and darker than average and (3) little detail and lighter than average. Quantisers were initially optimised under a mean-square-error criterion and the optimum balance between implementation and picture quality was found to be produced by the use of the same fine quantisation (512 levels) for all coefficients, combined with a Huffman code to generate the output code words (a refinement of the approach uses a different code for each coefficient, and produces a slight improvement). Optimisation was then carried out on the system with regard to the subjective quality of the reconstructed image. As far as error introduced by coefficient deletion is concerned, it was found that, in the absence of quantisation, each category generates the same amount of distortion when the number of retained coefficients in categories 2 and 3 is the same, and equal to half the number retained in category 1. Experiments on quantisation strategy were then carried out by dividing each retained coefficient (12, 6 and 6 in number, respectively) by a scale factor and using the same uniform quantiser for all coefficients. The various scale factors were then modified such that quantisation of each coefficient introduced approximately the same degree of subjective distortion. Applying the optimised system to different data produced results just as good as for the original data set, i.e., comparable to the originals at a rate of about 1 bit/element. Further, it was found that no noticeable effect on subjective quality resulted from the use of a single transformation for all three data classes. This latter result is in keeping with the general point mentioned elsewhere in this volume that variations in the quantisation and coding of transform coefficients have a more significant effect upon overall system performance than do alterations in the actual transform used.

At this point, historically, a convenient review of previous work, and a good introduction to the topic of transform coding in general is provided by Wintz (1972) who includes an extensive listing of material published by that date. His general conclusion is that adaptive intraframe schemes produce satisfactory quality using input images of moderate detail at about 1 bit/element, whilst non-adaptive schemes require a further bit for equivalent quality.

5.1.2.1.2 Later techniques

The application of a measure of block activity is further considered by Gimlett (1975) who suggests the use of the weighted sum of the AC transform coefficient amplitudes (or their squares) as a basis for classification. He allocates sub-blocks to one of four possible classes, on an equal total occupancy basis and, following Claire et al. (1971), employs a combination of zonal sampling and threshold coding in which in each class certain low-order coefficients are always coded, and adaptive thresholds applied to higher-order zones, in each of which the coefficient having the largest magnitude together with its address is transmitted. No experimental results are presented. Parsons and Tescher (1975) using the DCT compare a zonal coding scheme with an adaptive approach. Their zones take the form of bands of coefficients parallel to the opposing diagonal of the coefficient array, as a result of their observation that, typically, the coefficients in such bands have similar variances. Their adaptive scheme reorders the coefficients into a one-dimensional sequence by scanning in the way shown in Fig. 5.3. The mth coefficient (C_m) is then quantised using a variance estimate based on previously coded coefficients, thus

$$\sigma_m^2 = W\sigma_{m-1}^2 + (1 - W)C_{m-1}^2 \tag{5.1}$$

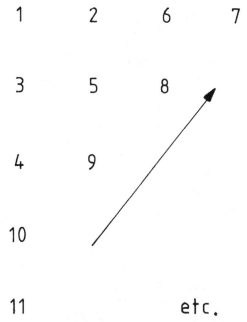

FIG. 5.3. Coefficient re-ordering scheme (Parsons and Tescher, 1975).

where W is a suitable weighting factor (chosen here to be 0.75). Since $W < 1$ this method assumes a continuous decrease in variance along the chosen scanning path modified only by the squared magnitude of the last quantised and coded coefficient. Results at approximately 1.5 bits/element indicate that the adaptive scheme has about half the mean square error of the non-adaptive system. The slant transform coder of Reader (1975) is typical, in basic outline, of the many approaches devised in the mid 1970s. Transform domain variances are estimated using a Markov data model and bits allocated proportionally. Before quantisation with a Max quantiser the coefficients are normalised, and Reader's first adaptive approach is to modify the normalisation factor in accordance with (sub-block AC energy)$^{1/2}$. Improved performance is obtained by reducing the horizontal and vertical adjacent element correlation coefficients (on which the transform domain variance modelling is based) from their actual values so that more coefficients are coded, albeit with fewer bits, on average, per coefficient. In fact, his published bit allocation maps appear to indicate that a separable correlation model was used, and better results could probably have been obtained with a non-separable model. It was also found that the extra complication of using a threshold/run-length coding technique to retain large magnitude coefficients outside the originally coded zone in an effort to improve performance was not justified, although it should be pointed out that the test image used is generally considered to have quite low activity, and the author's conclusion may not hold, therefore, for highly detailed input data. A final, and more successful, approach of his is to acknowledge that certain blocks are quite difficult to code and, for these (generally few in number but possessing the highest block AC energies), to widen the coded zone and increase the block coding rate to approximately 3 bits/element, reducing the rate for low activity blocks proportionately.

Increasing interest in the reliable recovery of data from deep space missions has given considerable impetus to the development of efficient coding schemes of all kinds, and it was for such an application that Rice's scheme was developed (Rice, 1975). In the context of an overall rate control/image fidelity strategy with extensive error control capabilities, his system codes an image with a user-specified number of bits which are allocated according to the 'normalised activity' of each sub-block by means of a set of multipliers which modify a notional uniform bit allocation per image. The transform itself is a cascade of 2×2 Hadamard transforms which are applied to the 64×64 sub-blocks of the image. Each of the six possible stages, of which four are used in the reported system, yields a $\frac{1}{4} \times \frac{1}{4}$ area array of 2×2 original coefficient averages, plus other coefficients. The former are passed to the next stage of the transform and the latter are stored. Entropy-reducing approximations and variable-length coding applied to the stored coefficient sets allow data rates down to 0.1 bit/element to be achieved, and adaptivity is extended to the inverse transformation by employing the correlation which exists between adjacent coefficients in order to reduce block edge effects. Space does not permit a detailed description of the scheme, for which the reader is referred to the original paper. Hsu and Savant (1976) suggest an optimum bit allocation and adaptive quantisation and coding scheme for Rice's system.

5.1.2.1.3   *The scheme of Chen and Smith*
One approach that has proved very popular for adaptive transform coding of both monochrome and colour image data is that of Chen and Smith (1976, 1977). Using the DCT and Max's method of optimum quantiser design, assuming Gaussian DC and AC coefficient pdfs, they allocate 16×16 sub-blocks of the original image to one of four classes, all of equal occupancy, on the basis of sub-block AC energy. (In passing it may be noted that, although most adaptive classification schemes utilise equal occupancy classes, there is no reason to suggest that this is an optimum choice from the point of view of coding efficiency, especially in the light of the results of Reader mentioned earlier, and an additional small occupancy class with relatively few, but very active, blocks may be advantageous.) The variance of

TABLE 5.1. Bit assignment, adaptive
scheme of Chen and Smith applied
to Image 1.

	Class			
N_B	1	2	3	4
8	1	1	1	1
7	2	—	—	—
6	3	2	—	—
5	7	4	3	—
4	13	8	4	1
3	27	23	8	3
2	44	29	24	13
1	85	82	73	57
Total	381	281	184	104

each coefficient in each class is calculated and used, together with the bit allocation technique of Eq. (4.73), to determine a 16×16 bit assignment map for each class. The assignment shown in Table 5.1 results in an overall rate of approximately 1 bit/element when a scheme of this type is applied to Image 1 (about 0.1 bit/element is reserved for overhead transmission and error protection, etc.). Tables 5.2–5.6 show the bit allocation maps and classification array, and the average class rates are 1.49. 1.10, 0.72 and 0.41 bit/element, respectively. The transform coefficients are normalised prior to quantisation (in order to use the same unit variance quantiser for any given bit allocation), and a corresponding inverse normalisation step is carried out at the decoder. In order not to have to send accurately a normalisation factor for each coefficient in each class it is desirable that the normalisation coefficient be derived, at both coder and decoder, from the bit allocation maps. The coefficient is thus set to be

$$k = c2^{N-1} \tag{5.2}$$

Where N is the number of bits allocated to any coefficient and c is a factor which is made equal to the maximum standard deviation of those coefficients allocated 1 bit at the assignment stage, in order to prevent coefficient clipping. It should be noted that choosing the appropriate normalisation coefficient is a matter of some significance, and a more detailed investigation into the factors influencing its determination has been carried out by Schaming and Bessette (1980). As a general comment, it can be deduced in a straightforward manner that, if the coefficients are divided by too large a number before quantisation, clipping will be avoided at the expense of the

TABLE 5.2. Bit allocation map, Image 1, class 1.

8	7	6	5	5	4	4	3	3	2	2	2	1	-	-	-
7	6	5	5	4	4	3	3	3	2	2	1	-	1	1	-
6	5	5	4	4	4	3	3	3	2	2	1	-	-	-	-
5	4	4	4	4	3	3	3	2	2	2	1	-	-	-	-
4	4	3	3	3	2	3	3	2	2	1	-	-	-	-	-
3	3	3	3	3	3	3	2	2	2	2	1	-	-	-	-
3	2	3	3	2	2	2	2	2	1	1	1	-	-	-	-
2	2	2	2	2	2	2	2	1	1	1	1	-	-	-	-
2	2	1	1	1	1	1	1	1	1	1	-	-	-	-	-
1	2	2	2	2	2	2	1	1	1	1	-	-	-	-	-
2	1	1	2	1	1	1	1	1	1	1	-	-	-	-	-
1	1	1	1	1	1	1	1	1	1	1	-	-	-	-	-
1	1	1	1	1	1	1	1	1	1	-	-	-	-	-	-
2	1	1	1	1	1	1	1	1	1	-	1	-	-	-	-
2	1	1	1	1	1	1	1	-	1	1	-	-	-	-	-
2	1	1	1	1	-	1	1	-	1	-	-	-	-	-	-

possible appearance of noise in those blocks in which the coefficient concerned is small, and vice-versa. The amount of overhead information that it is necessary to transmit is as follows; the sub-block classification map (four possible classes, i.e., 2 bits/block), the normalisation factor c and four bit allocation maps, the latter requiring, if Huffman coding is used, about 1.5 bits/entry. Leaving aside any additional error protection, the total is perhaps 0.05 bit/element for a 256×256 image. Excellent subjective results can be obtained with this method at an overall rate of 1 bit/element. Figure 5.4 shows the results of four-class adaptive transform coding as applied to Image

TABLE 5.3. Bit allocation map, Image 1, class 2.

8	6	5	5	4	4	4	4	3	3	3	3	3	2	2	1
6	5	4	4	3	3	2	2	2	2	2	1	1	-	-	-
5	4	3	3	3	3	3	2	1	1	1	1	-	-	-	-
4	3	3	3	3	3	2	2	1	1	1	-	-	-	-	-
3	3	3	2	2	2	2	2	2	2	1	-	-	-	-	-
3	2	3	2	1	2	2	1	2	1	1	-	-	-	-	-
3	2	2	2	2	2	1	1	1	1	1	-	-	-	-	-
2	1	1	1	2	1	1	1	1	1	1	-	-	-	-	-
1	1	1	1	1	1	1	-	-	-	-	-	-	-	-	-
1	1	1	1	1	1	1	1	1	1	-	-	-	-	-	-
1	1	1	1	1	1	1	-	-	-	-	-	-	-	-	-
1	1	1	-	1	-	1	-	1	1	-	-	-	-	-	-
1	1	-	1	1	-	1	1	1	1	1	-	-	-	-	-
1	1	1	1	1	-	1	-	-	1	-	-	-	-	-	-
1	1	-	1	-	-	1	-	-	-	-	-	-	-	-	-
1	1	-	-	-	-	-	-	-	-	-	-	-	-	-	-

TABLE 5.4. Bit allocation map, Image 1, class 3.

8	5	5	4	3	3	3	2	2	2	2	2	1	1	1	–
5	4	3	3	2	2	2	2	1	1	1	1	–	–	–	–
4	4	3	2	2	2	2	1	1	1	1	1	–	–	–	–
3	3	2	1	2	1	1	1	1	1	1	1	–	–	–	–
2	2	2	2	1	1	1	1	2	2	1	–	–	–	–	–
2	2	2	1	1	1	1	1	1	1	1	–	–	–	–	–
1	1	1	1	1	1	1	1	–	–	–	–	–	–	–	–
1	1	1	1	1	1	1	1	–	–	–	–	–	–	–	–
–	1	–	1	–	1	–	–	–	–	–	–	–	–	–	–
1	1	1	1	–	1	–	–	–	1	–	–	–	–	–	–
1	1	–	1	–	–	–	–	–	–	–	–	–	–	–	–
1	1	–	–	–	–	–	–	1	1	–	–	–	–	–	–
1	–	–	–	–	–	–	–	1	1	1	–	–	–	–	–
1	1	–	–	–	–	–	–	1	–	–	–	–	–	–	–
1	–	–	–	–	–	–	–	–	–	–	–	–	–	–	–
1	–	–	–	–	–	–	–	–	–	–	–	–	–	–	–

1 (the original picture is shown in Fig. 2.6), where the coding rates are 1, 0.5 and 0.25 bit/element respectively. Degradation is difficult to see at the highest rate, but becomes noticeable in the more active areas of the image at 0.5 bit/ element. At the lowest rate the block structure inherent in the coding process is easily visible and the result is unacceptable for all but the most undemanding of applications. Similar comments apply to the coding of the more active Image 2 (Fig. 5.5; original in Fig. 2.12), where the result at 0.25 bit/element must be considered unusable in any application. Figure 5.6 demonstrates the effect of coding the black and white typescript image of Fig. 2.16 (note that

TABLE 5.5. Bit allocation map, Image 1, class 4.

8	4	3	2	2	2	2	2	1	1	1	1	–	–	–
3	3	2	1	1	1	1	1	1	1	–	–	–	–	–
2	2	1	1	1	1	1	1	1	–	–	–	–	–	–
2	1	1	1	1	1	1	1	1	1	1	–	–	–	–
2	1	1	1	1	1	1	1	2	2	1	–	–	–	–
1	1	1	1	1	1	1	–	1	1	–	–	–	–	–
1	1	1	–	–	–	–	–	–	–	–	–	–	–	–
1	1	1	1	–	–	1	–	–	–	–	–	–	–	–
–	–	–	–	–	–	–	–	–	–	–	–	–	–	–
–	–	–	–	–	–	–	–	–	–	–	–	–	–	–
–	–	–	–	–	–	–	–	–	–	–	–	–	–	–
–	–	–	–	–	–	–	–	1	1	–	–	–	–	–
–	–	–	–	–	–	–	–	1	1	–	–	–	–	–
–	–	–	–	–	–	–	–	–	–	–	–	–	–	–
–	–	–	–	–	–	–	–	–	–	–	–	–	–	–
1	–	–	–	–	–	–	–	–	–	–	–	–	–	–

TABLE 5.6. Classification map, Image 1.[a]

3	3	3	2	3	2	2	3	2	1	1	1	2	1	4	4
3	3	3	2	2	1	1	1	2	4	3	4	1	1	4	4
3	2	3	2	3	1	2	3	4	4	4	4	1	1	4	4
3	2	3	2	4	1	1	1	2	1	1	2	1	1	4	4
2	3	3	2	4	1	1	1	2	1	1	2	2	1	4	3
3	3	3	2	4	3	1	1	3	3	3	4	3	2	4	2
3	3	3	2	4	2	2	1	1	3	3	4	3	3	4	2
3	3	3	2	4	2	2	1	1	2	2	4	3	3	4	2
1	2	3	2	4	3	1	1	2	3	3	3	3	4	4	2
2	2	3	3	4	4	2	1	1	1	2	3	1	2	4	3
3	3	3	3	3	1	2	1	2	2	2	1	1	3	1	3
4	4	2	1	2	2	1	4	1	1	2	4	1	4	3	1
2	2	2	3	2	2	1	1	1	1	1	1	3	4	4	2
3	4	4	4	2	4	2	2	1	1	2	1	4	4	3	4
4	4	4	4	4	4	2	3	1	1	1	1	4	4	4	4
4	4	4	3	4	4	2	3	1	2	1	2	4	4	4	3

[a] Block size = 16×16.

the jagged edges of some of the letters, visible most easily in the original picture, are a result of imperfections in the original scanning process and not of present procedures). As pointed out previously, there are much more efficient methods of coding such two-level information, and the results (theoretical and pictorial) presented here are only included to allow comparisons to be made over the widest possible range of source material. At this point a further, more general, comment is perhaps in order, and that is that the limitations on image reproduction imposed by the printing process mean that much subtle detail apparent on the video monitor screen cannot be properly demonstrated in the figures shown here.

5.1.2.1.4 *Other considerations*

As far as the application of adaptive transform coding to real-world image communication problems (as opposed to their investigation via computer simulation) is concerned, it is necessary to recognise that the inherent variable rate of generation of data by the coder must be buffered for transmission over a fixed rate channel. This requirement has been studied by Cox and Tescher (1976), who employ the DCT, together with conventional bit allocation/quantisation procedures. Division into eight equal occupancy classes is carried out (requiring 3 bits/block overhead) on the basis of the variance of the 16×16 sub-blocks, and eight standard deviation matrices are generated, one for each class. In order to control the data rate, information derived from either the input (reformatting) buffer, in which the scanned video data is placed 16 lines at a time prior to transformation, or the coder

FIG. 5.4. Image 1 coded using the discrete cosine transform in a four-class adaptive scheme with overall rates of (a) 1.0, (b) 0.5 and (c) 0.25 bit/element.

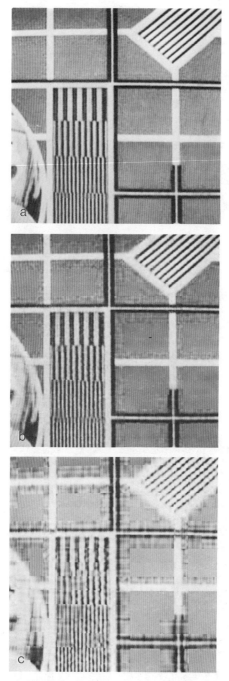

FIG. 5.5. Image 2 coded using the discrete cosine transform in a four-class adaptive scheme with overall rates of (a) 1.0, (b) 0.5 and (c) 0.25 bit/element.

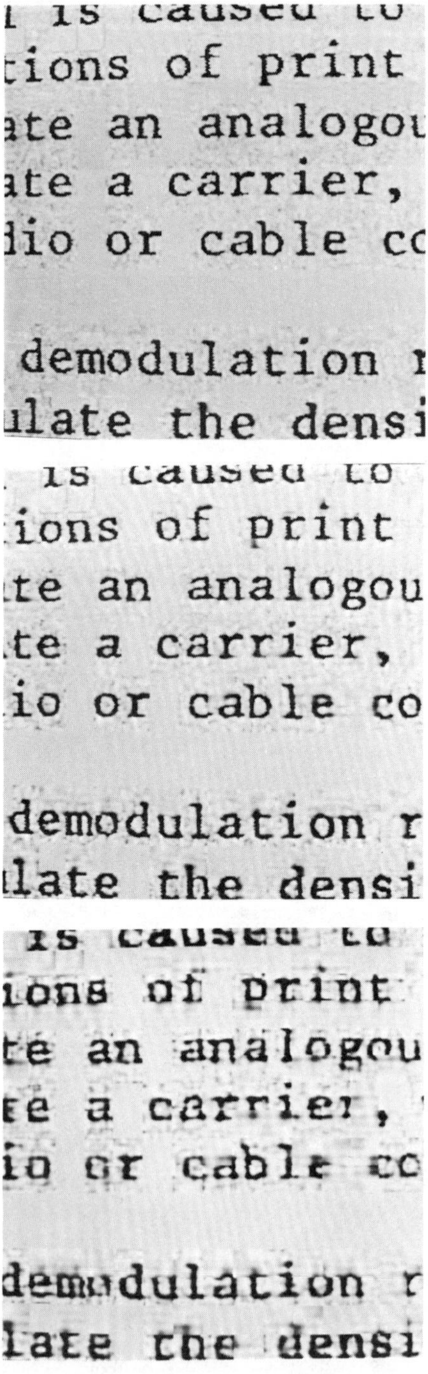

is caused to
tions of print
ate an analogou
ate a carrier,
lio or cable co

demodulation r
ulate the densi (a)

is caused to
ions of print
te an analogou
te a carrier,
io or cable co

demodulation r
ulate the densi (b)

is caused to
ions of print
te an analogou
te a carrier,
io or cable co

demodulation r
late the densi (c)

FIG. 5.6. Image 3 coded using the discrete cosine transform in a four-class adaptive scheme with overall rates of (a) 1.0, (b) 0.5 and (c) 0.25 bit/element.

output buffer, is utilised. In the first case the data rate is equalised over each data strip (32 sub-blocks, each 16×16 in extent, residing in the input buffer) by iterative determination of the distortion parameter D in the bit allocation equation [Eq. (4.73)], in conjunction with the relevant standard deviation matrix for each of the classified blocks. The quantisation error is thus approximately equal for all classes. In the second approach, the individual bit allocations are controlled by the output buffer status. A 'sliding window' is used, the blocks within the window being classified and coded, and D calculated based on these blocks and the current level of output buffer content. The next blocks are classified and coded using the calculated value of D, the blocks move sequentially past the window and the process is repeated. Changes in D are therefore made by the feedback system to maintain the overall average data rate. The two systems are considered to produce almost equivalent results, both subjectively and in terms of calculated mean square error.

The conjecture advanced earlier, in connection with the scheme of Reader, that improved performance is obtainable by making separate coding provision for relatively few, highly detailed blocks is borne out by H. Jones (1976), who found a significant subjective improvement with an image of moderate detail by processing only 0.6% of the total number of sub-blocks having the highest level of activity in this way. His scheme is part of a moving image transmission system, and so only the 'static' data compressor is relevant to the present discussion. The design uses a 4×4 Hadamard transform and three bit assignment modes, intended for high, medium and low correlation data blocks (i.e., a small, moderate or wide spread of significant transform domain coefficients, respectively). The two thresholds are set, not by the usual average block statistics (variance or coefficient magnitude), but by setting defined limits upon the magnitudes of various low-sequency coefficients. The spread of adaptivity is indicated by the fact that, for the image of lowest detail tested, the relative percentage occupancy of the highest and lowest correlation modes was 84 : 4, and for the image of highest detail 27 : 40. Data rate is maintained constant by simply reallocating a fixed total number of bits per block in accordance with the three mode bit allocation patterns.

In Chapter 3 it was suggested that, on theoretical grounds at least, the Haar transform performed poorly in comparison with other (Hadamard, cosine, Fourier, etc.) transforms, and that its only virtue lay in its extreme ease of implementation. Since, however, it is contended in the present chapter that adaptive coefficient processing can compensate for such deficiencies in performance, it is perhaps not surprising to find the fast two-dimensional Haar transform used in a practical design by Reis *et al.* (1976) for the transmission of RPV (remotely piloted vehicle) data. Again we are only concerned, for the moment, with the adaptive techniques employed. The image data is formatted into 8 vertical 'stripes', 240 elements deep and 32 elements wide, and a total of 30 16 × 16 transforms is thus needed per stripe. The adaptive coding process is a combination of zonal and threshold coding, in which a fixed number of low-order coefficients is always sent in each block, whilst other coefficients are tested against a threshold and only those exceeding it retained. The threshold for a given data stripe is that for the previous stripe plus a correction term which is a function of buffer content, the object being to maintain a content of 50% at the end of a stripe.

By 1977, adaptive image coding techniques (of all types, not exclusively transform) had reached a considerable degree of sophistication and a useful summary and review to that date is provided by Habibi (1977), who sets adaptive transform coding in the context of alternative schemes.

5.1.2.1.5   *Singular value decomposition and the discrete linear basis*

It is appropriate at this point to make brief reference to two transform techniques which lay rather to the side of the main trend of coder development in the 1970s. The first is singular value decomposition (SVD), which was referred to in Chapter 3 as being, in fact, the most efficient processing method, resulting in least square error on an image-by-image or block-by-block basis. This performance is not achieved without some complexity of implementation, however, and it has remained a technique investigated by few workers. In principle, to code an image or block of dimension $N \times N$, K (hopefully $\ll N$) singular values of significant magnitudes, and the pairs of singular vectors of length N must be transmitted, and attention has been directed towards doing this in the most efficient way. In general, the number of values representing an image block is $(2N + 1)K$, compared with N^2 for a conventional transform operation before coefficient deletion. Andrews and Patterson (1976c) point out that the process is inherently adaptive since decomposition is carried out on a block-by-block basis. If singular values are ordered by magnitude, significant components are always coded efficiently (in fact, the values typically have a very large dynamic range and require variable length coding). The singular values and vectors may then be coded by pulse code modulation (PCM) (or DPCM) with a linear quantiser for the former, and an optimum non-uniform (Max) quantiser for the latter. Another approach is to group together image sub-blocks with the same degree of detail, i.e., having similar singular values and vectors. For 16 × 16 sub-block coding, an overall rate of 1.5 bits/element resulted in a mean square error of approximately 1% with a detailed input image when the first four eigen-images are retained.

Garguir (1979) reports an adaptive SVD coding system in which the number of retained singular images is made a function of block activity by comparing the error produced by omitting an increasing number of singular images with a predetermined threshold. The total adaptive threshold over-head requirement is about 1 % of the data transmitted for a 256 × 256 image and 16 × 16 block decomposition. He concludes that the method is slightly better than a similar DCT scheme, and that the reconstruction time is much lower than for the latter approach. On the other hand Murphy (1981) compared the two-dimensional DCT with singular value decomposition in a class adaptive coding scheme using various one-dimensional (conventional) transforms to reduce the data rate necessary for the singular vectors. He found that the DCT performed best, with a mean square error of approxi-mately 0.5 % at a data rate of about 1 bit/element. The best SVD algorithm had a mean square error of twice this figure at the same rate. It was concluded that the necessity of coding the singular vectors (albeit by a variety of separate efficient techniques) cannot be compensated for by the gain in performance achieved by the use of the SVD and, as has been pointed out elsewhere in this volume, it is effective processing of the coefficients, rather than minor differences in transform efficiency, which determines the overall system quality. The second alternative approach to the use of more well-known transforms was made by Haralick and Shanmugam (1974) who employed the discrete linear basis (DLB) over a block size of 4 × 4, in conjunction with predictive coding, to process 64 × 64 6-bit images at data rates between 0.8 and 1.75 bits/element. Comparison with the K-L and Hadamard transforms was made, with the performance of the DLB being fairly close to that of the KLT, and that of both much better than that of the WHT. Griswold and Haralick (1976) have compared the performance of various transforms at rates of 1, 0.75 and 0.5 bit/element using 16 × 16 sub-blocks over a 6-bit 512 × 512 image. The DLB was found to have a performance lying between those of the slant and discrete cosine transforms and to produce good image quality at the lowest of the three rates.

5.1.2.1.6.   *Combining zonal and threshold sampling*

An interesting combination of zonal sampling (retaining those coefficients within a low-sequency, maximum variance zone) and threshold sampling (retaining those coefficients, wherever they may occur within a block, that exceed a predetermined or adaptively set threshold, necessitating, of course, suitable addressing information) is reported by Narasimhan *et al.* (1977). Using various transforms and a block size of 16 × 16, they progressively vary the method used, from 100% threshold to 100% zonal sampling. As the selection method is varied from the former to the latter, the mean square error increases relatively slowly until a 50%/50% combination is reached, after which it increases sharply to the figure for purely zonal sampling. For an input image of fairly low activity and the DCT, the corresponding figures are, at an output rate of 1 bit/element, 0.357, 0.398 and 0.845%, respectively.

Similar ratios hold for other transforms. These results show the benefit of using at least some threshold sampling in a transform coefficient block, even with an image of low activity, for which most high-magnitude coefficients naturally cluster into the low-sequence region in any case.

5.1.2.1.7.   'One-pass' schemes and block activity measures

An adaptive scheme such as that of Chen and Smith requires two 'passes' over the image, and thus incurs a one frame delay—whilst the 'present' frame is having its statistics measured for classification, etc., the previous one is actually being transmitted. The 16×16 scheme of Gonsalves et al, (1978) requires only one pass for the implementation of their adaptive technique. A new bit map is derived for each block, based upon an overall preset bit rate modified by an estimated coefficient variance. The latter is derived from the power spectral density representation of a separable first-order Markov model for the image correlation. For each block two parameters need to be sent as overhead data, the block AC energy and a factor defining the ratio of horizontal and vertical data correlation coefficients. Deviation of the latter ratio from unity allows the bit allocation map to be skewed in the direction of higher AC coefficient energy. Max quantisation is employed, and the scheme is compared with a simple threshold coding approach which retains a predetermined fraction of the total number of coefficients (together with addresses) which are each coded with 8 bits. Overall differences were not found to be significant at approximately 1–1.5 bits/element. The scheme reported by Hein and Jones (1979) is very similar to that of Jones described earlier, and again is a component part of an interframe system for coding moving images. This time an 8×8 WHT is used and five coefficient threshold maps determine the application of one of six bit allocations to the block to be coded. For the lowest five allocations the average block rates vary from 0.86 to 4.73 bits/element, whilst blocks of highest activity are allocated a full 8 bits per coefficient (see earlier comments regarding designs of Jones and Reader).

Up to this point, the majority of schemes discussed have employed block 'activity' measures calculated over the whole extent of any sub-block (the methods of Jones and Hein and Jones being notable exceptions). This method naturally does not represent accurately the detailed activity properties of the sub-block, since many patterns of luminance may have the same variance (thus 32 white, and 32 black, elements may be arranged in a variety of ways in an 8×8 block, ranging from one-half black, one-half white to a chess-board configuration; in each case the variance is the same but the transform coefficient distribution different). Mauersberger (1979b) has therefore suggested an alternative classification parameter based on the horizontal and vertical mean square differences, Δh, Δv between adjacent elements, thus, for example

$$\Delta h = \frac{1}{N(N-1)} \sum_{i=1}^{N} \sum_{j=1}^{N-1} (x_{i,j} - x_{i,j+1})^2 \qquad (5.3)$$

where i and j, respectively, are the row and column indices of elements in an $N \times N$ block. Differences in horizontal and vertical block structure are therefore acknowledged in this approach.

5.1.2.1.8 *Channel rate control*

Tescher (1979) discusses in comprehensive fashion his earlier work in conjunction with Cox on buffering requirements to allow variable rate coders to operate over fixed rate channels. He sets his review in the context of rate control, pointing out that it is not specifically related to transform coding [note that his Figs. 4.4 and 4.8 derive, in fact, from a paper on variable rate DPCM (Tescher and Cox, 1977) and are therein correctly captioned, which is not the case in the later reference]. In contrast to the measured results of Cox and Tescher (see the preceding) which indicate that, in terms of visual quality and mean square error there is little to choose between control based on the input (reformatting) buffer and on its output (rate equalisation) counterpart, Tescher suggests that control in the latter way is a more efficient approach for various reasons, including reduction in quality variations between different image regions, better memory utilisation (the rate equalising buffer has only to store the compressed data) and the fact that buffer control depends on previously transmitted data, thus requiring no overhead information to be transmitted to the receiver. His paper is well worth reading for its individual approach to what otherwise often tend to be somewhat entrenched attitudes with regard to the whole subject.

5.1.2.1.9 *Coefficient energy estimation*

Wong (1980) and Wong and Steele (1981) have carried out an extensive series of experiments using the 16×16 DCT and intended to establish methods of coefficient variance estimation to avoid the necessity of transmitting excessive overhead information. Initially employing a non-adaptive scheme they observed that the relationship between the logarithm of the variance of coefficient (m,n), $\sigma_{m,n}^2$, and of distance along the first row, first column and the diagonal of the coefficient array is approximately linear, at least for lower-order coefficients, and on this basis propose a model for the two-dimensional energy profile in the transform domain. Only the parameters defining the model need then be transmitted, instead of each individual coefficient variance. In fact their results show that, even if the latter course is taken, and the code words representing the variance values are error protected, uncertainties in the derivation of the energy estimate from the model cause the performance of the estimation scheme to be worse by about 0.1 bit/element at a rate of approximately 1 bit/element. Since the image they use is one with high correlation, i.e., good energy compaction into relatively few low-order coefficients and a rapid fall-off thereafter, this result must be considered disappointing, since the performance is likely to be worse still for more active images. Their scheme is subsequently made adaptive, by estimating, row by row, the energy of a given coefficient from the energies of several of its neighbours. This estimate is compared with a threshold and, if it falls below that value, that coefficient and all succeeding coefficients in the same row are deleted. Energies in the first row and column are estimated to begin with (the four lowest-order coefficients always being transmitted in order to start the coefficient selection process), and that of any arbitrary coefficient (m, n) is estimated as the average of the energies of coefficients $(m, n - 1)$, $(m - 1, n)$, $(m - 1, n - 1)$, i.e., the nearest three coefficients to have been estimated previously. The adaptive scheme produces the characteristic reduction in rate of something like 0.5 bit/element to a figure of 0.5–0.6 bit/ element, and its application together with that of the energy distribution model results in a level of performance which is about 0.3 bit/element better than that of the equivalent system in which error-protected coefficient variances are transmitted, instead of energy model parameters.

In employing different energy estimation schemes for bit assignment and for adaptive coefficient selection the preceding scheme is somewhat out of the ordinary, and when the method is compared with a more conventional approach in which the same energy estimation based upon knowledge of the first four coefficients is used for bit allocation also (this type of scheme has a 'built-in' coefficient selection mechanism, in that coefficients with less than a predetermined energy are automatically assigned zero bits), the results of the latter approach are about 15% better. In addition, if energy estimation is carried out at both coder and decoder based on previously quantised coefficient amplitudes, no transmission of overhead information is necessary. It remains to be seen, however, whether estimation schemes can be refined to the point where they can give reliable results with input data of widely varying degrees of activity.

5.1.2.1.10   *Adaptive quantiser selection, and threshold sampling re-examined*

Guglielmo *et al.* (1982) have investigated two different adaptive coding schemes, the first having a fixed bit assignment and eight sets of quantisers derived from non-adaptive counterparts (designed in the conventional way to minimise mean square error) by multiplying all decision and reconstruction levels by a scale factor varying from 0.05 to 64. The particular quantiser set used is selected to minimise the reconstruction error for each block, necessitation a small overhead of 3 bits/block. The second approach uses adaptive bit allocation, together with the scaled quantiser sets, with predetermined allowable block distortion and maximum/minimum total bit allocation. Both systems have a level of performance which is distinctly better than that of a non-adaptive approach employing a fixed quantisation/bit allocation strategy.

Historically, one of the first adaptive techniques to be implemented was threshold sampling, in which only those coefficients with amplitudes above a predetermined threshold are retained for subsequent quantisation and coding. Intuitively this should be the best of the simple approaches, but it has the disadvantage that address information is necessary for the location of significant coefficients, and therefore other techniques have usually been preferred. In a recent application of the method Kekre and Aleem (1983) have processed chest X-ray images, 128 × 128 elements in extent, and quantised to 16 levels. An eighth-order fast DCT is performed and adaptive amplitude bounds established, based on the input data and the properties of the DCT basis matrix, which are used for coefficient normalisation prior to linear quantisation. The authors report a normalised mean-square-error figure of 0.85% at a rate of 1 bit/element together with satisfactory image quality. Threshold coding has also been used by Turkington (1983) to code component colour images using the 8 × 8 DCT. In his scheme two zones are established, in the low- and high-sequency regions of the transform coefficient array, and thresholds set according to the visibility of image impairments. Coefficients in the two regions are quantised with 4- and 2-bit uniform Laplacian quantisers, respectively, and three AC coefficients of lowest order are allocated 6 bits each. Address information is efficiently encoded using a diagonal scanning and run-length coding technique. The overall rate required for a set of eight colour images to produce very good subjective quality lies between 1 and 3 bits/element. Threshold coding is also used in the design of Chen and Pratt (1984), which has the advantage that only a single pass over the image is necessary. Those coefficients greater than the threshold value first have the latter subtracted and are then scaled by a parameter dependent upon the status of the coder output buffer and the input data rate. Address information is retained by run-length coding along the diagonal scanning path of Fig. 5.3. Excellent reconstruction of colour images at an overall rate of 0.4 bit/element is reported, the chrominance signals being subsampled by a factor of 4 : 1 both horizontally and vertically prior to coding.

5.1.3 Hybrid coding

As will become apparent in Chapter 7 in the consideration of the complexity of implementation of transform coding schemes, one disadvantage of the technique, which has only relatively recently been mitigated by advances in the speed and processing power of microelectronic devices, is the computational load which it places upon the operating system, even when fast algorithms are employed. This problem is particularly severe, of course, where moving images are concerned, but it also exists, albeit to a lesser degree, in the case of two-dimensional transforms, and any means of reducing the volume of computation without compromising the efficiency of the technique is welcome. In order to describe the system of hybrid image processing it is initially necessary to return briefly to general image coding considerations in order to introduce the widely studied alternative method of data compression—predictive coding. (The technique is usually referred to as differential pulse code modulation—DPCM, but the former terminology is both more accurate and a better description of the nature of the process.) Predictive coding also operates efficiently when the data source has a high degree of inter-element correlation and neither approach, therefore, is necessarily restricted to image coding applications only. It has, however, found wide application in the video area, in both one- and two-dimensional forms, as well as in conjunction with transform processing (as is to be described here) and it has the advantage that it is considerably simpler than the latter scheme to implement. It can be shown (Habibi and Herschel, 1974) that the two approaches are mathematically related, although this feature is not relevant to the present discussion. Before examining the 'hybrid' coding schemes that have been proposed over the past decade, we shall first examine the basic theoretical foundations of predictive coding [good introductions to the method, described in more detail than is either possible, or necessary, here, can be found in O'Neal (1966) and Musmann (1979)].

In essence, the scheme is far more straightforward than transform coding. Observation of any typical scene shows immediately that much of the image is made up of areas of reasonably constant luminance, separated by discontinuities in the form of the edges of the various objects within the observer's field of view. When sequentially scanned and sampled, therefore, the members of the resulting train of data elements will, on average, be very similar in amplitude for much of the time, with occasional large positive or negative changes when edge detail is traversed. In its simplest form a predictive coding system uses the value of the previous element in the sequence as a prediction for that of the present one. The difference between the two will, on average, be small and that difference signal is quantised, coded and transmitted or stored. Of course, where the previous and present elements are on opposite sides of a luminance boundary the difference will be large, and its magnitude may approach the maximum data amplitude. In the context of image data processing, then, we have exchanged a signal which has, typically, a more or less uniform distribution (see the entropy values for Image 1 given in Chapter 2) and a permissible amplitude range of $0 \to x_{max}$ (image data is always non-negative) for a signal with a high probability of being small, and a low (but finite) probability of reaching an extreme value of $\pm x_{max}$. Such a highly peaked distribution will have a significantly reduced entropy (perhaps by as much as 3 bits/element) and a correspondingly reduced variance, resulting in a smaller transmission or storage requirement. At the decoder, the prediction (now generated within the decoder) is added to the error signal to regenerate the original data element. As far as the combination of this technique with transform processing is concerned, a one-dimensional transform carried out along the rows of the image, for example, results in a set of coefficients whose amplitudes correspond with the basis vector content for the original data vector in the usual way. We now assume that the picture detail is similar on successive image lines, and the members of the set of transform coefficients will therefore be alike (from line to line) also. This high degree of correlation, now between transform coefficients, rather than data elements, is reduced by the application of the predictive process in the column direction. In fact, predictive processing of all coefficient sequences is not worthwhile, although it usually seems to be carried out regardless (Clarke, 1984b). The reason is that whilst slowly varying image detail in the horizontal direction (corresponding, approximately at least, to the low-sequency coefficients) generally varies slowly in the vertical direction also, and so makes the prediction process efficient, this is not true of rapidly varying horizontal detail, which contributes to the magnitudes of the high-order coefficients. These vary quite sharply from line to line, therefore, and quite often the variance of the difference can be larger than that of the original coefficient sequences. It is better, therefore, to confine the predictive operation to the large-amplitude, highly correlated lower-sequency coefficients, where, in any case, the majority of the signal energy lies. The hybrid system thus consists of a transform operation of length N, say, followed by application of a set of at most N predictive coding stages, one to each coefficient, and subsequent coding of the difference (error) signal.

We now carry out a simple analysis of the predictive process before examining its application, in conjunction with transform coding, to hybrid image processing. Consider a sequence of data elements (or, in the present context, transform coefficients of a given order) $\ldots, x_2, x_1, x_0$ of variance σ^2 and known inter-element covariance r_{ij}. (Note that the sequence is assumed to be stationary and thus that $r_{00} = r_{11} = r_{22} = \cdots = \sigma^2$. The inter-element correlation coefficients are then $\rho_{ij} = r_{ij}/\sigma^2$.) We now attempt to predict the value of the present element, x_0, by using a weighted sum of previously observed values; see Fig. 5.7

$$\hat{x}_0 = a_1 x_1 + a_2 x_2 + \cdots + a_n x_n = \sum_{i=1}^{n} a_i x_i \qquad (5.4)$$

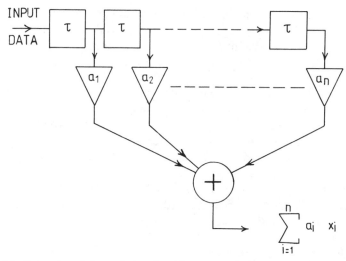

FIG. 5.7. Generation of the prediction signal from successive previous elements for the one-dimensional case. Here, a_i are weighting factors and τ is the element delay.

where increasing subscript value represents increasing distance into the 'past history' of the sample sequence, and $\hat{x}_0$ represents the prediction. The error signal

$$e_0 = x_0 - \hat{x}_0 \tag{5.5}$$

will subsequently be quantised and coded for transmission or storage. The various weighting coefficients $a_1, a_2, \ldots, a_n$ are now optimised in order to minimise the mean square error (or error signal variance)

$$\sigma_e^2 = E(e_0^2) = E((x_0 - \hat{x}_0)^2)$$

$$= E\left(\left(x_0 - \sum_{i=1}^{n} a_i x_i\right)^2\right) \tag{5.6}$$

The minimisation process results in n solutions of the equations

$$\frac{\partial \sigma_e^2}{\partial a_i} = 0 \qquad i = 1 \rightarrow n \tag{5.7}$$

i.e.,

$$-2E\left(\left(x_0 - \sum_{i=1}^{n} a_i x_i\right) x_i\right) = 0$$

or

$$E((x_0 - \hat{x}_0)x_i) = 0 \qquad i = 1 \rightarrow n \tag{5.8}$$

The value of σ_e^2 is given by Eq. (5.6)

$$\sigma_e^2 = E((x_0 - \hat{x}_0)(x_0 - \hat{x}_0))$$
$$= E(x_0(x_0 - \hat{x}_0) - \hat{x}_0(x_0 - \hat{x}_0)) \tag{5.9}$$

From Eq. (5.8) the second term is zero when all of the a_i are optimum, and therefore the minimum error signal variance is

$$\sigma_{e_{\min}}^2 = E(x_0(x_0 - \hat{x}_0)) \tag{5.10}$$

Knowledge of the various r_{ij} [i.e., $E(x_i x_j)$] enables the minimisation to be effected, i.e.,

$$E((x_0 - \hat{x}_0)x_i) = E((x_0 - a_1 x_1 - a_2 x_2 - \cdots - a_n x_n)x_i) = 0$$

or

$$r_{01} = a_1 r_{1i} + a_2 r_{2i} + \cdots + a_n r_{ni} \qquad i = 1 \to n \tag{5.11}$$

and the minimum error variance to be calculated,

$$\sigma_{e_{\min}}^2 = E(x_0(x_0 - a_1 x_1 - a_2 x_2 - \cdots - a_n x_n))$$
$$= \sigma^2 - \sum_{i=1}^{n} a_i r_{0i} \tag{5.12}$$

Hybrid coding schemes almost invariably confine the predictive step to the use of the previous element only, in which case the simple result is

$$r_{01} = a_1 r_{11} \qquad \text{or} \qquad a_1 = r_{01}/\sigma^2 = \rho \tag{5.13}$$

and

$$\sigma_{e_{\min}}^2 = \sigma^2 - a_1 r_{01} = \sigma^2 - (r_{01}^2/\sigma^2) = \sigma^2(1 - \rho^2) \tag{5.14}$$

where ρ is the adjacent element (one-step) correlation coefficient.

It can be seen that this result is intuitively correct for extreme values of ρ. If $\rho = 0$ there is no correlation between the elements of the data sequence and a knowledge of the amplitude of the previous element is of no use, on average, in trying to predict that of the present one. If $\rho = 1$ all element values are the same and it is not necessary to transmit any signal at all on an element-by-element basis; an initial code word specifying the actual element value will represent a vanishingly small amount of total transmission requirement as the sequence progresses.

At the decoder the received error signal is added to the predicted value to yield the output signal

$$x_0 = e_0 + \hat{x}_0 \tag{5.15}$$

In practice, of course, the received signal is not e_0 in the form derived in the preceding treatment, but its counterpart after quantisation, i.e., containing added quantisation error q_0, and the decoder predictor therefore operates on previously reconstructed samples which are in error by this quantity. Since it is desirable that the predictors in both coder and decoder perform identical operations, the coder takes on a rather more complex form than seems at first sight necessary. Specifically, this requirement brings the quantiser into the feedback loop, and thus it is only an approximation to optimise the prediction process whilst neglecting the presence of the quantiser (Musmann, 1979). Diagrams of the coder and decoder structure are given in Fig. 5.8 together with the various signal relationships.

Before considering the application of the predictive process in transform image coding systems, one or two general remarks on the method are in order. The first is that the use of the technique in conjunction with the transform process is a quite specific and specialised example of its employment. In its more general use in image coding in its own right the prediction

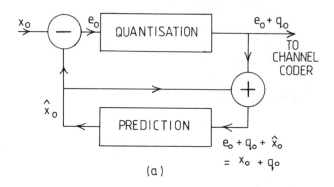

(a)

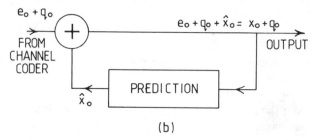

(b)

Fig. 5.8. Predictive coding scheme. (a) Coder and (b) decoder.

of the present sample value will be made from several previous samples, both on the same line (necessitating storage intervals of up to several element separations) and on previous line(s) (necessitating storage over at least one complete line interval). In the case of three-dimensional processing, prediction may take place between consecutive image frames also, if a frame delay is available. In the vast majority of intraframe coding applications the prediction is limited to the single equivalent element on the previous line (i.e., the same transform coefficient in the block vertically above the present one). In fact this procedure is almost optimum, the results of Wang and Jain (1979) demonstrating that the use of more than one previous coefficient for prediction produces only a very small reduction in the variance of the error sequence. The second point is that the method is extremely simple in comparison with the transform operation. Fewer multiplications are needed, and storage requirements are simplified also. A more general comparison based upon performance for a given bit rate (made subsequently in this chapter) and behaviour in the presence of transmission errors (see Chapter 8) will, however, redress the balance somewhat.

Finally, it useful to summarise briefly the ways in which the transform and predictive techniques may be combined. The most common combination is one-dimensional transformation using a block length of, say, 16, followed by previous element (coefficient) predictive coding in the mutually orthogonal direction [it is also possible to carry out the predictive step first and then transform blocks of prediction error samples—this approach, however, requires more complex implementation and has only been used infrequently (see Essman et al., 1976; Ericsson, 1983)]. In interframe processing, two-dimensional transform coding may be followed by predictive coding carried out in the temporal direction, necessitating a frame delay to generate the present sample prediction (see subsection 5.2.3). The only other alternative is to use two-dimensional transformation and predict between transform blocks on an intraframe basis. Unless the transform block size is very small, this method is not effective because of the reduced inter-coefficient correlation between neighbouring blocks.

5.1.3.1 Intraframe hybrid techniques

In terms of coding within a single image frame using hybrid techniques, the obvious method, mentioned at the end of the last section, is to employ a one-dimensional transform in the horizontal direction (processing a line, or more usually part of a line, at a time), followed by the application of the predictive operation in the vertical direction to the columns of transform coefficients; see Fig. 5.9. In principle, each vertical coefficient sequence will have a different value of correlation and of variance, and so will not only require its own specific values of prediction coefficient but a separate quantiser for the

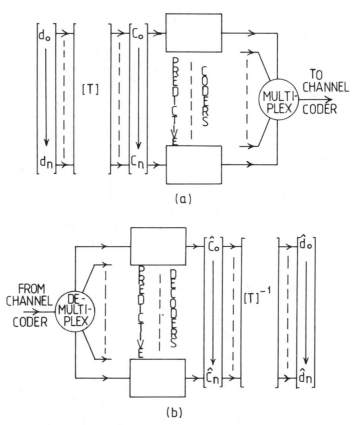

FIG. 5.9. Hybrid intraframe coding scheme. (a) Coder and (b) decoder. Here, $d_0, \ldots, d_n$ are elements of a one-dimensional data vector; $[T]$ is the transform; $C_0, \ldots, C_n$ the members of a one-dimensional coefficient vector; $\hat{C}_0, \ldots, \hat{C}_n$ the one-dimensional coefficient vector after predictive coding, transmission or storage and predictive decoding; $[T]^{-1}$ the inverse transform and, $\hat{d}_0, \ldots, \hat{d}_n$ the reconstructed data vector.

difference sequence generated. In fact, assumptions regarding the pdf of the difference sequences which, as in the case of predictive coding in its own right, are taken to be Laplacian for all sequences, including that generated by the vertical succession of DC coefficients (note the difference here compared with conventional transform coding) together with suitable scaling, allow the same quantiser to be used for most coefficients, and separate predictor optimisation is a nicety which is not, in these circumstances, justified. Should the transmission or storage medium result in errors in the coded difference signal, the selection of the prediction coefficient will be mainly influenced by the latter, rather than by a desire to minimise the difference sequence variance. The influence of such errors on coding system performance is considered in more detail in Chapter 8.

An alternative approach, which has been used occasionally, is to divide the image into small blocks, and then either carry out a standard two-dimensional transform operation, or re-order the data into a one-dimensional vector and carry out a one-dimensional transform, following which a predictive coding operation is performed on the coefficient sequences which result. Intuitively this should produce poorer results, as mentioned previously, since the correlation between coefficients is likely to be lower than that obtaining when the coefficients result from sequential one-dimensional transformation of successive lines (or parts of lines) of the data. Examples of both approaches are detailed in the following. It is worth mentioning here that although intraframe coding implies that the processing steps are carried out within a single image frame, this does not rule out its use as a technique for the coding and transmission of moving image sequences, and it has frequently been applied, together with frame rate reduction techniques, to the implementation of image communication schemes in hardware form, for example in RPV systems.

5.1.3.1.1 *Basic hybrid coding schemes*

Both of the basic approaches to hybrid coding are described by Habibi (1974). His scheme starts with a 6-bit 256×256 image which is subdivided into a collection of 16 element vectors either line by line (16 vectors per line giving 16 columns of 256 vectors per column for predictive processing) or as reordered 4×4 blocks, in which case a column of the image 256 lines deep by four elements wide yields a set of 64 16-element vectors. A variety of transforms is used and their relative efficiency in this application corresponds, naturally enough, with that in more conventional transform coding approaches detailed elsewhere in this volume. Employing an assumed first-order separable Markov model for image covariance with $\rho_h = 0.947$, $\rho_v = 0.880$ and single element prediction combined with conventional bit allocation to the Laplacian distributed error signal, results are found to be similar for the two schemes, with the one-dimensional approach having a slight advantage. As far as variations in block size are concerned. the one-dimensional scheme shows no change in performance once a vector of length 8 is reached, and for the two-dimensional method this condition obtains at a block size of 8×8. With a pure transform coding scheme we would expect a gradual, if not very significant, increase in performance with increase in block size (for both one- and two-dimensional coding), but in the case of hybrid coding the increase in transform efficiency with larger block sizes is offset by the fact that the predictive coder has a poorer performance, since it becomes increasingly unlikely that similarities between adjacent vectors (and thus between transform coefficients on neighbouring lines) will be maintained. Furthermore, no noticeable performance degradation results if all predictor coefficients are set, arbitrarily, to a value of 0.9. The one-dimensional scheme using the WHT has a better performance than a two-dimensional pure WHT system, and, in comparison with a purely predictive coding approach using prediction from three previous elements, the performance of the hybrid scheme is better at all bit rates. A similar two-dimensional 4 × 4 system is used by Haralick and Shanmugam (1974) applied to an ensemble of 64 × 64 element 6-bit images. In this case bits are assigned as a function of the coefficient variances, rather than of the variances of the difference sequences, and only the four most significant components out of the total of 16 are retained. A real-time moving image application is proposed by Means et al. (1974, 1975) using a 100 × 100 element format and a frame rate of $10 \, \text{s}^{-1}$, and is intended to produce a signal to noise rate ratio (SNR) of 30 dB at an average rate of 1 bit/element. An alternative system employs a vidicon camera and CCD/DCT implementation operating at a rate of 4.8 MHz, using a block size of 32. In a simulation experiment, no significant difference was found between two-dimensional transformation using the DCT and a combination of that transform with predictive coding. Further details of implementation are given by Whitehouse et al. (1975). The relaxation in computational requirement due to the use of hybrid schemes in place of the more conventional two-dimensional transform approaches has brought real-time video compression into the realm of microprocessor applications, and such a scheme is described by Murray (1977). The system is much the same as the Means/Whitehouse one described earlier, in which 32 element strips of a 256 × 256 image are processed, one per field, using a hybrid DCT scheme. An updated version of the second of the Means/Whitehouse systems is described by Whitehouse et al. (1977), with selectable rates per element between 0.4 and 3.2 and a frame rate of $7.5 \, \text{s}^{-1}$. Strips 32-elements wide are sequentially processed, one per field, using a 32-element DCT/single previous element predictive system and, since the image is 256 elements wide, eight input fields produce one processed field of dimension 256 × 262.5. The DCT coefficients are first scaled to equalise their variances before the predictive step is applied. This is carried out by multiplication by 1 for the DC, and by $k + 2$ for the AC, coefficients, where k is the coefficient order. Each difference signal is quantised to an accuracy of 6 bits, and the number of bits actually transmitted then depends on the overall desired data rate, with a maximum allocation of 5 to any one coefficient, At a data rate of 400 kbits/s (0.8 bit/element), a mean square error of 1.12 % is quoted for a reasonably detailed input image. The scheme of Dutta and Millman (1980) is similar, using a 16-point DCT and scaling of the coefficients by $(k + 2)/2$, where k runs from 0 to 15.

5.1.3.1.2   *An alternative approach*
Another RPV application is described by Essman et al. (1976). In passing he considers the hybrid system in which one-dimensional predictive coding

precedes the application of the one-dimensional transform in the mutually perpendicular direction, and demonstrates that, under the assumption that the errors produced by the separate processes of coefficient truncation and quantisation are uncorrelated, the order in which the two processing steps are carried out is immaterial. However, the input to the predictor of the coder consists of the predictor output $\hat{x}_0$ plus the quantised error $e_0 + q_0$ (see Fig. 5.8a) and so, if the prediction step is carried out first, the quantised output from the transform process must be inverse transformed at the coder to provide this latter signal. The transform followed by prediction system is, therefore, to be preferred, on the grounds of lesser complexity of implementation. Using the same values of ρ_h and ρ_v as Habibi (1974), a similar separable two-dimensional covariance model, and the same bit allocation relation, the results of Essman *et al.* follow those of Habibi very closely indeed. It should be noted, however, that different definitions of SNR are used, Essman effectively using definition (2) and Habibi definition (3) (see Appendix 7). The difference between the two is the ratio of peak-to-peak to mean-square signal power, typically about 17 dB (O'Neal, 1966). Unfortunately, ready comparison of results is often obscured in this way by the use of varying numerical criteria of comparison. The hybrid scheme is optimised by minimising the total system mean square error (including the effects of channel errors, if present) with respect to the predictor coefficients. The results show that there is little to choose between the hybrid system, two-dimensional transform coding and two-dimensional predictive coding, with the latter technique slightly better at higher rates (4 bits/element) and pure transform coding better at the lowest rates (0.5 bit/element). As far as coding in the presence of an errorless channel is concerned, it is shown that there is hardly any advantage at all to be gained by optimising the predictor coefficients for the separate coefficient sequences, confirming the earlier result of Habibi.

In view of this result, it is somewhat curious that R. Jones (1976) goes to some lengths to develop an algorithm which will sequentially update the predictor coefficient values based upon a minimisation of average difference sequence power over a given block length. Unfortunately no numerical results are presented, but it is demonstrated that periodic retransmission of predictor coefficients does mitigate the problem of channel errors. A further analysis is presented by Jones and Mix (1978), but no comparison with non-optimised predictor values is made.

5.1.3.1.3   *Later developments*

In the context of the transmission of multispectral imagery from Landsat satellites Habibi and Hung (1977) report the application of a one-dimensional 16-element Hadamard transform/previous element predictive coding scheme in which a single time-shared predictor loop selects one of three different predictor coefficients ($\frac{15}{16}, \frac{3}{4}, \frac{1}{2}$) and one of five bit allocations (5, 3, 2, 1, 0) according to coefficient order, optimised over typical multispectral sources. For a 512 × 512 image at a compressed rate of 1.85 bits/element, it is found that feature classification accuracy is actually slightly better than for the original image, due to high-frequency noise reduction resulting from the low-pass nature of the compression operation.

The vast majority of intraframe hybrid coding schemes carry out a one-dimensional 16- or 32-element transform followed by previous element prediction in the orthogonal direction. A somewhat different line of approach is taken by Netravali et al. (1977), who consider methods for the adaptive and predictive coding of transform coefficients obtained by taking successive Hadamard transforms of 2 × 2 blocks. It is shown that a more accurate prediction for a particular coefficient in a given block is possible than is obtained by simply taking the value of the corresponding coefficient in the previous block. Thus, considering adjacent blocks, as in Fig. 5.10, the WHT coefficients for the present block (X) will be (ignoring the scale factor)

$$H_1 = a + b + c + d$$

$$[H] = \begin{bmatrix} H_1 & H_2 \\ H_3 & H_4 \end{bmatrix} \qquad \begin{aligned} H_2 &= a - b + c - d \\ H_3 &= a + b - c - d \end{aligned} \qquad (5.16)$$

$$H_4 = a - b - c + d$$

[note that Netravali's notation differs from that of Eq. (5.16), his H_2 represents the first vertical AC coefficient, H_3 the first horizontal and vertical AC coefficient, and H_4 the first horizontal coefficient], and corresponding coefficients H'_1, H'_2, H'_3, H'_4 will have been generated by transformation of the previous block. The prediction for H_1 is then taken to be (we neglect quantisation effects for simplicity)

$$\hat{H}_1 = H'_1 - (H'_2 + H_2)$$

$$= 2(b' + d') + b + d - (a + c) \qquad (5.17)$$

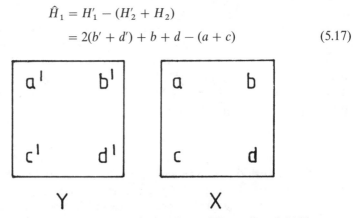

FIG. 5.10 Adjacent 2 × 2 data blocks in the scheme of Netravali et al. (1977).

and the resulting difference signal will be

$$e = H_1 - \hat{H}_1$$
$$= (a - b') + (c - d') + (a - b') + (c - d') \tag{5.18}$$

using H_1' alone as the estimate for H_1 results in

$$e' = H_1 - H_1'$$
$$= (a - b') + (c - d') + (b - a') + (d - c') \tag{5.19}$$

Now it is likely that $(b - a') + (d - c')$ will be greater than $(a - b') + (c - d')$ due to the greater relative separation of the elements concerned, and thus the prediction of Eq. (5.17) results in the lower average prediction error. Predictors for the other coefficients may be similarly developed and, of course, the adjacent block in the vertical direction may be used, if desired. These results illustrate a general principle to be observed in the application of any predictive technique, and that is that prediction should be made from the physically closest available elements previously processed, such that the correlation between them and the element whose value is to be predicted is as high as possible (in fact, this poses certain problems in the coding of composite colour television signals, due to the presence of the colour subcarrier, and this difficulty will be referred to again subsequently). This in turn explains why hybrid schemes involving two-dimensional intraframe transformation plus corresponding coefficient prediction are inefficient unless the block size is very small. In those cases a technique such as that just described will yield an improvement in performance. In the present instance a reduction of approximately 25% in the entropy of the difference signal is obtained for the improved predictor, and further advantage results if quantisation is made adaptive based upon block activity. For this purpose the greatest of the magnitudes of either the first horizontal (H_2) or vertical (H_3) AC coefficient is taken as an indication of local detail. It should be noted that, in this case, quantiser optimisation is carried out with respect to subjective criteria, and this procedure is discussed in more detail in Chapter 6.

In the previous section of this chapter, buffer control of adaptive two-dimensional coding schemes was discussed in the light of the work of Tescher *et al.* Habibi (1979, 1981) proposes a similar rate control strategy for adaptive hybrid coding, in which the buffer status is checked periodically. The coefficients generated by the transform stage are quantised before being predictively coded, and the accuracy to which this step is carried out is made to depend on buffer content. The system is thus adaptive in the sense that the data rate is constrained over a block size which is constant in the direction in which the one-dimensional transform is taken but which has a length which

depends on the time interval between buffer status checks, and, again, the
adaptivity is present to ensure a fixed output rate rather than to allocate
coding capacity according to image activity. In the present case the variable
rate coding arises from the entropy (Huffman) coding used to code the
discrete predictive difference signal. For this purpose both simple and block
coding schemes are proposed, and an advantage of some 3–4 dB in SNR at a
given rate compared with a non-adaptive hybrid technique is quoted.

5.1.3.1.4 *Hybrid coding at high data rates*

The successful application of data compression techniques to studio
quality television signals has long been a research goal, and an intraframe
hybrid scheme in this context is described by Kim and Rao (1979). The input
signal is a composite NTSC colour signal sampled at three times the colour
subcarrier frequency which, as a result of the presence of the subcarrier and of
conventional vertical interlace, has a correlation coefficient/element separation relation which shows a marked peak every third sample horizontally and
every other sample vertically. Two schemes are proposed, one-dimensional
Hadamard transformation horizontally followed by vertical predictive coding, and two-dimensional Hadamard transformation with a block size of
4×4 followed by interblock predictive processing of the transform coefficients, with both one- and two-dimensional block structures arranged to take
account of the spatial correlation relation. Standard bit allocation methods
are used based on transform domain variance mapping via a first-order
Markov image model. Over a variety of input material, image quality is
reported to be good at a rate of 4 bits/element. Unfortunately, since the
quoted formula for SNR is in error, the curves of SNR versus bit rate cannot
be relied on as a guide to the quantitative performance of the system. An
extension of the approach is described by Ploysongsang and Rao (1982) in
which the DCT replaces the WHT and inter-block (two-dimensional)
predictive coefficient decorrelation is now performed on an adaptive basis,
the previously processed neighbouring block either above, or to the left of, the
present one which has the closest average luminance (i.e., DC coefficient) to
the latter being used for prediction. It is found that, in this case, line-by-line
processing is markedly inferior to block processing, and this is assumed to be
due to the subcarrier/interlace correlation effects referred to previously. With
this form of processing, quality was unacceptable at rates below 3.5 bits/
element. With a modified block processing scheme, however, in which a
threshold applied to all prediction errors within a block determines whether
the block is active, and to be quantised and coded or inactive, in which case
reference in the processing to its inactivity and to the previous block used for
prediction is all that is necessary, better results were achieved, little image
degradation occurring with more than twice the degree of data compression.

Both of these schemes will be referred to again subsequently in the more specific context of colour signal coding.

5.1.3.1.5 *More complex techniques*

Roese (1979) reviews the topic and presents results which show that, with a zonal type of bit allocation, the performance of the typical one-dimensional transform, one-dimensional predictive coding scheme improves up to a block length of 16 for an overall rate of 1 bit/element. He also discusses an adaptive approach in which sub-block column (256 × 32) statistics are used to vary the bit assignment to the various difference signal sequences on a sub-block-by-sub-block basis, where the overall assignment to each sub-block remains the same. As the amount of image detail increases, the advantage of the adaptive scheme, in terms of normalised mean square error, decreases. Thus, for an image of moderate detail, the application of the adaptive approach reduces the error by approximately 50% at rates between 2 and 0.5 bit/element. The equivalent reduction for a more highly detailed image is about 10%. Obviously a reduction in sub-block size would be advantageous in this context, even at the cost of increased transmission overhead. An alternative is to use a classification technique (rather like the Chen and Smith approach in the case of two-dimensional transform coding) in which each vector to be transformed is allocated to one of four equal-probability classes on the basis of vector variance (Wang and Jain, 1979; Jain, 1981). For each class and coefficient index, the two necessary predictive coding parameters, the correlation coefficient and the difference sequence variance, are retained as 8-bit numbers. For a 16-element transform, the overhead requirement is therefore 16 × 4 × (8 + 8) bits for the parameters and 2 bits/vector to indicate the classification, i.e., 0.14 bit/element overall for a 256 × 256 image. A significant improvement in SNR can be achieved in this way (some 6–8 dB), but the scheme is complex, and a simplification can be made by assuming that the correlation coefficient for each predictive channel is the same for all classes, and that the variance parameter depends only upon the vector class variance and on a model of the unit variance prediction error. The results are then about 3 dB poorer than those of the optimum system. Here, as image detail increases the advantage of the adaptive scheme decreases, the vector variances become more similar, and overhead classification information is then transmitted to no effect. An alternative scheme is proposed which modifies the quantisation process in each channel according to an updated variance estimate; specifically, the error signal is normalised before quantisation by its updated standard deviation. In this case improvments of 2–4 dB are obtained for images of both low and fairly high detail. One further result of Wang and Jain is worth re-emphasising here, and that is that, at least for an image of low detail, using a predictor of order higher than one (i.e., using more than one previous element for prediction) results in a negligible improvement in performance.

5.1.3.1.6 *Predictor coefficient selection in a practical context*

The moving sequence transmission system of McWhirter *et al.* (1981) uses a conventional 16-element WHT combined with previous element prediction to code a 6-bit image 290 × 290 in extent. As has been mentioned previously, optimisation of the predictor coefficients is of little significance as far as system performance is concerned, and the effect of channel errors (see Chapter 8) influences the choice of value to a much larger degree. Here the value $\frac{7}{8}$ is selected. Non-uniform bit allocation with each component coded to the same accuracy is incorporated and average data rates of 1, 3 and 5 bits/element are available. It turns out that the same value of predictor coefficient is used in the predictive section of the video data compression scheme of Whiteman *et al.* (1981) and Chan and Whiteman (1983), who decide upon such a value on the basis of the average of the measured values for the low-sequency coefficients containing 95% of the total energy resulting from the use of a 16-element DCT on six typical input images. Optimum non-uniform quantisers are designed and a single quantiser used for all (pre-scaled) coefficient sequences assigned the same number of bits. The original image resolution is 8 bits, and overall rates of 2, 1 and 0.5 bit/element can be selected, greater degrees of compression being provided by such techniques as frame rate and resolution reduction. Thus, at 2 bits/element, using an input image of dimension 640 × 480, the frame rate is $7.5 \, \mathrm{s}^{-1}$, during which internal five parallel DCT processors operate four times upon two sequential 16-element wide input columns, generating four 160-element wide image strips which make up a full frame. At this value of compression the system data rate is 4.608 Mbits/s (the original rate, at 30 frames/s and 8 bits/element, being 73.728 Mbits/s). Actual frame rates are variable from $30 \, \mathrm{s}^{-1}$ over a range of 256:1, and the system produces an SNR of 32 dB, averaged over six test images, at an overall rate of 1 bit/element.

5.1.4 Two-component coding

It will be apparent to the reader that an efficient transform coding scheme depends for its operation on the similarity between low-order transform basis vectors and the detail present in the image sub-blocks. If such similarity exists, then relatively few coefficients will have large magnitudes, the majority of high-order coefficients may be deleted with little reconstructed image degradation, and satisfactory low-rate (high compression) coding results. If we consider, however, the structure of 'typical' images, it is soon appreciated that this is seldom the case. Images tend to consist of areas of relatively uniform luminance separated by abrupt transitions (objects against a background), and such sharp, high-magnitude changes result in upper-order coefficients of significant amplitudes, thus reducing the coding efficiency. As an attempt to overcome this problem, so-called 'two-component' coding has been investigated by several workers. In such a scheme, areas of relatively uniform (or slowly changing) luminance are approximated by straight-line segments whose properties can easily be coded with little channel capacity. The approximation is then subtracted from the actual luminance variation, to leave a residual signal of relatively small amplitude which (hopefully) may be coded efficiently by transform techniques. Thus Yan and Sakrison (1977) propose fitting such segments to an image on alternate lines (the intervening lines being similarly processed after the image detail has been suitably smoothed along the direction of substantial edges to eliminate line-to-line irregularities), on the basis of a limit placed upon the maximum error between segment and image luminance profile. The straight-line segment break points on the first line are run-length coded, as are the differences between those values and their equivalents on successive lines, rather than the actual values (in order to reduce the overall coding requirement). As is usual with the work of Sakrison, attention is paid to the properties of the human visual system (HVS), and the image is initially processed with a cube-root non-linearity (see Chapter 6) with a corresponding inverse operation at the decoder prior to reconstruction. Accurate coding of run length reflects the sensitivity of the viewer to the location of sharp luminance discontinuities. After subtraction of the piecewise linear approximation from the image field the residual signal is coded using a full-image (256 × 256) Fourier transform. At an overall rate of approximately 0.8 bit/element half of the coding capacity is used for each of the coding processes, and the reconstructed image quality is better than straightforward Fourier coding at the same rate, with (as might be expected) good reproduction of edge detail. A rate distortion analysis of the process is developed by Anastassiou and Sakrison (1979).

A further rationale for the approach is provided by Algazi and Ford (1980). Their work on filtering of high contrast images will be described in Chapter 6, and it suggests that low-pass filtering errors in image processing are most easily detectable at object boundaries. Thus any process (transform coding, for example) having a low-pass-like function will preferentially degrade edge detail and make a two-component technique desirable. The scheme of Garibotto and Micca (1981) uses such a model in an enhancement/restoration, as well as coding, context, in which the separation is carried out by non-linear, space variant filtering. Again, the response of the HVS is invoked as a justification of the procedure—the eye being sensitive to noise in the detail/texture component, whereas it is not noise, but rather low-pass filtering which degrades the background (i.e., luminance transition) signal.

Mitrakos and Constantinides (1983) propose an improvement of the basic two-component method in which the slowly varying edge signal is approximated by a polynomial, rather than straight-line, component (the latter is used experimentally). This signal is run-length coded without error, whilst the difference signal. which is of small magnitude and is assumed to have a Gaussian distribution, is coded using either the discrete cosine or Walsh–Hadamard transforms. To optimise the coding procedure dynamic programming is employed to achieve optimum separation of components such that the transmission rate is minimised for a given overall average distortion, and the operation of the algorithm is locally adaptive to variations in image structure.

5.1.5   Hierarchical transmission

Where moving images are concerned, a certain minimum system bandwidth is necessary in order that a satisfactory level of the illusion of motion be achieved, and will be a function of image size, resolution and frame rate. Where the transmission of still images is the objective, this criterion does not apply, and they may be conveyed to the recipient over channels of vanishingly small bandwidth provided that the viewer is prepared to wait for the result. Thus 'slow-scan' systems may be used (possibly employing predictive coding techniques) in which the image at the receiver is built up in just that way—slowly, line by line. The disadvantage of such an approach is that full resolution is available from the start of image display over only the first few lines (the rest of the image field remaining blank), and it may take minutes for a detailed region of the picture to appear, when it may subsequently be decided that (in a visual information provision service, for example) that particular image is not the one desired in any case. It would be very much more acceptable if the full image could initially be reconstructed at reduced resolution, with more and more detail being added with the passing of time, so that an 'accept/reject' decision could be made as soon as possible after the start of transmission. This is, of course, easily done in the case of transform coding schemes, since the higher the coefficient order, the greater degree of detail in the sub-block it represents. Such an approach is called 'hierarchical' transmission, and involves initial reconstruction of the image using the DC coefficients only, when it will appear to have a blockwise structure of regions of constant luminance. Obviously the smaller the blocksize the better the initial resolution but then more DC coefficients are needed to start the process. Transmission of higher-order coefficients allows the displayed resolution to improve with time, and the problem is now to decide upon the order in which these coefficients should be transmitted. Theoretically this is a formidable task since what we require at each step is transmission of the coefficient from the set of those remaining which results in the maximum increase in reconstructed image quality (it is possible, of course, that the determination of coefficient transmission order can be carried out off-line, when the image is first coded and stored on the data base, rather than at the actual time of transmission). Bypassing, for the purpose of the present argument, the matter of correlation of subjective quality with any numerical error measure, we might carry this out by searching for that coefficient which results in the greatest decrease in mean square error when added to those already transmitted. This should really be done on a block-by-block basis but, in practice, to reduce the search time, it can be carried out for a given coefficient added to the reconstruction of all blocks at the same time. Even this restricted approach might be abandoned in favour of the use of a simple predetermined scan path (perhaps along the reverse diagonals of the coefficient array, starting with coefficient (1, 2) or (2, 1) and working towards the lower right-hand corner, although it should be emphasised that there is no necessity for coefficient magnitudes to fall off monotonically along such a path, this just happens to be the case (approximately, at least) if the image is not highly detailed.

It is worth noting that this is not the only possible approach to hierarchical coding of images in a transform processing context. Yasuda *et al.* (1979) suggest dividing a 256 × 256 image into 8 × 8 sub-blocks and calculating the average luminance level of each block. Four such blocks are then coded using a 2 × 2 WHT and, if the reconstruction error is less than a predetermined threshold no further coding is carried out in that region. If not, the 8 × 8 regions are divided into four 4 × 4 sub-regions and the process is continued as necessary until coding is being performed on an element by element basis. Fairly good results at 1.5–2.0 bits/element are reported. A similar scheme is described by Bourbakis and Alexandridis (1982), and the specific application of the technique to the picture viewdata service of British Telecom (Prestel) is reported by Nicol *et al.* (1981).

5.1.6 Summary and comparison of intraframe techniques

In the previous subsections we have examined techniques for intraframe coding, i.e., coding on the basis of information contained within a single image frame. Whilst two-dimensional intraframe transform processing is more attractive from a conceptual point of view, interest in real-time image coding for RPV and surveillance applications has meant that, due to hardware processing constraints, systems combining a one-dimensional transform with mutually orthogonal predictive coding have received much attention in the past few years. The introduction of the latter step implies, of course, that the system has different properties from those of a pure two-dimensional transform process, particularly in connection with its sensitivity to transmission errors, which topic will receive more detailed attention later in this volume. For the present the techniques are compared on the basis of performance (nomalised mean square error and image quality) at various overall data rates, and reference is also made to pure predictive coding systems, which have the advantage of very simple implementation and minimal data storage requirements.

Habibi (1971) presents a comparison between transform coding and predictive approaches, in the latter case employing predictors of orders as high as 22 (i.e., up to 22 previous elements on the same or previous lines are included in forming the prediction of the present element). In this context, his results show that little is to be gained by increasing the order above a value of 3 or 4. In comparison with transform coding techniques, Habibi's optimised third-order predictive scheme, at a rate of 3 bits/element, surpasses the performance of two-dimensional K–L coding (with a block size of 16 × 16) to the extent of some 2 dB in SNR for a particular image. When the same system is used with a different image, however, the fall-off in performance is quite marked, whilst that for transform coding (both one- and two-dimensional) is not as great. This reduced sensitivity to image statistics in the case of transform processing is due, at least in part, to the assumption of a separable exponential correlation model on which the design of the system is based. Thus, the coding process is not matched optimally to the image to start with. One- and two- dimensional transform schemes differ in performance by approximately 3 dB, on average, in terms of SNR. On all other points of comparison, the predictive coding scheme is preferred, requiring only one line of delay or storage (the two-dimensional transform approach requiring, naturally, 16 lines), with easy implementation and low complexity, In this experiment none of the schemes is adaptive. Habibi (1974) later extends his comparison to hybrid transform coding and shows that one-dimensional K–L, WHT or Fourier transformation plus predictive coding is better in terms of SNR at all rates from 0.5 to 4 bits/element, and the relative improvement increases below about 1.75 bits/element. In this region two-dimensional WHT coding is better than third-order predictive coding and approaches the performance of the hybrid schemes as the data rate falls to 0.5 bit/element. In fact the more rapid relative degradation incurred by predic-tive coding methods when high levels of compression are required is a general feature of the technique. In addition, the visible effect of system errors is less objectionable in the case of pure transform coding than for hybrid processing, with predictive methods demonstrating the poorest performance in this sense.

The results of Essman et al. (1976) indicate that, subjectively, hybrid techniques are superior to two-dimensional transformation (with the excep-tion of the application of the KLT), at all rates above 0.25 bit/element, and that there is apparently a linear relation between subjective quality and the number of bits allocated overall per element which does not hold for the latter approach. Again, the adaptive/predictive Hadamard system of Netravali *et al.* (1977) which uses 2×2 blocks shows an advantage of approximately 1.25 bits/element, in terms of coefficient entropy, when compared with a non-adaptive two-dimensional predictive approach, for the production of excellent picture quality. The overall rate is about 1.8 bits/element. Gonsalves and Shea (1979) carried out an interesting experiment in which a block adaptive (16×16) DCT is combined with two-dimensional second-order predictive and entropy coding in order to restrict the appearance of significant numbers of large-magnitude errors. The difference signal generated by comparing the original image with a compressed and reconstructed version (i.e., transform coded at a rate of R_1 bit/element) is processed by the predictive algorithm at a rate R_2 and the result added to the transformed version of the image. In this way a total bit allocation $R = R_1 + R_2$ can be allotted to the transform system alone ($R_2 = 0$), the predictive system alone ($R_1 = 0$) or split between the two. For a total rate of 2 bits/element the results for either approach are almost identical. However, although rms errors tend to be similar as bits are preferentially allocated to one system or the other, the maximum error amplitudes are much smaller when the allocation favours the predictive technique, as shown in Table 5.7. Thus the superiority of the predictive approach at higher rates is demonstrated, whilst the results also show that, for a combined scheme, the transform method is more tolerant of low rates. In fact, it is reported that the difference in performance is not detectable when the images are subjectively assessed.

Habibi (1979, 1981) compares his adaptive hybrid coding strategy with an adaptive two-dimensional DCT system. Whilst adaptivity within the hybrid system produces an improvement of some 3–4 dB over a similar non-adaptive hybrid approach for a prespecified bit rate, his comparison bears out results demonstrated previously, i.e., that at higher rates (above 1 bit/element) the hybrid scheme is best, whilst the reverse is true if coding at lower rates is attempted.

TABLE 5.7. Relative maximum error of the scheme of Gonsalves and Shea (1979).[a]

Rate allocation DCT/predictive coding	Error amplitude
1.5/0.5	2.3
0.5/1.5	1.6
2.5/1.5	1.0
1.5/2.5	0.7
2.5/0.0	3.9
0.0/2.5	1.0

[a] Predictive coding alone at 2.5 bit/element = 1.0.

As a general overall summary of the properties of the three approaches the following conclusions may be drawn.

(a)   Two-dimensional transform coding requires the most complex implementation, is relatively insensitive to individual image statistics, has a reasonable performance in the presence of transmission or storage errors, needs a fair amount of storage and is the best system for very low data rates.

(b)   Predictive coding is simple, sensitive to data statistics, has a very poor error performance, needs little storage and produces better results at higher rates.

(c)   Hybrid coding has properties which are more or less the average of those of the two major approaches.

As a further, and no doubt gross oversimplification, it is possible to assert as earlier, that adaptive schemes, of whatever nature, have approximately double the performance (in terms of SNR) of similar, but non-adaptive, approaches.

5.2   Interframe coding

5.2.1   Introduction

Up to this point, we have been concerned with the coding of single, independent, images, consisting of an array usually, but not necessarily square, perhaps 256×256 or 512×512 elements in extent. A conventional two-dimensional transform operation will then process rectangular blocks of the image, or a one-dimensional transform/predictive hybrid scheme may process image strips maybe 16 or 32 elements wide and of length equal to the full height of the array, in the ways previously described. Both techniques can be applied to the coding of sequential frames of moving images and the second, particularly, has been used in the context of image transmission from RPVs. What distinguishes such methods of intraframe coding from those of interframe coding now to be described is that they take no account of the relationships which naturally exist between the separate frames of a moving image sequence, and which can be used within the coding process to make the transmission and/or storage of such sequences more efficient. There are, of course, well-known restrictions on the allowable time interval between successive frames of a moving sequence in order that the eye be persuaded of the illusion of continuous smooth motion, and this severely limits real-time processing techniques in terms of the allowable sophistication of adaptive classification and coding methods. In this regard predictive techniques are considerably easier to implement than transform processing, and this accounts for the popularity of the combination of the one-dimensional forms of both in intraframe hybrid coding of moving sequences, as described previously.

The fact remains, however, that it has long been realised that the correlation within sequences formed by taking the value of a given element at a fixed spatial location in successive frames may be just as great or, for restricted forms of motion, even greater, than that measured purely in the spatial domain within a given frame (in 'normal' image sequences, prolonged periods of rapid motion are relatively rare; Seyler, 1965). There is therefore a great temptation to use a correlation reducing procedure in the temporal direction as well as across the spatial plane to increase the overall efficiency of the coding process. It may be appropriate to mention here that the third dimension need not necessarily be time (although this is most usual, given the wide interest in the transmission of moving images), and could well be the path joining the 'same' spatial elements on successive images within a multispectral satellite picture. Although the same principles as those for the time domain apply, the situation is complicated by the fact that the inter-scan correlation behaviour is quite different from that of a moving image in the time domain, and also that there are relatively few spectral frames available for processing, which restricts the use of hybrid schemes (Habibi and Samulon, 1975).

The approaches which have actually been used for interframe transform coding are basically three in number. It has been pointed out earlier that the fundamental one-dimensional transform operation may readily be extended to two dimensions, and this is, of course, the usual form in which transform processing of still images is carried out, the horizontal and vertical operations reducing inter-element correlation in the same respective directions. A logical step, then, is to extend the operation to a further, mutually perpendicular, direction, and to carry out three-dimensional transform coding, the third stage of the process being a one-dimensional transform of the sequences formed by coefficients in the two-dimensional spectral domain having the same horizontal and vertical sequency indices. Since these coefficients are 'likely' to be similar, data compression in the third dimension results in exactly the same manner as for basic one-dimensional processing. This probable similarity of neighbouring coefficients along the third axial direction naturally prompts the application of an extended hybrid coding process, in which separate frames of an image sequence are coded by two-dimensional transform processing, and the coefficient sequences coded by predictive techniques in the third dimension in exactly the same way that one-dimensional coefficient sequences are processed predictively in the mutually perpendicular direction in intraframe hybrid coding. The third interframe coding method has its origins in a technique originally developed to reduce the data rate of moving sequences coded using conventional PCM. Called 'conditional replenishment', the scheme utilises a frame store at both transmitter and receiver. The first frame is transmitted normally to the receiver, and the next incoming frame compared element by element with the stored first frame at the transmitter to ascertain whether a significant element difference has occurred at the same spatial location between adjacent frames. If not, nothing is transmitted; if so, then the new value is sent to update the stored value at the appropriate location within the receiver store. In the present context, the scheme involves coding and transmitting to the receiver only those transform blocks which have changed significantly since the previous frame was coded, to update the information stored within the receiver.

Several workers have directed their attention towards the problems resulting from actual scene movement from frame to frame. As far as motion in a plane normal to the line joining the objects within the scene to the camera is concerned, it may frequently be approximated by a simple translational shift in location (i.e., an object moves, without rotation or change in shape or size, a certain distance across the image field in a direction which may be determined in some way). In this case, coding may be carried out by reference to the previous frame in which the detail has now been modified to account for such instances of translation. Such a process involves the techniques of motion prediction and compensation, which have over the past few years become increasingly important in the general area of the coding of moving images and which, of course, form an interesting link between the practical problems of efficient image coding and the more basic theoretical studies of the fundamental nature of still and moving pictures.

5.2.2   Three-dimensional transform coding

The theoretical development of Chapter 3 demonstrates that, whenever a 'random' variable (picture elements and transform coefficients are frequently considered to be random variables in quantitative terms, although whether this assumption is fully justified in a formal sense is not really clear) takes on a sequence of values which have a substantial degree of correlation, the application of a one-dimensional transformation results in a set of coefficient sequences which are only weakly correlated and in which the variance of the individual coefficients decreases markedly with increase in coefficient order. The one-dimensional relationship extends separably to two-dimensions [Eq. (3.34)], and three-dimensional processing requires a similar extension, where the coefficients are now functions of three mutually perpendicular independent variables. As mentioned briefly in the introduction, the third of these will be typically, but not exclusively, time. It can be seen, therefore, that not only does three-dimensional transform coding require an increased number of mathematical operations compared with its two-dimensional counterpart, but the storage requirement is similarly enlarged. Just as an $N \times N$ two-dimensional transform requires the storage of N lines from a single image frame, so an $N \times N \times M$ three-dimensional transform will require storage of those lines from M frames, making multiple frame storage a necessity. Since restriction of M to 2 greatly reduces the efficiency of the last (temporal) stage of the transform process, whilst employing a predictive system with simple previous element prediction still allows the achievement of much of the data compression inherent in the latter coding method, this difficulty has meant that the study of three-dimensional transform coding has, with one or two exceptions, been on the basis of computer simulation to determine the possible benefits that it might yield, rather than as an implementation in real time.

Following the generation of the coefficient set, which now exists in three-dimensional space and consists of values which, at least for images containing only moderate degrees of motion, decrease rapidly away from the origin (the DC coefficient), adaptive quantisation and coding techniques based upon spatial and/or temporal block activity can be applied in a way similar to that in which they are used in two-dimensional processing (subject, in a real-time application, to the availability of adequate processing time). Here, however, there are additional considerations which broaden the field of choice of coefficients to be retained and coded, since the spatial and temporal responses of the human eye are not separable. Thus following a sudden temporal disturbance, e.g., a scene change, the spatial sensitivity of the eye is reduced, and does not completely recover for 0.75–1 s (Seyler and Budrikis, 1965). Available coding capacity may therefore be allocated, on the basis of the output of a temporal change detector, to the task of accurately representing the temporal alteration, since the eye will not notice the transient reduction in spatial detail. This feature is incorporated into the real-time Hadamard compression system of Knauer (1976), in which four frames of video data are stored at an accuracy of 6 bits, and a $4 \times 4 \times 4$ Hadamard transform carried out. Just as, in the two-dimensional case, a 4×4 transform can be represented by 16 basis pictures similar to those shown in Fig. 3.2, so there will be 64 basis 'volumes' in the present case, and the original image volume (x, y, t) will be reconstructed by recombining the volumes each weighted by the sign and magnitude of its respective transform coefficient. Half of the total of 64 coefficients are set to zero, the DC term is retained at 7-bit accuracy, and the remaining 31 may be quantised using 2, 3 or 4 bits (of these, four have an alternative option of 7-bit resolution). In an adaptive mode spatial fidelity is exchanged for temporal fidelity as the coder senses an increasing degree of motion within the image. Up to four coefficients may be tested against three preset thresholds and, at a rate of 1 bit/element, approximately half the total allocation is used in representing static detail in the lowest motion option, whilst for higher degrees of motion, three-quarters of the allocation is used to represent temporal effects. In passing, two interesting effects resulting from the inclusion of interframe processing are reported. First, the probability distribution of the transform coefficients in the temporal spectral domain differs from that in the spatial spectral domain. Thus, whilst high-sequency spatial coefficients rarely have large amplitudes (typical moving images used containing little fine spatial detail), high-sequency temporal coefficients are more likely to have high amplitudes due to the relatively greater degree of motion detail encountered. The second effect results from the fact that, as with all television systems, the four frames stored for transformation are, in fact, eight fields, appropriately interlaced. This causes the highest-sequency vertical basis vector $[1 \ -1 \ \ 1 \ -1]^T$ to be sensitive to both fine horizontal stripe detail and motion between the pair of fields which make up a single frame.

Roese and Pratt (1976) and Roese et al. (1977) have considered the theoretical performance of three-dimensional transform coding based upon an assumed correlation model of the form

$$R(\Delta x, \Delta y, \Delta z) = e^{-\alpha \Delta x} e^{-\beta \Delta y} e^{-\gamma \Delta z} \qquad (5.20)$$

i.e., a straightforward separable extension into three-dimensions of the one- and two-dimensional models considered in Chapter 2. Variances are determined in a similar way to that described for two dimensions in sub-section 2.3.3 and bits allocated and quantisation carried out in the usual way, assuming Rayleigh and Gaussian distributions for the DC and AC coefficients, respectively. At an overall allocation of 0.25 bit/element and with a sub-block size of 16×16, the normalised mean square error for 1 (i.e, two-dimensional coding), 2, 4, 8 and 16 frames is 3.8, 1.9, 1.1, 0.75 and 0.6%, respectively, with an assumed inter-element correlation coefficient in all three directions of 0.96. Similar trends for other block sizes demonstrate that it is not worth going beyond, say, 8 frames in the temporal direction in an attempt to improve performance, particularly in view of the increasing computational load which high-order three-dimensional transform coding systems impose. An experiment to demonstrate the performance of the system using a real moving image sequence showed it to be superior to that of an interframe hybrid coder of the type to be described in the following section.

It has been mentioned previously in this volume that an alternative to two-dimensional processing of a single image frame using block size $N \times N$ is to re-order the block into a vector of dimension $N^2 \times 1$ and carry out a single transform operation. This procedure can, of course, be extended to three dimensions, and Natarajan and Ahmed (1977) use it to process a set of $4 \times 4 \times 4$ blocks taken from four frames of the luminance component of a standard NTSC video signal and reordered into the form of 64×1 data vectors. Both the DCT and WHT were used in the investigations, and uniform and exponential distributions assumed for the DC and AC coefficients, respectively. No degradation was observed, for scenes of differing activities, when the four frames were displayed repeatedly in real time and, as might be expected, the measured mean square error was slightly lower in the case of the DCT, the difference between the transforms, however, being only slight. Wong (1980) carried out experiments using the DCT on 48 frames (approximately 2 s) of two image sequences, one containing moderate, and the other, rapid, motion, with an image size of 96×128 elements. He found that, with an adaptive scheme and a block size of $16 \times 16 \times 8$, the possible reduction in bit rate for a given normalised mean square error over that for intraframe coding was by a factor of approximately 2 to 3. Satisfactory image quality was obtainable at an overall rate of about 0.25 bit/element.

A comprehensive three-dimensional DCT coding scheme has been reported by Götze and Ocylok (1982). A block size of $8 \times 8 \times 4$ was chosen, based upon a measured comparison with a two-dimensional 8×8 coder which yielded a 3 dB SNR improvement for the former scheme. The size is also considered to be a compromise between small blocks for good activity classification and low (temporal) delay, and large blocks for high coding efficiency. The coder stores both the four frames for the coding operation and the last frame from the previous set of four. A change detector monitors the differences between an element in the last frame and the corresponding elements in the four new frames in order that only changed sub-blocks be transmitted. This is carried out adaptively, according to the measured amount of temporal and/or spatial detail within the block. There are three allowable degrees of motion—the lowest of which allows block coding with very good spatial resolution, and, for both higher levels of movement, there are seven categories which include a direction (horizontal or vertical) dependent activity criterion. For each of these categories two bit allocation options are available—one for good subjective quality, the other with reduced quality to prevent output buffer overflow. The quantisation characteristics are matched to either a uniform (for the DC coefficient) or a two-sided gamma distribution for the AC coefficients (see Chapter 4). Data transmission is carried out in seven steps yielding gradually increasing quality, following an initial step of changed block detection and classification and calculation of the overall number of bits for the four-frame image block. If the calculated rate is too high, the reduced bit allocation is applied to those blocks showing the greatest change; if too low, unchanged blocks have their resolution increased according to a criterion taking into account block detail and the resolution already inherent in the block by virtue of previous transmission. The system operates at a design allocation of 0.4 bit/element

(576 kbits/s per complete frame). As with other schemes in which rate control is carried out by means of variable bit allocation (for example, the scheme of Tescher discussed earlier) the overall SNR (or distortion) will vary according to the initial frame block requirement. Thus, in the presence of strong activity the reduction from the required (i.e, greater than nominal) to the allowable allocation reduces the SNR by approximately 4 dB whilst in the opposite direction allocation of unused capacity to maintain the channel transmission rate will raise the SNR by approximately the same amount.

5.2.3   Hybrid interframe coding

Just as intraframe hybrid coding techniques reduce the data storage requirement from N lines (where N is the vertical dimension of the transform block) to one, all that is necessary for previous element prediction to be carried out, so interframe hybrid schemes involving the same predictive operation require the storage of only the previous frame. The prediction operation is then carried out in the temporal direction between the 'same' coefficients in equivalent blocks in successive frames (although some improvement may be obtained by using information from more than just the previous frame for prediction, the advantage gained does not offset the added storage requirement). The processing load is significantly reduced, compared with that for three-dimensional transform coding, and the method has proved attractive to several workers.

Roese and Robinson (1975) use either a 16×16 DFT or DCT spatially, combined with previous element predictive coding in the temporal direction. The frame-to-frame coefficient difference signal has a Laplacian distribution (a property common to all schemes which utilise a stage of data or coefficient element to element differencing) and is quantised using a companding/ uniform quantisation technique which minimises mean square error. Coding bits are allocated according to the block coefficient variance in the way described previously. It is assumed that the first frame of the moving sequence to be coded is available at the receiver (in a practical application periodic updating will be required, in any case, to remove the cumulative effects of system noise), and the coder then stabilises in 4–6 frames. Results for the DCT at 0.25 bit/element and for the DFT at twice that rate are approximately the same (0.2% normalised mean square error, 35 dB SNR). In a comparison with hybrid intraframe processing, the latter scheme required 2 bits/element for the same error, but it is pointed out that the performance of the scheme is strongly data dependent. The authors suggest that this is a result of scene motion, which conclusion is undoubtedly true, although we have seen previously that data dependence is a property which is characteristic of predictive techniques in general. In a later simulation, Roese and Pratt (1976) and Roese *et al.* (1977) compare two-dimensional hybrid and three-dimensional interframe coding in a way described in the previous section, where the reduction in variance of the coefficient sequences obtained following predictive coding is assumed to be that for the ideal first-order Markov case, i.e., by a factor $(1 - \rho^2)$, where ρ is the transform coefficient correlation coefficient. At a 32:1 bit rate reduction, with correlation coefficients in all three dimensions assumed to be 0.96, the hybrid coder has a performance, for a block size of 8 × 8, equivalent to that of a two-frame three-dimensional transform processor. At a block size of 16 × 16 the performance of the hybrid coder is better, coming midway between the three-dimensional results for 2 and 4 frames. There is thus an obvious trade-off between ultimate performance and complexity of implementation. The system can be made temporally adaptive by periodically recalculating time domain statistics to reoptimise the prediction and bit assignment procedures and, although this results in a significant improvement in performance, it naturally increases the complexity of the coder greatly, since in practice there is no way of measuring interframe parameters of actual data to be transmitted without a large amount of data storage.

In the context of broadcast television transmission, not only do network standards demand a very high level of reconstructed image quality, but rapid scene changes are probably more usual than in other, less demanding applications. Adaptive coding techniques are therefore mandatory, and one such hybrid interframe scheme has been investigated by Kamangar and Rao (1980, 1981) for NTSC component colour signals. A block size of 8 × 8 and the DCT are used, followed by the usual predictive operation in the temporal direction. The system is made adaptive in the spatial domain by monitoring the degree of intrablock (spatial) detail and in the temporal direction by monitoring the interfield difference between similarly located blocks. In the spatial domain each block is divided into four sub-blocks which are experimentally observed to have minimum correlation, and the detection of detail is carried out by observing the sub-block AC energy. Spatially active sub-blocks are assigned more bits when the threshold (set by the 50% point on the cumulative pdf of sub-block energy) is exceeded. In the temporal direction activity is determined by the block DC coefficient prediction difference signal. For temporally active blocks, more bits and increased normalisation factors are applied to the quantisation process for the low-sequency coefficients. Temporal activity always takes precedence over spatial activity, and prevents the allocation of more bits to the high-sequency coefficients of a spatially active block, in accordance with the temporal/spatial response of the human visual system already referred to. Results at 2 bits/element demonstrate that, as might be expected, the mean square error is lower than that of a similar but non-adaptive system and, perhaps more significantly, from the point of view of visual observation of the transmitted image, that the maximum reconstruction error is much less in the adaptive case.

At the other end of the spectrum of bit rate requirement for picture transmission is the scheme devised by May (1980) for image sequence transmission over mobile radio channels at 9.6 kbits/s. Obviously the illusion of normal scene movement cannot be sustained at such a low rate, since transmission of even a reduced-area image will take substantially more than a television frame interval. However, for surveillance applications, sending an image update every 1.5 s is judged to be satisfactory, and the basis of the system is the application of a two-dimensional 16×16 DCT together with interframe predictive coding to the sequence of 384×256 frames. Blocks are classified according to the prediction error energy averaged over the block and the appropriate prediction coefficient determined by a correlation measurement made, not in the temporal direction, as is usual, but between adjacent frames where the summation takes place spatially, it being observed that the optimum prediction coefficients for the various spectral coefficients within a block are normally strongly correlated. (There is thus not, as in the normal case, one optimum predictor coefficient per transform coefficient, but only one per block.) Unfortunately no numerical results are given to substantiate this conjecture since, not only is it unlikely on the basis of all other known results, but the idea of temporal correlation loses significance unless measured over a sequence of some extent in the temporal direction, for which 'parallel' element pairs taken from different coefficient prediction sequences within a block are no substitute. Four bit allocation classes are established using a large range of test input material, and quantisation is carried out accordingly. With a 25 % scene change, coding at 0.14 bit/element results in a normalised mean square error of approximately 0.2 %.

One advantage that derives from the usual method of subdivision of an image into smaller sub-blocks for the purpose of transform coding is that the intraframe coding process can be made spatially adaptive by allocating different numbers of bits to different blocks in accordance with some measure of block spatial detail. A concomitant disadvantage is the appearance in the reconstructed image of block structure at low coding rates. For full frame transforms the situation is reversed, and the advantage that there is no sub-block structure superimposed upon the image, whatever the transmission rate, is offset by the impossibilty of making the transform spatially adaptive. When interframe coding is considered, the trade-offs are not so clear-cut, for optimum bit allocation to a set of full frame transform coefficients still allows much of the intrinsic advantage of transform coding, whilst in the temporal direction full advantage is gained from the predictive coding step (which may, in principle at least, be made adaptive). Thus Pearlman and Jakatdar (1981) advocate just such a system as producing better results than those of Roese described earlier. They use a full-frame (256 × 256) DFT together with previous element prediction in which the predictor coefficient for each coefficient sequence is optimised separately. On the assumption that, for so large a block size, the transform coefficients are uncorrelated and have a Gaussian distribution, optimum bit allocation is carried out following the technique of Segall (see Chapter 4) for both real and imaginary components. At a rate of 0.2 bit/element reproduced quality is 'tolerable' and the SNR is 21.6 dB. The authors point out the visual superiority of their results compared with those of Roese et al. (1977), and spend some time discussing the equivalent SNR figures. It is unfortunate, however, that this comparison is invalidated by the fact that different SNR measures are used in each case, the authors using Eq. (2) and Roese using Eq. (3) of Appendix 7. Despite this fact, their investigation is significant in that it explores a rather different avenue en route to the goal of low-bit-rate coding of moving images, although a real-time 256 × 256 Fourier transform at a reasonable frame rate presents a severe problem in implementation.

5.2.4   Frame difference techniques

In the introduction to this section the technique of conditional replenishment was briefly described, and this has formed the basis of several interframe transform coding schemes. The ideal is, of course, that given a starting (reference) frame stored at both transmitter and receiver, a comparison is made with the next frame to be coded, and there is then no need to code and transmit any detail that has not changed. In traditional conditional replenishment this operates on an element-by-element basis, but the technique can equally well be applied to frames divided into sub-blocks for subsequent transform coding. There are, naturally, problems inherent in the scheme, and one of the most important is to decide just what constitutes a significant change in detail; i.e., on what basis do we decide whether or not to transmit a transformed block? Such a scheme is described by Reader (1975), and is based upon initial slant transformation followed by adaptive coding of an image divided into sub-blocks of dimension 16 × 16. It is found that for all degrees of motion apart from the slowest, detection of sub-block frame difference energy and subsequent comparison with a threshold to determine whether or not to transmit a sub-block results in a reasonably linear variation of mean square error with threshold. Careful setting of the latter quantity is needed to achieve good performance, and it is possible to ensure that block update due to detection of image noise is, for the most part, eliminated whilst allowing an additional degree of data compression (i.e., over and above the intraframe figure) of approximately 3:1. Raising the threshold by a factor of two causes the energy detector to miss blocks containing perceptible motion, producing impairments in the reconstructed image.

Another conditional replenishment system is reported by Jones (1977) [see also the static adaptive system of H. Jones (1976) described in a previous section]. Here the image is subjected to an 8 × 8 WHT and the block coefficient vectors compared with those stored from the same block in the previous field. There are two memories, one for even, and one for odd, fields. Although frame processing gives a better compression factor than field processing, the required memory size is doubled and, furthermore, at low rates frame transmission tends to average adjacent lines within the frame, and rapid motion between the individual fields making up the frame reduces the otherwise higher static correlation between adjacent lines in the frame. [For a fuller discussion of this point see Jones and Hofman (1978). As one memory is being updated, the contents of the second are being transferred to one of two output buffers after transmission rate determination through a knowledge of how many blocks per field are detected as having changed. To deal with an increasing number of changed blocks the sub-picture bit assignment is reduced. A block size of 8 × 8 is regarded as optimum in this application, as a trade-off between wasted area update for larger sizes and increased overhead for smaller blocks.

As mentioned earlier, the change detector is of crucial importance in a successful conditional replenishment system. In Jones's design a group of 20 transform coefficients is tested against a threshold, and if any coefficient is found to exceed it the block is considered to have changed. The coefficients employed are those in the first row and first column of the 8 × 8 block, plus (2, 2), (2, 3), (2, 4), (3, 2) and 4, 2). Even this test occasionally misses fine detail, whilst testing only the three lowest-order coefficients was found to be generally unsatisfactory, as might be expected. Dependent upon the average transmission rate and memory capacity, the threshold is made adaptive. In this way all changed blocks can be reproduced at full resolution on the first transmission. If this condition cannot be satisfied, then all changed blocks are updated at reduced resolution and, when a scene change occurs, all blocks are updated at the fixed average transmission rate. At a total allocation of 3 bits/element, the 192 available bits are divided into 12 groups of 16 (i.e., the minimum transmission rate is 0.25 bit/element) and then sequentially sent in groups of increasing order, this corresponding with the gradually increasing spatial resolution requirement of the eye after a scene change which has been mentioned previously. Overall performance, with 6-bit input data and 416 × 464 lines per frame sampled at 8.064 MHz gave high-quality graphics and adequate motion performance for teleconferencing (the latter including graphics and document input) at 0.5 bit/element. The scheme was subsequently modified by Hein and Jones (1979) to include block classification into one of six possible modes, one of which is a 'no compression' mode. In this case the lowest threshold tests 31 out of 64 coefficients arranged in a similar pattern to that of the 20 coefficients referred to earlier and at threshold three and above, all coefficients apart from the DC coefficient are included in the test, which consists of summing the squared difference between like coefficients in consecutive blocks, the numerical value of threshold used being determined experimentally. Again there is the problem of accurate setting of this parameter to ignore noise but detect as many real changes as possible, and a further significant point is well made, which is that small variations in the position of large-amplitude luminance transitions in the original image may give rise to large difference signals, even though they may not be perceptible visually. The scheme requires two 'passes' over a given data set, the first to determine overall coding rate and which blocks have changed, and the second to code the blocks to be transmitted and to determine how many (if any) frame repeats are needed. Should the total rate be less than the average set for transmission, the extra capacity is used to refresh unchanged areas of the image, which prevents buildup of errors in the reconstruction. During intervals of significant motion, when many blocks are changing, it is necessary for the receiver to display the last frame received until transmission of the changed frame is complete. At an overall rate of 1 bit/element no repeats are needed: at 0.5 bit/element approximately half of the frames are repeated once. At lower rates the large number of repeats introduces noticeable motion degradation. The scheme also includes a motion prediction/compensation algorithm, which is properly the subject of the following subsection.

As a general comment at this point, it is worth noting that any scheme of the kind described here has the problem of wide variation in overall generated data rate, which has to be buffered for transmission over a fixed rate channel. This is particularly serious with moving image systems, since there is no way in which extended periods of rapid motion can be catered for without some degree of reduction in performance. The best that can be done is to try to take advantage of the reduced spatial resolution of the eye during intervals of high temporal activity, and this transform domain conditional replenishment schemes can do very conveniently by preferentially transmitting lower-order coefficients.

5.2.5 Motion prediction and compensation

The obvious difficulties which accompany any attempt to code moving detail have prompted various workers to consider whether anything can be done in terms of the motion of picture areas themselves, i.e., whether there are properties inherent in that motion which may be used to improve the performance of a coding system (see, e.g., Cafforio and Rocca, 1976; Brofferio and Rocca, 1977). One property which is readily apparent upon examination of a wide variety of moving images is that much of the motion is, to a first approximation at least, pure translation; i.e., the object viewed moves across the background field in an arbitrary direction, but without rotation or size change. Even when either or both of those additional components is present, provided that the motion is not too violent in the short time interval between successive frames, the approximation may still hold. On this property have been based several schemes designed to predict interframe motion (from a knowledge of object location in earlier frames) and thus to compensate for its presence by using, for processing, elements or blocks in the previous frame(s) which have been suitably corrected. Thus Haskell (1974) points out, in this context, the well-known result that, in Fourier transformation, a data shift in the original time or space domain only affects the phase, and not the magnitude, of the resulting components. Thus (see Brigham, 1974), if (in one-dimension) $H(n)$ is the DFT of $h(k)$, then the DFT of $h(k - i)$, the discrete data $h(k)$ shifted by i increments, is $H(n)e^{-j2\pi ni/N}$, or the original transform multiplied by a phase factor $e^{-j\theta}$, say, where θ is the product of spatial frequency and data displacement. The separability of the Fourier kernel immediately allows us to generalise the result to arbitrary translational motion in the x, y plane. Haskell thus suggests that the two-dimensional DFT of a given frame difference signal (i.e., the signal obtained by taking element differences in the original data domain), modified by phase factors derived from horizontal and vertical displacement estimates, be used to predict the transform of the next frame difference signal which may then be inverse transformed to form a prediction of that frame difference signal. Changed image areas then have the difference between the actual signal and its prediction coded as has been previously described. The scheme may, with advantage, be applied to the image divided into sub-blocks. Although Haskell considers the scheme as a modification to the original idea of data domain conditional replenishment (his reference 1), it is apparent that it is applicable to transform image coding using the DFT (it should be recalled here that other transforms do not have an equivalent to the simple Fourier translation property), and the concept is discussed by Roese (1976). Thus, two-dimensional frame-to-frame phase differences are estimated for each transform block. Each is then used, together with the block transform, to provide an estimate for the set of block coefficients in the next frame, and so on.

The conditional replenishment scheme of Hein and Jones has already been briefly described, and we need only note here the algorithm introduced for motion detection. Each 8×8 block is first checked to determine whether or not replenishment is necessary. If so, a test is carried out, by determining the difference signal generated when the block is compared with all possible block locations within a 22×22 element window in the previous frame centred on the location of the block to be coded. If the difference signal is below the change threshold, the block is coded by sending an 8-bit word representing both horizontal and vertical displacements. Otherwise, the block is coded as previously described. Typically about one-third to one-half of the total number of changed blocks can be coded in this way and, since the average number of bits per element required for such blocks is very low (block field repeat is used at the receiver in such instances since the human visual system sensitivity to spatial detail is reduced in the presence of temporal activity, as has been mentioned previously), the overall rate can be reduced by approximately this amount. In this case no frame repeats are required at 0.5 bit/element, and over a range of lower rates, frame display time is reduced by about one-third by the introduction of motion prediction. The authors point out, as might be expected, that the compression gain produced is offset by a considerable increase in system complexity in order to carry out the 225 block comparisons needed. Netravali and Stuller (1979) have simulated two motion compensation algorithms for interframe hybrid image coding (note that the addition of transmitter and receiver stores, a thresholding operation and the transmission of address information suffice to convert a conventional interframe hybrid coder to a conditional replenishment transform coder). The first recursively estimates motion as a function of previously transmitted transform coefficients of the present and previous frames and thus has the advantage that no actual displacement data need be transmitted. A coefficient within a given block is calculated in the normal way, as is the corresponding one in the previous frame, where the data has been shifted by the displacement estimate. The error in estimating the displacement is then minimised by a steepest descent algorithm, under the initial assumption that the displacement of the leftmost block is zero, and that the starting estimate for any new block is based on the final estimate of the previous one. The recursion thus proceeds sequentially through the coefficients in any one block. If the error magnitude exceeds a predetermined threshold, it is quantised and transmitted, allowing both correction of the coefficient value and also a displacement update at the receiver. A block size of 2×4 is found to be optimum, in conjunction with the use of the DCT, and coefficient deletion and quantisation is less critical than is the case when motion compensation is omitted. A full theoretical development of the technique appears in Stuller and Netravali (1979). A second algorithm, due to Limb and Murphy (1975), was also investigated. In this case displacement estimates are made for 'displacement blocks' significantly larger than the transform block (for example, 8×16), and coefficients predicted by using either the displaced or non-displaced coefficient from the previous frame. Thus the usual overhead/blocksize trade-off operates, since small blocks are adaptive to localised image motion but require, overall, more overhead for the transmission of an increased number of displacement estimates, and vice versa. The improvements obtained by including motion compensation were found, for real-life sequences, to lie in the range 20–40%, with the recursive scheme having marginally the better performance. The figure agrees reasonably well with that quoted previously by Hein of 33–50%. It should be emphasised, of course, that the results are those of a computer simulation, and that hardware implementation will of necessity make the coder more complex than one which does not include such a scheme.

The problem of complexity of motion prediction and compensation algorithms, particularly with regard to the search routine, has been considered by Jain and Jain (1981). As before the image is segmented into small rectangular areas each assumed to be undergoing independent translation, and the objective is to determine a reliable search routine that, for shifts of $\pm r$ elements horizontally and vertically, can be implemented in substantially fewer than the $(2r + 1)^2$ separate steps that would otherwise be required. The assumption made is that the distortion measure (here taken to be mean square error) is a monotonically increasing function of distance from the location of the true minimum, and this holds providing that the image covariance relation is a decreasing function of displacement in all directions, which is usually true as long as the maximum displacement is no more than a few elements (here the search is made over horizontal and vertical displacements of up to ± 5 elements). By initially searching 5 locations spread within the 11×11 area and progressively reducing the search area until it is 3×3 in extent, when all 9 remaining locations are tested, the total search requirement is reduced to approximately 15% of the maximum possible. When applied to a 16×16 DCT hybrid interframe coding system in which blocks are classified into one of four groups based upon spatio–temporal block activity, a reduction in bit rate by a factor of 2 is possible when coding a moving head and shoulders sequence. A detailed review of the motion estimation problem is given by Wells (1983).

5.2.6 General comments on interframe coding

The satisfactory transmission of moving images has, because of the large amount of information within an image frame (of the order of $3–4 \times 10^5$ data points), combined with the requirement for retransmission 25–30 times per second, always needed large channel bandwidth. This is considerably increased if digital transmission is desired. Thus, the already 5.5-MHz wide

PAL colour television signal requires a total of 216 Mbits/s if represented in component form according to the recently introduced standard. At the other end of the scale, such applications as videoconferencing, reconnaissance and surveillance require the transmission of moving detail (albeit at reduced resolution, and most probably with detectable, though acceptable, levels of visible impairment) at rates up to perhaps 2 Mbits/s. Where very slow frame update is acceptable, rates may be reduced to the tens of kilobits per second region. There is thus ample scope for the application of interframe coding schemes which, on the one hand, reduce very high data rates by relatively modest compression factors, say 2 or 3 to 1, without visible degradation of any kind, or, on the other, allow the maximum possible fidelity of image reconstruction at high degrees of compression via highly adaptive techniques (including motion compensation) in cases where overall transmission capacity is severely constrained.

Whilst there is little doubt that the introduction of hybrid processing into intraframe coding brings with it advantages which are, at most, marginal, the same is not true for interframe coding. To employ transform processing in the third (temporal) dimension necessitates the storage of a number of frames equal to the order of the transform in that direction, which is extremely wasteful in a practical system—although the transform operation will, of course, produce high compression efficiency provided that the temporal correlation of the data remains high. Although it would by very unwise to predict the actual cost of such a system, in either financial or engineering terms, in a few years' time, it is nevertheless the case that the alternative scheme which employs two-dimensional transform coding together with previous element prediction has the virtue of relative simplicity of implementation as well as a reduced storage requirement. At low data rates the addition of motion compensation is feasible, which will improve efficiency by perhaps 50% or more. Unfortunately, it is difficult to make a simple system which is adaptive in the temporal direction, since multi-element estimation and updating of such parameters as the predictor coefficient are required.

Turning now to conditional replenishment schemes, these constitute an attractive means of implementing interframe coding, and the biggest problem seems to be in the design of an efficient change detector which reliably distinguishes between significant variations in block detail and spurious signals due to noise. Another drawback is that moving areas are unlikely to correspond, either in shape or size, with the preselected transform block, and so smaller blocks than usual are advantageous in this application. Again, these schemes may usefully include motion compensation, and it is that specific topic which, at the moment, is the focus of much interest in interframe coding. More efficient motion prediction and compensation algorithms will reduce the data transmission requirement for moving image sequences, and it is probably true to say that much remains to be done in this area. There seem to be two main avenues of approach to the problem. First, by generalising the treatment of interframe motion to include both rotation and scale change (Huang *et al.*, 1982), and second, by considering in greater depth the response of the human visual system to motion in images. The well-known reduction in perception of spatial detail in the presence of marked temporal change has been effectively employed in several of the schemes disussed in this section, but the fact remains that more knowledge of the behaviour of the eye in the general (non-separable) spatio–temporal case would greatly assist the design of efficient three-dimensional image coding systems.

5.3   Transform coding of colour data

5.3.1   Introduction

The previous sections of this chapter have considered the transform operation as applied to grey-scale images, i.e., those consisting of a rectangular array of single luminance values (typically of 8-bit accuracy). Whilst the majority of published studies in the field have related to such images, there is also now a reasonably extensive collection of results relating to the coding of colour data, which is the subject of this section. Obviously the colour coding process is more complex than that for black and white images, and the matter is further complicated by the fact that, whilst input data of the latter type can be produced by a wide variety of processes having various spatial and amplitude resolution standards, much colour input data is generated by broadcast television systems, either in component form (the separate chrominance and luminance signals, or basic colour channels, before modulation) or as a composite signal, in which the chrominance data has been modulated onto the colour subcarrier and added to the luminance signal. (Note that only those details of television systems pertinent to the present discussion are described here.) Indeed, the large bandwidths required for the transmission of digital television signals of broadcast quality (perhaps 120 Mbits/s for composite format and 216 Mbits/s for component format) have motivated efforts to apply transform compression techniques to them without, as yet, fully satisfactory results.

At first sight, coding of a colour signal appears to require three times the data rate for the corresponding monochrome image, since there are three input channels (R, G, B). In fact, a simple colour coordinate conversion step, as incorporated within the colour television process, converts the three original signals into one (usually) monochrome compatible wideband luminance component and two reduced bandwidth colour information carrying signals (which, in broadcast television, are transmitted within the luminance bandwidth, allowing satisfactory colour transmission with no increase in bandwidth over the equivalent monochrome requirement). The overall data rate, then, is only fractionally more than that for the monochrome signal. In the case of the composite colour format, the colour information signals are modulated onto a colour subcarrier and combined with the luminance data to give a complete baseband signal ready for modulation and transmission. Due to the location of the colour subcarrier and colour sidebands near to the upper end of the luminance spectrum, the coding requirements will differ from those applicable to monochrome signals (which have, typically, a reasonably smooth fall-off in energy with increasing frequency). Furthermore, the presence of the sinusoidal subcarrier modifies the otherwise more or less regular variation of data interelement correlation coefficient with element spacing, as does the phase relation between the subcarrier pattern on successive lines in the video field. All such factors tend to make the coding of composite colour data a more complex problem than that of the equivalent component signals (this also applies to other forms of compression, such as predictive coding, and to processing in general), and it is probably true to say that, in the future , more effort will be concentrated upon the processing of colour signals of the latter, rather than the former, type. A comprehensive review of the digital coding of colour signals is given by Limb *et al.* (1977).

5.3.2   Transform coding of component colour signals

Coding of the separate components of colour data differs in no essential way from that of monochrome images. Typically a two-dimensional transform of block size perhaps 16 × 16 is applied to the separate components, and the coefficients have bits allocated to them and are quantised according to the schemes described earlier. The main difference between colour component and monochrome coding is that the actual components coded are not the R, G and B signals as generated by the pick-up device, and so the coding system does not consist of three identical parallel processors each driven from the appropriate camera channel. It is, in fact, highly advantageous to precede the actual processing step by a transformation (usually, but not necessarily, linear) which has the effect of reducing the correlation between the R, G and B signals, of producing, if desired, a monochrome compatible luminance signal, as in broadcast television, and of allowing the three signals produced by the transformation to be allocated only such bandwidth as is required for adequate colour reproduction. [In practice, the colour carrying channels require only a fraction, perhaps 20%, of the bandwidth needed by the luminance signal if it is to reproduce spatial detail accurately. Thus Tescher (1980), suggests that 64 : 1 two-dimensional subsampling of colour components only produces small impairments, and that even 4 : 1 luminance subsampling is acceptable, provided that, following the interpolation process at the decoder necessary to reconstruct the missing samples, a spatial high-pass filter is applied to improve the appearance of the displayed image by enhancing edge detail.] A transformation of the type

$$\begin{bmatrix} T_1 \\ T_2 \\ T_3 \end{bmatrix} = \begin{bmatrix} a_{11} & a_{12} & a_{13} \\ a_{21} & a_{22} & a_{23} \\ a_{31} & a_{32} & a_{33} \end{bmatrix} \begin{bmatrix} R \\ G \\ B \end{bmatrix} \tag{5.21}$$

is therefore carried out to generate the signals which are to be coded. The NTSC transmission primary system is given by

$$\begin{bmatrix} Y \\ I \\ Q \end{bmatrix} = \begin{bmatrix} 0.299 & 0.587 & 0.114 \\ 0.596 & -0.274 & -0.322 \\ 0.211 & -0.523 & 0.312 \end{bmatrix} \begin{bmatrix} R \\ G \\ B \end{bmatrix} \tag{5.22}$$

where Y is the monochrome compatible luminance signal, and I and Q carry the colour information. In the PAL system a similar relationship applies to the Y signal, but the colour (difference) signals are directly derived as follows

$$U_d = 0.493(B - Y)$$

$$V_d = 0.877(R - Y) \tag{5.23}$$

the scale factors being introduced to limit the maximum excursion of the total instantaneous signal amplitude. From these the NTSC I and Q signals may be derived by applying a $33°$ rotation to the colour axes (the I and Q axes are thus oriented in the orange/cyan and green/magenta directions, respectively). An alternative transformation (CIE uniform chromaticity scale)

$$\begin{bmatrix} U \\ V \\ W \end{bmatrix} = \begin{bmatrix} 0.405 & 0.116 & 0.133 \\ 0.299 & 0.587 & 0.114 \\ 0.145 & 0.827 & 0.627 \end{bmatrix} \begin{bmatrix} R \\ G \\ B \end{bmatrix} \tag{5.24}$$

may be applied [note that the U and V signals are not the U_d and V_d of Eq. 5.23), in fact the V signal is the Y signal of Eq. (5.22)], together with a further conversion

$$u = \frac{U}{U + V + W} \tag{5.25}$$

$$v = \frac{U}{U + V + W} \tag{5.26}$$

to give a Y, u, v coordinate system (see Pearson, 1975, for a detailed discussion of this matter). It is also possible to employ a KLT coordinate rotation (see Chapter 3) to generate uncorrelated colour components. Thus Pratt (1971) has employed

$$\begin{bmatrix} K_1 \\ K_2 \\ K_3 \end{bmatrix} = \begin{bmatrix} 0.575 & 0.615 & 0.540 \\ 0.608 & 0.120 & -0.785 \\ 0.548 & -0.779 & 0.305 \end{bmatrix} \begin{bmatrix} R \\ G \\ B \end{bmatrix} \tag{5.27}$$

for one specific image source.

The colour signal bandwidths can now be reduced without significant image quality degradation. Thus the I signal is allocated approximately 1.3 MHz and the Q signal 0.5 MHz, the luminance bandwidth remaining at about 4 MHz (in the PAL system both colour difference signals are allocated about 1.3 MHz and the luminance bandwidth is 5.5 MHz). For the image source mentioned above Pratt determined the energy redistribution obtained by the use of an initial coordinate rotation, and the results are shown in Table 5.8. It can be seen that the YIQ system is very effective in redistribution the originally roughly equal energy spread of the R, G and B components. Pratt then investigated YIQ and Yuv coding of the original 6-bit colour image using both full-frame and 16×16 Fourier and Hadamard transformation and zonal sample deletion with uniform quantisation. The luminance sample reduction ratio was 2:1 and that for the colour signals 16:1, giving a total average rate of 3.75 bits/element. By employing KLT transformation of the luminance signal and a 10:1 threshold (i.e., adaptive) sample deletion, together with 16×16 WHT coding of I and Q signals, coding of the colour image at a rate of 1.75 bits/element was found possible.

The relationships between the various colour components has been studied by Rubinstein and Limb (1972) and Pirsch and Stenger (1976) and, although primarily concerned with the predictive processing of colour data, their results are relevant to the matter of the coding of colour signals in general. Thus, Rubinstein finds that a fixed rotation of $23°$ is optimum for the majority of a set of six colour pictures, being better than both $33°$ (I, Q), and

TABLE 5.8. Colour signal energy redistribution for various co-ordinate conversions.

System	Component		
	1 (%)	2 (%)	3 (%)
RGB	33.2	36.2	30.6
YIQ	93.0	5.3	1.7
$K_1 K_2 K_3$	94.0	5.1	0.9

$0°(U_d, V_d)$. In terms of required bit rate, however, the effect is relatively small. Pirsch points out that there is little relationship between the luminance and colour difference signals, and that any benefit in joint processing of those signals comes rather from the U_d/V_d interdependence. It is also shown that the U_d and V_d signals have significantly smaller dynamic range than the Y signal, in keeping with the results of Table 5.8. The benefits of even a substantial improvement in coding of the colour carrying signals will therefore represent only a small overall advantage when the luminance signal is taken into account.

Pratt *et al.* (1974) subsequently extended the work described earlier to the use of the 16×16 slant transform and conventional (variance dependent) bit allocation and non-linear quantisation techniques. He appears to use a slightly different version of the same image for his later work, which results in rather poorer energy redistribution performance of the YIQ and $K_1K_2K_3$ coordinate conversions, apparently because the original RGB distribution is less evenly spread than in Table 5.8. At an overall rate of 2 bits/element the optimum distribution to minimise the reconstructed mean square error is $Y - 1.25, I - 0.55$ and $Q - 0.20$ bits, which relative allocation is found to be reasonably independent both of the actual image used and of the total number of bits employed.

In the case of monochrome images it has been shown that the application of adaptive techniques results in an improvement in compression performance over a corresponding non-adaptive system by a factor of, very roughly, 2 : 1. Similar opportunities exist in relation to colour transform coding, and the scheme of Chen and Smith (1976, 1977), already described earlier in this chapter, has been employed by them, on the same 256×256 image as used by Pratt *et al.* (1974) to code the YIQ colour components. This time the 16×16 DCT is used, and satisfactory results are obtained at an overall rate of approximately 1 bit/element ($Y - 0.49, I - 0.23, Q - 0.12$) with 0.08 bit/element overhead, and there is no perceptible degradation at 2 bits/element ($Y - 1.07, I - 0.53, Q - 0.29$). A comparison of the Y, I and Q classification maps contained in Chen and Smith's (1976) paper is interesting in the light of the previous discussion in relation to common properties of luminance and colour carrying signals. Classification is carried out, as in the monochrome case, on the basis of the cumulative probability distribution of sub-block AC energy and the maps, although broadly similar, are by no means identical. Thus, blocks in the highest luminance activity category can have very low I and Q classifications and vice versa. Luminance energy, therefore, may not be a reliable guide to colour signal energy, and it would appear that added coding advantage cannot be gained by using the luminance classification for the colour signal blocks, even for an image of very low activity overall. The authors do suggest, however, that four levels of classification (used in the monochrome case and for the luminance signal) are excessive for the I and Q signals, for which 3 and 2, respectively, would suffice.

Frei (1976) and Frei and Baxter (1977) have used a modified version of the YIQ coordinate conversion (one component of which retains the conventional luminance signal, however), as a pre-processing stage in their model of the colour response of the human visual system for coding a 256 × 256 image at 1 bit/element. This approach is rather different from the majority of work described in this section as is that of Hall and Andrews (1978), which also uses an HVS model with a modified coordinate conversion to code colour images at total rates as low as 0.25 bit/element. Both are discussed in more detail in Chapter 6. Component coding of sequences of frames of broadcast television standard is described by Kamangar and Rao (1980, 1981). As mentioned earlier, their adaptive scheme consists of an 8 × 8 DCT followed by interfield predictive coding. The image sampling frequency is 8.064 MHz and the visible section of each frame consists of 464 lines each having 416 elements, linearly quantised to 6-bit accuracy. Each 8 × 8 block is divided into four sub-blocks to which, individually, more bits are allocated if it is considered that they are active on the basis of their AC energy. Although in the case of spatial detail, the Chen and Smith results show that luminance AC energy is not a certain guide to colour signal activity, in the temporal direction such a relation is more likely to hold, and Kamangar and Rao use the luminance DC coefficient prediction error to indicate increased I and Q activity, when extra bits are added to low-sequency allocations only (in accordance with the spatio–temporal HVS response). They suggest that, at approximately 2 bits/element (including overhead) their system is suitable for teleconferencing and industrial applications, and that at a rate of 2.5–3 bits/element, broadcast television signals could be coded with adequate quality. More recently, by the application of chrominance channel subsampling, the scene adaptive coder of Chen and Pratt (1984), described in subsection 5.1.2.1 has been used for intraframe coding of NTSC colour video signals at 1.5 Mbits/s.

5.3.3 Transform coding of composite colour signals

The composite video signal consists of a baseband luminance signal approximately 4 MHz wide in the NTSC system and 5.5 MHz wide in PAL, together with I and Q (or U_d and V_d) chrominance information which is suppressed-carrier modulated onto a colour subcarrier (thus in the absence of colour data the subcarrier will not be present). The subcarrier frequency is chosen according to a variety of considerations, such as visible patterning on a monochrome receiver display, interference between luminance and chrominance energy, etc., which are fully described in texts devoted to the theoretical aspects of colour television systems. The relevant figures are the following:

(a)   NTSC: Line rate $f_L = 15{,}734.264$ s^{-1}, with the colour subcarrier midway between harmonics 227 and 228, i.e, at $f_{SC} = 227.5 \times f_L = 3{,}579{,}545$ Hz.

(b)   PAL: Line rate $f_L = 15{,}625$ s^{-1}, with the colour subcarrier at $f_{SC} = (284 - 0.25) \times f_L + 25 = 4{,}433{,}618.75$ Hz.

The NTSC system has 525 lines per frame and therefore contains a non-integral number of subcarrier cycles per frame. Two frames, however (i.e., four fields), contain an integral number (238, 875) and the subcarrier pattern thus has a so-called 'four field' repeat, i.e., a specific location in the scanning raster has the same subcarrier phase angle every four fields. For the PAL system the equivalent distance is given by the relationship

$$(284 - 0.25) \times n \times 625 = \text{Integer} \qquad (5.28)$$

i.e, $n = 4$, and the repeat interval is 4 frames or 8 fields. It should be noted that the 25-Hz offset in the PAL relationship adds one complete cycle per frame to the total given by $(284 - 0.25)f_L$ and thus leaves the above result unaffected (the PAL frame rate is 25 s^{-1}). Furthermore, each NTSC line contains 227.5 subcarrier cycles, and thus successive samples lying on a given vertical line within the display have subcarrier phases differing by 180°. For PAL the equivalent figures are almost exactly 283.75 and 90° (the error incurred is that corresponding to a 1 cycle shift per frame, i.e, 1/625 cycle or approximately 0.5°). Depending upon the relation between sampling and subcarrier frequencies the interelement correlation when colour information is present will not be as high as for the equivalent monochrome image, and it is desirable that this should be allowed for if possible. Thus Enomoto and Shibata (1971) employ an 8th order one-dimensional Hadamard/slant transform with a sampling frequency of 10 MHz basically to code a monochrome television signal. They point out, however, that the NTSC chrominance information (for which f_{SC} is approximately 3.58 MHz, corresponding to a period of about 0.28 μs) lies at a sequency corresponding to vectors 6 and 7 $(+ - - + - + + -; + - + - - + - +)$ which should therefore have their bit allocations (originally either 1 or 2) increased by 3, making the overall rate 0.75 bit/element greater. Again Ohira et al. (1973) use a one-dimensional 8th order WHT and non-linear quantising at a sampling frequency of $3 f_{SC}$ (10.7 MHz) to code at 3.5 bits/element, with the allocation of vectors 6, 7 and 8 increased with respect to the monochrome case.

The matter was investigated in detail by C. K. P. Clarke (1976) who studied the application of a one-dimensional 32nd-order WHT to the coding of broadcast quality PAL television pictures as a possible means of reducing the data rate. Various coefficient truncation procedures are employed together with both linear and non-linear quantisation, and sampling to subcarrier frequency ratios of 3, $\frac{8}{3}$ and 2 (the last of these is, of course, below the Nyquist limit for sampling of a 5.5-MHz low-pass signal, and special techniques are necessary to remove the alias energy which would otherwise interfere with the upper frequency range of the signal; Devereux, 1975), in which circumstances the subcarrier and colour energy is located around Hadamard coefficients 21-23, 24-26 and 31-32, respectively (although the distribution of energy for the WHT is not well defined with regard to the sequency of the components; see R. J. Clarke, 1983b). Using critical test material consisting of saturated colour signals and alphanumeric characters (white lettering upon a black background) it was found that hardly any bit rate reduction was permissible before visible picture impairment appeared. Naturally, the test images used covered the widest possible range of input material with, of course, conflicting requirements, the saturated colour detail, in particular, generating high amplitude high-sequency coefficients which were very sensitive to the less accurate representation provided by non-linear quantisation. For a sampling to subcarrier frequency ratio of 3, every third sample is located at a point of similar phase on successive subcarrier cycles, and this suggests grouping 96 samples in three blocks of 32, formed by taking samples 1, 4, 7, 10, ..., 2, 5, 8, 11, ..., 3, 6, 9, 12, ..., so that each block contains samples of similar subcarrier phase. This is effective in transforming the colour energy to low sequencies, although it is not so efficient in terms of decorrelation, since the samples to be transformed are now three times farther apart than usual, and the energy distribution (sequency spectrum) will cover a wider range of coefficients. With this method it becomes possible to maintain reasonable picture quality over a wide range of picture material at a rate of 4.5 bits/element.

Although C. K. P. Clarke's work must be acknowledged as one of the most detailed and exacting examinations of a transform coding system in terms of its ability to satisfy the highest standards of reproduced image quality, its conclusions tend not to be borne out by many of the more optimistic studies published since, from which, however, it is only too evident that what constitutes an acceptably processed image varies very widely indeed (it is of course true that later studies have used sophisticated adaptive approaches, as well as two-dimensional transformations). Furthermore, comparison between systems is made more difficult by the differing bandwidth and resolution standards of, for example, NTSC and PAL. Naturally the results obtained by Clarke would have been different if a fully adaptive 8×8 or 16×16 DCT system had been investigated. Whether they would have been different enough to justify the application of such a scheme to practical compression of broadcast quality PAL signals is an interesting question which has not, to date, been answered.

As far as NTSC is concerned, Ohira *et al.* (1978) find that a 4×8 WHT/slant transform of the kind employed in one dimension by Enomoto (see the preceding) can be effectively employed to code colour images at 3 bits/element with fine, and at 2.25 bits/element with passable, quality (these rates allow, at sampling frequencies of 10.45 and 9,69 MHz respectively, transmission at approximately 32 and 22 Mbits/s). Non-linear quantisation and bit allocation procedures were based on both measurements on test images and subjective optimisation. The scheme is made adaptive by assigning blocks to one of three modes, emphasising (a) high contrast and medium frequency detail, (b) saturated colours and (c) vertical high-frequency detail (Netravali and Limb, 1980). As in Enomoto's scheme, more bits need to be assigned to those coefficients in the high horizontal sequency region which corresponds with the colour energy in the signal. However, as pointed out earlier, the subcarrier phase within a given field varies by 180° in a vertical direction from line to line and so, since the line structure effectively samples in a vertical direction, those coefficients are located in the highest vertical sequency row of the transform array (i.e., the last).

Kim and Rao (1979) examined one-dimensional 16- and 32-element Hadamard transformation combined with vertical predictive coding and also 4×4 two-dimensional Hadamard transformation plus interblock prediction, as applied to intrafield coding of colour images sampled at $3 \times f_{SC}$ (10.74 MHz). Conventional bit allocation/quantisation techniques were applied to the error signal, the presence of the colour energy resulting in a larger allocation for high-sequency coefficients than would otherwise obtain for a monochrome image (at an overall rate of 4 bits/element the highest 17 coefficients still require an allocation of 3 bits each). Overall image fidelity was found to be good. Their work exemplifies the effect of the colour coding process upon image data correlation, As can be seen from Table 5.9, every third correlation lag in the horizontal, and every second in the vertical, direction has a markedly higher value than is the case for the intervening

TABLE 5.9. Horizontal and vertical correlation coefficients for the composite colour signal.[a]

Lag	0	1	2	3	4	5	6	7
ρ_h	1.000	0.947	0.943	0.988	0.938	0.935	0.979	0.933
ρ_v	1.000	0.958	0.991	0.952	0.985	0.948	0.980	0.945

[a] From Kim and Rao (1979).

locations. The results are for a specific test image but the principle is, of course, valid generally.

A very similar, but adaptive, approach is taken by Ploysongsang and Rao (1982) who use either a 32nd-order one-dimensional DCT or a 16th-order DCT applied to a reordered 4×4 sample block, followed by a predictive coding stage to process separate fields of NTSC colour data sampled at $3f_{SC}$, with a view to transmission with negligible impairments at 44.7 Mbits/s. The data used is the same as that of Kim and Rao. For one-dimensional processing the reordering scheme discussed by C. K. P. Clarke is used, and blocks of 32 samples, each having the same subcarrier phase, are formed by taking every third element along an image line. It was found that, at 3.5 bits/element, the overall image quality was good, with the exception of colour defects in regions of sharp colour and luminance change. The disadvantage of using every third element over a distance of 96 samples, i.e., with reduced correlation and the likelihood that image detail may change significantly in such a length, motivated the authors to consider two-dimensional processing using blocks of 4 adjacent lines with 12 elements per line. Again, these 48 elements are subdivided into three 4×4 blocks each of which contains elements of the same subcarrier phase. The samples are then rearranged into a 16×1 vector and a 16th-order DCT applied, The DC coefficient of a given block is then compared with those of the four neighbouring blocks of similar phase which have been previously processed, and the block with the closest value of DC coefficient is used for predictive coding using block coefficient differences. Each block thus has a 2 bit overhead indicating which previous block was used for prediction and a further bit indicates whether at least one prediction error exceeds a predetermined threshold. If this is not the case then the block is completely described by the 3 bits (no prediction errors below the threshold need be transmitted). This scheme removed the difficulties associated with single-line processing and allowed detailed images to be coded at approximately 3.5 bits/element with virtually imperceptible degradation, Coding of less active images proved satisfactory at a rate of 2.5 bits/element.

5.3.4   Conclusions

It is readily apparent that there is, even before matters of implementation are considered, a significant difference between the transform coding of a still 256×256 monochrome image and that of a full resolution moving colour television picture containing over four times that number of data points per frame. Furthermore, in the latter case there is the choice of format (component or composite) of the image, each with its own disadvantages. Thus, in composite form the presence of the subcarrier and chrominance sidebands makes coding more complex, whilst in component form there are always three separate signals to be considered for any one complete video signal. Notwithstanding the latter factor, however, it is likely that interest will centre more on component coding techniques in the future, not purely with regard to compression methods but also because of the problems of programme exchange between countries having different television broadcasting standards. For still image material, the well-established techniques described elsewhere in this volume with regard to monochrome images can easily be applied to the component signals derived from a colour image. Thus the luminance signal can be coded in exactly the same way as the monchrome data, whilst the colour carrying signals can be similarly processed, but at markedly reduced resolution, without impairing the quality of the reconstructed image. Overall rates in the region of 1 bit/element and below may, according to various authors, be obtained in this way, with picture quality which is described by the use of one of a seemingly almost infinite set of adjectives, ranging from 'passable' to 'outstanding'.

Whereas the acceptable quality of a teleconference, surveillance or industrial video data compression system is very much an individual matter for the specific customer, the same is not true for broadcast television systems, which are not only subject to the most critical quality standards of all, but are also called upon to deal with the widest variety of input material. Even the most optimistic estimates of coding rate for satisfactory quality are of the order of 3.5 bits/element, and C. K. P. Clarke (admittedly using a non-adaptive one-dimensional WHT) has produced results that appear to demonstrate that the transform coding operation is not really suited to such an application since a reasonably substantial, rather than a minor, bit rate reduction would be needed to make its use worthwhile. Since a transform such as the now widely used DCT provides almost optimum energy packing, together with adequate correlation reduction, such an advance will only come with the development and implementation of more highly sophisticated adaptive processing and motion detection/compensation techniques.

Chapter 6

The Human Visual Response

6.1 Introduction

In contrast to the treatment of topics in the more analytical sections of this book, the discussion of the present chapter covers what has been, until quite recently, a relatively neglected area of image coding, although the topic has, in its own right, been the subject of intensive investigation for many years. The difficulty lies in the successful application of the results of those investigations to the design of efficient image coding systems, and it is the case that little of a useful general nature has yet emerged. It would be satisfying to report that the relation between the visual properties of the human viewer and the system which has processed the displayed image now stands upon a firm theoretical foundation, and that the mechanism by which those properties can be taken into account has been thoroughly investigated, but this is far from being the case in reality. Although our present knowledge of the operation of the human visual system (HVS) is reasonably detailed, at least for some well-defined viewing situations (detection of certain types of spatial patterns, for example), there are still large areas where the human visual response is much more difficult to account for (e.g., in higher-level perception, as opposed to detection, of spatial detail, or the response of the eye to complex scenes). The topic is of particular importance for image coding (compression) schemes, since the majority of such are not 'information preserving', i.e., only an approximation, and not an exact replica of the original image cannot be reconstructed at the receiver, and therefore some criterion of just how good, or poor, the reconstruction is, for a given transmission rate, is essential. The theoretical treatment of the relation between allowable degradation within the received signal and the transmission system capacity is properly the subject of rate distortion theory, which is dealt with in more detail in Chapter 9. Suffice it to say here that, in an application where a fairly simple numerical measure of distortion is applicable and the data has a well-defined probability distribution (the classic example being a mean square measure between original and decoded data and a Gaussian distribution), specification of either rate or distortion will allow calculation of the other quantity. In terms of purely numerical analysis (in situations where the decoded image is to be assessed solely on a quantitative basis), simple distortion measures may well be adequate, and thus we may set an upper limit to the mean square error (or possibly to the maximum error amplitude) generated by the coding–transmission–decoding process. Where the human viewer is concerned, the determination of just what the error measure should be has consistently proved to be the stumbling block in attempts to apply theoretical analyses to the relation between minimum transmission rate and an allowable level of perceived image degradation. The other problem of the ill-defined nature of the input data probability distribution is, in a sense, of secondary importance, since it is possible to upper-bound the transmission rate, even if it cannot be explicitly calculated.

It is possible, of course, to doubt whether a truly viewer-specific fidelity criterion (i.e., a functional relationship between the degree of annoyance felt by a particular observer and the measurable characteristics of the degraded image) will ever be definable, since what that viewer considers to be objectionable is a purely subjective matter—if interested in some aspect of spatial detail, accurate colour reproduction may be of no consequence, for example. Again, individual viewers concentrate their attention on particular areas of a display at any one time, and large distortions in other regions of the visual field may well be of little consequence. On the other hand, the attention of the casual observer, whose eye roams, initially at least, at will over the displayed image, will be caught by isolated large impairments, especially if each is caused by individual localised luminance errors which are correlated, i.e., form a pattern with readily recognisable structure. In such a situation a suitable error criterion will attempt to restrict the magnitude of the few large impairments, at the expense of dealing with many relatively small ones, perhaps by the use of a mean nth power measure of the form $E(x - \hat{x})^n$, where x is the original, and $\hat{x}$ the reconstructed, element amplitude and n is not 2, as in the case of mean square error but possibly 5 or 6. Furthermore, there is the problem of just what degree of 'realism' should be attempted in an image transmission system, for there is a marked contrast between such a system and one designed, say, to reproduce high-quality music. In the latter case, it is nowadays possible to generate, with good equipment, to the satisfaction of most listeners, the aural illusion of being subjected to the original sound field, i.e., of actually sitting in the concert hall. A true basis for an aural fidelity criterion is therefore the difference between what is to be coded (the original signal) and what is actually heard. Where images are concerned this is at present (and probably for the forseeable future) impossible. A small screen displays a two-dimensional representation of what, to the observer situated at the camera location, is a three-dimensional presentation of spatial and temporal detail spanning the whole of his visual field. It has been suggested, therefore, that a more appropriate comparison would be between the displayed image and the best possible photographic reproduction of the same scene. There is a further aspect of the matter, though, which concerns the divergence between laboratory tests of image coder performance and the actual use of such a system to reproduce images at a distant location. In the former situation, it is invariably the case that comparison is made between the input data (for example, a test slide scanned and digitised) and the reproduced image after decoding. The captive viewer of the real system output, however, makes no such comparison, and it would be possible to present him with an accurate spatial reproduction of the scene in which all the colours had been changed, or even a completely different high-quality image, for him to perceive no visible degradation. Under such conditions any distortion measure which is, in any sense, a function of the difference between input and displayed images would be meaningless. His criterion of fidelity would be only the absence of any impairments in an image which he compared, not with the original, but with what such scenes 'ought' to look like. As a less extreme example of such a discrepancy between numerical and perceived quality measures, it has frequently been demonstrated, in regard to both photographic and video display of images, that the viewer prefers reproduced scenes in which the edge detail has been artificially emphasised to the original data. As an interesting example of this effect in the present context Parsons and Tescher (1975) applied high sequency emphasis to a 16×16 array of DCT coefficients using the function

$$W(i,j) = 1 + \tfrac{1}{15}[(i-1)^2 + (j-1)^2]^{1/2}, \qquad i,j = 1 \rightarrow 16 \qquad (6.1)$$

and found that, at a coding rate of 2.6 bits/element, the processed image was preferred to the original.

There is also the influence of viewing conditions upon the perception of the displayed image. Although the luminance of a particular region in the display is an objective (measurable) quantity, the brightness which the observer detects is a subjective quantity dependent on both the luminance of surrounding picture areas and of the region around the display as a whole. It is effects such as these, combined with the basic non-linearity of the eye's amplitude response, which make even a simple visual distortion measure dependent not only upon the difference between original and reconstructed images but a function of the original and reconstructed element values also, i.e., $f((\hat{x}), x, \hat{x})$ which, only in the case when the actual distortion $f(x - \hat{x})$ is small, may be approximated by $f((x - \hat{x}), \hat{x})$. The severe difficulties associated with the development of a numerical fidelity criterion are responsible in part for the widespread use of subjective quality ratings in tests carried out by, for example, the broadcasting authorities (see, e.g., Pearson, 1975). Panels of skilled or unskilled (i.e., the 'average' viewer) subjects view, under closely controlled conditions, sets of displayed images and accord them various quality ratings. Such procedures require much time and effort, as well as detailed statistical analysis, if their results are to be consistent, but they do have the advantage that they provide a direct link between coding impairments and quality degradation of the displayed image. On a more modest level, informal viewing results are often reported, in conjunction with mean-square-error figures, by those involved with the simulation or implementation of coding schemes such as are described elsewhere in this volume, but lack of uniformity of testing procedures between research groups usually renders the results of little value except in the most approximate sense.

Inherent in the use of subjective tests of image quality is the problem of deciding just how bad one obviously impaired image is when compared with another. Tests based on comparison with otherwise good-quality images impaired by various levels of white noise, or with deliberately defocused images have been devised, but the results are still much more variable than those obtained when measurements are restricted to low levels of degradation. Such a restriction is less of a problem than might appear at first sight, since we may presume that, except under exceptional circumstances, heavily degraded images are unacceptable in any case, and any impairments resulting from the use of a satisfactory coding scheme will, of course, be held to a low level. In this connection, it is somewhat paradoxical that the least important signals (entertainment television, for example) are subject to the most stringent impairment criteria, compared with, say, military communications. Presumably the interpretation of 'information content' is different in two cases! Much attention has therefore been centred upon the threshold of detection of image degradation, and from these results extrapolation, with care, into the region of low levels of impairment ought to be possible. As far as utilising the results of research work dealing specifically with the operation of the HVS is concerned; this is a fortunate circumstance, since most of that work has been directed towards establishing the characteristics of threshold vision, rather than towards the operation of that system at levels well above threshold.

Turning now to the more specific matter of the influence of coding techniques on the presence of impairments in the reconstructed image, it is important to point out that different schemes necessarily generate different kinds of distortion. Thus images processed using predictive coding methods are subject to granular noise if the inner levels of the quantiser are too widely spaced, or to visible quantisation error if the quantisation of large values of the difference signal is too coarse (Mussman, 1979). It is particularly fortunate in this case that the masking property of the eye in the presence of a luminance edge in the original image (see the following) allows the determination of a 'visibility' function which determines whether or not an error in luminance value in such a location will be visible. The quantiser of a predictive coding scheme may then be designed on the subjective basis of visibility of luminance error (rather than, say, the analytical minimisation of mean square error) to ensure that such errors remain undetected. Where transform coding is concerned, the situation is not nearly so clear-cut. Errors in individual coefficients manifest themselves as incorrect basis picture amplitudes and therefore appear, with greater or lesser effect, over the whole of the relevant block. On the other hand, transform coding is a spatial frequency (or sequency) decomposition, and evidence is well established now that the eye operates in a similar way, analysing spatial detail according to the outputs of the analogues of a set of parallel band-pass filters (Campbell and Robson, 1968). It should be possible, therefore, to account for this characteristic of the HVS in terms of selective weighting of the various transform coefficients prior to bit-allocation and coding, with a complementary step following coefficient decoding, and before inverse transformation at the receiver. In spite of the fact that this technique is only theoretically correct in the case of the Fourier transform, recent experiments have shown that it is also successful with other transforms, and these are described subsequently.

In the following sections of this chapter the properties of the HVS which are relevant to image coding are first considered, and a model of the system is developed which takes them into account. It is then shown how the model may be applied to transform image coding schemes to improve their subjective performance. The development is carried out initially in terms of the still monochrome image, since it is in this area that the majority of research work has been carried out. Additional effects due to colour and motion are then included, although relatively little work has been carried out in connection with the latter. For further discussion on the interaction between the properties of the HVS and image compression schemes, the reader is referred to Pearson (1967, 1975), Limb (1967), Schreiber (1967), Stockham (1972), and Sakrison (1977).

6.2 Properties of the eye

Prior to the development of a model for the HVS, it is necessary to consider the physical characterisation of the eye and the observable effects to which these give rise. The treatment presented here is brief, and more detail can be found in Cornsweet (1970), Hall (1979), and Lindsay and Norman (1977).

Visible light covers the approximate wavelength range of 400 (violet) to 700 (red) nm, and is focused by the lens (which has an aperture variable over the range 2–8 mm, controlled by the iris) onto the light sensitive retina some 15 mm away. The incident light intensity is detected by means of a photochemical reaction with sensors of two kinds, 'rods' and 'cones', the former having the greatest sensitivity, although lacking colour response, and operating at very low light levels (scotopic vision), the latter being responsible for higher intensity (photopic), high resolution and colour vision, for which last mentioned purpose they occur in three main types, each having an absorption peak at a different location within the visible spectrum. Together, the rod/cone system allows operation of the eye over an intensity range of some 11 orders of magnitude and it is evident, therefore, that a very large degree of adaptation to background intensity takes place within the various stages of the process of visual perception. The distribution of both types of detector across the retina is highly non-uniform, with a total of approximately 6×10^6 cones concentrated at the fovea (a small area some 0.5 mm across on the retina near the optical axis of the lens) where the area density reaches perhaps $150,000/mm^2$—the fovea is the location of maximum visual acuity and gives a perceived area about $1.5°$ across upon which the viewer fixes his attention with maximum resolution. The area density of cones falls to one-tenth of the maximum value at about $7°$ off axis. The 10^8 rods are maximally concentrated to something like the same degree approximately $20°$ off axis, and the density has fallen to perhaps one-half at the visual periphery ($70–80°$ off axis) and to zero at the fovea. Since the network of sensor interconnections, neural cells (neurons) and optic nerve fibres lies between the photoreceptive elements and the lens, a blind spot is caused, containing neither rods nor cones, some $15°$ off axis, where the nerve fibre bundle leaves the eye. There are many fewer (roughly 8×10^5) optic nerve fibres than individual sensitive elements and so, although the ratio of fibres to sensors is approximately $1:1$ at the fovea, it falls to $1:100$ or lower at the visual periphery. Varying numbers of receptors are therefore interconnected, in different regions of the retina, before contact with the optic nerve is established, and this cross-coupling is responsible for the initial stage in the processing of visual information. Transmission of that information along the optic nerve fibres takes place in the form of impulses which occur at a rate which is variable, but is governed by the intensity of the stimulus, and has a maximum value of several hundred per second.

Any useful model of the operation of the HVS must take into account as many of the phenomena which are revealed by the everyday working of the eye as possible, and there is a long history of work in this area, carried out under controlled laboratory conditions, with the object of defining and explaining various perceptual effects. Basically there are four 'dimensions' to the operation of the eye which are of relevance in the present context, i.e., how it behaves as a function of the independent variables (a) intensity, (b) variation in spatial detail, (c) variation in temporal detail and (d) colour. Knowledge of these responses would then enable a complete model of the system to be constructed which would materially aid the attack on the fidelity criterion problem referred to in the preceding introduction. Unfortunately, whilst the methods of operation of certain mechanisms within the HVS are firmly established, others are more conjectural, and there is still debate over the appropriate forms of explanation and modelling. Again, the various responses are not separable, spatial and temporal acuity being linked, for example, and this inevitably adds to the complexity of the model. As far as the response to still monochromatic images is concerned, the matter is simplified to a consideration of the eye's characteristics with regard to intensity and variation in spatial detail, and these will allow us to generate a basic HVS model, which may subsequently be modified to attempt to account for motion and colour effects.

6.2.1 The amplitude response of the eye

It has already been pointed out that the eye is able to respond to an enormous range of intensities (of the order of 10^{11}), from starlight to the threshold of pain. Since the pupillary aperture can vary in diameter by only about $4:1$, it is apparent that a very large degree of adaptation to average scene luminance exists at the receptor level of visual processing, since it is inconceivable that the frequency of generation of the impulses which travel along the optic nerve could vary by a factor of 10^9–10^{10} [Estevez and Tweel, (1980) suggest that the fluctuation in impulse rate for constant stimulation lies in the range 1–10%]. Nor is this necessary in practice, since a much smaller dynamic range is adequate, within a given observation (i.e., average overall luminance level), in everyday life. Thus experiments to demonstrate the minimum noticeable difference between a visual target area and a small surrounding region produce results which depend critically upon the state of the main background area (see Fig. 6.1). As long as $L_B = L$, the just noticeable contrast ratio $\Delta L/L$ is approximately 2% (the Weber fraction) over a range of L some four orders of magnitude in extent. At lower and higher values of L the ratio is larger and the eye consequently less sensitive (curve a, Fig. 6.2). If L_B is held constant, however, the range over which $\Delta L/L$ is small is considerably less, as shown by curve b in the figure. Schreiber (1967) suggests that the dynamic range of the eye is about 2.2 logarithmic units, and various other estimates [for example, the results of Kretz (1975) on

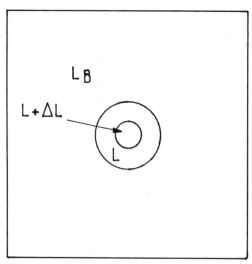

FIG. 6.1. Configuration of target, surrounding and background illumination. Here, $L + \Delta L$ is the target luminance, L the surrounding luminance and L_B background luminance.

subjectively optimal quantisation] confirm that, given an overall background (adapting) luminance, the number of distinguishable brightness levels is roughly 150–250.

The significant fact about the preceding experiment is that the minimum noticeable luminance difference is a constant fraction of the surround luminance rather than a constant value itself. The visual system thus

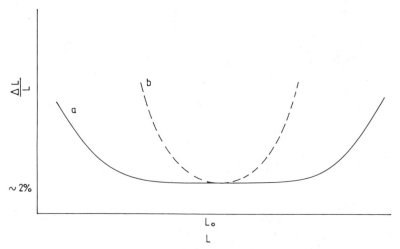

FIG. 6.2. Just noticeable contrast ratio $\Delta L/L$ as a function of relative displayed luminance. (a) $L_B = L$ and (b) $L_B = L_0$.

responds, at or near threshold at least, to fractional changes, i.e., the relation between response and stimulus is logarithmic, and perception of brightness depends on the ratio of object to surround luminance, rather than on its absolute value. This implies that a disturbance of a given magnitude (noise, for example) will be more noticeable in areas of an image that are dark than elsewhere. In fact this effect is considerably modified by the non-linearity of the display device

$$L = kE^{\gamma} \qquad (6.2)$$

where L is the displayed luminance, E the electrical input to the display tube, and γ is typically 2.5, which tends to cancel the logarithmic operation inherent in the eye's amplitude response (Limb, 1979) making the overall visual response an approximately linear function of the electrical signal produced by the system, i.e., where analogue or quantisation noise occurs. In fact, due to the presence of ambient illumination surrounding the display, degradation due to noise in very dark areas tends to be less visible than that occurring in regions of higher luminance. There is thus a more complex relationship between the visual luminance threshold and nearby and more distant illumination levels than appears at first sight (Netravali and Limb, 1980).

6.2.2 The spatial response of the eye

It is readily apparent that intricate spatial detail becomes more difficult to perceive, the smaller is the visual angle subtended by the component parts. Eventually, with increasing complexity, individual structure is no longer perceptible, and we are justified, in a qualitative way, in considering that the eye's spatial response falls to negligible values at a high enough spatial frequency (the number of complete cycles of a sinusoidally varying luminance pattern per degree subtended at the eye). Likewise, experiments have shown that the sensitivity of the eye to regions of constant luminance (i.e., zero spatial frequency) is also low and so, as Schreiber (1967) has pointed out, for us to be able to see at all the response must be substantial over some intermediate range of spatial frequencies. It turns out that, not only is this general frequency range well defined (albeit a function of both overall luminance level and temporal activity) but there is good experimental evidence that the visual system subdivides the spatial frequency range into individual narrow-band channels and detects visual events on the basis of the outputs of such channels (the exact width of such filters is a matter of some debate; see Stromeyer and Klein, 1975). This is particularly interesting from the point of view of transform coding, since it operates in a very similar way, converting the spatial detail in an image into frequency (or sequency) components and processing and coding them, rather than the original data.

Research into the operation of this mechanism of the HVS ought, therefore, to be able to guide the efficient manipulation of the spectral coefficients of such a system. As far as the overall spatial frequency response is concerned, we have the further opportunity of exchanging contrast fidelity for resolution, since in areas of high detail, where good resolution is required, the eye is more tolerant of inaccuracies in absolute luminance level.

It is worth noting here that the behaviour of the eye in general is governed by the operation of groups of receptors some of which have an 'excitation' type of response, in that their illumination causes an increase in the rate of generation of the impulses which travel along the optic nerve, and others which operate by an 'inhibition' mechanism, i.e., the corresponding impulse rate is decreased (Cornsweet, 1970). Such groups are often coupled in one of two ways, i.e., either 'on-centre, off-surround' or vice versa. The terminology is self-explanatory. Furthermore, the overall response is inhomogeneous, since the distribution of such groups is not uniform over the retinal area. Thus even the amplitude response, as described in the previous section, is modified by spatial effects, first by the influences upon different receptor groups of the background and surround luminances, and second by the fact that, for very small target areas, the luminance threshold becomes a function of target area (Lukas and Budrikis, 1982). An account of receptive field distribution and properties is given by Braccini *et al.* (1981), who consider, amongst other things, a processing step which would account for response invariance to changes in scale (i.e., a given object is detected as such whether it is nearby or far away). Again, the measurements of Limb (1976) and Limb *et al.* (1977) of the line spread function of the receptor field as a function of eccentricity (displacement from the visual axis of the eye) show that it more than doubles in width as the eccentricity changes from 0 to 8°.

The perceptual effects of spatial interactions are usually demonstrated via the phenomena of simultaneous contrast and Mach bands (both of which, incidentally, can be demonstrated in terms of colour response as well as monochrome effects). In the first of these, the perceived brightness of a target area of constant luminance changes as the surround luminance is varied, appearing darker the higher is the latter quantity. Furthermore, the magnitude of the effect varies according to the incident level of illumination. Thus, if the contrast between centre and surround is low, increasing the overall illumination increases the perceived brightness of the target region. If the contrast is high, increasing the illumination level makes the target area seem darker, and an intermediate value of contrast can be found for which the brightness of the target remains constant when the illumination is varied (Lindsay and Norman, 1977). The second effect appears at a sudden change in luminance, and is responsible for making the step appear sharper than it really is. Thus a region of high constant luminance level on one side of the boundary depresses the perceived brightness of the region of lower (but again constant) luminance next to it. The phenomenon responsible for these two effects is generally known as 'lateral inhibition' and, in terms of the spatial response of the eye, can be modelled as a high-pass filter which has sharply reduced sensitivity to regions of constant, and slowly varying, luminance and allows the selective detection of sharp changes (i.e., the edge structure of objects). In this connection it is relevant to refer to the phenomenon of spatial masking, which is related to, but different from, the Mach band effect (Limb, 1976). It is found that the luminance change threshold, as defined earlier in this chapter, is sensitive to the presence of a nearby luminance transition. Put another way, the threshold is higher than it would be if the transition were not present, and the transition is thus said to 'mask' small perturbations of luminance in the neighbourhood. Thus (Limb, 1967), for a transition amplitude of approximately 10 % of the maximum possible the threshold of a one-element wide vertical line one picture element from the transition (about 1 minute of arc) is already some four times that for the situation in which the boundary is not present. Furthermore, the effect is strongly dependent upon the spacing between line and transition, falling to a negligible level when the separation is doubled and rising by a factor of about 3 when the line and transition are coincident (Budrikis, 1972). Other experiments have confirmed this very narrow spread of the phenomenon (Lukas and Budrikis, 1982), which is in contrast with that of the occurrence of Mach bands by the latter's greater width (estimated at about 0.5°), and the fact that whereas the brightness increases on the high luminance side of the transition, it decreases on the other (Limb, 1976). The fact remains, however, that the observer in a masking experiment will inevitably be subject to the presence of the Mach effect, and the separate responses to the two effects are likely to be difficult to distinguish. A further significant feature of the spatial masking effect is that it is a function of the gradient of the luminance change against which it is measured (in a typical image it will therefore be dependent on localised picture detail), and this has been taken into account by Netravali and Prasada (1977) who have defined masking functions on the basis of weighted slopes of luminance values over an area a few picture elements in extent and used them to optimise the quantisation process in predictive coding systems (see also Sakrison, 1979). This is a fruitful instance of the application of HVS properties to the coding of images, since the quantisation error is now directly related to the displayed luminance value. In a transform coding system it is of course the transform coefficients which are subjected to quantisation error and their relation with the final reconstructed image is only indirect. It is not apparent, therefore, that the masking property of the eye can be employed to improve the performance of such schemes.

Before examining models of the human visual response in more detail, one factor which is independent of the operation of the retinal receptors should be mentioned, and that is the effect of the purely optical (pupil/lens) system. Westheimer and Campbell (1962) have measured the retinal distribution of light formed by the human eye and have found the line spread function to have the form.

$$h(\theta) = e^{-\alpha|\theta|} \tag{6.3}$$

where θ is measured in minutes of arc and α, for a pupil diameter of 3 mm, is 0.7. The Fourier transform of $h(\theta)$ produces the spatial frequency response

$$H(\omega) = 2\alpha/(\alpha^2 + \omega^2) \tag{6.4}$$

which has a 3-dB point at $f = \alpha/2\pi = 6.7$ cycles/deg. Incoming visual information is thus low-pass filtered by the optical system before any retinal/neural detection and processing can occur. In particular, this filter operates, of course, before the logarithmic non-linearity, and this influences the composition of the appropriate spatial model of the HVS (see the following).

The main elements of the human visual response, as just described, have now to be incorporated into a model which can be employed, for example, to enhance the efficiency of a data compression scheme, or, somewhat more conjecturally, to replace subjective testing as a method of assessing image quality. To the extent that refinement of the model then allows us to predict the response of the eye to more complex test conditions, it also enables us to learn more about the operation of the HVS per se.

6.3   Modelling the human visual system

The main features of the HVS to be modelled are a low-pass spatial response due to the physical properties of the system, a high-pass spatial response due to the interconnection of the various receptor regions (lateral inhibition), and an amplitude (point) non-linearity due to the adaptation mechanism that allows the system to operate over a wide range of background intensity. There is also the question of a detection mechanism to be 'connected ' to the output of the preceding stages in order to determine whether or not the stimulus has been perceived.

As far as the spatial response of the HVS is concerned there is reasonable agreement between the various published results. Overall measurements of the luminance threshold as a function of spatial frequency have been carried out by many workers and Mannos and Sakrison (1974) report several of these. Whilst there are differences in detail (due, no doubt, to variations in experimental conditions as well as differences in response from individual to individual), all results show similar general characteristics—a peak in the response at perhaps 4 to 7 or 8 cycles/deg (which, however, falls to a lower value at the periphery; Stromeyer and Julesz, 1972), with a fall-off to about

3 % of the maximum at 0.1 cycle/deg and at 30–40 cycles/deg on the low- and high-frequency sides, respectively (see Fig. 6.3). In circuit theory terms, the Q value of the band-pass response is, very roughly, 0.5. Kelly (1975) has approximated the contrast sensitivity function by

$$G(\omega) = \omega^2 e^{-\omega} \tag{6.5}$$

where the ω^2 term is responsible for a response increasing with increasing frequency (approximating the effect of lateral inhibition). The Fourier transform of $G(\omega)$ will then be the effective (circularly symmetric) receptive field.

The preceding measurements have been carried out using sinusoidal gratings having various orientations, with the result that the horizontal and vertical behaviour of the eye is found to be similar whilst, at a spatial frequency of 10 cycles/deg, the response in a diagonal direction is reduced by

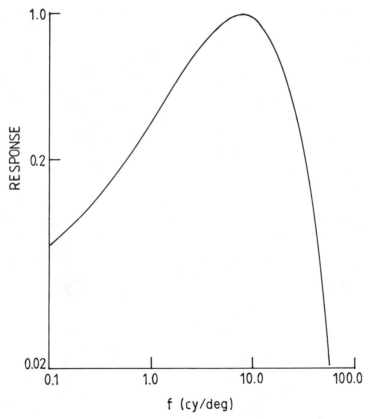

FIG. 6.3. Typical plot of the relative spatial frequency response of the eye.

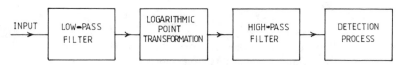

FIG. 6.4. Basic model of the human visual system.

about 15% (Hall and Hall, 1977). It appears then, that whilst the response of
the eye is anisotropic, the effect is small, under threshold viewing conditions,
at least.

We are thus led to the basic model of the form described by Hall and Hall
(1977) and shown in Fig. 6.4, which accounts for the gross characteristics of
the system. If measurements are confined to very small luminance increments,
then the model may be rearranged by replacing the low-pass filter after the
logarithmic non-linearity. For larger contrast ratios this is no longer acceptable, as the results of Davidson (1968) using exponential contrast gratings
indicate. Were the log–band-pass filter model adequate, the exponential and
logarithmic functions would cancel, leaving a linear filter system whose
response is independent of level. In fact Davidson's results were contrast
dependent at high, but not low, spatial frequencies, implying that the
cancellation is ineffective in that region, i.e., the correct location of the low-
pass filter was between the exponential and the logarithmic functions (at the
HVS system input). The model of Fig. 6.4 is analysed in some detail by Hall
and Hall (1977), who point out, in general, that it represents a band-pass filter
whose bandwidth is a function of image contrast, decreasing as the contrast
level increases [Cavonius and Estevez (1980) and Lloyd *et al.* (1982) suggest
the opposite, however]. Its application to image transform coding will be
described subsequently.

As mentioned earlier, the Q factor of the overall visual response is very low
and the question then arises as to the existence of fine structure within the
pass band of the filter. The results of Campbell and Robson (1968) on the
response to gratings of various spatial frequencies and profiles (sinusoidal,
square, sawtooth, etc.) provide evidence for the existence of individual,
narrow-band spatial frequency channels within the HVS, each with an
independent detection mechanism. A typical profile is defined by the relation

$$L(x) = L_0[1 + m \sin(2\pi f x + \varphi)] \tag{6.6}$$

where $m = (L_{max} - L_{min})/2L_0$ is the contrast, L_0 is the background luminance
and f is the spatial frequency. As far as overall filter behaviour is concerned,
the envelope of the separate spatial channel characteristics forms the total
response of Fig. 6.3. The individual channels have significantly reduced
sensitivity at frequencies one-half and two times that for which it is a

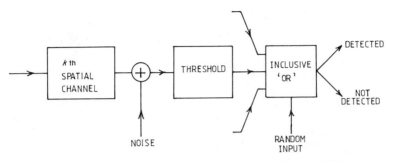

Fig. 6.5. Visual detection mechanism according to Sachs *et al.* (1971).

maximum. These results were substantiated by Sachs *et al.* (1971) who investigated the detection of both simple and compound gratings (i.e., those containing one, or two, sinusoids, in the latter case of different frequencies). The detection mechanism was taken to be of the form shown in Fig. 6.5, where the addition of noise represents the uncertainty of the detection mechanism and the random input accounts for the proportion of positive identification of stimuli when in fact none is present. In the case where $f/f' = 2$ (f and f' being the frequencies of the two components within a compound grating), independent detection could be assumed for values of f between 5.6 and 28 cycles/deg. In the lower-frequency region (below $f = 2.8$ cycles/deg) the evidence indicated that the channels were more broadly tuned (i.e., of lower Q), whereas the Q value of the higher-frequency channels seems to be approximately 3 or 4 (see also Stromeyer and Klein, 1975). A later experiment by Stromeyer and Julesz (1972) on the masking of sinusoidal gratings by narrow-band noise further reinforced the tuned spatial frequency detector hypothesis. As far as the mechanism producing the narrow-band response is concerned, Kelly (1975) argues that it may well be caused by the spatial distribution of receptive fields, rather than any higher-level neural processing.

The model developed by Sakrison *et al.* (1975) and Sakrison (1977, 1979), whilst broadly on the lines of that just described, differs from it in one or two points of detail. In this case the narrow-band spatial filters have a bandwidth of approximately ± 0.4 times the centre frequency and the filter output of the kth channel, $v_k(x, y)$, is weighted by a factor $a_k(x, y)$ which takes account of the increase in contrast sensitivity which takes place as the spatial extent of the observed grating is increased (Robson, quoted in Sakrison *et al.* 1975). To account for the observed depression of the luminance threshold due to the presence of background detail (the spatial masking phenomenon referred to earlier), the product $v_k(x, y)a_k(x, y)$ is divided by $(1 + s(x, y))$, where $s(x, y)$ is a measure of the local rms gradient (Netravali and Prasada, 1977). The detection process is represented by the operation of a nonlinearity, and the resulting function is integrated over the image to form the output

$$r_k = \int\int \left(\frac{a_k(x, y)v_k(x, y)}{1 + s(x, y)} \right)^n dx\, dy \qquad (6.7)$$

where the value $n = 6$ is in agreement with experimental observations (for the range of normally visible stimuli, as opposed to those being just detected, i.e., at threshold, n falls to 1). The various r_k are then subject to noise input and the remainder of the model of Fig. 6.5. As can readily be seen, the model has now become quite complicated, and Sakrison suggests simplification in order to make it easier to use, for example by dropping the weighting functions $a_k(x, y)$.

A similar narrow-band spatial filter model has been reported by Pearlman (1978), who relates the response of the eye to a luminance increment to the change in the probability of detection in order to develop a distortion measure for image restoration applications (see also Lloyd et al., 1982), and Limb (1979) has considered a model which involves filtering, masking and the application of the widely disparaged mean-square-error measure (amongst several other power law relations), in which the image is divided into areas subtending 1° of arc and the average of the two largest error values taken before a square-root operation to generate the rms error value. It is suggested that the rms measure can produce significant results since, for the majority of images, edge detail forms a relatively small fraction of the total area and so, although the effect of masking will allow a greater amount of edge noise to yield equal noise visibility over the image, that increased amount only forms a small fraction of the whole and so does not affect the rms error criterion greatly. It is the visible noise in 'flat' areas of the image, therefore, which dominates the assessment.

Masking is also included in the model of Lukas and Budrikis (1982) in which, in the spatial domain (temporal response is considered also), the outputs of parallel excitation and inhibition operations are combined in a non-linear fashion (Budrikis, 1972) to account for both high-pass filter response and adaptation to background luminance. The separate (linear) channels have outputs determined by the convolution of the input luminance distribution with the spatial spread function of inhibition and excitation responses. This processing is carried out for both the stimulus plus background signal (although the masking signal is derived from the background excitation response alone), and that due to the background only, the difference is taken and subjected to a masking operation dependent upon gradient magnitude (as referred to earlier) followed by threshold detection. In this case error powers of 3 or 4 gave the best results (compared with 2 in the rms case).

6.3.1   Effects due to motion

The previous section has described, in some detail, the development of models which attempt to account for the spatial and amplitude responses of the eye to stationary luminance patterns, the objective being (a) to obtain a numerical quality measure which is well correlated with observed image degradation, to obviate the need for elaborate subjective testing routines and (b) to improve the efficiency of image coding schemes by trying to concentrate the inevitable degradation associated with data compression of the present type in regions of the reconstructed image where it will be least visible.

These objectives apply equally well, of course, to moving image sequences, although now a further independent variable (time) has to be taken into account. In fact, although the spatial and temporal axial coordinates x, y and t are independent, the responses are not, and strong coupling exists between spatial and temporal effects, i.e., they must be regarded as non-separable. For example, just as in a still image the presence of a high degree of spatial detail increases the contrast threshold, so, where motion is concerned, the visibility of spatial detail falls as the velocity of moving objects increases. Furthermore, in the case of the most violent degree of motion, i.e., a change of scene (something confined to artificial image representation, i.e., foreign to nature), the spatial resolution can be reduced to perhaps 5–10% of normal, provided that it is restored within 0.5–1.0 s, without visible effect (Seyler, 1962, 1963; Seyler and Budrikis, 1965). Budrikis (1972) suggests that this phenomenon is due to temporal masking by the sudden scene transition—the counterpart of the spatial masking effect discussed earlier, and Ninoyima and Prasada (1979) propose that a moving object provides a significant degree of masking with respect to the newly uncovered background area from where it has just moved. Higher levels of distortion (i.e., less accurate coding) can therefore be allowed in that region. Spatio–temporal coupling is further illustrated by the results of Robson (Budrikis, 1972) who made measurements equivalent to those resulting in Fig. 6.3 but with gratings modulated temporally as well as spatially. Where the spatial effect is unimportant, the contrast sensitivity as a function of temporal frequency (hertz) follows a form similar to that of the spatial response (Fig. 6.3), starting from a relatively low value at low frequencies, reaching a peak at approximately 6 Hz and falling off rapidly thereafter. The low-pass response is due to the time delay involved in the photochemical reaction at the receptors, and the high-pass part of the response may be due to a delay in the inhibitory response compared with that of excitation (Hall, 1979; Limb, 1976). This response is illumination dependent, and the band-pass characteristic disappears, to be replaced by a low-pass response at low levels (Pearson, 1975). For spatial frequencies above about 5 cycles/deg the temporal response, likewise, changes from a band-pass characteristic to one which is simply low pass. A similar feature is present in the spatial response at temporal frequencies of approximately 6 Hz. Thus, above these frequencies, separability can be assumed. Otherwise, spatio–temporal coupling should be taken into account. In terms of a temporal response model Hall suggests a low-pass/logarithmic/high-pass interconnection similar to that proposed for the spatial response.

The spatial model of Lukas *et al.* described earlier also incorporates properties of the response to temporal stimuli. In order to simplify the analysis, they assume separability of spatial and temporal properties represented by (a) Gaussian point spread function and (b) an exponential impulse response, respectively. The temporal masking signal is obtained by differentiating the combined excitation/inhibition response with respect to time.

It will be apparent that, although the visual response to motion has been subjected to extensive research, its properties have not, in general, been incorporated into models of the HVS to anything like the extent to which spatial characteristics have been employed. Potentially, of course, the benefits of a comprehensive spatio–temporal model are very great, given the widespread use of television systems and their attendant degradations due not only to any coding operations, but also to the fundamental nature of the raster scan/field-frame interlace process.

6.3.2 Effects due to colour

The properties of the HVS referred to in earlier sections have all been described in terms of the response to monochromatic test fields. For levels of luminance of most interest for image coding (i.e., those corresponding to a typical television monitor display), colour response is important, and any model developed in the way previously discussed must be modified to take account of this. Again, only the properties of colour vision relevant to the use of HVS models in image coding are considered here; the general topic of colour display and vision is extremely wide ranging, and even that of colour representation in television systems far too detailed to be covered here (see, e.g., Pearson, 1975). In a slightly more general context, a comprehensive review of digital coding of colour signals is given by Limb *et al.* (1977).

Basically the HVS responds to three properties of a coloured area: hue (what is colloquially termed colour, i.e., red, green, etc.) dependent on wavelength; brightness—the perceived (subjective) intensity of the area; and saturation—the spectral purity of the colour, highly saturated colours consisting of narrow band radiation with little white content. Perception of colour is due to the presence in the retina of three types of cones whose responses peak at wavelengths of approximately 440, 550 and 580 nm, i.e., in the blue, green and green–yellow regions of the spectrum. The response of the latter receptors remains appreciable in the red region and is of approximately the same sensitivity as that of the green receptors whilst the blue receptors are considerably less sensitive (Lindsay and Norman, 1977). Intercoupling between colour receptors is responsible for the generation of output signals based upon what is known as the 'opponent process' system and is well supported by experimental evidence. Thus the four colours blue, red, green and yellow combine in two opponent pairs, blue–yellow and red–green, in addition to which there is a black–white channel responsible for brightness perception. Hue response results from combinations of the outputs of blue–yellow and red–green channels, and saturation from a comparison of the relative proportion of black–white output compared with that of blue–yellow and red–green (it is worth noting that there are other models for the perception of colour information; see Limb et al., 1977). The 'opponent' colours exist in complementary pairs, and thus a red area makes neighbouring areas seem greener, and so on. Furthermore, the previously described luminance properties of brightness constancy, simultaneous contrast and Mach bands can all be demonstrated as colour phenomena as well, and there is considerable evidence that, in both spatial and temporal domains, significant masking can occur, both of one colour signal by another, and of a colour signal by the associated luminance component (Limb et al., 1977; Dennis et al., 1979).

How, then, is the basic model of the HVS, previously developed, affected if its colour response is to be accounted for? As in the case of effects due to motion, where colour response is concerned, also, refinement of the model has not reached a very advanced stage, at least as far as image coding applications are concerned. Frei (1976) and Frei and Baxter (1977) propose a modified version of Fig. 6.4 (logarithmic function/band pass) of the form shown in Fig. 6.6 (see also Faugeras, 1979), where

$$\begin{bmatrix} T_1 \\ T_2 \\ T_3 \end{bmatrix} = \begin{bmatrix} 0.299 & 0.587 & 0.114 \\ 0.607 & 0.174 & 0.201 \\ 0 & 0.066 & 1.117 \end{bmatrix} \begin{bmatrix} R \\ G \\ B \end{bmatrix} \tag{6.8}$$

and

$$\begin{bmatrix} G_1^* \\ G_2^* \\ G_3^* \end{bmatrix} = \begin{bmatrix} 21.5 & 0 & 0 \\ -41.0 & 41.0 & 0 \\ -6.27 & 0 & 6.27 \end{bmatrix} \begin{bmatrix} \log T_1 \\ \log T_2 \\ \log T_3 \end{bmatrix} \tag{6.9}$$

The T_1 channel performs the task of generating a signal corresponding to luminance from the original R, G and B inputs (as in the conventional

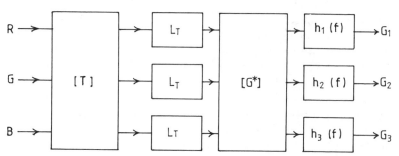

FIG. 6.6. Colour human visual response model according to Frei (1976). Here, R, G and B are colour inputs, $[T]$ the transformation of Eq. (6.8), L_T the logarithmic transformation, $[G^*]$ the transformation of Eq. (6.9), $h_i(f)$ the band-pass spatial filter operations and G_i the model outputs.

representation). The logarithmic and band-pass spatial filter $h_1(f)$ operations the follow in the same way as for the monochrome case. The opponent process colour signals are generated in channels T_2 and T_3, whose outputs are invariant to linear scaling of the R, G and B inputs. The characteristics of $h_2(f)$ and $h_3(f)$, corresponding, respectively, to the red–green and blue–yellow channels, have a similar form to that of $h_1(f)$ (i.e., the response of Fig. 6.3) but with peak frequencies of approximately 1.0 ($h_2(f)$), and 0.5 ($h_3(f)$) cycles/deg. One further interesting feature of the model is that it is very effective in 'compacting' the total R, G and B colour image energy selectively into the G_1^* channel (whilst leaving the other two channels significantly correlated, however). A similar model has been used by Hall and Andrews (1978), albeit with a rather different transformation. The results obtained when such models are applied in image coding schemes are described subsequently.

6.4 Application of visual models
to the assessment of image quality

The overriding reason for the development of HVS models, in the context of image storage and/or transmission, is the hope that sufficiently comprehensive representation of the way in which the system operates will enable quality assessment to be carried out on an objective (quantitative) basis, thus removing the necessity for subjective testing. In this respect, due to various considerations referred to in the introduction to this chapter, there is a distinct possibility that it will never be feasible completely to replace such tests but, rather, that large degrees of degradation, or those of a specific kind, might be detected or measured 'automatically'. Obviously, the larger any numerically measured degree of impairment becomes, the more likely is it that the corresponding visual effect will be perceptible (although there are exceptions to this generalisation, see the following), and thus common sense might initially dictate that automatic measurement of gross distortion in the reproduced image would be followed by a stage of subjective assessment. In fact, whether or not such a procedure might be acceptable will depend very much upon the specific coding application. Thus in low bit rate coding (large degrees of compression), some perceptible distortion is usually allowable and the use of even such a gross numerical measure as mean square error is helpful as a rough guide to likely image quality. On the other hand, a broadcast television system, for example, will demand the absence of any visible degradation (i.e., that any degradation that does occur will be below the threshold of perception), and any corresponding numerical measure will take on very small (and probably very variable) values. Although the first situation may appear to be most suited for numerical assessment of image quality, it is the second which, paradoxically, may give greater scope for simpler HVS models, the reason being that for very small degrees of perceptible degradation, the usual model at threshold is either valid, or its characteristics may be cautiously extrapolated to cover the situation, there being significantly less information available concerning the operation of the HVS at levels considerably above threshold. The majority of work has thus been concerned with the first step in establishing a visual model for the numerical assessment of image degradation, and that is to consider the case of still, grey-scale images in which the level of distortion lies approximately at the visual threshold. Thus early work by Sakrison and Algazi (1971) to determine the effect of moving from one- to two-dimensional encoding of random images in terms of the required transmission rate for a given distortion employs a simple model consisting of a logarithmic nonlinearity followed by spatial filtering and then by a mean square distortion measure as indicative of the 'distance' between original and reproduced image fields (the result of the comparison, incidentally, is that two-dimensional processing allows the rate to be reduced by a factor of 2–3 compared with the one-dimensional result; this aspect of their paper is discussed further in Chapter 9). The application of such a model is considered by Stockham (1972) who points out the justification for its use—it emphasises those features of the original image which are similarly emphasised by the visual system, and vice versa. He also makes a point which is crucial to the relationship between subjective and objective image assessment, i.e., those distortions considered significant by the eye may well be numerically relatively small. Thus minor degradation in areas of uniform luminance is likely to be more perceptible than numerically more serious errors in active regions.

In order to investigate the detailed applicability of a model of the preceding type to the determination of image degradation, Mannos and

Sakrison (1974), whilst still employing a mean-square-error measure (to enable straightforward calculation of the associated rate distortion function $R(D)$; see Chapter 9), varied both the parameter determining the non-linearity (which constitutes the first stage of processing) and those of the subsequent (linear) spatial filter to determine what the optimum functional relationships should be. Thus different images were coded (at a predetermined number of bits per element) in accordance with a model of the HVS emphasising and/or suppressing various characteristics of the image depending on the exact form of the non-linearity and spatial filter. Extensive subjective tests were then used to assess the reconstructed images on both a 'best image' and a quality scaling basis. The conclusions drawn by the authors were as follows: The most important parameter is the frequency at which the spatial filter has maximum response, and this was found to be approximately 8 cycles/deg, i.e., somewhat higher than in the majority of psychovisual experiments. It is possible that this might be accounted for by the preference of observers, in general, for images whose edges have been sharpened to some degree, as pointed out earlier in this chapter. The value of the low-frequency intercept was found to be less critical, as was the rate of fall-off in the response at high frequencies. The resulting filter response is given by

$$A(f) = 2.6(0.0192 + 0.114f) \exp[-(0.114f)^{1.1}] \qquad (6.10)$$

As far as the non-linearity is concerned, overall preference was shown for a cube root, rather than a logarithmic, relationship. The investigation of Mannos and Sakrison has been extended to colour images by Frei (1976) and Frei and Baxter (1977). Their colour HVS model has previously been described, and it was used to carry out comparisons between numerically calculated mean square distortion values (in the 'perceptual space' following the model) and subjectively determined image quality ratings. Good agreement was obtained, and the authors conclude that such a fidelity criterion is apparently consistent with human quality judgements. The use of a model of this kind in the discrimination of colour texture fields is reported by Gagalowitz (1980).

The application of the parallel band-pass spatial frequency model to the establishment of an image quality criterion has been considered by Sakrison et al. (1975) and Sakrison (1977, 1979). The major difference from the foregoing approaches (apart from the multiple filter channels) is the inclusion of the masking function of Eq. (6.7) and the value of the error power ($n = 6$), which is obviously very sensitive to the numerically largest errors present. This accords with the hypothesis that the attention of the eye is selectively drawn to the largest errors present in the reconstructed image. As far as the spatial filtering is concerned, Sakrison postulates a radially symmetric arrangement of wedge-shaped responses spaced approximately every $10°$ in angle and each extending radially to ± 0.5 of their individual centre frequencies, covering the range 1-25 cycles/deg. A similar approach is taken by Pearlman (1978), with the exception that the probability of detection at the output of each channel is used as the basis of the fidelity measure. The overall distortion measure is the average of the responses of each of the channels, where the response is taken to be the squared absolute difference between corresponding Fourier coefficients (equivalent to the band-pass filter outputs) of the true and distorted images weighted by a function of the amplitude of the true coefficient, where the weighting function accounts for the effect of changes in intensity on the detection probability. Experiments involving optimal linear filtering of images in noise suggest that the criterion is more effective than the conventional squared error measure.

Limb (1979) has considered the question of error power in more detail in the case in which the error signal is the difference between picture elements in the original and reconstructed images,

$$e_i = x_i - \hat{x}_i \qquad (6.11)$$

and the measure of image impairment EM_p is given by

$$EM_p = \left[\frac{1}{N} \sum_{i=1}^{N} \left| \frac{e_i}{W_i} \right|^p \right]^{1/p} \qquad (6.12)$$

where there are N elements in the image, and W_i represents the masking effect of local image activity around element i. He finds that rms error ($p = 2$) is a reasonably good criterion of visible image distortion. This conclusion is apparently borne out by the results of Girod (1981), although he finds that subjective quality is better correlated with the logarithm of the mean square error. Based on the results of his experiments, Limb postulates a model in which the error signal is filtered, subjected to masking, squared and integrated over a localised area of the image, as described earlier. It is interesting that it was consistently found that the preferred filtering function was low pass rather than band pass, and it is conjectured that it is insufficient simply to follow the filtering operation with a masking step, since high-pass effects due to inhibitory mechanisms may not occur until masking has taken place.

A similar model (apart from the fact that logarithmic transformation precedes masking) is applied by Algazi and Ford (1980) in a study of the degradation produced by low-pass filtering. In this case it is demonstrated that impairments occur preferentially at edges in the image and are of the same type as those which appear when only a piecewise constant approximation to the image (i.e., containing edge detail alone, without fine structure) is filtered. An ideal luminance edge [i.e., a (scaled) unit step function] therefore constitutes a worst case test image, and filters may be designed on the basis of minimisation of the response of the HVS model which have subjectively better performance when compared with equiripple Tchebyschev designs.

Carlson and Cohen (1980) have likewise used high contrast one-dimensional luminance edge transitions as one form of test image in order to generate a model which will predict the visibility of various characteristics of a displayed image—sampling structures, changes in modulation transfer function, and so on. They consider a set of octave wide filters, with centre frequencies between 0.5 and 48 cycles/deg, followed by the introduction of noise terms to represent (a) 'background' noise which determines the ultimate channel sensitivity and (b) the Weber-law response at high input levels. Square-law detection and spatial summation then follow. Their results are presented in graphical form as 'discriminable difference diagrams' (DDDs), which give the total number of 'just noticeable differences' (jnds) in the MTF of a display as a function of spatial frequency. For any particular set of circumstances the change in MTF required to produce, for example, 1 jnd may then be determined by inspection.

The model of Lukas and Budrikis (1982), as previously described, includes the effects of motion in a prediction of visual image quality. The distortion measure is given by an equation of the form of Eq. (6.12), only this time temporal variations are included:

$$N = \left[\int_X \int_Y \int_T |N(x, y, t)|^p \, dx \, dy \, dt \right]^{1/p} \tag{6.13}$$

where $N(x, y, t)$ is the output of the model. A detailed discussion of the effects of using various values of p and of different methods of error averaging is presented, and the conclusion is drawn that values of p in the region of 2–4 are appropriate, together with averaging the maximum local error in each frame over all frames, in a similar fashion to the approach of Limb referred to earlier.

6.5   Transform coding and the visual response

Apart from modelling the characteristics of the HVS as a means of supplementing, or eventually even supplanting subjective testing, they can also be taken into account more directly in the actual image coding process. This has been done successfully in the case of predictive coding by such workers as Netravali (1977) and Netravali and Rubinstein (1977), Sharma and Netravali (1977), Sharma (1978), and Limb (1978) to design quantisers whose displayed error is maintained below the threshold of visibility by making use of the masking properties of the eye in the presence of a sharp change in luminance (where the prediction error will naturally take on large values), or high levels of local activity more generally.

Since predictive coding is an element-by-element process, i.e., each individual data point is coded and subsequently reconstructed, this procedure is quite feasible. In the case of transform coding the situation is quite different, since not single data elements but one- two- or three-dimensional blocks are reconstructed at a time. The quantisation error incurred in coding an individual transform coefficient is therefore not simply reflected in the reconstructed value of a given data element; on the contrary, the quantisation error magnitudes of all coefficients coded in turn affect, in a complex way, the visible luminance values of all reconstructed elements within a particular image sub-block. Such subjective optimisation as has been carried out in this way has, therefore, of necessity been of limited scope. Other methods of subjective optimisation have proceeded on a rather *ad hoc* basis by modifying quantiser and bit allocation parameters in such a way as to improve the visible quality of the reconstructed image. Such approaches have, in fact, been successful, and they are discussed in more detail subsequently.

An alternative way of making use of the properties of the HVS in transform coding is to employ the model as a pre- and post-processing step, before the coefficient quantisation and bit allocation stage, and after reconstruction of the transform coefficients from the decoded data at the receiver. It thus takes on the role of a pre-emphasis/de-emphasis operation, in which those signal properties to which the eye is most sensitive are artificially increased in magnitude, and the inevitable processing error added. After decoding, the complementary de-emphasis stage at the receiver reduces the desired signal to its correct level and, in so doing, also reduces the magnitude of the introduced error. Since transform coding is basically a spatial frequency (sequency) decomposition, and the eye has a reasonably well-defined spatial frequency response, the latter can be used for the process as applied to the transform coefficient set, and encouraging results have been obtained in this way. The non-linear amplitude response of the eye can also be made use of in a similar fashion. The process is known as 'perceptual' or 'psychovisual' coding, and the actual coding operation is considered to take place in a 'perceptual' space formed by the action of the HVS model upon the input image in the same way that the 'mechanistic' part of the eye's operation affects the data prior to interpretation by the brain.

6.5.1   Subjective optimisation of coding parameters

The adaptive coding scheme of Tasto and Wintz (1971) has been described elsewhere (Chapter 5), and here reference is made only to the techniques used for subjective optimisation of the coding parameters with respect to reconstructed image quality. The 6×6 image sub-blocks were divided into three categories: (I) highly detailed blocks, (II) blocks with little detail and darker than average and (III) as category II but lighter than average. Initial experiments with unquantised coefficients indicated (for a specific data set) that it was necessary to retain the largest one-third of the 36 coefficients of category I blocks, and one-sixth of the coefficients of blocks in categories II and III. Determination of the maximum quantisation step size (initially the same for all coefficients) that was subjectively tolerable followed, and this was then allowed to increase with increasing coefficient order (a linear relation between order and magnitude of the quantisation scaling constant was found to be optimum) to correspond with the fall-off in HVS response with spatial frequency. Adjustments of quantiser step size and the actual number of coefficients retained enabled a balance to be maintained between truncation distortion and that due to quantisation. It was found that, for a given coding rate, images processed with the subjectively optimised system had a higher quality than those processed with the system optimised for minimum mean square error and, for a given quality, subjectively optimised images had a significantly higher mean square error.

Jones (1979) made a somewhat similar investigation into the drawbacks of transform compression system design based upon minimisation of mean square error and the assumption of first-order Markov statistics for the data source. An 8×8 WHT was used, and comparison made between standard design procedures and an experimental approach intended to cater specifically for edge detail (which causes some transform coefficients to take on ranges of values much greater than the Markov assumption would indicate), and for low contrast blocks. Thus bits were preferentially added to the assignments for coefficients in the first row and column, to account for the presence of horizontal or vertical luminance transitions at the expense of the theoretical allocations for coefficients of smallest variance. To deal with blocks of low contrast (where quantisation errors are likely to be most visible) the quantisers were arranged to have one reconstruction level (and not a decision level, as is more usual) at, and several reconstruction levels near, zero. It is interesting that, in this case, the modified design has not only better subjective performance, but lower mean square error also, in contrast to that of Tasto and Wintz.

It was suggested earlier that, due to the complex relation between coefficient quantisation error and image element reconstruction, quantiser optimisation based upon subjective criteria is likely to prove much more difficult than in the case of predictive coding. An experiment of this kind has been carried out by Mounts et al. (1977), however, using a small (2×2) WHT to make use of perceptual redundancies dependent on local picture detail. In fact, the time and effort involved in carrying out the experiment for each coefficient of a more usual (8 × 8 or 16 × 16) block size is likely to prove a deterrent to a wider application of the method. The experiment consists of adding noise (simulating quantisation error) to an AC coefficient (H_2, H_3 or H_4), whenever that coefficient (which represents, in some sense, a difference in picture element amplitudes within a block and thus constitutes a masking signal) exceeds a threshold, and the same procedure is applied to the difference of successive horizontal block DC coefficients (masking over two adjacent blocks). The generated impairment is then compared subjectively with additive white noise impairment of the same image. Functional relationships are then plotted relating the visibility of noise to the coefficient threshold. It was found that the diagonal term was unimportant and could be ignored in this context. On the basis of these results quantisers were designed using standard techniques (Chapter 4) but weighting the quantisation error according to its subjective visibility before minimisation. Such quantisers were found to have more widely spaced decision and reconstruction levels than the equivalent minimum mean-square-error quantisers, and required fewer levels (for example, 24 compared with 30) for equivalent picture quality. Their further application is described by Netravali *et al.* (1977).

6.5.2   'Perceptual' transform coding

In this approach to efficient image coding an attempt is made, more or less systematically, to take into account the properties of the HVS in the design of a processing scheme, rather than simply carrying out an *ad hoc* experimental variation of parameters in order to improve subjective quality. There are three basic characteristics which can be used in this way—the non-linear amplitude response, the varying spatial frequency response, and the variation in spatial resolution requirement following a violent (scene-change) alteration in image detail. Most work has concentrated on the second of these factors, and it will soon become apparent that more can yet be done to take the detailed nature of the HVS response into account in transform coding in particular and in image coding in general.

Thus Anderson and Huang (1971) performed the coding operation on the logarithm of the input picture brightness (see also Pratt, 1971), and compensated for this step by an exponentiation at the decoder before the reconstructed image is displayed, the object being to distribute the effects of any error occurring in the coding process more evenly across the luminance range of the image, rather than allowing them to appear selectively in low-brightness regions. In fact, of course, the strong non-linearity of the display device will tend to carry out such a compensation step, independent of decoder exponentiation, and the exact nature of the benefit to be gained is then dependent upon the relation between input luminance and pick-up device electrical output (if this is relatively linear, and is followed, as in a television system, by gamma correction, then the addition of the non-linearity of the display device to the coding/decoding chain will imply that an approximate logarithmic/exponentiation type of amplitude-dependent processing is being carried out in any case). As far as spatial response is concerned, Anderson and Huang note that the sub-block width (one-sixteenth of a picture width) viewed at a distance of four times picture height has a period corresponding to a frequency of approximately peak response in the spatial frequency characteristic, and so higher-order Fourier components are naturally weighted by smaller and smaller factors as the spatial frequency increases, in accord with the reduced accuracy with which a conventional transform processing scheme operates on such coefficients. The spatial frequency characteristic of the eye is also taken into account by Enomoto and Shibata (1971) who employ a visual weighting function when determining the numbers of bits to be allocated to the various coefficients of an 8th order one-dimensional Hadamard or slant transform to be used in a television application. Another worker to employ a weighting function of this kind is Ghanbari (1979). The visual weighting function used by Zvi-Meiri (1976) for bit allocation following a 16×16 pinned sine transform is of a similar nature and is obtained by fitting an approximate visual spatial model to the 16×16 coefficient set under the interesting assumption that the viewing distance is not fixed but that the observer will tend to sit at that distance at which single elements are just below the visual threshold of resolution (say, 1.25 minutes of arc). The 16×16 block then subtends an angle of $16 \times 1.25 = 20$ minutes, which corresponds to three block widths per degree, i.e., 1.5 cycles/deg since the lowest term in the DST response (in contrast to that of the Fourier transform) is one-half cycle. Transform coefficients thus span the visual spatial frequency range 1.5–24 cycles/deg.

Perhaps the first real exploitation of an HVS model in the context of coding is that of Mannos and Sakrison (1974) already referred to. Although their experiments were intended to determine an amplitude non-linearity and spatial frequency model which would lead them towards an improved numerical fidelity criterion, the system employed was basically a Fourier transform coder operating at a predetermined rate, and they point out the benefits to be gained by using pre- and post-processing operations based upon the HVS model. In fact, the degree of improvement to be obtained from such a procedure is very much a matter for discussion. O'Neal and Natarajan (1977) used Mannos and Sakrison's weighting function [Eq. (6.10)], though not the accompanying point non-linearity, in connection with experiments using 8×8 and 4×4 DCT, DFT and WHT processing and found the resulting bit allocations little altered by its application. On the other hand, the visual model of Frei (1976) again described previously has been used to code images at an overall rate of 1 bit/element. The addition of uncorrelated Gaussian noise at various points in the coding process (at the input, after the logarithmic transformation and after the spatial filtering) demonstrated that its introduction at the final stage (i.e., in the 'perceptual' domain) produced a reconstructed image which had the lowest perceived visual noise and distortion. Further, the results of Hall and Andrews (1978; see also E. L. Hall, 1979; C. F. Hall, 1980) with both monochrome and colour images suggest that there are substantial advantages to be gained by perceptual or psychovisual processing. They use a logarithmic non-linearity and a two-dimensional isotropic version of Mannos and Sakrison's spatial frequency response, together with the DFT, and determine the bit allocation by modifying the power spectrum of an input process assumed to be first-order Markov by the spatial frequency weighting function, in order to calculate the coefficient variances. A similar procedure is followed in the case of colour images, in which the appropriate filter responses (see Fig. 6.6) are used. For a black and white image, rates of 0.1 bit/element were obtained and colour images could be coded at 1 bit/element with no visible degradation, and at 0.25 bit/element (total) with minor distortions. It is suggested that rates an order of magnitude lower than those previously employed will, with the aid of perceptual processing, produce images of comparable quality. In this case, and in contrast to the results of O'Neal, the bit allocation map changes its form appreciably, more bits being assigned to the middle-order coefficients, as would be expected. As compared with the more usual small sub-block transforms, a full-image DFT was apparently used for this experiment, and this seems to give much greater flexibility to the application of the spatial model to the coefficient set, which may account for the improved results (other benefits to be gained from such an approach have previously been mentioned in a different context; see Chapter 5). The application of the point non-linearity to the data luminance values will also tend to modify the variance distribution used in the bit-allocation step—a process not included in O'Neal's experiments.

A somewhat different approach is suggested by Algazi and Ford (1980) based upon their visual model described earlier. Since in their work the worst case image for processing is one which contains a high contrast edge, they initially determine a threshold by applying their model to the difference signal generated between the input image (a luminance step) and its approximate reconstruction obtained via the orthogonal (transform) expansion. Blocks are then coded retaining sufficient terms in the expansion to ensure that the error signal, again processed by the model, does not exceed the threshold.

Hall's work, as described earlier, was restricted to the Fourier domain, for the very good reason that it is the transform that, by definition, provides an exact spatial frequency representation of the properties of the input data. The Fourier coefficients can then be processed directly with the spatial visual model. Where other transforms are concerned, the data domain/coefficient domain equivalence is only approximate and, where the WHT and DCT, etc., have been employed for psycho-visual coding, a rough equivalence in terms of sequency has been assumed. As far as the DCT is concerned the problem has been investigated by Griswold (1980), who defines a cosine domain energy function related to the slope of the image correlation function. Thus when the latter slope is large, the energy function is allowed to maintain a significant amplitude over a wider coefficient range, corresponding to a wide *frequency* response for data of lower correlation, as would be expected. The distribution function is then modified by the (Mannos and Sakrison) spatial filter response and bit-allocation follows in the usual way. Again the process allocates rather more bits (i.e., more accurate quantisation) to those coefficients corresponding to important areas of the HVS spatial frequency response. Coding of the same image as used by Hall using a 16×16 DCT resulted in acceptable images at rates of 0.5–1.0 bit/element, and higher values of signal-to-noise ratio than those obtained without pre-processing, results which are by no means as remarkable as those of Hall, possibly again due to the relatively small block size.

In fact, in its application of the Mannos and Sakrison weighting function to DCT coefficients based upon the coefficient order [i.e., the independent variable in Eq. (6.10) is replaced by $(i^2 + j^2)^{1/2}$, where i and j are the two-dimensional coefficient indices within a 16×16 block], Griswold's approach bypasses the problem of where, given a specific spatial *frequency* component in the image, the equivalent energy resides in terms of the *sequency* of the transform coefficients. This has been investigated by Clarke (1983b) who measured the transform domain energy distribution for the 8×8 and 16×16 DCT and WHT as a function of sine-wave data input of arbitrary phase. It was found that, no matter what the phase relation between the input sine wave and the transform window, energy in the DCT domain resided almost exclusively in three neighbouring coefficients centred at the location of the frequency component corresponding to the DCT basis vector. Thus, for example, with $N = 16$ the fourth basis vector is a sampled approximation to two complete cycles of a sine wave. For sinusoidal data having a period equal to one-half the window width, therefore, whatever the input phase relation with the transform window, the energy always appears predominantly in coefficients 3, 4 and 5. Since the usual weighting function is fairly broadly peaked, pre-emphasis is naturally applied to not just one, but to several adjacent coefficients, and this is sufficient to justify, at least in an approximate sense, the application of the spatial HVS model to the perceptual coding of DCT coefficients. Where the WHT is concerned this result no longer holds, and energy appears at seemingly unrelated locations amongst the coefficients. Furthermore, the use of a small block ($N = 8$) is not advisable since it allows only a very coarse approximation of the weighting operation to be carried out, and this lends support to the apparent superiority of full frame (256×256 or 512×512) transforms in this application. Subsequent work on the other transforms described in Chapter 3 has yielded the general conclusion that those transforms whose basis vectors are approximately similar in shape to sinusoidal waveforms (sine, cosine and Fourier) are successful in the present application, and those whose basis vectors are of a rectangular nature (WHT, Haar, slant, etc.) are not. This result is probably to be expected intuitively on the interpretation of the transform coding operation as one of correlation between a basis vector and detail of a similar form within the image.

On the question of the application of the HVS model to the transform coding of moving images, very little work has been reported, and it remains a largely unexplored area. One well-documented property, however, is the reduction in sensitivity to spatial detail which occurs after a violent scene change (Seyler and Budrikis, 1965). The coding scheme of Jones (1977) has been described previously, and it suffices here to point out that the update procedure for changed sub-pictures initially adds only low-sequency coefficients, followed by those of higher order, in accordance with this particular property of the eye. In a similar way the scheme of Kamangar and Rao (1980, 1981) preferentially allocates extra coding bits to the low-sequency coefficients within a sub-block that is considered to be temporally active. No further bits are added to the high-sequency coefficients of the sub-block even if it is considered to be spatially active also. It remains to be seen whether less extreme forms of temporal masking can be accommodated within the transform coding process as applied to moving images and, even then, just what the benefits will be.

6.6 Conclusions

This chapter has considered, briefly, the operation of the human eye specifically as the endpoint of the visual communication chain which starts with the original scene and opto-electronic pick-up device. It has been shown how a model for the most elementary viewing situation, that of threshold detection of impairments in a still achromatic image, can be developed, and how that model has been modified, albeit in a rudimentary way, to account for the effects of colour and motion. It goes without saying, of course, that such models will continue to be developed and refined in the future to take account of more complex viewing situations (for example, supra-threshold visibility of impairments, chrominance/chrominance and luminance/chrominance masking in spatial and temporal domains), and the use of such models will enable both improved quality measures and fidelity criteria to be generated. In addition, the application of such models to the actual coding process may be expected to become more widespread and in this context the apparent advantage of large block sizes, compared with small, will bear more investigation. Again, not nearly enough attention seems to have been directed towards satisfactory control of the relationship between image size and viewing distance. Since the application of a spatial frequency 'preemphasis' operation, by its nature, renders, as does the eye itself, certain spatial frequencies more important than others, it is at first sight vital that those emphasised components should appear of the correct spatial frequencies to the viewer, i.e., there is only one correct value for the viewing distance/image dimension ratio; and yet this matter is only occasionally mentioned in reported work on the topic. In fact the broadness of the characteristic does allow some relaxation in this requirement, and yet this itself argues that very large reductions in coding rate are not to be obtained in this way. Another feature that merits more detailed study is that of system non-linearity. As already mentioned, a television system employing gamma correction already places the coding process in a 'perceptual' domain as far as the amplitude response is concerned (when the display device luminance/electrical input relation is taken into account). Further non-linear processing will then tend to over-compensate for the otherwise increased visibility of errors in picture areas of low luminance. More often than not, scenes are 'observed' by devices whose values of gamma are nowhere near the inverse of that of the typical display device, leaving the relation between scene luminance and displayed luminance markedly non-linear. Again, many processed images are initially produced photographically, and subsequently electro-optically scanned, and this leads to unspecified degrees of luminance/output signal non-linearity even before any further processing is carried out. In fact, the eye is, as a whole, remarkably tolerant to gross defects of this nature, and manipulation of the display monitor brightness and contrast controls too easily covers a host of imperfections with regard to correct displayed response. Major advances in the application of HVS models to image transform coding and quality measure development must therefore rest, to a large degree, upon the use of more tightly controlled experimental standards, data scanning linearity, display device linearity, surround viewing conditions, etc., which have been evident, so far, in little of the published material in the field.

Chapter 7

Fast Transforms and System Implementation

7.1 Introduction

It is no exaggeration to say that, over the space of the last 20 years two developments, one general and one more specific, have revolutionised the practice of signal analysis and manipulation. The first of these has been the move from analogue to digital signal representation, which itself has been fostered by the explosive growth in the application of the digital computer to problems in signal theory and communications. Since such computers are unable to process real numbers represented with an arbitrary degree of accuracy, and are also incapable of accepting data which is a continuous function of some independent variable (time or space, for example), this application has prompted the representation of signals determined at specific points in time or space (i.e., necessarily band limited and sampled at the appropriate rate), and with an accuracy limited by that of the analogue-to-digital converter or by computer word length (the former being more usually the case). Analysis now proceeds on a discrete basis using, for example, z transform methods, in which the integrals which fill the older texts on signal and communication theory are replaced by summations, and the result must then be considered in the light of its correspondence with the exact (analytical) result. This has given rise to many extensive analyses in, for example, the case of the Fourier transform and its discrete approximation, the DFT (see, for example, Brigham, 1974). The fact that the results so produced *are* inexact implies that particular care must be taken in their production using discrete techniques and, of course, in their interpretation. Thus, again, a large body of

291

literature has built up over the years dealing with reliable techniques for the estimation of power spectra, to quote but one example.

Hand in hand with the development of discrete signal manipulation has gone the rapid advance in hardware with which to carry out such tasks. The widespread application of complex high-speed integrated circuits containing hundreds of thousands of, individually, very simple circuit elements needs no further comment, save to say that, until recently, even 'state-of-the-art' hardware of this kind has not been advanced enough to cope with real-time operations upon high-resolution images. Such is the pace of hardware development, however, that difficulties in implementation are rapidly becoming insignificant, allowing the application of increasingly sophisticated adaptive real-time processing algorithms. Unfortunately, of course, a description of the very latest hardware techniques is inevitably rendered impossible in the context of a volume of this nature because of the rapid changes which occur, but an attempt will subsequently be made to survey the progress made in implementing transform coding systems, which, by their nature, are much more demanding in terms of processing complexity than, say, the predictive coding approach.

The more specific development referred to previously concerns the algorithmic details of carrying out the discrete calculation. The basic operation of signal analysis is the conversion between temporal (or spatial) and frequency domains by the use of the forward and inverse Fourier transforms, an operation which involves many complex multiplications and additions. Even with discrete signal representation and high-speed manipulation, the sheer volume of computation involved in multiplying a vector of N by an $N \times N$ matrix meant until fairly recently that Fourier transforms were non-real-time operations involving huge amounts of computer time. In the mid-1960s, however, came the realisation that there were in existence (but known to relatively few workers) methods of decomposing a matrix, such as that employed in the Fourier transform, into a product of sparse matrices (i.e., those containing a significant number of zero entries). A single, large calculation was thereby converted into a sequence of much simpler operations with the result that the number of multiplications was greatly reduced. Typically, by the use of the method, the number of operations necessary fell from N^2 to approximately $N \log_2 N$. The historical background to this 'rediscovery' is intriguing and is discussed by Cooley et al. (1967). Various forms of the 'fast Fourier transform' (FFT) were soon generated and are detailed in many books, for example those by Brigham (1974) and Elliott and Rao (1983), and also in the extensive professional literature on the subject. The technique was (and is) applied to what seem purely time (or spatial) domain processes, for convolution and correlation can be carried out by product manipulation in the Fourier domain followed by inverse transformation, and the application of the FFT and its inverse made this approach more efficient than the equivalent, purely time or space domain, operations. As far as image transform processing is concerned, the FFT allowed Fourier image coding to be carried out much more speedily and also prompted the development of fast versions of other transforms, until now almost all of the transforms discussed in Chapter 3 have true fast routines for their execution.

The following section of this chapter, then, is devoted to a discussion of the generation of fast routines for the various transforms which have been employed in image coding, and in this respect in particular one or two points are worth emphasising. First, the basic FFT routine which has received by far the most attention is that in which the length of the data vector N is an integral power of 2. Versions exist in which this restriction is relaxed, first to the situation in which N is highly composite (i.e., a product of several factors) and second to the case in which N may take on any value (it turns out, however, that the use of base 2 is reasonably efficient and, in any case, a data sequence of arbitrary length can usually be 'padded out' to a length equal to 2^g, where g is an integer, without difficulty). In image transform coding the dimensions of the block to be coded are almost invariably powers of 2 (8, 16, 32, etc., 8×8, 16×16, occasionally 8×4, and so on), and whilst there is no strict requirement that this be the case, since the actual block size used does not strongly determine coding efficiency, such a choice, which makes digital implementation straightforward, is normal. The second point is that there is a distinction between the use of a transform in the estimation, say, of power spectra, and its use in image coding. In the former application, due to the inexact correspondence between the discrete and analytical Fourier transforms, the application of some form of smoothing or windowing technique to improve the reliability of the estimate is necessary, and this has led to the development of an extensive array of window types each with its advantages and disadvantages (Harris, 1978). In transform coding, the transform is employed to generate a domain in which the original spatial data is represented exactly by the spectral coefficients, and inverse transformation will allow its precise reconstruction (of course the gain in coding derives from the application of approximations, i.e., deleting small coefficients and more or less accurately quantising the remainder, but the fact remains that the initial transform representation is exact, and the information content of the two domains is the same; see Andrews, 1968). Windowing and smoothing techniques therefore have no place in transform coding schemes (any post-reconstruction filtering carried out to improve the visual appearance of the displayed image is naturally a different matter unconnected with the basic transform process). Finally, the reader comparing the examples of fast

Fourier (FFT) and fast Walsh–Hadamard (FWHT) decomposition in this chapter will notice a strong similarity between them. In fact they are both members of a family of orthogonal transforms generated via matrix factorisation. The detailed treatment of this topic is not directly relevant to the theme of this volume, however, and the interested reader is referred to the work of, for example, Ahmed and Rao (1975) and Fino and Algazi (1977). Since the development of the fast Fourier algorithm has received most attention over the past 20 years or so, we begin with a review of that transform, although others discussed subsequently (the DCT, for instance) have been of wider interest in the field of transform coding per se.

7.2   Fast Fourier transform

The algorithm to be described here initially is that due to Cooley and Tukey (1965) [based upon the work of Good (1958) who considered the sparse matrix factorisation method for calculating the N vector/$N \times N$ matrix product], and used by them to compute complex Fourier series. Although their development is general, it is clearer and more convenient (and of direct application to transform coding) to consider the specific numerical example in which the one-dimensional block length $N = 8 = 2^g$, where $g = 3$. The development for other values of g then follows the same lines.

The calculation of the DFT of a set of data points f_k requires the evaluation of the sum [see Eq. (3.80)]

$$C_p = \frac{1}{\sqrt{N}} \sum_{k=0}^{N-1} f_k e^{(-2\pi jpk)/N} \qquad p = 0 \rightarrow N - 1 \qquad (7.1)$$

in which we note that the factor $1/\sqrt{N}$ is merely an overall scaling factor used in the development to ensure equivalence, for theoretical convenience, between data and transform domains. In a practical coding system its use is unnecessary, and it need not be included in determining the computational requirement for Eq. (7.1). Furthermore, it is conventional to write

$$W = \exp\left(-\frac{2\pi j}{N}\right) \qquad (7.2)$$

and therefore Eq. (7.1) may be rewritten as

$$C_p = \sum_{k=0}^{N-1} f_k W^{pk} \qquad (7.3)$$

where in this example $N = 8$ and p and k range from 0 to 7.

The calculation becomes, in matrix form, that shown in Eq. (7.4) (note that the matrix entries denote powers of W),

$$
\begin{bmatrix} C_0 \\ C_1 \\ C_2 \\ C_3 \\ C_4 \\ C_5 \\ C_6 \\ C_7 \end{bmatrix} =
\begin{bmatrix}
0 & 0 & 0 & 0 & 0 & 0 & 0 & 0 \\
0 & 1 & 2 & 3 & 4 & 5 & 6 & 7 \\
0 & 2 & 4 & 6 & 8 & 10 & 12 & 14 \\
0 & 3 & 6 & 9 & 12 & 15 & 18 & 21 \\
0 & 4 & 8 & 12 & 16 & 20 & 24 & 28 \\
0 & 5 & 10 & 15 & 20 & 25 & 30 & 35 \\
0 & 6 & 12 & 18 & 24 & 30 & 36 & 42 \\
0 & 7 & 14 & 21 & 28 & 35 & 42 & 49
\end{bmatrix}
\begin{bmatrix} f_0 \\ f_1 \\ f_2 \\ f_3 \\ f_4 \\ f_5 \\ f_6 \\ f_7 \end{bmatrix}
\tag{7.4}
$$

and, if we consider the vectorial representation of W^s,

$$
W^s = \cos(2\pi s/N) - j \sin(2\pi s/N) \tag{7.5}
$$

it is evident that the following relations hold,

$$
W^0 = W^{rN} = 1 \tag{7.6}
$$

$$
W^{s \pm (N/2)} = -W^s \tag{7.7}
$$

$$
W^{s+rN} = W^s \tag{7.8}
$$

where r and s are integers. These relationships are exemplified in Fig. 7.1. The matrix in Eq. (7.4) may thus be written

$$
[T] =
\begin{bmatrix}
1 & 1 & 1 & 1 & 1 & 1 & 1 & 1 \\
1 & W^1 & W^2 & W^3 & -1 & -W^1 & -W^2 & -W^3 \\
1 & W^2 & -1 & -W^2 & 1 & W^2 & -1 & -W^2 \\
1 & W^3 & -W^2 & W^1 & -1 & -W^3 & W^2 & -W^1 \\
1 & -1 & 1 & -1 & 1 & -1 & 1 & -1 \\
1 & -W^1 & W^2 & -W^3 & -1 & W^1 & -W^2 & W^3 \\
1 & -W^2 & -1 & W^2 & 1 & -W^2 & -1 & W^2 \\
1 & -W^3 & -W^2 & -W^1 & -1 & W^3 & W^2 & W^1
\end{bmatrix}
\tag{7.9}
$$

and there are now only 14 distinct complex products to be evaluated.

The Cooley-Tukey formulation begins by writing p and k in binary notation as

$$
p = 2^{g-1}p_{g-1} + 2^{g-2}p_{g-2} + \cdots + p_0
$$

$$
= 4p_2 + 2p_1 + p_0 \tag{7.10}
$$

$$
k = 2^{g-1}k_{g-1} + 2^{g-2}k_{g-2} + \cdots + k_0
$$

$$
= 4k_2 + 2k_1 + k_0 \tag{7.11}
$$

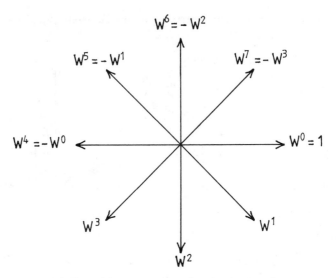

FIG. 7.1. Vectorial representation of W^s for the case of $N = 8$.

since in the present example $N = 8$ and so $g = 3$. Note that the p_i and k_i only take on the values 0 or 1. Equation (7.3) can then be written

$$C_{(p_2, p_1, p_0)} = \sum_{k_0=0}^{1} \sum_{k_1=0}^{1} \sum_{k_2=0}^{1} f_{(k_2, k_1, k_0)} W^{(4p_2 + 2p_1 + p_0)(4k_2 + 2k_1 + k_0)} \qquad (7.12)$$

We now separate the W exponent in terms of k, making use of the relation of Eq. (7.8) to obtain

$$(4p_2 + 2p_1 + p_0)4k_2 \equiv 4p_0 k_2$$
$$(4p_2 + 2p_1 + p_0)2k_1 \equiv (2p_1 + p_0)2k_1$$

thus Eq. (7.12) may be written as three nested summations

$$f_{1(p_0, k_1, k_0)} = \sum_{k_2=0}^{1} f_{(k_2, k_1, k_0)} W^{4p_0 k_2} \qquad (7.13)$$

$$f_{2(p_0, p_1, k_0)} = \sum_{k_1=0}^{1} f_{1(p_0, k_1, k_0)} W^{(2p_1 + p_0)2k_1} \qquad (7.14)$$

$$f_{3(p_0, p_1, p_2)} = \sum_{k_0=0}^{1} f_{2(p_0, p_1, k_0)} W^{(4p_2 + 2p_1 + p_0)k_0} \qquad (7.15)$$

where $f_{3(p_0, p_1, p_2)}$ is the desired set of output coefficients $C_{(p_2, p_1, p_0)}$ in *bit-reversed* order.

From Eq. (7.13) we see, for example, that, setting $p_0 = k_1 = k_0 = 0$

$$f_{1(0)} = \sum_{k_2 = 0}^{1} f_{(k_2, 0, 0)} W^0 = f_{(0)} + f_{(4)}$$

and, setting $p_0 = k_1 = 0, k_0 = 1,$

$$f_{1(1)} = \sum_{k_2 = 0}^{1} f_{(k_2, 0, 1)} W^0 = f_{(1)} + f_{(5)}$$

and so on.

There are thus g ($= 3$ here) stages in the computation, at each of which each newly calculated value is a function of two previously determined ones. The result is usually depicted in the form of a signal flow diagram, as shown in Fig. 7.2, where BR represents the bit reversal (relocation) operation. It can be seen that, in this example, the data appear in 'natural' order, and the coefficients in bit-reversed order. Furthermore, the original data array can be used to store the intermediate coefficients as they are generated, since each pair such as $f_{1(3)}$ and $f_{1(7)}$ is a function of f_3 and f_7 only. Many variations upon this basic approach are possible and are described by Brigham (1974). An upper bound to the number of multiplications needed is $2N$ per stage, with $g = \log_2 N$ stages, i.e., $2N \log_2 N$, although the number is significantly lower, since many multiplications are by factors W^0 ($= 1$) or $W^{N/2}$ ($= -1$). Furthermore, although separate products of the form $+ W^i$ and $- W^i$ emanate from the same intermediate node, they constitute (together with a sign change) only one actual procuct. In the case of a one-dimensional transform carried out on real data, the coefficient set between $p = N/2$ and $N - 1$ will be the complex conjugates of that between $p = 0$ and $N/2 - 1$, and so need not be explicitly computed, and this further reduces the number of computations required. Where two-dimensional transformation is concerned, however, the input data to the second stage of transformation will have a generally complex form, and this property will no longer hold. It is perhaps worth pointing out here that, for small values of N, the advantage of employing the FFT is not nearly so great as it is for larger block sizes (i.e., for a full frame transform, for example). Since there is only one complex product to be formed per node, the relevant comparison is between the quantities $N \log_2 N$ and N^2 for a one-dimensional operation, and the ratio is 4:1 if $N = 16$, rising to 32 for $N = 256$. In fact the products involving ± 1 occurring in practice distort this simple comparison of upper bounds, the example of Fig. 7.2 only requiring five distinct complex products instead of

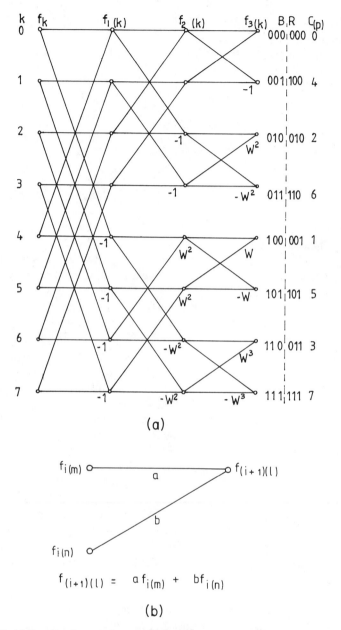

$$f_{(i+1)(l)} = a\,f_{i(m)} + b\,f_{i(n)}$$

(b)

FIG. 7.2. (a) Fast Fourier transform signal flow diagram; $N = 8$. Here k is the data element order, p the coefficient order and **BR** represents the bit-reversal (relocation) operation. (b) Explanation of the notation in (a) and similar diagrams. If no multiplier is indicated this implies that a, b, etc. $= 1$.

the 24 indicated by the expression $N \log_2 N$. Nevertheless, the real advantage in applying the FFT comes in the area of data analysis when vectors hundreds or thousands of elements long are transformed, which situation does not apply to transform image coding, except in the relatively few examples of full-frame coding.

As far as the inverse transform is concerned, the structure of the algorithm will be exactly the same as in the forward case, with the exception that the complex conjugate of W is employed and, depending upon the precise form of the calculation, an overall scaling operation may or may not be needed for transform domain/data domain equivalence.

The signal flow diagram in Fig. 7.2 may be viewed as a sequential sparse matrix multiplication of the type discussed by Good (1958, 1960, 1971) and referred to briefly in the introduction to this chapter. This formulation is considered in more detail by Ahmed and Rao (1975), Theilheimer (1969), Ahmed and Cheng (1970), and Kahaner (1970). The first stage is

$$
f_{1(k)} \qquad\qquad\qquad\qquad\qquad f_k
$$

$$
\begin{bmatrix} 0 \\ 1 \\ 2 \\ 3 \\ 4 \\ 5 \\ 6 \\ 7 \end{bmatrix}
=
\begin{bmatrix}
1 & 0 & 0 & 0 & 1 & 0 & 0 & 0 \\
0 & 1 & 0 & 0 & 0 & 1 & 0 & 0 \\
0 & 0 & 1 & 0 & 0 & 0 & 1 & 0 \\
0 & 0 & 0 & 1 & 0 & 0 & 0 & 1 \\
1 & 0 & 0 & 0 & -1 & 0 & 0 & 0 \\
0 & 1 & 0 & 0 & 0 & -1 & 0 & 0 \\
0 & 0 & 1 & 0 & 0 & 0 & -1 & 0 \\
0 & 0 & 0 & 1 & 0 & 0 & 0 & -1
\end{bmatrix}
\begin{bmatrix} 0 \\ 1 \\ 2 \\ 3 \\ 4 \\ 5 \\ 6 \\ 7 \end{bmatrix}
\qquad (7.16)
$$

the second

$$
f_{2(k)} \qquad\qquad\qquad\qquad\qquad f_{1(k)}
$$

$$
\begin{bmatrix} 0 \\ 1 \\ 2 \\ 3 \\ 4 \\ 5 \\ 6 \\ 7 \end{bmatrix}
=
\begin{bmatrix}
1 & 0 & 1 & 0 & 0 & 0 & 0 & 0 \\
0 & 1 & 0 & 1 & 0 & 0 & 0 & 0 \\
1 & 0 & -1 & 0 & 0 & 0 & 0 & 0 \\
0 & 1 & 0 & -1 & 0 & 0 & 0 & 0 \\
0 & 0 & 0 & 0 & 1 & 0 & W^2 & 0 \\
0 & 0 & 0 & 0 & 0 & 1 & 0 & W^2 \\
0 & 0 & 0 & 0 & 1 & 0 & -W^2 & 0 \\
0 & 0 & 0 & 0 & 0 & 1 & 0 & -W^2
\end{bmatrix}
\begin{bmatrix} 0 \\ 1 \\ 2 \\ 3 \\ 4 \\ 5 \\ 6 \\ 7 \end{bmatrix}
\qquad (7.17)
$$

and the third

$$
\begin{matrix} f_{3(k)} & & & & & & & & & f_{2(k)} \end{matrix}
$$

$$
\begin{bmatrix} 0 \\ 1 \\ 2 \\ 3 \\ 4 \\ 5 \\ 6 \\ 7 \end{bmatrix} = \begin{bmatrix} 1 & 1 & 0 & 0 & 0 & 0 & 0 & 0 \\ 1 & -1 & 0 & 0 & 0 & 0 & 0 & 0 \\ 0 & 0 & 1 & W^2 & 0 & 0 & 0 & 0 \\ 0 & 0 & 1 & -W^2 & 0 & 0 & 0 & 0 \\ 0 & 0 & 0 & 0 & 1 & W & 0 & 0 \\ 0 & 0 & 0 & 0 & 1 & -W & 0 & 0 \\ 0 & 0 & 0 & 0 & 0 & 0 & 1 & W^3 \\ 0 & 0 & 0 & 0 & 0 & 0 & 1 & -W^3 \end{bmatrix} \begin{bmatrix} 0 \\ 1 \\ 2 \\ 3 \\ 4 \\ 5 \\ 6 \\ 7 \end{bmatrix} \tag{7.18}
$$

the total product resulting in Eq. (7.4). The location of the five separate complex products can easily be seen in the second and third matrices.

Apart from the various re-orderings of input and output data and coefficients which result in modifications of the basic Cooley–Tukey algorithm many workers have sought to improve the efficiency of the calculation itself. Thus the Winograd–Fourier transform (WFT) (Silverman, 1977; Winograd, 1978) assumes that the value of N is decomposable into small mutually prime factors for each of which an efficient 'small-N' FFT exists (i.e., one with a minimal number of multiplications). Thus for $N = 8$ only two real multiplications and 26 summations are required, whilst for $N = 16$ the corresponding figures are 10 and 74 (see also Burrus, 1981). It is also possible to determine the Fourier transform of a set of data points via the Walsh transform (to be described later in this chapter); see the work of Kitai and Siemens (1979), Blachman (1974), Abramson (1977) and Tadokoro and Higuchi (1978). In fact this latter paper provided an interesting exchange with Kitai and Siemens [see Tadokoro and Higuchi (1979)] on the distinction (real or imagined) between the two approaches. As far as the efficient calculation of the DFT is concerned, Tadokoro and Higuchi (1981) returned to the attack with an algorithm which computes all N Fourier coefficients via the Walsh transform with $(N^2 - 4)/6$ multiplications and L of the N coefficients with approximately $NL/9$ multiplications. This property could be useful in a one-dimensional transform or in the second stage of a two-dimensional transform where it has previously been decided to delete several high-order coefficients.

The development of ever more efficient algorithms for determining Fourier coefficients in the general case, and the unification of the several approaches are topics which are still of much interest (Mersereau and Speake, 1981; Moharir and Varma, 1981; Speake and Mersereau, 1981). An approach to the implementation of such algorithms which has become popular in the last few years is via the so-called number theoretic transform (see Hall, 1979, for an introduction), although since such transforms have no obvious regular relationship between spatial (input) and transform domains in terms of spatial frequency or sequency they cannot be employed directly in transform coding (i.e., by truncating the coefficient set, for example) but rather offer an improved means of implementation of more conventional transforms.

7.3 Fast Walsh–Hadamard transform

The rediscovery of the application of factorisation techniques in the development of an efficient method for the numerical calculation of Fourier transforms was widely welcomed since it enabled one-dimensional transforms of vectors containing perhaps several thousand data values to be carried out in computer time measured in minutes rather than hours. The reason for the reduction in execution time was, of course, the decrease in the number of multiplications which the fast algorithm required, which far outweighed any benefit incurred through a reduction in the number of additions, due to the difference in time required for the two operations. In the case of the WHT, of course, multiplications are not necessary in any case (save for an optional final overall scaling operation) and so, in terms of processing speed, the transform started out with a decided advantage, despite its worse theoretical performance, which accounted for its popularity during the years when transform processing was becoming an established image coding technique. Even so, there was still an interest in minimising the number of operations required, and it was found that fast routines similar to those used to calculate the FFT could reduce that number from approximately N^2 to, again, something of the order of $N \log_2 N$. We begin here by examining the application of factorisation techniques to the Hadamard matrix.

The basic lowest-order Hadamard matrix is (see Chapter 3)

$$H(2) = \begin{bmatrix} 1 & 1 \\ 1 & -1 \end{bmatrix} \tag{7.19}$$

omitting, as before, the orthonormalisation constant as not being directly relevant to the present discussion. It has been shown that successive higher-order matrices can be generated by combining lower-order ones by the use of the 'direct' or Kronecker matrix product, thus

$$H(4) = H(2) \otimes H(2) = \begin{bmatrix} H(2) & H(2) \\ H(2) & -H(2) \end{bmatrix}$$

$$= \begin{bmatrix} 1 & 1 & 1 & 1 \\ 1 & -1 & 1 & -1 \\ 1 & 1 & -1 & -1 \\ 1 & -1 & -1 & 1 \end{bmatrix} \tag{7.20}$$

and

$$H(8) = H(2) \otimes H(4)$$

$$= \begin{bmatrix} 1 & 1 & 1 & 1 & 1 & 1 & 1 & 1 \\ 1 & -1 & 1 & -1 & 1 & -1 & 1 & -1 \\ 1 & 1 & -1 & -1 & 1 & 1 & -1 & -1 \\ 1 & -1 & -1 & 1 & 1 & -1 & -1 & 1 \\ 1 & 1 & 1 & 1 & -1 & -1 & -1 & -1 \\ 1 & -1 & 1 & -1 & -1 & 1 & -1 & 1 \\ 1 & 1 & -1 & -1 & -1 & -1 & 1 & 1 \\ 1 & -1 & -1 & 1 & -1 & 1 & 1 & -1 \end{bmatrix} \begin{matrix} S \\ 0 \\ 7 \\ 3 \\ 4 \\ 1 \\ 6 \\ 2 \\ 5 \end{matrix} \qquad (7.21)$$

is the 8×8 Hadamard ordered Walsh–Hadamard matrix (S indicating the number of sign changes in each basis vector—note that S is not the sequency of the various vectors but is often stated colloquially to be so). The coefficient order is determined (Ahmed and Rao, 1975) by a bit reversal and Gray/binary code conversion process. Thus the index of the second row of the matrix is, in bit-reversed and converted form, $001 \to 100 \to 111$ i.e., 7; for the fifth row $100 \to 001 \to 001$, i.e., 1, and so on.

Good (1958, 1971) pointed out that a matrix such as that of Eq. (7.21), written as the direct product of lower-order matrices, could also be expressed as the ordinary matrix product of a set of sparse matrices. Thus

$$H(8) = [A] \times [A] \times [A] \qquad (7.22)$$

where

$$[A] = \begin{bmatrix} 1 & 1 & 0 & 0 & 0 & 0 & 0 & 0 \\ 0 & 0 & 1 & 1 & 0 & 0 & 0 & 0 \\ 0 & 0 & 0 & 0 & 1 & 1 & 0 & 0 \\ 0 & 0 & 0 & 0 & 0 & 0 & 1 & 1 \\ 1 & -1 & 0 & 0 & 0 & 0 & 0 & 0 \\ 0 & 0 & 1 & -1 & 0 & 0 & 0 & 0 \\ 0 & 0 & 0 & 0 & 1 & -1 & 0 & 0 \\ 0 & 0 & 0 & 0 & 0 & 0 & 1 & -1 \end{bmatrix} \qquad (7.23)$$

[Note that Good (1971) points out several typographical errors in the matrix given on p. 363 of his 1958 paper, and there are in fact six incorrect signs in the printed version.] In each stage there are therefore a total of eight additions or subtractions and, since there are three stages, the total number of operations is 24 (i.e., $N \log_2 N$, where $N = 8$). Since all three stages are identical, one single stage can be used sequentially three times to carry out the

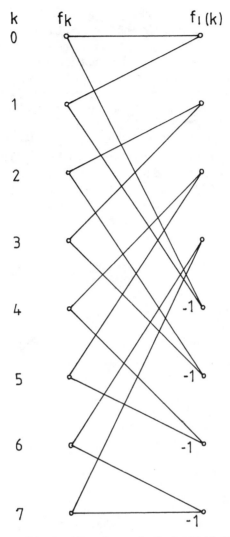

FIG. 7.3. Single stage of the signal flow diagram for the fast Walsh–Hadamard transform as defined by Eqs. (7.22) and (7.23); $N = 8$.

transform operation. The flow diagram of one stage is shown in Fig. 7.3. This structure has been used by Carl and Swartwood (1973) and Bacchi and Moreau (1978) for transform implementation, and a similar approach has been employed by Noble (1975).

An alternative development in the form of a matrix partitioning operation has been applied by Ahmed and Cheng (1970) and Ahmed and Rao (1975) to generate a Cooley–Tukey type of algorithm having a signal flow diagram identical to that of Fig. 7.2 with the exception that all powers of W are replaced by unity. The same then applies to the sequential decomposition depicted in Eqs. (7.16)–(7.18). The fact that the output coefficients of the Hadamard-ordered computation described earlier require both bit reversal and a code conversion operation to reorganise them into a sequence ordered according to an increasing number of zero-crossings has prompted the development of algorithms which do not require one or both of these steps. Thus that of Pratt *et al.* (1969) has the flow diagram shown in Fig. 7.4, corresponding to a factorisation of the matrix of Eq. (7.21) but with the rows arranged in order of increasing number of zero crossings. Other factorisations are also possible; see, for example, Ghanbari and Pearson (1982). Again Manz (1972) has developed a Cooley–Tukey type of algorithm which calculates the coefficients in this order but requires bit reversal of the input

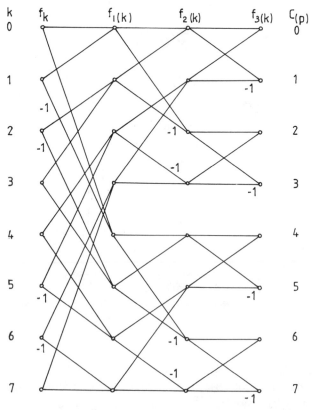

FIG. 7.4. Signal flow diagram for the sequency ordered fast Walsh–Hadamard transform; $N = 8$; k and p are defined in Fig. 7.2.

indices and also reversal of the addition/subtraction operation at certain locations within the flow diagam. The same result may be achieved in principle, of course, by using the flow diagram of the Hadamard-ordered algorithm (i.e., Fig. 7.2 with powers of $W = 1$) followed by a further matrix product for the reordering process.

Since the Hadamard transform is unitary and symmetric, the form of the algorithm is the same for both forward and inverse operations, with an optional overall scaling step if orthonormality is desired.

7.4   Fast Haar transform

The Haar transform (see Chapter 3) has an initial advantage in terms of implementation in that it already has a sparse form (although, again, its efficiency in data compression terms is not particularly good). Nevertheless it may still be more efficiently carried out with a fast algorithm. Thus Andrews and Caspari (1970) show that the Haar matrix for $N = 8$, given in Eq. (7.24), can be written as the product of three matrices [Eq. 7.25)]

$$
HA(8) = \begin{bmatrix}
1 & 1 & 1 & 1 & 1 & 1 & 1 & 1 \\
1 & 1 & 1 & 1 & -1 & -1 & -1 & -1 \\
\sqrt{2} & \sqrt{2} & -\sqrt{2} & -\sqrt{2} & 0 & 0 & 0 & 0 \\
0 & 0 & 0 & 0 & \sqrt{2} & \sqrt{2} & -\sqrt{2} & -\sqrt{2} \\
2 & -2 & 0 & 0 & 0 & 0 & 0 & 0 \\
0 & 0 & 2 & -2 & 0 & 0 & 0 & 0 \\
0 & 0 & 0 & 0 & 2 & -2 & 0 & 0 \\
0 & 0 & 0 & 0 & 0 & 0 & 2 & -2
\end{bmatrix} \tag{7.24}
$$

$$
HA(8) = [A_1] \times [A_2] \times [A_3] \tag{7.25}
$$

where

$$
[A_1] = \begin{bmatrix}
1 & 1 & 0 & 0 & 0 & 0 & 0 & 0 \\
1 & -1 & 0 & 0 & 0 & 0 & 0 & 0 \\
0 & 0 & \sqrt{2} & 0 & 0 & 0 & 0 & 0 \\
0 & 0 & 0 & \sqrt{2} & 0 & 0 & 0 & 0 \\
0 & 0 & 0 & 0 & \sqrt{2} & 0 & 0 & 0 \\
0 & 0 & 0 & 0 & 0 & \sqrt{2} & 0 & 0 \\
0 & 0 & 0 & 0 & 0 & 0 & \sqrt{2} & 0 \\
0 & 0 & 0 & 0 & 0 & 0 & 0 & \sqrt{2}
\end{bmatrix} \tag{7.26}
$$

$$[A_2] = \begin{bmatrix} 1 & 1 & 0 & 0 & 0 & 0 & 0 & 0 \\ 0 & 0 & 1 & 1 & 0 & 0 & 0 & 0 \\ 1 & -1 & 0 & 0 & 0 & 0 & 0 & 0 \\ 0 & 0 & 1 & -1 & 0 & 0 & 0 & 0 \\ 0 & 0 & 0 & 0 & \sqrt{2} & 0 & 0 & 0 \\ 0 & 0 & 0 & 0 & 0 & \sqrt{2} & 0 & 0 \\ 0 & 0 & 0 & 0 & 0 & 0 & \sqrt{2} & 0 \\ 0 & 0 & 0 & 0 & 0 & 0 & 0 & \sqrt{2} \end{bmatrix} \tag{7.27}$$

and

$$[A_3] = \begin{bmatrix} 1 & 1 & 0 & 0 & 0 & 0 & 0 & 0 \\ 0 & 0 & 1 & 1 & 0 & 0 & 0 & 0 \\ 0 & 0 & 0 & 0 & 1 & 1 & 0 & 0 \\ 0 & 0 & 0 & 0 & 0 & 0 & 1 & 1 \\ 1 & -1 & 0 & 0 & 0 & 0 & 0 & 0 \\ 0 & 0 & 1 & -1 & 0 & 0 & 0 & 0 \\ 0 & 0 & 0 & 0 & 1 & -1 & 0 & 0 \\ 0 & 0 & 0 & 0 & 0 & 0 & 1 & -1 \end{bmatrix} \tag{7.28}$$

It should be noted that, in this form the transform requires multiplications by $\sqrt{2}$ and 2. Since these can be regarded simply as basis vector scaling operations, in actual implementation they are not essential [although Bacchi and Moreau (1978) combine $\sqrt{2}$ scaling at transmitter and receiver into one operation of a multiplication by 2, i.e., a binary shift, at the transmitter], and the orthogonal Haar [HA(8)] transform can be carried out without multiplications in $2 + 4 + 8 = 14 = 2(N - 1)$ addition/subtractions. Maintenance of orthonormality requires an additional 10 multiplications. In its original form it requires 24 addition/subtractions. If the orthonormal form is desired, then Shore (1973) has pointed out that multiplication by $\sqrt{2}$ can be implemented in three binary shifts and three additions by the approximation $1 + \frac{1}{4} + \frac{1}{8} + \frac{1}{16} = 1.4375$.

The relation between the Haar and Walsh–Hadamard matrices is demonstrated by Fino (1972) who also gives a signal flow diagram for the transform and demonstrates how, by the application of re-ordering within the fast algorithm, it can be used to generate the WHT coefficients. The Haar computation for $N = 8$ is given by the flow diagram of Fig. 7.5, which corresponds to the factorisation of Eqs. (7.26–7.28). The Haar transform can also be computed using an algorithm of the Cooley–Tukey type together with $\log_2 N$ bit reversals (Ahmed and Rao, 1975). Again, Rao *et al.* (1975) have

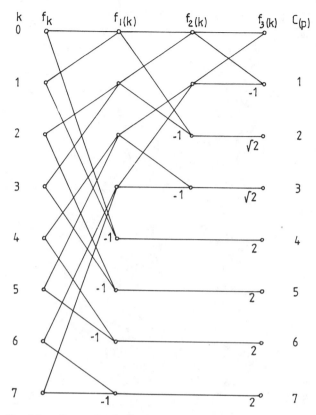

FIG. 7.5. Signal flow diagram for the fast Haar transform; $N = 8$; k and p are defined in Fig. 7.2.

defined a Hadamard–Haar transform in which the basis vectors are linear combinations of Haar functions, and Fino and Algazi (1977) define rules for recursive generation of Haar matrices leading to the fast algorithm. It is worth reiterating, however, that, because of its relatively poor performance, the Haar transform has not received much attention of late, in comparison with better transforms, even though the latter require more complex processing.

7.5   Fast slant transform

The slant transform (Pratt *et al.*, (1972, 1974), described in Chapter 3, is, unlike the Haar transform, reasonably efficient in terms of data compression performance and can be computed with the fast algorithm whose flow

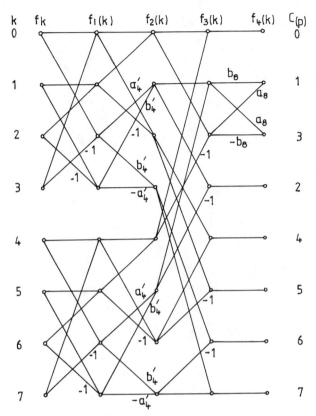

FIG. 7.6. Signal flow diagram for the fast slant transform; $N = 8$; k and p are defined in Fig. 7.2.

diagram is shown in Fig. 7.6, which corresponds to the factorisation

$$S(8) = [A_1] \times [A_2] \times [A_3] \times [A_4] \qquad (7.29)$$

in which

$$[A_1] = \begin{bmatrix} 1 & 0 & 0 & 0 & 0 & 0 & 0 & 0 \\ 0 & b_8 & a_8 & 0 & 0 & 0 & 0 & 0 \\ 0 & 0 & 0 & 1 & 0 & 0 & 0 & 0 \\ 0 & a_8 & -b_8 & 0 & 0 & 0 & 0 & 0 \\ 0 & 0 & 0 & 0 & 1 & 0 & 0 & 0 \\ 0 & 0 & 0 & 0 & 0 & 1 & 0 & 0 \\ 0 & 0 & 0 & 0 & 0 & 0 & 1 & 0 \\ 0 & 0 & 0 & 0 & 0 & 0 & 0 & 1 \end{bmatrix} \qquad (7.30)$$

$$[A_2] = \begin{bmatrix} 1 & 0 & 0 & 0 & 1 & 0 & 0 & 0 \\ 0 & 1 & 0 & 0 & 0 & 1 & 0 & 0 \\ 1 & 0 & 0 & 0 & -1 & 0 & 0 & 0 \\ 0 & 1 & 0 & 0 & 0 & -1 & 0 & 0 \\ 0 & 0 & 1 & 0 & 0 & 0 & 1 & 0 \\ 0 & 0 & 1 & 0 & 0 & 0 & -1 & 0 \\ 0 & 0 & 0 & 1 & 0 & 0 & 0 & -1 \\ 0 & 0 & 0 & 1 & 0 & 0 & 0 & 1 \end{bmatrix} \tag{7.31}$$

$$[A_3] = \begin{bmatrix} 1 & 1 & 0 & 0 & 0 & 0 & 0 & 0 \\ 0 & 0 & a_4' & b_4' & 0 & 0 & 0 & 0 \\ 1 & -1 & 0 & 0 & 0 & 0 & 0 & 0 \\ 0 & 0 & b_4' & -a_4' & 0 & 0 & 0 & 0 \\ 0 & 0 & 0 & 0 & 1 & 1 & 0 & 0 \\ 0 & 0 & 0 & 0 & 0 & 0 & a_4' & b_4' \\ 0 & 0 & 0 & 0 & 1 & -1 & 0 & 0 \\ 0 & 0 & 0 & 0 & 0 & 0 & b_4' & -a_4' \end{bmatrix} \tag{7.32}$$

$$[A_4] = \begin{bmatrix} 1 & 0 & 0 & 1 & 0 & 0 & 0 & 0 \\ 0 & 1 & 1 & 0 & 0 & 0 & 0 & 0 \\ 1 & 0 & 0 & -1 & 0 & 0 & 0 & 0 \\ 0 & 1 & -1 & 0 & 0 & 0 & 0 & 0 \\ 0 & 0 & 0 & 0 & 1 & 0 & 0 & 1 \\ 0 & 0 & 0 & 0 & 0 & 1 & 1 & 0 \\ 0 & 0 & 0 & 0 & 1 & 0 & 0 & -1 \\ 0 & 0 & 0 & 0 & 0 & 1 & -1 & 0 \end{bmatrix} \tag{7.33}$$

The coefficients are given by Eqs. (3.112) and (3.113) and are

$$a_4' = 3/\sqrt{5} \qquad b_4' = 1/\sqrt{5}$$
$$a_8 = 4/\sqrt{21} \qquad b_8 = \sqrt{5/21}$$

(note that a_4' and b_4' depend upon a_4 and b_4 via the relations $a_4' = a_4 + b_4$ and $b_4' = a_4 - b_4$). The result, when scaled by $1/\sqrt{N}$, is that of Eq. (3.114).

The total number of operations is

$$8 + 8 + 8 + 2 = N \log_2 N + N/2 - 2 = 26 \quad \text{additions}$$

and

$$0 + 8 + 0 + 4 = 2N - 4 = 12 \qquad \qquad \text{multiplications}$$

An alternative algorithm (Fino and Algazi, 1977) generates slant transform coefficients in 'natural' order, rather than in the order of increasing numbers of zero crossings, and with a reduced number of multiplications, and, as was the case with the Walsh–Hadamard and Haar transforms, Fino and Algazi (1974) have defined a slant–Haar transform which is, like the Haar transform, sparse even in its original form and which also has some computational advantage in terms of a smaller number of multiplications.

7.6   Fast Karhunen–Loève transform

As was pointed out in Chapter 3 the optimum transform under the criterion of minimum mean square error is the KLT. In order to carry out a Karhunen–Loève transform it is necessary to determine the covariance matrix of the data source. In practice, this will mean measuring the various covariance products for a single image, or a set of images judged, in some way, to be representative of the source output, which is a task not lightly undertaken. Alternatively, a model for the image generating process may be assumed, and the eigenvectors of the associated covariance matrix calculated, as was done for the first-order Markov model in Chapter 3. In either case, it is evident that the elements constituting the transform basis matrix are functions of the data properties, and so the matrix, unlike all those examined so far in this chapter, does not necessarily possess any underlying structure and cannot, in general, be decomposed into sparse matrix products to generate an algorithm with a reduced number of multiplications. It should be noted that, even when the eigenvectors can be expressed analytically, as for the Markov process just mentioned, the equation is still inharmonic, and an underlying periodic structure is absent. A true 'fast' algorithm for the KLT does not exist, therefore. Its marginally superior theoretical performance in data compression applications has, however, prompted the development of approximate fast forms of the transform.

The first of these is that reported by Haralick et al. (1975; see also Shanmugam and Haralick, 1973). Their treatment begins by generating the covariance matrix of the (two-dimensional) image in the manner described in Chapter 2. The image is assumed to be stationary and isotropic, under which conditions the submatrix partitions of the main covariance matrix turn out to be (approximately) multiples of one another. Under this condition, each submatrix has the same eigenvectors, and the eigenvectors of the covariance matrix of the image as a whole are formed by the direct product of the submatrix eigenvectors and those of the matrix of eigenvectors. A submatrix is therefore generated such that the squared difference between the best multiple of its elements and those of a submatrix of the covariance matrix is minimised when averaged over all the submatrices. Each submatrix is then replaced with the best multiple of the new submatrix. The direct product representation then allows decomposition of the transform operation into an equivalent fast process. Results using a 4×4 block size show that the true KLT is well approximated by the 'fast' version, but also that the difference between the true KLT and the slant transform, for example, in terms of rms error is only a few tenths of 1 %.

The second approach to the 'fast' KLT is that of Jain (1976b) and is based upon the separation of a data vector $\mathbf{X} = x_0 \cdots x_{n+1}$ into a boundary response x_b defined by x_0 and x_{n+1}, and a partial sequence $\mathbf{X}' - x_b$, where $\mathbf{X}' = x_1 \cdots x_n$. Jain then shows that if $\mathbf{X}$ is a first-order stationary Gauss-Markov sequence, the sequence $\mathbf{X}' - x_b$ has, as its KLT, the sine transform (see Chapter 3). In this, or the more general two-dimensional, case the partial sequence (or field) is regarded as having been 'pinned' at the boundary, giving rise to the so-called 'pinned' KLT (Zvi-Meiri, 1976). Thus the 'fast' KLT is in fact not so much a fast algorithm as such, but a decomposition of an image field into sub-fields, for one of which the KLT is a (sinusoidal) fast transform.

An alternative approach to the 'fast' KLT has also been reported by Jain (1976a, 1979). He points out that each member of the family of sinusoidal transforms discussed in Chapter 3 is the KLT of a sequence having a particular $[J]$ matrix as its covariance matrix. Since the transforms all have sinusoidal basis vector components, they are decomposable into fast algorithm structures. The success of the method rests upon the assumption that the measured image covariance matrix for the image or image sequence can be modelled as a simple function of a $[J]$ matrix for which a fast transform exists (see the discussion in Chapter 3).

It can be seen, therefore, that it is not possible to produce a fast computational algorithm for the KLT in the general case. This would remain an unfortunate circumstance were it not for the fact that the difference in performance between the KLT and the transform to be described in the next section, which does have a true fast algorithm is, for the majority of typical images, negligible.

7.7 Fast discrete cosine transform

Although a multiplicity of orthogonal transforms has been employed in the development of transform coding systems one in particular is outstanding as being very nearly optimum for typical image data having reasonably high values of inter-element correlation coefficient, and that is the DCT, introduced by Ahmed *et al.* (1974). It is, unlike the KLT, a data independent (co)sinusoidal transform, and therefore can be decomposed into a fast algorithmic structure. Its basis vectors are very similar to those of the KLT of a first-order Markov process for values of correlation coefficient approaching unity and this is hardly surprising since, in the limit as the coefficient becomes one, the analytical expressions for both become identical (Clarke, 1981a). It is not unexpected, therefore, that much effort has been expended upon the development of a fast algorithm for its calculation (unlike the WHT, of course, it does require real multiplications for its computation, which is a disadvantage for very high-speed applications). In view of the extensive body of literature the introduction of this transform has provoked, we shall briefly review here the development of fast algorithms for the DCT over the past few years and also examine one or two of them in more detail.

The basic computation to be carried out is (see Chapter 3)

$$C_p = \sqrt{\frac{2}{N}} \sum_{k=0}^{N-1} f_k \cos\left\{ p\left(k + \frac{1}{2}\right)\frac{\pi}{N} \right\} \qquad p = 0 \to N - 1 \qquad (7.34)$$

It should be noted that this is not the scaled real part of the (complex) discrete Fourier transform

$$\text{DFT}_p = \frac{1}{\sqrt{N}} \sum_{k=0}^{N-1} f_k \exp\left(-j\,\frac{2\pi pk}{N} \right) \qquad (7.35)$$

i.e.,

$$\text{DFT(RE)}_p = \frac{1}{\sqrt{N}} \sum_{k=0}^{N-1} f_k \cos\frac{2\pi pk}{N} \qquad (7.36)$$

However, if we carry out a DFT of length $2N$, then

$$\text{DFT}(2N)_p = \frac{1}{\sqrt{2N}} \sum_{k=0}^{2N-1} f_k \exp\left(-j\,\frac{2\pi pk}{2N} \right) \qquad (7.37)$$

whilst C_p in Eq. (7.34) can be written as

$$C_p = \sqrt{\frac{2}{N}}\,\text{RE} \sum_{k=0}^{N-1} f_k \exp\left[-jp\left(k + \frac{1}{2}\right)\frac{\pi}{N} \right] \qquad (7.38)$$

$$= \sqrt{\frac{2}{N}}\,\text{RE}\,\exp\left(-j\frac{\pi p}{2N} \right) \sum_{k=0}^{N-1} f_k \exp\left(-j\frac{\pi pk}{N} \right) \qquad (7.39)$$

We can therefore carry out a DFT of length $2N$ (appending zeros to the data sequence of length N) to give

$$C_p = \sqrt{\frac{2}{N}} \, \text{RE} \exp\left(-j\frac{\pi p}{2N}\right)\sqrt{2N} \, \text{DFT}(2N)_p$$

$$= 2 \, \text{RE} \exp\left(-j\frac{\pi p}{2N}\right)\text{DFT}(2N)_p \qquad (7.40)$$

i.e., the N length DCT is given by twice the real part of a rotated DFT output vector of the original sequence, where the factor $\exp(-j\pi p/2N)$, of course, implies rotation without change in magnitude. This decomposition is the basis of several methods of implementation of the FDCT (fast DCT) via the FFT. For example, Haralick (1976) suggests that the implementation in the case of a real data sequence may be improved by the application of the N length FFT to two sequences of the original length (N), where one is the original data and the other is a complex sequence derived from the data. Tseng and Miller (1978) pointed out, however, that the single $2N$ method is to be prefered in an algorithm which turns the N length data into a real, even sequence $f_0, f_1, \ldots, f_{2N-1}$ satisfying the condition $f_k = f_{2N-1-k}$, for which only the real parts of the coefficients are calculated, followed by a real scaling operation. In a somewhat similar vein Narasimhan and Peterson (1978) decompose the input sequence into two parts and calculate a rotated Fourier transform over $\frac{1}{2}N + 1$ points, followed by separation of real and imaginary parts. Generalisation to the two-dimensional case is considered by Makhoul (1980).

Other algorithms for the DCT also exist in which the coefficients are derived from a rotation applied to the output of a Fourier transform operation, the emphasis being placed on implementing the latter in the most efficient way. Thus Nussbaumer (1980) computes the two-dimensional DCT via partial decomposition using a polynomial transform followed by a one-dimensional FFT, and Nasrabadi and King (1983) describe a similar scheme. Both report a reduction in the number of multiplications compared with the conventional (two-dimensional) method of employing a $2N \times 2N$ FFT, by a factor of 8. A somewhat different approach is taken by Ward and Stanier (1983) who employ a $4N$-point Winograd–Fourier transform algorithm to calculate the N-point DCT.

The original fast factorisation of the DCT matrix is due to Chen *et al.* (1977). They demonstrate that the DCT matrix of order N, $[A_N]$, may be written as

$$[A_N] = [P_N]\begin{bmatrix} A_{N/2} & 0 \\ 0 & R_{N/2} \end{bmatrix}[B_N] \qquad (7.41)$$

where $[P_N]$ is an $N \times N$ matrix whose function is solely to convert bit-reversed coefficients to natural ordering; the basic $[A]$ matrix is

$$[A_2] = \frac{1}{\sqrt{2}} \begin{bmatrix} 1 & 1 \\ 1 & -1 \end{bmatrix} \qquad (7.42)$$

$[R_{N/2}]$ is decomposed into $2 \log_2 N - 3$ matrices containing, in general, sine and cosine coefficients and unit elements, and $[B_N]$ is composed of identity, or opposite diagonal identity, matrices of order $N/2$. The signal flow diagram for the case $N = 8$ is given in Fig. 7.7 and corresponds to the following matrix factorisation (the recursive form of the algorithm allowing easy extension to

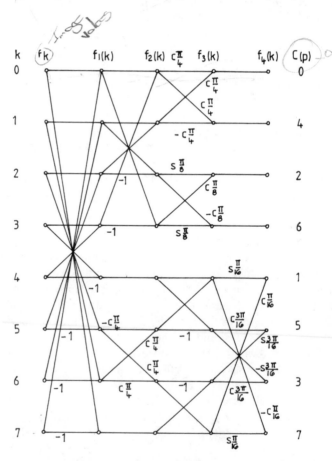

FIG. 7.7. Signal flow diagram for the fast discrete cosine transform; $N = 8$; k and p are defined in Fig. 7.2; $s(\cdot)$ represents the sine and $c(\cdot)$ the cosine function.

higher integral powers of 2), for convenience omitting $[P_N]$

$$R_{4(1)} = \begin{bmatrix} 1 & 0 & 0 & 0 & 0 & 0 & 0 & 0 \\ 0 & 1 & 0 & 0 & 0 & 0 & 0 & 0 \\ 0 & 0 & 1 & 0 & 0 & 0 & 0 & 0 \\ 0 & 0 & 0 & 1 & 0 & 0 & 0 & 0 \\ 0 & 0 & 0 & 0 & s\dfrac{\pi}{16} & 0 & 0 & c\dfrac{\pi}{16} \\ 0 & 0 & 0 & 0 & 0 & c\dfrac{3\pi}{16} & s\dfrac{3\pi}{16} & 0 \\ 0 & 0 & 0 & 0 & 0 & -s\dfrac{3\pi}{16} & c\dfrac{3\pi}{16} & 0 \\ 0 & 0 & 0 & 0 & -c\dfrac{\pi}{16} & 0 & 0 & s\dfrac{\pi}{16} \end{bmatrix} \tag{7.43}$$

$$R_{4(2)} = \begin{bmatrix} c\dfrac{\pi}{4} & c\dfrac{\pi}{4} & 0 & 0 & 0 & 0 & 0 & 0 \\ c\dfrac{\pi}{4} & -c\dfrac{\pi}{4} & 0 & 0 & 0 & 0 & 0 & 0 \\ 0 & 0 & s\dfrac{\pi}{8} & c\dfrac{\pi}{8} & 0 & 0 & 0 & 0 \\ 0 & 0 & -c\dfrac{\pi}{8} & s\dfrac{\pi}{8} & 0 & 0 & 0 & 0 \\ 0 & 0 & 0 & 0 & 1 & 1 & 0 & 0 \\ 0 & 0 & 0 & 0 & 1 & -1 & 0 & 0 \\ 0 & 0 & 0 & 0 & 0 & 0 & -1 & 1 \\ 0 & 0 & 0 & 0 & 0 & 0 & 1 & 1 \end{bmatrix} \tag{7.44}$$

$$R_{4(3)} = \begin{bmatrix} 1 & 0 & 0 & 1 & 0 & 0 & 0 & 0 \\ 0 & 1 & 1 & 0 & 0 & 0 & 0 & 0 \\ 0 & 1 & -1 & 0 & 0 & 0 & 0 & 0 \\ 1 & 0 & 0 & -1 & 0 & 0 & 0 & 0 \\ 0 & 0 & 0 & 0 & 1 & 0 & 0 & 0 \\ 0 & 0 & 0 & 0 & 0 & -c\dfrac{\pi}{4} & c\dfrac{\pi}{4} & 0 \\ 0 & 0 & 0 & 0 & 0 & c\dfrac{\pi}{4} & c\dfrac{\pi}{4} & 0 \\ 0 & 0 & 0 & 0 & 0 & 0 & 0 & 1 \end{bmatrix} \tag{7.45}$$

$$B_8 = \begin{bmatrix} 1 & 0 & 0 & 0 & 0 & 0 & 0 & 1 \\ 0 & 1 & 0 & 0 & 0 & 0 & 1 & 0 \\ 0 & 0 & 1 & 0 & 0 & 1 & 0 & 0 \\ 0 & 0 & 0 & 1 & 1 & 0 & 0 & 0 \\ 0 & 0 & 0 & 1 & -1 & 0 & 0 & 0 \\ 0 & 0 & 1 & 0 & 0 & -1 & 0 & 0 \\ 0 & 1 & 0 & 0 & 0 & 0 & -1 & 0 \\ 1 & 0 & 0 & 0 & 0 & 0 & 0 & -1 \end{bmatrix} \tag{7.46}$$

In the above arrays 'c' and 's' represent, respectively, cosine and sine terms. The required number of multiplications is

$$N \log_2 N - \tfrac{3}{2} N + 4 = 16 \tag{7.47}$$

and of summations is

$$\tfrac{3}{2} N (\log_2 N - 1) + 2 = 26 \tag{7.48}$$

for the case of $N = 8$. Furthermore, an overall scaling operation (multiplication of all coefficients by $\sqrt{2/N}$) is necessary if orthonormality is desired. It should be noted that, since all of the 2×2 stages at each point in the flow diagram are unitary, calculation of the inverse transform (apart from scaling) can be performed by introducing the coefficients at the output points, when the data vector will be reproduced at the input.

Chen et al. consider that the advantage in their method in terms of the reduction in the number of multiplications compared with the $2N$-point FFT technique is by a factor of approximately 6. In fact the advantage is not as great as this, since a real $2N$-point FFT can be computed in fewer than something of the order of $N \log_2(2N)$ multiplications using an efficient algorithm. Makhoul (1980) suggests, in fact, that the advantage is only a factor of 2. An interesting comparison here is with the scheme of Murray (1977). He uses an FFT/rotation approach to compute the one-dimensional 32-point DCT. The total number of operations needed to carry out these two procedures is 194 additions and 115 multiplications, whereas the equivalent figures for Chen's method are 194 and 116.

The symmetric cosine transform of Kitajima (1980), described in Chapter 3 can be computed with fewer multiplications by the application of a modified Chen-type fast decomposition. In this case the required number is $(N + 3)\log_2 N - \tfrac{7}{2} N + 5$, i.e., 10 for $N = 8$.

In Chapter 3 it was pointed out that as an alternative to the sequential application of horizontal and vertical one-dimensional N-length transformations to carry out a two-dimensional ($N \times N$) transform, the data array could be re-ordered into a vector of length N^2 and a one-dimensional transform performed using an $N^2 \times N^2$ transform matrix derived from the original $N \times N$ form. Using this approach, Kamangar and Rao (1982) employ a sparse matrix decomposition somewhat similar to that of Chen *et al.* For the basic one-dimensional DCT in the case $N = 8$ Chen's method requires 16 multiplications (see the preceding) and thus a sequential two-dimensional transform will require $2N \times 16 = 256$ multiplications. Kamangar's algorithm requires just one-half that number, with about the same number of summations (approximately 400).

So far two methods of calculating the coefficients of the DCT using fast algorithms have been described. The ease with which FWHT operations may be carried out has prompted the development of FDCT routines using Walsh–Hadamard matrices, for example, by Hein and Ahmed (1978) who write

$$\hat{C} = [\hat{\Lambda}]\mathbf{X} \tag{7.49}$$

where C is the DCT coefficient vector, Λ the DCT matrix and $\mathbf{X}$ the data vector, ' $\hat{\ }$ ' denoting bit-reversed ordering. Since all correctly scaled Hadamard matrices are orthonormal, i.e.,

$$[\hat{H}][\hat{H}] = [I] \tag{7.50}$$

where $[H]$ is the Hadamard matrix ordered according to increasing numbers of zero crossings and $[I]$ the identity matrix (of course, all Hadamard matrices are symmetric and so are their own transposes), Eq. (7.49) can therefore be written as

$$\hat{C} = [\hat{\Lambda}\hat{H}][\hat{H}\mathbf{X}] \tag{7.51}$$

where $[\hat{H}\mathbf{X}]$ will be a bit-reversed Walsh-Hadamard transform of $\mathbf{X}$ and

$$[\hat{\Lambda}\hat{H}] = \begin{bmatrix} 1 & 0 & 0 & 0 & 0 & 0 & 0 & 0 \\ 0 & 1 & 0 & 0 & 0 & 0 & 0 & 0 \\ 0 & 0 & 0.923 & 0.923 & 0 & 0 & 0 & 0 \\ 0 & 0 & -0.383 & 0.923 & 0 & 0 & 0 & 0 \\ 0 & 0 & 0 & 0 & 0.907 & -0.075 & 0.375 & 0.180 \\ 0 & 0 & 0 & 0 & 0.214 & 0.768 & -0.513 & 0.318 \\ 0 & 0 & 0 & 0 & -0.318 & 0.513 & 0.768 & 0.214 \\ 0 & 0 & 0 & 0 & -0.180 & -0.375 & -0.075 & 0.907 \end{bmatrix} \tag{7.52}$$

in the case $N = 8$. The calculation of the DCT coefficients here requires 20 multiplications. An approximation for this exact result employs only integer arithmetic and, together with its extension to $N = 16$, has been described by Srinivasan and Rao (1983). A further extension to $N = 32$ is reported by Kwak *et al.* (1983). This approach has also been used by Ghanbari and

Pearson (1982) to generate a fast DCT algorithm for $N = 8$ with the emphasis placed upon ease of implementation.

It can be seen that the efficiency of the DCT in terms of energy packing and decorrelation has stimulated intense interest in making the computational structure of the transform amenable to high-speed operation. Later in this chapter we shall examine the more practical aspects of transform implementation.

7.8   Fast discrete sine transform

As was the case with the DCT, it is possible to employ a modified FFT to calculate the coefficients of the sine transform, which are given by (see Chapter 3)

$$C_p = \sqrt{\frac{2}{N+1}} \sum_{k=1}^{N} f_k \sin \frac{\pi pk}{N+1} \qquad p = 1 \rightarrow N \qquad (7.53)$$

where the indexing has been modified to allow the sine argument to correspond with the Fourier kernel. If we carry out a DFT of length $2(N + 1)$ we obtain

$$\text{DFT}(2N + 2)_p = \frac{1}{\sqrt{2(N+1)}} \sum_{k=0}^{2(N+1)-1} f_k \exp\left[-j\frac{2\pi pk}{2(N+1)} \right] \qquad (7.54)$$

Taking the negative imaginary part gives

$$\text{IM}(\text{DFT}(2N + 2))_p = \frac{1}{\sqrt{2(N+1)}} \sum_{k=0}^{2N-1} f_k \sin \frac{\pi pk}{N+1} \qquad (7.55)$$

and therefore the sine transform coefficients are

$$C_p = 2 \, \text{IM} \, \text{DFT}(2N + 2)_p \qquad p = 1 \rightarrow N \qquad (7.56)$$

where $f_k = 0$ for $k = 0$ and $k \geqslant N + 1$.

For reasons explained elsewhere in this volume, the sine transform has excited nothing like the interest which has surrounded the DCT since its introduction. Yip and Rao (1980) have, however, developed a fast algorithm, using a recursive sparse matrix factorisation approach similar to that of Chen et al. in the case of the DCT. Due to the fact that the denominator of the sine argument is not N but $N + 1$ in this case, the factorisation is valid for values of $N = 2^i - 1$, where i is an integer, i.e., $N = 7, 15$, etc. Yip and Rao suggest that 8 multiplications are required for $N = 7$, but taking into account the fact that $\sin \pi/4 = \cos \pi/4$, the total is actually 6, compared with 16 for the DCT

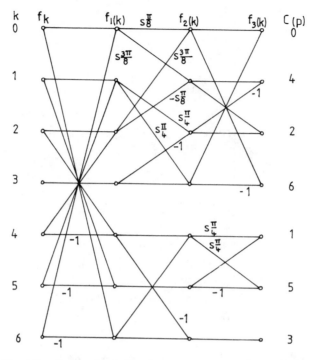

FIG. 7.8. Signal flow diagram for the fast discrete sine transform; $N = 7$; k and p are defined in Fig. 7.2; $s(\cdot)$ represents the sine function.

with $N = 8$. An alternative flow diagram is shown in Fig. 7.8, and corresponds to the factorisation

$$DST(8) = SI_1 \times SI_2 \times SI_3 \tag{7.57}$$

where

$$SI_1 = \begin{bmatrix} 1 & 0 & 0 & 1 & 0 & 0 & 0 \\ 0 & 1 & -1 & 0 & 0 & 0 & 0 \\ 0 & 1 & 1 & 0 & 0 & 0 & 0 \\ 1 & 0 & 0 & -1 & 0 & 0 & 0 \\ 0 & 0 & 0 & 0 & s\dfrac{\pi}{4} & 1 & 0 \\ 0 & 0 & 0 & 0 & s\dfrac{\pi}{4} & -1 & 0 \\ 0 & 0 & 0 & 0 & 0 & 0 & 1 \end{bmatrix} \tag{7.58}$$

$$SI_2 = \begin{bmatrix} s\dfrac{\pi}{8} & 0 & s\dfrac{3\pi}{8} & 0 & 0 & 0 & 0 \\ s\dfrac{3\pi}{8} & 0 & -s\dfrac{\pi}{8} & 0 & 0 & 0 & 0 \\ 0 & s\dfrac{\pi}{4} & 0 & -1 & 0 & 0 & 0 \\ 0 & s\dfrac{\pi}{4} & 0 & 1 & 0 & 0 & 0 \\ 0 & 0 & 0 & 0 & 1 & 0 & 1 \\ 0 & 0 & 0 & 0 & 0 & 1 & 0 \\ 0 & 0 & 0 & 0 & -1 & 0 & 1 \end{bmatrix} \tag{7.59}$$

$$SI_3 = \begin{bmatrix} 1 & 0 & 0 & 0 & 0 & 0 & 1 \\ 0 & 1 & 0 & 0 & 0 & 1 & 0 \\ 0 & 0 & 1 & 0 & 1 & 0 & 0 \\ 0 & 0 & 0 & 1 & 0 & 0 & 0 \\ 0 & 0 & 1 & 0 & -1 & 0 & 0 \\ 0 & 1 & 0 & 0 & 0 & -1 & 0 \\ 1 & 0 & 0 & 0 & 0 & 0 & -1 \end{bmatrix} \tag{7.60}$$

A slightly different factorisation is presented by Bisherurwa and Coakley (1981), who point out that the published version of Yip and Rao's flow diagram is incomplete (in fact it contains other typographical errors also).

7.9   Fast high-correlation transform

This transform was developed as a compromise between the ease of implementation of the WHT and the efficiency of the DCT (Cham and Clarke, 1983). The basis vectors consist of those of the WHT modified to 'resemble' those of typical image vectors, but by the use of the elements $+1, +\frac{1}{2}, -\frac{1}{2}$ and -1 only so that the only multiplications necessary (apart from overall scaling operations) may be implemented by binary shifts. The transform is described further in Chapter 3. The basis matrix for the case $N = 8$ is

$$HCT(8) = \begin{bmatrix} 1 & 1 & 1 & 1 & 1 & 1 & 1 & 1 \\ 1 & 1 & \frac{1}{2} & \frac{1}{2} & -\frac{1}{2} & -\frac{1}{2} & -1 & -1 \\ 1 & \frac{1}{2} & -\frac{1}{2} & -1 & -1 & -\frac{1}{2} & \frac{1}{2} & 1 \\ \frac{1}{2} & \frac{1}{2} & -1 & -1 & 1 & 1 & -\frac{1}{2} & -\frac{1}{2} \\ 1 & -1 & -1 & 1 & 1 & -1 & -1 & 1 \\ 1 & -1 & -\frac{1}{2} & \frac{1}{2} & -\frac{1}{2} & \frac{1}{2} & 1 & -1 \\ \frac{1}{2} & -1 & 1 & -\frac{1}{2} & -\frac{1}{2} & 1 & -1 & \frac{1}{2} \\ \frac{1}{2} & -\frac{1}{2} & 1 & -1 & 1 & -1 & \frac{1}{2} & -\frac{1}{2} \end{bmatrix} \tag{7.61}$$

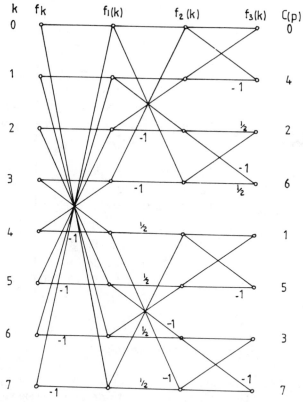

Fig. 7.9. Signal flow diagram for the fast high-correlation transform; $N = 8$; k and p are defined in Fig. 7.2.

and its fast algorithm is represented by the flow diagram of Fig. 7.9, which corresponds to the following matrix factorisation,

$$\text{HCT}(8) = \text{HCT}_1 \times \text{HCT}_2 \times \text{HCT}_3 \tag{7.62}$$

where

$$
\text{HCT}_1 = \begin{bmatrix}
1 & 1 & 0 & 0 & 0 & 0 & 0 & 0 \\
1 & -1 & 0 & 0 & 0 & 0 & 0 & 0 \\
0 & 0 & \frac{1}{2} & 1 & 0 & 0 & 0 & 0 \\
0 & 0 & -1 & \frac{1}{2} & 0 & 0 & 0 & 0 \\
0 & 0 & 0 & 0 & 1 & 1 & 0 & 0 \\
0 & 0 & 0 & 0 & 1 & -1 & 0 & 0 \\
0 & 0 & 0 & 0 & 0 & 0 & 1 & 1 \\
0 & 0 & 0 & 0 & 0 & 0 & -1 & 1
\end{bmatrix} \tag{7.63}
$$

$$
HCT_2 =
\begin{bmatrix}
1 & 0 & 0 & 1 & 0 & 0 & 0 & 0 \\
0 & 1 & 1 & 0 & 0 & 0 & 0 & 0 \\
0 & 1 & -1 & 0 & 0 & 0 & 0 & 0 \\
1 & 0 & 0 & -1 & 0 & 0 & 0 & 0 \\
0 & 0 & 0 & 0 & \frac{1}{2} & 0 & 0 & 1 \\
0 & 0 & 0 & 0 & 0 & \frac{1}{2} & 1 & 0 \\
0 & 0 & 0 & 0 & 0 & -1 & \frac{1}{2} & 0 \\
0 & 0 & 0 & 0 & -1 & 0 & 0 & \frac{1}{2}
\end{bmatrix}
\tag{7.64}
$$

$$
HCT_3 =
\begin{bmatrix}
1 & 0 & 0 & 0 & 0 & 0 & 0 & 1 \\
0 & 1 & 0 & 0 & 0 & 0 & 1 & 0 \\
0 & 0 & 1 & 0 & 0 & 1 & 0 & 0 \\
0 & 0 & 0 & 1 & 1 & 0 & 0 & 0 \\
0 & 0 & 0 & 1 & -1 & 0 & 0 & 0 \\
0 & 0 & 1 & 0 & 0 & -1 & 0 & 0 \\
0 & 1 & 0 & 0 & 0 & 0 & -1 & 0 \\
1 & 0 & 0 & 0 & 0 & 0 & 0 & -1
\end{bmatrix}
\tag{7.65}
$$

7.10   General comments on fast transforms

It is undoubtedly the case that the area of fast transforms has generated a high and sustained level of interest amongst workers in the signal processing field ever since the reintroduction of the basic idea in the mid 1960s, and it has been shown here how transform matrices which exhibit some underlying structure may be decomposed into a set of sequential operations enabling the total computational load of the calculation to be significantly reduced. The fact remains, however, that such a procedure increases in efficiency with data block size, and the very large relative improvements in computing speed obtainable for long data vectors are not achievable in the case of image transform processing (unless full frame operations are carried out) since the block size rarely exceeds 32 × 32. Furthermore, fast routines may bring with them complexities of storage and internal organisation of the algorithm, whether or not intermediate coefficients are stored 'in-place' in the appropriate locations of the preceding vector. Again, with a fast operation, incoming data cannot be processed on an element-by-element basis; i.e., multiplied by the N appropriate basis matrix coefficients and accumulated as the N partial sums forming the transform coefficient vector. Typically, two data values (which may be located anywhere within the N length data vector) are needed to calculate a subsequent pair of values, and so on, and the data must be regarded as being processed in parallel fashion.

Nevertheless, until very recently, interframe transform image processing, for example, has been an application which (particularly with real number transforms) makes extreme demands upon system design techniques, and even modest improvements in speed of computation via the use of fast transforms have been welcome. Of course, the influence of advances in hardware processing capability are naturally bound up closely with the matter of transform implementation using either fast, or more conventional, methods, and this point is considered further at the end of the following section.

7.11 Implementation of transform coding schemes

The eventual objective of the extensive investigation of transform (and indeed many other) image coding schemes which has taken place over the past 15 years is, of course, the practical reduction of data transmission rates or storage requirements whilst retaining an acceptable level of reconstructed image fidelity. In this context there are two separate stages to be considered and the first, not surprisingly, given the developments of recent years, is computer simulation of the various schemes which have been devised for the purpose. One factor tending to make simulation more attractive than actual hardware construction for test purposes is that, given due attention to such matters as rounding and truncation errors, the (digital) simulation of a digital coding scheme should produce results which can be used, with confidence, to predict the actual performance of the scheme when implemented in hardware. The latter more involved and time and finance consuming operation, which is the second stage of the design and development process, may therefore often be simplified.

There are therefore many transform coding simulation schemes which have been reported in the literature, whilst the number of actual hardware coders, although by no means negligible, is much smaller. It is the latter, of course, which are of most interest, since the specific details of a particular coding simulation, highly dependent as they are upon both the actual computer and language used, as well as the idiosyncracies of the programmer, are rarely of general significance. It is for this reason that in this section we concentrate upon those matters concerning hardware implementation which have been dealt with in the literature. Naturally implementation at real-time television rates imposes the greatest load upon the available hardware, and the design of such systems has exercised the ingenuity of several workers in the transform coding field. It is doubtful if the application of transform coding schemes will ever become widespread in this area, however, and lower rate approaches are probably of more significance. Both kinds of application are considered here, but first of all we examine an interesting theoretical concept concerned with the transform process itself which turns out to have an elegant form of implementation—the chirp-z transform algorithm.

7.11.1 Implementation using the chirp-z transform algorithm

Implementation of the discrete Fourier transform relation

$$C_p = \frac{1}{\sqrt{N}} \sum_{k=0}^{N-1} f_k \exp\left(-j\frac{2\pi pk}{N}\right) \qquad p = 0 \rightarrow N-1 \qquad (7.66)$$

can obviously be carried out by forming the products between the digitally represented data values f_k and the real and imaginary parts of the Fourier kernel which have been pre-calculated and stored. There is another approach to the calculation, however, and that is via the so-called 'chirp-z transform' algorithm (Bluestein, 1970; Rabiner and Schafer, 1969). The name arises from the fact that the algorithm basically computes the z-transform along a path more general than that corresponding to that for the DFT (the unit circle) and defined by a linearly increasing (complex) frequency, the term 'chirp' arising from the applications of such types of signal in radar. By expanding Eq. (7.66) using the identity

$$2pk = p^2 + k^2 - (p^2 + k^2 - 2pk)$$
$$= p^2 + k^2 - (p-k)^2 \qquad (7.67)$$

we obtain

$$C_p = \frac{1}{\sqrt{N}} \exp\left(-j\frac{\pi p^2}{N}\right) \sum_{k=0}^{N-1} f_k \exp\left(-j\frac{\pi k^2}{N}\right) \exp\left(j\frac{\pi(p-k)^2}{N}\right) \qquad (7.68)$$

If we define

$$g(k) = f_k \exp\left(-j\frac{\pi k^2}{N}\right) \qquad k = 0 \rightarrow N-1 \qquad (7.69)$$

Then it is apparent that

$$G(p) = \sum_{k=0}^{N-1} g(k) \exp\left(j\frac{\pi(p-k)^2}{N}\right) \qquad p = 0 \rightarrow M-1 \qquad (7.70)$$

where M is an arbitrary integer, is the discrete convolution of $g(k)$ and the sequence

$$r(k) = \exp\left(j\frac{\pi k^2}{N}\right) = W^{-k^2/2} \qquad (7.71)$$

where, as usual, $W = \exp(-j2\pi/N)$. Thus

$$G(p) = \sum_{k=0}^{N-1} g(k)r(p-k) \qquad (7.72)$$

A further rotation and scaling operation gives

$$C_p = (1/\sqrt{N})W^{p^2/2}G(p) \qquad (7.73)$$

as the coefficient sequence. The calculation of the DFT of Eq. (7.66) has therefore been converted into three sequential operations;

(1)   Rotation by $W^{k^2/2}$
(2)   Convolution with $W^{-k^2/2}$
(3)   Rotation by $W^{p^2/2}$

Since $W = \exp(-j2\pi/N)$, $W^\theta = \cos(2\pi\theta/N) - j\sin(2\pi\theta/N)$ and the rotation kernel is thus

$$W^{m^2/2} = \cos(\pi m^2/N) - j\sin(\pi m^2/N)$$

where $m = k$ or p, according to operations (1) or (3). The convolution kernel is

$$W^{-k^2/2} = \cos(\pi k^2/N) + j\sin(\pi k^2/N)$$

and we can represent the above sequence of operations by the flow diagram of Fig. 7.10 where the input data is allowed to be complex (although image data is real, a multidimensional DFT will have complex input data, in general, after the first stage of the transform).

Since the DCT can be computed via a DFT operation of length $2N$, it may be implemented in a similar way. Thus the DFT version of the DCT given in Eq. (7.39)

$$C_p = \sqrt{\frac{2}{N}}\,\mathrm{RE}\,\exp\!\left(-j\frac{\pi p}{2N}\right)\sum_{k=0}^{N-1} f_k \exp\!\left(-j\frac{\pi pk}{N}\right) \qquad (7.74)$$

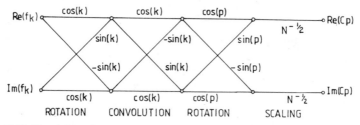

FIG. 7.10. Signal flow diagram for the chirp-z transform implementation of the Fourier transform. Here, $\cos(m) = \cos(\pi m^2/N)$ and $\sin(m) \equiv \sin(\pi m^2/N)$.

can, using the identity of Eq. (7.67), be written as

$$
C_p = \sqrt{\frac{2}{N}} \, \text{RE} \exp\left(-j\frac{\pi p}{2N}\right) \exp\left(-j\frac{\pi p^2}{2N}\right)
$$

$$
\dot{\times} \sum_{k=0}^{N-1} f_k \exp\left(-j\frac{\pi k^2}{2N}\right) \exp\left[j\frac{\pi(p-k)^2}{2N}\right] \tag{7.75}
$$

in this case there is an additional output rotation to be made, the transform is of length $2N$, the imaginary part input and output ports are redundant, and the scale factor becomes $\sqrt{2/N}$ rather than $1/\sqrt{N}$.

The odd form of the DCT (ODCT), referred to briefly in Chapter 3 has a similar interpretation over a block length of $2N - 1$ and may be implemented in a similar way, where the data term f_0 must be halved to account for the fact that making the data vector symmetrical by imaging it in the vertical axis and making the two elements f_0 coincide now doubles the effective value (Whitehouse et al., 1975; see also Fig. 3.9). Thus,

$$
C_p = \frac{1}{\sqrt{2N-1}} \sum_{-N+1}^{N-1} f'_k \exp\left(-j\frac{2\pi pk}{2N-1}\right) \qquad p, k = 0 \to N - 1 \tag{7.76}
$$

where $f'_k = f_k$, $k = 1 \to N - 1$; $f'_k = f_{-k}$, $k = -N + 1 \to -1$, and $f'_0 = \frac{1}{2}f_0$. Since the data is now real and even,

$$
C_p = \frac{2}{\sqrt{2N-1}} \sum_{k=0}^{N-1} f'_k \cos\frac{2\pi pk}{2N-1}
$$

$$
= \frac{2}{\sqrt{2N-1}} \, \text{RE} \sum_{k=0}^{N-1} f'_k \exp\left(-j\frac{2\pi pk}{2N-1}\right)
$$

$$
= 2 \, \text{RE} \, \text{DFT}(2N - 1)_p \tag{7.77}
$$

in analogy with Eq. (7.40). The ODCT may be implemented, therefore, via the relation

$$
C_p = \frac{2}{\sqrt{2N-1}} \, \text{RE} \exp\left(-j\frac{\pi p^2}{2N-1}\right)
$$

$$
\times \sum_{k=0}^{N-1} f'_k \exp\left(-j\frac{\pi k^2}{2N-1}\right) \exp\left[j\frac{\pi(p-k)^2}{2N-1}\right] \tag{7.78}
$$

Here there is no additional output rotation, the transform length is $2N - 1$, and the scale factor is $2/\sqrt{2N - 1}$.

Transform implementation via the CZT using charge transfer (i.e., sampled analogue) devices has been suggested by Means et al. (1974, 1975) and Whitehouse et al. (1975) using the ODCT with a block length of 32. Conventional previous element predictive coding follows the transform to complete the hybrid scheme, in which the sampling rate is 4.8 MHz and the image size 240 lines × 256 elements with a field rate of $60 \, \text{s}^{-1}$. Multiplications in the implementation are carried out conventionally and the reference functions are stored in read only memory. Buss et al. (1975) consider the electrical characteristics of the device in more detail (see also Cheek et al., 1978). It is also possible to use surface acoustic wave devices for Fourier transform processing of this type, and a comprehensive review of their operation is given by Jack et al. (1980).

Charge transfer devices (CTDs) can also be used to implement transforms in more conventional ways. Thus Roberts et al. (1977) have described a tapped CTD structure of length $2N - 1$ (where N is the length of the data vector) in which N^2 resistors are used to determine the weighting coefficients (i.e, basis vector elements). They demonstrate results for the WHT and slant transforms, for $N = 16$, using discrete silicon chip resistors or thick film structures at a rate of approximately 10^5 data points/s and suggest that, at rates two orders of magnitude higher than this, a single-chip version of their techniques offers advantages in size and power consumption compared with a computational approach. For large N, of course, the necessity for N^2 weighting resistors makes the approach unattractive, but this is no problem in the present application, where a block size of 16 is adequate.

A two-dimensional WHT scheme intended to process 512 × 480 element 6-bit video input at 7.5 frames/s (corresponding to 3.7 Mbits/s at an output rate of 2 bits/element), with a variety of lower rate and resolution options also is described by Spencer (1979). The 8 × 8 transform is carried out in the form of a 64-element one-dimensional operation, and the implementation is interesting in the present context in that it employs monolithic LSI digital CTDs, which operate at a clock rate of 2.5 MHz. There are $\log_2 N = 6$ stages, in parallel 12-bit format for each digital input word. At the output, the word length is rounded to 9 bits, which is considered to be the minimum if the fidelity of the reconstructed image is not to be affected. Kapur et al. (1980) use a 64-tap programmable CCD transversal filter to compute the ODCT using a prime transform algorithm. The ODCT relation is that of Eq. (7.77). For this approach to the transform $2N - 1$ must be a prime number, and is here made 127 (i.e., $N = 64$). The algorithm involves re-ordering of the data before, and of the coefficients after, transformation, the latter consisting of a circular convolution operation between the re-ordered data and the set of DCT weighting coefficients stored in read only memory.

In a digital implementation of the transform operation, errors arise from the effects of finite word length and coefficient roundoff. Where the data amplitudes are processed in analogue form other sources of inaccuracy (non-linearity and noise) are present, and these have been considered by Wrench (1976), who compared the implementation of the DCT in three forms—the CZT discussed earlier, the prime transform algorithm and a fast digital algorithm. The CZT was used to implement the ODCT for $N = 32$, and the prime algorithm for $N = 31$ (note that, for $N = 32$, $2N - 1$ is not prime). Assuming that $\pm 1\%$ accuracy is obtainable from the analogue devices, the prime algorithm was found to be about an order of magnitude better than the CZT. Using a 6-bit image, a digital implementation via an FFT-type algorithm with 9-bit computational accuracy was found to be superior to both of the other forms on implementation.

Shaw and Westgate (1980) point out that fast computational algorithms generally require data re-ordering stages in their implementation and are thus basically unsuited to simple processing using serial access CTDs. They suggest a 4×4 Hadamard implementation (extendable to larger values of N) which uses external microprocessor control to generate the appropriate timing sequence. To overcome the problem of subtraction in the processing (corresponding to the -1 entries in the basis matrix) they decompose the matrix

$$[H] = \begin{bmatrix} 1 & 1 & 1 & 1 \\ 1 & 1 & -1 & -1 \\ 1 & -1 & -1 & 1 \\ 1 & -1 & 1 & -1 \end{bmatrix} \tag{7.79}$$

into the difference

$$[H] = [A] - [B]$$

where

$$[A] = \begin{bmatrix} 1 & 1 & 1 & 1 \\ 1 & 1 & 0 & 0 \\ 1 & 0 & 0 & 1 \\ 1 & 0 & 1 & 0 \end{bmatrix} \tag{7.80}$$

and

$$[B] = \begin{bmatrix} 0 & 0 & 0 & 0 \\ 0 & 0 & 1 & 1 \\ 0 & 1 & 1 & 0 \\ 0 & 1 & 0 & 1 \end{bmatrix} \tag{7.81}$$

so that the data array can be separately processed by $[A]$ and $[B]$ to form two output arrays, the difference between which (taken subsequent to transform processing) forms the desired output. Implementation of the FFT and the FWHT in their basic Cooley–Tukey form derived by conventional matrix factorisation is proposed by Yarlagadda and Hershey (1981). They suggest that the application of the CTD is particularly suitable when the ultimate in processing speed is not the main criterion, but rather low cost and simplicity.

7.11.2 Implementation at television data rates

As a result of the wide bandwidth requirement for transmitting moving television image sequences, there has been, for many years, much interest expressed in the application of data compression techniques in this area, although it is one in which the problems are particularly severe. First of all, the data rate is very high, with sampling frequencies of at least 10 MHz, and images of (original) resolution at least 6 and usually 8 bits. Second, the advent of colour has made the video signal more difficult to code, basically because it contains more information, and bit allocations for composite coding need to be adjusted accordingly. Third, the greatest bar to the application of significant amounts of data compression to entertainment-type television signals is that there must be no perceptible degradation in the reconstructed image. This matter has been discussed at length in Chapter 6.

Nevertheless, there has been much work carried out in the past 10 years on the application of transform coding to real-time television signals and, at the time of writing, the problems of implementation remain severe, though not insurmountable. The advantages of reduced rate television signal coding were realised in Japan in the mid-1960s and are exemplified in the work of Enomoto and Shibata (1971). They describe the implementation of a slant transform of order 8 to reduce the data rate by approximately one-half for a 6-bit image sampled at 10 MHz. The actual transform operation is carried out via a tapped delay line/resistor matrix combination, with 8 parallel outputs sampled at $\frac{10}{8} = 1.25$ MHz for PCM coding. A similar scheme has been reported more recently by Jain and Delogne (1981) using the WHT with $N = 8$ to code the 625-line, 625-element 25-frame/s (European) system. It is found to be better in many respects (power consumption, complexity and compression capability) than an equivalent digital scheme. The slant trans-form implementation of Enomoto has also been extended by Ohira et al. (1978) to two dimensions using a block size of 8 × 4, with an output rate of 3 bits/element corresponding to a transmission rate of 32 Mbits/s. In this digital implementation it is, of course, necessary to approximate certain basis vector elements by their nearest binary equivalents (thus, for example, $1/\sqrt{5} = 0.4472136$, approximated by $[0.011100100111]_2$).

There are naturally advantages in the sampled analogue technique (at least from the point of view of implementation) when a transform requiring real number multiplications is employed. As far as digital implementation is concerned the WHT is attractive, and has been thoroughly investigated in regard to its possible (non-adaptive) benefits for real-time television by C. K. P. Clarke (1976) whose work has been commented on in Chapter 5. A digital real-time implementation for standard broadcast PAL colour television with a sampling frequency of 13.5 MHz and a word length of 8 bits is described by Walker (1974) and Walker and Clarke (1974). The scheme carries out a fast WHT decomposition of order 32, of the kind shown for the FFT earlier in this chapter for $N = 8$, where powers of W are replaced by unity. Summation and differencing of data (or subsequent fast algorithm intermediate coefficients) are carried out using shift registers of the appropriate length. Thus, for $N = 8$, successive operations would require input elements at spacings of 4, 2 and 1 element, respectively. At clock pulse 5 the output of the shift register of length 4, x_1, is added to the incoming data sample x_5 to give the partial sum $x_1 + x_5$, which is passed to the next stage of the algorithm. At the same time the difference $x_1 - x_5$ is also formed and fed back to the register input, from the output of which it emerges at clock pulse 9, followed by $x_2 - x_6, x_3 - x_7$ and so on. Two further stages complete the process. The scheme is very similar to that suggested for a pipeline FFT implementation described by Groginsky and Works (1970). The 'transformer' operates in parallel on each bit of the input word and the overall clock rate is therefore the input sampling frequency. The equivalent data rate is approximately 106 Mbits/s.

Because of its ease of implementation the WHT has been found attractive for operation at real-time television rates by several workers. Alexandridis and Klinger (1972) have suggested an implementation in which the N columns of an $N \times N$ image are processed separately, but simultaneously. The N partial transforms are then added in parallel to give the $N \times N$ WHT matrix. Noble (1975) points out that a configuration similar to the flow diagram of Fig. 7.3, i.e., in which the same set of computations is carried out $\log_2 N$ times can carry out a 16-point pipeline transform at rates well above those required for real time NTSC video (512 elements $\times$ 525 lines $\times$ 30 frames $= 8 \times 10^6$ elements/s). Furthermore, since each of the $\log_2 N$ stages is of the same form, a single hardware stage plus feedback requires only N arithmetic elements, operating at $(\log_2 N)^{-1}$ times the pipeline rate, which may still be greater than the actual rate needed. For $N = 8$ a single 25-ns ECL element could process data at a rate of about 13 MHz (24 arithmetic operations in 600 ns, in which time 8 elements are transformed, i.e., at a rate of $8 \times 10^9/600 = 13.3$ MHz).

Image data is naturally of at least two-dimensional form and a one-dimensional algorithm such as that described earlier has to be applied twice to carry out a two-dimensional transform. Bringing in the third dimension for true three-dimensional transform processing creates the requirement for multiframe storage, as in the real-time WHT video processor described by Knauer (1976), the theoretical aspects of which design have been discussed previously elsewhere (Chapter 5). In this system seven fields are stored on a disc and read out simultaneously with the incoming eighth field. The image block then consists of the 64 elements in a 4 × 4 area extending over four frames which are transformed, processed and the coefficients then decoded and the image reconstructed in a similar way. With this method coding schemes can be tested in a laboratory environment on standard NTSC video input sequences.

Bacchi and Moreau (1978) have used the fast algorithm shown in Fig. 7.3 to implement the WHT, and that of Fig. 7.5 to perform the Haar transform, in one or two dimensions at real-time rates with colour television signals, with the aim of reducing the basic (composite) rate of approximately 120 Mbits/s to that recommended by the CCITT of 34 Mbits/s. Their input data is an 8-bit luminance signal sampled at 12 MHz, and two 8-bit colour difference signals sampled at 3 MHz. The signal is formed into blocks of 16 elements, and an image line consists of 39 luminance and 2 × 10 colour difference words, where one word contains $16 \times 8 = 128$ bits. Therefore 16 lines contain a total of 59, 16 × 16 blocks. Each block must be transformed in $16 \times 64/59 = 17.35\,\mu s$ (where the video line period is $64\,\mu s$). The one-dimensional transform operation takes $8\,\mu s$ and so each vector/matrix product requires 500 ns. Thus 125 ns is available for each of the four cycles (with feedback) through the single hardwired stage of the fast algorithm. Intermediate storage between the two one-dimensional operations is carried out using TTL random access memory. The 16 outputs of the one-dimensional transform appear every 500 ns, corresponding to a serial data rate of $16/0.5 = 32$ MHz before storage.

Where processing with real-number transforms is concerned, there is naturally a problem with the implementation of the many multiplications necessary. Hein and Ahmed (1978) whose DCT/WHT algorithm has previously been described, suggest a 'look-up' table approach, in which the products of the basis matrix coefficients and all members of the range of input values are predetermined and stored in a read only memory. In the case $N = 8$, with 12-bit input words, the capacity required is a few kilobytes. By using the C-matrix transform (CMT), an approximation to the DCT devised by Srinivasan and Rao (1983), the storage requirement can be reduced by 20–30%. A similar procedure has also been reported by Bisherurwa and Coakley (1982). In fact, should this method be selected for a transform coding system, it is unlikely nowadays that look-up table capacity will be a problem.

Despite the greater complexity involved in the implementation of the more efficient transform processes, there have been several approaches reported more recently, mainly using the DCT. The scheme of Alker and Andreassen (1982), however, employs the two-dimensional Fourier transform, in a hybrid coding scheme for television signal transmission with a pipeline architecture using custom-designed NMOS technology. The Fourier transform is chosen because of the ease with which motion compensation can then be carried out (see Chapter 5), and edge blocking effects are mitigated by extending the data block before transformation. The processing is carried out by a set of bit-serial arithmetic elements, suitable for LSI implementation, six of which, plus one stage of multiplication, produce the one-dimensional row transform, followed by reformatting and then a similar operation for the column transform. The real and imaginary parts of the output coefficients are then converted to magnitude/phase form. This approach forms an interesting departure from the more usual trend of using off the shelf digital components but the suggested overall compression rate of 40:1 for broadcast quality colour television signals is perhaps a trifle optimistic.

The processor of Ghanbari and Pearson (1982) employs matrix factorisation of the DCT with $N = 8$ for real-time broadcast television signal transformation at a sampling rate of 11 MHz. Like that of Hein and Ahmed discussed earlier, the factorisation involves Hadamard sparse matrices, which of course are particularly easy to implement. The system is of modular form, each unit performing the 2-point transform of one of the stages in the matrix decomposition, using TTL shift registers and Schottky TTL adders as arithmetic units. As in the coder of Ohira, binary approximations are necessary for the various sinusoidal weightings used in the transform. A modular, pipeline configuration is a feature of the coder designed by Jalali and Rao (1982) for real-time processing of the composite NTSC colour signal sampled at $3f_{sc}$ (10.7 MHz). The fast algorithm used is the original one of Chen and Smith, chosen for its advantages of (a) easy extension to larger block sizes and (b) straightforward implementation of the inverse transform. In this case it is pointed out that look-up table techniques require far too much memory space and discrete monolithic multipliers, carrying out a 16×16 bit operation in 140 ns, are used instead. Memory read/write operations and access to the trigonometrical coefficients stored in random access memory are in each case carried out in a period of 35 ns.

With the present day emphasis on implementation of complex signal processing functions using LSI or VLSI techniques, structures consisting of identical elementary processing stages, coupled together in a regular lattice formation, have generated considerable interest (Kung, 1980). The application of such a 'systolic' array in transform processing is reported by McCanny and McWhirter (1982) who describe a pipeline 4-point bit-sliced matrix/vector product operation (i.e, each lattice involves only 1 bit of the digital word representing a matrix element). The process is particularly simple in the case of the WHT, but Ward and Stanier (1983) have described an implementation of this type for the DCT. The N-point DCT is calculated using a DFT over $4N$ points, where the N data elements are situated in the first N odd locations of the $4N$ length vector, all other elements being zero. The DCT terms (apart from scaling constants) are then given by

$$C_p = \text{RE} \sum_{k=0}^{4N-1} f'_k \exp\left(-j\frac{2\pi pk}{4N}\right) \qquad p = 0 \rightarrow N - 1 \qquad (7.82)$$

where f'_k is the modified data sequence. The Fourier algorithm is due to Winograd, and is carried out using arrays which contain $+1$, -1 or 0, and a set of predetermined multipliers. The authors suggest that an implementation of this algorithm via systolic array processing would be adequate for real-time television images.

7.11.3   Other systems for transform implementation

There are, of course, good reasons, (discussed in other places in this volume) why real-time broadcast television is not the best application for a compression scheme such as transform coding. At lower rates, however, it is a valuable and efficient means for the compression of image data, and many systems have been designed for such applications as surveillance, videophone and RPV image transmission. With the lower rates come, naturally, reduced spatial and/or temporal resolution, and simplified hardware requirements. Furthermore, even at relatively low data rates, a fast algorithm implemented in hardware can greatly ease the computational load imposed when extensive simulation of coding schemes is required. Thus the scheme of Carl and Swartwood (1973) implements the flow diagram shown in Fig. 7.3 for $N = 8$, in a hybrid analogue/digital realisation in which the single stage is used $\log_2 N$ times in a feedback configuration.

To transmit a 1-MHz videophone signal using a 6.3-Mbits/s PCM channel, Fukinuki and Miyata (1973) have designed a 3-bits/element Hadamard transform coder, using a sampling frequency of approximately 2.1 MHz, which carries out either a 1×8 or 2×4 transform. The processing stages use shift register delays, inverters and adders and operate in a two-dimensional mode on blocks taken in a staggered pattern from the original image and re-ordered into a one-dimensional sequence to minimise the number of delay elements needed. A similar scheme is used in Ohira's real-time television coder discussed in the previous section. In that section also, the work of Noble on high speed WHT implementation was considered. He also, in the same paper, considers real-time implementation at lower rates

(<7.5 frames/s) or lower resolution (256×256), of an 8×8 WHT without the use of a fast algorithm, using two 8-point stages with input shift registers and intermediate fast random access memory in which to store the first stage output coefficients.

In an RPV application, Reis *et al.* (1976) have implemented a two-dimensional fast Haar transform via sparse matrix factorisation in a predictive configuration. The stages consist simply of delay elements and summing junctions and can operate at a data rate of 120 Mbits/s. Since such an application places a premium on power consumption and hardware simplicity, a reduced rate version processes only one-eighth of a line per field (giving an input data rate of 4.8 Mbits/s), in which read only memories control the operation of the latches, summation elements and memory. The scheme of Murray (1977) also processes input data at a reduced rate in much the same way. In this case one-eighth of a field at a time (32 elements $\times$ 256 rows) is processed using a hybrid FDCT/predictive coding arrangement. Three AM2901 4-bit slice Schottky TTL microprocessor chips are used in the model 1240 processor to give 12-bit word length, and a pipeline configuration containing a fast multiplier allows a 12×12 product to be formed in 150 ns. The microcode programs employed in the system are described in detail in the paper. Whitehouse *et al.* (1977) describe a similar RPV system utilising SOS–LSI and hybrid circuit technology, pointing out that integer rather than floating point computation is desirable and that 8 bit plus sign representation is adequate for acceptable picture quality.

The one-dimensional transform/predictive coding hybrid scheme has proved very popular from the point of simplicity and ease of implementation, and another version of the approach is reported by McWhirter *et al.* (1981), with a block length of 16 and 6-bit input data 290×290 elements in extent. In this case the internal accuracy of the coding scheme is 10 bits. The WHT vectors are stored in read only memory and the 16 transformation elements themselves are implemented, two at a time, on 225-cell Ferranti ULAs. The coder is intended for low power, remote surveillance applications at an on-line selectable output rate between 0.2 and 1Mbits/s. Whiteman *et al.* (1981) and Chan and Whiteman (1983) have reported a similar system using a hybrid DCT/predictive technique operation on 8-bit input data of maximum extent 640 elements $\times$ 480 lines at 7.5 frames/s, giving a maximum data rate of 4.6 Mbits/s at an output rate of 2 bits/element. As in earlier schemes, reduced resolution and frame rate options are also available. Since the input frame rate is 30 s^{-1}, every fourth input frame is processed in four 160-element wide stripes. Thus in the time of one horizontal line period, five parallel DCT pipelines process 32 elements in two sequential $N = 16$ operations. A single predictive coding stage is applied on a time sharing basis to all the DCT coefficients. In this case multiplication in the DCT implementation is avoided by using a 2K × 8-bit programmable read only memory in a look-up table format. Quantiser tables are stored in a similar way. The compression unit employs a total of six LSI circuits and is designed with a view to minimising size, weight and power consumption.

7.12   General comments on implementation

This section has been concerned with the practical aspects of implementing transform coding systems in hardware form, and it is in this area that the greatest advances in transform coding will probably come, directly or indirectly, in the future. It is unlikely that new transforms will be discovered or invented which improve coding efficiency by any significant amount, nor is the removal of most of the multiplications, even if it were possible in, for example, the DCT, going to increase the performance of present day designs very much. Where benefits will come is in the ability to carry out statistical measurements on, say, sequential image frames in real time, in order to be able to implement very flexible adaptive bit allocation and area classification techniques, coupled with 'intelligent' receivers and decoders, which can make use of already transmitted information for decoding in order to minimise the overhead requirement, and also can apply, again in real time, enhancement and restoration techniques to the reconstructed image.

The ultimate limits in this field are, of course, those which apply to that of digital image processing in general. For an informative review of these, the paper by Keyes (1981) is recommended.

Chapter 8

Error and Noise Effects

8.1 Introduction

In all forms of communication, it is necessary to take account of the possible influence of undesired effects which may render the received data at best, impaired and, at worst, useless. Such effects may arise from a variety of causes, both external to the coding/decoding operation and inherent within it. The former are produced by the non-ideal nature of any practical communication channel and, in terms of the digital systems with which we are dealing, result in the incorrect decoding of received data. In the binary case this amounts to the replacement of the symbol '1' by '0', and vice versa. The severity of the degradation produced then crucially depends upon the exact location of the error in any code word. The result of an error in a bit of low significance in a word which represents a small, high-order transform coefficient may not even be perceptible in the reconstructed image; an error in a significant bit of a low-order coefficient may result in the appearance of the corresponding basis picture (see Chapter 3) in the image, or an error in a synchronisation code word may result in the complete failure of the decoding process. Again, hybrid processing involves a prediction/reconstruction operation, and this brings with it the specific problem of error propagation (i.e., incorrect coefficient values) over a possibly significant length in the direction of prediction. The influence of channel errors upon an 'efficient' coding scheme is therefore likely to be more serious than in the case of conventional PCM, where only the specific word is affected, and the exact effect will be dependent on the type of system used and the bit error rate (ber). An obvious solution is channel error protection, as in the scheme described by Rice (1975) for deep space communication, and there is an interesting interaction between the allocation of available coding capacity to the compressed data, on the one hand, and to error protection on the other, which is discussed further later. Furthermore, schemes have been developed which are able to detect and correct, or at least ameliorate, the effects of errors purely by operations carried out at the receiver.

In addition to external sources of error, the coding operation naturally involves manipulations which are only approximate, and thus contribute to image degradation. It is in this way, of course, that data compression is actually achieved, since the 'output' of an orthonormal transform, per se, contains exactly the same amount of information as the input data, but presented in a form which makes it more amenable to transmission or storage at a lower rate. Thus the basic form of approximation introduced in a transform coding scheme is that of deleting small magnitude coefficients. Generally speaking, images which can be successfully coded at low rates have high inter-element correlation, which implies that the transform coefficients will have magnitudes which decrease rapidly as their order increases. Therefore, omitting small coefficients amounts to not coding those lying towards the lower right-hand corner of the (two-dimensional) variance map. As something of an oversimplification, such coefficient deletion is rather like low-pass filtering, and sharp detail in the original image tends to be smoothed out by such a procedure. The resulting numerical value of the error will be relatively small, if reasonable visual quality of the reconstructed image is to be preserved, but the relation between the two is complex (see Chapter 6).

As well as the effects of the deletion of small transform coefficients, an additional source of error is the quantisation process needed to allow the transmission of the coefficients in digital form (frequently, of course, the deletion and bit allocation steps are combined into a single operation—coefficients smaller than a predetermined level being allocated zero bits, i.e., being deleted). This factor will be determined by the overall coefficient variance, the number of bits allocated to any particular coefficient (naturally, increasing the bit allocation will raise the data rate whilst reducing the quantisation error) and its pdf. The total quantisation error may then be calculated fairly easily if a particular data model and coefficient pdf are assumed, using the techniques described in Chapter 4.

In the case of actual image data, even when the separate coefficient variances are known, it is hardly worthwhile attempting to calculate the overall deletion/quantisation error by the use of analytical techniques—pdf estimation, and so on, in the transform domain, especially when the coding scheme is adaptive, and optimisation operations usually proceed by more or less *ad hoc* adjustment of the various class bit allocations, based upon visual quality of the reconstructed image and an overall mean square error or signal-to-noise ratio figure calculated by the equations contained in Appendix 7. Thus, for a given overall bit rate, we may choose to retain many coefficients, relatively coarsely quantised, or to quantise a smaller number of coefficients more accurately. Such a trade-off between noise and resolution has been described by Parsons and Tescher (1975). The low resolution image is relatively noise free, and vice versa.

The other 'internal' source of image degradation in transform coding schemes is that resulting from the finite accuracy with which the various mathematical operations are carried out. The multiplication and addition or subtraction manipulations involved in the transform calculation result in a greatly increased dynamic range of the coefficients compared with that of the original data (see Chapter 4), and although the coefficients need not be retained at full accuracy (16 bits, for example, for 8-bit data and a two-dimensional 16×16 transform), care must be taken to ensure that the resulting truncation or round-off errors do not reach unacceptable levels. For this reason (amongst others) it is dangerous to assume that results obtained via simulation using long word-length computations will necessarily carry over without modification to a practical, reduced word-length, implementation. Again, there is the problem of accuracy when analogue devices are used to carry out the transform (Wrench, 1976; see also Chapter 7).

To summarise, then, there are four basic sources of error in the transform coding process: finite computational accuracy, errors due to coefficient deletion, those due to the quantisation of the remaining coefficients and errors introduced externally into the communication channel or storage operation. Each of these is now discussed separately.

8.2   Requirements of implementation

We have seen in an earlier chapter that the transform operation expands the possible range of values within the data by a factor of the order of N^c, where N is the transform order and c its dimension. Obviously for a large two-dimensional transform this effect is very significant and must be taken into account during subsequent processing. As a simple example, a one-dimensional WHT of order 8 has a maximum DC coefficient of $256 \times \sqrt{8}$ when all of the data elements are 256 and $1/\sqrt{8}$ when one element is unity and the remainder zero. The input data thus requires 8, and the coefficient set 11, bits for correct representation. On inverse transformation, in the absence of any intermediate processing, only the upper 8 bits of the reconstructed data output are of any significance and can be appropriately relabelled. In the present example, the smallest coefficient value is $1/\sqrt{8}$, and Walker and

Clarke (1974) suggest that, in the critical environment of broadcast television, the corresponding number of bits, on average, may be deleted from the coefficient representation, since they are the equivalent of not more than the smallest input quantisation step. The reduction is therefore $\log_2 N^{1/2}$, i.e., $\frac{1}{2} \log_2 N$ bits. Further reduction may be achieved by selective removal of some of the most significant bits since coefficients of the maximum possible amplitude occur relatively rarely (Clarke, 1976). As another television coding example, the application of the slant transform to real-time coding by Ohira et al. (1978) maintains an internal coefficient accuracy, prior to bit reduction, of 10 bits for 8-bit data and $N = 32$. The transform, however, requires the binary representation of several awkward real weighting factors $(1/\sqrt{5}$, $\sqrt{5/21}$, for example) and for this purpose the accuracy is 16 bits.

As has been mentioned earlier, the use of a transform coding scheme to process an arbitrary television image satisfactorily (i.e., without visible degradation) is an extremely critical and stringent test of such a system, and one, moreover, which it does not pass with any degree of consistency. For less exacting applications, restrictions upon the truncation of less significant bits in the transform operation are somewhat eased, and Knauer's (1976) approach is a typical one—with 6-bit input data and a Walsh–Hadamard transform of order 64, the word length is allowed to grow to 8 bits in the first two of the six $(\log_2 64)$ stages, and then maintained at that figure by truncating the least significant bit in the following four, instead of being allowed to increase to the theoretical value of 12 bits. Knab (1977) has investigated this point more specifically, using a 6-bit image, the WHT of block size 8×8 and a compressed data rate of 2 bits/element by considering different degrees of round-off error to be permissible in the horizontal and vertical transforms. The theoretical maximum accuracy required (the horizontal transform is carried out first) is 9×12 bits, and it was found that 8-bit precision in both stages was the minimum which would allow acceptable image reconstruction in both uncompressed and compressed cases. However Spencer (1979), finds that, in the same situation, 9 bits is the minimum number required to prevent visible image degradation.

The problems of approximate transform implementation have been studied by Gonsalves and Johnson (1980) who considered a two-dimensional hybrid coding scheme utilising a one-dimensional WHT of order 32. Random noise of zero mean and variance 0.1 was added to the basis elements (of magnitudes ± 1) and the inverse transform was carried out using either the noise-free Hadamard transform or the matrix inverse. It was demonstrated that the use of the Hadamard inverse produced unacceptable results, even with the bit rate increased from an original 2 to 2.5 bits/element. The situation was corrected by the use of the exact matrix inverse for image reconstruction, but the rate necessary was still 2.5 bits/element. It is thus apparent that inaccuracies of this nature in forward processing can be removed, provided that the resulting values in the forward basis matrix can be determined accurately and the matrix inverse calculated for reverse transformation at the decoder, an interesting but probably not very realistic situation.

As far as analogue implementation is concerned, Wrench (1976) has examined the effect of computational accuracy on the application of the cosine transform, as mentioned in the chapter on fast transforms, the 9-bit digital approach being found superior to chirp-z and prime transform techniques.

8.3   Coefficient deletion errors

The data compression capabilities of a transform coding scheme derive from the deletion or coarse quantisation of those coefficients in the transform domain which are considered to be 'small' in some more or less definable way. Mathematically, there is little to be said concerning the contribution of the deleted coefficient energy to the overall system error. We know that, for the orthonormal transform, the total energy in the data and coefficient domains is identical, and so the error induced by the omission of coefficients will simply be that given by their energy relative to the whole. If, as has been suggested earlier, the coefficient set is normalised to the variance of the input data, then the sum total of the energy of the coefficients will be equal to N in the case of one-dimensional, and N^2 for two-dimensional, transforms. Two points should be noted here. First, if as is usually the case, the data to be transformed has a finite mean value, then the mean value of the transform DC coefficient is excluded from the preceding calculation; second, for transforms usually employed in coding schemes, all AC basis vectors have zero mean values, and thus the mean value of the coefficient sequences is very close (but not identical to) zero. (Chapter 3 exemplifies these considerations.) To be strictly accurate, therefore, deleting an AC coefficient not only increases the error incurred by the variance of that coefficient, but by its mean energy also. As can be seen from Table 4.1, however, the energy residing in the (normalised) mean value is very small, and so this contribution is, for practical purposes, negligible.

Formally, therefore, for unit variance input data (or the normalised case), the deletion error is given by

$$e_{d} = 1 - \frac{1}{N} \sum_{R} \sigma_{r,s}^2 \qquad (8.1)$$

TABLE 8.1. One-dimensional transform coefficient variances for various transforms.[a]

Transform	Variance							
KLT	6.358	0.931	0.298	0.148	0.093	0.068	0.055	0.049
DCT	6.344	0.930	0.312	0.149	0.094	0.068	0.055	0.049
WHT	6.344	0.796	0.275	0.226	0.094	0.094	0.092	0.080

[a] $N = 8$, $\rho = 0.91$.

in one dimension, and

$$e_d = 1 - \frac{1}{N^2} \sum_R \sigma_{r,s}^2 \tag{8.2}$$

in two, where R indicates the region over which coefficients are retained.

For the separable first-order Markov model these results may easily be demonstrated. In two dimensions, the variance array is simply given by the product of the row–column transform coefficient variances (see Chapter 2). Thus for $N = 8$ and inter-element correlation coefficient of 0.91 the (one-dimensional) variance vectors are shown in Table 8.1 for the KLT, DCT and WHT. If, therefore, we choose to omit the smallest 50% of the two-dimensional coefficients, the error incurred will be

$$e_{KLT} = 0.470\%$$

$$e_{DCT} = 0.483\%$$

$$e_{WHT} = 0.806\%$$

(It should be noted that, in general, the n coefficients of smallest variance are not simply those located in a square region in the lower right of the array.) Although it is unwise to draw confident conclusions as to the appearance of the reconstructed image from such figures as those just given, both the good performance of the DCT and the worse behaviour of the WHT in a quantitative sense are obvious.

As a final comment it is worth mentioning that the error resulting from coefficient deletion is obviously quite independent of the dimension of the transform coding process and of whether true transform coding or a hybrid technique is being employed.

8.4   Coefficient quantisation errors

The coefficients which remain after those with sufficiently small variances have been deleted must, of necessity, now be quantised and coded for transmission or storage. The question of bit allocation has been dealt with in

Chapter 4, and we may make use of the relations developed therein to set the inevitable degree of quantisation error so generated in the context of overall system error. The relations are slightly different in the cases of the DC and of the AC coefficients since the latter are assumed to be symmetrical about zero whilst the former, of necessity, are always positive. Quantisation of the DC coefficient with a number of bits $b_{(0,0)}$ results in an error

$$e_{q(0,0)} = \sum_{i=1}^{2^{b(0,0)}} \int_{x_i}^{x_{i+1}} (x - y_i)^2 p(x)\, dx \qquad (8.3)$$

[the notation of Chapter 4 has been retained here for clarity, thus x represents the DC coefficient to be quantised, x_i, x_{i+1} decision and y_i reconstruction levels and $p(x)$ the DC coefficient pdf]. Since the DC coefficient is simply the (scaled) block average of the original luminance values, its distribution will have an entropy little smaller than that of the original image (Chapter 2), and it is therefore not worthwhile assuming $p(x)$ to be anything other than a uniform distribution. Following the analysis in Chapter 4, the quantisation error for the DC coefficient can be written

$$e_{q(0,0)} = \sum_{i=1}^{2^{b(0,0)}} \int_{x_i}^{x_{i+1}} x^2 p(x)\, dx - y_i^2 p_i \qquad (8.4)$$

If we assume that the DC coefficient is uniformly distributed then $p_i = 1/L$, where $L = 2^{b(0,0)}$, and so

$$e_{q(0,0)} = E(x^2) - \frac{1}{L} \sum_{i=1}^{L} y_i^2 \qquad (8.5)$$

For the uniform quantiser $y_i = (A/2L)(2i - 1)$, where A is the maximum coefficient amplitude and, for a uniform distribution, $\sigma^2 = A^2/12$. Thus

$$e_{q(0,0)} = \frac{1}{A} \int_0^A x^2\, dx - \frac{A^2}{4L^3} \sum_{i=1}^{L} (2i - 1)^2$$

$$= \frac{A^2}{3} - \frac{A^2}{4L^3} \frac{4L^3 - L}{3}$$

$$= \sigma_{(0,0)}^2/L^2 = \sigma_{(0,0)}^2 2^{-2b(0,0)} \qquad (8.6)$$

This is the approximate error incurred in quantisation of the DC coefficient, having variance $\sigma_{(0,0)}^2$, with a uniform $b_{(0,0)}$ bit quantiser.

In the case of the AC coefficients the quantisation error for the r, sth coefficient is

$$e_{q(r,s)} = \sigma_{(r,s)}^2 - 2 \sum_{i=2}^{2^{b(r,s)}/2} y_i^2 p_i \qquad (8.7)$$

In this case the error is somewhat difficult to determine explicitly, since the coefficient pdf is not well defined. On the assumption of, say, a Laplacian or gamma ($\frac{1}{2}$) distribution the actual value of mean square error may be obtained from the data of Chapter 4. As far as coefficient deletion is concerned, this may be accounted for in Eq. (8.7) by the assumption of zero bit allocation. The error is then, as before, just equal to the coefficient variance.

The total error due to quantisation is

$$e_Q = \frac{1}{N}\left(e_{q(0)} + \sum_{r=1}^{N-1} e_{q(r)} \right) \tag{8.8}$$

for a one-dimensional transform of order N, and

$$e_Q = \frac{1}{N^2}\left(e_{q(0,0)} + \sum_{\substack{r=0 \\ r=s\neq 0}}^{N-1} \sum_{s=0}^{N-1} e_{q(r,s)} \right) \tag{8.9}$$

for the two-dimensional ($N \times N$) version.

As far as practical coding systems are concerned it is rare for the deletion and quantisation errors to be determined separately, performance normally being assessed by a value for the overall image reconstruction mean square error. The experiments of Parsons and Tescher (1975) referred to previously have demonstrated the separate effects of the two processes, and the authors make the pertinent point that although equalising the errors resulting from deletion and quantisation ought to result in minimum overall error, altering the balance between the two on a more or less *ad hoc* basis is likely to lead to better visual reproduced quality.

In the case of a hybrid coding system the situation is rather different. Here all of the transform coefficients generated are subsequently processed by the predictive step and there is no longer any difference, in principle, between the DC and AC coefficient difference sequences. Thus all sequence elements may now be either positive or negative, and the pdf of all sequences is, to a good approximation, Laplacian [although Ploysongsang and Rao (1982) consider the DC term to be more critical, and use a uniform quantiser with a large number of levels]. Furthermore, the quantisation error will be determined relative to the separate sequence variances, and of course the predictive coding process does not have the property, as does the transformation step, of energy invariance. If we consider a one- or two-dimensional coefficient array coded by using a single previous element predictor (in the latter case, of course, interframe coding is implied), it is easy to show that the relation between the variance of the error sequence $\sigma^2_{e(r,s)}$ and that of the original coefficient sequence $\sigma^2_{(r,s)}$ is (Clarke, 1984b)

$$\sigma^2_{e(r,s)} = \sigma^2_{(r,s)}(1 + \alpha^2 - 2\alpha\rho) \tag{8.10}$$

where α is the one-step predictor coefficient and ρ the inter-element correlation. In the often quoted optimum first-order Markov case, $\alpha = \rho$, and so

$$\sigma^2_{e(r,s)} = \sigma^2_{(r,s)}(1 - \rho)^2 \tag{8.11}$$

(it is worth noting that this relation hardly ever holds, in practice, for transform coefficients). Equation (8.7) may then be used to determine the overall quantisation error, with $\sigma^2_{e(r,s)}$ replacing $\sigma^2_{(r,s)}$ and $b_{(r,s)}$ being the appropriate bit allocation to the coefficient error sequence. Equations (8.8) and (8.9) will then be replaced by

$$e_Q = \frac{1}{N} \sum_{r=0}^{N-1} e_{q(r)} \tag{8.12}$$

and

$$e_Q = \frac{1}{N^2} \sum_{r=0}^{N-1} \sum_{s=0}^{N-1} e_{q(r,s)} \tag{8.13}$$

respectively.

8.5   Channel error effects

In the case of system performance degradation caused by incorrect coefficient deletion or quantisation procedures, the remedy naturally lies within the control of the designer—either the overall transmission rate must be increased, or possibly a more judicious trade-off between errors induced by deletion and coarse quantisation may suffice. In the case of errors produced by the transmission or storage process, however, the interaction between their effects and the overall system design requirements is not nearly so straightforward. Thus, when channel error rates become quite high, the reconstructed image quality will generally improve if the transmission rate is reduced. Furthermore, there is an alternative form of trade-off of which advantage can be taken, and that exists between the allocation of transmission bits, on the one hand, to the actual coding of the source material and, on the other, to channel error protection. These considerations will be dealt with in a later part of this section, but first it is necessary to examine the influence of errors on the basic performance of both pure transform and hybrid coding schemes. In this context a channel error is regarded as inverting an individual code-word digit, i.e., converting a '0' into a '1', and vice versa.

As far as pure transform coding is concerned, a channel error will necessarily result in a wrong coefficient value being decoded at the receiver. The effect of this incorrect value will depend on both the significance of the coefficient itself; i.e., whether it is a DC, or low-order or high-order AC term;

and on the location of the error within the actual code word. Thus, whilst errors in even the low-significant bits of the DC or low-order AC coefficients may cause intolerable image degradation, those in high-order terms may not cause noticeable effects, no matter what the significance of the bit in error, and it is, of course, impossible to predict exactly where the errors will fall. For this reason workers have usually depended more on experimental results for given channel error rates than on analytical calculations of mean square error due to channel effects. [Zelinski (1979) however, has analysed the effect of channel errors on the mean-square-error performance of transform coding systems in connection with speech transmission, finding that, at least for Gaussian data, the technique is no more sensitive than PCM without error protection, and less so if similar error protection is used. However, the subjective effects of errors in speech communication are quite different from those where image transmission is concerned, and it would be dangerous to carry over any conclusions drawn in the one situation to the other.]

It is a natural property of bandwidth compression schemes that they are more susceptible to transmission error effects than uncompressed methods of transmission (in spite of the conclusions of Zelinski), particularly where adaptive schemes are considered, since errors in the communication to the receiver of overhead information, which is required for correct decoding, will naturally cause catastrophic breakdown in the operation of the system. It is usual, therefore, to invoke channel error protection for such vital information, even if the actual coded image transform coefficients are left unprotected (Chen and Smith, 1976). We shall shortly have occasion to consider the error behaviour of the predictive process, in the context of hybrid coding, and since predictive coding is an alternatively widely studied form of data compression in its own right, the comparison between differential pulse code modulation (DPCM), the commonly used name for the application of predictive techniques to a PCM signal, and transform coding is frequently made. As far as pure transform coding is concerned, the basis picture interpretation of two-dimensional coding is valuable in considering the effect of incorrect coefficient values (caused by any factor, including channel errors), since that particular basis picture will be added to the reconstruction of the block in question in direct proportion to the (correct or incorrect) coefficient value. The result is that the spread of the influence of a digit error is restricted to a given block (as is not the case with DPCM) and, furthermore, since an error in one coefficient affects the reconstructed values of *all* data elements in the block, the resulting error 'averaging' property is held to be an advantage of the transform coding approach compared with the direct effect of incorrect values in the uncoded data domain. In fact the illustrations provided by Clarke (1976) for a ber of 10^{-3} demonstrate that this is not necessarily always the case. The usual result, in the event of a gross error in a coefficient value, will be the appearance of the actual corresponding basis picture in the reconstructed image.

The usual range over which channel error effects have been examined is 10^{-4}–10^{-2}. Thus Wintz (1972) shows the effects of ber of 10^{-3} and 10^{-2} on a 16×16 DFT at 2 bits/element. In the first case occasional large coefficient errors result in the presence of obviously incorrect basis picture contributions; at the higher rate the effect is, as might be expected, very much greater. The results of Habibi (1974) using the 16×16 WHT bear this conclusion out, and also show that, at the higher error rate, transmission at 1 bit/element gives a better overall reconstructed image quality, and signal-to-noise ratio, than at 2 bits/element. Similar results at the same error rates and using the 8×8 WHT at 1 and 0.5 bit/element are reported by Essman et al. (1976).

Chen and Smith (1976, 1977) choose to protect only the overhead component (as mentioned briefly earlier) in their compression system and report no visible degradation at ber 10^{-4}, whilst Reis et al. (1976) using the 16×16 Haar transform in an adaptive system, send a fixed number of (usually large-magnitude) low-order coefficients lying in a predetermined zone of the transform array as an ordered data block in a known transmission sequence with respect to the synchronisation signals so that they may always be easily identified. Possible incorrect amplitude values resulting from channel errors are then dealt with by adding a parity bit over the four or five most significant bits, and then, when necessary, replacing an incorrect coefficient by its corresponding value from the previous frame, which has possibly been compensated for motion effects. In the NTSC compression system of Ohira et al. (1978) tests are carried out on each bit of each coefficient remaining after the data reduction step to determine which has most influence upon reconstructed picture quality. Eleven such bits exist in the 4×8 block of coefficients, consisting of the most significant bits of the lower-order AC coefficients, one most significant bit for one of the coefficients corresponding approximately to the colour subcarrier frequency, and the four most significant bits (out of eight) for the DC coefficient. These bits are error protected by a (15, 11) single error correcting Hamming code. Four parity check bits are obtained by removing least significant bits from certain high-order coefficients where they do not influence picture quality. A few errors are visible at ber 10^{-4}, and more at 10^{-3}, at a transmission rate of 32 Mbits/s.

It will be noticed from the preceding figures that the broadcast television system is, as might be expected, a more critical test of error visibility than a surveillance or RPV application. Clarke (1976) investigated the influence of errors on a WHT of order 32 applied to the coding of PAL broadcast television pictures, under the constraint that a maximum of 1 error/word was allowed. Subjective tests showed that visible impairment was approximately the same as that in conventional PCM, with noticeable effects occurring in the ber range around 10^{-6}. Two mitigating features were suggested by the author: first, as the compression factor is increased, the removal of high-significance bits and the use of non-linear quantisation will reduce the average effect of errors; second, negligible increase in the overall rate would be required to protect the 16 bits of highest significance at a data rate of $4\frac{1}{2}$ bits/element.

Modestino *et al.* (1980, 1981) and Modestino and Daut (1980) have analysed the effect of channel errors on the performance, in a mean-square-error sense, of two-dimensional transform coding schemes employing the DCT. They show that the total system error can be written as the sum of three terms, i.e.,

$$e_T^2 = e_Q + e_C + 2e_M \qquad (8.14)$$

where e_Q is the quantisation error (previously defined), e_C a term resulting from the presence of channel errors and e_M a mutual term due to coupling between the quantisation and channel error effects. For a picture having any reasonable degree of reconstructed fidelity, both e_Q and e_C will be quite small, and the authors find that the mutual term is negligible when compared with the other two. They studied the effect of channel signal-to-noise ratio (using BPSK coding and additive white Gaussian noise) on that of the reconstructed image, with uniform Gaussian quantisation and average bit rate as a parameter. Their results clearly show the benefit of low data rates when the channel noise level is significant, as can be seen from Table 8.2 (this point will be taken up again subsequently).

In the case of predictive coding, errors in transmission or storage are likely, in the absence of effective protection schemes, to have a very damaging effect upon the quality of the reconstructed image. The scheme is, of course, a useful and easily implemented data compression technique in its own right,

TABLE 8.2. Reconstructed image
signal-to-noise ratio (dB) as a function
of channel signal-to-noise ratio
and bit rate.

Bit rate/element	Channel SNR	
	20 dB	10 dB
2.5	33	2
0.5	16	16

[a] From Modestino *et al.* (1981).

producing good-quality images at rates in the region of 2–3 bits/element. It is, of course, sensitive to the effects of errors, whose presence in the received data causes bright or dark streaks in the direction of coding (in one dimension) which gradually decrease in intensity as the system recovers. These do not propagate from line to line since the system is usually reset at the beginning of each new scan line. In two dimensions, however, such propagation does occur, causing areas of incorrect luminance which, again, gradually recover towards the correct values. The degree of error propagation is a direct function of the prediction coefficient(s) of the system, and so there is conflict between good compression efficiency, which requires (in the basic one-step case) a coefficient equal to the data inter-element correlation coefficient which will, in the case of images, naturally be quite high, and good error recovery, which demands a low value of predictor coefficient. It is easy to analyse this effect in the usual hybrid coding situation, making use of the development of Subsection 5.1.3 and, for simplicity, ignoring quantisation effects. Thus element x_n is predicted by the value

$$\hat{x}_n = \alpha x_{n-1} \tag{8.15}$$

i.e., the predictor coefficient multiplied by the previous element. The transmitted or stored signal is

$$e_n = x_n - \hat{x}_n = x_n - \alpha x_{n-1} \tag{8.16}$$

and the reconstruction at the decoder is given by

$$x_{n(r)} = e_n + \hat{x}_n = e_n + \alpha x_{n-1} \tag{8.17}$$

(plus, in practice, the quantisation error attaching to e_n). Equation (8.17) is generally true, and so, for example,

$$x_{n-1(r)} = e_{n-1} + \alpha x_{n-2}$$

We may therefore write the reconstructed element as

$$x_{n(r)} = e_n + \alpha(e_{n-1} + \alpha(e_{n-2} + \cdots + \alpha(e_1 + \alpha x_0)))$$
$$= e_n + \alpha e_{n-1} + \alpha^2 e_{n-2} + \cdots + \alpha^n x_0 \tag{8.18}$$

If e_{n-k} is received with error δ, therefore, the influence upon $x_{n(r)}$ will be $\alpha^k \delta$, and thus, k elements after the error has occurred, the magnitude of the effect remaining will be determined by α^k. If $\alpha = 0.95$, decay of the error influence to 1 % of its initial value will take a distance equal to that occupied by about 90 elements, if $\alpha = 0.6$, then about one-tenth of that distance is needed, but in that case the compression efficiency is very poor. Another reason for using a value of α close to unity is that the maximum magnitude of the recovered signal is inversely proportional to $(1 - \alpha)$, since the first received value will be an error signal equal to the maximum allowable channel amplitude A_{max}, say; the prediction for the next element in the receiver is then αA_{max} and the recovered signal increases as

$$(((\alpha A_{max} + A_{max})\alpha + A_{max})\alpha + \cdots +) = A_{max}(1 + \alpha + \alpha^2 + \cdots + \alpha^n)$$
$$\rightarrow A_{max}/(1 - \alpha) \qquad (8.19)$$

This property obviously determines the behaviour of the system in response to large changes in input signal.

Despite the improved error performance obtained by using low values of α, the fact that such values seriously reduce the degree of compression obtainable has meant that practical schemes have used coefficients in the region of 0.95 for both hybrid intra- and inter-frame coding. The significant feature of the error behaviour of such a system is that the errors occur, not as is the case with DPCM in the luminance values but in the one- or two-dimensional transform coefficients, since it is they that form the separate input sequences of the predictive coding operation. An error thus causes a sequence of incorrect terms in a particular location within the coefficient array, which in turn (as is the case with pure transform coding) causes the relevant basis vectors or pictures to be added to the image reconstruction in the wrong proportion.

These effects are demonstrated by Habibi's (1974) results for intraframe coding at 1 and 2 bits/element and with channel error rates of 10^{-4}, 10^{-3} and 10^{-2}. Degradation is clearly visible at ber 10^{-3} and a rate of 2 bits/element, and is reduced when the rate is lowered to 1 bit/element, an effect remarked on previously in regard to pure transform coding systems. For both approaches, in a multispectral imaging context, it is found that the effects of channel errors are minimal at ber less than 10^{-4} (Habibi and Samulon, 1975), whilst the interframe two-dimensional Fourier or DCT plus temporal predictive coding systems described by Roese and Robinson (1975) have essentially the same numerical values of normalised mean square error and signal-to-noise ratio up to a ber of 10^{-3}. At 10^{-2} degradation gradually increases from frame to frame (at rates of both 1 and 0.25 bit-element) until corrected by a frame resetting operation. Again, with interframe coding a random ber of 10^{-4} gives results indistinguishable from those obtained for the error-free case (Roese et al., 1977).

Essman et al. (1976) have compared the two-dimensional WHT and a one-dimensional transform/predictive coding scheme in an RPV application and their results highlight the danger of using numerical evaluation as a guide to image quality; although at rates between 0.25 and 1 bit/element and ber of 10^{-3} and 10^{-2} the measured mean square error is less for the hybrid scheme, the visual appearance is much poorer, with noticeable streaking in the direction of prediction. An interesting feature of their approach is the

**CHANNEL SIGNAL
TO NOISE RATIO** ⟶ **7 dB**

5

3

1

↑

**CODING RATE
BITS/ELEMENT**

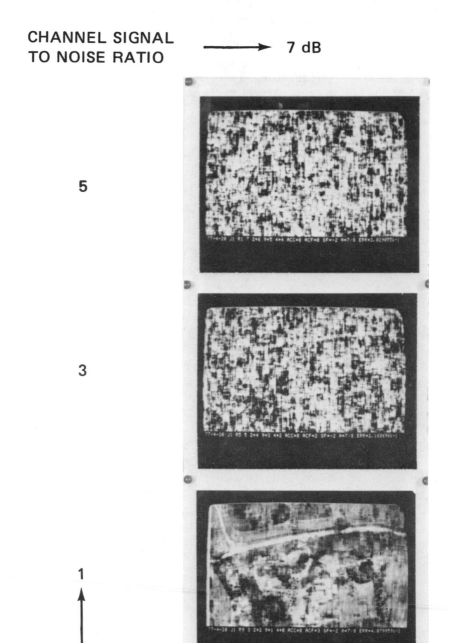

FIG. 8.1. The relation between reconstructed image quality, coding rate and channel signal-to-noise ratio for the hybrid coding scheme of McWhirter *et al.* (1981). British Crown copyright 1981. Reproduced with the permission of the Controller of Her Majesty's Stationery Office.

12 dB

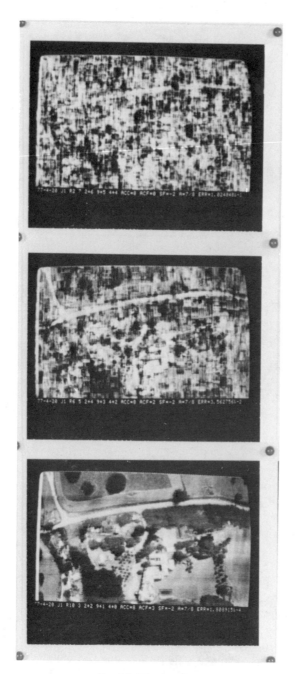

Fɪɢ. 8.2 (Continued)

minimisation of the overall numerical measure with respect to the individual predictor coefficients as a function of the individual transform coefficient sequence bit assignments. The optimum values tend to fall from around 0.85–0.90 at 1 bit to something of the order of 0.75 at 7 bits, and a considerable improvement in image quality at higher error rates is obtained.

It has been mentioned earlier that a small amount of error protection judiciously applied can improve the situation in regard to channel errors considerably, with little increase in overall transmission rate. This result is borne out by Essman's experiments in which such protection was applied to the DC coefficient with success at ber 10^{-2}, but it was found that, at ber 10^{-3}, periodic resetting (every 16 lines) was a superior technique and produced images of better quality in the presence of channel errors than two-dimensional transform coding.

An interesting application of two-dimensional transform/predictive coding is discussed by May (1980), in which the system is used for transmission of image sequences over a 9.6-Kbits/s mobile radio channel. In the context of error effects it was required to have minimal degradation for ber less than 10^{-3} (80% of the transmission time), acceptable quality up to ber 10^{-2} (15% of the time) and to retain the previously transmitted (and acceptable) image in the case of an intense error burst. The scheme is described in Chapter 5 and only the error protection techniques are relevant here. Thus overhead information for the adaptive system is protected with a 128-bit BCH code able to correct 6 errors/block, giving a residual error rate of 3.3×10^{-4} at a channel error rate of 10^{-2}. The DC coefficients of sub-blocks in moving areas are also protected and the decoder error message is used to indicate the presence of error bursts, in which case the previously transmitted image is retained. At the other end of the scale, Kamangar and Rao (1981) suggest the same degree of protection (overhead and DC coefficient error sequence) for their adaptive hybrid coding scheme for NTSC component television signals, but they do not give specific figures for comparison, whilst the similar application of hybrid coding reported by Ploysongsang and Rao (1982) also requires protection of the same terms. Naturally, in this last area of application, the satisfactory operation of the system with respect to channel errors is vital. On the other hand, it is an environment in which the error behaviour is likely to be very much more amenable to the transmission of compressed signals than that of mobile radio, for example.

As a final example of the interaction between channel errors and hybrid transform coding system performance, we examine briefly the one-dimensional WHT/predictive system of McWhirter et al. (1981). The relation between reconstructed image quality, bit rate and channel signal-to-noise ratio is much the same as that in the case of pure transform coding as described by Modestino (see Table 8.2). Thus, as the (binary FSK) channnel signal-to-noise ratio falls from 20 to 10 dB the recovered image signal-to-noise ratio is unaltered at approximately 23 dB when the rate is 0.5 bit/element, whilst at a rate of 2.5 bits/element it falls from 30 to 17 dB. The results are perhaps more striking visually where, for a channel signal-to-noise ratio of 12 dB the images at rates of 5 and 3 bits/element are almost completely chaotic in nature, whilst at 1.0 bit/element the image detail is clearly visible; see Fig. 8.1. Naturally, the overall quality at the latter rate is no better than that in the error-free case, but the results for both pure transform and hybrid coding do suggest that, if the bit rate is increased in the presence of channel errors in order to improve reconstructed image quality, then the extra bit allocation ought not to be made exclusively to the coding of image elements but rather split between that application and the introduction of error protection coding. Such 'source–channel' coding is the subject of the next section.

8.6 Source–channel coding

The effect of channel errors on both pure transform and hybrid coding schemes described earlier suggests the inclusion of bit allocation to error protection as well as to source coding directly in the total system data rate. In the absence of error protection, for a given error rate, coding at a high source allocation (say 2–3 bits/element or more) will be subject to many errors and the reconstruction may well be unusable. At very low rates (perhaps 0.5 bit/element) the numerical error measure will increase due to the approximate coding and again more or less severe image degradation will occur. We might therefore expect a peak in the relationship between output signal-to-noise ratio and coded rate (bit/element), with channel signal-to-noise ratio as a parameter, which moves to lower overall rates as channel signal-to-noise ratio decreases. Such an effect is clearly evident in the results of Bowyer (1971) and McWhirter *et al.* (1981). Consideration has been given, therefore, to so-called 'source–channel' coding as a means of optimising performance of a transform coding system in the 'real' (i.e., error-prone) environment of transmission or storage. Jain and Jain (1979) suggest minimisation of mean square error in the case where error protection coding is included in the overall bit allocation (i.e., protection is not simply applied to every coded bit regardless of its significance in coefficient decoding at the receiver). At 1 bit/element and ber 10^{-3} results are only 0.5 dB different from those in the error-free case and some 5 dB better than when no protection is included. A similar approach is described by Götze (1979), again in the context of transmission over a binary symmetric channel, and results are given for both the number of most sensitive bits to be protected and the overall (minimised) mean square error.

Extensive work has been carried out on the subject of source–channel coding by Modestino *et al.* (1980, 1981) and Modestino and Daut (1980). Their results on the influence of channel errors on two-dimensional 16 × 16 DCT coding have already been mentioned, and it can be seen that the use of coding bits for error protection results in a marked improvement in performance for low values of channel signal-to-noise ratio. At higher values performance degradation occurs since the allocation of bits to error protection is effectively wasted. Thus at an overall rate of 1 bit/element using a rate one-half code, 0.5 bit/element is used for actual coding of the source data and the rest for error protection. At a channel signal-to-noise ratio of 3 dB, this increases the output signal-to-noise ratio from 3 dB to a value of 16 dB, but does not allow that value to improve at higher values of channel signal-to-noise ratio, whereas employing the total of 1 bit/element for source coding alone would increase the output signal-to-noise ratio to 23 dB. The authors experimented with several different codes and methods of error protection coding at low values of channel signal-to-noise ratio. They found that the most efficient approach was to use a convolutional code with constraint length 9, in the case when the modulation/coding scheme was kept the same for all bits of all coefficients. Alternative techniques are (a) to protect selectively several most significant coefficients (those with larger variances) or (b) to protect the most significant bits of any quantiser output word. In this way some of the practical constraints on code construction which obtain in the case of identical modulation/coding of all bits of all coefficients can be circumvented.

It is evident that, in the situation in which channel noise parameters can be estimated reasonably well, an optimum trade-off between source and channel coding bit allocations at a given overall data rate is not difficult to achieve. In the case of the transmission of transform coded images over the PSTN, however, results using the additive white Gaussian noise channel model are unlikely to be valid in the presence, for example, of error bursts. Whether or not a source–channel trade-off can be established for such an application remains to be seen.

8.7 Error correction techniques

As an alternative to the use of channel coding techniques including error protection of significant elements in the data stream, an 'intelligent' decoder might possibly be devised which could correct the effects of errors by carrying out a sequence of tests on the received data. Such a scheme is described by Fenwick and Steele (1977) in the case of the one-dimensional Walsh–Hadamard transformation of image data, with not more than 1 error/block. The success of the method depends on the fact that the total reconstructed data vector is the sum of the correct vector (obtained in the absence of error) and the basis vector corresponding to the coefficient in error. In the simple case $N = 4$ using the unscaled (orthogonal but not orthonormal) WHT, with an error e occurring in the third coefficient, the inverse transform gives the reconstructed vector $\mathbf{X}'$ as

$$\mathbf{X}' = \begin{bmatrix} 1 & 1 & 1 & 1 \\ 1 & 1 & -1 & -1 \\ 1 & -1 & -1 & 1 \\ 1 & -1 & 1 & -1 \end{bmatrix} \begin{bmatrix} c_1 \\ c_2 \\ c_3 + e \\ c_4 \end{bmatrix} \tag{8.20}$$

$$= 4 \begin{bmatrix} x_1 \\ x_2 \\ x_3 \\ x_4 \end{bmatrix} + e \begin{bmatrix} 1 \\ -1 \\ -1 \\ 1 \end{bmatrix} \tag{8.21}$$

Since

$$\mathbf{C} = \begin{bmatrix} c_1 \\ c_2 \\ c_3 \\ c_4 \end{bmatrix} = \begin{bmatrix} 1 & 1 & 1 & 1 \\ 1 & 1 & -1 & -1 \\ 1 & -1 & -1 & 1 \\ 1 & -1 & 1 & -1 \end{bmatrix} \begin{bmatrix} x_1 \\ x_2 \\ x_3 \\ x_4 \end{bmatrix} \tag{8.22}$$

If we now (artificially) set x_1, say, to zero, the magnitude and sign of the coefficient error are simply those of the decoded value of x_1 (appropriately scaled). What remains unknown is the actual location of the error, and to determine this a planar prediction technique is employed over coefficients of the same order in four neighbouring blocks. Thus, in Fig. 8.2 if an error is detected in block k, i, the values of all $c_{j(k, i)}$ for $j = 1 \rightarrow N$ are predicted from those of corresponding c_j using the relation

$$\hat{c}_{j(k, i)} = c_{j(k, i-1)} + c_{j(k-1, i)} - c_{j(k-1, i-1)} \tag{8.23}$$

where the estimate of $c_{j(k, i)}$ is made on the assumption that the change between coefficients on line $k - 1$ is the same as that between coefficients on line k (i.e., a plane is fitted to the three predictor locations and its ordinate at

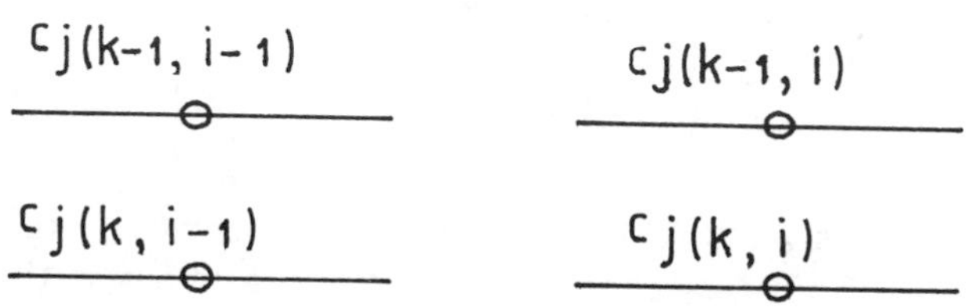

FIG. 8.2. Location of coefficient c_j in four neighbouring one-dimensional transform blocks. [After Fenwick and Steele (1977).]

the location of $c_{j(k,i)}$ forms the prediction). The poorest prediction (largest value of $|c_{j(k,i)} - \hat{c}_{j(k,i)}|$) is then taken to indicate the coefficient in error. There is naturally a trade-off in this system between blocklength and accuracy of error detection since for large data blocks the data loss (setting each $x_1 = 0$) is minimal, but the prediction is likely to be poorer, and vice versa. One drawback the system has is that higher-order coefficients will tend to be much smaller than those of lower order and so the detection sensitivity will depend upon the location of the error. It is suggested by the authors that normalisation of the prediction error by the magnitude of either the coefficient in the same block on the previous line, or the average magnitudes of the three coefficients used for prediction, will improve the efficiency (Fenwick *et al.*, 1978).

Another one-dimensional approach has been reported by Wong and Steele (1978). In this case the absolute difference between like coefficients on succeeding lines is tested against a threshold which is a function of the rms values of the differences for the present and previous lines. Two refinements are incorporated within the system. First, since the low-order coefficients are very likely to be much larger than the higher-order ones, the coefficients are separated into groups (5 in the case $N = 32$), each having a different value of threshold; second, the thresholds are dependent also upon the change in rms difference from line to line, i.e., the activity of the image from block to block vertically. When an error is detected, the relevant coefficient is replaced by the average of the preceding and succeeding similarly located coefficients. The scheme is effective in reducing the mean square error by a factor of approximately 20 dB for error rates below 3×10^{-2}, and has a similar performance in the presence of 2 errors/block.

If we return for a moment to the representation of a reconstructed data vector [Eq. (8.21)] we can see the basis of another method of error correction. Suppose that the data changes only relatively slowly from line to line, and that the preceding line is either error free or has had an error successfully corrected. Then the reconstructed data vectors on succeeding lines will be $4[x_1, x_2, x_3, x_4]^T$, approximately, and $4[x_1, x_2, x_3, x_4]^T + e[1, -1, -1, 1]^T$. If we form the difference vector it will be approximately $e[1, -1, -1, 1]^T$ and, if we now take its transform

$$
E = e \begin{bmatrix} 1 & 1 & 1 & 1 \\ 1 & 1 & -1 & -1 \\ 1 & -1 & -1 & 1 \\ 1 & -1 & 1 & -1 \end{bmatrix} \begin{bmatrix} 1 \\ -1 \\ -1 \\ 1 \end{bmatrix} = \begin{bmatrix} 0 \\ 0 \\ 4e \\ 0 \end{bmatrix} \tag{8.24}
$$

and the result indicates that the third coefficient was in error (more simply, we could just identify the appropriate zero-crossing pattern in the difference vector). This is the basis of the 16×16 DCT error correction scheme of

Mitchell and Tabatabai (1981). The four-edge difference vectors between a given block and its four neighbours are generated and then transformed to give four coefficient vectors which are examined for dominant components. On the assumption that the data does not vary very rapidly across the block boundaries, such transformation will result in a large magnitude component corresponding to the column location in the case of the two horizontal, and the row location in the case of the two vertical, vectors of the coefficient in error (the error, of course, corresponding to the inclusion of the incorrect 'amount' of the relevant basis picture in the reconstructed block). Tests of significance are then carried out to confirm the presence of the error, whose sign and magnitude may be estimated, and the coefficient subsequently corrected. It is found that the dominant error is still often corrected when there is more than 1 error/block, and the scheme is effective in reducing the mean square error by an average factor of about 3.7 at a ber of 10^{-2}, and 1.6 at 10^{-3}, at rates between 0.5 and 2 bits/element.

In all such schemes, of course, the basic problem is reliably to detect all errors which will cause noticeable impairment of the reconstructed image whilst not detecting (and correcting!) errors which are not really there. This is a particular problem when luminance changes happen to coincide with block boundaries in two-dimensional schemes, and a possible solution is to detect such changes by more detailed examination of regions perhaps 2-3 elements deep in neighbouring blocks. In one-dimensional schemes it is usual for the higher-order coefficients to have low correlation from line to line (this is what makes predictive coding of high-order coefficients in hybrid coding not worthwhile) and the presence of an error is therefore more difficult to determine. On the other hand, errors in those coefficients have less effect on overall picture quality and it is probably sufficient to employ some simple limiting or smoothing process to combat high-order coefficient errors, whilst applying more sophisticated techniques to those of lower order. In general such schemes have the distinct advantage that no extra transmission capacity is required and, as more complex decoder processing becomes feasible, we may expect to see them used more widely in the future.

8.8 Summary

Any practical communications system introduces some distortion, however, small, into the transmitted data. In the case of coding schemes which attempt to achieve significant degrees of data rate compression, such distortion, at least in part, is introduced knowingly as an integral part of the operation. In addition there are those uncontrolled errors which occur in the channel and cause corruption of the received material. In this chapter all such sources of degradation of the reconstructed image have been considered, and one or two approaches to the mitigation of the channel error problem outlined.

As far as the computation involved in the transform operation is concerned, retaining coefficient values to the requisite degree of accuracy presents little difficulty, at least in an all-digital implementation. Where analogue system components are introduced, however, this may not be the case, and maintaining required device tolerances may be a problem. Such is the overwhelming rate of advance of digital technology nowadays, though, that the analogue approach is likely to account for a very small part of coding system design.

The basic data reduction process in transform coding is the deletion and/ or coarse quantisation of small energy coefficient sequences, and both of these operations admit of relatively simple mathematical formulation. In spite of this, however, overall coding performance is usually specified numerically by a global value of mean square or absolute magnitude error, which naturally includes varying contributions from both sources. Indeed, the visual quality of the reconstructed image is critically dependent upon the balance between coefficient deletion and quantisation at a given overall bit rate, and can be optimised by *ad hoc* adjustments which are not subject to clearly defined mathematical relationships.

The final contribution to the problem, and the one over which the system designer has little control, is the error performance of the channel. As far as this alone is concerned, there is little to say with the exception that performance tests usually make use of additive white Gaussian noise and show visible degradation at bit error rates having a very wide range of values and crucially dependent upon the stringency of the criteria set by the observer. Two approaches to the solution of the channel error problem (apart from the obvious one of the 'static' protection of significant bits, especially in overhead information—essential for correct decoding) are described here. The first is to share dynamically the total available number of bits between error protection and coding, depending upon the channel signal-to-noise ratio. This naturally requires knowledge of the channel error parameters, and is perhaps more suited to lower-quality low-rate systems (surveillance links, for example) than to high-quality channels (where the SNR may perhaps be expected to be adequate, anyway) where the 'separation' between source and channel coding is large. The second possibility is to carry out error correction purely as a receiver function, testing received element values against other received data taken to be correct or having previously been corrected. Good results are possible in this way, although, since no system is perfect, there will inevitably be occasions when corrections are made to values which are, in fact, not in error. This is a difficulty which will, of course, diminish in importance as decoder sophistication increases.

Chapter 9

Rate Distortion Theory
and Image Coding

9.1 Introduction

The move from analogue to digital signal processing and manipulation that has occurred over the past 20 years or so has brought many advantages in its train. Thus there is the possibility of transmitting a signal, even in the presence of channel imperfections, over virtually unlimited distances with no degradation in quality; the convenience of being able to group signals of varying bandwidth requirements into a hierarchy having a common 'integrated' format; the ease with which complex and yet precise operations upon the signal may be carried out; and so forth. One disadvantage which the digital format has, however, is that it requires a much wider channel bandwidth than its analogue equivalent. A rather more subtle point is that, given the increase in quality which digital format can provide, a desire for even higher quality and for new system functions intensifies the pressure for even greater transmission capacity. A good example of this effect is colour television. In its analogue form it requires a bandwidth of $5\frac{1}{2}$ MHz, inside which the luminance and both chrominance signals are neatly fitted so that there is no bandwidth requirement in excess of that originally provided for the monochrome service. Albeit with a certain degree of visible impairment, the system operates very successfully. In its equivalent digital format, sampled at a frequency of three times that of the colour subcarrier and digitised to an accuracy of 8 bits, the signal needs a channel capacity in excess of 100 Mbits/s. In a move towards higher-quality standards and the possibility of greater flexibility and ease of exchange of programme material between broadcasting networks, it turns out that it is more convenient to retain the colour signal in its component, rather than composite, form, in which case the luminance and each chrominance channel are sampled at 13.5 and 6.75 MHz, respectively. The total data rate now becomes $27 \times 8 = 216$ Mbits/s. At the present there is a rapidly developing interest in high-definition television, which in terms of the preceding figures would require, for a doubling of horizontal and vertical resolution alone, a channel capacity approaching 1 Gbits/s. At the other end of the scale, there is increasing interest, too, in the transmission of low-resolution images over low-band-width channels as rapidly as conveniently possible for surveillance, videoconference and viewdata-type information provision systems, for example.

Throughout the whole of the video spectrum, therefore, much time and effort has been and is being expended upon transmitting images at the lowest possible rate whilst retaining an adequate level of reproduced quality. As the reader of Chapter 6 will be aware, the greatest problem in this context is that of specifying a numerical criterion of quality (or fidelity to the original image), the development of which would then allow the extensive mathematical theory which now accompanies the subject of data compression to be brought to bear in a specific way. In spite of this continuing problem, however, it is possible to specify, for fairly simple measures of image (or, in general, signal) degradation, the functional relationship between the channel transmission rate and the numerical value of the criterion. Thus, if the value of distortion is D and the rate R we are able, in some cases, to specify the rate distortion $R(D)$, or distortion rate $D(R)$ function, and so determine either the necessary rate for a given level of degradation or, conversely, the amount of distortion produced by transmission at a predetermined rate. The development of the theory is an offshoot of Shannon's original work on information theory, and can be seen taking shape in two fundamental papers of his (Shannon, 1948, 1959) which will be referred to again subsequently. Since then a vast body of literature has appeared on the subject, much of it, it has to be said, extremely abstruse and not specifically intended for the engineer who simply wishes to design, or appreciate the fundamental theoretical basis of, data compression systems. The more general literature on the topic is somewhat sparse—there is only one book dedicated to the subject (Berger, 1971), although Gallager (1968) does consider the matter in some detail. A general introductory article (Davisson, 1972) contains much of the substance of the topic in a concise form, and Pearson (1967) has considered the problem specifically in the context of visual communication systems, but all material on the subject requires (a) the prerequisite of a reasonable knowledge of information theory and, (b) what is far less likely to be possessed by the average worker in the field, time for careful study and reflection. A general, and more recent, helpful review of the topic of information theory is given by Wyner (1981).

In this chapter we shall avoid as much of the detailed mathematical analysis as possible and concentrate upon, first, formulating the general rate distortion problem and second examining those areas where the theory has produced results of relevance to transform coding. In essence these are three in number. The first concerns the overall advantage of block coding and the comparison of transformations, which can be carried out on the basis of the rates needed for the separate transform coefficient sequences. The second is that of quantiser design and comparison with the theoretical limits provided by the theory, and the third is bit allocation, where a frequently quoted theoretical result is widely used (and which has already been referred to in Chapter 4). We begin with the general problem.

9.2   Rate distortion function

At the outset, it is worth clarifying one matter concerning the application of the theory to data compression schemes of the kind dealt with in this volume. The original theory considered the transmission of members of a finite set (i.e., time discrete and amplitude discrete) symbols from transmitter to receiver, where reproduction of input letter j as output letter i incurred a penalty in the form of a prespecified, non-negative 'cost' function. Subsequently it was generalised by Shannon to apply to continuous input and output distributions. In the context of transform coding, it is this latter theory which is employed, although some reflection will indicate that the signals emanating from the transform operation do not really fall into this category, since the input signal is in digitised (i.e., integer) form, and the product of a set of integers with the various real numbers in the transform basis set does not form a true continuous distribution. Nevertheless, as will be seen later, the approximations and assumptions necessary to allow the application of rate distortion theory in the present situation are such as to render this point of little significance and, as far as transform coding is concerned, we shall apply only the theoretical results for time discrete (sampled), continuous amplitude, distributions.

We begin by considering generally the relation between rate and distortion. Intuitively we expect that, the more information which we transmit, the better the reproduced quality will be. As a simple example, consider the operation of quantisation using differing accuracies (numbers of bits). Clearly, if we decide to quantise with an accuracy of 10 bits, the approximate version of the signal will be much closer to the original than if we choose a 3-bit quantiser. However, in any given sampling interval, we pay the penalty (in

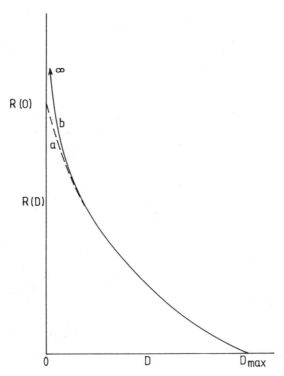

FIG. 9.1. General form of the rate distortion relation $R(D)$. (a) Discrete case and (b) continuous case.

terms of transmission capacity) of having to transmit ten digits instead of three to achieve the higher quality. In general, the central region of the curve relating rate and distortion (or, loosely, the penalty we pay for inaccurate representation) will have a negative slope, as shown in Fig. 9.1. For very low rates of information transmission the distortion reaches a maximum value D_{max}, which, in the case of the continuous distribution, will be the total signal energy. Clearly, if the allowable distortion in the received signal is equal to the signal energy (or greater), then we may as well not bother to transmit the signal at all, and the rate will then be zero (this point is of relevance to transform coding, of course, where we do not, in fact, transmit those coefficients with very small variances; this will be expanded upon later). At the other end of the distortion scale, as we require better and better reproduced signal quality (lower and lower distortion), then the rate must increase and, in the continuous case, become infinite if perfect reproduction is desired. In the discrete case (i.e., when the input amplitude assumes any of a finite number of separate levels), we know that perfect reproduction is obtainable, in principle, provided that we code at a rate not lower than the source entropy $H(x)$ and thus, providing that the source symbol set is 'imaged' in that of the receiver, and that the penalty for correct reception (i.e., symbol j sent and received as such) is zero (Shannon, 1959; Berger, 1971), then $R(0) = H(x)$. In the discrete case, other penalty functions may allow more than one correct decoding of a given input symbol, so that, generally, $R(0) \le H(x)$ in these circumstances. It is worth pointing out here that, as far as the present purpose is concerned, it is only necessary to appreciate the general form of the relationship, and that these comments on the rate–distortion interaction are given a rigorous foundation in the references by Berger and Gallager.

We now consider formulation of the $R(D)$ function in terms of information theory, which we have already used in a simple way to characterise image properties in Chapter 2. Again, the references quoted may be consulted for more details of the present topic, and a convenient and concise review of the fundamental equations in information theory is given by Berger. Using Eqs. (2.1) and (2.5), the self-information of the event $x = X$, $i(x)$, is given by

$$i(x) = -\log p(x) \tag{9.1}$$

As before, the logarithmic base defines the unit of information. The average value of $i(x)$ is the entropy

$$H(x) = -\sum p(x) \log p(x) \tag{9.2}$$

where the summation is taken over all allowable values of x. In a similar fashion,

$$H(y) = -\sum_y p(y) \log p(y) \tag{9.3}$$

where $y = Y$ represents the occurrence, at the receiver, of the variable y taking on the value Y. The joint distribution of the variables x and y is $p(x, y)$, and the separate marginal distributions are obtained by summing out, respectively, y and x from $p(x, y)$, i.e.,

$$p(x) = \sum_y p(x, y) \tag{9.4}$$

$$p(y) = \sum_x p(x, y) \tag{9.5}$$

and the conditional distributions are defined by

$$p(x/y) = p(x, y)/p(y) \quad \Rightarrow P(x,y) = P(y)P(x/y) \tag{9.6}$$

$$p(y/x) = p(x, y)/p(x) \Rightarrow P(x,y) = P(x) P(y/x) \tag{9.7}$$

can be proved, see notes.

Interpreting Eq. (9.6), the probability of the joint event $(x = X, \ y = Y)$, $p(x, y)$, is the probability of the occurrence of the event $y = Y$, $p(y)$, multiplied by the probability of the event $x = X$ given that $y = Y$ has already occurred. A similar interpretation applies to Eq. (9.7).

In terms of the communication of information through a channel, or the reconstruction of an image after coding and processing, we can regard x as the transmitted, or original, and y as the received, or reconstructed, quantities, respectively. The question is then: How much does the actual occurrence of the event $y = Y$ tell us about the state of the input $x = X$? Before we knew that $y = Y$, the probability of x taking on the value X was the *a priori* probability $p(x)$. After we know that $y = Y$, we have the *a posteriori* probability $p(x/y)$. The equivalent quantities in terms of information content are

$$i(x) = -\log p(x) \qquad\qquad (9.8)$$

and

$$i(x/y) = -\log p(x/y) \qquad\qquad (9.9)$$

The difference is the mutual information

$$i(x; y) = i(x) - i(x/y)$$
$$= \log \left[p(x/y)/p(x) \right] \qquad\qquad (9.10)$$

If we now average this quantity over the joint distribution $p(x, y)$, we have

$$I(x; y) = \sum_{x} \sum_{y} p(x, y) \log \frac{p(x/y)}{p(x)} \qquad\qquad (9.11)$$

Under normal circumstances we would naturally wish to maximise $I(x; y)$, i.e., make the mutual information between transmitter and receiver as great as possible. However, in the present application, the requirement is rather different, and that is due to the operation of an alternative set of constraints. In this case the source is predetermined; i.e., we wish to transmit, for example, a given image or set of images or, at least, those having a certain class of statistical properties (it will become evident, in fact, that this is a nicety which cannot be observed in practice). Furthermore, we require that, given a definable fidelity criterion, transmission takes place at the *minimum* rate. The problem is thus to *minimise* Eq. (9.11) subject to that criterion. If we allow the input distribution to be variable, then the maximum of $I(x; y)$ will be the capacity C of the channel, or system, relating x and y. In the former case it will be the transition probability distribution which will be variable in the determination of the rate distortion function.

We now have to consider, in more detail, the nature of the allowable distortion. Under ideal conditions we expect that the input and output symbols (we restrict the analysis, for the moment, to the discrete case) will always be identical, i.e., when $x = X$ then $y = X$ also. When distortion is allowable this is not true, and so the distortion function measures the 'distance' between x and y and can be written $d(x, y)$. We shall see subsequently that this form of relation is too general for simple valuation. We would naturally expect, of course, that $d(x, x) = 0$. If the separate source symbols $x_1, x_2, \ldots, x_n$ are grouped into words of length n, then a so-called 'single-letter' fidelity criterion is given by

$$\rho_n(\mathbf{x}, \mathbf{y}) = \frac{1}{n} \sum_{k=1}^{n} d(x_k, y_k) \tag{9.12}$$

i.e., the average over the word length of the individual symbol distortions. Over the whole of the joint distribution the distortion will be

$$D_{p(y/x)} = \sum_x \sum_y p(x, y)\, d(x, y)$$

$$= \sum_x \sum_y p(x)p(y/x)\, d(x, y) \tag{9.13}$$

This form is convenient since the source distribution $p(x)$ is fixed in the analysis. Then $D_{p(y/x)}$ is the average distortion for the transition probability distribution $p(y/x)$. In general, there will be more than one distribution which achieves less than the allowable distortion D, and they will form the set

$$P_D = \{p(y/x): D_{p(y/x)} \le D\} \tag{9.14}$$

Rewriting Eq. (9.11) we have

$$I_{p(y/x)} = \sum_x \sum_y p(x)p(y/x) \log \frac{p(y/x)}{p(y)} \tag{9.15}$$

and the rate distortion function $R(D)$ is defined as

$$R(D) = \min I_{p(y/x)} \qquad p(y/x) \in P_D \tag{9.16}$$

i.e., the minimum of the average mutual information for all those transition probability assignments $p(y/x)$ which result in a distortion not greater than D. In terms of the distortion rate interpretation mentioned earlier, we could alternatively fix the mutual information and seek that assignment $p(y/x)$ which minimises the distortion. In this case $R(D)$ takes the place of the source entropy in Shannon's coding theorem making it necessary, in order that distortion D be not exceeded, that the channel capacity C is at least equal to

$R(D)$. In other words, $R(D)$ is the effective rate at which the source produces information.

The difficulties associated with analytical approaches to the minimisation problem are dealt with in detail by Berger (1971). In practical situations numerical techniques of the type described by Blahut (1972) can be employed, but there remains the problem of (a) the source distribution, which must be known, and (b) the distortion criterion, which should suit the coding problem in hand. An alternative approach is to try to set ever more tight upper and lower bounds to the rate distortion function in particular cases (see, e.g., Gerrish and Schultheiss, 1964; Anastassiou and Sakrison, 1979). Again a solution may be sought over a restricted range of distortion (Jelinek, 1967) or class of sources (Sakrison, 1969, 1970; Tasto and Wintz, 1971).

As mentioned at the beginning of this section the output of the transformation stage of the transform coding operation is usually considered to be a continuous distribution, and so it is now of importance to generalise the rate distortion concept to cover the continuous-amplitude case. We cannot directly apply the basic equations of information theory, however, since if we consider the set of input and output symbols to be continuous (i.e., contain an infinite number of members) then the (absolute) entropy defined by Eq. (9.2) becomes infinite. Instead we define the differential entropy

$$h(x) = -\int_{-\infty}^{\infty} p(x)\log p(x)\,dx \tag{9.17}$$

which turns out to be no longer independent of the coordinate system (Berger, 1971; Kolmogorov, 1956). A simple example will demonstrate this feature. Consider a uniform distribution of width $\pm a$; $p(x)$ is then $1/2a$ and

$$h(x) = -\frac{1}{2a}\log\frac{1}{2a}\int_{-a}^{a} dx = \log 2a$$

It will be convenient for later discussion to write $h(x)$ as a function of the distribution variance, here $a^2/3$, i.e.,

$$h(x) = \log 2a = \tfrac{1}{2}\log 4a^2 = \tfrac{1}{2}\log 12\sigma^2 \tag{9.18}$$

It is similarly easy to show that, for a double-sided triangular distribution of total width $\pm a$

$$h(x) = \tfrac{1}{2}\log 6e\sigma^2 = \tfrac{1}{2}\log 16.310\sigma^2 \tag{9.19}$$

For a Laplacian distribution of variance $\sigma^2 = 2/\alpha^2$,

$$h(x) = \log(2e/\alpha) = \tfrac{1}{2} \log 2e^2\sigma^2 = \tfrac{1}{2} \log 14.778\sigma^2 \qquad (9.20)$$

and for a Gaussian distribution

$$h(x) = \tfrac{1}{2} \log 2\pi e\sigma^2 = \tfrac{1}{2} \log 17.079\sigma^2 \qquad (9.21)$$

In fact, it can be shown that, for a fixed value of variance, the Gaussian distribution has the largest value of differential entropy $h(x)$.

In spite of the relative nature of differential entropy, however, it turns out that, since mutual information is still defined in terms of the difference of (albeit) differential information measures [see Eq. (9.10)], the relations generated in the discrete case carry over to the continuous situation in differential form. Thus,

$$I_p = \iint p(x)p(y/x) \log \frac{p(y/x)}{p(y)} \, dx \, dy \qquad (9.22)$$

$$D_p = \iint p(x)p(y/x) \, d(x, y) \, dx \, dy \qquad (9.23)$$

and the rate distortion function is defined in the same way as for the discrete case [Eq. (9.16)]. In this case, of course, $R(0) = \infty$, and since in the usual image coding situation we can only tolerate small amounts of distortion (very roughly below 1 %, measured in terms of mean square error) we may expect R to be a fairly sensitive function of D (see Fig. 9.1).

In order that analytic solutions be obtainable, it is necessary to limit severely the possible forms of $p(x)$ and $d(x, y)$, although this should not be taken to imply that there is not interest in the development of new criteria for specific applications (Rickard, 1979). As far as cost functions are concerned, so-called 'difference' distortion measures have received much attention, i.e., those of the form

$$d(x, y) = (x - y)^2 \qquad (9.24)$$

or

$$d(x, y) = |x - y| \qquad (9.25)$$

The former, particularly, has been extensively used since its average over the whole joint distribution [Eq. (9.13)] is the usual mean-square-error measure defined elsewhere in this volume for image coding and reconstruction. If now we also assume that $p(x)$ is Gaussian (and zero mean)

$$p(x) = (1/\sqrt{2\pi\sigma^2}) \exp(-x^2/2\sigma^2) \qquad (9.26)$$

and that the source is stationary and memoryless (i.e., the samples are generated independently), then we find that the expression for the rate-distortion function becomes

$$R(D) = \begin{cases} \frac{1}{2}\log(\sigma^2/D) & 0 \le D < \sigma^2 \\ 0 & \sigma^2 \le D \end{cases} \qquad (9.27)$$

a result derived by Shannon (1959) which is frequently applied to the coding of transform coefficients, which are at least closely zero mean if not truly Gaussian in distribution (see Chapter 4). It turns out that, just as the Gaussian distribution is that having the maximum differential entropy, so the value of $R(D)$ for the Gaussian source is an upper bound for that of those sources of different distribution but of equal variance. Again, the relation can be used to lower bound the rate if the variance is replaced by the 'entropy power' Q of the distribution, where Q is the variance of a Gaussian distribution having the same differential entropy as the distribution in question, i.e.,

$$h(\cdot) = \frac{1}{2}\log 2\pi e Q \qquad (9.28)$$

Naturally, for a Gaussian distribution, upper and lower bounds are identical. It is interesting to note, in passing, that for the simple types of distribution usually assumed, the difference between the bounds is not great in absolute terms. Thus, comparing uniform and Gaussian results, for the mean-square-error measure and unit variance,

$$h_U(x) = \frac{1}{2}\log 12 \; = 1.792 \quad \text{bit} \qquad (9.29)$$

$$h_G(x) = \frac{1}{2}\log 2\pi e = 2.047 \quad \text{bit} \qquad (9.30)$$

a difference of 0.255 bit ($\frac{1}{2}\log_2 \pi e/6$). Whether this is a significant amount depends, of course, upon the overall coding rate. Again, if we compare Laplacian and Gaussian results,

$$h_{LA}(x) = \frac{1}{2}\log 2e^2 = 1.943 \quad \text{bits} \qquad (9.31)$$

and the rate difference is 0.104 bit.

From Eqs. (9.27) and (9.28), the lower bound is

$$R_L(D) = \frac{1}{2}\log(Q/D) = \frac{1}{2}\log Q - \frac{1}{2}\log D$$

$$= h(\cdot) - \frac{1}{2}\log 2\pi e D \qquad (9.32)$$

and Berger shows that the upper bound may be tightened from the general Gaussian result to

$$R_U(D) = R_L(D) - \frac{1}{2}\log(1 - (D/\sigma^2)) \qquad (9.33)$$

Thus as D tends to zero the bounds converge and, for distortions of a few percent, the difference is minimal. Results for Laplacian and gamma distributions have been examined by Abut and Erdol (1979) and for the generalised Gaussian distribution by Szepanski (1980). As was pointed out in Chapter 4, the latter distribution is useful because it covers not only the usual (uniform, Gaussian and Laplacian) cases, but also those which are more sharply peaked than the last mentioned and represent certain transform coefficient distributions quite well. Szepanski has calculated $h(\cdot)$ as a function of the generalised Gaussian parameter r and finds that, for all r greater than 0.74 the differential entropy is always within 0.255 bit of the absolute maximum (Gaussian) value. For smaller values of r it falls off quite sharply [if $r = 0.3$, $h(\cdot)$ is approximately 0.4 bit], which implies that care in matching quantiser characteristics with actual coefficient distributions might bear fruit. How robust the resulting system would be is, as yet, an open question.

Before turning to examine the more interesting subject of the rate distortion relation for sources with memory, it is perhaps worth summarising briefly the ground covered so far. The function results from an attempt to minimise the necessary coding rate, expressed in terms of mutual information, of an input signal for a given value of average distortion between input and output. Both the source distribution and the distortion criterion must be specified, and it is only possible to produce an analytical result for a very limited range of such parameters. For the frequently used mean-square-error criterion, the Gaussian result, for a given signal variance, forms an upper bound to the value of $R(D)$. Furthermore the source must be memoryless (i.e., the samples must have been generated independently) and it should be stationary.

9.2.1 Rate distortion function for sources with memory

The reader who has been somewhat perturbed by the theoretical development of the previous section may be reassured that, in the context of transform image coding (specifically, the comparison of transforms on a rate distortion basis, and the allocation of coding bits to the transform coefficients), he need appreciate little more than the result of Eq. (9.27). Furthermore, it turns out that, for stationary Gaussian sources with memory (the only case which admits of a simple treatment, we can directly apply the results obtained in Chapter 3, together with Eq. (9.27), to determine the rate for the process with little further effort. The approach is to make use of the correlation between samples of the source output to produce, via a K–L transform coding operation, a set of independent sequences which may then be individually coded. Just as was found in Chapter 4 that, for a given bit allocation, lower distortion resulted following such an operation, so we shall find that a reduction in overall rate is possible in the theoretical sense of the present analysis. Furthermore, we are assured that the information content of the original data carrries over, directly, via the unitary transform, to the coefficient sequences (Andrews, 1968).

We begin by selecting a blocklength N over which to carry out the transform, and then define the rate distortion function with respect to N, $R_N(D)$ as the average over the block length of the smallest value of I_p in Eq. (9.22), as before (ignoring one or two minor mathematical subtleties). The function is then defined as the limiting value of $R_N(D)$ as the blocklength grows to infinity, i.e.,

$$R(D) = \lim_{N \to \infty} R_N(D) \tag{9.34}$$

As far as the (mean square) distortion measure is concerned, the theory developed in earlier chapters will show that such a quantity is invariant to the transform operation and so, like the information content, also carries over to the coefficient domain. We now recall that, if our source sequence has variance σ^2, two possibilities are open to us according to the relative magnitudes of σ^2 and D, the allowable distortion,

(a)　If $D < \sigma^2$ we code the sequence and incur a distortion D.

(b)　If $D \geq \sigma^2$ there is no point in coding the sequence and we incur a distortion σ^2.

Since we wish to reserve the symbol D for its conventional meaning of overall distortion, it is usual to introduce the parameter θ in connection with the various individual output sequences of the transformation. Thus, the latter operation produces (using the optimum transform) a set of coefficient sequences whose variances are the eigenvalues of the data covariance matrix, i.e., λ_i, $i = 1 \to N$. Applying the preceding principles for a given value of θ, we find that the individual distortion contribution is θ, if $\theta < \lambda_i$, and λ_i otherwise, i.e., the overall block average distortion is

$$D(\theta) = \frac{1}{N} \sum_{i=1}^{N} \min(\theta, \lambda_i) \tag{9.35}$$

and the individual rate contribution is $\frac{1}{2} \log \lambda_i/\theta$ if $\theta < \lambda_i$, and 0 otherwise, i.e., the average rate is

$$R_N(D) = \frac{1}{2N} \sum_{i=1}^{N} \max\left(0, \log \frac{\lambda_i}{\theta}\right) \tag{9.36}$$

Since the optimum transform (KLT) has been used to generate the λ_i, we expect the preceding rate to be the lowest achievable for a given N. In fact, substituting the coefficient variance sets for other transforms allows us to make a direct comparison of their efficiency in a rate distortion context (see Subsection 9.3.1). One or two points are worth noting about the relations of Eqs. (9.35) and (9.36):

(1) Suppose that $\theta < \lambda_i$ for all i. This is defined as the small distortion region, for which

$$D(\theta) = \frac{1}{N} \sum_{i=1}^{N} \theta = \theta \tag{9.37}$$

$$R_N(D) = \frac{1}{2N} \sum_{i=1}^{N} \log \frac{\lambda_i}{\theta}$$

$$= \frac{1}{2N} \sum_{i=1}^{N} \log \lambda_i - \frac{1}{2} \log \theta \tag{9.38}$$

If no transform were applied all $\lambda_i = 1$, and we would have

$$R_N(D) = -\tfrac{1}{2} \log \theta \tag{9.39}$$

which is, of course, the basic result [Eq. (9.27)] for the unit variance case. The magnitude of the first term in Eq. (9.38), then, represents the coding 'gain' at low distortion due to the application of the transform of order N

$$R_{G(N)} = \frac{1}{2N} \sum_{i=1}^{N} \log \lambda_i \tag{9.40}$$

(2) If $\theta = 0$, $D(\theta) = 0$ and $R_N(D) = \infty$.
(3) If θ is greater than the largest λ_i then

$$D(\theta) = \frac{1}{N} \sum_{i=1}^{N} \lambda_i = 1 \tag{9.41}$$

(note that this is normalised to the input sequence variance) and

$$R_N(D) = 0 \tag{9.42}$$

9.3 One-dimensional spectral representation and the rate for the first-order Markov source

In order to determine the limit in Eq. (9.34) we must allow the block size N to tend to infinity. Since the eigenvalues are, after all, 'spectral' coefficients, it is not surprising that this results in an equivalent spectral representation of the rate distortion function. We quote here the limiting results without proof (Berger, 1971):

$$D(\theta) = \frac{1}{2\pi} \int_{-\pi}^{\pi} \min(\theta, P(\omega)) \, d\omega \qquad (9.43)$$

$$R(D) = \frac{1}{2\pi} \int_{-\pi}^{\pi} \max\left(0, \frac{1}{2} \log \frac{P(\omega)}{\theta}\right) d\omega \qquad (9.44)$$

where $P(\omega)$ is now the power spectral density of the source. Equations (9.43) and (9.44) can be seen to be close parallels of Eqs. (9.35) and (9.36), respectively, and to apply then we need to know the spectral density $P(\omega)$ for the source in question. Furthermore, if we wish to employ a weighted mean-square-error criterion (as perhaps in psychovisual coding) we can use the spectral weighting function $W(\omega)$, say, directly to modify $P(\omega)$ before using the preceding equations (Sakrison, 1968; Davisson, 1972; Mannos and Sakrison, 1974).

In Chapter 2 we determined the spectrum of the first-order Markov source of inter-element correlation coefficient ρ as

$$P(\omega) = (1 - \rho^2)/(1 + \rho^2 - 2\rho \cos \omega) \qquad (9.45)$$

the motivation being that such a model is very widely used to describe the simple spatial statistical properties of image sources, and therefore that the model and source properties ought to show similarities in the spectral domain also. We can now use this model to determine the theoretical rate for the source by substitution of Eq. (9.45) into the rate and distortion equations. We first of all calculate the maximum and minimum values of the spectral function $P(\omega)$. The maximum and minimum values of $\cos \omega$ are ± 1 and so

$$P(\omega)_{\max} = (1 - \rho^2)/(1 + \rho^2 - 2\rho) = (1 + \rho)/(1 - \rho) \qquad (9.46)$$

and

$$P(\omega)_{\min} = P(\omega)_{\max}^{-1} \qquad (9.47)$$

In the case where $\theta < P(\omega)_{\min}$ (i.e., $\theta < P(\omega)$ for all ω), the small distortion condition,

$$D(\theta) = \frac{1}{2\pi} \int_{-\pi}^{\pi} \theta \, d\omega = \theta \qquad (9.48)$$

and

$$R(D) = \frac{1}{4\pi} \int_{-\pi}^{\pi} \log \frac{P(\omega)}{D} \qquad (9.49)$$

which, with a little manipulation, may be written as

$$R(D) = \frac{1}{2}\left(\log \frac{1 - \rho_1^2}{D(1 + \rho_1^2)} - \log \frac{1 + \sqrt{1 - k^2}}{2} \right)$$

where $k = 2\rho/(1 + \rho^2)$, and we employ the standard integral

$$\int_0^\pi \log(1 - k \cos \omega) = \pi \log\left(\frac{1 + \sqrt{1 - k^2}}{2} \right)$$

Thus, in this region,

$$R(D) = \tfrac{1}{2} \log \left[(1 - \rho^2)/D \right] \tag{9.50}$$

It is interesting to note that this result would be produced by optimum one-step predictive coding, for which the error signal variance is $1 - \rho^2$, given that the variance of the source sequence is unity [see Eq. (5.14); see also Davisson, 1972; Elias, 1951].

For the general case, where $P(\omega)_{max} \geq \theta \geq P(\omega)_{min}$

$$D(\theta) = \frac{1}{\pi} \int_0^\pi \min(\theta, P(\omega)) \, d\omega \tag{9.51}$$

and the interpretation of the relation between θ and $P(\omega)$ is similar to that for the discrete spectral case except that, of course, $P(\omega)$ is now a continuous function. Thus the spectral domain divides into two parts, as shown in Fig. 9.2, and we retain all components where $P(\omega) > \theta$, incurring a distortion θ, and omit the remainder, incurring distortion $P(\omega)$. In this general case, and the more so where $P(\omega)$ is not a smooth function of ω, the so-called 'water-filling' analogy is invoked, in which the area below level θ is likened to that below the surface when water fills an irregularly shaped container (in fact, the two-dimensional interpretation of this analogy is probably easier to appreciate, and is described subsequently). Thus

$$D(\theta) = \frac{1}{\pi} \int_0^\alpha \theta \, d\omega + \frac{1}{\pi} \int_\alpha^\pi P(\omega) \, d\omega \tag{9.52}$$

which, by the use of the previous substitution for k and that of $t = \tan(\omega/2)$, results in

$$D(\theta) = 1 + \frac{\theta\alpha}{\pi} - \frac{2}{\pi} \tan^{-1}\left[\frac{1 + \rho}{1 - \rho} \tan \frac{\alpha}{2} \right] \tag{9.53}$$

The integral for $R(D)$ is difficult, although Berger suggests a procedure for its evaluation. In the present case, it has been determined numerically, for various values of ρ, and the results are shown in Fig. 9.3. It should be noted that the curves are in fact straight (on a logarithmic basis) up to the small

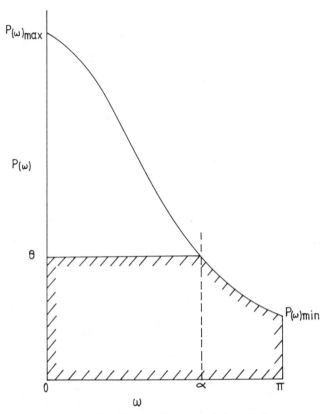

FIG. 9.2. Spectral interpretation of the rate distortion relation; $P(\omega)$, power spectral density; ω, normalised frequency; θ, distortion level and α, frequency corresponding to θ.

distortion limit, which for high values of inter-element correlation is quite low (1 % for $\rho = 0.98$). The curves of Pratt (1978) are in error in this respect, in that they continue the small distortion result into a region in which it is no longer valid. All curves must, of course, pass through the point $D/\sigma^2 = 1$, $R(D) = 0$.

To conclude this section, we may make use of the earlier results to produce the following comparison. With the optimum transform, in the limit of infinite blocklength, and assuming a stationary first-order Markov source of inter-element correlation coefficient ρ, the relation between data rate reduction and ρ in the small distortion region is as shown in Table 9.1, where $R_G(D)$ is the reduction in rate (compared with the memoryless case) required for the same value of distortion when inter-element correlation is taken into account. Significant reductions may only be realised by transformation and optimum coding alone, therefore, when the data correlation coefficient is very close to

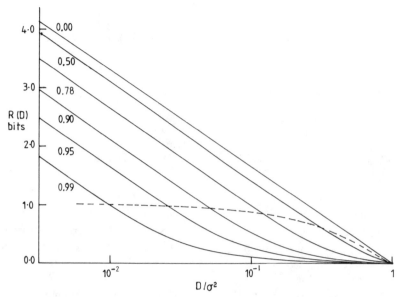

FIG. 9.3. Rate distortion relation for the one-dimensional first-order Markov source for different inter-element correlation coefficients ρ. Dashed line represents the locus of the 'small' distortion limit.

one (note that the figures in the table are, or course, theoretical limiting maxima and will not be attained in practice).

9.3.1   One-dimensional transform comparison on a rate distortion basis

Several authors (Ahmed and Rao, 1975; Andrews, 1971; Pearl, 1971a,b; Pearl et al., 1972; Ahmed et al., 1974; Mauersberger, 1980) have employed rate distortion theory to compare the performance of various transforms. The approach is simply to substitute the spectral variances in Eqs. (9.35) and (9.36) and compute the resulting rate as a function of the transform used with block size and correlation coefficient as parameters (Mauersberger considers two-dimensional coding but employs a separable covariance model, and so

TABLE 9.1.   Rate reduction as a function of inter-element correlation
for the stationary first-order Markov source.

ρ	0	0.19	0.36	0.51	0.64	0.75	0.84	0.91	0.96	0.99
$R_G(D)$	0	0.027	0.100	0.218	0.380	0.597	0.882	1.271	1.837	2.826

TABLE 9.2. Rate reduction $R_{G(N)}$ due to the application
of various transforms over different block lengths
for the first-order Markov source, $\rho = 0.91$.

Transform	Block length						
	4		8		16		∞
KLT	0.953	(0.158)	1.111	(0.080)	1.191	(0.079)	1.27
	(0.004)		(0.005)		(0.005)		
DCT	0.949	(0.157)	1.106	(0.080)	1.186		—
	(0.060)		(0.133)		(0.190)		
WHT	0.889	(0.084)	0.973	(0.023)	0.996		—

his results are a straightforward combination of those for two one-dimensional processes). In general it is difficult to deduce detailed results from the curves presented by the authors since all lie fairly close together, with the KLT best and, when comparing the four or five most popular transforms, the WHT worst. In the circumstances it is clearest to examine one or two particular cases, therefore, in the context of the infinite blocklength lower limit provided by the KLT.

We use Eq. (9.40) to determine $R_{G(N)}$, the low distortion coding 'gain' due to the application of the transform. If we consider a blocklength of 8 and a correlation coefficient of 0.91, the spectral variances have already been given in Chapter 3 for several transforms, of which here we compare the KLT, DCT and WHT. Thus we find that the gain under these conditions for the three transforms is, respectively, 1.111, 1.106 and 0.973 bits, the advantage of the first two over the last stemming not so much from the fact that the lower-order terms are rather larger than that the highest-order terms are significantly smaller.

If we widen the basis of comparison to include different blocklengths the results are as shown in Table 9.2, where the figures in parentheses are the differences between the values in the table on either side. As expected, the DCT and KLT have performances which are very similar for all blocklengths, the WHT is conspicuously worse, and in a practical sense it does not appear worthwhile employing a blocksize larger than 16 in an attempt to reduce the coding rate still further.

9.4   Two-dimensional rate distortion representation

In general, the majority of data sequences which we wish to process, code, transmit or store and subsequently reconstruct at a given level of fidelity are one-dimensional, consisting of a set of values obtained by sampling what was originally probably continuous data at a sufficiently high rate. For such sequences the theory developed earlier holds and, given fairly stringent constraints on the source probability distribution and the error criterion, will allow us to determine the required coding capacity. Where image data is concerned, the representation is at least two dimensional, and the additional interdependence between elements in the vertical, as well as the horizontal direction, can be taken advantage of in two-dimensional coding further to reduce the necessary rate. In the same way, the rate distortion analysis can be extended to two dimensions to furnish appropriate bounds upon coding performance. This extension is referred to briefly by Hayes *et al.* (1970) and more detailed treatment can be found in Sakrison and Algazi (1971) and O'Neal and Natarajan (1977). The general one-dimensional spectral representation of Eqs. (9.43) and (9.44) may be rewritten in two-dimensional form as follows:

$$D(\theta) = \frac{1}{4\pi^2} \int_{-\pi}^{\pi} \int_{-\pi}^{\pi} \min(\theta, P(\omega_h, \omega_v)) \, d\omega_h \, d\omega_v \qquad (9.54)$$

$$R(D) = \frac{1}{4\pi^2} \int_{-\pi}^{\pi} \int_{-\pi}^{\pi} \max\left(0, \frac{1}{2} \log \frac{P(\omega_h, \omega_v)}{\theta}\right) d\omega_h \, d\omega_v \qquad (9.55)$$

where $P(\omega_h, \omega_v)$ is now the two-dimensional power spectral density. More generally, it may be multiplied by a spatial weighting function $W(\omega_h, \omega_v)$ exactly as in the one-dimensional case, to take account of, say, the two-dimensional HVS response. The 'water-filling' analogy referred to in the case of one-dimensional coding is again useful in appreciating the rate distortion behaviour of the two-dimensional process. Over the square area $(-\pi \rightarrow \pi)^2$ a constant level of distortion is defined and is equivalent to the 'water' level. The general spectral distribution then appears as a set of one or more 'islands', where 'ground' level (representing $P(\omega_h, \omega_v)$ may either be above or below the liquid level. In the first case we encode the signal and incur distortion θ; in the second we delete the signal and thereby incur distortion $P(\omega_h, \omega_v)$. The determination of $R(D)$ and $D(\theta)$ now depend crucially upon the assumptions made regarding $P(\omega_h, \omega_v)$. The first is to consider the correlation properties of the image to be separable. Daut (1978) has analysed this situation for the first-order Markov model with covariance function

$$R_{(x, y)} = \sigma^2 \rho_h^{|x|} \rho_v^{|y|} \qquad (9.56)$$

where ρ_h and ρ_v are, respectively, the horizontal and vertical inter-element correlation coefficients. For the unit variance process, the two-dimensional spectrum is then defined by

$$P(\omega_h, \omega_v) = \frac{(1 - \rho_h^2)(1 - \rho_v^2)}{(1 + \rho_h^2 - 2\rho_h \cos \omega_h)(1 + \rho_v^2 - 2\rho_v \cos \omega_v)} \qquad (9.57)$$

i.e., the product of the horizontal and vertical spectral distributions. As Daut points out, and as will be evident from a moment's consideration of the two-dimensional water-filling analogy, in the case where the distortion is greater than $P(\omega_h, \omega_v)_{min}$ the regions of integration in the evaluation of the relevant equations must be carefully defined. In the small distortion region $\theta < P(\omega_h, \omega_v)_{min}$ for all ω_h, ω_v, the one-dimensional analysis developed earlier may be followed to show that

$$D(\theta) = \theta \tag{9.58}$$

and

$$R(D) = \tfrac{1}{2} \log[(1 - \rho_h^2)(1 - \rho_v^2)/D] \tag{9.59}$$

(see also Davisson, 1972). In this case $P(\omega_h, \omega_v)_{min}$ is the analogous result to that of Eq. (9.47), i.e.,

$$P(\omega_h, \omega_v)_{min} = \frac{(1 - \rho_h)(1 - \rho_v)}{(1 + \rho_h)(1 + \rho_v)} \tag{9.60}$$

and the advantage of two-dimensional over one-dimensional processing is

$$R_{G(2D)} = -\tfrac{1}{2} \log(1 - \rho_v^2) \tag{9.61}$$

For $\rho_v = 0.95$, this represents 1.68 bits/element.

An alternative approach is to consider the power density spectrum to be isotropic (Sakrison and Algazi, 1971; O'Neal and Natarajan, 1977). In this case,

$$R_{(x,y)} = \sigma^2 \exp[-\alpha(x^2 + y^2)^{1/2}] \tag{9.62}$$

where

$$\alpha = -\ln \rho_h \tag{9.63}$$

(see Chapter 2). The unit variance two-dimensional power spectral density is then

$$P(\omega_h, \omega_v) = \frac{2\pi\alpha}{(\alpha^2 + \omega_r^2)^{3/2}} \tag{9.64}$$

where $\omega_r^2 = \omega_h^2 + \omega_v^2$, and has circular symmetry defined by the radial frequency ω_r. For this spectral representation the region to be coded is contained inside a circle whose radius is defined by the relation

$$P(\omega_h, \omega_v) = \theta \tag{9.65}$$

9.4.1 Comparison between two-dimensional and one-dimensional processing

Based upon the two spectral distributions just described, it is possible to compare the limiting transmission capacity requirements of one- and two-dimensional forms of coding. On the basis of the separable model of Daut or Davisson, the advantage of two-dimensional processing is given by Eq. (9.61), and, typically, lies in the region of 1 to 2 bits/element. Again, it should be stressed that this is a theoretical asymptotic limit for a tightly defined source model and error criterion. Sakrison and Algazi (1971) have specifically compared line-by-line and two-dimensional image coding rates in the context of the complexity of the system implementation. Their two-dimensional coding results impose no constraint upon how complicated the coding operation may be, and are compared with those of independent line coding obtained with the simpler one-dimensional approach. Nowadays, of course, the allowable degree of complexity of coding is much less of a restriction upon system design and their results are of more interest for the information they provide in a wider sense with respect to image properties and coding efficiency. Their overall conclusions are that the rate decrease obtainable with two-dimensional coding is by something like a factor of 2–3, and that for one-dimensional coding the correct selection of linewidth is very important, a point that does not seem to have been given serious attention since. They apply their theoretical results to the isotropic case discussed earlier, with a radial spectral weighting function corresponding to that of the HVS. The inclusion of such weighting has a significant effect at low values of distortion (around 1%), where the rate is at least 20 times less for the weighted case. When the weighting is omitted there is a factor of 2 relating the rates required for one- and two-dimensional processing. This rises to approximately 3 when the weighting is reintroduced, provided that the optimum (image dependent) line spacing can be achieved. If not, then the improvement resulting from the use of two-dimensional processing is likely to be greater.

9.5 Quantisation and rate distortion theory

We have already seen how the formulation of rate distortion theory can serve as a guide to the efficiency of various systems for coding signals on a one- or two-dimensional basis, and also for comparing the efficiency of various transforms in a way complementary to that described in Chapter 3. Generally speaking, of course, any situation in which there is a 'trade-off' relation between the allocation of coding capacity, on the one hand, and the allowable system distortion level, on the other is amenable, at least in principle, to the application of the theory. The classic example of this is quantisation, and interest in this topic has been very great over the past 20 or 30 years, owing to the development of digital, instead of analogue, means of processing and coding signals. During the 1960s many papers were written on the theory of quantisation, most, although not all, employing a mean-square-error measure, and showing what sort of techniques would enable the minimum rate for a given distortion to be achieved. In terms of transform coding, the quantisation procedures which have been applied to date have been relatively simple. It was realised early on (Andrews and Pratt, 1968) that uniform quantisation (without further coding) was an inefficient way to deal with transform coefficients having strongly non-uniform distributions, and practically all recent work on transform compression techniques has employed minimum mean-square-error quantisation based upon the design of Max (1960) coupled with the assumption of uniformly distributed DC, and Laplacian-distributed AC, coefficients. Very occasionally the gamma distribution has been investigated as a model for the latter. Setting aside, for the moment, the question of subjective distortion in the reconstruction of the image, it may be that the efficiency of compression systems can still be increased by a more careful consideration of the relationship between the pdf of the AC coefficients and the optimum quantiser. It is therefore the purpose of this section to review the performance of various approaches to quantiser design in relation to their ultimate theoretical performance as given by the rate distortion function.

The basic problem is, given the input signal (i.e., transform coefficient) distribution, determine decision and reconstruction levels subject to one (or more) of the various possible criteria—minimum overall error, number of output levels, output entropy, etc. For the uniform distribution, the optimum quantiser is obviously uniform itself, every output (reconstruction) level is equally used, and can be coded with a fixed word length. This does not apply, generally, to the more interesting and important case of the AC coefficients. Typically the pdf will fall off steeply as the coefficient amplitude increases (see Chapter 4), and yet it is observed epxerimentally that the tails of the distributions are very long, i.e., there are always a few coefficients with very large amplitudes. If we apply a uniform quantiser to such a distribution, the inner levels will be used very frequently, the outer ones hardly at all and, in order to code the output efficiently, a variable length (entropy) code must be used, with short code words for the inner levels, and vice versa. The sharply peaked output distribution leads us to expect a relatively low value of entropy, and this turns out to be the case in practice. In fact, the optimum quantiser under the constraint of minimum rate for a given level of error can be shown to be asymptotically uniform and, furthermore, to have a performance which is within about $\frac{1}{4}$ bit of the rate bound (Goblick and Holsinger, 1967). The calculation which leads to this result is fundamentally that of Eqs.

(9.29) and (9.30), based on the comparative entropy power of the uniform and Gaussian distributions together with the bounding property of the rate for a Gaussian distribution itself. The minimum rate is of course, obtained when the outputs (of strongly differing probabilities) are entropy coded. Any attempt to reduce the entropy further (by widening the inner levels at the expense of the outer ones) will result in an increase in quantisation error. Gish and Pierce (1968) have carried out an interesting calculation which shows how the rate difference depends upon the error exponent: 0.255 bit for the mean square measure ($n = 2$); it falls to 0.059 bit for $n = 10$ and rises to 1.624 for $n = 0.1$. Since the superiority of the uniform quantiser brings with it the necessity of using a large number of quantisation levels, Gish and Pierce have also shown that the entropy increase in moving from the asymptotically ideal situation to one where a constraint exists upon both mean square error and number of levels (i.e., requiring that the entropy is a minimum given both mean square error and the number of levels) is not large for 'usual' types of distribution. The optimal property of the uniform quantiser is substantiated by Wood (1969), who reiterates that, in practice, the better performance obtainable from optimum (uniform) quantisers is subject to the necessity of variable-word-length coding and subsequent buffering, if transmission is to be carried out at a fixed rate.

The alternative, and more popular, method of quantiser design is to employ the technique of Max and, for a given number of levels, select decision and reconstruction levels so that, for a given distribution, the (mean square) error is minimised. This approach results in the quantisers discussed in Chapter 4. In this case the level separations are highly non-uniform, the probability of occupancy much less non-uniform, and the entropy consequently greater, though always less than $\log_2 N_L$ where N_L is the number of levels, implying that the occupancy is never truly equi-probable (see the tables in Chapter 4). Thus entropy coding can still bring an advantage, although a smaller one than in the case of the uniform quantiser. Comparative results for the two approaches are shown in Figs. 9.4 and 9.5 for Gaussian and Laplacian data and compared with the respective rate bounds. It can be seen that the different methods produce differences in rate which are greater in the case of the Laplacian distribution, reflecting its more sharply peaked character. Thus the usual (minimum mean square error, non-uniform) quantisation method is about $\frac{3}{4}$ bit from the rate bound in the Gaussian case and about $1\frac{1}{4}$ bit for the Laplacian distribution.

There is yet one more constraint which may be applied to the design of quantisers, and that is of a predetermined entropy. This situation has been investigated by Berger (1972) and Noll and Zelinski (1978), and it is shown that the uniform quantiser is, under this constraint, truly optimum for the mean-square-error criterion and a Laplacian pdf. In terms of our previous

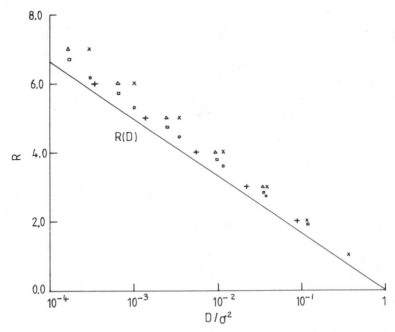

FIG. 9.4. Rate distortion performance of various quantisers for Gaussian data; x, optimum uniform quantiser; ○, optimum uniform quantiser (coded); △, optimum non-uniform quantiser; □, optimum non-uniform quantiser (coded) and +, entropy constraint (Noll, 1978).

theoretical development of quantiser characteristics, addition of a further constraint makes the optimisation problem more difficult. Using Eqs. (4.36) and (4.37) of Chapter 4, we have the total mean square error

$$e = \sum_i \int_{x_i}^{x_{i+1}} (x - y_i)^2 p(x)\, dx \qquad (9.66)$$

and, from Eq. (4.61), the quantiser entropy

$$H_N = \sum_i p_i \log p_i \qquad (9.67)$$

where the p_i are functions of x_i only (where the reconstruction levels are placed does not affect the occupancy of the quantisation interval and they are set to minimise e alone).

We therefore determine

$$G = e + \lambda H_N \qquad (9.68)$$

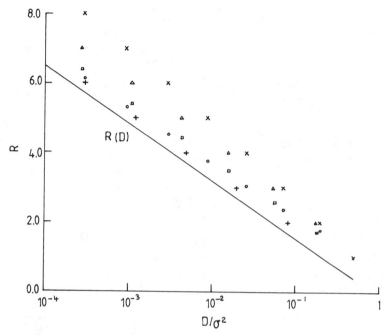

FIG. 9.5. Rate distortion performance of various quantisers for Laplacian data. Symbols are defined in Fig. 9.4.

and set $\partial G/\partial x_i = 0$, giving the set of equations

$$(x_i - y_{i-1})^2 - (x_i - y_i)^2 - \lambda(\log p_{i-1} - \log p_i)$$
$$= (x_i - y_{i-1})^2 - (x_i - y_i)^2 + \lambda \log(p_i/p_{i-1}) = 0 \qquad (9.69)$$

where λ determines the entropy H_N. It is found (Noll and Zelinski, 1978) that the decision levels tend to become uniformly spaced, but that the reconstruction levels (unaffected by entropy considerations) are still determined by the original relation of Chapter 4. Results for this constraint are also shown in Figs. 9.4 and 9.5, and it can be seen that there is a slight improvement over the performance of the optimum uniform (coded) quantiser which, in the case of the Laplacian distribution, increases as the bit rate falls.

In this case the number of levels is unrestricted, and usually is very large. Since, in any practical quantisation situation, the number of levels has to be finite, Noll has considered this point also. The output rate for a restricted number of levels will, of course, exceed the minimum obtainable when the number is unconstrained, but the difference turns out to be very small indeed provided that we allow the minimum entropy quantiser to have at least twice the number of levels of the corresponding minimum mean square error quantiser. The problem of variable rate coding remains, however. Results are also presented for the gamma distribution, which is of interest because it does frequently approximate the actual distribution of a wide range of transform coefficients. Not only does the gamma distribution have a very long tail, but many higher-order coefficients tend to be allocated small numbers of bits (which circumstance is considered in detail by the authors) as the maps of Tables 5.2–5.5 demonstrate. Under these conditions (uncoded) minimum mean-square-error quantisation is quite inefficient and some form of coding will certainly improve the performance of the quantiser, although this will necessarily add to the complexity of implementation.

9.6   Application to practical coding schemes

In view of the difficulties associated with the determination of the rate distortion function in practical circumstances (i.e., when the source pdf departs from the narrow range of distributions for which calculations are possible) it is not surprising that the associated theory has not helped with the design of efficient coding schemes as much as had originally been hoped when it was first developed; indeed this applies generally to attempts to use the theory in any branch of signal coding, of which transform coding is just one. There are three areas of the present topic where the relationships previously developed in this chapter have been invoked—bit allocation, HVS coding at a given rate and straightforward comparison between the mean-square-error performance of a coding scheme with the rate distortion bound. The first of these, in fact, does not really use the theory at all, but simply employs Eq. (9.27) to allocate coding bits to the coefficients produced by the transform operation, as described in Chapter 4. Under the assumption that the coefficients are uncorrelated and have a Gaussian distribution then D in the equation represents the mean square error resulting from the coding process. As we have seen, of course, neither assumption is true. The approach then taken is to assert that, since the Gaussian case forms an upper bound to the coding capacity needed for a given mean square error in practice we shall achieve better performance (lower error) for a given rate. In this case D no longer represents mean square error, and is simply used as a convenient (adjustable) parameter to arrive at the desired overall bit allocation. In fact, as has been pointed out earlier, in such a poorly defined situation we could have arrived at such a relation intuitively by allocating bits to coefficients on the basis of proportionality between the number of levels and their amplitude (standard deviation) using an expression of the form

$$N_{L(i)} = K\sigma_i \qquad (9.70)$$

where, since b_i, the allocation for the ith coefficient equals $\log_2 N_{L(i)}$,

$$b_i = \log_2 K\sigma_i = \tfrac{1}{2}\log_2 (\sigma_i^2/D) \tag{9.71}$$

where $D = K^{-2}$. This application of Shannon's Gaussian/mean-square-error rule can hardly be described as rigorous, therefore.

The second application of the theory is in the setting up of a simulation experiment which codes at a predetermined rate for the purpose of comparison between different approaches to some aspect of the coding operation. The experiments of Mannos and Sakrison (1974), Frei (1976) and Frei and Baxter (1977) fall into this category, although it is of more general applicability. In those cases just mentioned, the object is to compare HVS models as applied to both the determination of a suitable distortion weighting measure and as an adjunct to the basic coding operation and, since these aspects have been discussed in Chapter 6, we shall here confine discussion to the rate distortion aspect of the simulation. Basically, the approach is to employ the same development that led to Eqs. (9.54) and (9.55), but for practical, rather than idealised, source distributions. Thus, the spectrum of the input process (after a point non-linear transformation) is estimated using conventional techniques under the isotropic assumption $\omega_r = (\omega_h^2 + \omega_v^2)^{1/2}$. Following spatial filtering, $P(\omega_h, \omega_v)$ is then substituted into Eq. (9.55) to determine the parameter θ corresponding to the desired rate $R(D)$. The transform operation is then carried out (a full-image FFT, in the case of Mannos and Sakrison) and the coefficients spectrally weighted before deletion of those with a variance less than θ. Inverse transformation and reconstruction then follows in the usual way. Thus, although the actual input two-dimensional power spectrum is estimated, both the rate and distortion determinations are based upon the mean-square-error/Gaussian development (albeit applied to a non-linearly transformed and spatially weighted signal), again since analysis is highly involved in the general case and also since, as pointed out earlier, the Gaussian result will upper bound the error obtained in any practical situation.

The third, and probably most obvious, application of the theory to transform coding is simply the comparison of actual performance with the rate distortion bound. Again this is complicated by the fact that, for an arbitrary source distribution, we do not know what the rate bound will be in any case, and so comparison usually proceeds by assuming a source model (of separable or isotropic distribution) with given correlation for which the bound can be calculated, with which actual performance is then compared. Thus Habibi and Wintz (1971), whose experiments have been discussed elsewhere, compare K–L, Fourier and Hadamard two-dimensional coding with $N = 16$ on the basis of (a) the actual performance with a moderately detailed picture, (b) the theoretical performance with a Gauss–Markov source model with the same (separable) correlation parameters as the actual image and (c) the Gaussian rate bound. Their theoretical results show the expected relative 'ratings' of the transforms and the bound; thus, $R(D)$ is 0.83, KLT 1.11, DFT 1.27, WHT 1.39 bits/element at a mean square error of 4%. When the actual image is coded, results are similar in the 3–4% distortion region, but are worse than the theoretical ones for D below 2% and are significantly better when D reaches 10 or 20%, the practical rate for the KLT lying well below the Gaussian rate bound. Habibi points out here that the image chosen is apparently not a good example of a Gauss–Markov process, and this illustrates well the difficulties of applying a theoretical result to a practical situation in which the criteria upon which that result are based are not valid. In this case the comparisons between theoretical results are useful, as are those between various transforms applied to the same picture, but not those between theory and practice, at least, not with any consistency.

In an attempt to tighten the Gaussian bound to $R(D)$ in image coding, Tasto and Wintz (1972) have considered partitioning the source output into a group of subsets, such that the local rate is a minimum. In practice, there is a trade-off between the number of partitions and the need for adequate computation time. Thus three equiprobable partitions were chosen, which were found to have the following characteristics: (a) high detail, (b) low detail and darker than average and (c) low detail and lighter than average. Furthermore, it was the case that the partition optimised on an image of moderate detail worked well on images of much greater and lesser detail also, and was therefore very insensitive to actual image content. The resulting bound turns out to be significantly tighter than the Gaussian bound and the corresponding rate is 0.6 bit/element for two-dimensional 6 × 6 processing with a mean square error of 1%. Optimum coding results in a rate approximately 0.2 bit/element higher than this for this block size, and practical implementations with entropy coding of the coefficients (Tasto and Wintz, 1971) approach this figure to within 0.1 bit/element. In this case, of course, the figures are specific to the set of input images used. O'Neal and Natarajan (1977) have considered various rate distortion coding simulations for the isotropic case and an adjacent element correlation coefficient of 0.95 with unweighted and frequency-weighted mean-square-error criteria, and find that the addition of weighting alters the relative performance of the coders tested very little. Thus a sixth-order predictive coder performs as well as an 8 × 8 DCT down to (unweighted) rates of 1 bit/element, and both are about 1 bit from the rate bound at a mean square error of 1%. In fact it is by no means certain that the predictive coder will produce an acceptable visual output at such a low rate (the experiment did not deal with actual image data). The 4 × 4 WHT coding turned out to be only about $\frac{1}{4}$ bit worse than the coders already mentioned. In this (isotropic) case the rate bound is higher than that for the separable case as given by Eq. (9.59) (by approximately 0.9 bit in the low-distortion region). The latter bound is also presented by Pratt (1978) but, as in the one-dimensional case, is in error outside the small distortion region. Where it is valid it indicates that the 16×16 DCT has a performance within 0.5–0.6 bit of the bound.

In general it is probably true to say that this figure represents roughly what an adaptive two-dimensional transform coder should achieve. The difficulty remains, of course, in actually determining the bound in any specific situation, and it is doubtful if rate distortion theory can really be of any more help in determining image coder performance beyond the establishment of approximate rate targets. Any more definitive rate distortion performance criteria seem to be, at least at present, beyond our reach.

9.7 Summary

In this chapter an attempt has been made to introduce, in the context of image coding, the work which has been carried out over the past 35 years or so on a fundamental problem of communication theory: How much system capacity is necessary to transmit a signal given a predetermined allowable degree of impairment in its reconstruction at the receiver? The rate distortion relation $R(D)$ answers this question, given that one or two quite stringent constraints are satisfied but, as might be expected, practical image (or transform coefficient) properties, and the difficulty of numerically specifying a visual distortion measure mean that it is useful as an approximate indication only of the channel rate or bandwidth required.

Notwithstanding the difficulties mentioned earlier, the theory can still be fruitfully applied in other directions, one of which is the comparison of various orthogonal transforms in a way complementary to that of Chapter 3, and this procedure confirms the earlier results with regard to the efficiency of the DCT and the suitability of a block size in the range 8–16. Again, it is possible in this way to gain some idea of the advantage of two- over one-dimensional processing and also of the relative merits of various approaches to the problem of quantisation—a topic which is at once of general interest in digital communication system design and of great relevance to the development of efficient transform image coding schemes.

Finally, the difficulty of rigorous analysis by which the application of rate distortion theory is beset has not deterred several workers from making the best of the situation and using it, in any case, as an aid to system development. Thus the general form of the relation for the Gaussian case has frequently been used to allow the bit allocation process to be influenced by transmission rate considerations via the distortion parameter D (although, as we have seen, this has no specific connection with formal rate distortion theory). Alternatively, the performance of any particular design may be compared with the rate distortion bound although, given the ever recurrent problem of valid distortion criteria, this is probably of limited use to the designer of practical image transmission systems, and it is likely that, in spite of the attractions of the elegant mathematical formulation of the theory, more *ad hoc* approaches to coder/decoder design will be with us for some time yet.

Appendix 1

Calculation of First- and Second-Order Entropies

Suppose that the image contains Q elements, each of which may assume one of L levels. The probability of occurrence of the ith level is

$$p(i) = n_i/Q \qquad i = 1 \to L$$

where there are n_i occurrences of level i. Then using Eq. (2.5),

$$H(x) = -\sum_{i=1}^{L} p(i) \log_2 p(i) = \sum_{i=1}^{L} \frac{n_i}{Q} \log_2 \frac{Q}{n_1}$$

$$= \sum_{i=1}^{L} \frac{n_i}{Q} \log_2 Q - \sum_{i=1}^{L} \frac{n_i}{Q} \log_2 n_i$$

$$= \log_2 Q - \frac{1}{Q} \sum_{i=1}^{L} n_1 \log_2 n_i \qquad (A.1.1)$$

If all levels are equiprobable, $p(i) = 1/L$ and $n_i = Q/L$. Therefore,

$$H(x) = \log_2 Q + \frac{1}{Q} \sum_{i=1}^{L} \frac{Q}{L} \log_2 \frac{L}{Q}$$

$$= \log_2 Q + \frac{1}{L} \sum_{i=1}^{L} \log_2 L - \frac{1}{L} \sum_{i=1}^{L} \log_2 Q$$

$$= \log_2 L \qquad (A.1.2)$$

Now consider the image to contain Q pairs of elements (this quantity will in fact be $Q - 1$, taking pairs in a predetermined direction throughout the image, but for all practical purposes the difference between this and Q will be negligible). Each element of the pair may assume one of L levels, and the probability of occurrence of pair (i, j) is

$$p(i, j) = n_{ij}/Q \qquad i, j = 1 \to L$$

where there are n_{ij} occurrences of pair (i, j). Using Eq. (2.7),

$$H(x, y) = - \sum_{i=1}^{L} \sum_{j=1}^{L} p(i, j) \log_2 p(i, j)$$

$$= \sum_{i=1}^{L} \sum_{j=1}^{L} \frac{n_{ij}}{Q} \log_2 Q - \sum_{i=1}^{L} \sum_{j=1}^{L} \frac{n_{ij}}{Q} \log_2 n_{ij}$$

$$= \log_2 Q - \frac{1}{Q} \sum_{i=1}^{L} \sum_{j=1}^{L} n_{ij} \log_2 n_{ij} \tag{A.1.3}$$

If all pairs are equiprobable $p(i, j) = 1/L^2$ and $n_{ij} = Q/L^2$. Therefore,

$$H(x, y) = \log_2 Q + \frac{1}{Q} \sum_{i=1}^{L} \sum_{j=1}^{L} \frac{Q}{L^2} \log_2 \frac{L^2}{Q}$$

$$= \log_2 Q + \frac{1}{L^2} \sum_{i=1}^{L} \sum_{j=1}^{L} \log_2 L^2 - \frac{1}{L^2} \sum_{i=1}^{L} \sum_{j=1}^{L} \log_2 Q$$

$$= \log_2 L^2 = 2 \log_2 L \tag{A.1.4}$$

These forms are more convenient than the original defining equations [Eq. (2.5) and (2.7)] for the purposes of numerical evaluation of entropy.

Appendix 2

Statistical Relationships

A technique such as transform coding operates upon the input (image) in a manner determined by the statistical properties of the data. Thus coefficients are processed subsequent to transformation according to their means and variances determined over the whole image, in the case of non-adaptive, or over distinct block classes in the case of adaptive, coding, and these properties are shown in Chapter 2 to be deterministic functions of those of the original image. The advantage of dealing with any signal manipulation task in a statistical sense is that there is a very substantial body of random process theory which can be brought to bear when such data is specified in terms of overall averages of various quantities. One accompanying disadvantage, however, lies in the extent to which such theory can be consistently interpreted in terms of quantities which can actually be measured with some degree of confidence. The purpose of this appendix is to note briefly the relation between the two. Although the general theory is couched in terms of the set of real numbers, for the present purpose we consider the (real) data to be discrete in both amplitude and time (or space) domains, i.e., sampled and quantised. Furthermore, it should be noted that, via the operation of the scanning process, there will be a correspondence relation between time and space domains in the practical situation of image pickup or display. A comprehensive treatment of the theory is to be found in many standard texts, for example, Papoulis (1965, 1977).

Under a statistical interpretation, then, we consider the scanned image to be represented by the output of a device which produces, at regular intervals determined by the sampling frequency in the horizontal, line density in the vertical and frame repetition rate in the temporal, directions, one of 2^B numbers, where B is the number of bits with which the amplitude range of the luminance signal is quantised. Typically, therefore, at each instant we can record one of 256 different numbers ($B = 8$). The process has two independent variables, the discrete sampling instant k and the actual instance of the source output P, where P may be a generated image frame, an individual image sub-block, or an image sequence. In the most general sense, the domain of P is infinite, i.e., by directing the camera towards enough different scenes over a very long period of time, *any* combination of amplitude value/sample locations will be observed to form a realisation of P. In practice, of course, the useful domain of P is restricted by the requirement, in the present image coding context, that reasonable correlation exist along the direction(s) in which the transform is to be taken. Furthermore, it would be possible to design an efficient coding scheme for the restricted class of images consisting of head and shoulders views which, without modification, would perform poorly if used to code detailed crowd scenes, for example.

There are, in general, four possible quantities which are represented by the function describing the process, $x(k, P)$:

(a) With both k and P variable, it represents the ensemble of time (space) functions made up of individual realisations of the picture generation process (i.e., the frames, sub-blocks or sequences referred to earlier).

(b) Fixing P produces an individual sample function defining a particular instance of the relation between amplitude values and time (space) coordinate(s)—$x(k)_P$.

(c) Fixing k results in a random variable which is that defined by the amplitude values (one per instance of P) taken at a given sampling instant (spatial location) within each sample function—$x(P)_k$.

(d) The result of fixing both k and P is the single amplitude value existing at the kth sample instant in the Pth frame, sub-block, etc.

The expected value of the random variable x is defined as

$$E(x(k)) = \sum_{\text{all } i} X_i p_i \qquad (A.2.1)$$

where X_i is the value taken on by x in the ith realisation of P and p_i is the probability of the outcome $x = X_i$. The autocorrelation of the process is

$$R(k, l) = E(x(k)x(l)) \qquad (A.2.2)$$

and the autocovariance

$$C(k, l) = E[(x(k) - E(x(k))(x(l) - E(x(l))]$$
$$= R(k, l) - E(x(k))E(x(l)) \qquad (A.2.3)$$

The average power is

$$R(k, k) = E(|\mathbf{x}(k)^2|) \tag{A.2.4}$$

and the variance is

$$C(k, k) = R(k, k) - (E(\mathbf{x}(k)))^2 \tag{A.2.5}$$

The process is strict-sense stationary if its statistical properties are unaffected by a displacement of the time (space) origin. It is stationary of order U if the Uth order probability density and, thus, lower-order densities are so unaffected. If its expected value is constant and its autocorrelation is a function of $|k - l|$ only, it is termed wide-sense (weakly) stationary, i.e.,

$$E(\mathbf{x}(k)) = E(\mathbf{x}) = \text{const} \tag{A.2.6}$$

$$R(k, l) = R(|k - l|) = R(\Delta)$$

$$= E(\mathbf{x}(k)\mathbf{x}(k + \Delta)) \tag{A.2.7}$$

$$C(k, l) = C(\Delta)$$

$$= R(\Delta) - (E(\mathbf{x}))^2 \tag{A.2.8}$$

$$E(|\mathbf{x}(k)^2|) = R(0) \tag{A.2.9}$$

and

$$C(0) = R(0) - (E(\mathbf{x}))^2 \tag{A.2.10}$$

is the process variance. The process is sometimes called quasistationary if $R(\Delta)$ is in fact a slowly varying function of k (Papoulis, 1977).

The basic problem is the extent to which measurements made on an individual outcome of the image generation process truly represent the statistical properties as defined by ensemble averages, i.e., those of case (c). Thus the quantities most easily measured are those over an individual realisation of P [case (b)], i.e, the time average

$$\bar{x}_K = \frac{1}{K} \sum_{k=1}^{K} \mathbf{x}(k) \tag{A.2.11}$$

or, in spatial form

$$x_K = \frac{1}{MN} \sum_{m=1}^{M} \sum_{n=1}^{N} \mathbf{x}(m, n) \tag{A.2.12}$$

where the dimension of the image, sub-block, etc., is $M \times N$ and there is, by virtue of the scanning process, a direct relation between K and (m, n), i.e., at sampling instant k the scan location is $x = m$, $y = n$, and, of course, $K = M \times N$. Similarly we may calculate

$$R_K(\Delta) = \frac{1}{K - \Delta} \sum_{k=1}^{K-\Delta} \mathbf{x}(k)\mathbf{x}(k + \Delta) \qquad (A.2.13)$$

In the case of the equivalent spatial form a variety of expressions is possible depending upon the direction in which we wish to determine the autocorrelation. The preceding will suffice for our present needs.

If we allow K in Eqs. (A.2.11) and (A.2.13) to tend to infinity, we may use the equations as alternative definitions of mean and autocorrelation. Since each is an average over a set of random variables, however, they are themselves random variables, and do not necessarily result in the same values as the ensemble definitions of Eqs. (A.2.1) and (A.2.7). Their expected values, in turn, are $E(\bar{x}_K)$ and $E(R(\Delta))$, and if these quantities tend, respectively, to those of Eqs. (A.2.1) and (A.2.7), with the variances of $\bar{x}_K$ and $R(\Delta)$ tending to zero as $K \to \infty$, then the process is said to be ergodic in mean and autocorrelation. These statistics, derived from a single realisation of the process, are then true of the process as a whole. If parameters up to order V can be so treated, the process is termed ergodic in V. An ergodic process is necessarily both strict- and wide-sense stationary, and, loosely, it is said that time (in the present context, space) averages and ensemble averages are equal or (Shannon, 1948) that each sample function is typical of the ensemble.

As far as images are concerned, it is apparent that a single realisation is very unlikely to have spatial properties which are those of the whole ensemble (although a moderate length sequence might have—approximately, at least—we could then select a reasonably varied sample of images to represent the properties of the totality of images which it is desired to code). In more restricted terms, a single image frame is often spoken of as non-stationary in that its local statistics (i.e., measured over a 16×16 sub-block, for instance) vary from location to location within the image, independent of the degree to which that image 'represents' the totality of pictures to be coded. In practical terms this is not such a problem as it at first seems. Adaptive coding schemes (see Chapter 5) collect together sub-blocks with similar statistics into one of a number of classes, each of which has its own optimised coding parameters, and recently work has been directed (see, e.g., Strickland, 1983) towards mapping initially non-stationary image data into a stationary form.

Appendix 3

The Inverse Transform

It is instructive to demonstrate the forward and inverse transform relationships in the simple case $N = 2$ by direct evaluation. Thus, consider the transform

$$\begin{bmatrix} C_1 \\ C_2 \end{bmatrix} = \begin{bmatrix} t_{11} & t_{12} \\ t_{21} & t_{22} \end{bmatrix} \begin{bmatrix} f_1 \\ f_2 \end{bmatrix} \tag{A.3.1}$$

i.e.,

$$\begin{aligned} C_1 &= t_{11} f_1 + t_{12} f_2 \\ C_2 &= t_{21} f_1 + t_{22} f_2 \end{aligned} \tag{A.3.2}$$

giving

$$\begin{aligned} t_{22} C_1 &= t_{11} t_{22} f_1 + t_{12} t_{22} f_2 \\ t_{12} C_2 &= t_{21} t_{12} f_1 + t_{12} t_{22} f_2 \end{aligned}$$

and so

$$f_1 = (t_{22} C_1 - t_{12} C_2)/(t_{11} t_{22} - t_{21} t_{12}) \tag{A.3.3}$$

and similarly

$$f_2 = (-t_{21} C_1 + t_{11} C_2)/(t_{11} t_{22} - t_{21} t_{12}) \tag{A.3.4}$$

If now

$$\begin{bmatrix} f_1 \\ f_2 \end{bmatrix} = \begin{bmatrix} s_{11} & s_{12} \\ s_{21} & s_{22} \end{bmatrix} \begin{bmatrix} C_1 \\ C_2 \end{bmatrix} \tag{A.3.5}$$

i.e.,

$$f_1 = s_{11}C_1 + s_{12}C_2$$
$$f_2 = s_{21}C_1 + s_{22}C_2 \tag{A.3.6}$$

then

$$s_{11} = \frac{t_{22}}{t_{11}t_{22} - t_{21}t_{12}}$$

$$s_{12} = \frac{-t_{12}}{t_{11}t_{22} - t_{21}t_{12}}$$

$$\tag{A.3.7}$$

$$s_{21} = \frac{-t_{21}}{t_{11}t_{22} - t_{21}t_{12}}$$

$$s_{22} = \frac{t_{11}}{t_{11}t_{22} - t_{21}t_{12}}$$

If the matrices are orthogonal, $t_{11}t_{21} + t_{12}t_{22} = 0$ and $t_{11}^2 + t_{12}^2 = t_{21}^2 + t_{22}^2 = A$ [see Eq. (3.14)], and a similar relation holds for the s terms also. Simple substitution then results in

$$s_{11} = t_{11}/A \qquad s_{12} = t_{21}/A$$
$$s_{21} = t_{12}/A \qquad s_{22} = t_{22}/A \tag{A.3.8}$$

and so, representing the transform matrices by $[T]$ and $[S]$, respectively,

$$[S] = \frac{1}{A}[T]^{\mathrm{T}} \tag{A.3.9}$$

If the matrix $[T]$ is orthonormal, then $A = 1$, and the inverse transform is

$$\begin{bmatrix} f_1 \\ f_2 \end{bmatrix} = \begin{bmatrix} t_{11} & t_{21} \\ t_{12} & t_{22} \end{bmatrix} \begin{bmatrix} C_1 \\ C_2 \end{bmatrix}$$

$$= C_1 \begin{bmatrix} t_{11} \\ t_{12} \end{bmatrix} + C_2 \begin{bmatrix} t_{21} \\ t_{22} \end{bmatrix} \tag{A.3.10}$$

The data vector is therefore reconstructed from 'C_1' of the first basis vector plus 'C_2' of the second.

In the case of the unitary inverse the terms are, in general, complex. The orthogonality relationships are

$$(r_{11} \pm jd_{11})(r_{21} \mp jd_{21}) + (r_{12} \pm jd_{12})(r_{22} \mp jd_{22}) = O$$

$$(r_{11} + jd_{11})(r_{11} - jd_{11}) + (r_{12} + jd_{12})(r_{12} - jd_{12}) = A \quad \text{(A.3.11)}$$

$$(r_{21} + jd_{21})(r_{21} - jd_{21}) + (r_{22} + jd_{22})(r_{22} - jd_{22}) = A$$

where r and d represent, respectively, the real and imaginary terms in the elements of $[T]$. Further manipulation gives $s_{11} = (r_{11} - jd_{11})/A$, $s_{12} = (r_{21} - jd_{21})/A$, and so on.

Appendix 4

Gradients of Vector and Matrix Functions

Consider the transform relation

$$C = \mathbf{t}_j^{\mathrm{T}} [A] \mathbf{t}_j \qquad (A.4.1)$$

where $\mathbf{t}_j$ is the jth basis vector (written, as convention dictates, in column form) i.e.

$$\mathbf{t}_j^{\mathrm{T}} = t_{j1} \quad t_{j2} \quad t_{j3} \quad \cdots \quad t_{jN} \qquad (A.4.2)$$

and $\mathbf{t}_j^{\mathrm{T}} \mathbf{t}_j = 1$.

For simplicity suppose $N = 2$. Then we have

$$
\begin{aligned}
C &= \begin{bmatrix} t_{j1} & t_{j2} \end{bmatrix} \begin{bmatrix} a_{11} & a_{12} \\ a_{21} & a_{22} \end{bmatrix} \begin{bmatrix} t_{j1} \\ t_{j2} \end{bmatrix} \\
&= \begin{bmatrix} t_{j1} & t_{j2} \end{bmatrix} \begin{bmatrix} a_{11}t_{j1} + a_{12}t_{j2} \\ a_{21}t_{j1} + a_{22}t_{j2} \end{bmatrix} \\
&= a_{11}t_{j1}^2 + a_{12}t_{j1}t_{j2} + a_{21}t_{j2}t_{j1} + a_{22}t_{j2}^2 \qquad (A.4.3)
\end{aligned}
$$

The gradient of C with respect to $\mathbf{t}_j$ will have N (here 2) components

$$\frac{dC}{dt_{j1}} = 2a_{11}t_{j1} + a_{12}t_{j2} + a_{21}t_{j2} \qquad (A.4.4)$$

$$\frac{dC}{dt_{j2}} = a_{12}t_{j1} + a_{21}t_{j1} + 2a_{22}t_{j2} \qquad (A.4.5)$$

In the case that $[A]$ is a symmetric matrix (e.g., a covariance matrix) $a_{21} = a_{12}$ and so

$$\text{GRAD}_{(\mathbf{t}_j)}C = \begin{bmatrix} \dfrac{dC}{dt_{j1}} \\[2mm] \dfrac{dC}{dt_{j2}} \end{bmatrix} = 2\begin{bmatrix} a_{11}t_{j1} + a_{12}t_{j2} \\ a_{21}t_{j1} + a_{22}t_{j2} \end{bmatrix}$$

$$= 2[A]\mathbf{t}_j \qquad\qquad\qquad (A.4.6)$$

where $\text{GRAD}_{(\mathbf{t}_j)}C$ denotes the gradient of C with respect to $\mathbf{t}_j$. Furthermore,

$$\mathbf{t}_j^{\mathrm{T}}\mathbf{t}_j = t_{j1}^2 + t_{j2}^2$$

and

$$\text{GRAD}_{(\mathbf{t}_j)}(\mathbf{t}_j^{\mathrm{T}}\mathbf{t}_j) = \begin{bmatrix} 2t_{j1} \\ 2t_{j2} \end{bmatrix} = 2\mathbf{t}_j. \qquad\qquad (A.4.7)$$

Decorrelation and Energy-Packing Properties of the Walsh–Hadamard Transform

For small values of block size one or two interesting properties of the WHT can be deduced analytically. Thus, consider the general covariance matrix for $N = 4$,

$$[D] = \begin{bmatrix} 1 & \rho_1 & \rho_2 & \rho_3 \\ \rho_1 & 1 & \rho_4 & \rho_5 \\ \rho_2 & \rho_4 & 1 & \rho_6 \\ \rho_3 & \rho_5 & \rho_6 & 1 \end{bmatrix} \tag{A.5.1}$$

which is constrained to be symmetric and have stationary (unit) variance. Applying the two-dimensional WHT to generate the transform domain covariance matrix results in

$$\text{COV}(Y) = [B][D][B] \tag{A.5.2}$$

Where $[B]$ is the WHT basis matrix. Thus, after a little manipulation

$$\text{COV}(Y) = \frac{1}{2} \begin{bmatrix} 2y_1 & \rho_1 - \rho_6 & \rho_3 - \rho_4 & \rho_2 - \rho_5 \\ \rho_1 - \rho_6 & 2y_2 & \rho_5 - \rho_2 & \rho_4 - \rho_3 \\ \rho_3 - \rho_4 & \rho_5 - \rho_2 & 2y_3 & \rho_6 - \rho_1 \\ \rho_2 - \rho_5 & \rho_4 - \rho_3 & \rho_6 - \rho_1 & 2y_4 \end{bmatrix} \tag{A.5.3}$$

and

$$y_1 = 1 + \tfrac{1}{2}(\rho_1 + \rho_2 + \rho_3 + \rho_4 + \rho_5 + \rho_6)$$
$$y_2 = 1 + \tfrac{1}{2}(\rho_1 - \rho_2 - \rho_3 - \rho_4 - \rho_5 + \rho_6)$$
$$y_3 = 1 + \tfrac{1}{2}(-\rho_1 - \rho_2 + \rho_3 + \rho_4 - \rho_5 - \rho_6) \tag{A.5.4}$$
$$y_4 = 1 + \tfrac{1}{2}(-\rho_1 + \rho_2 - \rho_3 - \rho_4 + \rho_5 - \rho_6)$$

The matrix COV (**Y**) is diagonal, in general, if

$$\rho_1 = \rho_6 \qquad \rho_2 = \rho_5 \qquad \rho_3 = \rho_4 \tag{A.5.5}$$

i.e., if the properties which hold for $[D]$ about the main diagonal hold about the opposing diagonal also.

There are two interesting applications of the preceding development.

The 2 × 2 WHT. Consider a 2 × 2 data block extracted from a stationary, unit variance image sequence

$$[X] = \begin{bmatrix} x_{11} & x_{12} \\ x_{21} & x_{22} \end{bmatrix} \tag{A.5.6}$$

which may be reordered into a 4 × 1 data vector

$$\mathbf{X'} = [x_{11} \quad x_{12} \quad x_{21} \quad x_{22}] \tag{A.5.7}$$

The (4 × 4) covariance matrix of $[X]$ will be

$$\text{COV}(\mathbf{X}) = \begin{bmatrix} 1 & \rho_h & \rho_v & \rho_d \\ \rho_h & 1 & \rho_d & \rho_v \\ \rho_v & \rho_d & 1 & \rho_h \\ \rho_d & \rho_v & \rho_h & 1 \end{bmatrix} \tag{A.5.8}$$

where ρ_h, ρ_v, and ρ_d are the one-step correlation coefficients in the horizontal, vertical and diagonal directions, respectively.

Comparing Eq. (A.5.8) with Eq. (A.5.1) we see that the conditions of Eq. (A.5.5) obtain, and therefore COV (**Y**) is diagonal, i.e., the 2 × 2 WHT is the optimum (KL) transform of the data block. The diagonal terms are

$$y_1 = 1 + \rho_h + \rho_v + \rho_d$$
$$y_2 = 1 + \rho_h - \rho_v - \rho_d$$
$$y_3 = 1 - \rho_h - \rho_v + \rho_d \tag{A.5.9}$$
$$y_4 = 1 - \rho_h + \rho_v - \rho_d$$

Analytical calculation of decorrelation and energy packing performance. In the first-order Markov case the covariance matrix of the data will have

$$\rho_1 = \rho_4 = \rho_6 = \rho$$

say,

$$\rho_2 = \rho_5 = \rho^2$$
$$\rho_3 = \rho^3$$

and the covariance matrix in the transform domain will not be diagonal. Simple substitution gives

$$\text{COV}(\mathbf{Y}) = \frac{1}{2}\begin{bmatrix} 2y_1 & 0 & (\rho^3 - \rho) & 0 \\ 0 & 2y_2 & 0 & -(\rho^3 - \rho) \\ (\rho^3 - \rho) & 0 & 2y_3 & 0 \\ 0 & -(\rho^3 - \rho) & 0 & 2y_4 \end{bmatrix} \quad (A.5.10)$$

where this time

$$y_1 = 1 + \tfrac{1}{2}(3\rho + 2\rho^2 + \rho^3)$$
$$y_2 = 1 + \tfrac{1}{2}(\rho - 2\rho^2 - \rho^3)$$
$$y_3 = 1 + \tfrac{1}{2}(-\rho - 2\rho^2 + \rho^3) \quad (A.5.11)$$
$$y_4 = 1 + \tfrac{1}{2}(-3\rho + 2\rho^2 - \rho^3)$$

Thus, taking the case $\rho = 0.91$,

$$\text{COV}(\mathbf{Y}) = \begin{bmatrix} 3.5699 & 0 & -0.0782 & 0 \\ 0 & 0.2501 & 0 & 0.0782 \\ -0.0782 & 0 & 0.0937 & 0 \\ 0 & 0.0782 & 0 & 0.0863 \end{bmatrix} \quad (A.5.12)$$

The energy packing efficiency (retaining $N/2$ terms) is [Eq. (3.50)]

$$\eta_E = (2 + 2\rho)/4 = (1 + \rho)/2 \quad (A.5.13)$$

and the decorrelation efficiency, using Eq. (3.49)

$$\eta_C = 1 - [(1 - \rho^2)/(3 + 2\rho + \rho^2)]$$
$$= \begin{cases} 1 & \text{when } \rho = 1 \\ \tfrac{2}{3} & \text{when } \rho = 0 \end{cases} \quad (A.5.14)$$

The latter figure is approached as a limit when ρ becomes very small.

Inner and Outer Products

(a)   The inner (scalar) product of the vectors

$$\mathbf{X}_N = \begin{bmatrix} x_1 \\ x_2 \\ \vdots \\ x_N \end{bmatrix} \qquad \mathbf{Y}_N = \begin{bmatrix} y_1 \\ y_2 \\ \vdots \\ y_N \end{bmatrix}$$

is the number

$$\mathbf{X}_N^{\mathsf{T}}\mathbf{Y}_N = \begin{bmatrix} x_1 & x_2 & \cdots & x_N \end{bmatrix} \begin{bmatrix} y_1 \\ y_2 \\ \vdots \\ y_N \end{bmatrix}$$

$$= x_1 y_1 + x_2 y_2 + \cdots + x_N y_N$$

$$= \sum_{i=1}^{N} x_1 y_i \qquad\qquad (A.6.1)$$

(b)   The outer product of the vectors

$$\mathbf{X}_N = \begin{bmatrix} x_1 \\ x_2 \\ \vdots \\ x_N \end{bmatrix} \qquad \mathbf{Y}_M = \begin{bmatrix} y_1 \\ y_2 \\ \vdots \\ y_M \end{bmatrix}$$

is the $N \times M$ matrix

$$\mathbf{X}_N \mathbf{Y}_M^T = \begin{bmatrix} x_1 y_1 & x_1 y_2 & \cdots & x_1 y_M \\ x_2 y_1 & x_2 y_2 & \cdots & x_2 y_M \\ \vdots & \vdots & & \vdots \\ x_N y_1 & x_N y_2 & \cdots & x_N y_M \end{bmatrix}. \qquad \text{(A.6.2)}$$

Appendix 7

Mean-Square-Error Measures

There is considerable confusion in the literature concerning the relationships between (a) compressed bit rate, (b) mean square error and (c) subjective quality. Acknowledging the difficulties with regard to the latter assessment (see Chapter 6), there is still no consistent agreement between (a) and (b), due partially, of course, to the various data sets used by different workers. Even when the same data is employed, however, there are still discrepancies, and it is not always evident just what basis of comparison has been used. Thus at least three different error definitions have been quoted in connection with the work discussed in Chapter 5 as follows.

$$\sum \sum (x - \hat{x})^2 / \sum \sum x^2 \qquad \text{(A.7.1)}$$

$$\sum \sum (x - \hat{x})^2 / \sigma^2 N^2 \qquad \text{(A.7.2)}$$

$$\sum \sum (x - \hat{x})^2 / (N^2 x_{\text{max}}^2) \qquad \text{(A.7.3)}$$

where the image is of dimension $N \times N$, x is the amplitude of an arbitrary input element, $\hat{x}$ its reconstructed counterpart, σ^2 the input data variance and x_{max} the maximum amplitude of the input data. The summation is taken over all image elements.

In each case there is unanimity in the choice of numerator in the expressions, the difference between input and reconstructed element amplitudes being squared and summed over the whole extent of the image. This quantity is then compared with one of three possible measures of total data 'energy'. The first [Eq. (A.7.1)] is the sum of the squares of the data element

TABLE A7-1. Mean square error/rate comparisons
for various intraframe coding schemes.

Author	Rate (bit/element)	Mean square error (%)	Equation
Tasto	1.0	1.0	
Parsons	1.5	0.08 adaptive	
		0.17 non-adaptive	1
Reader	1.5	0.05–0.08	
Andrews	1.5	0.5–1.0	
Chen	1.0	0.05	3
Cox	1.0	1.5	2
Reis	1.0	0.6	1
Narasimhan	1.0	0.4–0.8	1

amplitudes. This is the conventional mean-square-error measure and is defined on an element-by-element basis, which becomes more evident when both numerator and denominator are divided by the total number of elements N^2. Alternatively the denominator may use the data variance [Eq. (A.7.2)] in which circumstance the numerical value will be larger than for [Eq. A.7.1)], since the variance (AC energy) of even quite active images is typically not a very significant fraction of their total energy [i.e., the denominator in Eq. (A.7.1)]. Again, the squared error may be determined on a per element basis [Eq. (A.7.3)] and the resulting figure divided by the square of the maximum data amplitude. This will make the mean-square-error measure very small numerically, for the usual range of bit rates encountered (a similar procedure resulting in very small values of error was mentioned in Chapter 2, and arose due to the erroneous inclusion of synchronising and blanking pulses in the normalisation process). Equation (A.7.3) is, of course, when inverted, equivalent to a statement about the signal-to-'noise' ratio for the reconstructed signal.

To show how the use of these different error measures affects published results of performance/bit rate Table A.7–1 contains details of several intraframe rate/error comparisons, together with the relevant definition used, where specified.

References

Abramson, R. F. (1977). The sinc and cosinc transform. *IEEE Trans Electromagn. Compat.* **EMC-19**, 88–94.

Abut, H., and Erdol, N. (1979). Bounds on R(D) functions for speech probability models. *IEEE Trans. Inf. Theory* **IT-25**, 225–228.

Adams, W. C., Jr., and Giesler, C. (1978). Quantising characteristics for signals having a Laplacian p.d.f. *IEEE Trans. Commun.* **COM-26**, 1295–1297.

Ahmed, N., and Cheng, S. M. (1970). On matrix partitioning and a class of algorithms. *IEEE Trans. Educ.* **E-13**, 103–105.

Ahmed, N., and Rao, K. R. (1975). "Orthogonal Transforms for Digital Signal Processing." Springer-Verlag, Berlin and New York.

Ahmed, N., Natarajan, T., and Rao, K. R. (1974). Discrete cosine transform. *IEEE Trans. Comput.* **C-23**, 90–93.

Alexandridis, N. A., and Klinger, A. (1972). Real-time Walsh–Hadamard transformation. *IEEE Trans. Comput.* **C-21**, 288–292.

Algazi, V. R. (1966). Useful approximations to optimum quantisation. *IEEE Trans. Commun.* **COM-14**, 297–301.

Algazi, V. R., and Ford, G. (1980). Quality measures in the processing of high contrast images. *SPIE Semin. Proc.* **249**, 54–60.

Alker, H. J., and Andreassen, K. (1982). A hardware digital processor for image bandwidth compression, *ICASSP Proc.* pp. 1207–1210.

Anastassiou, D., and Sakrison, D. J. (1979). New bounds to R(D) for additive sources and applications to image encoding. *IEEE Trans. Inf. Theory* **IT-25**, 145–155.

Anderson, G. B., and Huang, T. (1971). Piecewise Fourier transformation for picture bandwidth compression. *IEEE Trans. Commun.* **COM-19**, 133–140.

Andrews, H. C. (1968). Entropy considerations in the frequency domain. *IEEE Proc.* **56**, 113–114.

Andrews, H. C. (1971). Walsh functions in image processing, feature selection and pattern recognition, *Proc. Symp. Appl. Walsh Funct.*, *Washington, D.C.* AD 727000, pp. 26–32.

Andrews, H. C., and Caspari, K. (1970). A generalised technique for spectral analysis. *IEEE Trans. Comput.* **C-19**, 16–25.

Andrews, H. C., and Patterson, C. (1976a). Outer product expansions and their uses in digital image processing. *IEEE Trans. Comput.* **C-25**, 140–148.

Andrews, H. C., and Patterson, C. (1976b). Singular value decomposition (SVD) image coding. *IEEE Trans. Commun.* **COM-24**, 425–432.

Andrews, H. C., and Patterson, C. (1976c). Singular value decomposition and digital image processing. *IEEE Trans. Acoust., Speech, Signal Process.* **ASSP-24**, 26–53.

Andrews, H. C., and Pratt, W. K. (1968). Television bandwidth reduction by encoding spatial frequencies. *J. SMPTE* **77**, 1279–1281.

Bacchi, H., and Moreau, A. (1978). Real time orthogonal transformation of colour television pictures. *Philo. Tech. Rev.* No. 4/5, pp. 119–130.

Barnett, S. (1979). "Matrix Methods for Engineers and Scientists." McGraw-Hill, New York.

Baronetti, G., Guglielmo, M., and Riolfo, B. (1979). A frozen picture transmission system employing orthogonal transformations. *Picture Coding Symp. Proc. Ipswich, Engl.* Pap. 3.3.

Beauchamp, K. G. (1984). "Applications of Walsh and Related Functions." Academic Press, London.

Beauchamp. K. G., and Yuen, C. K. (1979). "Digital Methods for Signal Analysis." Allen & Unwin, London.

Berger, T. (1971). "Rate Distortion Theory." Prentice-Hall, Englewood Cliffs, New Jersey.

Berger, T. (1972). Optimum quantisers and permutation codes. *IEEE Trans. Inf. Theory* **IT-18**, 759–765.

Bisherurwa, E., and Coakley, F. (1981). New fast discrete sine transform with offset. *Electron. Lett.* **17**, 803–805.

Bisherurwa, E., and Coakley, F. (1982). Improvements in the quality of pictures reproduced from a few low sequency DCT and DST coefficients. *Proc. Int. Conf. Electron. Image Process. York, Engl.* p. 230. (IEE Conf. Publ. No. 214).

Blachman, N. M. (1974). Sinusoids versus Walsh functions, *IEEE Proc.* **62**, 346–354.

Blahut, R. (1972). Computation of channel capacity and rate-distortion functions. *IEEE Trans. Inf. Theory* **IT-18**, 460–473.

Bluestein, L. (1970). A linear filtering approach to the computation of the Discrete Fourier transform. *IEEE Trans. Audio Electroacoust.* **AU-18**, 451–455.

Booton, R., and Ready, P. (1976). Inadequacies of the Markov model in linear predictive coding of images. *SPIE Semin. Proc.* **87**, 204–210.

Bourbakis, N. G., and Alexandridis, N. A. (1982). An efficient, real time method for transmitting Walsh–Hadamard transformed pictures. *ICASSP Proc.* pp. 452–455.

Bowyer, D. (1971). Walsh functions, Hadamard matrices and data compression. *Proc. Symp. Appl. Walsh Funct., Washington, D.C.*, AD 727000, pp. 33–37.

Braccini, C., Gambardella, G., and Sandini, G. (1981). A signal theory approach to the space and frequency variant filtering performed by the human visual system. *Signal Process.* **3**, 231–240.

Brigham, E. O. (1974). "The Fast Fourier Transform." Prentice-Hall, Englewood Cliffs, New Jersey.

Brofferio, S., and Rocca, F. (1977). Interframe redundancy reduction of video signals generated by translating objects. *IEEE Trans. Commun.* **COM-25**, 448–455.

Bucklew, J. A. and Gallagher, N., Jr. (1979). Quantisation schemes for bivariate Gaussian random variables. *IEEE Trans. Inf. Theory* **IT-25**, 537–543.

Budrikis, Z. L. (1972). Visual fidelity criterion and modelling. *IEEE Proc.* **60**, 771–779.

Burrus, C. S. (1981), A new prime factor Fast Fourier transform algorithm. *ICASSP Proc.* pp. 335–338.

Buss, D., Broderson, R., Hewes, C., and Tasch, A., Jr. (1975). The technology of charge-coupled devices for video bandwidth reduction. *SPIE Semin. Proc.* **66**, 48–56.

Cafforio, C., and Rocca, F. (1976). Methods for measuring small displacements of television images. *IEEE Trans. Inf. Theory* **IT-22**, 573–579.

Campanella, S., and Robinson, G. (1971). Comparison of orthogonal transforms for digital speech processing. *IEEE Trans. Commun.* **COM-19**, 1045–1049.

Campbell, F. W., and Robson, J. G. (1968). Application of Fourier analysis to the visibility of gratings. *J. Physiol. (London)* **197**, 551–556.

Carl, J., and Swartwood, R. (1973). A hybrid Walsh transform computer. *IEEE Trans. Comput.* **C-22**, 669–672.

Carlson, C. R., and Cohen, R. W. (1980). A simple psychophysical model for predicting the visibility of displayed information. *SID Proc.* **21/3**, 229–246.

Cavonius, C., and Estevez, O. (1980). Applications of signal processing methods in visual psychophysics. *In* "Signal Processing Theories and Applications" (M. Kunt and F. de Coulon, eds.), pp. 343–349. North-Holland Publ., Amsterdam.

Cham, W. K., and Clarke, R. J. (1983). Simple high efficiency transforms for image coding. *Proc. Int. Picture Coding Symp. Davis, Calif.* 66–67.

Chan, L. C., and Whiteman, P. (1983). Hardware-constrained hybrid coding of video imagery. *IEEE Trans. Aerosp. Electron. Syst.* **AES-19**, 71–83.

Chatfield, C. (1980). "The Analysis of Time Series: An Introduction," 2nd Ed. Chapman & Hall, London.

Cheek, T., Eversole, W., Barton, J., and Bush, D. (1978). Digital CCD memories for signal processing applications. *SPIE Semin. Proc.* **154**, 120–126.

Chen, W., and Pratt, W. K. (1984). Scene adaptive coder, *IEEE Trans. Commun.* **COM-32**, 225–232.

Chen, W., and Smith, C. (1976). Adaptive coding of colour images using the cosine transform, *Int. Commun. Conf. Proc.* pp. 47-7–47-13.

Chen, W., and Smith, C. (1977). Adaptive coding of monchrome and colour images. *IEEE Trans. Commun.* **COM-25**, 1285–1292.

Chen, W., Smith, C., and Fralick, S. (1977). A fast computational algorithm for the discrete cosine transform. *IEEE Trans. Commun.* **COM-25**, 1004–1009.

Claire, E., Farber, S., and Green, R. (1971). Practical techniques for transform data compression/coding. *Proc. Symp. Appl. Walsh Funct., Washington, D.C.* AD 727000, pp. 2–6.

Clarke C. K. P. (1976). Hadamard transformation: assessment of bit-rate reduction methods. BBC Res. Rep. 1976/28.

Clarke, R. J. (1981a). On the relation between the Karhunen–Loève and Cosine transforms. *IEE Proc. Part F: Commun. Radar Signal Process.* **128**, 359–360.

Clarke, R. J. (1981b). – Unpublished memorandum.

Clarke, R. J. (1983a). Application of the sine transform in image processing. *Electron. Lett.* **19**, 490–491.

Clarke, R. J. (1983b). Spectral response of the discrete cosine and Walsh–Hadamard transforms. *IEE Proc., Part F: Commun., Radar Signal Process.* **130**, 309–313.

Clarke, R. J. (1983c). Performance of the Karhunen–Loève and discrete cosine transforms for data having widely varying values of intersample correlation coefficient. *Electron Lett.* **19**, 251–253.

Clarke, R. J. (1984a). The application of image covariance models to transform coding. *Int. J. Electron.* **56**, 245–260.

Clarke, R. J. (1984b). Hybrid intraframe transform coding of image data. *IEE Proc., Part F: Commun. Radar Signal Process.* **131**, 2–6.

Clarke, R. J. (1985). On the dynamic range of coefficients generated in the transform processing of digitised data. *Proc. IEE Part F: Commun. Radar Signal Process.* **132**, 107–110.

Cooley, J. W., and Tukey, J. W. (1965). An algorithm for the machine calculation of complex Fourier series. *Math. Comput.* **19**, 297–301.

Cooley, J. W., Lewis, P. A. W., and Welch, P. D. (1967). Historical notes on the fast Fourier transform. *IEEE Trans. Audio. Electroacoust.* **AU-15**, 76–79.

Cornsweet, T. N. (1970). "Visual Perception." Academic Press, New York.

Courant, R., and Hilbert, D. (1953). "Methods of Mathematical Physics." Wiley (Interscience), New York.

Cox, R., and Tescher, A. (1976). Channel rate equalisation techniques for adaptive transform coders. *SPIE Semin. Proc.* **87**, 239–246.

Daut, D. G. (1978). Rate distortion function for a two-dimensional image model. Report, Rensselaer Polytech. Inst., Troy, New York (Unpublished).

Davidson, M. (1968). Perturbation approach to spatial brightness interaction in human vision. *J. Opt. Soc. Am.* **58**, 1300–1308.

Davisson, L. (1972). Rate distortion theory and application. *IEEE Proc.* **60**, 800–808.

Dennis, T. J., Hackett, A. D., and Pearson, D. E. (1979). Chrominance masking in temporal colour transitions. *Pict. Coding Symp. Proc. Ipswich, Engl.* Pap. 2.4.

Devereux, V. G. (1975). Digital video: sub-Nyquist sampling of PAL colour signals. BBC Res. Rep. 1975/4.

Dutta, K., and Millman, M. (1980). Dynamic simulation of hybrid video compression. *SPIE Semin. Proc.* **249**, 21–27.

Elias, P. (1951). A note on autocorrelation and entropy. *Proc. (IRE)* **39**, 839.

Elias, P. (1970). Bounds on the performance of optimum quantisers. *IEEE Trans. Inf. Theory* **IT-16**, 172–184.

Elliott, D. F., and Rao, K. R. (1983). "Fast Transforms: Algorithms, Analyses, and applications." Academic Press, New York.

Enomoto, H., and Shibata, K. (1971). Orthogonal transform coding system for television signals. *Proc. Symp. Appl. Walsh Funct., Washington, D.C.* AD 727000, pp. 11–17.

Ericsson, S. (1983). Fixed and adaptive predictors for hybrid predictive transform coding. Tech. Rep. TRITA-TTT-8305, *R.* Inst. Technol., Stockholm.

Essman, J., Hua, Q., and Griswold, N. (1976). Video link data compression for remote sensors. *SPIE Semin. Proc.* **87**, 55–77.

Estevez, O., and Tweel, L. v. d. (1980). Signal processing in vision. *In* "Signal Processing Theories and Applications" (M. Kunt and F. de Coulon, eds.), pp. 335–341. North-Holland Publ., Amsterdam.

Faugeras, O. D. (1979). Digital colour image processing within the framework of a human visual model. *IEEE Trans. Acoust., Speech, Signal Process.* **ASSP-27**, 380–393.

Fenwick, D. M., and Steele, R. (1977). Predictable sample error detector and a planar prediction corrector for removal of isolated transmission errors in Walsh–Hadamard transformed pictures, *Electron Lett.* **13**, 8–10.

Fenwick, D. M., Steele, R., and Vasanji, N. (1978). Partial correction of DPCM video signals using a Walsh corrector, *Radio Electron. Eng.* **48**, 271–276.

Fino, B. (1972). Relations between the Haar and Walsh–Hadamard transforms. *IEEE Proc.* **60**, 647–648.

Fino, B., and Algazi, V. R. (1974). Slant–Haar transform. *IEEE Proc.* **62**, 653–654.

Fino, B., and Algazi, V. R. (1975). Computation of transform domain covariance matrices. *IEEE Proc.* **61**, 1628–1629.

Fino, B., and Algazi, V. B. (1977). A unified treatment of discrete fast unitary transforms. *SIAM J. Comput.* **6**, 700–717.

Fox, B., (1966), Discrete optimisation via. marginal analysis. *Manage. Sci.* **13**, 210–216.

Frei, W. (1976). Rate-distortion coding simulation for colour images. *SPIE Semin. Proc.* **87**, 197–203.

Frei, W., and Baxter, B. (1977). Rate-distortion coding simulation for colour images. *IEEE Trans. Commun.* **COM-25**, 1385–1392.

Fukinuki, T., and Miyata, M. (1973). Intraframe image coding by cascaded Hadamard transforms. *IEEE Trans. Commun.* **COM-21**, 175–180.

Fukunaga, K. (1972). "Introduction to Statistical Pattern Recognition." Academic Press, New York.

Gabrielli, C., Keddam, M., and Raillon, L. (1979). Random signals: third order correlation measurement. *J. Phys. E* **12**, 632–636.

Gagalowitz, A. (1980). Visual discrimination of stochastic colour texture fields. *In* "Signal Processing Theories and Applications" (M. Kunt and F. de Coulon, eds.), pp. 335–341. North-Holland Publ. Amsterdam.

Gallager, R. G. (1968). "Information Theory and Reliable Communication." Wiley, New York.

Gallagher, N., Jr. (1978). Quantising schemes for the DFT of a random time series. *IEEE Trans. Inf. Theory* **IT-24**, 156–163.

Garguir, N. (1979). Comparative performance of SVD and adaptive DCT in coding images. *IEEE Trans. Commun.* **COM-27**, 1230–1234.

Garibotto, G., and Micca, G. (1981). Image processing through a two-component model. *Signal Process.* **3**, 241–246.

Gerrish, A. M., and Schultheiss, P. M. (1964). Information rates of non-Gaussian processes. *IEEE Trans. Inf. Theory* **IT-10**, 265–271.

Ghanbari, M. (1979). Real time transform coding of broadcast standard television pictures. Ph.D Thesis, Univ. of Essex.

Ghanbari, M., and Pearson, D. (1978). Probability density functions for Hadamard coefficients in transformed television pictures. *Electron. Lett.* **14**, 252–254.

Ghanbari, M., and Pearson, D. (1982). Fast cosine transform implementation for television signals. *IEE Proc., Part F: Commun., Radar Signal Process.* **129**, 59–68.

Gimlett, J. (1975). Use of activity classes in adaptive transform coding. *IEEE Trans. Commun.* **COM-23**, 785.

Girod, B. (1981). Objective quality measures for the design of digital image transmission systems. *ICASSP Proc.* pp 1132–1135.

Gish, H., and Pierce, J. (1968). Asymptotically efficient quantising. *IEEE Trans. Inf. Theory* **IT-14**, 676–683.

Goblick, T., and Holsinger, J. (1967). Analog source digitisation—a comparison of theory and practice. *IEEE Trans. Inf. Theory* **IT-13**, 323–326.

Götze, M. (1979). Channel encoding of transform coded pictorial data, *Picture Coding Symp. Proc., Ipswich, Engl.* Pap. 11.5.

Götze, M., and Ocylok, G, (1982). An adaptive interframe transform coding system for images. *ICASSP Proc.* pp. 448–451.

Golub, G. H., and Reinsch, C. (1970). Singular value decomposition and least squares solutions. *Numer. Math.* **14**, 403–420.

Gonsalves, R. A., and Johnson, G. (1980). Image compression with approximate transform implementation. *SPIE Semin. Proc.* **249**, 138–145.

Gonsalves, R. A., and Shea, A. (1979). Bounded error coding of cosine transformed images. *SPIE Semin. Proc.* **207**, 291–298.

Gonsalves, R. A., Shea, A., and Evans, N. (1978). Fixed error encoding for bandwidth compression. *SPIE Semin. Proc.* **149**, 27–42.

Good, I. J. (1958). The interaction algorithm and practical Fourier analysis. *J. R. Stat. Soc., Ser. B* **20**, 361–372.

Good, I. J. (1960). The interaction algorithm and practical Fourier analysis: addendum. *J. R. Stat. Soc., Ser. B* **22**, 372–375.

Good, I. J. (1971). The relationship between two fast Fourier transforms. *IEEE Trans. Comput.* **C-20**, 310–317.

Goodman, L. (1967). A binary linear transformation for redundancy reduction. *IEEE Proc.* **55**, 467–468.

Gray, R. (1972). On the asymptotic eigenvalue distribution of Toeplitz matrices. *IEEE Trans. Inf. Theory* **IT-18**, 725–730.

Gray, R., and Davisson, L. (1975). Quantiser mismatch. *IEEE Trans. Commun.* **COM-23**, 439–443.

Gray, R., and Gray, A. (1977). Asymptotically optimal quantisers. *IEEE Trans. Inf. Theory* **IT-23**, 143–144.

Griswold, N. (1980). Perceptual coding in the Cosine transform domain. *Opt. Eng.* **19**, 306–311.

Griswold, N., and Haralick, R. (1976). A critical comparison of fast transforms for image data compression. *SPIE Semin. Proc.* **87**, 180–188.

Groginsky, H., and Works, G. (1970). A pipeline Fast Fourier Transform. *IEEE Trans. Comput.* **C-19**, 1015–1019.

Guglielmo, M., Marion, R., and Sciarappa, A. (1982). Subjective quality evaluation of different intraframe adaptive coding schemes based on orthogonal transformations. *ICASSP Proc.* pp. 467–470.

Haar, A. (1910). Zur theorie der orthogonalen funktionensysteme. *Math. Ann.* **69**, 331–371; **71**, 38–53 (1912).

Habibi, A. (1971). Comparison of n-th order DPCM with linear transformations and block quantisation techniques. *IEEE Trans. Commun.* **COM-19**, 948–956.

Habibi, A. (1974). Hybrid coding of pictorial data. *IEEE Trans. Commun.* **COM-22**, 614–624.

Habibi, A. (1977). Survey of adaptive image coding techniques. *IEEE Trans. Commun.* **COM-25**, 1275–1284.

Habibi, A. (1979). Adaptive hybrid coding of images. *SPIE Semin. Proc.* **207**, 233–239.

Habibi, A. (1981). An adaptive strategy for hybrid image coding. *IEEE Trans. Commun.* **COM-29**, 1736–1740.

Habibi, A., and Herschel, R. (1974). A unified representation of DPCM and transform coding systems. *IEEE Trans. Commun.* **COM-22**, 692–696.

Habibi, A., and Hung, A. Y. (1977). Classification consistency of bandwidth compressed multispectral scanned images using a Bayes supervised classifier. *SPIE Semin. Proc.* **119**, 79–84.

Habibi, A., and Samulon, A. (1975). Bandwidth compression of multispectral data. *SPIE Semin. Proc.* **66**, 23-35.

Habibi, A., and Wintz, P. (1971). Image coding by linear transformation and block quantisation. *IEEE Trans. Commun.* **COM-19**, 50–62.

Hall, C. F. (1980). Perceptual coding in the Fourier transform domain. *Nat. Telecommun. Conf. Proc.* pp. 36.1.1–36.1.7.

Hall, C. F., and Andrews, H. C. (1978). Digital colour image compression in a perceptual space. *SPIE Semin. Proc.* **149**, 182-188.

Hall, C. F., and Hall, E. L. (1977). A non-linear model for the spatial characteristics of the human visual system. *IEEE Trans.* **SMC-7**, 161–170.

Hall, E. L. (1979). "Computer Image Processing and Recognition." Academic Press, New York.

Hamidi, M., and Pearl, J., (1976). Comparison of the cosine and Fourier transforms of Markov I signals. *IEEE Trans. Acoust., Speech, Signal Process.* **ASSP-24**, 428–429.

Haralick, R. (1976). A storage efficient way to implement the discrete cosine transform. *IEEE Trans. Comput.* **C-25**, 764–765.

Haralick, R., and Shanmugam, K. (1974). Comparative study of a discrete linear basis for image data compression. *IEEE Trans.* **SMC-4**, 16–27.

Harlick, R., Griswold, N., and Kattiyakulwanich, N. (1975). A fast two-dimensional Karhunen–Loève Transform. *SPIE Semin. Proc.* **66**, 144–159.

Harmuth, H. F. (1977). "Sequency Theory: Foundations and Applications." Academic Press, New York.

Harris, F. (1978). On the use of windows for harmonic analysis with the discrete Fourier transform. *IEEE Proc.* **66**, 51–83.

Haskell, B. (1974). Frame to frame coding of television pictures using two-dimensional Fourier transforms. *IEEE Trans. Inf. Theory* **IT-20**, 119–120.

Hayes, J., Habibi, A., and Wintz, P. (1970). The rate-distortion function for a Gaussian source model of images. *IEEE Trans. Inf. Theory* **IT-16**, 507–509.

Hein, D., and Ahmed, N. (1978). On a real time Walsh Hadamard/Discrete cosine transform image processor. *IEEE Trans. Electromagn. Compat.* **EMC-20**, 453–457.

Hein, D., and Jones, H. (1979). Conditional replenishment using motion prediction. *SPIE Semin. Proc.* **207**, 268–277.

Hotelling, H. (1933). Analysis of a complex of statistical variables into principal components. *J. Educ. Psychol.* **24**, 417–441, 498–520.

Hsu, Y., and Savant, C. (1976). Adaptive quantisation and coding in the RM2 transform. *In* "Image Science Mathematics" (C. O. Wilde and E. Barrett, eds.), pp. 193–197. Western Period. North Hollywood, California.

Huang, J. J. Y., and Schultheiss, P. M. (1963). Block quantisation of correlated Gaussian random variables. *IEEE Trans. Commun.* **COM-11**, 289–296.

Huang, T. S., Hsu, Y. P., and Tsai, R. Y. (1982). Interframe coding with general two-dimensional motion compensation. *ICASSP Proc.* pp. 464–466.

Huffman, D. A. (1952). A method for the construction of minimum redundancy codes. *Proc. IRE* **40**, 1098–1101.

Hunt, B. (1980). Non-stationary statistical image models and application to image data compression. *Comput. Graphics Image Process.* **12**, 173–186.

Hunt, B., and Cannon, T. (1976). Non-stationary assumptions for Gaussian models of images. *IEEE Trans.* **SMC-6**, 876–882.

Jack, M. A., Grant, P. M., and Collins, J. H. (1980). The theory, design and applications of surface acoustic wave Fourier-transform processors, *IEEE Proc.* **68**, 450–468.

Jain, A. (1976a). A fast KLT for a class of random processes. *IEEE Trans. Commun.* **COM-24**, 1023–1029.

Jain, A. (1976b). Some new techniques in image processing. *In* "Image Science Mathematics" (C. O. Wilde and E. Barrett, eds.), pp. 201–223. Western Period., North Hollywood, California.

Jain, A. (1977). Partial differential equations and finite difference methods in image processing: Part 1, Image representation. *J. Opt. Theor. Appl.* **23**, 65–91.

Jain, A. (1979). A sinusoidal family of unitary transforms. *IEEE Trans.* **PAMI-1**, 356–365.

Jain, A. (1981). Image data compression: a review. *IEEE Proc.* **69**, 349–389.

Jain, J. R., and Jain, A. (1979). Optimisation of transform coding for transmission of images over noisy channels. *Picture Coding Symp. Proc. Ipswich, Engl.* Pap. 12.4.

Jain, J. R., and Jain, A. (1981). Displacement measurement and its application in interframe image coding. *IEEE Trans. Commun.* **COM-29**, 1799–1808.

Jain, P., and Delogne, P. (1981). Real time Hadamard transform coding for television signals. *IEEE Trans. Electromagn. Compat.* **EMC-23**, 103–107.

Jalali, A., and Rao, K. R. (1982). A high-speed FDCT Processor for real time processing of the NTSC colour TV signal. *IEEE Trans. Electromagn. Compat.* **EMC-24**, 278–286.

Jelinek, F. (1967). "Probabilistic Information Theory." McGraw-Hill, New York.

Jenkins, G. M., and Watts, D. G. (1968). "Spectral Analysis and its Applications." Holden-Day, San Francisco, California.

Jones, H. (1976). A real time adaptive Hadamard transform video compressor. *SPIE Semin, Proc.* **87**, 2–9.

Jones, H. (1977). A conditional replenishment Hadamard video processor. *SPIE Semin. Proc.* **119**, 91–98.

Jones, H. (1979). A comparison of theoretical and experimental video compression designs. *IEEE Trans. Electromagn. Compat.* **EMC-21**, 50–56.

Jones, H., and Hofman, L. (1978). Comparison of video fields and frames for transform compression. *SPIE Semin. Proc.* **149**, 214–221.

Jones, R. (1976). Adaptive hybrid picture coding. *SPIE Semin. Proc.* **87**, 247–255.

Jones, R., and Mix, D. (1978). A rate-distortion analysis of adaptive hybrid picture coding. *SPIE Semin. Proc.* **149**, 10–17.

Kac, M., Murdock, W., and Szego, G. (1953). On the eigenvalues of certain Hermitian forms. *J. Rational Mech. Anal.* **2**, 767–800.

Kahaner, D. K. (1970). Matrix description of the fast Fourier transform. *IEEE Trans. Audio Electroacoust.* **AU-18**, 442–450.

Kamangar, F., and Rao, K. R. (1980). Adaptive coding of NTSC component video signals. *Nat. Telecommun. Conf. Proc.* pp. 36.4.1–36.4.6.

Kamangar, F., and Rao, K. R. (1981). Interfield hybrid coding of component colour television signals. *IEEE Trans. Commun.* **COM-29**, 1740–1753.

Kamangar, F., and Rao, K. R. (1982). Fast algorithms for the two-dimensional discrete cosine transform. *IEEE Trans. Comput.* **C-31**, 899–906.

Kanefsky, M., and Thomas, J. B. (1965). On polarity detection schemes with non-Gaussian inputs. *J. Franklin Inst.* **280**, 120–138.

Kapur, N., Mavor, J., and Jack, M. A. (1980). Discrete cosine transform processor using a CCD programmable transversal filter. *Electron. Lett.* **16**, 139–141.

Kay, S. M., and Marple, S. L., Jr. (1981). Spectrum Analysis—a modern perspective. *IEEE Proc,* **69**, 1380–1419.

Kekre, H. B., and Aleem, S. A. (1983). Adaptive linear quantisation and reconstruction scheme in the discrete cosine transform domain. *Int. J. Electron.* **54**, 31–45.

Kelly, D. H. (1975). Spatial frequency selectivity in the retina. *Vision Res.* **15**, 665–672.

Keyes, R. W. (1981). Fundamental limits in digital information processing. *IEEE Proc.* **69**, 267–278.

Kim, E. S., and Rao, K. R. (1979). Walsh–Hadamard/DPCM processing of intraframe colour video. *SPIE Semin. Proc.* **207**, 240–246.

Kim, N. C., and Kim, J. K. (1983). Behaviour of a generalised covariance model in image coding. *Electron. Lett.* **19**, 260–261.

Kitai, R., and Siemens, K. (1979). Discrete Fourier transform via the Walsh transform. *IEEE Trans. Acoust., Speech, Signal Process.* **ASSP-27**, 288.

Kitajima, H. (1980). A symmetric cosine transform. *IEEE Trans. Comput.* **C-29**, 317–323.

Kitajima, H., and Shimono, T. (1980). Some aspects of the fast Karhunen–Loève transform. *IEEE Trans. Commun.* **COM-28**, 1773–1776.

Klema, V., and Laub, A. (1980). The singular value decomposition, its computation and some applications. *IEEE Trans. Autom. Control* **AC-25**, 164–176.

Knab, J. (1977). Effects of round-off noise on Hadamard transformed imagery. *IEEE Trans. Commun.* **COM-25**, 1292–1294.

Knauer, S. C. (1976). Real time video compression algorithm for Hadamard transform processing. *IEEE Trans. Electromagn. Compat.* **EMC-18**, 28–36.

Kolmogorov, A. (1956). On the Shannon theory of information transmission in the case of continuous signals. *IRE Trans. Inf. Theory* **IT-2**, 102–108.

Kretz, F. (1975). Subjectively optimal quantisation of pictures. *IEEE Trans. Commun.* **COM-23**, 1288–1292.

Kung, H. T. (1980). The structure of parallel algorithms. *Adv. Comput.* **19**, 65–112.

Kurtenbach, A., and Wintz, P. (1969). Quantising for noisy channels. *IEEE Trans. Commun.* **COM-17**, 291–302.

Kwak, H. S., Srinivasan, R., and Rao, K. R. (1983). C-Matrix transform *IEEE Trans. Acoust., Speech, Signal Process.* **ASSP**, 1304–1307.

Lanfer, H. (1978). Quantisierungsvorshrift für maximales signal/rausch verhältnis bei signalen mit Laplace-verteilten amplitudendichten. *NTG–Fachber.* **65**, 48–52.

Limb, J. (1967). Source–receiver encoding of television signals. *IEEE Proc.* **55**, 364–379.

Limb, J. (1968). Entropy of quantised television signals. *IEE Proc.* **115**, 16–20.

Limb, J. (1976). Visual perception applied to the encoding of pictures. *SPIE Semin. Proc.* **87**, 80–87.

Limb, J. (1978). On the design of quantisers for DPCM coders—a functional relationship between visibility, probability and masking. *IEEE Trans. Commun.* **COM-26**, 573–578.

Limb, J. (1979). Distortion criteria of the human viewer. *IEEE Trans.* **SMC-9**, 778–793.

Limb, J., and Murphy, J. A. (1975). Estimating the velocity of moving images from television signals. *Comput. Graphics Image Process.* **4**, 311–327.

Limb, J., Rubinstein, C., and Thompson, J. (1977). Digital coding of colour signals—a review. *IEEE Trans. Comput.* **C-25**, 1349–1385.

Lindsay, P. H., and Norman, D. A. (1977). "Human Information Processing." Academic Press, New York.

Lloyd, R. O., Baker, K. D., and Sullivan, G. D. (1982). Image transform modelled on visual processing mechanisms of the brain. *Proc. Int. Conf. Electron. Image Process. York, Engl.* pp. 31–37.

Lukas, F., and Budrikis, Z. L. (1982). Picture quality prediction based on a visual model. *IEEE Trans. Commun.* **COM-30**, 1679–1692.

Lynn, P. A. (1982). "An Introduction to the Analysis and Processing of Signals," 2nd Ed. Macmillan, New York.

McCanny, J. V., and McWhirter, J. G. (1982). Implementation of signal processing functions using 1-bit systolic arrays. *Electron. Lett.* **18**, 241–243.

McWhirter, J., Roberts, J., Simons, R., and Watson, D. (1981). A compact low power coder for extreme bit rate reduction of television pictures. *Proc. IERE Conf. Digital Process. Signals Commun., Loughborough Univ. Technol.* pp. 435–457.

Makhoul, J. (1980). A fast discrete cosine transform in one- and two-dimensions. *IEEE Trans. Acoust., Speech, Signal Process.* **ASSP-28**, 27–34.

Mannos, J. L., and Sakrison, D. J. (1974). The effects of a visual fidelity criterion on the encoding of images. *IEEE Trans. Inf. Theory* **IT-20**, 525–536.

Manz, J. (1972). A sequency ordered fast Walsh–Hadamard transform. *IEEE Trans. Audio Electroacoust.* **AU-20**, 204–205.

Mauersberger, W. (1979a). Experimental results on the performance of mismatched quantisers. *IEEE Trans. Inf. Theory* **IT-25**, 381–386.

Mauersberger, W. (1979b). An adaptive transform coding system based on two-dimensional classification. *Picture Coding Symp. Proc., Ipswich, Engl.* Pap. 12.1.

Mauersberger, W. (1979c). Generalised correlation model for designing two-dimensional image coders. *Electron. Lett.* **15**, 664–665.

Mauersberger, W. (1980). Comparing orthonormal matrices for two dimensional image coding by means of the gain-distortion function. *Signal Process.* **2**, 67–70.

Mauersberger, W. (1981). An analytic function describing the error performance of optimum quantisers. *IEEE Trans. Inf. Theory* **IT-27**, 519–521.

Max, J. (1960). Quantising for minimum distortion. *IEEE Trans. Inf. Theory* **IT-16**, 7–12.

May, F. (1980). Hybrid coding of picture sequences for transmission over narrowband mobile radio channels. *In* "Signal Processing Theories and Applications" (M. Kunt, and F. de Coulon, Eds.), pp. 283–288. North-Holland Publ., Amsterdam.

Means, R., Whitehouse, H., and Speiser, J. (1974). Television encoding using a Hybrid DCT and DPCM in real time. *Nat. Telecommun. Conf. Proc.* pp. 61-66.

Means, R., Whitehouse, H., and Speiser, J (1975). Real time television image redundancy reduction using transform techniques. *In* "New Directions in Signal Processing in Communications and Control" (J. Skwirzynski, ed.), pp. 83-98. Noordhoff, Leiden.

Melzer, S. (1978). An image transform coding algorithm based on a generalised correlation model. *SPIE Semin. Proc.* **149**, 205-213.

Mersereau, R., and Speake, T. (1981). A unified treatment of Cooley-Tukey algorithms for the evaluation of the multidimensional DFT. *IEEE Trans. Acoust., Speech, Signal Process.* **ASSP-29**, 1011-1018.

Miller, J. H., and Thomas, J. B. (1972). Detectors for discrete-time signals in non-Gaussian noise. *IEEE Trans. Inf. Theory* **IT-18**, 241-250.

Mitchell, O., and Tabatabai, A. (1981). Channel error recovery for transform image coding. *IEEE Trans. Commun.* **COM-29**, 1754-1762.

Mitrakos, D. K., and Constantinides, A. G. (1983). Non-linear image processing for optimum composite source coding. *IEE Proc., Part F: Commun., Radar Signal Process.* **130**, 441-451.

Modestino, J., and Daut, D. (1980). Block transform image coding in the presence of channel errors. *SPIE Semin. Proc.* **249**, 112-122.

Modestino, J., Daut, D., and Vickers, A. (1980). Combined source-channel coding of images using the block cosine transform. *Nat. Telecommun. Conf. Proc.* pp. 50.4.1-50.4.7.

Modestino, J., Daut, D., and Vickers, A. (1981). Combined source-channel coding of images using the block cosine transform. *IEEE Trans. Commun.* **COM-29**, 1261-1274.

Moharir, P., and Varma, S. (1981). A new class of orthonormal transforms. *IEEE Trans. Acoust., Speech, Signal Process.* **ASSP-29**, 452-454.

Mounts, F. W., Netravali, A., and Prasada, B. (1977). Design of quantisers for real-time Hadamard transform coding of pictures. *Bell Syst. Tech. J.* **56**, 21-48.

Murphy, M. S. (1981). Comparison of transform image coding techniques for compression of tactical imagery. *SPIE Semin. Proc.* **309**, 212-219.

Murray, G. G. (1977). Microprocessor system for television imagery compression. *SPIE Semin. Proc.* **119**, 121-129.

Musmann, H. (1979). Predictive image coding. *In* "Image Transmission Techniques" (W. K. Pratt, ed.), pp. 73-112. Academic Press, New York.

Narasimhan, M., and Peterson, A. (1978). On the computation of the discrete cosine transform. *IEEE Trans. Commun.* **COM-26**, 934-936.

Narasimhan, M., Rao, K. R., and Raghava, V. (1977). Image data processing by hybrid sampling. *SPIE Semin. Proc.* **119**, 130-136.

Nasrabadi, N., and King, R. (1983). Computationally efficient discrete cosine transform algorithm. *Electron. Lett.* **19**, 24-25.

Natarajan, T., and Ahmed, N. (1978). On interframe transform coding *IEEE Trans. Commun.* **COM-25**, 1323-1329.

Natarajan, T., and Ahmed, N. (1978). Performance evaluation for transform coding using a non-separable covariance model. *IEEE Trans. Commun.* **COM-26**, 310-312.

Netravali, A. (1977). On quantisers for DPCM coding of picture signals. *IEEE Trans. Inf. Theory* **IT-23**, 360-370.

Netravali, A., and Limb, J. (1980). Picture coding—a review. *IEEE Proc.* **68**, 366-406.

Netravali, A., and Prasada, B. (1977). Adaptive quantisation of picture signals using spatial masking. *IEEE Proc.* **65**, 536-548.

Netravali, A., and Rubinstein, C. (1977). Quantisation of colour signals. *IEEE Proc.* **65**, 1177-1187.

Netravali, A., and Saigal, R. (1976). Optimum quantiser design using a fixed point algorithm. *Bell Syst. Tech. J.* **55**, 1423-1435.

Netravali, A., and Stuller, J. (1979). Motion compensated transform coding. *Bell Syst. Tech. J.* **58**, 1703–1718.

Netravali, A., Prasada, B., and Mounts, F. W. (1977). Some experiments in adaptive and predictive Hadamard transform coding of pictures. *Bell Syst. Tech. J.* **56**, 1531–1547.

Nicol, R. C., Fenn, B. A., and Turkington, R. D. (1981). Transmission techniques for picture Prestel. *Radio Electron. Eng.* **51**, 514–518.

Nicol, R. C., Fenn, B. A., Clarke, R. J., Ngan, K. N., and Cham, W. K. (1983). Method and apparatus for transmitting an image. Eur. Pat. Appl. No. 82303825.2; Publ. No. EP 0 072 117 A1.

Ninoyima, Y., and Prasada, B (1979). Some qualitative results on temporal masking in television pictures. *Picture Coding Symp. Proc. Ipswich, Engl.* Pap. 2.5.

Noble, S. (1975). A comparison of hardware implementations of the Hadamard transform for real time image coding. *SPIE Semin. Proc.* **66**, 207–211.

Noll, P., and Zelinski, R. (1978). Bounds on quantiser performance in the low bit-rate region. *IEEE Trans. Commun.* **COM-26**, 300–304.

Nussbaumer, H. (1980). Fast multidimensional discrete cosine transforms. *IBM Tech. Disclosure Bull.* **23**, 1976–1981.

Ohira, T., Hayakawa, M., and Matsumoto, K. (1973). Picture quality of Hadamard transform coding using nonlinear quantising for the colour television signal. *Proc. Symp. Appl. Walsh Funct., Washington, D.C.* AD 763000, pp. 127–131.

Ohira, T., Hayakawa, M., and Matsumoto, K. (1978). Orthogonal transform coding system for NTSC colour television signals. *IEEE Trans. Commun.* **COM-26**, 1454–1463.

O'Neal, J. B., Jr. (1966). Predictive quantising systems (Differential Pulse Code Modulation) for the transmission of television signals. *Bell Syst. Tech. J.* **45**, 689–721.

O'Neal, J. B., Jr., Natarajan, T. (1977). Coding isotropic images. *IEEE Trans. Inf. Theory* **IT-23**, 697–707.

Paez, M., and Glisson, T. (1972). Minimum mean square error criterion quantisation in speech PCM and DPCM systems. *IEEE Trans. Commun.* **COM-20**, 225–230.

Panter, P. F., and Dite, W. (1951). Quantisation distortion in pulse-count modulation with non-uniform spacing of levels. *Proc. IRE* **39**, 44–48.

Papoulis, A. (1965). "Probability, Random Variables, and Stochastic Processes." McGraw-Hill, New York.

Papoulis, A. (1977). "Signal Analysis." McGraw-Hill, New York.

Parsons, J., and Tescher, A. (1975). An investigation of m.s.e. contributions in transform image coding schemes. *SPIE Semin. Proc.* **66**, 196–206.

Pearl, J. (1971a). Basis restricted transformations and performance measures for spectral representations. *IEEE Trans. Inf. Theory* **IT-17**, 751–752.

Pearl, J., (1971b). Walsh processing of random signals. *Proc. Symp. Appl. Walsh Funct. Washington, D.C.* AD 727000, pp. 137–141.

Pearl, J. Andrews, H. C., and Pratt, W. K. (1972). Performance measures for transform data coding. *IEEE Trans. Commun.* **COM-20**, 411–415.

Pearlman, W. (1978). A visual system model and a new distortion measure in the context of image processing. *J. Opt. Soc. Am.* **68**, 374–386.

Pearlman, W., and Jakatdar, P. (1981). Hybrid DFT/DPCM interframe image quantisation. *ICASSP Proc.* pp. 1121–1124.

Pearson, D. (1967). A realistic model for visual communication systems. *IEEE Proc.* **55**, 380–389.

Pearson, D. (1975). "Transmission and Display of Pictorial Information." Pentech Press, London

Pettofrezzo, A. J., and Lacatena, M. M. (1970) "Analytic Geometry with Vectors." Scott, Foresman, Glenview, Illinois.

Pierce, J. R. (1962). "Symbols, Signals and Noise." Hutchinson, London and New York.

Pirsch, P., and Stenger, L. (1976). Statistical analysis and coding of colour video signals. *Acta Electron.* **19**, 277–287.

Ploysongsang, A., and Rao, K. R. (1982). DCT/DPCM processing of the NTSC composite video signal. *IEEE Trans. Commun.* **COM-30**, 541–549.

Pratt, W. K. (1971). Spatial transform coding of colour images. *IEEE Trans. Commun.* **COM-19**, 980–992.

Pratt, W. K. (1975). Vector space formulation of two-dimensional signal processing operations. *Comput. Graphics Image Process.* **4**, 1–24.

Pratt, W. K. (1978). "Digital Image Processing." Wiley (Interscience), New York.

Pratt, W. K., Kane, J., and Andrews, H. C. (1969). Hadamard transform image coding. *IEEE Proc.* **57**, 58–68.

Pratt, W. K., Welch, L., and Chen, W. (1972). Slant transforms for image coding. *Proc. Symp. Appl. Walsh Funct., Washington, D.C.* AD 744650, pp. 229–234.

Pratt, W. K., Chen, W., and Welch, L. (1974), Slant transform image coding. *IEEE Trans. Commun.* **COM-22**) 1075–1093.

Rabiner, L. R., and Schafer, R. W. (1969). The chirp z-transform algorithm, *IEEE Trans. Audio Electroacoust.* **AU-17**, 86–92.

Rademacher, H. (1922). Einige Sätze von allgemeinen Orthogonalfunktionen. *Math. Ann.* **87**, 122–138.

Rao, K. R., Narasimhan, M., and Revuluri, K. (1975). Image data processing by Hadamard/Haar transform. *IEEE Trans. Comput.* **C-24**, 888.

Ray, W., and Driver, R. M. (1970). Further decomposition of the K-L series representation of a stationary random process. *IEEE Trans. Inf. Theory* **IT-16**, 663–668.

Reader, C. (1975). Intraframe and interframe adaptive transform coding. *SPIE Semin. Proc.* **66**, 108–117.

Reis, J. J., Lynch, R., and Butman, J. (1976). Adaptive Haar transform video bandwidth reduction system for rpv's. *SPIE Semin. Proc.* **87**, 24–35.

Rice, R. (1975). An advanced imaging communication system for planetary exploration. *SPIE Semin. Proc.* **66**, 70–89.

Rickard, J. (1979) New fidelity criteria for discrete time source encoding. *IEEE Trans. Inf. Theory* **IT-25**, 275–282.

Roberts, J. B., Darlington, E. H., Edwards, R. D., and Simons, R. F. (1977). Transform coding using charge-coupled devices. *Electron. Lett.* **13**, 277–278.

Roe, G. M. (1964). Quantising for minimum distortion. *IEEE Trans.* **IT-10**, 384–385.

Roese, J. (1976). Interframe coding of digital images using transform and hybrid transform/predictive techniques. Tech. Rep. No. 700 (AD A035 083), Image Process. Inst., Univ. of Southern California, Los Angeles.

Roese, J. (1979). Hybrid transform-predictive image coding. *In* "Image Transmission Techniques" (W. K. Pratt, ed.), pp. 157–187. Academic Press, New York.

Roese, J., and Pratt, W. K. (1976). Theoretical performance models for interframe transform and hybrid transfrom/DPCM coders. *SPIE Semin. Proc.* **87**, 172–179.

Roese, J., and Robinson, G. (1975). Combined spatial and temporal coding of digital image sequences. *SPIE Semin. Proc.* **66**, 172–180.

Roese, J., Pratt, W. K., and Robinson, G. (1977). Interframe cosine transform image coding. *IEEE Trans. Commun.* **COM-25**, 1329–1339.

Rubinstein, C., and Limb, J. (1972). Statistical dependence between components of a differentially quantised colour signal. *IEEE Trans. Commun.* **COM-20**, 890–899.

Sachs, M. B., Nachmias, J., and Robson, J. (1971). Spatial frequency channels in human vision. *J. Opt. Soc. Am.* **61**, 1176–1186.

Sakrison, D. J. (1968). The rate-distortion function of a Gaussian process with a weighted square error criterion. *IEEE Trans. Inf. Theory* **IT-14**, 506–508; see also addendum, *IEEE Trans. Inf. Theory* **IT-15**, 610–611 (1969).

Sakrison, D. J. (1969). The rate-distortion function for a class of sources. *Inf. Control* **15**, 165–195.

Sakrison, D. J. (1970). The rate of a class of random processes. *IEEE Trans. Inf. Theory* **IT-16**, 10–16.

Sakrison, D. J. (1977). On the role of the observer and a distortion measure in image transmission. *IEEE Trans. Commun.* **COM-25**, 1251–1267.

Sakrison, D. J. (1979). Image coding applications of vision models. *In* "Image Transmission Techniques" (W. K. Pratt, ed.), pp. 21–71. Academic Press, New York.

Sakrison, D. J., and Algazi, V. R. (1971). Comparison of line by line and two-dimensional encoding of random images. *IEEE Trans. Inf. Theory* **IT-17**, 386–398.

Sakrison, D. J., Halter, M., and Mostafavi, H. (1975). Properties of the human visual system as related to the encoding of images. *In* "New Directions in Signal Processing in Communications and Control" (J. Skwirzynski, ed.), pp. 83–98. Noordhoff, Leiden.

Schaming, W. B., and Bessette, O. (1980). Empirical determination of processing parameters for a real-time two-dimensional DCT video bandwidth compression system. *SPIE Semin. Proc.* **249**, 78–84.

Schreiber, W. F. (1956). The measurement of third order probability distributions of television signals. *IRE Trans. Inf. Theory* **IT-2**, 94–105.

Schreiber, W. F. (1967). Picture coding. *IEEE Proc.* **55**, 320–330.

Segall, A. (1976). Bit allocation and coding for vector sources. *IEEE Trans. Inf. Theory* **IT-22**, 162–169.

Seyler, A. J. (1962). The coding of visual signals to reduce channel capacity requirements. *IEE Proc. Monogr. Ser.* No. 535E, pp. 676–684.

Seyler, A. J. (1963). Real time recording of television frame difference areas. *IEEE Proc.* **51**, 478–480.

Seyler, A. J. (1965). Statistics of television frame differences. *IEEE Proc.* **53**, 2127–2128.

Seyler, A. J., and Budrikis, Z. L. (1965). Detail perception after scene change in television image presentations. *IEEE Trans. Inf. Theory* **IT-11**, 31–43.

Shanmugam, K., and Haralick, R. (1973). A computationally simple procedure for imagery data compression by the Karhunen–Loève method. *IEEE Trans.* **SMC-3**, 202–204.

Shannon, C. (1948). The mathematical theory of communication. *Bell Syst. Tech. J.* **27**, 379–423, 623–656.

Shannon, C. (1959). Coding theorems for a discrete source with a fidelity criterion. *IRE Natl. Conv. Rec.* pp. 142–163.

Sharma, D. (1978). Design of absolutely optimal quantisers for a wide class of distortion measures. *IEEE Trans. Inf. Theory* **IT-24**, 693–702.

Sharma, D., and Netravali, A. (1977). Design of quantisers for DPCM of picture signals. *IEEE Trans. Commun.* **COM-25**, 1267–1274.

Shaw, V. M., and Westgate, C. R. (1980). A CCD image processor for Hadamard transform operations. *IEEE Proc.* **68**, 939–940.

Shore, J. (1973). On the application of Haar functions. *IEEE Trans. Commun.* **COM-21**, 209–216.

Silverman, H. (1977). An introduction to programming the WFTA (Winograd Fourier transform algorithm). *IEEE Trans. Acoust., Speech, Signal Process.* **ASSP-25**, 152–165.

Smith, B. (1957). Instantaneous companding of quantised signals. *Bell Syst. Tech. J.* **36**, 653–709.

Speake, T., and Mersereau, R. (1981). Evaluation of two-dimensional Fourier transforms via. generalised FFT algorithms. *ICASSP Proc.* pp. 1006–1009.

Spencer, D. (1979). Video data processor: a real time video data compressor. *SPIE Semin. Proc.* **207**, 284–290.

Srinivasan, R., and Rao, K. R. (1983). An approximation to the discrete cosine transform for $N = 16$. *Signal Process.* **5**, 81–85.

Stockham, T. (1972). Image processing in the context of a visual model. *IEEE Proc.* **60**, 828–842.

Strickland, R. N. (1983). Transforming images into block stationary behaviour. *Appl. Opt.* **22**, 1462–1473.

Stromeyer, C. F., and Julesz, B. (1972). Spatial frequency masking in vision: critical bands and spread of masking. *J. Opt. Soc. Am.* **62**, 1221–1232.

Stromeyer, C. F., and Klein, S. (1975). Evidence against narrow-band spatial frequency channels in human vision: the detectability of frequency modulated gratings. *Vision Res.* **15**, 899–910.

Stuller, J., M and Netravali, A. (1979). Transform domain motion estimation. *Bell Syst. Tech. J.* **58**, 1673–1702.

Szepanski, W. (1980). Δ entropy and R(D) bounds for generalised Gaussian information sources and their application to image signals. *Electron. Lett.* **16**, 109–111.

Tadokoro, Y., and Higuchi, T. (1978), Discrete Fourier transform computation via. the Walsh transform. *IEEE Trans. Acoust., Speech, Signal Process.* **ASSP-26**, 236–240.

Tadokoro, Y., and Higuchi, T. (1979). Comments on 'Discrete Fourier transform computation via. the Walsh transform.' *IEEE Trans. Acoust., Speech, Signal Process.* **ASSP-27**, 295–296.

Tadokoro, Y., and Higuchi, T. (1981). Another discrete Fourier transform computation with small multiplications via. the Walsh transform. *ICASSP Proc.* pp. 306–309.

Tasto, M., and Wintz, P. (1971). Image coding by adaptive block quantisation. *IEEE Trans. Commun.* **COM-19**, 957–972.

Tasto, M., and Wintz, P. (1972). A bound on the rate distortion function and application to images. *IEEE Trans. Inf. Theory* **IT-18**, 150–159.

Tenenbaum, J. M., Fischler, M. A., and Barrow, H. G. (1981). Scene modeling: A structural basis for image description. *In* "Image Modeling" (A. Rosenfeld, ed.), pp. 371–389. Academic Press, New York.

Tescher, A. (1979). Transform image coding. *In* "Image Transmission Techniques" (W. K. Pratt, ed.), pp. 113–155. Academic Press, New York.

Tescher, A. (1980). Adaptive transform coding of colour images at low rates. *Nat. Telecommun. Conf. Proc.* pp. 36.3.1.–36.3.4.

Tescher, A., and Cox, R. (1977). Image coding—variable rate DPCM through a fixed rate channel. *SPIE Semin. Proc.* **119**, 147–154.

Theilheimer, F. (1969). A matrix version of the fast Fourier transform. *IEEE Trans. Audio Electroacoust.* **AU-17**, 158–161.

Tseng, B., and Miller, W. (1978). On computing the discrete cosine transform. *IEEE Trans. Comput.* **C-27**, 966–968.

Turkington, R. D. (1983). Two-dimensional transform coding of colour television pictures using the discrete cosine transform. *IEE Colloq. Transform Tech. Image Process.* Dig No. 1983/50.

Walker, R. (1974). Hadamard transformation—a real time transformer for broadcast standard PCM television. BBC Res. Rep. 1974/7.

Walker, R., and Clarke, C. K. P. (1974). Walsh–Hadamard transformation of television pictures. BBC Res. Rep. 1974/13.

Walsh, J. L. (1923). A closed set of orthogonal functions. *Am. J. Math.* **45**, 5–24.

Wang, S. H., and Jain, A. (1979). Applications of stochastic models for image data compression. Res. Rep. Dep. Electr. Eng., Univ. of California, Davis.

Ward, J. S., and Stanier, B. J. (1983). Fast discrete cosine transform algorithm for systolic arrays. *Electron. Lett.* **19**, 58–60.

Wells, S. C. (1983). Motion estimation algorithms and their application to adaptive hybrid coding. Tech. Rep., Digital Syst. Lab., Dep. Elect. Electron. Eng., Heriot-Watt Univ., Edinburgh, Scotland.

Westheimer, G., and Campbell, F. W. (1962). Light distribution in the image formed by the living human eye. *J. Opt. Soc. Am.* **52**, 1040–1045.

Whitehouse, H., Means, R., and Wrench, E. (1975). Real time television image bandwidth reduction using charge transfer devices. *SPIE Semin. Proc.* **66**, 36–47.

Whitehouse, H., Wrench, E., Weber, A., Claffie, G., Richards, J., Rudnick, J., Schaming, W., and Schanne, J. (1977). A digital real time intraframe video bandwidth compression system. *SPIE Semin. Proc.* **119**, 64–78.

Whiteman, P., Beckwith, F., Couey, F., Bistarkey, D., and Chan, L. (1981). Hardware systems design of an airborne video bandwidth compressor. *SPIE Semin. Proc.* **309**, 93–103.

Winograd, S. (1978). On computing the discrete Fourier transform. *Math. Comput.* **32**, 175–199.

Wintz, P. (1972). Transform picture coding. *IEEE Proc.* **60**, 809–820.

Wintz, P., and Kurtenbach, A. (1968). Waveform error control in PCM telemetry. *IEEE Trans. Inf. Theory* **IT-14**, 650–661.

Wong, W. (1980). Adaptive transform coding of viewphone signals. Ph.D. Thesis, Loughborough Univ. of Technol.

Wong, W., and Steele, R. (1978). Partial correction of transmission errors in Walsh–Hadamard image coding without recourse to error correction coding. *Electron. Lett.* **14**, 298–300.

Wong, W., and Steele, R. (1981). Adaptive discrete cosine transformation of pictures using an energy distribution logarithmic model. *Radio Electron. Eng.* **51**, 571–578.

Wood, R. C. (1969). On optimum quantisation. *IEEE Trans. Inf. Theory* **IT-15**, 248–252.

Wrench, E., Jr. (1976). The effects of finite computational accuracies on several cosine transform architectures. *SPIE Semin. Proc.* **87**, 229–237.

Wyner, A. (1981). Fundamental limits in information theory. *IEEE Proc.* **69**, 239–251.

Yan, J., and Sakrison, D. J. (1977). Encoding of images based on a two-component source model. *IEEE Trans. Commun.* **COM-25**, 1315–1322.

Yarlagadda, R., and Hershey, J. (1981). Architecture of the fast Walsh–Hadamard and Fourier transforms with charge transfer devices. *Int. J. Electron.* **51**, 669–681.

Yasuda, Y., Takagi, M., and Awano, T. (1979). Hierarchical coding of still images. *Picture Coding Symp. Proc. Ipswich, Engl.* Pap. 3.2.

Yip, P., and Hutchinson, D. (1982). Residual correlation for generalised discrete transforms. *IEEE Trans. Electromagn. Compat.* **EMC-24**, 64–68.

Yip, P., and Rao, K. R. (1980). A fast computational algorithm for the discrete sine transform. *IEEE Trans. Commun.* **COM-28**, 304–310.

Zelinski, R. (1979). Effects of transmission errors on the mean square error performance of transform coding systems. *IEEE Trans. Acoust., Speech, Signal Process.* **ASSP-27**, 531–537.

Zvi-Meiri, A. (1976). The pinned Karhunen–Loève transform of a two-dimensional Gauss–Markov field. *SPIE Semin. Proc.* **87**, 155–163.

Zvi-Meiri, A., and Yudilevich, E. (1981). A pinned sine transform image coder. *IEEE Trans. Commun.* **COM-29**, 1728–1735.

Supplementary material

Proceedings of the Symposia on the Applications of Walsh Functions:
(1) 1970   Rep. No. AD 707431.
(2) 1971   Rep. No. AD 727000; also *IEEE Trans. Electromagn. Compat.* **EMC-13**, No. 3 (1971).
(3) 1972   Rep. No. AD 744650.
(4) 1973   Rep. No. AD 763000.
(5) 1974   IEEE Publ. No. 74CHO861-5EMC. New York.

Relevant Special Issues:
(1) 1977   Image Bandwidth Compression. *IEEE Trans. Commun.* **COM-25**, No. 11.
(2) 1981   Image Processing. *IEEE Proc.* **69**, No. 5.
(3) 1981   Picture Communication Systems. *IEEE Trans. Commun.* **COM-29**, No. 12.

Supplementary References

Books

Andrews, H. C. (1970). "Computer Techniques in Image Processing." Academic Press, New York.

Davisson, L. D., and Gray, R. M., eds. (1976). "Data Compression."

Dowden, Hutchinson & Ross, Stroudsburg, Pennsylvania.

Gonzalez, R. C., and Wintz, P. (1977). "Digital Image Processing." Addison-Wesley, Reading, Massachusetts.

Harmuth, H. F. (1972). "Transmission of Information by Orthogonal Functions," 2nd Ed. Springer-Verlag, Berlin and New York.

Huang, T. S., ed. (1979). "Picture Processing and Digital Filtering," 2nd Ed. Springer-Verlag, Berlin and New York.

Huang, T. S., and Tretiak, O. J., eds. (1972). "Picture Bandwidth Compression," Proceedings of the Symposium on Picture Bandwidth Compression, Cambridge, Massachusetts, 1969. Gordon & Breach, New York.

Rosenfeld, A., ed. (1981). "Image Modeling." Academic Press, New York.

Stucki, P., ed. (1979). "Advances in Digital Image Processing," Proceedings of the International Symposium on Advances in Digital Image Processing, Fed. Rep. Germany, 1978. Plenum, New York.

Image properties and models

Biemond, J., Links, L., and Boekee, D. (1979). Image modelling and quality criteria. *IEEE Trans. Acoust., Speech, Signal Process.* **ASSP-27**, 649–652.

Deriugin, N. G. (1957). The power spectrum and the correlation function of the television signal. *Elektrosvyaz* No. 7, pp. 3–14 [*Telecommunications (Engl. Transl.)* No. 7, pp. 1–12 (1957)].

Franks, L. E. (1966). A model for the random video process. *Bell Syst. Tech. J.* **45**, 609–630.

Jain, A. (1981). Advances in mathematical models for image processing. *IEEE Proc.* **69**, 502–528.

Keskes, N., Kretz, F., and Maitre, H. (1979). Statistical study of edges in television pictures. *IEEE Trans. Commun.* **COM-27**, 1239–1247.

Kretzmer, E. R. (1952). Statistics of television signals. *Bell Syst. Tech. J.* **31**, 751–763.

Links, L., and Biemond, J. (1979). On the non-separability of image models. *IEEE Trans.* **PAMI-1**, 409–411.

Narayanan, S., and Franks, L. E. (1971). Spectra of digitally encoded video signals. *IEEE Trans. Commun.* **COM-19**, 459–466.

Nishikawa, S., Massa, R. J., and Mott-Smith, J. C. (1965). Area properties of television pictures. *IEEE Trans. Inf. Theory* **IT-11**, 348–352.

Stuller, J., and Kurz, B. (1976). Two-dimensional representations of sampled images. *IEEE Trans. Commun.* **COM-24**, 1148–1152.

Wong, E. (1968). Two-dimensional random fields and representation of images. *SIAM J. Appl. Math.* **16**, 756–770.

Woods, J. W. (1972). Two-dimensional discrete Markov fields. *IEEE Trans. Inf. Theory* **IT-18**, 232–240.

The Karhunen–Loève transform

Algazi, V. R., and Sakrison, D. J. (1969). On the optimality of the Karhunen–Loève Expansion. *IEEE Trans. Inf. Theory* **IT-15**, 319–321.

Chien, Y., and Fu, K. (1967). On the generalised Karhunen–Loève Expansion. *IEEE Trans. Inf. Theory* **IT-13**, 518–520.

Fukunaga, K., and Koontz, W. (1970). Application of the Karhunen–Loève expansion to feature selection and ordering. *IEEE Trans. Comput.* **C-19**, 311–318.

Karhunen, K. (1947). Über lineare methoden in der Wahrscheinlichkeitsrechnung. *Ann. Acad. Sci. Fenn., Ser. A: Math.-Phys.* **137**. Transl. by I. Selin, "On Linear Methods in Probability Theory," Doc. T-131. Rand Corp., Santa Monica, California, 1960.

Kremer, H. P., and Mathews, M. V. (1956). A linear coding for transmitting a set of correlated signals. *IRE Trans. Inf. Theory* **IT-2**, 41–46.

Sequency theory and the Walsh–Hadamard transform

Chien, T. (1975). On representations of Walsh functions. *IEEE Trans. Electromagn. Compat.* **EMC-17**, 170–175.

Crowther, W. R., and Rader, C. M. (1966). Efficient coding of vocoder channel signals using linear transformation. *IEEE Proc.* **54**, 1594–1595.

Harmuth, H. (1968). A generalised concept of frequency and some applications. *IEEE Trans. Inf. Theory* **IT-14**, 375–382.

Kennedy, J. (1971). Walsh function imagery analysis. *Proc. Symp. Appl. Walsh Funct., Washington D.C.* AD 727000, pp. 7–10.

Kitajima, H., and Shimono, T. (1983). Residual correlation of the Hadamard transforms of stationary Markov-I signals. *IEEE Trans. Commun.* **COM-31**, 119–121.

Lyle, W., Jr., and Forte, F. (1980). A useful property of the coefficients of a Walsh–Hadamard transform. *IEEE Trans. Acoust., Speech, Signal Process.* **ASSP-28**, 479–480.

Ohnsorg, F. (1971). Spectral modes of the Walsh–Hadamard transform. *Proc. Symp. Appl. Walsh Funct., Washington, D.C.* AD 727000, pp. 55–59.

Paley, R.E.A.C. (1932). A remarkable series of orthogonal functions. *Proc. London Math. Soc.* **34**, 241–279.

Paley, R.E.A.C. (1933). On orthogonal matrices. *J. Math. Phys.* **12**, 311–320.

Pratt, W. K. (1971). Linear and non-linear filtering in the Walsh domain. *Proc. Symp. Appl. Walsh Funct., Washington, D.C.* AD 727000, pp. 38–42.

Sinusoidal transforms and their coding applications

Bertocci, G., Schoenherr, B. W., and Messerschmitt, D. G. (1982). An approach to the implementation of a discrete cosine transform. *IEEE Trans. Commun.* **COM-30**, 635–641.

Chen, W., and Fralick, S. (1976). Image enhancement using cosine transform filtering. *In* "Image Science Mathematics" (C. O. Wilde, and E. Barrett, eds.), pp. 186–192. Western Period., North Hollywood, California.

Clarke, R. J. (1984). Relation between the Karhunen–Loève and sine transforms. *Electron. Lett.* **20**, 12–13.

Hayes, M. H. (1981). Multidimensional signal reconstruction from phase or magnitude. *ICASSP Proc.* pp. 1014–1017.

Jain, A., and Angel, E. (1974). Image restoration, modelling and reduction of dimensionality. *IEEE Trans. Comput.* **C-23**, 470–476.

Marano, P., and Schwartz, P. (1970). Compression d'information sur la transformée de Fourier d'une image. *Onde Electr.* **50**, 908–919.

Ngan, K. N., and Clarke, R. J. (1982). Filtering and subsampling using transform coding techniques. *Proc. Int. Conf. Electron. Image Process. York, Engl.* pp. 220–224.

Pearl, J. (1973). On coding and filtering stationary signals by discrete Fourier transforms. *IEEE Trans. Inf. Theory* **IT-19**, 229–232.

Pearlman, W., and Gray, R. (1978). Source coding of the discrete Fourier transform. *IEEE Trans. Inf. Theory* **IT-24**, 683–692.

Pohlig, S. (1980). Fourier transform phase coding of images. *IEEE Trans. Acoust., Speech, Signal Process.* **ASSP-28**, 339–341.

Reininger, R. C., and Gibson, J. D. (1983). Distributions of the two-dimensional DCT coefficients for images. *IEEE Trans. Commun.* **COM-31**, 835–839.

Shanmugam, K. (1974). Comments on the discrete cosine transform. *IEEE Trans. Comput.* **C-23**,759.

Tadokoro, Y., and Higuchi, T. (1983). Conversion factors from Walsh coefficients to Fourier coefficients *IEEE Trans. Acoust., Speech, Signal Process.* **ASSP-31**, 231–232.

Wang, Z. (1983). Reconsideration of "A fast computational algorithm for the discrete cosine transform" (Chen, Smith and Fralick, 1977). *IEEE Trans. Commun.* **COM-31**, 121–123.

The generalised transform

Ahmed, N., Rao, K. R., and Schultz, R. (1971). The generalised transform. *Proc. Symp. Appl. Walsh Funct., Washington, D.C.* AD 727000, pp. 60–67.

Ahmed, N., Rao, K. R., and Schultz, R. (1971). A generalised discrete transform. *IEEE Proc.* **59**, 1360–1362.

Andrews, H. C., and Caspari, K. (1971). Degrees of freedom and modular structure in matrix multiplication. *IEEE Trans. Comput.* **C-20**, 133–141.

Cheng, D., and Liu, J. (1979). A generalised orthogonal transformation matrix. *IEEE Trans. Comput.* **C-28**, 147–150.

Rao, K. R., Mrig, L., and Ahmed, N. (1973). A modified generalised discrete transform. *IEEE Proc.* **61**, 668–669.

Transform properties and comparisons

Ahmed, N., and Rao, K. R. (1970). Discrete Fourier and Hadamard transforms. *Electron. Lett.* **6**, 221–224.

Andrews, H. C. (1971). Multidimensional rotations in feature selection. *IEEE Trans. Comput.* **C-19**, 1045–1051.

Delp, E., and Mitchell, O. R. (1979). Image compression using block truncation coding. *IEEE Trans. Commun.* **COM-27**, 1335–1342.

Hamidi, M., and Pearl, J. (1975). On the residual correlation of finite dimensional discrete Fourier transforms of stationary signals. *IEEE Trans. Inf. Theory* **IT-21**, 480–482.

Kekre, H., and Solanki, J. (1978). Comparative performance of various trigonometric unitary transforms for transform image coding. *Int. J. Electron.* **44**, 305–315.

Nawrath, R. (1977). Vergliechende betrachtung von präediktive verfahren und transformations-methoden in der bildcodierung. *Arch. Elektron. Uebertragungstech.* **31**, 217–224.

Olsen, J. D., and Heard, C. M. (1977). A comparison of the visual effects of two transform domain encoding approaches. *SPIE Semin. Proc.* **119**, 137–146.

Pearl, J. (1975). Asymptotic equivalence of spectral representations. *IEEE Trans. Acoust., Speech, Signal Process.* **ASSP-23**, 547–551.

Yemeni, Y., and Pearl, J. (1979). Asymptotic properties of discrete unitary transforms. *IEEE Trans.* **PAMI-1**, 366–371.

General transform processing

Andrews, C. A., Davies, J. M., and Schwartz, G. R. (1967). Adaptive data compression. *IEEE Proc.* **55**, 267–277.

Haralick, R., Griswold, N., and Paul, C. (1976). An annihilation transform compression method for permuted images. *SPIE Semin. Proc.* **87**, 189–196.

Haskell, B., and Steele, R. (1981). Audio and video bit-rate reduction. *IEEE Proc.* **69**, 252–262.

Kumar, N., Chakraborti, N., and Mukherjee, A. (1980). Transform domain spectrum extrapolation for efficient picture processing. *Electron. Lett.* **16**, 198–199.

Landau, H., and Slepian, D. (1971). Some computer experiments in picture processing for bandwidth reduction. *Bell Syst. Tech. J.* **50**, 1525–1540.

Reininger, R. C., and Gibson, J. D. (1983). Soft decision demodulation and transform coding of images. *IEEE Trans. Commun.* **COM-31**, 572–577.

Robinson, G., and Reis, J. (1978). Spectral extrapolation with spatial constraints. *SPIE Semin. Proc.* **149**, 91–104.

Tam, T. O., and Stuller, J. (1983). Line-adaptive hybrid coding of images. *IEEE Trans. Commun.* **COM-31**, 445–450.

Tasto, M., and Wintz, P. (1973). A note on the error signal of block quantisers. *IEEE Trans. Commun.* **COM-21**, 216–219.

Watson, L. T., Haralick, R. M., and Zuniga, O. A. (1983). Constrained transform coding and surface fitting. *IEEE Trans. Commun.* **COM-31**, 717–726.

Wilson, R., Knutsson, H. E., and Granlund, G. H. (1983). Anisotropic non-stationary image estimation and its applications: Part II—Predictive image coding. *IEEE Trans. Commun.* **COM-31**, 398–406.

Subjective effects and the human visual response

Allen, C., and Schindler, R. (1980). Determining image quality from electronic or digital signal characteristics. *SPIE Semin. Proc.* **249**, 179–184.

Goodman, J. S., and Pearson, D. (1979). Multidimensional scaling of multiply impaired television pictures. *IEEE Trans.* **SMC-9**, 353–356.

Huang, T. S. (1965). The subjective effect of two-dimensional pictorial noise. *IEEE Trans. Inf. Theory* **IT-11**, 43–53.

Limb, J., and Rubinstein, C. (1977). A model of threshold vision incorporating inhomogeneity of the visual field. *Vision Res.* **17**, 571–584.

Stockham, T. (1976). The role of psychophysics in the mathematics of image science. *In* "Image Science Mathematics" (C. O. Wilde, and E. Barrett, eds.), pp. 57–66. Western Period., North Hollywood, California.

Fast transforms and system implementation.

Algazi, V. R., and Fino, B. (1982). Performance and computation ranking of fast unitary transforms in applications. *ICASSP Proc.* pp. 32–35.

Andrews, H. C., and Kane, J. (1970). Kronecker matrices, computer implementation and generalised spectra. *J. Assoc. Comput. Mach.* **17**, 260–268.

Arambepola, B. (1980). The general discrete Fourier transform and the fast Fourier transform algorithm. *In* "Signal Processing Theories and Applications" (M. Kunt, and F. de Coulon, eds.), pp. 583–588. North-Holland Publ. Amsterdam.

Buijs, H., Pomerleau, A., Fournier, M., and Tam, W. (1974). Implementation of a fast Fourier transform for image processing applications. *IEEE Trans. Acoust., Speech, Signal Process.* **ASSP-22**, 420–424.

Fino, B., and Algazi, V. R. (1976). Unified matrix treatment of the fast Walsh–Hadamard transform. *IEEE Trans. Comput.* **C-25**, 1142–1146.

Gaertner, W., Reddi, S. S., Retter, C., and Singh, I. (1976). Computational complexity and parallelism in image processing algorithms. *In* "Image Science Mathematics" (C. O. Wilde, and E. Barrett, eds.), pp. 224–228. Western Period., North Hollywood, California.

Gerard, H. (1978). Surface acoustic wave transform techniques for analogue signal processing. *SPIE Semin. Proc.* **154**, 164–173.

Jack, M. A., Park, D. G., and Grant, P. M. (1977). C.C.D. spectrum analyser using prime transform algorithm. *Electron. Lett.* **13**, 431–432.

Shanks, J. (1969). Computation of the fast Walsh–Fourier transform. *IEEE Trans. Comput.* **C-18**, 457–459.

Information and rate-distortion theory

Berger, T., and Yu, W. (1972). Rate-distortion theory for context dependent fidelity criteria. *IEEE Trans. Inf. Theory* **IT-18**, 378–384.

Bunin, B. (1969). Rate-distortion function for Gaussian Markov processes. *Bell Syst. Tech. J.* **48**, 3059–3074.

Goblick, T. (1965). Theoretical limitations on the transmission of data from analogue sources. *IEEE Trans. Inf. Theory* **IT-11**, 558–567.

Gray, R. (1970). Information rates of autoregressive sources. *IEEE Trans. Inf. Theory* **IT-16**, 412–421.

Gray, R., Neuhoff, D., and Omura, J. (1975). Process definitions of distortion-rate functions and source coding theorems. *IEEE Trans. Inf. Theory* **IT-21**, 524–532.

Haskell, B. (1969). The computation and bounding of rate-distortion functions. *IEEE Trans. Inf. Theory* **IT-15**, 525–531.

Jelinek, F. (1967). Evaluation of distortion-rate functions for low distortions. *IEEE Proc.* **55**, 2067–2068.

Kellogg, W. (1967). Information rates in sampling and quantisation. *IEEE Trans. Inf. Theory* **IT-13**, 506–511.

Macdonald, R. A., and Schultheiss, P. M. (1964). Information rates of Gaussian signals under criteria constraining the error spectrum *IEEE Proc.* **52**, 415–416.

O'Neal, J. B. (1967). A bound on signal to quantising noise ratios for digital encoding systems. *IEEE Proc.* **55**, 287–292.

Sakrison, D. J. (1969). An extension of the theorem of Kac, Murdock and Szego to N dimensions. *IEEE Trans. Inf. Theory* **IT-15**, 608–610.

Index